Winfield Scott Hancock

Winfield Scott Hancock (*Matthew Brady Collection, National Archives*).

Winfield Scott Hancock

★ ★ ★

A SOLDIER'S LIFE

David M. Jordan

Indiana
University
Press

BLOOMINGTON AND INDIANAPOLIS

First paperback edition 1996

© 1988 by David M. Jordan

Manufactured in the United States of America

Library of Congress Cataloging-in-Publication Data

Jordan, David M., date.
Winfield Scott Hancock : a soldier's life.
Bibliography: p.
Includes index.
1. Hancock, Winfield Scott, 1824-1886. 2. Generals—
United States—Biography. 3. United States Army—
Biography. 4. United States—History—Civil War,
1861-1865—Campaigns. I. Title.
E467.1.H2J67 1988   973.7'092'4   87-46091
ISBN 0-253-36580-5 (cloth)
ISBN 0-253-21058-5 (paper)

3 4 5 6 7 00 99 98 97 96

To Diana

CONTENTS

Illustrations

Winfield Scott Hancock   Frontispiece

Following Page 74

Major General Hancock
Almira Russell Hancock
Henry Heth, C.S.A.
Hancock and Division Commanders, 1864
William B. Franklin
William Farrar Smith
Hancock of the Postwar Army
William A. Wallace
Thomas F. Bayard
Hancock in 1880
James A. Garfield

MAPS

Preface

Hancock the Superb. No other general in the Civil War, Union or Confederate, attracted such a nickname; few could have merited it as much as the soldier from Norristown, Pennsylvania, who was one of the outstanding leaders of the war. The story of Hancock's career, from the Mexican War to his death in 1886, is a unique reflection of America's history for much of the nineteenth century: war in Mexico, expansion to California, the bloody sectional war, the struggle with the Indians of the plains, reconstruction and reconciliation, the great railroad strikes, the postwar campaigns for the presidency. That Winfield Scott Hancock was at or near the center of all these makes his life an integral and important part of the history of the period.

With the help of many who will be mentioned shortly, I have located a great number of Hancock's letters, written in his peculiarly elegant yet sometimes illegible hand. It seems clear to me, however, after laborious search, that one sizable body of his correspondence no longer exists. Donal Henahan, writing in the *New York Times* on September 23, 1984, about Constanze Mozart, said, "The widows of famous men are history's worst enemies." Into this category, unfortunately, we must cast Almira Hancock, who published her reminiscence of the general a year after his death. In her book she quoted from a few of his letters to her, and then she undoubtedly destroyed them, having determined that no one else should read what she decided not to print. Hancock's longest periods of separation from Allie came during the Civil War, which was certainly the time of the greatest number of his letters to her. One regrets deeply not having them but turns to what is available. For a prominent figure in the American Civil War, of course, that is considerable.

In telling Hancock's story, I have had much help, which I should like to acknowledge. First, of course, the great historians of the Civil War—Catton, Nevins, Palfrey, Freeman, and others of similar stature, some mentioned in my bibliography, some not, to whom anyone studying in this field owes a sizable debt. Next, those with whom I worked on a more personal level, members largely of that community of librarians, researchers, archivists, and historians who remain dedicated to the preservation and transmission of knowledge of our past. My thanks for their assistance to Richard J. Sommers and Valerie Metzler of the United States Army Military History Institute; the staff of the various divisions of the Library of Congress, particularly the Manuscript Division; Marie T. Capps, the warmhearted Map and Manuscript Librarian at the United States Military Academy Library; Robin W. Smith of the Manuscript Department, Alderman Library, University of Virginia; Jim Trimble, Still Picture Branch, National Archives, together with other members of the staff of that institution, especially William E. Lind and Michael E. Pilgrim of the Military Services Branch; Laurel G. Bowen, Curator of Manuscripts, Illinois State Historical Library; Linda F. White of the Carnegie Public Library, Clarksdale, Mississippi; Alice Smith and Florence Young of the Historical Society of Montgomery County, Pennsylvania (whose artifacts on display include the ball removed from Hancock's thigh after Gettysburg); Elizabeth Stege Teleky at the Joseph Regenstein Library,

University of Chicago; Denise Whitten of the Mississippi Library Commission; Forrest R. Blackburn, Newspaper-Census Division, Kansas State Historical Society; Laura V. Monti, Keeper of Rare Books and Manuscripts, Boston Public Library; Robert L. Byrd, Manuscript Department, William R. Perkins Library, Duke University; Vicki Denby of the Houghton Library, Harvard University; Elaine Pease, who permitted me to examine the letters of her great-grandfather, Captain T. W. Kelly of the 164th New York, who was captured at Reams' Station; Patricia Adams (St. Louis) and Kathleen McIntyre and Darrell Garwood (Columbia) of the Western Historical Manuscript Collection, University of Missouri; Wilbur E. Meneray, Manuscripts Librarian, Tulane University Library; Harry F. Parker, Division of Archives and Manuscripts, Pennsylvania Historical and Museum Commission; Harriet McLoone, Assistant Curator for American History, Huntington Library; Merna Whitley, Department of Archives, Louisiana State University; Judith A. Schiff and Mary C. LaFogg, Manuscripts and Archives, Sterling Memorial Library at Yale University; Susan Ravdin, Assistant, Special Collections, Bowdoin College Library; Robert Sink, Manuscript Specialist, New York Public Library; Janice L. Fox, Archival Assistant, Missouri Historical Society; Joyce Baur and Edith Prout of the Jenkintown (Pennsylvania) Library; George Miles, Western Americana Collection, Beinecke Rare Books and Manuscripts Library, Yale University; the staffs of Firestone Library of Princeton University, the Historical Society of Pennsylvania, the Maryland Historical Society, the Massachusetts Historical Society, the library of the Military Order of the Loyal Legion in Philadelphia, the New-York Historical Society, the Van Pelt Library of the University of Pennsylvania, the Louisiana room of the New Orleans Public Library, the Mississippi Department of Archives and History, and the Paterson (New Jersey) Public Library; Marjorie Wilmington Mastro, for research assistance related particularly to the Kansas expedition; the Honorable Alfred L. Taxis, Jr.; C. Howard Nichols, Southeastern Louisiana University; Lawrence H. Curry, Philadelphia College of Art; Robert F. Looney, Free Library of Philadelphia; George C. Corson, Jr.; William Ivy Hair, Georgia College; H. Scott McMillin, Cornell University; James Williams; Kirke Bryan; Joseph R. Strayer, Princeton University; and Joe Gray Taylor, McNeese State University. In addition, recognition should be given to those selfless employees of the National Park Service who preserve and enhance the old battlefields of Antietam, Gettysburg, Fredericksburg, Chancellorsville, the Wilderness, Spotsylvania, and Petersburg and the sites of the fighting around Richmond.

I extend special thanks to Janice Milam, who typed the manuscript for me; to my daughter Diana, who accompanied me in retracing the path of Hancock's expedition across Kansas and who tracked down documents at the Historical Society of Pennsylvania; to my daughters Laura and Sarah, who walked the battlefields with me; and, most of all, to my wife, Barbara, who encouraged, listened, suggested, but never complained, except when she felt I was not pushing ahead fast enough.

Finally, one last personal word: nowhere does the Civil War become more alive for me than at the crossing of the Brock and Orange Plank roads in the Wilderness. Stand there on a warm spring day, half-close your eyes and gaze westward out the plank road, and in your mind's eye you too should see Hill's rebels coming up through the dust as Hancock pushes his weary men out after Getty's to stop them. A magical moment, before the killing starts.

Winfield Scott Hancock

ONE

Hancock the Superb

Saturday, February 13, 1886, dawned cold and rainy in New York City. On Governor's Island, out in the harbor, a detachment of 114 soldiers lined up at 8:30 a.m., in front of the commanding general's house. Inside, forty-five minutes earlier, the steel casket holding the body of Major General Winfield Scott Hancock, U.S.A., still in the bedroom where he had died four days before, had been closed after the general's distraught widow had placed a final kiss upon the cold features.

The casket was carried out of the house and, accompanied by the honor guard, through the rain to the boat landing. At precisely 9 a.m. the casket and the military escort boarded the government steamer *Chester A. Arthur* for the trip to the Battery, at the foot of Manhattan Island. A cannon was fired, once every minute, from Castle William, as the steamer made its way through the dense fog, repeatedly blowing its whistle. At 9:15 the steamer reached the barge office, and fifteen minutes later the casket and the escort had been disembarked.

The contingent from the island was met by fourteen pallbearers, led by Secretary of State Thomas Francis Bayard. Among the pallbearers were four men who had been or who would be commanding general of the United States Army—William Tecumseh Sherman, Philip H. Sheridan, John M. Schofield, and Nelson A. Miles—and other distinguished generals, relics of the Civil War, such friends of the deceased as Alfred H. Terry, William B. Franklin, William F. Smith, James B. Fry, Orlando Willcox, who had stood up for Hancock at his wedding, and Francis A. Walker, his adjutant in the Second Corps and now president of the Massachusetts Institute of Technology. The pallbearers, all wearing heavy white sashes and black rosettes, formed in front of the casket and escorted it out to the street, where they entered carriages for the ride up Broadway.

A sizable crowd stood in the rain to watch the funeral procession; Broadway was lined with people all the way to Trinity Church, where the throng was particularly dense. The entourage was led by a large platoon of New York police, followed by the military honor guard and six carriages containing the pallbearers. After these came the hearse bearing the casket, with a military escort on either side, a dozen more carriages with family and friends of General Hancock, and, on foot, five posts of the Grand Army of the Republic, a detachment of the Legion of Honor, and a delegation from Tammany Hall, led by one-legged General Daniel E. Sickles.

1

Trinity Church was packed, and many persons stood during the brief Episcopal funeral service, conducted by the Reverend Doctor Morgan Dix and Chaplain E. H. C. Goodwin of Governor's Island. A Beethoven funeral march served as the processional, "Rock of Ages" was sung during the service, and the casket was removed from the church to the strains of the Dead March from Handel's *Saul.* The procession then moved back to the barge office, followed by some two to three thousand persons as far as the police would permit.

The guns at Castle William resumed their firing, and bells in the vicinity of the Battery tolled solemnly as the casket was reembarked on the steamer for a trip across the harbor to Jersey City. There, eighty policemen were needed to hold back the crowd as the funeral party transferred to the special train which would carry Hancock's body to his hometown, Norristown, Pennsylvania.

The tracks in Jersey City and all across New Jersey—at Elizabeth, New Brunswick, Princeton, and Trenton—were lined with people, standing in the drizzle to pay their final respects to Winfield Scott Hancock. On the other side of the Delaware, in the general's native state of Pennsylvania, the crowds were larger and the tributes even more marked. At Fifty-second Street in Philadelphia, three carloads of local dignitaries, led by Governor Robert Pattison, were added to the train for the final leg of its journey. At 2:45 p.m. the train drew up at the DeKalb Street Station in Norristown.

"All Norristown," wrote the reporter for the *New York Times,* "came out to witness the soldier's final return home." The procession, led by the fourteen distinguished pallbearers, marched out Main Street to Montgomery Cemetery, to the modest granite vault which Hancock himself had designed and in which his daughter was already entombed. After a simple ceremony, the undertaker closed the vault, the five thousand persons present bared their heads, the salute to a major general was fired, and a bugler played "Taps."

Winfield Scott Hancock was laid to rest.[1]

It was twenty-one years since the end of the Civil War, five and a half years since Hancock's unsuccessful run for the presidency. Yet the outpouring of affection and respect for Hancock at his death, marked by the thousands standing in the rain to watch his funeral procession pass as well as by the organizations and individuals all over the country, north and south, who sent or adopted messages of sympathy and mourning, was startling in its depth of feeling. The general's widow had asked that the funeral be kept as simple as possible; she herself was emotionally unable to participate in it. One reporter called it "the least pretentious funeral ever given to a great soldier." Still, it grew beyond Mrs. Hancock's conception because she failed to realize that her husband belonged to the nation as much as or more than he belonged to his family.

One fact became evident in the wake of the general's death: Winfield Scott Hancock was beloved by the American people. Part of this, of course, was because of his achievements during the war. He was one of the great soldiers of the Civil War. His exploits of generalship at Williamsburg and Chancellorsville, at Gettysburg and Spotsylvania won him this recognition and guaranteed him history's attention. He has been called the greatest Union general of the war, save only Grant and Sherman, though obviously partisans of Thomas and Sheridan and a handful of others might dispute that opinion.[2]

Hancock never commanded an independent force, except at the very end of the war, in West Virginia, not really in the presence of the enemy. This fact, of course, makes comparisons with other generals more difficult. He was not called on to devise strategy. But what he was called on to do, he did peerlessly. George Gordon Meade once said that Hancock was "the only one of my corps commanders who will always go right in when I order him." Perhaps it is best simply to read what Grant wrote in his memoirs (after a long estrangement from Hancock):

> Hancock stands the most conspicuous figure of all the general officers who did not exercise a separate command. He commanded a corps longer than any other one, and his name was never mentioned as having committed in battle a blunder for which he was responsible. . . . His genial disposition made him friends, and his personal courage and his presence with his command in the thickest of the fight won for him the confidence of troops serving under him. No matter how hard the fight, the 2d corps always felt that their commander was looking after them.[3]

John M. Schofield called him "the almost incomparably gallant Hancock, the idol of his soldiers and of a very large part of the people"; Henry W. Slocum "looked upon him as one of the very best of our generals"; and Sherman called Hancock "one of the greatest soldiers in history." These were generals; the men in the ranks loved Hancock too. One of them, signing himself "A Soldier," wrote in 1868 that Hancock, "instinct with quick determination and energetic movement," could "infuse his own being, vitality, force, and fire into his soldiers." The colonel of a Maine regiment who served with Hancock said "his presence always inspired the troops with enthusiasm" and spoke of "the cheers [which] would run down the line as he dashed past the soldiers to some point where his presence was needed." And Hugh McCulloch, Lincoln's secretary of the treasury, said of Hancock: "In uprightness, in a keen sense of honor, in kindness of heart, in generosity, in genuine manliness, he had no superior in the army."[4]

But the Civil War ended in 1865, and Hancock lived on to 1886. For all of that time he served as a general officer in the United States Army, participating in all sorts of varied activities, military and otherwise. He fought Indians, served as a reconstruction commander in Louisiana and Texas, suppressed railroad strikes, supervised great national ceremonies, and ran for president. He did not shrink from taking controversial positions, and he was at times at odds with the leadership of the military establishment. Not everyone loved him, and obviously not everyone agreed with him. Yet it was during this period that Hancock's high place in the affections of his country-

men was secured. When he died, the editor of the *New York Evening Post,*
who had not supported Hancock during the presidential contest of 1880,
wrote: "No soldier on either side of the late great conflict of arms commanded more fully the admiration and love of his fellow-countrymen than
he who entered into rest at Governor's Island yesterday."[5]

Though Hancock was a tough soldier and a demanding leader, he was
clearly a genuine human being. A warm friend and a devoted family man,
he was kind and considerate to acquaintances and strangers alike. Hancock
was a notoriously "soft touch," particularly with old soldiers. This trait often
placed a strain upon his family budget, funded as it was by a meager
military salary. He worked hard, and he did his duty. His postwar endeavors
were frequently frustrated by events and opposing forces, but Hancock bore
his disappointments with apparent equanimity and serenity. The self-
discipline that he always exhibited, produced by his sturdy upbringing and
military training, enabled him to conceal from public view the sentiments
he must have felt when the Cheyennes went on the warpath after his
"peace" mission, when Grant turned around his initiatives in New Orleans,
and when John Kelly's blind selfishness lost the state of New York and
made Garfield president. Hancock soldiered on and did his job to the end.

At Williamsburg, early in the Civil War, McClellan had labeled Hancock
"superb," and the word was frequently assigned to him thereafter. Few
soldiers at any time could have borne such a cognomen without having it
turn into an embarrassment or a mark of derision. In Hancock's case,
however, as the years passed, the American people attached the nickname
to him naturally, and "Hancock the Superb" became simply a common
description of the man.

TWO

The Lawyer's Son

Winfield Scott Hancock was born on February 14, 1824, in the hamlet of Montgomery Square, some three miles east of the small town of Lansdale, Pennsylvania, approximately twenty miles or so northwest of Philadelphia. He was, obviously, named for the hero of the battles of Chippewa and Lundy's Lane in the War of 1812. Winfield had an identical twin brother, who received the more prosaic name Hilary; one wonders just what inspiration caused the Hancocks to give the martial name to the babe who would grow to be a mighty soldier while his twin became a lawyer in Minneapolis, afflicted with a drinking problem.

Winfield and Hilary were the sons of Elizabeth and Benjamin Hancock. Elizabeth was a Hoxworth (or Hawkesworth), and her grandfather John Hoxworth had come to Montgomery County in 1728, settling in Hatfield Township, near Lansdale. He married a Jenkins (whose family had been the original settlers of the area) from the adjoining farm. Their son Edward was Elizabeth's father. Richard Hancock, Benjamin's father, was a seaman who wed a Scottish lass named Anna Maria Nash and settled a couple of miles from the Hoxworth farm. The union of Elizabeth and Benjamin furnished their children with a solid English, Welsh, and Scottish heritage.

A year after the birth of the twins, Benjamin moved his family to another house in Montgomery Square, where he taught school. Two years later, the Hancocks removed to Norristown, some eight or nine miles distant, the county seat of Montgomery County. Here the elder Hancock taught in a local school and read law in the office of John Freedley, Esquire. While her husband trained for the bar, Elizabeth Hancock opened a milliner's shop in her home to help make ends meet. In August 1828, Benjamin was admitted to the bar, though he had to struggle to make a living for some years. Winfield and his brothers (including a younger son named John, born six years later) grew up in Norristown, a small town which had developed at the site of a ferry across the Schuylkill River and had spread to the hills overlooking the river.[1]

Benjamin Franklin Hancock was a deacon in the Baptist Church at Norristown and a firm and lifelong Democrat, a man who was to be elected town burgess in 1841. Winfield the lawyer's son had instilled in him from an early age respect and reverence for the law, for Blackstone and Coke, for the concept of due process, for the Almighty, and for the principles and tenets of the Democratic party, as they matured in the age of Jackson and Van Buren.

5

These principles of course included the rights of the sovereign states, limited government, and opposition to such innovations as a protective tariff and the national bank. For the chief justice of the United States, John Marshall, there was less reverence; his Federalist expansion of national power and grasp was anathema to any good Democrat. The young man listened and absorbed. "I never knew a man whom I respected as much as my father," Winfield said, years later. "It was due to his character, his appearance and the method of his life."[2]

Montgomery County in those days was a sparsely settled but growing area, much wooded but increasingly cultivated, watered by the Schuylkill and its tributaries, and populated by people of Welsh, English, Swedish, and German descent. There was no longer an Indian threat to worry its inhabitants, and the county offered great promise to a denizen of Philadelphia who might be seeking more open spaces and opportunities. It was not a frontier, but frontier virtues were still useful to its citizens. Agriculture was its major business, but there were thriving mining and quarrying industries, concentrating on iron ore, limestone, and marble. Within the county's borders, in 1830, were some 39,000 souls.

Norristown itself was described by a traveler as possessing "an agreeable site on the Schuylkill" with "wonderful improvements since the opening of the Schuylkill canal." With two or three excellent inns and a new bridge across the river, the town was thriving, though the visitor complained that there was "no reading room or Athanaeum." The business from the canal, the establishment of mills and factories, and the gathering of folk from across the county during court sessions, he concluded, "must conduce to render the town flourishing, and the inhabitants enterprising and wealthy."[3]

In such a society and subject to such influences, young Winfield passed his childhood and adolescent years. He and Hilary, inseparable and almost indistinguishable as boys, were sent to the Norristown Academy, of which Benjamin was a trustee. Here they came under the tutelage of one Eliphalet Roberts, who, nearly fifty years later, remembered Winfield with these words: "I never found a knife-mark on his section of the long, old-fashioned, white pine desk, nor was I ever obliged to speak to him about its condition." When Pennsylvania established the system of free public schools, Benjamin, who was to serve on the Norristown School Board for thirty years, took his sons out of the academy and sent them to the new public school. Winfield, though a high-spirited boy, getting into a normal amount of trouble, did well at his studies. He and Hilary were also exemplars at the Baptist Sunday School, the superintendent of which was their father. They made frequent visits to Grandfather Hoxworth's farm, and when they did their grandfather made sure to get them over to the Baptist Church in Montgomery Square on Sundays. Years later the general remembered the young men sitting on the fence outside the church ("looking like so many crows") while the "good boys like myself" went inside. "They had not strong-minded mothers or fathers, I imagine." The results of having strong-minded parents were gratifying, however. Winfield, at the age of fifteen, was given the signal honor of selection to read the Declaration of Independence at the town's Fourth of July celebration in 1839, evidence surely that he was considered among the very brightest of Norristown's youth.[4]

In the following year, Congressman Joseph Fornance, one of Benjamin Hancock's brethren at the county bar and a fellow Democrat, applied to Secretary of War Joel R. Poinsett for the appointment of Winfield to the United States Military Academy at West Point, stating his belief "that he possesses all the necessary qualifications under the rules of the department." There are several stories about the motivating factors behind this appointment, so fateful to the future of the young man, so fruitful to the nation. One of his boyhood friends, B. E. Chain, told a story many years later of young Winfield's organizing a marching company of his schoolmates in Norristown, which may or may not have indicated a military bent. Benjamin Hancock, as a devout Christian, is said to have hesitated over permitting a military education for his son. John B. Sterigere, the local Democratic leader, urged him to accede; Benjamin's doubts were resolved by the Reverend David Bernard, the Baptist pastor, who said that since soldiers were necessary it was best that they should be good Christians. Benjamin sat down, on Winfield's sixteenth birthday, and, as requested by the congressman, wrote a letter to the secretary of war describing his son:

> He is five feet five inches high, well built and has a persevering mind, and is entirely free from any deformity, disease, or infirmity, which would render him unfit for the military service, and from any disorder of an infectious or immoral character. He can read and write well and perform with facility and accuracy the various operations of the four ground rules of arithmetic, of reduction of simple and compound proportions and of vulgar and decimal fractions, so that he is well acquainted with all the rules of arithmetic, he has done something at mathematics, and has paid much attention to natural philosophy, chemistry, algebra, English grammar, geography, and has been for some time past and is now engaged in learning Latin. . . .[5]

A month later, Fornance had to write again to Poinsett, begging that the vacancy from the Montgomery County district be filled with his nominee: "There can be no objection to Winfield Hancock, he is a native and resident of my district and in every respect qualified." Within days the appointment came through, and on March 31, 1840, Winfield S. Hancock wrote to the secretary, advising that he accepted the conditional appointment as a cadet. The boy's father signed his assent to the acceptance and also consented to Winfield's signing articles agreeing to eight years of service from his date of admission.[6]

The step was taken. Though not irrevocable at the time, it committed Winfield Hancock to his life's work. He remained in the United States Army from the time of his admission to West Point to the day of his death, over forty-five years later.

The decision to attend West Point, of course, meant for Winfield separation, for the first time but, in a very real sense, for good, from his twin brother. Difficult as this was for the young cadet, it was no doubt harder on the twin left behind. Winfield was also separated from his father. This may well have been a good thing. That Benjamin Hancock had a great influence on his son is sure; that this influence might in time have become suffocating is a clear possibility. Everywhere that Winfield might turn, at home, in school, in the church, in the court house, and in the town hall, he saw the shadow of Benjamin Hancock. He was proud of his father, respected and loved him. He was also growing into a young man of self-confidence and assertiveness. His father, he knew, intended that he become a lawyer; at Benjamin's request, the young cadet took Chitty's *Blackstone* to West Point and read it through six times. Still, he planned to make his own way. In Norristown, Winfield must eventually have rebelled against the paternal dominance; at West Point and in the army, he was far enough removed from home that he could maintain an ideal relationship with Benjamin Franklin Hancock.[7]

Appointment to the military academy was not the same as admission. Winfield arrived on the great plain in the Hudson Highlands, some one hundred feet above the river, in June 1840, facing a stern test before he became a cadet. The incoming aspirant was called "a conditional thing," wore his own clothes, learned the rudiments of military order, and prepared for the entrance examination. Five young men shared a room, their beds blankets on the floor. Sophomores (third classmen) instructed them in marching, drill, the manual of arms, and the knowledge they needed for the entrance exam. They moved from place to place to the roll of drums. Sixty percent of the appointees failed the entrance examination, even though it was based on subjects generally taught in the rural common schools; of those who passed, some fifty-five percent would not graduate for one reason or another. Winfield could take some comfort in the knowledge that boys from the East, where there were more accomplished preparatory schools, fared somewhat better than those from the West and the South. On the other hand, at sixteen he was younger than most of his fellows and "looked even younger," according to a first classman named Don Carlos Buell.[8]

The day came, at the end of June, and the would-be class of 1844 took its entrance examination. Hancock was among those who passed. The first great hurdle behind him, he then marched off with the entire corps of cadets (except for the old third class, which went on furlough) to the annual summer encampment on the northeast corner of the plain, there to pass July and August in a simulation of a soldier's life. Winfield Hancock, as his father's son, must have been thrilled when President Martin Van Buren arrived to review the corps of cadets.[9]

With the issuance of uniforms, Winfield could finally doff the civilian clothes he had brought from Norristown and become accustomed to cadet gray, called by one old West Pointer "such a felicitous average of the be-sullying contingencies of real life, that it never shows dirt, even when threadbare." Hancock learned that cadets received a nominal pay of about $28 per month, but they never saw it; practically everything they needed to live on was deducted from the pay. He found that one of the easiest things to do at the Point was to pick up demerits; an accumulation of 200 of these in a year was a ticket home. Hancock was careful never to exceed 140 demerits in any year.[10]

The summer encampment ended and the new plebes started their academic life at West Point. It was a difficult regimen, starting at 5 a.m. in the summer, 6 a.m. in the winter. Beds had to be made, barracks scrubbed, boots polished, uniforms and equipment tended to, proper deference extended to upper classmen. Eventually the plebes were marched off to class. Here they encountered the legacy of Major Sylvanus Thayer, "the father of West Point," superintendent until 1833. Among Thayer's many innovations were the system of daily marks and the routine of blackboard recitations. The course of study covered two years of mathematics, French, and drawing, and one year of chemistry, construction of fortifications, English, mental and moral philosophy, elementary law, and infantry and artillery tactics. Civilian educators were not much impressed by West Point's schooling; one observer estimated that four years in the military academy brought a student "about as far as the end of the Freshman year in Yale, Harvard, or Princeton."[11]

The cadets got to know the superintendent, Major Richard Delafield, a pudgy, bustling New Yorker, called "Dicky the Punster" behind his back. Delafield that fall introduced new cadet pantaloons with buttons in the front rather than on the side, so that he was temporarily in the good graces of the cadets. They got to know Delafield's two adjutants, Lieutenant Irvin McDowell and Lieutenant Joseph Hooker, and the members of the faculty.[12]

Finally, of course, the cadets got to know each other, first those in their own class, then, as time went on, those in the classes ahead of them.

The class of 1844 was not one of the most distinguished of West Point classes. Fifty-four young men passed the entrance examination. Of the twenty-five who graduated four years later, only five served in the Union army during the Civil War; two indeed resigned from the army at the very start of the war to return to civilian life. Five members were killed in the Mexican War, five others died prior to the Civil War, and three served in the Confederate army. The remaining five entered civilian life before the war, including the top-ranked graduate, William G. Peck, who became a well-known Columbia University mathematics professor. Of the five Union army soldiers, besides Hancock, one was a cavalry major, one a quartermaster colonel, one was Alfred Pleasonton, who led the cavalry of the Army of the Potomac for a time, and one was Alexander Hays, a big, strapping fellow, twenty-one years old and already a graduate of Allegheny College when he came to the Point. Hays led both a brigade and a division under Hancock and died in the Wilderness. Of the three Confederates, only Simon Bolivar Buckner of Kentucky became prominent; one, Francis J. Thomas, was killed at Bull Run.[13]

Eventually Hancock became acquainted with the members of the classes ahead of his. The corps of cadets was small and homogeneous, and everyone knew everyone else. The star student in the class of 1843 was William B. Franklin, a fellow Pennsylvanian who became a close friend. One of those fairly far down the list in that class was a taciturn cadet from Illinois named Sam Grant, a young man not very happy at the Point except when riding a horse. In the class of 1842 were such future notables as William Rosecrans, John Pope, D. H. Hill, George Sykes, Lafayette McLaws, Earl Van Dorn, and, down near the bottom of the class, James Longstreet.[14]

Young Hancock's career at the military academy was undistinguished, but he made many friends, both in his own class and in those ahead of and behind him. "His handsome face and figure and pleasing manners," said a cadet in the class behind him, "made him a favorite with his brother cadets and the officers of the institution." He made many friends among southerners, who found Hancock's views on states' rights and other political issues similar to those with which they had been inculcated. Buell said Hancock was "one of the few 'Plebes' who are at once taken into good fellowship by the older class." And Orlando Willcox, a plebe during Hancock's final year, remembered the good will with which the older cadet treated plebes.[15]

It was at a summer encampment that Hancock first met his namesake, General Winfield Scott. Scott and his two eldest daughters were in the custom of visiting the Point each summer, and the general loved to gather the cadets around him and tell war stories. When he met Hancock and was told of the young cadet's promise, Scott was much pleased, because, he said, nearly all of his other namesakes that he had heard about had turned out to be great scamps.[16]

As new classes came to the Point, Hancock made new friendships. In the class behind him, William Farrar Smith, later called "Baldy," became a friend, as did the ill-starred Charles P. Stone; others in the group were Fitz John Porter, Edmund Kirby Smith, and Gordon Granger. In the class of 1846 one of the leaders was a brilliant young man named George B. McClellan, and other members of that class were Darius Couch, a dour Virginian named Thomas Jackson, George Stoneman, and the last man in the class, George E. Pickett.[17]

Hancock was secretary of the cadet literary society, "The Dialectic," but this was not emblematic of any scholarly merit. As his friend Baldy Smith said of Hancock, "his progress through the course of study was not conspicuous in any way." Indeed not, for Winfield finished eighteenth in his class of twenty-five graduates. His best marks came in drawing, geology, and infantry tactics, but the rest of his course was relentlessly mediocre.

Hancock was younger than his fellows, and his work may have been affected by the fact that he was still growing throughout his college years. Five feet five when his application for the Point went in, Hancock was more than six feet tall when he graduated and well able to take care of himself. Early in his career at the academy, Hancock was bullied by a big Kentuckian named Crittenden. Alex Hays intervened and took on Crittenden in a long and bloody fight. As a senior, however, Hancock himself engaged in a celebrated fistfight that increased his esteem among the cadets. Franklin, a year ahead, spotted Hancock when he arrived, "a small boy scarcely of the regulation height," but three years later, "as manly a fellow as the Academy ever produced." Hancock enjoyed West Point: the military discipline, the camaraderie, even clandestine visits to the famous Benny Havens's saloon, off limits but very popular with the cadets. He made friends, applied himself, and accomplished enough to make it through.[18]

Winfield even had time for a little rebellion in his senior year, when he conspired with a Boston clothier named John Earle to have that worthy make postgraduation uniforms for Hancock and his classmates, against the explicit denial of Major Delafield, who said that the commissary of clothing at the Point could make the uniforms. "I exerted myself all I could for the purpose of obtaining the Major's permission for you to take our measures," Hancock wrote. "But it was labor lost." After detailing Delafield's opposition, Hancock said, "I have spoken to nearly all of the first class on the subject— and they are very anxious that you should make us a visit. I am confident that all of them will patronize you, and I hope you will not disappoint us."[19]

This uncharacteristic insubordination on Hancock's part was produced no doubt by his realization that Delafield had gone beyond his authority in trying to force patronage of his own man (who Hancock said was a relative of the superintendent) for the purchase of the uniforms which all the graduates would require for their next assignment. Hancock could always become touchy when he felt that his rights were being infringed.

Graduation for Hancock's class came on June 30, 1844. Those near the top of the class could make their choice of the branch of the service in which they wished to serve, with the top one or two going into the Corps of Engineers. The other branches, in declining order of desirability, were the topographical engineers, ordnance, artillery, dragoons, and infantry. With his ranking in the bottom third of the class, Hancock had no choice in the matter and was assigned to the infantry. He was designated a brevet (temporary) second lieutenant in the Sixth Infantry Regiment. Congress so severely restricted the size of the peacetime military establishment that there were not sufficient available commissions to take care of the military academy's entire graduating class. Hancock would wait two years to receive his commission as a regular second lieutenant—in the infantry.

Winfield Hancock came out of the military academy with definitely mixed credentials. He had a brevet commission and many friends who would be his military contemporaries over the years. He had attracted the favorable attention of Scott, the general-in-chief. But his mediocre record in a lackluster class did not mark him as one of brilliant promise, so that his career before the Civil War would not be highlighted by rapid advancement.

THREE

To Mexico

Brevet Lieutenant Hancock was detailed to the Indian Territory, to Fort Towson on the Red River and later to Fort Washita, on the Washita. Here he served with units of the Sixth Infantry on what was then regarded as the "Permanent Indian Frontier," helping to keep a watchful eye on the Indian tribes, both those indigenous to the area and those which had been forcibly removed from east of the Mississippi.

The "Permanent Indian Frontier" was never much more than a chimera, but relations between the races were comparatively calm during the period that Hancock was stationed in the Red River region. Without a large influx of whites through the area, there were not the constant frictions that usually resulted in trouble. Consequently, Hancock had the leisure to work at learning his trade. It was of course true that little in the duties of a subaltern prepared him for the responsibilities of leading large bodies of men in combat. Nevertheless, he sought to develop competence in all the tasks a young officer must perform. He was involved in recruiting duties, among others, and his commanding officer on at least two occasions required reimbursement for funds expended in this service by Hancock.[1]

In the spring of 1846, the administration of President James Knox Polk had either blundered or planned its way into war with Mexico, depending on one's point of view. While the war was not universally popular with American citizens, it was regarded as a great opportunity by almost all those in the United States Army, and Winfield Hancock was no exception.

Unfortunately, Hancock had to work very hard to get himself included in the fighting. In June 1846 the young officer received from the adjutant-general's office a form sent out to learn which officers would be willing to be transferred to a mounted riflemen's unit. Hancock misconstrued the import of the communication and, on June 30, wrote to Washington, answering the question "whether or not I desired to be transferred to another Regiment" with the reply "that I do wish to be transferred, and to the army in Mexico." When he found that he had inadvertently brought about his transfer to the mounted riflemen, Hancock wrote to the adjutant-general again, explaining that he had "misunderstood the intention" of the earlier communication. He managed to avoid transfer to the mounted riflemen, but he was no closer to Mexico. Finally, in September 1846, he received his long-awaited commission as a regular second lieutenant.[2]

One of Hancock's problems was that he unknowingly made himself very useful to the recruiting service. Early in 1847 he was sent to Newport Barracks, Kentucky, to take charge of a body of recruits destined for the Sixth Infantry. On March 16 Hancock left Cincinnati with the detachment of sixty recruits headed for Jefferson Barracks, outside St. Louis. Upon arrival there, he was directed to conduct his troop to Fort Scott, Missouri, to the great unhappiness of his superior back in Cincinnati, who said the young officer's "services are much wanted here."[3]

Arriving at Fort Scott, Hancock was ordered, not to his company, but back to the recruiting service, at Newport Barracks. He promptly went to work again on getting to Mexico, though he was gloomy about his prospects. He wrote to Hilary on May 5: "The only thing that grieves me is that I cannot get to Mexico. I made an application today to join the army going to the front," but he thought it "doubtful" that the adjutant-general would "favor it." He was busy, he said, as superintendent of the recruiting service for the western division and as assistant inspector general; "but, though my services are said to be useful, I still want to go to Mexico."[4]

Hancock wrote to the colonel commanding at Newport Barracks, pointing out that his company of the Sixth Infantry had been ordered to Mexico and asking that he be directed to join it: "I am exceedingly anxious to go, as I have not been there, and, by waiting I see no chance of getting there at all." If the colonel could not grant his application, Hancock said, he asked that it be forwarded to the adjutant-general. The colonel rejected his request, on the ground that Hancock was too valuable to the recruiting service. In frustration, the young lieutenant forwarded to the adjutant-general his application as thus denied and a letter pointing out that he was not even supposed to be part of the recruiting service but had been sent to Newport originally simply to take charge of a detachment of recruits to be conducted to his company. Something worked, whether Hancock's correspondence or his name's being on a list of officers whom General Scott asked to be sent forward to Mexico from the States. On May 31, 1847, the adjutant-general ordered that Second Lieutenant Winfield Hancock conduct a body of recruits to Mexico and then rejoin his regiment.[5]

Accordingly, Hancock left Cincinnati on June 21, to proceed via New Orleans to Vera Cruz, where he arrived with his 73 men on July 13. Scott's army, of course, was now at Puebla, Mexico's second city, having taken Vera Cruz, moved inland over the National Road, and devastated the Mexican army at Cerro Gordo. Puebla, a city of 80,000 people, was much higher and healthier than the port city, with its annual visitation of yellow fever, and Scott waited there for the arrival of reinforcements to his tiny army before he marched against Mexico City.[6]

Hancock did not linger in Vera Cruz. The day after he arrived, attached temporarily to a regiment in a column of reinforcements of about 2,500 men under Brigadier General Franklin Pierce, he marched off toward Puebla. There were some half-dozen skirmishes with guerrillas along the way, "in all of which I can truly say I have endeavored to do my duty," as Hancock wrote his brother. Pierce's force reached Puebla on August 6, bringing the size of Scott's army to little more than 10,000 men. The Americans were set for the march on the Mexican capital. Hancock had made it in time.[7]

Scott's little army began its departure from Puebla on August 7; two days later, Brigadier General William J. Worth moved out his division, which included Hancock's Sixth Infantry. A three-day march brought the American army into the Valley of Mexico without opposition, but Scott and his soldiers knew that Antonio López de Santa Anna, the wily Mexican leader, waited for them with a vastly larger army in strong defensive positions.[8]

The Valley of Mexico, a basin about thirty-two by forty-six miles, was formerly a large lake, which had been drying up over the centuries. The few roads through the marshy valley were usually elevated causeways on which it was easy to arrange defensive positions. Santa Anna's plan of defense was much simpler to devise than was Scott's plan of attack. Nevertheless, it was Scott who managed to catch his adversary off balance, whose army hung on to win hard-fought battles, and who ultimately occupied the Mexican capital. In these battles in the Valley of Mexico, Winfield Hancock received his first taste of fighting, carried himself with credit and distinction, and learned of himself that it was an experience he enjoyed.

Scott surprised the Mexicans by making his attack from the south of Mexico City, rather than from the east or the southeast as was expected. On the morning of August 20, 1847, a force under Brigadier General Persifor Smith surprised and routed a larger Mexican force near the village of Contreras. Worth's division was posted near San Antonio, a few miles to the east, a strong point held by a large force under General Nicholas Bravo. When Contreras fell, Santa Anna ordered Bravo to fall back to a fortified convent at Churubusco, about a mile to the north. Before Bravo could do so, Worth sent Colonel Newman S. Clarke's brigade around the enemy's right, through an almost impassable lava field called the Pedregal. Clarke's objective was to reach the causeway ahead of the Mexican retreat; while he could not quite accomplish that, he was able to cut the retreating Mexican column in two. The rear half fled eastward across the marshes and was effectively out of the fight; the front half headed for Churubusco. A portion of Clarke's force, primarily the Sixth Infantry, pushed on without orders after the fugitives and became fully engaged at Churubusco. Whether Scott wanted one there or not, he now had a battle in full swing.[9]

Churubusco was an excellent defensive position. The village itself was an insignificant scattering of houses 100 yards south of the Rio de Churubusco, but just to the west of the village was the massive stone Convent of San Mateo, effectively turned into a fortress with embrasures and platforms for artillery and crenellated walls for musketry. About 350 yards to the east, where the causeway from San Antonio crossed the river, was a strong *tête-de-pont,* a fortified bridgehead. Behind both the convent and the *tête-de-pont* was the river itself, straight, deep, and wide, with its banks artificially raised to prevent flooding, thus affording more good cover for troops. General Manuel Rincon, with 3,000 men, was under orders to hold out at Churubusco as long as possible.[10]

San Antonio had been Hancock's baptism of fire, aside from the skirmishing on the road to Puebla, but that had been nothing compared with the hard fighting of the afternoon at Churubusco. The Mexican defenders fought with fierce desperation, and they hurled back charge after charge of the Americans. Hancock was heavily engaged in the fray, sustaining a minor wound, which was hardly noticed in the clamor of combat. He was with a portion of the Sixth Infantry which worked its way around behind the *tête-de-pont,* crossed through a deep, wet ditch, and carried the strongpoint with a bayonet charge, just as some of Worth's other units forced their way over the parapet with hand-to-hand fighting. The fall of the *tête-de-pont* effectively sealed the fate of Rincon's force, for American artillery placed there tore up the convent and brought about surrender. Churubusco was Scott's, and the road to Mexico City was open to his army. Hancock received a brevet promotion to first lieutenant "for gallant and meritorious conduct" at Churubusco.[11]

A few days later, while the army enjoyed an ill-advised armistice which Scott had entered into with Santa Anna, Hancock wrote home to his father, telling him that "we have had to fight desperately to get here. It has been the theatre of a sanguinary battle." There were, it might be noted, no regrets; Winfield Scott Hancock enjoyed a good fight.[12]

On September 7 Scott brought the armistice to a close. The peace negotiations never really accomplished anything. It finally became clear to him that the armistice was being used mainly for Santa Anna to rebuild his army and the defenses of his capital. The Americans would have to fight their way into Mexico City.

Scott ordered Worth to attack and to clear out a series of large stone buildings, called the Molino del Rey, about 1,100 yards west of the great rock and castle of Chapultepec. Five hundred yards farther west was another fortified stone building, the Casa Mata, with the Mexican line extending there from the Molino. Worth, with some 3,700 men, attacked at dawn and isolated the enemy force in the two building complexes, although he had to withstand several ferocious attacks down the hill from Chapultepec. Clarke's brigade attacked the Casa Mata, while the balance of the division fought at the Molino. After some two hours of fierce hand-to-hand combat and the loss of one-fourth of his command, Worth took the position. Clarke's brigade lost half of its officers and close to one-third of its men; Lieutenant Hancock wound up in command of his company. Again, in this fiery struggle, Hancock distinguished himself as a natural fighter.[13]

The final move against Chapultepec was not made until September 13. Hancock, lying sick in his tent with chills and fever, missed the fight. "I shall always be sorry that I was absent," he wrote to Hilary. Once he heard the sounds of battle, though, nothing could keep him in his tent. "Wrapping my blanket around me," he wrote, "I crept to the top of the roof of the nearest house, watched the fight, and had strength enough to cheer with the boys when the castle fell." Winfield was particularly thrilled to see the colors of his own Sixth Infantry hoisted over the captured castle; "my heart beat quick at the glorious sight."[14]

With the fall of Chapultepec and the subsequent forcing of the gates of the city, the conquest of Mexico City was complete. Hancock was back on his feet when the army marched into the ancient city of Montezuma, but there was to be no more fighting in the Valley of Mexico and little more in the rest of the country. Scott's army was to remain in Mexico for nine more months while the politicians and diplomats tried to work out a means of concluding the war.

In the meantime, of course, the American army had no alternative to settling in for garrison duty. First Lieutenant Lewis A. Armistead, a Virginian, had been named to the command of Hancock's company, in place of the severely wounded Captain W. H. T. Walker. Armistead, who had led the impetuous pursuit that began the battle of Churubusco, was a kindred spirit with Hancock and became a very dear friend. Among the other officers in the regiment with whom Winfield became close were First Lieutenant Edward Johnson, another Virginian, and Hancock's West Point classmate, Simon Bolivar Buckner of Kentucky. Shortly after Mexico City was taken, a new second lieutenant, fresh from the military academy, joined the regiment. This was Henry Heth, also a Virginian and a kinsman of Armistead. Harry Heth had missed the fighting, but he was determined to savor life in Mexico to the fullest. And he found a willing accomplice in Winfield Hancock. "Armistead, Hancock and I were messmates," Heth said, "and never was a mess happier than ours."[15]

Heth, not quite so well favored by nature as was the tall and handsome Pennsylvanian, soon learned to stick close to Hancock to share in the available social action. "Hancock," Heth said, "was then a magnificent specimen of youthful beauty, as he afterwards was of manly looks. He was tall, graceful, a blonde, with light hair, the style of all others that at once captivated the Mexican girls." The two officers were frequently invited to entertainments given by the senoritas of Mexico City; Heth admitted, "I owed my invitations to Hancock with whom these senoritas were in love." After paying their respects to the hostess, Heth explained, they were free to pick out the young ladies they preferred. "We only knew a few words of Spanish, they less of English," he said, but this lack hardly seemed a barrier to Hancock's conquest of the young lovelies of Mexico.[16]

Hancock, of course, was writing home about the wonders of Mexico, of the "most beautiful and very fertile" valley of Toluca, of the magnificence of the Almada, and of the astonishing "variety of fruits produced here," over fifty different kinds at one market. "Think of opening a fine, fresh, ripe watermelon, in the month of January." He neglected to mention his amorous adventures in his letters, but Heth took great delight in recording them.[17]

A couple of months after the fighting closed, Clarke was ordered with 2,000 men to Cuernavaca, some sixty miles south of Mexico City, to assist in the collection of taxes. Hancock by this time was the acting regimental quartermaster, and he shared a mess at Cuernavaca with Colonel Clarke, Heth, and the regimental adjutant. One day Clarke and his staff were invited to breakfast at a large plantation formerly owned, it was said, by Cortez himself. Their host, the duke of Monte Leon, served them a sumptuous meal, its many courses washed down with fine wines and champagne. Though the ladies of the place did not appear at breakfast, Hancock and Heth spotted one beauty, the daughter of their host. After breakfast the two young officers walked in the garden and sighted again the lovely girl they had seen earlier.

"Now is your chance, old fellow," Heth said. "Pluck a rose and go for her. I will remain here, gather flowers and watch; if her duenna comes I will be seized with a coughing spell. You must do a heap of lovemaking in a short time for you may never have such a chance again."

"I will," Hancock responded, and off he went. Heth watched him make a deep bow, present his rose, and take the girl's hand.

The rest of the story Hancock told Heth back in Cuernavaca. "When I took her hand, I squeezed it just a little, and she returned it," he related. "I said, 'Usted as me amante;' she said, 'Lieutenant, I speak English, and my father is going to take me to England to finish my English education.' "[18] Hancock saw his chance: "I told her pure English was only spoken in America, to come to America, complete her education there, and we would be married." She said she would persuade her father to change his plans. "Heth, I looked and your back was turned towards us; I kissed her and told her that I had never loved before."

Heth said: "How could you have told such a story? I know you have said the same thing to half a dozen girls in the city of Mexico and God knows how many in the States."

Winfield's father would have been proud of his son's legalistic answer: "We are at war with Mexico, peace has not yet been made, and you know all is fair in love and war." He then said that an assignation had been made for the day after next.

Snorted Heth: "That Spanish beauty was in love with Hancock the moment she saw him." He asked his friend: "What is her name—did she tell you?" "Yes," Hancock said, "she gave me her card; Isabella Garcia is her name; Isabella is a beautiful name, don't you think so?"

Heth reported no more about Hancock's conquest, if such it was, of Isabella Garcia, and of course Hancock himself did not mention it. But it was clear that the two young subalterns were making garrison duty less onerous than it might have been.[19]

Finally, the Treaty of Guadalupe Hidalgo was signed and eventually ratified, restoring peace between the two countries. Preparatory to leaving Mexico, the army moved back toward the coast. It camped in the hills around Jalapa until the transports were ready. Here, while they waited for transportation for the Sixth Infantry, Hancock, Armistead, and Heth reestablished their old mess. They got along very well, though Hancock and Heth tended to tease the older officer. On June 30, 1848, Clarke made official his provisional appointment of Hancock as regimental quartermaster.[20]

In his new eminence, Hancock got himself into some trouble when the orders came to move out from Jalapa to the boats at Vera Cruz. The soldiers of the Second Dragoons, who had many close friendships with the Sixth Infantry, were camped along the road out of Jalapa. They mixed up buckets of juleps, which they placed on tables along the roadside for their buddies in the Sixth. When one bucket disappeared, it was speedily replaced by a full one. "In short," as Harry Heth wrote, "all got more or less under the influence of julep." And the road, as might be expected, quickly became congested in front of the dragoons, with traffic hopelessly snarled.

Lieutenant Colonel Gustavus Loomis, newly arrived to command the Sixth Infantry, came along, saw the jumble, mainly of Hancock's quartermaster wagons, and became very angry. In the presence of some officers of the regiment he exclaimed: "This is all Hancock's fault; if he had attended to his duty, this blockage would not have occurred; he has *shamefully* neglected his duty."

Hancock, hearing of this outburst, corralled Heth and dragged him off for a confrontation with Loomis, whom they found in his tent, reading his Bible. Heth did not realize just how much of the dragoons' whiskey Hancock had consumed.

Hancock said: "Colonel Loomis, you said today in the presence of several officers that I had shamefully neglected my duty. Now, sir, by———I will not permit anyone to say I neglected my duty."

Loomis replied: "Don't swear in my presence, young man"; to which the irate young lieutenant sputtered: "I will be God damned if I don't swear."

Loomis put an end to the interview: "Go to your tent, sir, under arrest." Heth took his friend back to his tent and put him to bed, where he soon fell fast asleep.

The next morning Heth related what had happened, and Hancock realized an apology was urgently needed. When Loomis said he would accept Hancock's apology, it was quickly made and the incident ended.[21]

Chastened and with, no doubt, an aching head, Winfield Scott Hancock moved onto the transport at Vera Cruz that would take him and the Sixth Regiment to New Orleans. His less than glorious departure, however, could not obscure the fine record he had made in Mexico.

FOUR

Between Two Wars

The excitement, the strangeness, the danger of fighting and loving in Mexico was over. The Sixth Infantry shipped out for New Orleans, arrived there without incident, and then moved upriver by steamer to Jefferson Barracks, south of St. Louis. Soon the Seventh and Eighth infantry regiments joined it there.

Everyone knew that in a very short time the regiments would be split up and scattered over the western frontier, their brief existence as actual units ended except on paper in the War Department. A company here, a company there, and the thrill of fighting a real war would fade, living only in memories of the battles with Santa Anna's force. In the meantime, however, each of the regiments gave a ball for its officers and the ladies of St. Louis, a final fling before the deadening routine of the peacetime army fastened its grip again.

Hancock, as acting regimental quartermaster, had to spend a lot of time in St. Louis, making arrangements for the ball. Harry Heth recalled that Hancock would say to him, "Heth, get permission from old Loomis, and let us go to St. Louis and make some calls." The colonel usually gave Heth a difficult time but eventually relented. The two young officers maintained as active a social life in St. Louis as they had had in Mexico, though Heth, when he fell in love with a young beauty in the city, had to scheme for ways to see her alone—without Hancock. "I knew," Heth said, "if Hancock accompanied me, my cake would be all dough; she would never look at me."[1]

Eventually, of course, the regimental balls came and went, and the time came for the Sixth Infantry to move north. With a portion of the regiment shipping out on a Saturday afternoon, the headquarters contingent remained in St. Louis for the night to take on supplies. Heth cooked up a plan to take the regimental band into town "to serenade our sweethearts." When Colonel Loomis understandably refused permission, Heth persisted until Loomis yielded on the condition that Hancock had to be with the party. Since Hancock was included from the beginning, of course, Heth got his band, and all the young officers still in town spent the evening marching around with the band, serenading young ladies. They were about to return to quarters when a localite who had attached himself to the party told them that a young lady, "the most beautiful girl in the west," had just returned home after spending the summer in the East. Would not Heth have the band play her just one tune? The band was marched over to the young lady's home, appropriate music was played, and, according to Heth, "the window shutters . . . were slightly opened and something white was thrown out." Heth picked up the object, a kid glove, and handed it to Hancock. The name of the young lady was Almira Russell.[2]

Winfield had no more time for romance at that point. The Sixth Infantry moved up the Mississippi to Fort Crawford, at Prairie du Chien, Wisconsin, with Hancock as regimental quartermaster. Hardly had he had time to take up his duties, however, when Harry Heth reentered his life. Heth had been assigned to Fort Atkinson in Iowa, but a serious case of dysentery, which he had contracted in Mexico, flared up. He was transferred to Crawford, with its better medical facilities, but the doctors soon despaired of his life. They decided to send him home to Richmond to die. Because Heth was too weak to travel alone, Hancock volunteered to accompany him. The two young officers traveled down the Mississippi and up the Ohio to Cincinnati. Heth's condition improved, and Hancock saw to some urgent business in Covington, Kentucky; a young lady in Covington apparently had expectations of marriage with Winfield Hancock, and things had to be straightened out. In a couple of days, Hancock "had adjusted matters to his satisfaction . . . he and the lady were to be friends for life, nothing more."[3]

In Cleveland (hardly on a direct line from Cincinnati to Richmond, it will be noted), Heth suffered a bad setback; "but from prompt attention given me by Hancock I believe I should have died." When the Virginian was strong enough to travel, the two wayfarers left Cleveland and headed for New York City. On the night of May 10, 1849, with three other Sixth Infantry officers, they went to the Astor Opera House to see the noted English actor William C. McCready. They hardly suspected what they were getting into. The year before, in London, the American actor Edwin Forrest had been given a poor reception, which Forrest's friends attributed to the jealousy of McCready. Accordingly, upon McCready's appearance in New York, there was a riot outside the theater, and twenty-two persons were killed before order was restored. Hancock, Heth, and their colleagues became separated, had a good fright, but managed to get away unscathed.[4]

The next morning, somewhat shaken from the episode at the opera house, Hancock suggested a call to pay their respects to General Scott at his headquarters in the city. They made the visit, and as they were leaving the general told them he wished them to dine with him that evening. The two young men had plans to meet a couple of young ladies that night, but Scott's invitation was a virtual command. He served them shad and potatoes—"the finest potatoes in the United States," he told them, "sent to me by a friend residing in New Jersey where they are raised." Scott considered himself a gourmet; Hancock, on the other hand, never knew, said Heth, "when satisfying his hunger, whether he was eating fish, flesh or fowl." When Hancock was served his portion of the marvelous potatoes, he began to mash them with his fork. Scott, aghast, exclaimed: "My God, my young friend, do you mash your potatoes? You can't tell the taste of a potato when mashed." Hancock, abashed, replied, "I like my potatoes mashed." Heth, however, watched to see how the general manipulated his potato and imitated him. Scott noticed and commented approvingly. "Yes, General," Heth answered, "I cannot tell the taste of a potato when mashed." Hancock shot him a murderous glance.

After dinner Scott announced that they would play whist. The two young officers, while adept at draw poker, knew little about whist, but Heth assured the general that Hancock played a beautiful game. With the cards running heavily in his favor, Hancock managed to win four straight games, while Scott became very angry and berated Hancock for knowing nothing about whist. Eventually the luck of the cards changed, Scott started winning, and he became affable again. Finally, the game and the visit ended, though it was far too late to make the planned visit on the ladies. Outside, Hancock spluttered in impotent rage at his friend while Heth laughed merrily. For thirty years, he later said, he never failed to tell the potato story on Hancock.[5]

From New York, Hancock escorted Heth to Philadelphia and Washington. Heth, much better, went on from the capital to Richmond alone, and Hancock returned to Fort Crawford.[6]

Later in the year, regimental headquarters were transferred back to St. Louis, and Hancock had the opportunity to meet the young lady of the white kid glove. Major Don Carlos Buell, a West Point friend, introduced Hancock to Almira Russell, a golden-haired beauty who was the daughter of a prominent merchant named Samuel Russell. The young officer wasted little time in wooing Miss Russell, and on January 24, 1850, they were married. Almira was eighteen and Winfield seven years her senior when they said their vows, at her father's residence, before the Reverend William Greenleaf Eliot, eminent Congregational divine and founder of Washington University in St. Louis. Although violent weather marked the day of the wedding, with hail, wind, lightning, and thunder, and three times all the lights in the house were extinguished, the ceremony was carried off with solemn dignity. Buell, Orlando Willcox, and Anderson D. Nelson stood for Hancock, and General and Mrs. William Harney gave a reception for the bridal couple, "as handsome a pair as can be imagined," as Willcox said.[7]

William Hyde, a prominent resident of St. Louis, recalled Almira Russell Hancock:

> A woman of fine physique and striking comeliness of face, an accomplished musician, sparkling in conversation, ready with gems of repartee, and boun-teously endowed with a kind and generous nature, she was universally admired and beloved.[8]

Harry Heth was on convalescent leave in Richmond when Hancock got married, so that he was unable to accept an invitation to be one of his friend's groomsmen. Heth came back to Jefferson Barracks in 1852, and he found Hancock a changed man. No more would he accompany the likes of Heth on nocturnal escapades; Winfield Scott Hancock was happily married and thoroughly domesticated, a one-woman man for the rest of his days. His marriage to Allie Russell prospered through the stresses of travel, separation, and military life, and she proved to be a strong support for her soldier-husband. On October 29, 1850, in St. Louis, Allie gave birth to their first child, a boy, who was given the family name, Russell.

Since October 1, 1849, Hancock had been regimental adjutant and aide-de-camp to General Newman S. Clarke, the Sixth Infantry commander. In 1851 Clarke transferred his headquarters from the city to Jefferson Barracks, with the Hancocks necessarily following along. Once there, the young couple found the quarters assigned them to be dilapidated, with no hinges or keys for the doors. Lieutenant Hancock sought help from the post commander, Colonel Braxton Bragg, a man notable for his surly disposition and lack of tact. Bragg said that since the previous occupant, a major, had considered the quarters habitable, he saw no reason why a second lieutenant could not occupy them as they were. This response precipitated a lively correspondence on the part of Hancock, halted only when Clarke interceded on his behalf, thereby diverting Bragg's wrath.[9]

After their quarters were fixed up, Allie later wrote, "our garrison life at the barracks was generally quiet and uneventful." An exception was a cholera epidemic which took the lives of many men in the garrison, with few of those entering the post hospital leaving it alive. Hancock prepared and kept in his quarters some kind of "cholera specific," which seemed to work if applied early enough. The result was that the Hancocks were besieged by sufferers who begged that they not be sent to the hospital but be ministered to with the adjutant's medicine.[10]

A letter Hancock wrote to his clothier in Boston in early 1852 describes him at the time as six feet and one-half inch in height, weighing 169 pounds, with a hat size of 7⅛. Finally promoted to first lieutenant at the start of 1853, he was concerned about the chances of moving up to captain, to the point where an inquiry from his old traveling companion in Mexico, Franklin Pierce, now president of the United States, led Hancock to write to Pierce asking for a commission in one of the new regiments being organized. Nothing came of this overture, nor of Hancock's candidacies for promotion in the Adjutant-General's and the Subsistence departments.[11]

In 1855, when Harry Heth, then at Fort Leavenworth, received a letter notifying him of his promotion to captain in the newly organized Tenth Infantry, his first reaction was that it was a hoax perpetrated by Hancock. Alas, it was all too true; Heth got his promotion while Hancock, with his seniority and fine record in Mexico, stayed a lieutenant. Heth, who visited the Hancocks at Jefferson Barracks, wrote of Winfield's being "much disappointed at not being promoted," and Allie remembered "how severe was the wound to his professional pride." Still, Hancock took the trouble to write letters of congratulations to his brother officers who had received the promotions he thought he deserved.[12]

Hancock had another run-in with a superior officer early in 1855 when the Sixth Infantry was ordered to Leavenworth for an expedition against the Sioux, to be led by General William Harney. Clarke, disappointed at having his regiment ordered away without him, was soon directed to remove his headquarters to St. Louis, leaving Colonel Edwin V. Sumner in charge at Jefferson Barracks. Sumner, a veteran known in the army as "Old Bull," from his loud voice and blunt manner, remarked one day, in the presence of a number of officers, that Clarke's and Hancock's quarters were available to any officer who wished to claim them. Hancock, always sensitive to slights and particularly sore at being bypassed for promotion, fired off a letter to Sumner the same day, complaining of the latter's breach of "military courtesy and propriety." Hancock wrote: "I have rights here, and one of them is the privilege of occupying quarters so long as I am on duty." He asserted that Sumner's right to quarters at the post was no greater than his and Clarke's, and then concluded: "I will not run the risk of subjecting myself or family to further indelicate treatment by remaining here, but I have sufficient manliness to let you know that I resent it." Clarke once again intervened and took the heat of Sumner's ire against his touchy adjutant; "after a short time," Mrs. Hancock said, "the friendly intercourse between Colonel Sumner and my husband was resumed." Still, one wonders about the effect on Hancock's career of these epistolary flare-ups against high-ranking officers. Sumner was the kind of man who could forgive and forget, but Bragg, as we know from his ill-starred career in the Confederate army, was hardly likely to overlook the quarrel Hancock had with him. It is possible that the well-connected Braxton Bragg may have had something to do with Hancock's being ignored when the four newly created infantry regiments were staffed in 1854 and 1855.[13]

Hancock moved back to St. Louis with Clarke on June 19, 1855, to serve as assistant adjutant-general for the Department of the West, a position he held until that November. On November 5, he was appointed a captain in the Quartermaster's Department, which he accepted since the expected promotion in the Adjutant-General's Department never came through. "The disappointment was great," Allie said, "as he very much disliked quartermaster duties." But he could not afford to decline a promotion.[14]

Though Winfield Hancock did not want to be a quartermaster, the Quartermaster's Department wanted him. He already had in that small and close-knit army "a wide reputation for his mastery of army business and his knowledge of the regulations." Too, most of those who encountered Hancock remarked on his "generous and genial nature." So a quartermaster he became, ordered to Florida in February 1856.[15]

Winfield, Allie, and young Russell duly departed for Fort Myers, on the Caloosahatchee River in Florida, not knowing until they arrived that hostilities were shortly to begin with the Seminole Indians. This, called the Billy Bow-legs Campaign, was actually the third effort of the United States Army to subdue and remove the Seminoles. Fort Myers was the base for the army's operations in the swamps of southern Florida. It was tough country in which to campaign, and it was a tough job for a quartermaster. Hancock's prior service had been as a garrison quartermaster; the supplying of troops in the field, and such a field, was a far more arduous task. The commanders, first Colonel John Munroe and then Harney, were most concerned about their supply situation. But Hancock handled the job with apparent ease, with complete competence, and with entire satisfaction to those in authority.[16]

The assignment to Fort Myers was not a comfortable one, and Allie found herself the only woman on the post. Mail and supplies came down the coast by sailboat from Tampa once a week, provided the wind cooperated. Hancock tried to have a cow shipped from Tampa, to supply fresh milk for his family, but the cow failed to survive the first three efforts; only on a fourth try did Hancock's cow make it. Walks or rides away from their home were forbidden because of the danger of hostile Indians; when they went boating on the river, Allie and Russell were compelled to lie in the bottom of the boat covered with a heavy rubber blanket if Indians were spotted on the shore. Still, the Hancock home quickly became a cherished rendezvous for the officers in Florida. "A perfect oasis in the desert to the rest of us," Orlando Willcox called it, "and the liberal hospitality and genial cordiality of Captain and Mrs. Hancock shed a glow of sunshine over our precious visits."[17]

On February 24, 1857, the Hancocks' second child was born, a lovely little girl to whom they gave the name Ada. She bore the distinction of being the first white child known to be born in Fort Myers, Florida. Ada was a child with whom her father always had a very special relationship.[18]

With some degree of success achieved in Florida, the army ordered Harney to Fort Leavenworth, to help keep the lid on the disorders in "Bleeding Kansas." Harney specifically requested Hancock, who was happy "to turn his back upon the discomforts and unrestful life which had been ours, during fifteen months of toil and anxious watchfulness. . . ." Hancock and his family were in Kansas for about nine months, long enough to experience the bitterness and inflamed feelings the slavery issue had brought to that frontier.[19]

During the last few months at Fort Leavenworth, Hancock helped to prepare the military expedition which President James Buchanan was sending forth to chastise Brigham Young and his contumacious Mormons in Utah. The Latter-Day Saints refused to recognize the authority of the non-Mormon governor whom Buchanan had sent to Utah; late in 1857 the president sent General Albert Sidney Johnston with a force of 1,500 men to bring Young and his people into line. Johnston's expedition bogged down in winter weather, and reinforcements, under Harney, were sent to him in the spring. The expedition marched out in mid-May 1858. Hancock was quartermaster, with responsibility for a train of 128 wagons, 5 ambulances, and 1,000 mules. The first night out, having trouble sleeping in a tent after so long a time of sleeping in a marital bed, he wrote in his journal: "I now feel sad enough. We are *en route,* indeed, and I am finally separated from my wife and children, and yet I feel that our expedition will probably result in nothing, and we will return this fall."[20]

Captain Hancock's prediction was partly right and partly wrong. The government patched up a peaceful settlement with Brigham Young, and when Johnston's force reached Salt Lake City, on June 26, 1858, it simply marched through the town and out again, going into bivouac at Camp Floyd. Hancock erred, however, in thinking he was to return to Kansas. He was ordered to turn over the property in his charge to his successor and to report to Fort Bridger, in the southwestern corner of what is now Wyoming. At Bridger he found his entire regiment, the Sixth Infantry, united for one of its rare occasions, preparing to move west. Originally headed for Oregon, it had been ordered to California. Hancock resumed the duties of regimental quartermaster and set to work organizing the expedition. Provisioning such a march from the meager supplies at remote Bridger was a far more difficult task than doing it at Leavenworth; on top of that, the wagons were broken down and the draft animals half-starved from the journey already accomplished. Nevertheless, Hancock managed to conjure up from somewhere the things that were needed, and by August 21 the column was in motion. Hancock and the Sixth had one major piece of good fortune: though starting late in the season, they managed to cross the formidable ranges of the Sierra Nevada without encountering heavy snowstorms.[21]

Winfield even had time to attend a party given by the "vigilante" faction of residents in the Carson River Valley in Nevada; he danced a quadrille with one of the local matrons. The next night, other officers of the regiment attended a ball given by the "anti-vigilantes." The army wanted to demonstrate its impartiality and, incidentally, get a brief respite before it tackled the mountains. When the regiment arrived on November 15 at its destination, Benicia, California, the former state capital on the Carquinez Strait northeast of San Francisco, the troops and trains were said to be in better condition than when they had started the 1,119-mile journey. Hancock presented to the quartermaster-general a report filled with well-ordered information on the country traversed, with notations on practicable routes of travel, availability of water and grass, and distances from place to place. All in all, the conduct of the march and the comprehensive report reflected much credit on Hancock, and it was so noted in the upper echelons of the army.[22]

As soon as he arrived at Benicia, Hancock obtained a leave of absence so that he could go back east and bring his family out to California. He crossed the Isthmus of Tehuantepec, in southern Mexico, and sailed for the East Coast, where Allie was awaiting him in Washington. When she hesitated at the idea of going to California, Colonel Robert E. Lee took her aside and told her that her "post" was "by your husband's side." Lee warned her that it was often fatal to the future happiness of young married couples "upon small provocation, to live apart," because then "they cease to be essential to each other." Allie took Lee's advice and agreed to make the trip.[23]

In the meantime, however, the handsome young couple enjoyed several weeks of the Washington social whirl. With the Democrats in power, of course, those close to the administration, with its strong southern bias, dominated the scene, both politically and socially. Hancock, with his own sympathies for the South and the Democratic party, found this a congenial situation. Among those with whom the Hancocks mingled were Miss Harriet Lane, the president's sister and hostess, Senator and Mrs. Jefferson Davis, and Colonel and Mrs. Joseph E. Johnston. "Our happiness that winter was complete," Allie recalled, "and we left Washington with sincere regret and the most agreeable impressions."[24]

On April 4, 1859, the young family left New York City on the long trip back to California. The journey was a nightmare. They sailed in an overcrowded steamer to the Isthmus of Panama, were detained at the Chagres River during the transit of the isthmus in one-hundred-degree heat with no water for fourteen hours, and were plagued with rumors that all the passengers on a preceding steamer had been massacred by the natives. "We found the guards very insolent and unbearable," Allie said, "but the gentlemen were fully armed and prepared for an assault." Once on the Pacific side of the isthmus, they sailed on the *Golden Gate,* which was dangerously overcrowded, with the steerage passengers marauding over the whole boat. When a group of them molested eight-year-old Russell, Hancock drove them off with his bare hands and stated that he would kill any man who approached him or touched his child. No one called him on the threat, and the rest of the voyage passed in comparative calm.[25]

On May 23 Winfield, Allie, Russell, and Ada arrived in San Francisco. Instead of moving to Benicia, however, they found orders awaiting them directing Captain Hancock to travel to Los Angeles. They boarded a coastal steamer, the *Senator,* which was ready to sail that afternoon.

FIVE

In California

Hancock arrived on the West Coast to find that he had been appointed chief quartermaster for the southern district of California, with his headquarters at Los Angeles. He and his family steamed south for thirty-six hours, then anchored three miles off the coast at San Pedro to await a smaller vessel, which carried them to shore. Following a wild coach ride of eighteen miles, they reached the small town of Los Angeles.[1]

As a duty post, Los Angeles had both good and bad points. The town had about four thousand residents, all but a dozen or so Spanish-speaking. The main street was lined with adobe houses, but there were not many of them. The town was, as Allie said, "too small to attract or sustain public amusements of any kind," since she did not include gambling halls and saloons in her definition of the term. Sometimes Allie and a lady friend organized a drive to the seashore, but it was that same eighteen miles away, and the coachman carried a shotgun to frighten off coyotes. The Spanish inhabitants disapproved of the establishment of a Protestant church, but a retired minister from Philadelphia who had come west for his health held Sunday morning services in his home for his tiny flock. From San Francisco came a small organ, which Allie played during the services. On the other hand, the climate was delightful, and the town was in a setting of great beauty, with hills and valleys, the fertile fields of vast ranches, and the snow-capped mountains in the distance.[2]

Ada had picked up a dangerous fever during the transit of Panama, and she suffered from this for six weeks. Allie, too, became ill, probably from the fatigue and strain of the long journey. The Hancocks were to find, however, that the illnesses brought them new friends, as their neighbors came around to help and to care for them through those difficult early days.

Once his family's health was restored, Hancock settled into the routine of his job. From his quartermaster's office on Main Street near Third, he had charge of all government property in southern California and at Yuma, in the Arizona Territory. He bought whatever the army needed and sold that which was no longer of use. He had the opportunity as well to make acquaintances among the local residents. It was the first time since he had left for West Point nineteen years earlier that he found himself in a predominantly civilian setting; to this time almost all of his friends were fellow army officers. In Los Angeles he broadened his horizons and, with his naturally gregarious disposition, developed an interesting circle of friends, men who included him freely in their plans and projects. These were men, the leaders of the American community, with the vision to take the steps needed to set southern California on the road to its future prosperity.

One of the closest friendships Hancock formed was with Joseph Lancaster Brent, a lawyer from Louisiana. Brent had arrived in California in 1850, aiming to make his fortune in the practice of law, not in the hunt for gold. When he became ill, his doctor told him to leave San Francisco and to go to Los Angeles. He did so and quickly recovered his health. Though he was at first "rather disappointed in the quiet aspect of the place," Brent persevered. He made friends among the Californians, the Spanish-speaking people who were there long before the Americans started arriving, and these friendships formed the basis of a lucrative practice. He also became the Democratic political leader of southern California, because the Californians chose to vote in a bloc for the candidates he selected. Brent served on a couple of occasions in the state legislature, but for the most part he preferred to wield his influence behind the scenes. During the Civil War he returned east and secured a commission in the Confederate army, eventually rising to the rank of general. After the war Brent spent several years in Baltimore before returning to settle in Louisiana.[3]

Another friend was Benjamin D. Wilson, a Tennessean who had made his way west originally as a fur trapper. He prospered in Sante Fe and then moved on to California, where he acquired a vineyard and a ranch near San Bernardino, the first properties in what became a huge landholding. Though largely uneducated, Wilson acquired great political influence and served as mayor of Los Angeles in 1851 and later as a state senator. Affectionately called "Don Benito" by the Californians, he amassed a fortune from viniculture, citrus fruits, and sheep, and was a leader in attracting railroads to the area.[4]

Phineas Banning was an ambitious and hard-driving young man from Delaware who had arrived in Los Angeles in 1851. Sizing up the area, he determined that a port would be essential for the land-locked city, and he set to work to develop one. With the aid of Benjamin Wilson, Banning created a port on San Pedro Bay, at the two towns of San Pedro and Wilmington, which he named after his native city. He then organized stage and rail lines between the port and Los Angeles. He became a close friend of the Hancocks and named a son Hancock in Winfield's honor. Many years later, in 1880, Banning, by then a leader of the Republican party, deserted his party to lead the effort which swung California's electoral votes to his old friend.[5]

Other close friends included Henry Hancock, no relation but a lawyer and surveyor who had come from New England in 1849 and accumulated large holdings of land and a sizable fortune; Matthew Keller; and Judge Isaac K. S. Ogier.[6]

Had Winfield Hancock chosen to resign from the army while in California, there is little doubt that he could, with the connections he quickly acquired, have made himself wealthy there. (Ironically, he could probably have done so and *still* have secured a high commission when the war started.) But there is no evidence that he ever even considered such a step. From the day he set foot on the plain at West Point, Hancock was an army man, and he rarely gave thought to any other possible way of life. He was not a man of great and daring imagination, and his mind did not run to the "might-have-been" or "could-be" of a career outside the army. Change was not particularly appealing to Hancock; he knew what he had in the army. He had security, and he could provide adequately, though certainly not luxuriously, for his family. Hancock stuck to what he knew, worked hard at his profession, and trusted that his merits would ultimately be recognized in the military. Besides, he had savored in Mexico the joy of combat; the prospect of encountering it again in the future helped to keep him in the army.

Hancock and Brent became close. "I got to know him very well indeed," Brent said, "and to like him very much. His wife was with him and she was a charming woman, and I became a friend of his household." Brent included Hancock in several business deals which held some promise, though nothing much ultimately came to them. About five miles out of town there was "a large spring, of what the Californians called Brea, and which in English is asphalt." Brent thought it could be of value, and it was thought to be in the public domain. He convinced Hancock to join with Wilson, Keller, Banning, and a few others to form a venture which obtained school land warrants from the state for some 640 acres and located these warrants upon the asphalt spring and its environs.

During the Civil War, after word of the discovery of petroleum at Titusville, Pennsylvania, had filtered west, the group was reorganized into the Pioneer Oil Company, with Banning as president and with Wilson, Keller, and Hancock among the trustees, or directors. It bought land for oil drilling in the area of present-day Pasadena and the San Fernando Valley. Unfortunately for Hancock, he was associated with one of the few unsuccessful ventures that Banning and Wilson were involved in. Eventually a court decision restored title to the asphalt spring to the original Spanish settlers, and the other efforts of the Pioneer Oil Company were, on balance, unprofitable.[7]

Another company was formed by Hancock, Wilson, Keller, and Judge Ogier for the purchase of land on the Rio del Llano. Again, there is no evidence that anything came of this venture except more losses, although from New York during the 1870s Hancock was still trying to track down his title deeds.[8]

Among the things which Brent said drew him and Hancock together were "the identical views we held upon the slavery question." This question, of course, was forced more and more to the fore as the election year of 1860 developed—the slavery question and the even more crucial one of union and secession. As a young officer trying to make his way in the army, Hancock had been relatively passive regarding the political issues which were agitating the country. Now, however, living in a civilian community, with friends who were political activists, he became alarmed as the very real crisis of the Union approached. Hancock, a good Democrat who believed the Federal government had no right to interfere in a domestic institution such as slavery, was much concerned about the possible victory of a sectional party such as the Republicans. "The situation," he felt, "was pregnant with danger in the event of Mr. Lincoln's success," an opinion "which he did not hesitate to express." That success, he realized, became all the more likely as the Democratic party fragmented in its two 1860 conventions. All he could do about it, though, was what he did—vote for the Breckinridge electors and wait for the news of the election to work its way out to California.[9]

Back east, of course, it was quickly recognized that Abraham Lincoln had been elected. Not long after, the states of the Deep South, led by South Carolina, began enacting their ordinances of secession. The Union was crumbling, and saddened men and women, north and south, watched to see if the dissolution would lead to war. When forces under General Pierre G. T. Beauregard fired on and captured Fort Sumter in Charleston Harbor, the question was decided.

In California, of course, at the end of a lengthy and very tenuous line of communication from "the States," news of what was happening in Washington and South Carolina and Maryland and Virginia was very long in coming. But interest in the events back east was keen. The greater part of the Americans in southern California was probably in sympathy with the southern cause, as most of the immigration to Los Angeles, San Bernardino, and the other lower counties had come from slave states. The most influential newspaper in the area was the *Los Angeles Star*, whose editor, Henry Hamilton, was an ardent secessionist who urged the southern counties to secede from the rest of the state and to seek admission to the Confederacy. As early as autumn 1860, disunion sentiment appeared, in the form of flying the "Bear Flag," the symbol in California of rebellion and independence. In addition, the governor told the legislature in 1860 that California would set itself up as an independent republic in the event of a split, and two western senators, William M. Gwin of California and Joseph Lane of Oregon, advocated a Pacific Republic stretching from Canada to Mexico.[10]

News of the firing on Sumter reached San Francisco by Pony Express on April 24, 1861. General Edwin V. Sumner arrived on the same day with orders to replace General Albert Sidney Johnston as commander of Federal troops in California. Johnston, though he had forwarded his resignation from the army when his adopted state of Texas seceded, had continued to serve with fidelity, and he was deeply hurt by the secretive way in which the government sent Sumner to supersede him. What Johnston did not realize was that he paid the price for certain other southern officers, most notably General David Twiggs in Texas, who first surrendered their commands to the Confederates and then themselves joined the southern cause.[11]

On April 29 Sumner decided that steps must be taken in regard to Los Angeles, where Hancock was almost literally holding the fort by himself. Sumner worried about "a number of influential men . . . who are decided secessionists" in Los Angeles; presumably he did not know that many of them were friends of Captain Hancock. Feeling that there was "more danger of disaffection at this place than any other in the state," Sumner ordered that Fort Mojave on the Colorado River be abandoned and that its garrison and material be moved to Los Angeles. Hancock was directed to send a train to Mojave to bring in the equipment there and at the same time to select an appropriate campsite for the troops coming in, a site which was as near to the town as possible and which afforded "perfect protection" to Hancock's supply depot.[12]

Several days later, on May 3, Sumner directed Major James H. Carleton, commanding at Fort Tejon, northwest of Los Angeles, to leave that post and to march his dragoons to the camp Hancock was establishing. The next day Hancock advised Sumner that he was in the process of carrying out his orders; he further reassured the harried general that "if there is trouble here I will be able to defend the public property with the supporters of the Federal Government to be had on my call from among the citizens of Los Angeles."[13]

By May 7 Hancock was able to advise San Francisco that his encampment site had been established, and he detailed the advantages of the spot selected. He reported that the "Bear Flag" had been paraded with a mounted escort through the streets of El Monte, twelve miles to the east, a couple of days earlier but that, despite rumors, it had not yet made its appearance in Los Angeles. He felt that the pro-secession political leaders did not want force used because, as he said, "they are men of property." Still, the sooner troops arrived, the better; Sunday, May 12, was rumored as the day for trouble to start.[14]

By May 11 Hancock was anxious for the arrival of troops and concerned about the possible activity on the morrow. Nevertheless, he was able to report that the Union men he was in contact with were organizing "and I think will soon be formidable enough to control matters." By the next evening, Hancock was happy to describe a great fizzle: "There was no trouble here whatever today. . . . Those intending to parade . . . thought better of it." The secessionist leaders, he said, "found that they were being compromised in an affair for which they were not prepared." With the organized pro-Union men, well-placed reports of approaching troops, and a confident attitude, Hancock had faced down those secessionists who wanted trouble. On May 14 he reported that Carleton's dragoons would arrive the next morning, and, he exulted, "there need be no anxiety concerning matters at this place." On May 25 Banning and Hancock, with the backing of the troops, organized a pro-Union parade through the streets of Los Angeles. Thanks in good part to the efforts of Winfield Scott Hancock, southern California was still safely under the control of the Federal government.[15]

Hancock had not hesitated in standing by the Union. In his view the course of the government was misguided, but this in no way could justify a failure to stand behind it. Brent said Hancock told him that he was sure there would be war, "and he was a northern man and would adhere to his people, even though he knew they were wrong." There was more to it than that: Hancock was, by heredity and conviction, a staunch believer in the integrity of the Union; he had been educated and trained as a soldier by the Federal government; the time had come for him to offer his sword and, if necessary, his life in defense of that Union. It was as simple as that, and his political disagreements with the administration's policies were of no consequence at all. Indeed, when he arrived in Washington that autumn, he was reported to have said, in answer to a query: "My politics are of a practical kind; the integrity of my country, the supremacy of the federal government, and an honorable peace, or none at all."[16]

As soon as he heard of Fort Sumter's fall, Hancock requested transfer to the East; he was only too aware that California was three thousand miles from the probable fighting. He wrote to General Scott, he wrote to Postmaster-General Montgomery Blair (to use his influence with Lincoln), and, hearing nothing, he even wrote to Governor Andrew G. Curtin of Pennsylvania, offering his services. Finally, to his immense relief, he received orders from San Francisco on August 3, 1861, to go there immediately and from there to proceed to Washington and report to the quartermaster-general.[17]

As commentary on Hancock's stay in southern California, the *Los Angeles Star* printed an editorial after he left, saying:

> While resident here, Captain Hancock took great interest in our citizens, the development of our resources, and the welfare of this section of the country; and as a public-spirited, enterprising gentleman, he will be missed from among us, and his most estimable lady will long live in the hearts of her many friends. We desire their prosperity, happiness, and long life, wherever their lot may be cast.[18]

While he was waiting for some word on his own destiny, Hancock commiserated with his southern friends in the Sixth Infantry, old army colleagues who found themselves wrenched from the normal course of their lives by state loyalties when their states joined the Confederacy. George Pickett, Richard B. Garnett, and Hancock's old messmate Lewis Armistead all sought comfort and advice from Hancock. The advice was unyielding—"I shall not fight upon the principle of state-rights, but for the Union, whole and undivided"—but the sympathy he extended them for their plight was genuine. These were men, after all, who had served the government of the

United States for most of their adult lives. In the end, each of them made his decision to go with his state, but none did so happily.[19]

A bittersweet party was held at the Hancock home the night a half-dozen of these southern officers, all of whom had resigned their commissions, were to depart on their journey back to the East. Albert Sidney Johnston asked his wife to sing some of the sentimental old songs, such as "Mary of Argyle" and "Kathleen Mavourneen." Mrs. Johnston did so reluctantly, saying with deep emotion that she felt her music days were over. "Those songs," Allie wrote, "will ever be remembered by the survivors of that mournful gathering." Hearts, she said, "were filled with sadness over the sundering of life-long ties." Armistead was the most dejected of all; he placed his hands on Hancock's shoulders, looked him in the eye, and said, "Hancock, good-bye; you can never know what this has cost me, and I hope God will strike me dead if I am ever induced to leave my native soil, should worse come to worst." He gave Hancock a new major's uniform, for which he himself would have no further use, and he gave Allie a prayer book, inscribed "Lewis A. Armistead. Trust in God and fear nothing." Then the party ended, and the separation began.[20]

SIX

The Brigadier

Winfield Scott Hancock and his family departed from San Francisco late in August 1861, returning east by the same long, tedious route whieh had taken them to the West Coast two years earlier. They recrossed the Isthmus of Panama and then sailed for New York. The day they arrived there they took the first train to Washington. Hancock was designated quartermaster on the staff of General Robert Anderson—the late defender of Fort Sumter—at Louisville, Kentucky, where troops were being organized. Though he recognized that such service was essential, he felt that it was not essential that *he* perform it. Hancock was determined to free himself from the continuing assignment in the Quartermaster's Department; he knew what he had done in Mexico, knew that he was a fighter, that he was a leader of men. Once settled into a quartermaster's post, with the competence that would make him valuable there (it would be the Mexican War recruiting service all over again), he would find it virtually impossible to get away to the fighting army.

The regular army, at the start of the hostilities, consisted of about 16,000 men and officers. The great majority of the enlisted men remained loyal, but some 313 officers, about a third of the total, resigned their commissions, most to take service with the Confederacy. Some of these defections were made good by such officers as McClellan, Hooker, and Grant, who had previously resigned their commissions and who now accepted appointments in the Union army, but these additions were probably offset by those officers who remained loyal but who were simply too old for effective wartime duty. It was clear that the government did not have a surplus of trained, competent officers on hand.

In Hancock the army had a special kind of officer, if only it recognized the fact. In Mexico Hancock had proved that he was courageous and that he could lead men in battle. More important, he had used the period between the wars to learn his trade, to prepare himself, as all professional soldiers should but not all do, for the eventuality of war. Hancock had been given the opportunity on several occasions to serve under William Harney, the crusty Tennessean who was one of the best soldiers in the prewar army; it could almost be said that he was a protégé of Harney. Hancock watched, listened, and learned from Harney; he even picked up much of that general's famed profanity. Hancock read widely in military subjects, immersing himself in the campaigns of Caesar, Wallenstein, Napoleon, Wellington, and Frederick the Great, and learning among other things the great lesson that battles are lost because of commanders who fail to get their force into place on time. In the various assignments given to him, at Jefferson Barracks and Fort Crawford, at Fort Myers and Los Angeles, Hancock worked hard and intensely. One writer, indeed, doubted that any other officer in the United States Army learned so much in the period between the wars as did Hancock, who absorbed from the varied duties assigned to him the methods of sustaining and moving an army. When the war came, Hancock was ready.[1]

There is a school of thought that holds that Union generals, particularly those in the East, were psychologically undone by a massive inferiority complex vis-à-vis their opposite numbers in the Confederacy and that this factor, growing out of the feeling that the South was a more martial, physical, violent environment than the North, contributed to many southern military successes in the war. Whether this was so for such generals as McClellan, Pope, and Hooker, for example, there is no evidence whatever that such feelings afflicted Hancock. He knew many southerners well— Heth, Armistead, Buckner, and Pickett, among others—but he knew that he was just as good at soldiering as they were. Hancock was always self-confident; he was good at his profession, and he knew it.[2]

Hancock came to Washington at that time during which General George B. McClellan was maneuvering successfully to move Winfield Scott out of his position as general-in-chief. Arriving in Washington from Ohio on July 26, 1861, to take command of the forces around the capital, McClellan had set to work with great energy to whip them into an army. When McClellan, who had known Hancock both at West Point and in Mexico, learned of Hancock's presence in the capital, he sent his chief of staff to warn the new man to keep out of sight at Willard's Hotel until a brigade could be procured for him. That same evening, Hancock had a most satisfactory interview with McClellan for several hours, and on September 23 he was appointed brigadier general of volunteers and given command of a brigade in the division of General William Farrar Smith. The danger of Hancock's being immured in the Quartermaster's Department was averted, and he had what he wanted, a meaningful infantry command.[3]

General Smith was the same "Baldy" Smith who had been a year behind Hancock at West Point. The new brigadier did not realize it at first, but he soon learned that he was outranked by many newly created generals, a number of them political appointees, whose military competence was far inferior to his own. Smith was one of these. The combination of Hancock's relative lack of rank in the prewar army and his distance from Washington at the outbreak of the fighting produced this disparity, and its consequences cropped up from time to time throughout the war.

Hancock's new brigade was the Third in Smith's division, and it consisted originally of four regiments, the 5th Wisconsin, the 43rd New York, and the 47th and 49th Pennsylvania. It was in camp on the Virginia side of the Chain Bridge when Hancock first met with it. Shortly, the 47th Pennsyl-

vania was transferred away, and its place was taken by the 6th Maine.
Winfield Scott Hancock sized up his men and went to work.[4]

And work he did. He had an idea, as his young volunteers did not, of
what lay ahead. He knew, from his long talk with McClellan, that there
would be no combat in the immediate future, but while the "On to Richmond" pressure was temporarily abated there was not unlimited time to
train the recruits. Training commenced promptly, and it was hard and
tough. From the day Hancock took over, Smith later wrote, "he was unremitting in giving military instruction of all kinds to his officers, and in his
attention to the comforts and welfare of his men." Hancock was a stern
disciplinarian, because he knew that many times men's lives would depend
on prompt, unquestioning obedience to orders. But he was not a martinet;
he had no taste for the kind of senseless brutalities which some regular
officers inflicted upon their volunteer regiments during the early part of the
war. His troops recognized that Hancock was tough but fair, and they came
to have feelings of respect and affection for him as they got to know him.[5]

One of the means by which Hancock enforced discipline was a vocab-
ulary that was one of the most colorful and sulphuric in the whole Union
army. A staffer called it "an extravagant indulgence, at times, in harsh and
profane speech." Full-blooded profanity was an old if not honored tradition
in the army, and Winfield Hancock was soon recognized as one of its most
proficient and imaginative practitioners, a true heir to his old mentor
Harney. Even the swearing, though, served to endear him further to his
soldiers, who would recall fondly, in later years, Hancock's more vivid
eruptions.[6]

More important than his mastery of oaths, curses, and imprecations was
Hancock's mastery of army regulations. His years of service as an adjutant
and a quartermaster taught him the methods and necessity of supplying the
basic wants of his men and his units, and he exerted himself constantly to
make sure that these wants were met. He handled with ease the mountains
of paper which descended on a commander, and he understood as many of
his colleagues never did that proper administration of his paperwork gave
him another means of enforcing order upon the units under his command.
He knew the procedures appropriate to each department of the army as well
as to every occasion which might arise, and he was at home with all the
proper forms of military records and correspondence. It was written of
Hancock that he felt it "no less important a part of his duty to study the state
of his command through the morning reports and the monthly returns than
on parade or review." No one was Hancock's superior in the fine art of
handling his "papers."[7]

Hancock recognized early that a force of citizens in arms could become a
mighty weapon of war, and he drew no invidious distinctions between
volunteers and regulars. Many regular officers constantly talked about the
old days, sneered at the volunteers, compared them unfavorably to regulars,
and bemoaned the fact that they were cursed with such ill-favored clods.

Hancock would have none of this. He felt it important to build the self-confidence of his volunteer regiments and to make their members think they were the equals of any soldiers on earth. Hancock made the volunteers feel, "by his evident regard, his hearty greeting, his warm approval of everything they did well," that, as far as he was concerned, they were soldiers, just as much as anyone in the old Sixth Infantry. As a result of the way Hancock treated his regiments, and of the training he prescribed for them, Smith related, "no brigade in the Army was better fitted than his for a campaign when the movement to the Peninsula began, in the spring of 1862."[8]

Allie and the children lived that fall and winter in a rented house in Washington. While Hancock had no way of knowing how long the war would last, he could surely see that separation from his family was in prospect for him when the campaigning started, so that he insisted they stay near him for as long as possible. Winfield and Allie participated to some extent in Washington's social life, but it was a completely different group of people from their friends of 1859. Davis, Johnston, Lee, and so many others had departed for the Confederacy, and it was a coarser, less gracious society in the wartime capital. In addition, the gregarious new brigadier had to be careful about expressing views on politics, since his Democratic theories, if publicized, would have been anathema to the Republicans now in power. But Hancock was always discreet about his politics, and he seems not to have aroused any ill feeling about his Democratic leanings.

The Hancocks went to a soiree for regular army officers one evening, and on another they attended a "very exclusive ball" at the White House. Invitations were restricted to the Cabinet, the Senate, the diplomatic corps, and the major-generals of the army. Hancock was the only exception to the guest-list limitation, and no one understood why. Mary Todd Lincoln, however, explained to Allie that members of the Todd family had frequently been hospitably received by Mrs. Russell in St. Louis, and this was the first opportunity to reciprocate that any Todd had been afforded.[9]

Eventually, of course, the sociable winter came to an end, and the time for fighting drew near. Lincoln, with much difficulty, finally prodded his army commander into action; McClellan, over great misgivings in the White House and the War Department, won grudging approval for his plan to move his army by water to Fort Monroe and then by land up the peninsula between the York and the James rivers.

Before the Army of the Potomac left the Washington area, Lincoln arbitrarily divided it into army corps and named the corps commanders. Smith's division was assigned to the Fourth Corps, under General Erasmus D. Keyes of Maine, a graduate of the class of 1832 at the military academy who had served for many years on the frontier, had been Scott's aide-de-camp, and had taught cavalry and artillery at West Point. A brave old soldier, Keyes had now risen above his level of competence and would, after the close of the present campaign, be shuffled out of important command.

Smith's division comprised three brigades: a Vermont brigade led by William T. H. Brooks of Ohio; one consisting largely of New Yorkers, commanded by John W. Davidson, a Virginian who spurned a Confederate commission to remain with the Union; and Hancock's. Four artillery batteries completed the division.[10]

On March 23, 1862, the day his corps embarked from Alexandria, Hancock wrote to Allie: "I am off at last, and it is a matter of great pain to me that I am unable to see you again before we part—God alone knows for how long. I rode all last night, and while I rode, did not cease to think of how and where all this unhappiness is to end."[11]

SEVEN

Up the Peninsula with McClellan

The first of McClellan's twelve divisions started down the Potomac on March 17, 1862, headed for Fort Monroe, on Old Point Comfort, where the James meets the Chesapeake. The fort had not been taken by the rebels, and there McClellan was able to land his army with its supplies and equipment.

"Little Mac," meticulous and cautious as always, waited until he had all of his army (except Irvin McDowell's corps, held back by the president to protect the capital) and all of his stores in hand. Artillery, baggage wagons, ammunition wagons, pontoon trains, food, and forage—everything McClellan knew was needed to support an army of 140,000 was unloaded and packed onto the plain surrounding Fort Monroe. Finally, McClellan started his army toward the enemy on April 4—up the Peninsula.

The first day's march toward Yorktown was a good one, considering the lack of marching experience of the Army of the Potomac. Keyes's corps was on the left, near the James, and it made some ten or twelve miles that first day, meeting with no serious resistance. For Hancock and his men, it was good to be out of camp at last, on the road.[1]

April 5 was a different story. It rained—hard. The roads were of light, sandy soil over a subsoil of heavy clay, all underlain by a bed of shell marl through which water would not drain. Heavy rain gave it all "the consistency of soft mortar"; once the topsoil was broken through, by an artillery wagon or even a heavily laden mule, there was nothing to stop an object from sinking in "until it reaches the hard clay." The march of the Army of the Potomac bogged down.[2]

It came to a stop when Keyes encountered opposition at Lee's Mills, some six miles from his start, on Warwick Creek. He ordered a halt, and his column went no farther that day. The corps of General Fitz John Porter made no more than four miles. McClellan went out and looked at the situation, thought about what could be done, thought about the losses he might suffer, and, after a couple of days, decided that Yorktown would have to be taken by siege. McClellan was surprised to find a defensive line all the way across the Peninsula, mostly along the Warwick, and it apparently messed up his plans. The Confederates had 17,000 men to hold an eight-mile front; the two leading Union corps had at least 60,000, with more on the

Eastern Theater of the Civil War

way. An immediate assault could have overwhelmed the defenders, but McClellan settled down to a siege.[3]

Incredibly, he was there for a month. General Joseph E. Johnston was in command of the Confederate forces around Richmond. Johnston's plan was simply to delay McClellan's march up the Peninsula while Confederate defenses could be strengthened around Richmond. McClellan could not have been more cooperative. It was not even a complete siege, since the rebel defenders could move out to the northwest—up the Peninsula—any time they chose. Finally, on May 3, as McClellan's big siege guns were being wheeled into place, Johnston deemed his defenses to be in order and directed that Yorktown be abandoned.

Hancock's brigade, during this wasted month, participated in a number of skirmishes and reconnaissances, making itself as useful as possible in a basically useless endeavor. Smith and Keyes took turns commending Hancock for thoroughness and competence, even "great skill and daring," in his assignments, but he had done nothing yet to set him apart from other useful brigadiers.[4]

On the morning of May 4, McClellan was able to send his cavalry under General George Stoneman after the retreating Confederates. It took longer to get the infantry going, because the troops had settled in comfortably for a siege. By 4 p.m. Stoneman had caught up with Johnston's rear guard and come up against a defensive line in front of the old capital city of Williamsburg. This line was anchored by a substantial earthwork fortification called Fort Magruder, at the junction of two roads running north up the Peninsula, and a series of six small redoubts on either side extended the line to the two rivers. Reaching Fort Magruder, Stoneman sat down to await the infantry columns which were hurrying forward, Hooker's and Smith's divisions.

Johnston, feeling the Federal pursuit, determined to occupy the Fort Magruder line in order to fight a delaying action, so that his trains and equipment could be gotten safely away. His troops had expected only to rest at Williamsburg, not to fight there, and the line was not particularly formidable. Johnston put General Lafayette McLaws in charge of the defense; the next day McLaws was replaced by General James Longstreet.

When the Federal infantry arrived at the Confederate line, the two divisions were accompanied by Sumner, who, as the senior officer in the absence of McClellan, took command. Sumner ordered an attack, although it was getting dark, and sent Smith's divisions through a dense wood—"thick and tangled, and difficult to penetrate in the darkness," according to Hancock—to deliver the assault. Smith's brigades became completely mixed up in the woods, and Hancock took it upon himself to order a halt so that they could sort themselves out, much to Smith's relief. Sumner then came upon the scene, withdrew the order to attack, and ordered the troops to bivouac where they were.[5]

The next morning, in steady rain, the battle of Williamsburg opened with Hooker's attack upon Fort Magruder. One observer called it "a battle fought without a plan, with inadequate numbers, and at a serious sacrifice without compensating result." McClellan was not even present; he was back at Yorktown seeing to some logistical details. Though Sumner commanded, his tactical dispositions seemed aimless and haphazard. The only redeeming feature of the battle, aside from the bravery shown by Hooker's and Philip Kearny's troops in front of Fort Magruder, was Hancock's action on the far right.[6]

From 7 a.m. until about noon, Hooker's division, with little support, fought alone. The corps commanders, Sumner, Keyes, and Samuel K. Heintzelman, paid little attention to Hooker's fight; they were thinking about some kind of movement around the enemy's left flank. At 11 a.m. Hancock was summoned to meet with Smith and Sumner, who had been informed of an abandoned redoubt on the left of the rebel line. Sumner ordered Hancock "to take four or five regiments of infantry and a battery of artillery . . . crossing Cub Dam Creek . . . and to take possession, if possible, of the enemy's work on the opposite side of the creek." Smith later told him he could advance farther if "any advantage could be obtained" and to send back for reinforcements if needed.

Hancock took five regiments, three of his own and two of Davidson's, a battery of artillery, and a young officer on Smith's staff, George Armstrong Custer, who was looking for some excitement. Slogging through the rain, Hancock moved off about a mile to the right, within sight of the York River, then turned to the left until he came to Cub Dam Creek, passable only by the roadway on top of a dam across the creek. The dam was 75 yards in length and was commanded by the redoubt on the other side. After posting artillery to cover the advance, Hancock sent the 5th Wisconsin, guided by Lieutenant Custer, across the dam and into the redoubt, which was found to be unoccupied as reported. Hancock then spotted another work some 1,200 yards ahead. He sent word back to Smith and was told he would be reinforced by four regiments and a battery, and on the strength of this he felt he could move ahead to the next redoubt. It was also found to be abandoned. With the promise of help to protect his rear and right flank, Hancock determined to advance to the crest at his front, deploying skirmishers 1,000 yards ahead. "From my position here," he said, "Fort Magruder with all its surroundings could be distinctly seen and all portions of the enemy on the plain between us."

Two additional enemy redoubts were seen about 300 and 400 yards, respectively, from Hancock's skirmishers. He opened fire with his artillery, and the rebels moved back from these two works. While awaiting the promised reinforcements and preparing for an attack when they should arrive, Hancock was startled to receive orders from Sumner to "fall back to my first position." He sent back to Smith with word that the best thing would be to reinforce him, not to withdraw, but Smith replied that he could not send more troops and that Hancock must fall back.

"Never at a loss for expletives . . . ," Custer observed, "Hancock was not at all loath to express his condemnation" of orders which appeared to him (and were in fact) wrongheaded and foolish. He sent an engineer officer to Sumner to explain his situation, to let the general know that he held the key to Fort Magruder and the whole Confederate line, to beg him for the help he needed to make that position secure. Sumner was to be told that should no answer arrive within a reasonable time, Hancock would obey the order to fall back. At 4:20 Hancock wrote to Smith that he would wait a reasonable time for an answer. Of course, he was reserving to himself the interpretation of "reasonable time." Almost an hour later, at 5:10, with no reinforcements and no change in Sumner's order, at the very brink of insubordination and disobedience of orders (if indeed he had not already gone over that brink), Hancock prepared to pull back to the first redoubt. At that moment, he spotted enemy infantry advancing toward him, and all thoughts of a pullback vanished. Hancock was on the spot now; with his failure to obey Sumner's order, a defeat would be extremely damaging to his career.[7]

Longstreet had yielded to the importunities of Generals D. H. Hill and Jubal A. Early that an attack should be made to clear out the interlopers on the Confederate left. Early's brigade consisted of the 24th and the 38th Virginia and the 5th and the 23rd North Carolina; in the assault Early led the two Virginia regiments and Hill the North Carolinians. When the Confederates charged out of the woods into the open, they found Hancock's force on their left and had to wheel in that direction, a maneuver which was not done well in the muddy field. Then Early took a Minié ball in his shoulder and had to retire. Still, thinking they saw their enemy retreating, the Confederates hurried forward.[8]

In actuality, Hancock had feigned a withdrawal, pulling his regiments back behind the crest of the hill. When the rebels were within thirty paces, Hancock, riding along his lines, ordered his men forward to the crest, where they fired two effective volleys, and then sent them charging down the slope, with the bellowed order "Gentlemen, charge with the bayonet!" Several of "the leading spirits of the enemy were bayoneted," Hancock said; "the remainder then broke and fled." Hancock's troops, basically untried until now, responded very well to a task which would have tested veterans; the exhaustive training they had received paid its first dividend.[9]

It was a complete victory for Hancock, and it settled Williamsburg. By next morning Johnston had abandoned the now untenable position, although he had intended to do so in any event. Early lost at least 600 men in the attack; the 5th North Carolina was annihilated. Hancock lost 126, and his near-insubordination was forgotten. McClellan announced "Hancock's brilliant engagement" in his dispatch to Secretary of War Edwin M. Stanton, and he wired his wife on May 6 that "Hancock was superb yesterday." The adjective was picked up by the press, which was anxious to find legitimate Union heroes, and regularly applied to Hancock thereafter. Hancock wrote to *his* wife, saying, "On this occasion my men behaved beautifully, and captured the first color yet taken."[10]

Baldy Smith reported that he could not "pretend to do justice" to Hancock's engagement: "The brilliancy of the plan of battle; the coolness of its execution; the seizing of the proper instant for changing from the defensive to the offensive; the steadiness of the troops engaged, and the completeness of the victory" were all matters for which he recommended just praise. There was more in the same vein by Keyes and McClellan and others.[11]

The only real problem with Williamsburg was that, while Hancock's heroics were genuine enough, the battle was still just a badly managed collision with the rear guard of the retreating Confederates. McClellan inflated Hancock's performance in the press because his victory obscured the mishandled fighting around Fort Magruder, because Hancock was one of "his" generals, and because any kind of success lessened the pressure back in Washington and in the North.

There was, inevitably, some reaction among the officers of the Army of the Potomac to the commanding general's glorification of Hancock. One officer said they were "somewhat sore at all the glory going to Hancock, who did but very little fighting," and another complained of Hancock's being put "far in advance of all other participants in the engagement." A third asked whether McClellan's report did not make it appear "that Hancock was the only one who had been engaged?" Of course, the officers of this army soon brought the art of backbiting and complaining to a high level, and targets much more vulnerable than Hancock offered themselves.[12]

McClellan naturally took a couple of days to recover from the fighting at Williamsburg and then on May 8 resumed a leisurely pursuit of Johnston. On May 18 he received word from President Lincoln that he could reorganize the Army of the Potomac; in the resulting shuffle, Smith's division, along with that of Henry W. Slocum, was placed in the new Sixth Corps, under General William B. Franklin, another old friend of Hancock's from West Point.[13]

McClellan drew to within eight or ten miles of the Confederate capital, but then he stopped. On May 23 Hancock wrote to his mother: "I am well; and so, also, is brother John. We are not in Richmond yet, but trust we shall be there, all in good time. I hope that God, in his good mercy, will permit both your sons to reach that city, in safety and in honor." The Deity may have been willing, but the problem was McClellan.[14]

Eventually, the two armies locked in combat once again. On May 31 Johnston found and struck Keyes's Fourth Corps, isolated from the rest of McClellan's army, south of the Chickahominy River at Fair Oaks. The resulting two days of fighting, in a battle called both Fair Oaks and Seven Pines, was essentially a standoff. Johnston was severely wounded and was succeeded in command by Robert E. Lee. Franklin's corps, on the north of the Chickahominy, did not participate in the fight, so that Hancock listened to the sounds of battle off in the distance.

After Fair Oaks, McClellan sat down again, waiting for McDowell's corps (part of which was busy trying to trap Stonewall Jackson in the Shenandoah Valley) and engaging in acrimonious correspondence with Stanton. During the period June 12 to 15, General J. E. B. Stuart took his Confederate cavalry and rode completely around McClellan's army, making the Federals look foolish but alerting McClellan to the need to move his main base away from White House on the Pamunkey River. On June 26, with the Army of the Potomac still astraddle the Chickahominy, a swampy, sluggish stream with a tendency to spread over the countryside after a rain, Lee threw most of his army upon the Federal right flank at Mechanicsville, on the north side of the river. This was the first of the Seven Days' battles, a series of hard fights as Lee pressed fiercely while the Army of the Potomac retreated across the peninsula, changing its base from the Pamunkey to the James.

On June 27 the major battle was at Gaines's Mill, north of the river, where Fitz John Porter's Fifth Corps spent all afternoon fighting off Longstreet, A. P. Hill, and Jackson, until just before dark, when the Union line was broken. South of the river, where Lee had weakened his forces in order to make his main attack elsewhere, General John B. Magruder, the Confederate commander, maintained a threatening posture to discourage McClellan from moving forward. Magruder's effort was, given the nature of his opponent, completely successful; McClellan was now thinking defensively and had no thoughts of attacking.

One of the moves Magruder ordered was a demonstration, by G. T. Anderson's brigade, late in the afternoon of June 27, against Smith's division, which held the south bank of the Chickahominy. At the same time, the adjacent brigade commanded by the fiery Georgian Robert A. Toombs, formerly a United States senator and Confederate secretary of state, was to move forward cautiously when Anderson did, near the Garnett and Golding farms. Anderson, probing, found the line strongly held and broke off the movement, but Toombs, an amateur soldier with contempt for the caution of West Pointers, lunged ahead with more valor than discretion. His brigade collided with that of Hancock and suffered a severe repulse; "the fight lasted about forty-five minutes," Franklin reported, "when the enemy retired, not having been able to gain an inch of ground." It was a futile effort by Toombs, to no real purpose, and Hancock's men inflicted heavy casualties upon him.[15]

By the next day, McClellan was fully committed to the retreat toward the James, a retreat that was euphemistically called "a change of base," and Smith's division was ordered away from its position near the Chickahominy. As the division was withdrawing, it was attacked again by Toombs in another ill-advised action. Hancock easily halted the rebel thrust, killing or wounding over 100 and capturing 50, including two colonels.[16]

The night of June 28, McClellan gathered his corps commanders and told them his plans for the retreat. Franklin's corps was one of three which constituted the rear guard in McClellan's scheme, and on June 29 it was engaged in another fight at Savage's Station, on the York River Railroad, some two or three miles southeast of its prior position. The line at Savage's Station, designed to cover the crossing of White Oak Swamp (a tributary of the Chickahominy), was assailed late in the afternoon by Magruder. The Confederates charged gallantly but were easily stopped by elements of Franklin's and Sumner's corps. Hancock's brigade was held in reserve and did not participate in the fighting at Savage's Station.

The Union rear guard moved out the night of June 29–30 in a heavy rain, leaving huge quantities of supplies and 2,500 wounded men behind. Franklin's corps crossed White Oak Swamp at about three in the morning, and Smith's division deployed on the east side of the road south of the swamp. This swamp was a dismal and forbidding place, a dark and silent jungle. Not a difficult stream to cross in dry weather, in rainy weather as on this day it spread quickly from its bed and became virtually impassable. At 10 a.m. the Second Corps division of General Israel B. "Dick" Richardson demolished the White Oak Bridge behind it and then went into position alongside Smith, on the west side of the road. The Union army was now some five or six miles from the James, and Lee made his strongest effort on this day, June 30, to try to cut McClellan off, only to be balked by faulty execution on the part of his Confederate generals.

Longstreet and Hill engaged in a fierce and bloody battle with the divisions of Hooker, George McCall, and Kearny at Frayser's Farm, but they were unable to break the Union line. Three other rebel forces, under Generals Theophilus Holmes, Benjamin Huger, and Magruder, never got into the fight at all. And back at White Oak Swamp, Jackson simply quit. He reached the crossing at about 11 a.m. and laid down a heavy artillery barrage on the Federals across the stream, particularly on Hancock's brigade. After a couple of halfhearted efforts to cross, easily thwarted by the Union defenders, Jackson concluded that the swamp was impassible and then went to sleep under a tree. The rest of the day was marked by inconclusive artillery exchanges, but Jackson declined to try to reach any of the upper fords of the swamp. He simply sat down and conceded that he could not cross in the face of the opposition. Thus June 30, the crucial day of the Seven Days, passed with Lee unable to halt or to intercept the Army of the Potomac in its move to the James; it was a tactical victory for McClellan, although, strategically, each step took him farther from his original objective, the Confederate capital.[17]

On July 1 McClellan established his army on Malvern Hill, near the James, a height which Porter and General Henry J. Hunt, the artillery commander, had strongly posted with 250 guns. Smith's and Slocum's divisions of Franklin's Sixth Corps were sited on the extreme right of the Federal line and were not engaged in the battle. They were hardly needed. The Union position, on top of a long, gradual slope, covered a field of fire of 300 to 400 yards. The Confederate infantry, moving up this slope in its late afternoon attack, was slaughtered and thrown back in confusion. Despite this, passing up a chance for a counterattack which might have won him a decisive victory, McClellan withdrew that night to Harrison's Landing, on the James, where he established his new base, under the protection of Union gunboats in the river.[18]

The Peninsula campaign was over. McClellan sat at Harrison's Landing for a month and a half, clamoring for Washington to send him more troops, until he was finally ordered to evacuate. McClellan's defenders, at the time and since, have claimed that the government failed to support him, by keeping McDowell's 40,000 men from him, and by forcing him to straddle the Chickahominy in hopes that McDowell would come. His critics have pointed out that he had, even without McDowell, clear superiority in numbers and matériel and that it was McClellan's inadequacy and timidity, not any policy of Abraham Lincoln, which caused the failure of the campaign.

One of those who came out of the campaign with an enhanced reputation was Winfield Scott Hancock. Oddly, he and his brigade had seen far less action than many others—his total casualties for the Seven Days were only 200, a very low figure—but this was caused by the happenstance of position when actions or movements started. Whatever Hancock was called upon to do, he did, with alacrity and competence, and his fights at Williamsburg and Golding's Farm, though small, were among a limited number of Union victories.[19]

EIGHT

A Division at Antietam

While McClellan was awaiting reinforcements at the hot and noisome camp at Harrison's Landing on the James, the administration in Washington was moving ahead with plans to take his army away from him. At the end of June, the bombastic General John Pope was called east and placed in command of the newly created Army of Virginia, made up largely of the forces which had marched vainly up and down the Shenandoah Valley, trying to catch Jackson. To them was added McDowell's corps, formerly of the Army of the Potomac but detached from McClellan.

On August 3, 1862, McClellan received orders from Washington to withdraw his army from the James and ready it to be shipped off to Pope. By August 20 the units of the Army of the Potomac were on their way north, gradually passing out of McClellan's control. Franklin's Sixth Corps left Harrison's Landing on August 16 and arrived at Newport News on August 21. It embarked that day and the next for Aquia Creek, off the Potomac, but upon arriving there on the afternoon of August 24, it was sent on by McClellan to Alexandria. The wharves at Aquia were congested with the artillery and baggage of the corps of Ambrose E. Burnside and Porter, and one more army corps was one too many.[1]

In the meantime, Lee, once he knew that McClellan's army was being withdrawn by water, pounced on the hapless Pope. Lee's strategic concepts, Jackson's tactical daring, the sledgehammer attack of Longstreet, Pope's ineptitude, and the disinclination of McClellan and some of his subordinates to help Pope "to get out of his scrape" combined to produce the staggering defeat of Second Bull Run on August 29 and 30.

Franklin's corps did not participate in Pope's battle. Indeed, Franklin's failure to go to Pope's assistance was one of the items in the indictment of McClellan for his conduct during this period. It is no doubt too harsh to say that McClellan actively worked for Pope's failure, but the correspondence among McClellan and his favorites such as Porter and Franklin, combined with McClellan's lack of interest in forwarding help to the embattled Army of Virginia, lends credence to the assertion that Pope's success was certainly not one of McClellan's highest priorities.[2]

Hancock's role in the battle was necessarily a peripheral one, but it demonstrates vividly the difference between him and McClellan as a soldier.

About midnight on August 27, Hancock was roused from his sleep by Colonel Herman Haupt, a West Pointer who had resigned from the army shortly after graduation and who had become the most famous railroad man in the country. Placed now in charge of transportation and construction of military railroads, Haupt had planned and gotten approval from General Henry W. Halleck at the War Department for a subsistence train of rations, to be sent from Alexandria to Pope, whose supply depot at Manassas had been destroyed by Jackson. Halleck's approval was conditioned on the train's being adequately guarded; he told Haupt to see McClellan if possible, to procure an infantry escort for the train when it left at 4 a.m. The whole idea was distressing to McClellan, who found the situation around Manassas to be too murky and unclear to risk sending any of his soldiers; let Pope fend for himself. Haupt had in his pocket a dispatch from Halleck addressed to any general officer he could find, urging aid for the project, and about midnight, desperate, the railroad man got on his horse and rode some four miles to where he understood Hancock was camped. "I found General Hancock in bed in his tent," Haupt said. "He arose immediately and cheerfully agreed to give me the force I required, promising that they should be on hand at 4 a.m. punctually." At 4 a.m., the 2nd New Jersey showed up as ordered and went off with Haupt and his train. Also on hand were the 11th and the 12th Ohio. That the commander of the New Jersey troops exceeded his orders and got himself and many of his men killed was regrettable but beside the point. The important thing was the continued demonstration that Winfield Scott Hancock had an instinct for war and no hesitation in making the necessary decisions to act on it.[3]

Pope, of course, was defeated and driven back toward Washington. With extreme reluctance, President Lincoln reinstated McClellan in the command which had been effectively but unofficially taken from him, and John Pope was sent back out west, out of the way, where he did no further damage.

Lee moved quickly to exploit his victory and the presumed confusion in the Union ranks by carrying the war across the Potomac and into Maryland. One of the tenets of the Confederate faith was that Maryland was being held in the Union by force, that its citizens would respond to the rebel army as liberators. The arrival of Lee's Army of Northern Virginia would, it was expected, bring out many new recruits from among the Marylanders. Further, the invasion would relieve the ravaged state of Virginia by carrying the war away from it, and it would perhaps exploit northern dissatisfaction with the war. Lee was willing to give it a try.

McClellan did not start his army after Lee until the latter was known to be in Frederick, Maryland. He had to sort out and reequip the disordered and demoralized troops who had streamed back toward Alexandria and Washington after Pope's defeat. Such activity was always McClellan's greatest strength, anyway. And things were not going quite as Lee had expected. The hoped-for rising of sympathetic Marylanders had not materialized; most of them looked upon Lee's ragged troopers with disdain. But the

Confederates had replenished their stores in Maryland, and Lee saw a great prize awaiting him. Halleck had failed to order the garrison away from Harpers Ferry, at the confluence of the Potomac and the Shenandoah, and 12,000 men and a large quantity of supplies sat there as a great temptation to Lee. He decided to divide his army, move Jackson and six divisions south in three converging columns, and capture Harpers Ferry. Longstreet would march with three divisions over South Mountain. After the capture of Harpers Ferry, the two wings of the army could be reunited.

On September 9 Lee issued Special Orders No. 191, detailing the precise manner in which Harpers Ferry would be bottled up from three directions, while the remainder of the army crossed the mountain and assumed a waiting posture near Boonsboro. The Army of Northern Virginia would then be brought together again either at Boonsboro or at Hagerstown, as seemed best. The success of Lee's plan depended on its speedy execution and McClellan's customary slowness; it was a daring plan, but the unexpected was as characteristic of Lee as the dilatory was of his opponent.[4]

This time, however, destiny turned its back on Robert E. Lee. On September 13 a copy of the special order was found (wrapped around three cigars) when the Union army camped in the same area near Frederick where the Confederates had been a few days before. The order was brought late that morning to McClellan, who suddenly had before his eyes a clear picture of the dispositions of his enemy on the other side of the mountains. And an inviting picture it was, with the Confederates split into at least five parts, Longstreet near Hagerstown, D. H. Hill at Turner's Gap in South Mountain, and the three divided forces, under Jackson, McLaws, and John Walker, converging on Harpers Ferry. Rarely would a general be presented with such an opportunity: "here is a paper," McClellan, waving the lost order, told General John Gibbon, "with which if I cannot whip Bobbie Lee, I will be willing to go home."[5]

What he did with the opportunity, of course, constitutes the final sad chapter of McClellan's command of the Army of the Potomac. At 6:20 p.m., already over six hours after Lee's order was brought to him, McClellan directed Franklin, with his Sixth Corps of two divisions and with one division of the Fourth Corps, to "move at daybreak in the morning" toward Crampton's Gap, a more southerly pass in South Mountain, with an eye to relieving Harpers Ferry. Franklin was at Buckeystown, some twelve miles from Crampton's Gap; why he was not ordered to move that evening from Buckeystown is a serious question. The Confederates did not even know of the existence of Crampton's Gap or have it defended until the morning of September 14. If Franklin had moved to the foot of South Mountain on the evening of the thirteenth, he could have taken Crampton's Gap early the next morning, virtually without opposition, and been in excellent position to move the five miles to the relief of Harpers Ferry before noon on September 14. As the historian Francis W. Palfrey said, McClellan's failure to move

Franklin at once on the thirteenth was a mistake "which made his Maryland campaign a moderate success, bought at a great price, instead of a cheap and overwhelming victory."[6]

As it was, Franklin reached Crampton's Gap at about noon on September 14 and found the mountain lightly defended by about two brigades of infantry, an artillery battery, and a brigade or two of cavalry. After another long delay, Slocum's division attacked the defensive line, broke the Confederates, and captured the gap. Smith's division was behind, on the east side of the mountain, with Hancock's brigade once again in reserve, at the base of the hill. Franklin could be just as slow as McClellan, and he showed it here. He considered that Crampton's Gap was "the completest victory gained up to that time by any part of the Army of the Potomac," and he was satisfied to sit down and savor it. With time of the essence, Franklin incredibly ordered no further advance but had his men encamp overnight on the mountain.[7]

The next morning, Franklin sent Smith's division down the west side of the mountain, into Pleasant Valley, "to begin the movement toward Harper's Ferry." As he was crossing the mountain, Franklin observed a Confederate line across the valley and, after consultation with Smith, "concluded that it would be suicidal to attack it," though in fact he well outnumbered the defenders. A couple of hours later, Franklin heard the firing stop around Harpers Ferry and deduced, correctly, that the garrison there had surrendered. It was some 45 or 46 hours after McClellan's receipt of Lee's order, but Harpers Ferry had still fallen, with the relief force yet five miles away. A large number of prisoners and a vast amount of supplies fell into the hands of the Confederates.[8]

With the loss of the passes over South Mountain, Lee felt it was urgent that he reunite his army. He had now learned of the discovery of the lost order, which seemed to account for McClellan's unwonted energy, such as it was. Lee even contemplated a retreat back into Virginia, until Jackson assured him that the capture of Harpers Ferry was imminent. Lee pulled the force under Longstreet back to the little town of Sharpsburg, between Antietam Creek and the Potomac, and sent word to Jackson and the units at Harpers Ferry to hasten northward to join him. And while Lee frantically worked to end the division of his forces before he could be defeated in detail, Franklin sat at Crampton's Gap from the morning of September 15 until daylight on the seventeenth, when he was ordered to the Antietam, and McClellan wasted a whole day, September 16, when he was within striking distance of Lee's understrength army at Sharpsburg.[9]

The bloody battle of Antietam was fought on September 17, 1862. After it was all over, George McClellan wrote his wife: "Those in whose judgment I rely tell me that I fought the battle splendidly and that it was a masterpiece of art." Most other observers would have disagreed, violently, with this arrogant, self-satisfied assessment. They considered that McClellan squandered his huge advantage in manpower by attacking in piecemeal, scattered assaults and by holding back a substantial part of his army; they felt that he conducted the fight poorly and threw away his victory by failing to attack the severely damaged Army of Northern Virginia the following day.[10]

Antietam divides itself into three, almost separate battles—the early morning attacks of Hooker's First Corps and Joseph K. Mansfield's Twelfth Corps on the far right of the Union army, the mid-morning movements of Sumner's Second Corps in the center, and the afternoon activity of the Ninth Corps under Burnside on the left of the line. These assaults were virtually independent of one another, were without any meaningful coordination, and were so timed that Lee was able to move regiments from one part of the field to another as the Union emphasis slowly moved from one area to another. In this way Lee could negate to some degree his fearful inferiority in numbers, which according to best estimates was something like 40,000 against a Union force of 85,000.

Franklin's corps did not even arrive on the field until 10 a.m., at which time the fighting on the right had already ended. Sumner's poorly planned assault in the center was well under way: an unsupported attack by John Sedgwick's division across the Hagerstown Turnpike had been smashed on the left flank by McLaws and Walker (back from Harpers Ferry), while his other two divisions, those of William H. French and Dick Richardson, had charged into Longstreet and D. H. Hill along a depressed lane which would be ever after known as the Sunken Road or Bloody Lane. Behind Sedgwick was a line of unprotected Second Corps batteries, and Baldy Smith was told to send a brigade to cover them. Since Hancock was in the advance of the corps, his brigade handled the job by placing a regiment of infantry between each two of the three batteries. The rebels shelled the line briefly and then turned their attention elsewhere. Hancock's brigade suffered very light casualties.[11]

In the ghastly fighting at Bloody Lane, Dick Richardson, the very able commander of the First Division of the Second Corps, an unpretentious man but a hard fighter, was hit and carried from the field with a fatal wound. Early in the afternoon McClellan came to see Hancock and ordered him to take command immediately of Richardson's division, then holding a key spot in the center of the fight. When Richardson fell, the battle seemed to come almost to a standstill, and it was some time before Hancock could assume command. Longstreet and other Confederate leaders feared that if McClellan were to throw his reserves at the rebel center at that point the Confederates would be utterly routed and Lee's army irreparably sundered. But "Little Mac" never understood this and "Old Bull" Sumner had lost his nerve; the orders the two of them gave Hancock as the latter took over his new responsibility were to dig in and to throw back any attacks upon his position.[12]

Winfield Scott Hancock led his personal staff across the torn battlefield, galloping a half-mile or so from his brigade to where his new division was huddled along Bloody Lane. He arrived dramatically about 3 p.m. and immediately took charge, as if commanding a division was a perfectly natural thing to him. As he placed one of his regiments, he shouted, "Now, men, stay there until you are ordered away; this place must be held at all hazards." "A fine, soldierly looking officer," one staffer observed as Hancock arrived and met his division.[13]

One of the finest divisions in the army, the First was reduced at this time to little more than 2,100 men by the attrition of two major campaigns and the awful struggle for Bloody Lane. Its three brigades were led by General John C. Caldwell of Maine; General Thomas F. Meagher, "Meagher of the Sword," the famous Irish revolutionary; and Colonel John R. Brooke of Pennsylvania, a fine soldier who was to have a long and distinguished career in the army. Brooke was standing in for another excellent soldier, General Samuel K. Zook. The divison's regimental commanders, probably the best in the army, included such hard fighters as Edward E. Cross, Francis C. Barlow, Nelson A. Miles, H. Boyd McKeen, Patrick Kelly, and Paul Frank. Meagher's command was the picturesque and renowned Irish Brigade, made up predominantly of Irish regiments from New York City. Meagher and other Irish leaders in New York organized the brigade originally with the design of gaining martial experience in America's war for eventual use in a war to free Ireland from England. The brigade's regiments carried green flags along with the national colors, and they fought with tenacity and fiery enthusiasm. The soldiers of the Irish Brigade acquired much experience in warfare, as planned, but for great numbers of them the path led to graves in Virginia, Maryland, and Pennsylvania, not to the Emerald Isle across the sea.

When Hancock took over the division, he found it occupying "one line of battle in close proximity to the enemy." A dangerous interval existed between Caldwell and the Irish Brigade, and he filled it with two regiments from the division reserve. Finding no artillery, he applied to the commander of nearby units for guns, but "none could be spared at that time." His men were suffering under a continual bombardment, but they had to sit and take it. Some time later, Hancock spotted a column of rebels moving toward his left; he procured a battery of artillery from Slocum's division of his old corps and was able to drive the southerners back. Otherwise, the division settled down to watching for an attack that did not come, until night fell and the battle of Antietam was over.[14]

The sun rose on September 18 on two armies, bloodied, battered, and sorely hurt, still in line of battle facing one another over a field littered with thousands of corpses of men and horses. McClellan had Porter's Fifth Corps and Franklin's Sixth Corps, virtually unengaged the day before, fresh and ready for action. Lee, having started with greatly inferior numbers, had nothing but the regiments which had fought to exhaustion the day before. McClellan's position, achieved at the cost of so much blood, was a strong one for a further advance; Lee stood practically with his back to the Potomac. And yet McClellan did nothing. Hancock wrote that he had "been directed in the morning, by orders from the commander-in-chief, not to precipitate hostilities, as he expected some re-enforcements to arrive before he desired to recommence movements to the front." Similar orders went to other front-line commanders. Thus nothing was done on September 18, and that night Lee pulled his men out of their lines and retreated unmolested into Virginia.[15]

Antietam was, for those who tote up such things, a drawn battle, tactically. It was a strategic victory for the Union, because it forced the termination of Lee's Maryland campaign. On the basis of that strategic victory, Lincoln issued his preliminary Emancipation Proclamation. But Antietam was more than that: it was a missed opportunity of tremendous proportions. McClellan had numerous chances, from the time he intercepted Lee's order on September 13 to the time he declined to renew the fight on September 18, to overwhelm his opponent. He could perhaps have obliterated the Army of Northern Virginia and, if he had done so, might have shortened the war by more than two years.

After the battle the Army of the Potomac stayed at Sharpsburg while Lee took his army into the Shenandoah Valley for recuperation and replenishment. Lincoln tried to get his general to move—he even came to visit the army on October 1—but he was frustrated in his effort. Eventually, McClellan prepared to move. On October 16 he directed Hancock to take his division and 1,500 additional men, cross the river at Harpers Ferry, and make a reconnaissance up the Shenandoah Valley to Charles Town, to determine whether the rebels were still lingering in the vicinity of Bunker Hill and Winchester. General Andrew A. Humphreys, of Porter's corps, made a similar reconnaissance north of Hancock's, from Shepherdstown to Kearneysville. "We anticipated a jolly time of it," one young officer wrote, but first they met with heavy rain and then with Confederate cavalry and artillery. Hancock took Charles Town after chasing out the rebels, and then was visited by McClellan. From the opposition aroused, the general-in-chief was satisfied that the Confederates had not moved away, and he directed Hancock (and Humphreys) to return.[16]

Finally, on October 26, McClellan felt that all of his preparations were complete, and he started his army across the Potomac, back into Virginia. More than five weeks of good campaigning weather had been squandered, five weeks of which Robert E. Lee took advantage to bolster his army with new recruits and renewed equipment. It took the Army of the Potomac eight days to cross the river, but by November 2 it was all in Virginia. On that day Hancock moved his division into Snicker's Gap, the northernmost of the Blue Ridge gaps, drove out the enemy's cavalry, and then beat off a Confederate effort to retake it with 5,000 to 6,000 infantry.[17]

McClellan moved cautiously down the eastern side of the Blue Ridge, carefully sealing off each gap as he came to it. Still, Lee was able to interpose his army between McClellan and Richmond, and Abraham Lincoln had finally had enough. On November 5, 1862, the midterm elections took place in the North, and they went badly for the administration, largely because of dissatisfaction with the course of the war. Two days later, orders from the War Department arrived at the headquarters of the Army of the Potomac, relieving McClellan from command and replacing him with Burnside. McClellan was effectively shelved for the rest of the war. He went away quietly, though there was a lot of muttering in the Army of the Potomac, and a small amount of wild talk about marching on Washington. "Little Mac" was still popular with his troops, but some of them could see the opportunity to destroy Lee which had been thrown away at Antietam, and they knew that his kind of generalship was not going to win the war.

Hancock was of two minds about the change. McClellan was his friend and had been instrumental in getting him an infantry command. Hancock was always loyal to his friends. But Hancock was a fighter, and he would have had to be blind not to recognize that McClellan was not. Thus when he wrote to Allie about the change, he was careful to set forth the views of "the army," not necessarily his own. "The Army are not satisfied with the change," he wrote, "and consider the treatment of McClellan most ungracious and inopportune." He went on with his own views about possible resistance to the firing of McClellan: "Yet I do not sympathize in the movement going on to resist the order. 'It is useless,' I tell the gentlemen around me. 'We are serving no one man: we are serving our country.' "[18]

McClellan never strayed from character. He was slow outside of Washington in the fall of 1861 and the winter of 1862. He was slow at Yorktown. He was slow moving up the Peninsula. He sat down outside Richmond after Seven Pines. He was timid when Lee seriously weakened his Richmond defense to hit his right at Mechanicsville. He was timid when he retreated to Harrison's Landing and stayed there. He was slow to the point of willful culpability in forwarding troops to Pope's rescue at Second Bull Run. He was unforgivably slow in taking advantage of Lee's "lost order" in the Antietam campaign. And he was slow in following Lee's retreat and even in crossing the Potomac. Lincoln probably stayed with him far longer than he should have. In the end, it was Lincoln's assessment which hit the mark: McClellan would not do, because he was fatally afflicted with "the slows."

NINE

"A Chicken Could Not Live on That Field"

Thirty-eight years old as he took command of his division, Winfield Scott Hancock was tall and well built, with straight hair now light brown, a mustache and a tuft on his chin of the same color, with well-cut features, a firm jaw, deep blue eyes, and, as one observer put it, "a very mobile, emotional countenance." He was always neatly dressed, and one of the wonders of the Army of the Potomac was the fact that Hancock always wore a clean white shirt, well pressed, even in the midst of a long march or a protracted battle. When the fighting started, he was always in the thick of the action. During a fight Hancock kept the members of his staff ("and every other staff, which happens to be near him," wrote an aide to one of his brigade commanders, somewhat ruefully) on the go with messages and orders to his subordinates. "He is magnificent in appearance, lordly, but cordial, and is remarkably generous, giving every one ample credit for what he does," a staffer wrote. Hancock had such an air of command, another felt, that if he appeared in civilian clothes and gave commands to an army unit which did not know him, "he would be likely to be obeyed at once, and without any question as to his right to command."[1]

Hancock, as befitted his years of quartermaster and adjutant training, was meticulous and thorough. "There was no detail too minute to escape his attention," said Nelson Miles, one of his regimental (and, later, brigade and division) commanders. Major E. W. Clark of Hancock's staff affirmed this, but emphasized that "he did not magnify the minor things to the exclusion of the weightier matters." This care for details made him "a terror to adjutants," one such officer wrote, as did his penchant for showing up, two or three times a week, for an 11 p.m. visit to his own adjutant's tent. Hancock would ask to see all the books, papers, and correspondence. "From whatever brigade a paper may come from that is not to his mind," a frequent victim of this procedure wrote, "he immediately sends for its adjutant, who must get out of bed, order his horse, dress himself, and report without delay to the irate general. . . . The general usually pitches into us right and left, utterly indifferent to choice of language, and will sometimes keep us an hour or more." When the business is taken care of, however, "he is sure to calm down in the end and become very gracious." It was a procedure which, rough as it was on the adjutants, tended to concentrate the mind most forcefully; error, sloppy work, and improper procedures disappeared, if only for the sake of a good night's sleep.[2]

While Hancock was severe and businesslike in military matters, he was gracious, kind, and genial when off duty. He took care to learn and use the names of every officer in his command, a small habit of consideration which was nevertheless rare in the army. Those who served under him spoke of "his considerate kindness," of his being "always sensitive of the feelings of others, and never allowing himself to do what might seem to be an unkind act." Baldy Smith, while speaking of Hancock's stern demeanor on duty, said, "In his social hours he was kind and gentle."[3]

William Franklin, his corps commander until Antietam, said that no one combined so well as Hancock "the prudence which cherished the lives of his command, with the dash which was his distinguishing characteristic." Hancock, he said, did not court danger, "but when an order was given that involved a fight, the precise thing that was ordered was done, his brigade without exception behaving admirably."[4]

It should be added as well that Hancock took care to cultivate the reporters covering the Army of the Potomac. He was almost invariably well treated by the press, and it came as a rude jolt to him later in the war when he was portrayed unfavorably and, as he thought, unfairly by a *New York Tribune* writer over the failure to take Petersburg. His reaction at the time, a demand for the reporter's arrest, should be seen in the context of the growing conflict between the press and the high command under George Gordon Meade; it can also be seen as consistent with a story told by a well-known correspondent who said he fell into disfavor at Hancock's headquarters for his failure to mention the general's name prominently enough in his stories. In any event, it is apparent that Winfield Hancock was concerned that the story of his command—and its commander—should be properly presented to the public.[5]

To that end, later on, Hancock was even willing to take on a reporter as a member of his staff. He first offered a commission and appointment as adjutant to Sylvanus Cadwallader, a correspondent for the *New York Herald* attached to Grant's headquarters, and when that offer was declined, he extended the same invitation to Finley Anderson, a young reporter also with the *Herald* who had been released early in 1864 from a Confederate prison. Anderson, who was fearless in battle, a trait which obviously appealed to Hancock, accepted the position and served with the general to the end of the war. Hancock steered clear of the controversies among the generals of the Army of the Potomac, but he certainly considered that the proper care for his public image was essential to protect his flanks.[6]

And so, Winfield Scott Hancock, clearly one of the rising officers of the Army of the Potomac, marched with his division across northern Virginia. Behind them were McClellan, the Peninsula, and Antietam. Behind them was John Pope. Behind them, too, was the Emancipation Proclamation, a political act which was unpopular with Hancock and with a large part of the eastern army but which Hancock and that army nevertheless took in stride. The proclamation offended Hancock's constitutional beliefs, but the whole war, with secession, coercion, and a quasi-sovereign Confederacy, was becoming, if not unconstitutional, then extraconstitutional, beyond what was contemplated by the Constitution, and Hancock tacitly recognized this. He was fighting to restore the Union; if that struggle necessarily evolved into a war against slavery, he would not welcome the change, but he would accept it. Behind Hancock and his men, finally, was the idea, the possibility, that the war could be a short or an easy one. There were, it was now clear, no deals which could be made to patch up differences. The Confederacy was fighting for its life, without realistic hope, now, of foreign intervention. The war would be bitter and hard and bloody, and, unless the people of the North tired of it, it would go on to the end.

But first there was Burnside. Darius Couch, who had replaced Sumner as commander of the Second Corps after Antietam, said, "Those of us who were well acquainted with Burnside knew that he was a brave, loyal man, but we did not think that he had the military ability to command the Army of the Potomac." In fact, no one who was acquainted with Burnside thought he was up to the job, and this included Burnside himself. He was handsome and martial-looking, with full side-whiskers worn in a style to which was given his name, though inverted. He had a frank and ingratiating manner and a warm smile. "It is probably true," wrote one officer in the army, "that that man's manners made his fortune, for he remained long in the service in high places, and yet his presence was an element of weakness where he was a subordinate, and was disastrous when he held a great command." Primarily responsible for the failure on the Union left at Antietam, Burnside was selected by Lincoln to succeed McClellan as leader of the Army of the Potomac only because the choices were very limited. After Pope, the president dared not bring in another western general; of the other corps commanders in the east, Sumner was too old and tired, Porter and Franklin were too close to McClellan and suffered from some of the same faults as the ousted commander, and Hooker, the only other possibility at the time, had too many disquieting elements to him, including overweening ambition, frequent disloyalty to his superiors, and a tendency to grandstand for the Radicals in Washington. Burnside it was, and the Army of the Potomac would pay a great and unnecessary price for the choice.[7]

Burnside revamped the command structure of his army by creating a new level between himself and the corps commanders. He divided the army into three "grand divisions," with two corps each, and appointed Hooker, Franklin, and Sumner to lead them. The "grand division" idea was not a bad concept, but Burnside gave it a bad name. Although the "grand divisions" were abolished formally after Burnside's relief, his successors, Meade particularly, put the idea, or variants of it, into practice at such battles as Gettysburg and the Wilderness.

Burnside then went to work on a plan of campaign. McClellan, slow as he was in advancing down the east side of the Blue Ridge, had placed the Army of the Potomac in an advantageous position to strike Longstreet's corps near Culpeper, as Jackson was more than a day's march away in the Shenandoah Valley. Whether McClellan would have done anything with this advantage is, of course, a different question; just before his relief he had been talking about moving his army to the Peninsula once again. In any event, Burnside chose to abandon this position. He received reluctant consent from Lincoln to march secretly and rapidly down the north bank of the Rappahannock River, to cross at Fredericksburg, and move swiftly on Richmond before Lee could catch up. Lincoln's approval, emphasizing the necessity of speedy execution, came on November 14, and Burnside started his army the next day.

Late in the day of November 17, Hancock's division, at the head of Sumner's grand division, arrived at Falmouth, across the river from Fredericksburg, and found there only a few rebel cavalrymen. Burnside had indeed surprised Lee, and Fredericksburg was virtually undefended. Unfortunately, the pontoon boats Burnside had directed be sent from Washington for bridging material had not yet arrived. Sumner was all for fording the river, but Burnside demurred. Should rains cause a rise in the river, Sumner's force could be marooned on the opposite side, cut off from the rest of the army; it would be better to sit down and wait for the pontoons. "To our surprise," wrote Samuel Zook's adjutant, the division was "directed to establish camps and picket lines."[8]

Incredibly, because of unforgivable negligence in Washington, the first pontoons did not show up until November 25, by which time Longstreet was well entrenched in Fredericksburg and Jackson would soon be on his way there. The element of surprise was gone, as was any strategic merit Burnside's plan might have possessed when first hatched. Nevertheless, Burnside, whose most notable character trait may have been obstinacy, chose to push ahead with his plan: he would cross the river and move on Richmond.

Time passed. While Burnside waited for the rest of his pontoon train to arrive and for everything else to be arranged in proper order, November faded into December. Jackson arrived from the Valley, and the Army of Northern Virginia worked on creating a nearly perfect defensive position on the other side of the Rappahannock. The Federal soldiers settled in on their side of the river, increasingly sure that the commander would not now dare to attack the entrenched Confederates, particularly as the lateness of the season would work against any extended campaign. When rumors circulated that Burnside still intended to attack, the army concluded that the rumors must be untrue.[9]

While at Falmouth, Hancock got some good news. Within the space of two days, he received two promotions. On November 29 he became a major general of volunteers, commensurate with his new responsibility as a division commander. On November 30 he was promoted from captain to major (in the Quartermaster Corps) in the regular army. The latter promotion was not important at the time, obviously, but would be become meaningful at the end of the war, when the inflated wartime ranks disappeared.[10]

It soon became apparent that the rumors about Burnside's intentions were all too accurate. He still planned to cross the river and to assault at Frederickburg, with no allowance made for the difference in circumstances brought about by the long time lag and the fortification of the town by Robert E. Lee.

The Rappahannock here ran northwest to southeast, with Falmouth on the northeast side and Fredericksburg on the southwest. The latter town sat on a bench of land, above the water and something less than a mile wide. Behind the town rose a line of hills known as Marye's Heights, now crowned with Confederate artillery. Below Fredericksburg the hills were farther back, some 4,500 yards, and there was more room to maneuver on the flat land. It appears to have been Burnside's plan to attack with Franklin's Left Grand Division below the town, with Sumner's Right Grand Division coming through Fredericksburg to seize the heights beyond.

On the night of December 9, Sumner convened a meeting of the corps, division, and brigade commanders in his command, to review what was going to be done. The discussion was a frank one, and it soon became clear that there was virtual unanimity as to the foolishness of Burnside's plan. Sumner alone, most likely out of misguided loyalty to his commander, professed to find the plan workable. Wind of the meeting got to Burnside, and he called the same officers together again the next evening at his own headquarters. He was angry, and he was especially severe with Hancock, who had not, according to Darius Couch, been as outspoken at Sumner's as he himself had been. Burnside said he had made his plans and all he wanted was that they be loyally carried out. Hancock explained that he meant no personal discourtesy but still thought it would be very difficult to take the line of fortified heights which he knew awaited them on the other side of the river. Couch got up and said they would do everything they could; while he was talking, French walked in and asked, "Is this a Methodist camp-meeting?" On this note, the gathering broke up, but it had enhanced no one's confidence in Ambrose E. Burnside.[11]

That evening Hancock was directed to send two regiments, the 57th and the 66th New York, to serve as supports for the engineers who were to put the pontoon bridges across the Rappahannock. The next morning a detachment of Mississippi sharpshooters, concealed on the Fredericksburg side, took a terrible toll of both the engineers and the infantry supports as the effort to put the bridges together languished. Burnside ordered an artillery barrage, which reduced much of Fredericksburg to rubble but failed to flush out the snipers. Eventually a force of infantrymen rowed across in the pontoon boats and drove the rebels away; the bridges were finally completed late on December 11. There were 150 men killed and wounded in the two New York regiments, including both regimental commanders. But Burnside had his bridgehead at Fredericksburg.[12]

The next morning, at 8 o'clock, Hancock's division began its passage of the river, joining forces in Fredericksburg with the other divisions of the corps, those of French and O. O. Howard. Nothing much was accomplished that day, December 12, although at one point Burnside ordered the Second Corps to march down the Rappahannock to where Franklin's grand division was gathering, a march which Couch wrote "was the only proper move to make." But the direction to move down the river was revoked. "The orders that were given by Burnside," Couch snorted, "showed that he had no fixed plan of battle." The troops of the two corps which made up Sumner's grand division, the Second and the Ninth, were told to bivouac that night in the streets of the ruined town, with no fires. It was a miserable night, made worse for the generals by thought of the fuzzy-headed plan for the morrow.[13]

In his thinking for the assault on December 13, Burnside intended Franklin's force below the town to make the major effort against Lee's right, with Sumner simply making a demonstration against Marye's Heights. He was on the right track; if there was any chance of success, it was with his left. But the orders Burnside sent out were vague and confusing. Instead of reinforcing Franklin with Hooker, he kept the latter in reserve behind Sumner. He directed Franklin to attack with "not less than a division," and Franklin, who never took two steps when one would meet the letter of his orders, sent in just one division, Meade's, which was repulsed after initial success. Gibbon's division gave support on Meade's right but was also driven back.[14]

Assuming that the assault on the left was going well and thinking, perhaps, that Lee had weakened his force behind the town, Burnside ordered Sumner to attack Marye's Heights with a column of a division. Couch soon received orders from Sumner, detailing how the attack was to be made. Accordingly he directed French to prepare his division in three brigade lines for the advance, with Hancock's division to follow in the same order, with intervals of 200 yards between the lines. The stated objective of the assault was simply to seize "the heights in rear of the town."[15]

Neither Burnside, nor Sumner, nor Couch knew what really faced these two divisions of the Second Corps as they prepared to attack. The difficulty of capturing the fortified heights had been foreseen by Hancock at Burnside's headquarters a few nights earlier, and this would indeed be a hazardous undertaking. Longstreet, commanding on Marye's Heights, came upon an idle cannon and suggested to Porter Alexander, his chief of artillery, that it be utilized. Alexander replied, "General, we cover that ground now so well that we will comb it as with a fine-tooth comb. A chicken could not live on that field when we open on it." To the known danger of Marye's Heights, bristling with Confederate artillery and infantry, was added a danger unknown. The Telegraph Road ran south from Fredericksburg to the North Anna River; where it skirted the base of Marye's Heights, it ran in a trough between two stout stone walls. The attack of the Second Corps would head directly for the stone wall at the base of the hill, some 40 feet below the crest. And behind that stone wall, unseen by the Federals, was a brigade of Confederate infantry under Colonel Thomas Cobb, perfectly placed to fire point-blank upon attacking troops while being almost fully protected from return fire themselves.[16]

About 11 a.m. Couch received the order to move out with French's division. Hancock and his officers silently shook hands and then prepared to follow. The Federals filed out of town on two roads which led to Marye's Heights. Even before they left the town, the blue-clad soldiers came under bombardment from the artillery on the hill. As they emerged onto the plain, sloping up toward the stone wall, they were confronted with an unexpected obstacle, a millrace, or canal, which was too wide and too deep to be negotiated except by the two bridges on which the roads crossed it. On one of the bridges the planking had been torn up, and the attackers had to cross it in single file on the stringers. The canal ruined whatever formation had been preserved up to then, with bursts of artillery shells tearing great holes in the Union ranks as they moved forward. Fortunately, the depression through which the canal flowed was at this point deep enough that the troops who had crossed it were sheltered from direct fire and could deploy somewhat before resuming their advance. French's brigades reformed as best they could and moved forward, still under the murderous shelling of the artillery on Marye's Heights, and then were met with a devastating and unexpected blast of musketry from behind the stone wall. A windrow of dead and wounded Federal soldiers lay about 40 or 50 yards in front of the wall, and those not hit went reeling back for shelter.[17]

Just behind the three brigades of French's division came Zook's brigade, the first of Hancock's lines. Hancock gave them the word to move out, and on they came into a storm of bursting shells. "We marched rapidly forward," one of Zook's men said, "passing a huge pile of bricks, which the round shot was scattering in every direction, then came a mill race, and on the other side of it a high board fence." With these obstacles behind they marched forward, toward the strongest part of the enemy line. "It seemed a terrible long distance, as with bated breath and heads bowed down, we hurried forward, the rebel guns plowing great furrows in our ranks at every step; all we could do was close up the gaps and press forward." Three hundred yards from the stone wall, Zook's men burst into a cheer and charged, and then Cobb's troops behind the wall opened fire. "Before we knew it," wrote Zook's adjutant, "our momentum was gone, and the charge a failure. Within one hundred yards of the base of the hill we dropped down, and then flat on our bellies, opened fire." Those who got closest to the wall, about 25 or 30 yards, were in the 53rd Pennsylvania, under Colonel John R. Brooke. Zook's brigade, in passing the farthest advance of French's division, lost 527 of the 1,532 men it took into battle.[18]

Next came the Irish Brigade. Meagher had exhorted his men to do their duty "nobly to the last"; he ordered each man to wear a sprig of green boxwood in his cap. By the malevolent irony of war, the Confederates who faced them, Cobb's Georgians, were almost all Irishmen too. They groaned when they recognized Meagher's troops with their green insignia and green battle flags coming at them, but they did their duty. They poured forth a blast of rifle fire, and Meagher's men went down. They got to within 40 yards of the wall, a few closer, with some of Robert Nugent's men of the 69th New York dying only 25 yards from it. The rest of them moved slowly back or flopped down on the ground, anything to get out of that murderous fire. Of Meagher's 1,200 men, 545 were casualties.[19]

On behind Meagher came the men of Caldwell's brigade, with the same results. Some of Cross's men of the 5th New Hampshire got to the same line, 25 yards from the wall, which marked the greatest advance of the earlier brigades, but no one could get closer. Caldwell went down, wounded in the shoulder, and Hancock ordered Colonel George von Schack, of the 7th New York, to take over the brigade. Hancock was everywhere, helping to dispose the troops, holding them firm, trying to make the most of an impossible task. Caldwell's brigade lost more than 950 men, and those who were left, except the 145th Pennsylvania, which broke and ran when its colonel was shot, held doggedly to the position they had achieved. It was only twenty minutes from the time Zook's men started forward until Caldwell's were stopped; during this brief time, the division lost more than 2,000 of its 5,000 men, 156 of them officers. "These were veteran regiments," a saddened Hancock said, "led by able and tried commanders, and I regret to say that their places cannot soon be filled."[20]

Hancock formed his men in a single line of battle across the field and held this line for the rest of the day and the following morning. "This line was held for hours after the troops had exhausted their ammunition," Hancock wrote, "and after the ammunition of the killed and wounded within reach had been expended." Howard's division was thrown in after the repulse of Caldwell's brigade, with no better results. Then, when Burnside should have pushed Franklin forward again on the left, the only sector where success was possible, with all the reinforcements he could send him, the general commanding instead ordered Hooker to send his grand division to the support of Sumner, against the stone wall and Marye's Heights. Hooker came to look at the situation, talked with Couch, and talked with Hancock. He then recrossed the river to tell Burnside that the effort was futile. Burnside, however, who despised Hooker (the feeling was mutual), stubbornly adhered to his original plan and insisted on another attempt to take the hill. The divisions of Charles Griffin and then Andrew Humphreys were sent forward, followed by that of George Getty, but all that was accomplished was the killing and maiming of many more Union soldiers. None of them got any closer to the stone wall than Hancock had, and by now there were so many blue-clad bodies on the field that it became difficult to negotiate a way through them.[21]

Darkness fell on a torn and bleeding Army of the Potomac, the survivors of what a reporter called "a slaughter the most bloody and the most useless of the war." Burnside, apparently realizing, finally, what he had done, became almost incoherent in his despair; he decided that the next day he would lead, personally, his old Ninth Corps in an assault on the stone wall. The other generals talked him out of this lunatic plan. They recognized that, while Burnside might seek death on the battlefield as a form of atonement for his errors, it would involve the useless death of too many soldiers with him. The army stayed in position on December 14, and during the night of December 15 it was able to retire safely across the Rappahannock.[22]

The battle of Fredericksburg accomplished nothing for the Union cause, and it cost more than 12,000 casualties. "It was a desperate undertaking, and the army fought hard," Hancock wrote to his wife. But the army never had a chance, under the feeble and incompetent leadership of Ambrose E. Burnside. He had only the sketchiest plan of battle in mind: get across the river and send men forward and somewhere there should be success. The orders he gave his subordinates were vague and garbled, and he gave only a tap at the Confederate line at the place where he should have hit it hard, on the left, with Franklin. On the right, where the rebels held an impregnable position, he hurled wave after wave of his soldiers against Marye's Heights, holding stubbornly to an obviously unsound plan. It was a failure of Burnside, however, not of his troops, who fought for the most part with valor and dedication. After the war an officer in the Army of Northern Virginia, hearing someone cite Pickett's charge at Gettysburg as the most heroic effort of the war, said "I was with Lee's army from the beginning and surrendered at Appomattox, and . . . I never saw anything that surpassed the charge made by Hancock and Humphreys at Fredericksburg."[23]

Shortly after the army recrossed to Falmouth and went into what it thought was winter quarters, Hancock got a leave of absence and went to St. Louis to spend well-earned time with Allie and the children. Thus he missed the vicious internecine squabbling which took place among Burnside, Hooker, Franklin, Baldy Smith, and other generals as scapegoats were sought for the disaster at Fredericksburg. He missed the "mud march," Burnside's last futile offensive in January 1863, an offensive which simply bogged down in the mud created by an unseasonable heavy rain. On January 25 the president relieved Burnside and replaced him with Hooker, at the same time retiring Sumner and removing Franklin from his command. The Army of the Potomac would try it again in 1863, with a new man at the helm.[24]

TEN

The Failure of
Fighting Joe

Over the winter, three excellent young officers were added to Hancock's staff. Major George Washington Scott was a New Yorker who rose by the end of the war to command a brigade in the Second Corps. Captain Henry H. Bingham, a Pennsylvania native, won a brevet as brigadier general on the last day of the war and, in 1893, was awarded the Medal of Honor for his heroism on the second day of the Wilderness; he served after the war as a Republican congressman. The third young man was Lieutenant William P. Wilson, also a Pennsylvanian. Wilson served five years on Hancock's personal staff; he later wrote that he remembered his trepidation on first entering the general's office "and how quickly it was dispelled by his cordial greeting." His feelings for Hancock "deepened into love and respect that increased with the passing years, for he honored me with his friendship until the day of his death." Hancock was blessed with good staff members—intelligent, industrious, and loyal—but he helped immeasurably to develop their good qualities. He returned their loyalty, too. When Zook's official report on Chancellorsville was found to contain what Hancock felt was an unfair reflection on Major Scott, for allegedly posting one of Zook's regiments in an improper position, Hancock asked Zook to change it; when Zook refused to do so, Hancock simply declined to send the report on to the War Department.[1]

During those early months of 1863, Hancock occasionally drilled the division, to the delight of the troops and the other officers. When he did so, he turned the air around him blue with his swearing. He took great joy in aiming a barrage of profanity at Zook. That brigade commander's young adjutant reported that, "as swearing is contrary to the regulations, Zook, who cannot easily be beaten in that line, always gives as good as he gets without fear of consequences, and the officers think it great fun." Hancock, he wrote, "is very hot headed; sometimes goes off at half cock, but is a magnificent soldier." Out of all the whooping and shouting, the marching and the swearing, however, was forged one of the very best divisions of the Union army.[2]

On St. Patrick's Day, 1863, the Irish Brigade threw a party. Meagher and his staff put on a steeplechase race on the division parade ground, followed by a reception, featuring an immense bowl of very strong punch. Hancock and most of the general officers of the army, along with a large crowd of ladies, attended, and it was a very festive affair. Several of Hancock's aides made themselves particularly conspicuous, and there was much drunkenness and a number of fights. It was considered a highly successful party.[3]

In the meantime, "Fighting Joe" Hooker put his impress on the Army of the Potomac. Hooker was a strange combination of strengths and weaknesses. A Massachusetts man, he graduated from West Point in 1837. After good service in Mexico, where he publicly and loudly criticized Winfield Scott, Hooker resigned from the army, becoming a farmer in California. When the war started, back he came to the army, but Scott ignored him and he had to await McClellan to get a brigade, and shortly a division, in the Army of the Potomac. He was a capable commander and a brave soldier, and he received one very lucky break. A newspaper headline mistakenly called him "Fighting Joe Hooker," and the name stuck. Hooker professed to dislike the name, but it set him apart from his fellows and made him a public favorite. The people did not know that the nickname was a typographical error; they assumed that Hooker had earned it. Hooker was handsome and affable, one of the few clean-shaven generals in the army, with a florid complexion, light hair, and blue eyes. He was also a hard drinker, an egotist, and one who delighted in the company of ladies of dubious repute. He was very much involved with the Radical faction in Congress. Hooker was, said John Gibbon, "essentially an intriguer" who "sacrificed his soldierly principles whenever such sacrifice could gain him political influence to further his own ends."[4]

When Hooker took over his new command, he made a number of administrative changes. He abolished Burnside's "grand divisions," probably simply because that concept was his predecessor's idea. Hooker was left with direct responsibility for seven infantry corps and one of cavalry (after he consolidated all the cavalry into one corps under George Stoneman), and these, as it turned out, were more than Hooker could handle. While consolidating the cavalry, Hooker removed from Henry J. Hunt overall command of the army's artillery; this was a mistake, for Hunt was easily the best gunnery commander in the Union army. Hooker, in cooperation with the army's medical director, took steps to correct deficiencies in diet, sanitation, and hygiene, and the health of the troops improved measurably. He made changes in procedures governing leaves and furloughs, putting things on an orderly basis, thereby reducing substantially the number of desertions and causing many absentees to return to the army. So long as soldiers had a fairly certain idea of when they could expect a few weeks' leave to go home, there was much less incentive to desert. Finally, Hooker and his chief of staff, Daniel Butterfield, adopted an idea which Philip Kearny had put into play at Fair Oaks, that of a unit insignia to be worn on the cap. Each corps was given a basic design, and the badge for the first division of each corps was red, the second white, and the third blue. Their new badges—the Second Corps sported the trefoil—soon helped to develop

greater unit pride; the insignia also helped materially in identifying stragglers and getting them back to their proper places. One staffer, looking back
on this productive period after Hooker took up the reins of the Army of the
Potomac, wrote: "Whatever his merits or his shortcomings as a commander,
Hooker was surely an ideal inspector-general."[5]

Not everyone was enthralled by Hooker, or by the people around him.
Butterfield, the chief of staff, was particularly disliked; Andrew Humphreys,
a tough division commander in the Third Corps, called Butterfield "the most
detested and most despised man in the Army, false, treacherous, and
cowardly." But Hooker had 140,000 men, he had a plan to defeat Lee, and he
was ready to go. Reflecting the ambivalent feelings about Hooker, a reporter
wrote: "Every one . . . feels that the new General will do one of two things
and that right speedily—destroy the rebel army, or our own."[6]

Hooker had a plan, and it was a good one. With an advantage in numbers
of more than two or one, he would divide his army, leaving Sedgwick with
most of three corps and more than 50,000 men to cross the Rappahannock at
Fredericksburg, pinning Lee's force to that position, while the balance of
the Army of the Potomac moved swiftly upriver, crossed behind Lee, and, if
all went well, crushed the southern army. The cavalry under Stoneman was
to ride far to the south, threatening Lee's communcations with Richmond.

On April 27, 1863, Hooker set his plan in motion. The Eleventh and
Twelfth Corps started for Kelly's Ford, twenty-five miles up the Rappahannock, and the next day Meade, with his Fifth Corps, also moved toward
Kelly's Ford. They then crossed the Rappahannock, moved their commands
south to the fords of the Rapidan River, and crossed that potential obstacle.
They accomplished all this without difficulty and by the evening of April 30
had encamped at Hooker's point of concentration, in the vicinity of a road
crossing called Chancellorsville. In the meantime, Couch had moved two of
his three divisions (Hancock's and French's; the third division, now under
John Gibbon, was back at Fredericksburg with Sedgwick) upriver on April
28, had reached United States Ford on the Rappahannock on the twenty-
ninth, and had crossed the river on pontoon bridges on the afternoon of the
thirtieth. That evening the Second Corps also reached Chancellorsville. The
men were "in exuberant spirits" at passing the river barrier without having
to fight a bloody battle to do so, and Hooker issued a grandiloquent proclamation that "the operations of the last three days have determined that our
enemy must ingloriously fly, or . . . give us battle on our ground, where
certain destruction awaits him."[7]

Already, however, Hooker had made his first big mistake. He had halted
the Eleventh and Twelfth corps at Chancellorsville at 3 p.m. on April 30,
when they should have kept going. Chancellorsville was simply a clearing in
a dense and impenetrable forest called the Wilderness, and it was of urgent
importance for Hooker to get his army free of this encumbrance. A few
miles to the east, the Wilderness ended; at this point Hooker would enjoy
ease of maneuver and could make effective his great preponderance in

numbers. It was also crucial that the Union army take Banks's Ford, on the Rappahannock just upriver from Falmouth, which would shorten appreciably the line of communications between the two wings of Hooker's army. A force should have pushed on for that key point. But Fighting Joe let his men stop at Chancellorsville on the afternoon of April 30.

On May 1 the Union army was once more in motion, although the precise orders for movement were not received until well after daylight. There were three roads by which Hooker could move toward Fredericksburg: the Orange and Fredericksburg Turnpike, which was the most direct; the Orange Plank Road, which ran to the south of the turnpike before joining with it some five miles east of Chancellorsville; and the river road by way of Banks's Ford. Slocum's Twelfth Corps, followed by Howard and the Eleventh, was to move on the plank road, while George Sykes's division of regulars, in the Fifth Corps, marched out the turnpike. Meade took the rest of his corps toward Banks's Ford. Couch was ordered to send Hancock's division out the turnpike to support Sykes.

Suddenly, everything went into reverse. "Having arrived on the ground," Hancock later wrote in his report, "orders were received to withdraw all the troops." Hooker had made a costly blunder, one his generals could hardly believe. He had abandoned Banks's Ford, abandoned the position Meade had gained on Lee's flank, abandoned the high ground out in the open won by Sykes, and pulled all his troops back into the Wilderness, to take up positions around Chancellorsville.[8]

What had happened to the overconfident Union commander? When Lee realized what Hooker's strategy was, he did not hesitate. He left 10,000 men under Early at Fredericksburg and faced the rest of his army about to march toward Chancellorsville. Jackson got his men into position by the morning of May 1, and at 11 a.m. he ordered McLaws forward on the turnpike. When Sykes's men emerged from the woods, they found McLaws's Confederates in their front. The situation was still advantageous for the Federals, particularly with the opportunity which would shortly develop to deliver a flank attack from the river road. Sykes quickly drove the enemy from the high ground in front, a ridge which ran across all three roads and which was ideal for artillery. But when Hooker heard from Sykes of the opposition, which apparently showed up sooner than he had anticipated, he lost his nerve and ordered a withdrawal. Couch and Hancock had just gotten the latter's division into position when Hooker's order arrived. They were dumbfounded. One observer later wrote: "The field was exactly such a one as the men of the Army of the Potomac had always been crying out for—one on which they could see the enemy they were called to fight." Sykes and Gouverneur K. Warren, chief topographical engineer of the army, were with Couch and Hancock when the order was received, and they were of the unanimous opinion that the position then held should not be yielded. Couch sent an aide back to Hooker to recommend staying put, but the aide returned in half an hour "with positive orders to return." Though Warren suggested disobedience, Couch saw no alternative but to carry out the directive. Sykes's division moved back, followed by Hancock's. Later, Hancock, testifying before the Joint Committee on the Conduct of the War, said: "I have no doubt that we ought to have held our advanced positions, and still kept pushing on, and attempt to make a junction with General Sedgwick."[9]

In any event, Sykes was pulled back, and after him came Hancock. When the withdrawal was almost completed, Couch received a third order from Hooker, to hold on until 5 o'clock. Couch angrily snapped at the courier: "Tell General Hooker he is too late, the enemy are already on my right and rear. I am in full retreat." Given up to the Confederates was the high ground east of Chancellorsville which Sykes had taken; Lee found it a fine site for his guns.[10]

Hancock's division was posted some distance in front of the Chancellor mansion looking east, on the left of Sykes. Three-quarters of a mile east of Chancellorsville was a bushy ravine, through which ran a little brook called Mott's Run; two regiments under Colonel Nelson Miles occupied this ravine as skirmishers. The rest of the afternoon, until darkness came on, Hancock's lines were subjected to sporadic pressure from Confederates under the command of his old buddy, Harry Heth, now commanding a division under A. P. Hill.[11]

In the meantime, Darius Couch had stormed back to see Hooker, who assured him, "It is all right, Couch, I have got Lee just where I want him; he must fight me on my own ground." Hearing this fatuous statement, Couch withdrew, convinced "that my commanding general was a whipped man." Chancellorsville was no place for a defensive battle, with little open country and few good sites for artillery, but Hooker had lost his taste for the initiative. From the decision to fall back into the tangled Wilderness followed all the misfortune to come.[12]

The next morning, Sykes's division was withdrawn and Hancock's line adjusted, with the right resting on the left of John W. Geary's division of the Twelfth Corps, near the plank road, and angling back along the road that led to United States Ford. French's division connected on the left. Rifle pits were dug in front of Hancock's line, protected by an abatis, an obstacle of felled trees; Miles's skirmishers were posted in these pits. Throughout that day of May 2, there were periodic attacks on Hancock's lines, but they were all repulsed by Miles and his force. It was during this fighting that Hancock turned to an aide and said, "Captain Parker, ride down and tell Colonel Miles he is worth his weight in gold." Miles was a natural soldier, and Hancock had quickly recognized it. A former store clerk back in his native Massachusetts, Nelson Miles had no formal military education or training, but he rose rapidly in rank once the fighting began. Hancock, in sending him reinforcements, was careful to send regiments whose colonels were junior to Miles, thus making sure that the latter kept the front-line command. Lee made several efforts against the Union left, but the strongest ones were against Hancock.[13]

All of the rebel attacks on the Union left, however, were demonstrations to divert Hooker's attention from the real Confederate movement. Lee and Jackson, in an audacious decision, had split the Confederate army again, and Jackson took the larger part in a long march through the woods, to emerge late in the day on the unprotected right flank of the Union army, far down the turnpike. Jackson's march did not go wholly undetected, but Hooker chose to believe that the enemy was retreating; he did little except to try to hurry it along. Certainly neither Hooker nor O. O. Howard, whose Eleventh Corps constituted the Union right, took any measures to guard against a flank attack. Consequently, when Jackson's men burst out of the woods at about 5 p.m., they swarmed over an Eleventh Corps which was totally unprepared. Their rifles stacked, many of Howard's men were cooking dinner, writing letters, or otherwise relaxing. The Eleventh Corps was driven back nearly two miles. But the rest of the Army of the Potomac stood firm, and the triumphant Confederates soon became jumbled and disorganized, as so often happened after successful assaults. It was in trying to sort out his men and form them for further action in the forest twilight that Stonewall Jackson was shot and mortally wounded by his own men. A. P. Hill was also wounded, and a saddened Lee summoned Jeb Stuart from his cavalry to lead Jackson's men on the morrow.

The dismal story of the next day, May 3, at Chancellorsville is that of a demoralized general, moving from mistake to blunder to mistake, and an army that was defeated only because its commander believed that it was. The Eleventh Corps, which had been shattered by Jackson's attack the evening before, was made up primarily of German troops, part of the force which had panted up and down the Valley in vain efforts to catch Jackson the year before, and the soldiers of the Army of the Potomac regarded them with scorn. Hancock told Hooker, on the morning of May 3, that there was no reason to be despondent, "for the 11th Corps had never been considered a part of the original Army of the Potomac, and not much dependence had been placed upon it." Hooker, Hancock thought, was unduly depressed. Hancock, of course, was right: despite the collapse of the Eleventh Corps, the Federals were in a good position to defeat the Army of Northern Virginia, whose two wings, under Lee and Stuart, were widely separated and were much inferior to the Union army in numbers. Hooker, unfortunately, did not view the Confederates as being divided; he regarded himself as nearly surrounded.[14]

The evening before, the Third Corps under General Daniel Sickles had occupied Hazel Grove, a high point almost a mile south of Chancellorsville. Artillery on Hazel Grove commanded both wings of the Confederate army, but Hooker, on the morning of May 3, ordered Sickles to pull back from the position. When the Federals were gone, Lee promptly moved his guns onto the hill, from where they had easy shots at Chancellorsville and the Union lines. But Fighting Joe Hooker was bent on withdrawing his army to the Rappahannock; when Meade and John F. Reynolds, neither of whose corps had been seriously engaged, suggested to Hooker that they attack Stuart's exposed flank, Hooker refused. He continued to pull back.

When the fighting commenced on the morning of May 3, three corps were in action for the Federals—Sickles's Third Corps around Hazel Grove, Slocum's Twelfth between Hazel Grove and the turnpike, and Couch's Second in front of the road junction at Chancellorsville. In fact, it was Hancock's division that was at Chancellorsville, as French's division was farther up the road to United States Ford, not immediately confronted by the enemy. The firing began early, just after 5 a.m., with a forward movement by Stuart. As the morning wore on, Sickles's corps, as mentioned, was pulled back from Hazel Grove and eventually out of the action after the commander of the Second Division, General Hiram G. Berry, was killed. At 9:15 the pillar of the Chancellor mansion against which Hooker was leaning was struck by a shell, and the commanding general was hit on the head and back by the pillar as it fell. For the rest of the day, Hooker was dazed and somewhat incoherent, but he refused to yield the control of his army to the next senior general, Darius Couch. The Twelfth Corps, its divisions under Alpheus Williams and Geary, was slowly pushed back, Geary's men fighting stubbornly despite a vulnerable flank. Soon all that was left at Chancellorsville was the division of Winfield Scott Hancock.

Hancock had prepared for the morning's action by strengthening his front line, still under the command of Miles. He felt, "from the experience of the previous day and the well-known ability and gallantry of Colonel Miles," that the line could be held. And it was, even though it was subjected to heavy assaults by the rebels under McLaws and even though Miles was severely wounded and carried from the fray. Then, as Hancock later testified, "the whole front appeared to pass out. First the Third Corps went out; then the Twelfth Corps, after fighting a long time; and there was nothing left on that part of the line but my own division." Hancock was ordered to hold on until he was notified that the rest of the army had all gotten away.[15]

The division was formed in two lines, but, with Stuart and Anderson behind him and no other Federals on the field, Hancock, as he said, "had to face about the troops in the rear line, so as to be ready for the enemy in that direction, who were coming on." Hancock's two lines, about half a mile apart, were fighting in opposite directions, one line facing east toward Fredericksburg, the other west toward Gordonsville. Shelling from both front and rear tore up his ranks, but they held firm. "Notwithstanding that my flank, which had been covered by General Geary, was entirely exposed," Hancock reported, "our fourteen pieces of artillery prevented him [the enemy] from advancing, although his battle-flags were within a few hundred yards of us." Hancock's division, the last Federals on the field, held its ground, gaining time while the disordered troops were reformed and Hooker established a new defensive perimeter back toward the Rappahannock. Finally, after 10 a.m., the word came down to Hancock to retire. He moved his artillery batteries back first and then directed the withdrawal of his infantry. Save for one regiment which misunderstood its orders and blundered into the enemy, the division's pullback was accomplished in good order and completed by 11 a.m.[16]

Of Hooker's subsequent movements, little need be said. After the abandonment of the position at Chancellorsville, the breakout of Sedgwick from Fredericksburg, so long delayed by timidity and the vagueness of Hooker's orders, took place; Lee calmly turned his back on Hooker, faced about, and defeated Sedgwick at Salem Church, on the turnpike about halfway between Fredericksburg and Chancellorsville. The baffled troops back at the United States Ford, who knew they had not been whipped but simply outgeneraled, were still ready to fight; Hancock wrote to Allie early on May 4: "The battle is not through yet by a long ways. . . . We will, I suppose, have another fight today." He could hardly comprehend the craven tactics of the army's commander. Later he said that, in his opinion, "even at the moment the fight stopped on Sunday if we had pushed in all our troops we might have won that battle." But not with Hooker in command: Fighting Joe had no fight left in him, and early in the morning of May 6, he crossed his army over the Rappahannock and returned to the camp at Falmouth.[17]

Hooker's initial strategic success and his vainglorious boasting simply magnified the abysmal conduct which produced an ignominious defeat. He failed to put a large part of his army into action, he gave up strong positions for weak ones, he sent the cavalry under Stoneman off on a distant mission which kept it out of the battle altogether, and he badly misused his artillery. Most of all, the battle marked a failure of will, courage, and moral strength on Hooker's part. Lee's admirers consider Chancellorsville one of the high points of his career, but he had a great deal of cooperation from Fighting Joe Hooker.

Hancock later told the Joint Committee on the Conduct of the War that the real mistake was "in ever stopping at Chancellorsville at all." He went on:

> There was the cause of the whole trouble. General Hooker did not arrive there until Thursday night, about the same time we did. If his troops had marched on even on Thursday afternoon, and opened Banks's Ford, we would then have been within three miles of Fredericksburg, and would have been practically connected with the force under General Sedgwick. . . . There, no doubt, was the mistake. That movement might have been made on Thursday afternoon, or even on Friday morning. . . . I believe if we had . . . marched right down to Banks's Ford, the whole movement would have been a perfect success.[18]

In private, Hancock had other thoughts about Hooker's defeat. He wrote to Allie that the day before the battle Hooker had said, "God Almighty could not prevent me from winning a victory tomorrow." Hancock was a man of conventional religious views, and he did not believe in challenging the Deity. "Pray," he wrote, "could we expect a victory after that?"[19]

Despite the defeat of the Army of the Potomac, the star of Winfield Scott Hancock continued to rise at Chancellorsville. His conduct of the division, particularly in the harrowing rearguard action, was exemplary. At the end he held off McLaws, Anderson, and Stuart with one division where seven divisions had earlier been posted (although even Hancock realized that the Confederates by then were probably exhausted). His division lost over 1,100 killed, wounded, or missing, one of the heaviest losses in the whole army. Couch remarked on Hancock's "gallantry, energy, and his example of marked personal bravery." Hancock, though not wounded in this battle, was struck several times by shell fragments, and his horse was killed under him.[20]

An officer on Zook's staff noted Hancock and Zook riding by in the midst of the artillery duel at the Chancellor house, shortly before the division was pulled back. It was at a spot where a Confederate battery had the exact range, and shells were flying all about:

> It was interesting to see General Hancock ride along amidst this rain of shells utterly indifferent, not even ducking his head when one came close to him, which is a difficult thing to do, for one seems to do it involuntarily. General Hancock is in his element and at his best in the midst of a fight. . . .[21]

Hancock as a new major general (*Matthew Brady Collection, National Archives*).

Almira Russell Hancock (*Library of Congress*).

General Henry Heth, C.S.A., one of Hancock's oldest friends (*Matthew Brady Collection, National Archives*).

Hancock *(seated)* and his division commanders *(from left)*
Francis Barlow, David Birney, and John Gibbon in Virginia,
1864 *(Matthew Brady Collection, National Archives).*

Hancock as a distinguished leader of the postwar army (*Matthew Brady Collection, National Archives*).

William B. Franklin (*left*) and William Farrar "Baldy" Smith, compatriots of Hancock at West Point, in the Union army, and in postwar politics (*Matthew Brady Collection, National Archives*).

Senator William A. Wallace of Pennsylvania (*left*) and Senator Thomas F. Bayard of Delaware, Hancock's leading rival in the 1880 convention (*Library of Congress*).

Hancock (*left*) as the 1880 Democratic presidential candidate and his Republican rival, James A. Garfield (*Matthew Brady Collection, National Archives*).

ELEVEN

North to Pennsylvania

Darius Couch was disgusted by Hooker's conduct at Chancellorsville. A quiet, competent West Pointer himself, Couch had observed from all too close a vantage point the blundering in the abortive campaign south of the Rapidan. On May 22, when Lincoln consulted him, Couch recommended that Meade be placed in command of the Army of the Potomac. When nothing happened, Couch decided that he could no longer serve under Hooker, sacrificing his troops to no apparent purpose. He asked to be transferred to another command and on June 10 left the Second Corps.[1]

Hancock, too, was sorely depressed by Chancellorsville. He wrote to Allie: "I do not know what will be the next turn of the wheel of Fortune, or what Providence has in store for this unhappy army. I have had the blues ever since I returned from the campaign." He described to his wife Hooker's bumbling, and he assured her that "Hooker's day is over." He worried over a probable successor, citing two generals named as possibilities by the New York papers who, he said, "would be too much. I should ask to be relieved at once." And he revealed: "I have been approached again in connection with the command of the Army of the Potomac." There is nothing further to indicate whence came such an approach, although there were always intriguers and kingmakers enough at large in the parlors and corridors of Washington, and Stanton had long been an admirer of Hancock. It is hard to believe, however, that serious consideration could be given to vaulting a division commander over the seven corps commanders then with the army. Still, we must assume that there was some substance to this feeler for Hancock to pass it on to his wife. In any event, he had little taste for the political infighting which accompanied command of the Army of the Potomac. To Allie he concluded: "Give yourself no uneasiness—under no conditions would I accept the command. I do not belong to that class of generals whom the Republicans care to bolster up. I should be sacrificed."[2]

There was no doubt as to Couch's successor in the Second Corps. There had been a movement afoot, before Couch's departure, to place Hancock in command of the cavalry corps; Hancock, an infantryman to the bone, did not desire such a position but had finally agreed to the change if it had to be made. When the vacancy in the Second Corps developed, however, Hancock was the immediate choice; "his appointment to the command of the Corps," wrote the chief of staff of that unit, "was a matter about which there could have been no question." He was easily the outstanding division commander in the Second Corps and was generally recognized to be the best division commander in the Army of the Potomac. No other officer in the army, it was said, was so well regarded by the troops, so that Hancock's promotion was as popular as it was logical and well deserved.[3]

The men loved to tell the story of the time Hancock, with his staff behind him, galloped after three or four members of the Irish Brigade who were about to kill a sheep, in violation of explicit orders. By the time the general got to them, all but one of the malefactors had scattered, leaving behind their comrade, who had the sheep on the ground and his bayonet at the animal's throat. After a string of curses, Hancock roared, "How dare you? How dare you kill that sheep?" When the terrified soldier, seeing Hancock waving his sword, pleaded his innocence, Hancock shouted, "You infernal liar, what do you mean by telling me that? I saw you, you scoundrel! I'll teach you to disobey orders! I'll teach you to kill sheep!" At that the subject of the controversy gave a loud "baaaa," struggled to its feet, and bounded away, to the hoots and laughter of Hancock's staffers and of the general himself.[4]

His officers knew that Hancock appreciated their services and did his best to bring those services to the attention of others. On two occasions that spring, for example, Hancock wrote to Governor Horatio Seymour of New York, to acquaint him with the merits of Colonels Paul Frank and George von Schack, both regimental commanders; "New York," he wrote, "will do well to cherish such soldiers," and, incidentally, to fill up their regiments.[5]

John Caldwell succeeded Hancock as commander of the First Division, while Gibbon continued with the Second, and French, for the time being, with the Third. The new corps commander inherited a most useful officer in the corps chief of staff, Lieutenant Colonel Charles H. Morgan. A native of New York, Morgan was an 1857 graduate of West Point and a veteran of Albert Sidney Johnston's Utah expedition. Sumner had made him chief of artillery of the Second Corps, and Couch, finding him there, had moved him up to chief of staff. Hancock cited Morgan's "rare intelligence, activity, and gallantry," and Francis Walker, who as corps adjutant had the opportunity to watch Morgan on a daily basis, summed up what he did for the Second Corps: "Wherever the corps went he literally led the way."[6]

In any event, whatever adjustments Hancock needed to make in shifting from divisional to corps command would have to be made on the march; Robert E. Lee was already on the road north again.

It was time, Lee felt, to give Virginia some relief from the everlasting drain of the war and the demands that two armies made upon the state. Pennsylvania and Maryland could be tapped for replenishment of the Confederate army's depleted stores. After the victory at Chancellorsville, a successful Confederate campaign on northern soil might give a substantial or even decisive boost to the peace movement in the loyal states. Lee received permission from Jefferson Davis to take the Army of Northern Virginia across the Potomac again.

The movement began on June 3, when Lee commenced the withdrawal of his army from Fredericksburg. Over the next couple of days, leaving A. P. Hill with 30,000 men at Fredericksburg, Lee concentrated the bulk of his army at Culpeper Court House, some thirty miles to the northwest and halfway to the Shenandoah Valley. Hooker, by June 4, realized that Lee was moving, but he was unable to figure out where the Confederates were going. Over the next week, as the Army of Northern Virginia, with Richard S. Ewell in the lead, moved down the Valley toward the Potomac, Hooker with his imperfect sources of information attempted to fathom his opponent's whereabouts and intentions.[7]

By the end of the second week of June, Hooker knew that Longstreet and Ewell had passed through Culpeper and into the Valley, and he began the process of disengaging the Army of the Potomac from the Rappahannock. The men were happy to be on the move; they had had their fill of the camps around Falmouth. On the night of June 13–14, the Second Corps began its march, under its new commander, forming the right flank of the army as it moved over the next seven days, by way of Aquia Creek, Dumfries, Wolf Run Shoals, and Sangster's Station, to Centreville, northeast of Manassas. "These marches were devoid of particular incident," Colonel Morgan wrote, "those of the first and second day, however, being marches of excessive fatigue, on account of the dust and heat." So miserable was the hot weather that there were far more than the usual number of stragglers. Hancock recognized that most of these were victims of heat exhaustion or loss of sleep, not shirkers or malingerers, and he took pains to have his corps ambulances bring up the rear of his march, to pick up those who had fallen out of line. The commander of the provost guard wanted to utilize an old army trick, firing artillery toward the stragglers to cause them to think the enemy was behind them, but Hancock refused permission.[8]

The Second Corps rested at Centreville until June 21, when it marched across Bull Run to take position in Thoroughfare Gap, the pass between the Bull Run and Pignut mountains. That afternoon Hancock reported to Hooker that he was established in the gap: "I think you need have no fears of this position." The corps held the gap, "monotonously undisturbed by anything of interest," as Gibbon said, until recalled on June 25 to move back toward Gainesville and from there north to the Potomac. As the Second Corps approached the little village of Haymarket, it was fired upon by Confederate dismounted cavalry. When the rebels saw the size of the Federal unit, of course, they quickly made themselves scarce.[9]

The Confederate cavalry force was that of Jeb Stuart, who had obtained from Lee permission for a wide-ranging reconnaissance in the Union rear. Because, as Stuart reported, "Hancock had the right of way on my road," he was forced to alter his plans, cross the Bull Run lower down than expected, and make a wider circuit to get around the Army of the Potomac. It was this ride of Stuart's, thus pushed farther away from the rest of the Confederate army, that deprived Lee of Stuart's services when he most needed them, as the two armies groped toward each other near Gettysburg.[10]

Hancock's corps, leaving the Confederate cavalry to go its own way, marched on to Gum Springs. There it was joined by a brigade commanded by General Alexander Hays, made up of four New York regiments which had been captured at Harpers Ferry during the Antietam campaign of 1862. Hays, a native of Franklin, Pennsylvania, and one of Hancock's closest friends at West Point, was an officer celebrated for his "headlong courage," and Hancock quickly found better use for him. French's application for a separate command had been granted, and he was sent on June 24 to take over at Harpers Ferry. Hays was then named French's successor in the Third Division, with Colonel George L. Willard taking over the brigade. On the same day, General Alexander S. Webb showed up, with a new briga-dier's commission, looking for an assignment. Webb, a New Yorker, had graduated from the military academy in 1855 and had been serving in artillery and staff assignments thus far in the war. Hancock, who knew him, quickly latched onto Webb and placed him in command of the Philadelphia Brigade, in Gibbon's division. June 25 at Gum Springs was a busy day, but a profitable one.[11]

On June 26, in an all-day drizzle, the Second Corps marched to Edwards Ferry, crossed the Potomac on the pontoon bridge there, and went into camp about a mile from the river. By the next day the whole of the Army of the Potomac was north of its namesake river, while Ewell's corps of Lee's army had penetrated deep into Pennsylvania, driving toward Harrisburg, York, and the Susquehanna. On June 27 Hancock's corps marched to Sugar Loaf Mountain, and the next day it marched twenty-five miles—"with few stragglers and in excellent condition," as one officer wrote—to Monocacy Junction, near Frederick, Maryland. The Union soldiers were pleased to be in rich, abundant farm country, virtually untouched by the war, with friend-ly inhabitants who were, however, disturbed by Lee's invasion.[12]

While the Union army was moving up into Maryland, its command problem was suddenly resolved. It had been considered highly unlikely that the Army of the Potomac would go into another major battle under Hooker, and Lincoln had sounded out Couch and Reynolds on the possibility of their taking the top position. It was at this time that Hancock, too, received the feelers earlier described. Couch had demurred, suggesting Meade, and Reynolds categorically declined after he could not be assured of freedom from political interference. There the matter had rested, as Lee began a new campaign and as Hooker slowly put the army in motion after him. By the last week of June, Hooker was on Lee's trail while still protecting Washing-ton, and removing Fighting Joe under these circumstances would have involved unacceptable political risks. At that point, however, in a stroke of good fortune for the administration, Hooker removed himself. He squabbled with Henry Halleck over his authority to evacuate the garrison from Harpers Ferry and to add it to his army; when Halleck told him he had no such authority, he fired off a telegram to Washington on June 27, stating that he could not carry out his assigned mission "with the means at my disposal" and requesting "that I may at once be relieved from the position I occupy."[13]

Fighting Joe Hooker may have been bluffing, and he probably felt confident that no change in command could take place when a big battle was obviously imminent. Much to his surprise, however, his resignation was instantly accepted, and George Gordon Meade was named to command the Army of the Potomac. "Considering the circumstances," Halleck told Meade, "no one ever received a more important command." Meade, a competent but colorless officer with a choleric disposition, was not overjoyed with the new responsibility thus thrust upon him. John Gibbon noted that when he and Hancock visited Meade on the evening of June 28 the new commander appeared "very anxious." Still, he was no Burnside; he was confident of his ability to handle the army and he respected but did not fear Robert E. Lee.[14]

The Second Corps was directed to march at 4 a.m. on June 29, heading northeast toward Frizzellburg. The order, unfortunately, was delivered by an orderly who simply left it on a desk at Hancock's headquarters, with a staff officer who neglected to tell anyone in authority of its receipt. Hancock did not learn of the order until 6 a.m., with the result that the corps was not in motion until 8 a.m. "I regret the delay," Hancock advised Meade. "I shall try to make up the most of it by short cuts and rapid marching." The Second Corps did not stop until 10 p.m., when it was beyond Uniontown, Maryland, more than thirty miles from its starting point. This may have been the longest march made by any infantry unit in one day during the war. One member of the Second Corps looked back on this march and recalled "the perfect discipline in the ranks, the cheerfulness with which the enlisted men with their loads of fifty pounds weight—musket and ammunition, knapsack and cartridge-box, shelter tent and blanket, canteen and rations—trudged along under the broiling sun in the hottest month of our year." It was a hard, brutal march, hot and dusty, but the Second Corps took it almost in stride.[15]

When he arrived at Uniontown, Hancock was told by some of the locals that Stuart and his rebel cavalry were in camp at Westminster, some four miles away. Hancock sent this startling news to Meade by special messenger, so that steps could be taken to bag such a glittering prize. Unfortunately, Alfred Pleasonton, the Union cavalry commander, assured Meade that the report was all wrong: there were two brigades of Pleasonton's cavalry at Westminster, and the native informants must have gotten confused. Actually, there was no Union horse anywhere near Westminster, and Stuart, who *was* there, unaware of the arrival of the Second Corps at Uniontown, might easily have been captured or destroyed by Hancock in the morning. This great opportunity was squandered by the ignorant posturing of Pleasonton.[16]

Hancock's corps remained at Uniontown on June 30, resting while the Fifth Corps, delayed by the Second's late start the day before, caught up. It then moved northwest to Taneytown on the morning of July 1, going into bivouac at about 11 a.m. Hancock rode over to Meade's headquarters to advise him of the arrival of the Second Corps, and Meade discussed with him fully and frankly his plans and contingencies for the impending battle, as well as the general situation then existing, so far as Meade could ascertain it.

Lee's army was all in Pennsylvania. Two columns, under Ewell and Early, had gone as far east as Carlisle and Wrightsville, beyond York. Until June 28 Lee had not been aware that the Union army was north of the Potomac. He had assumed that Stuart would notify him when it crossed the river, but Stuart was off on his misadventure and out of contact with Lee. When Lee learned that the Federals were in Maryland and moving north, he quickly ordered his army's concentration, calling Ewell and Early back toward Chambersburg, Cashtown, and Gettysburg. In the meantime, three Federal corps, the First, the Third, and the Eleventh, under the overall direction of John Reynolds, in whom Meade had the utmost confidence, were fanned out toward Gettysburg, with a cavalry screen under the capable leadership of General John Buford. The other Union corps were working their way slowly toward the same point.[17]

Reynolds was directed to be cautious in bringing on a general battle; he was to examine the terrain and learn what he could of Confederate dispositions. If a collision with rebel forces occurred, Reynolds was expected to fight a delaying action until the Union army could be concentrated. Indeed, Meade had a position in mind for a battle, and it was not in the Gettysburg area. That very morning, July 1, Meade had issued what has come to be called the "Pipe Creek Circular" to his corps commanders, though it is doubtful that the paper itself was ever seen by Reynolds. Asserting that the army's movements had already accomplished the relief of Harrisburg and prevented an attack against Philadelphia, Meade wrote that it was "no longer his intention to assume the offensive" but, if the enemy should attack, to withdraw the army from its present position and form a line of battle along a small stream called Pipe Creek. Moving to this line would have involved a pullback of about fifteen miles from Gettysburg, back into Maryland, and lesser distances from the other places occupied by Meade's scattered corps. The Pipe Creek line would have been a formidable one, very difficult to assault or to turn, but there were disadvantages to Meade's plan as well. There was nothing to guarantee that Lee would choose to attack there, and the defensive strategy involved, with the lengthy retreats required, might have been demoralizing to the Union army. As it turned out, even though Meade briefed Hancock on it, the Pipe Creek plan was never more than a piece of paper. Events at Gettysburg soon took care of that.[18]

Hancock had hardly returned to his own headquarters from his discussion with Meade when he received an order dated 12:30 p.m. from Daniel Butterfield, whom Meade had inherited from Hooker as chief of staff, to move his corps out the road from Taneytown to Gettysburg until he should learn that Reynolds was withdrawing by that road, thus keeping the Union center covered. When this coverage was assured, Hancock was to withdraw to the position fixed for his corps in the Pipe Creek Circular.[19]

This order was almost immediately rendered obsolete by the arrival of Meade and Butterfield at Hancock's tent. Meade had learned two things of great import, first, that a fight had broken out at Gettysburg, involving at least the First and Eleventh corps and Buford's cavalry, and, second, that Reynolds had been severely or perhaps mortally wounded. With the loss of Reynolds, Meade had at the scene of battle no surrogate in whom he had faith and confidence; he directed Hancock to go to Gettysburg at once, to take command of the fighting, and to act as Meade's eyes and ears. Butterfield quickly wrote out an order, dated 1:10 p.m., and handed it to Hancock:

> The major-general commanding has just been informed that General Reynolds has been killed or badly wounded. He directs that you turn over the command of your corps to General Gibbon; that you proceed to the front, and, by virtue of this order, in case of the truth of General Reynolds' death, you assume command of the corps there assembled, viz, the Eleventh, First and Third, at Emmitsburg. If you think the ground and position there a better one to fight a battle under existing circumstances, you will so advise the general, and he will order all the troops up. You know the general's views, and General Warren, who is fully aware of them, has gone out to see General Reynolds.[20]

Hancock pointed out that both Howard, the Eleventh Corps commander, and Sickles of the Third outranked him; he was not sure that Meade could do what he was doing. (Gibbon, too, was not the senior division commander in the Second Corps, he added.) Meade told him that Stanton had authorized him to make such changes among his commanders as he saw fit, and he would be supported. Hancock was the best man for the emergency, he said, particularly since he had received a full briefing by Meade a few minutes earlier. Unspoken was the thought that neither Howard nor Sickles was a good enough soldier to carry the weight of authority in such a crisis as was now developing. Hancock, with some reservations about how this procedure would be received, raised no further questions and prepared to leave. At about 1:30 p.m. he set out with his personal staff for Gettysburg, riding the first two or three miles in an ambulance so that he could study available maps of the area and the instructions contained in the Pipe Creek Circular. He covered the rest of the journey on horseback, taking note of available defensive positions along the way, just in case. Midway between Taneytown and Gettysburg, he met an ambulance bearing the remains of a dead officer: General John F. Reynolds.[21]

TWELVE

Gettysburg

Winfield Hancock arrived on Cemetery Hill, just south of the town of Gettysburg, to find a scene of confusion and turmoil. He reached the battlefield in the latter part of the afternoon, probably about 3:30 p.m.; there is no precise agreement on the time. He found an army which was reeling back in defeat.[1]

As the first day of July began, Buford's division of cavalry was on patrol to the north and west of the town of Gettysburg, a town distinguished principally by the fact that a number of major roads met there—the turnpikes to Chambersburg, Baltimore, and York, as well as the highways to Emmitsburg, Taneytown, and Middletown. The Confederates, who were gathered mainly around Cashtown, some eight or nine miles to the northwest, had heard of a large supply of shoes which could be had in Gettysburg. On June 30 James J. Pettigrew's brigade of Harry Heth's division had approached Gettysburg to look for those shoes, but it had discovered Buford's troopers and withdrawn without a fight. Though Pettigrew expressed the opinion that he had encountered a portion of the Army of the Potomac, neither Heth nor his superior, A. P. Hill, believed that any portion of that army had yet gotten so far north. Heth received permission from Hill to return to Gettysburg on July 1. When the rebels marched in from Cashtown on the morning of the first, they were met by Buford and his men on a crest called McPherson's Ridge and brought to a halt. As the Confederates threw in additional units to try to overcome the impediment Buford presented, John Reynolds with his First Corps hurried forward to Buford's support. As he came forward, Reynolds sent off two messages, one to Howard directing him to bring up his Eleventh Corps, the other to Meade to let the army commander know that serious fighting had broken out to the west of Gettysburg.

Not long after getting his corps into action, Reynolds was shot through the head and killed instantly. Abner Doubleday succeeded to the corps command, but seniority placed Howard in command of the wing of the army represented by the three forward corps. The First Corps fought gallantly and doggedly in the lines west of the town, and Buford's troopers were brilliant. Howard moved his corps out to the north of the town, with the exception of one division which was left as a reserve on an elevation south of the town, the rise called Cemetery Hill. Eventually, however, the weight of Confederate numbers made the difference. Jubal Early, coming back from York, by sheer chance hit the flank of the Eleventh Corps at an odd angle, and the ill-fated Eleventh, the victims of Jackson at Chancellorsville, broke again.

In the meantime, the First Corps, outnumbered but not outfought, was pulling back slowly into the town. Unfortunately, when the disorganized Eleventh Corps units came streaming into the streets of the town, with Early's men hot on their heels, they overwhelmed the orderly lines of the First Corps and turned the entire pullback into a rout. Nearly 3,000 Union soldiers were taken prisoner in the tangled streets of Gettysburg, while the survivors, more as individuals than as units, swarmed southward, out of the town, toward Cemetery Hill, where the Union reserve might furnish a temporary sanctuary. At 3:20 p.m., just before Hancock arrived, Buford sent a message back to headquarters describing the disordered scene and ending: "In my opinion there seems to be no directing person. . . . We need help now." It was into this situation that Winfield Hancock was introduced.[2]

Hancock arrived on the scene just as the early waves of fugitives were struggling up Cemetery Hill from Gettysburg. The sight of Hancock, with his natural air of command and authority, proved to be an inspirational one for the worn, discouraged survivors of the First and Eleventh corps. In years to come, the thing which most veterans of that day remembered first was the comforting and heartening view of Winfield Scott Hancock on that field, because everyone in the army knew him to be a gallant, accomplished, fighting soldier; if he was there in charge, things should be all right after all.[3]

There was the inevitable encounter with O. O. Howard, when Hancock advised that general of his assignment to take command, superseding Howard. Several versions of this meeting exist. Hancock himself later wrote that

> as soon as I arrived on the field . . . I rode directly to the crest of the hill where General Howard stood, and said to him that I had been sent by General Meade to take command of all the forces present; that I had written orders to that effect with me, and asked him if he wished to read them. He replied that he did not, but acquiesced in my assumption of command.[4]

Howard, on the other hand, wrote that Hancock rode up to him and Doubleday, commanding the First Corps:

> General Hancock greeted me in his usual frank and cordial manner, and used these words: "General Meade has sent me to represent him on the field." I replied, "All right, Hancock. This is no time for talking. You take the left of the pike and I will arrange these troops to the right." He said no more, and moved off in his peculiar gallant style to gather scattered brigades and put them into position. . . . It did not strike me then that Hancock, without troops, was doing more than directing matters as a temporary chief of staff for Meade.[5]

But Doubleday recounted that Hancock rode up and said he had been "placed in command of both corps." And a First Corps adjutant, Major E. P.

Halstead, said that he heard the exchange between Hancock and Howard. He said that Howard appeared rattled and flustered in the bad situation then prevailing, with disordered units and individual soldiers pouring out of the town onto the hill and beyond and no one knowing when the rebels might appear. Hancock arrived at a gallop, saluted, and said that Meade had sent him to take command. Howard replied that he was senior. Hancock said, "I am aware of that, General, but I have written orders in my pocket from General Meade, which I will show you if you wish to see them." Stubbornly, Howard responded, "No; I do not doubt your word, General Hancock, but you can give no orders here while I am here." Hancock, as Halstead then reported, broke the impasse by saying, "Very well, General Howard, I will second any order that you have to give."[6]

It appears most likely that Hancock did advise Howard that he was placed in command and that Howard made some difficulty about the fact, an incredible bit of pettiness given the situation. Regardless, it is clear that Hancock then took charge of the field, organizing the dispirited troops into cogent defensive positions and generally breathing new life into a beaten army. He looked at the height called Culp's Hill on the right of the field and knew he had to occupy it; he ordered James S. Wadsworth's division of the First Corps and a battery of artillery to Culp's Hill and thus seized a key point of the whole battle. When Geary's division (Twelfth Corps) arrived on the field, Hancock ignored the fact that his orders did not specifically authorize him to command Twelfth Corps troops; he sent Geary's division to secure the left of the line, already threatened by enemy cavalry, protecting another strategic height called Little Round Top. Buford, one of the heroes of the day, wrote that Hancock "in a few moments . . . made superb disposition to resist any attack that might be made." Hancock, of course, was not alone: Howard, Doubleday, Warren, and Buford assisted in forming the new defensive position. But there is no real doubt that it was Hancock's presence and direction which governed the rallying of the Army of the Potomac on Cemetery Hill that afternoon.[7]

While he made the army temporarily secure, Hancock also looked into the second part of his assignment, in effect to choose whether or not to fight a major battle at Gettysburg. Hancock had not been on the field long before he pronounced it "the strongest position by nature upon which to fight a battle that I ever saw." At the northeast was Culp's Hill, rocky and heavily wooded; to its west was Cemetery Hill, of the same height but with a flat top which could be utilized for a concentration of artillery. Southward from Cemetery Hill was a slightly lower crest, Cemetery Ridge, which ran in that direction for about a mile and a half, flattening out as it approached Little Round Top. To the south and southwest of Cemetery Ridge, the terrain became more irregular, with outcroppings of huge boulders here and there; the largest of these outcroppings was a jumbled mass sixty feet high known as Devil's Den. South of Little Round Top was a very high, steep, and heavily wooded hill called Big Round Top; this height was far enough from

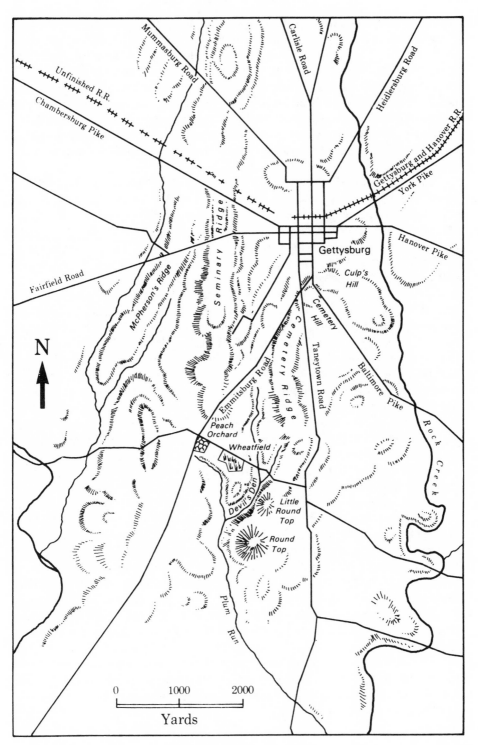

N

Unfinished R.R.

Chambersburg Pike

Mummasburg Road

Carlisle Road

Heidlersburg Road

Gettysburg and Hanover R.R.

York Pike

Hanover Pike

Gettysburg

Culp's
Hill

Fairfield Road

McPherson's Ridge

Seminary Ridge

Cemetery
Hill

Cemetery Ridge

Taneytown Road

Baltimore Pike

Rock Creek

Emmitsburg Road

Peach
Orchard

Wheatfield

Devil's Den

Little
Round
Top

Round
Top

Plum Run

0   1000   2000

Yards

Gettysburg, July 1–3, 1863

the battle lines and sufficiently inaccessible that it played no significant part in the fight. Of a much different nature was Little Round Top: this hill could easily be climbed by both infantry and artillery, and it dominated the left flank and rear of any line which might be laid out on Cemetery Ridge as well as the valley of a small stream called Plum Run at its western base and Devil's Den one thousand feet farther west. By the very nature of the dispositions he made, Hancock took advantage of the opportunities offered by the terrain south of Gettysburg: he occupied Culp's Hill, Cemetery Hill, Cemetery Ridge, and the base of Little Round Top and found that he had a strong position for a defensive battle.[8]

Hancock promptly dispatched his aide Major William G. Mitchell back to Meade, to describe the position, to tell him that Hancock would hold it until nightfall in order to give Meade the chance to decide whether to bring the rest of the army there, and to tell him it was a good place for a fight. Mitchell left Gettysburg about 4 p.m. and reported to Meade at Taneytown before 6 p.m. After Mitchell delivered his message, he understood Meade to reply, "I will send up the troops."[9]

Some time thereafter, Hancock wrote out a message to Meade, which he sent off at 5:25 p.m. by another aide, Captain I. B. Parker. Hancock said that the position in the cemetery "cannot well be taken. It is a position, however, easily turned." He said that Slocum's Twelfth Corps, which was coming onto the ground, would further protect the right, and that the Third Corps, not yet up, would by the direction of its march from Emmitsburg tend to protect the left. He recommended that the Second Corps take a position in the rear for the time being, since it was not possible to tell for sure where Lee's army would strike. "The battle is quiet now," he said. "I think we will be all right until night. I have sent all the trains back. When night comes, it can be told better what had best be done. I think we can retire; if not, we can fight here, as the ground appears not unfavorable with good troops."[10]

Close to 6 p.m. Hancock found Slocum (who had been hanging back from the developing battle because apparently he did not want the responsibility of commanding it) and turned over the command to him. Hancock then rode back to Taneytown to report in person to Meade, who told him that he had ordered the whole army to join at Gettysburg. Worn by his exhausting day, Hancock stretched out for a couple of hours of sleep while Meade rode off to Gettysburg. After midnight Hancock was up again, back in the saddle to rejoin the Second Corps just outside Gettysburg.[11]

In the meantime, while everyone else was working to prepare for the promised battle on the next day, Howard was writing to Meade that "General Hancock's order . . . to assume command . . . has mortified me and will disgrace me. Please inform me frankly if you disapprove of my conduct today, that I may know what to do." Unfortunately for Howard, George Meade had more pressing things to do than to soothe the troubled spirits of mortified generals.[12]

Another general who would be mortified by the first day of Gettysburg was Richard S. Ewell, commanding the corps which had formerly been Stonewall Jackson's. Lee had no more intention of committing to a major battle at Gettysburg on July 1 than Meade had. With no word from Stuart, Lee did not really know where the Army of the Potomac was; he was still in the process of pulling his army together when Harry Heth's shoe-foraging expedition triggered the fight. The Confederates combined their advantage in numbers present, the death of Reynolds, less-than-satisfactory troop placement by the Eleventh Corps, and Early's devastating attack into a substantial victory. The question southerners asked then and later was why on July 1 the demoralized, retreating Federals were not followed and annihilated as they fled through and out of the town.

Many years later Hancock wrote a letter to Fitzhugh Lee, a Confederate general, stating that had the rebels pushed the pursuit of Howard's men they would have driven them "over and beyond Cemetery Hill." This is no doubt true; Hancock watched the beaten Federals as they came panting up Cemetery Hill, their units broken up, their spirits crushed, winded and weary from their fight and flight. He had to be concerned, as he pulled them together into a defensive line, with how much time he had before the gray-clad men, shouting their infernal "rebel yell," burst upon them in a renewed attack. He could not see the Confederate soldiers, similarly winded and weary from the same hard fighting, milling about in the streets of Gettysburg, their organizations also torn and confused, the usual result of most successful assaults here magnified by the trap of the streets of town. The time required by the southern officers to regroup their men, round up thousands of prisoners, distribute ammunition and water, and find out what the higher command wanted done next was the same time utilized by Hancock and Howard and Warren to occupy Culp's Hill, organize a defensive line on Cemetery Hill and send Geary down toward Little Round Top. At that point, of course, Hancock advised Meade that the position could be held; in his 1878 letter to Fitz Lee, he said that by 4 p.m., when he had made his defensive dispositions, "I do not think the Confederate force then present could have carried it out."

Meanwhile, Robert E. Lee, still hoping to avoid a general engagement until all of his army should be up, suggested to Ewell an assault on Cemetery Hill if Ewell thought it was "practicable." After casting about for troops with which to make such an assault and finding insufficient numbers of men fresh enough, Ewell exercised the discretion vested in him by Lee's message and found a further attack that day to be impracticable. Since it was considered a heinous act of disloyalty to "the cause" for southerners to criticize Robert E. Lee, then or after the war, all of the onus for the failure to follow through to overwhelming victory on July 1 fell on Ewell. He it was who had been timorous, hesitating, and slow, and thereby a great opportunity for greater glory for "Marse Robert" was lost. In fact, by the time Ewell had regrouped a sizable portion of his force, the Union defense was consolidated and a further rebel assault would have been quite risky.[13]

One other matter of minor controversy arising from the events of July 1 was the question whether Meade's decision to fight at Gettysburg was the result of Hancock's advice. Hancock's friends always claimed that it was, because that fact would add greater luster to Hancock's Gettysburg laurels. Meade, after first stating that his decision was based on Hancock's information, changed his story, perhaps reflecting that if he did not claim credit for choosing the site of battle there was precious little that his critics would permit him *to* claim. Hancock, of course, did not know one way or the other, since he was at Gettysburg, directing troop dispositions and sending messages back to Taneytown. On March 5, 1864, Meade told the Committee on the Conduct of the War that early in the evening of July 1, 1863, "I should suppose about 6 or 7 o'clock," he "received a report from General Hancock, I think in person, giving me such an account of a position in the neighborhood of Gettysburg, which could be occupied by my army, as caused me at once to determine to fight a battle at that point." It is presumed that this report was the one delivered, not by Hancock, but by Mitchell. A week later, on March 11, Meade was back before the committee with a slightly different tale to tell. "From information received from the field, from officers returning," Meade said, "I became satisfied that the enemy were in such force there that it was evident that General Lee was about to concentrate his army there. I therefore did not wait for the report from General Hancock, as I can prove from staff officers who took my orders, but immediately commenced to move my troops to the front, being determined to fight a battle there." Mitchell, however, told Morgan, the Second Corps chief of staff, that after he delivered his message to Meade, just before 6 p.m., the army commander said to him, "I will send up the troops."[14]

This is one of those questions of minor import which will probably never be settled. At 6 p.m. Meade sent a message addressed to Hancock and Doubleday, stating that "Sedgwick is moving up here, and will be pushed forward in the night, if required." "It seems to me," Meade went on, "we have so concentrated that a battle at Gettysburg is now forced on us, and that, if we get up all our people, and attack with our whole force tomorrow, we ought to defeat the force the enemy has." There is little in the tone or content of this message to indicate one way or another whether it was sent before or after Mitchell's arrival and report. Given Meade's conflicting testimony to the committee and the inconclusive nature of the evidence from Mitchell's story and from the messages Meade sent at 6 p.m., it must be stated that whether Hancock's advice was decisive in Meade's conclusion to move to Gettysburg is not clear. What *is* clear is that Hancock's activities on the field at Cemetery Hill had to have been the decisive factor in whatever reports officers returning from the front brought to Meade. In one way or another, then, Hancock was responsible for the determination to fight at Gettysburg as well as the strong position in which the Army of the Potomac would fight.[15]

Hancock was also responsible for the position of the Second Corps on the night of July 1. The corps, under the temporary command of Gibbon, had moved up the road from Taneytown to Gettysburg during the afternoon, but Hancock sent word for it to halt two or three miles from Gettysburg, just to the southeast of Big Round Top, and to take position for the night between that landmark and the Taneytown road. His reason for so placing the corps was to protect against a possible effort by Lee to turn the Cemetery Hill–Cemetery Ridge line by moving around it to the southwest. Early the next morning, Hancock resumed command of the Second Corps when it arrived on the field and was positioned along Cemetery Ridge.[16]

It was a warm, sultry morning that July 2, the sky overcast with low-hanging clouds. There had been skirmishing earlier between Ewell's corps and Federals on Cemetery Hill, but that had died away by 8 a.m. Meade's soldiers sweated as they got into the positions designated for them, but then they had a chance to rest, as the anticipated morning's fight failed to develop. The Second Corps stretched from a group of trees called Ziegler's Grove on the right, where the corps connected with the Eleventh Corps, south for about a mile to its connection with the Third Corps. The Third Division, under Hays, was at the right of the line, around Ziegler's Grove, with Gibbon's division in the center and the First, that of Caldwell, on the left, a fateful placement which would give Caldwell's brigades a crucial role in the fighting of that day.[17]

As the day wore on, and as the expectancy of battle grew upon everyone there, Meade started having trouble with Daniel Sickles, the Third Corps commander. Sickles had been ordered to occupy the position Geary had held the evening before, connecting his right with the Second Corps and anchoring his left on Little Round Top. But Sickles did not like his position. He complained that he could not learn where Geary had been; the Third Corps had, in its usual fashion, been so dilatory the morning of July 2 that Geary's division had already moved away to its new position when the Third Corps arrived. But it should not have been difficult for Sickles to ascertain where a division of soldiers had camped the night before and a portion of the morning. In addition, Sickles thought the Cemetery Ridge line which he was ordered to occupy was a weak one, and indeed Cemetery Ridge south of the Second Corps position tended to flatten out so that it was not much of a ridge where Sickles stood. He felt there was a much stronger position out in front, near the Emmitsburg road, and he wanted to occupy that position, about three-quarters of a mile west. He talked about it to Meade, who was distracted with other matters, and he talked about it to Meade's son (the general's aide), to Hunt, the artillery commander, and to Warren. No one gave him permission to move to a new position, but finally, in mid-afternoon, Dan Sickles simply moved his corps out to the position he wanted, in violation of his orders and without telling anyone.[18]

Daniel E. Sickles was an original, even in this army of unusual characters. A New York City lawyer before the war, he had been a flamboyant Democratic congressman who sympathized and voted with the South. In 1859, learning that his wife was engaged in an affair with Philip Barton Key, son of the author of the "Star-Spangled Banner," Sickles ambushed Key in front of his Washington home and shot him to death. Acquitted on the basis of temporary insanity, Sickles found himself ostracized when he took his erring wife back. When war broke out, he raised the Excelsior Brigade in New York and won appointment as brigadier general, though he had no military training or background. Still intensely political, Sickles had become a favorite of the Radicals in Washington. He was undoubtedly brave and a fighter, but Dan Sickles had only rudimentary understanding of the concepts of military tactics and discipline, as he demonstrated so clearly on the afternoon of July 2.[19]

The new line to which Sickles had moved his two divisions was a quarter of a mile longer than the one he had abandoned, and yet both flanks were exposed. Humphreys' division, which had previously connected with the left of the Second Corps, was now in line on the Emmitsburg road, and a gap of three-quarters of a mile existed between Humphreys and the Second Corps. The division's line followed the Emmitsburg road south until it met the right of General David Birney's division at a peach orchard, soon to be known forever as *the* Peach Orchard. Birney's line then bent back at an obtuse angle, facing almost south, and continued along in front of a large field of wheat, shortly to become famous as *the* Wheatfield, until it ended in the rocky jumble of Devil's Den. Unfortunately, this was still a quarter of a mile short of Little Round Top; the valley of Plum Run between Devil's Den and Little Round Top offered easy access to an enemy force. The Third Corps was too thinly spread, its flanks were "in the air," and its center formed a salient, always a vulnerable formation. In addition, Sickles had broken up the defensive line which was the key to Meade's battle plan, and he had left Little Round Top, which dominated the entire Union position, wholly unprotected. It was truly amazing what one amateur general, cocksure in his ignorance, could do.[20]

On top of everything, of course, Sickles never told Hancock, with whom he was supposed to connect, that he was planning to move forward. Hancock and Gibbon were riding in front of their troops when they suddenly observed with astonishment the movement of Humphreys' division toward the Emmitsburg road, leaving a position which the two generals thought was supposed to be the battle line. "We could not conceive what it meant," Gibbon wrote later, "as we had heard of no orders for an advance and did not understand the meaning of making this break in our line." Hancock told the Committee on the Conduct of the War: "I recollect looking on and admiring the spectacle, but I did not know the object of it." He added that he expected a fight momentarily and thought Sickles's move "would be disadvantageous to us."[21]

At about the time the forward movement was completed, Meade arrived at what had been his left and was appalled to see what Sickles had done with the Third Corps. Sickles, after a weak explanation which Meade scorned, offered to pull his men back. At that moment the attack of the Confederates burst upon the hapless corps, and Meade said that the enemy would no longer permit a pullback. It was 4:00 p.m. when General John B. Hood's division of Longstreet's corps charged across the fields southwest of Devil's Den, striking Birney's Federals a heavy blow. Despite the fierce resistance offered by the brigade of General J. H. Hobart Ward, the situation on the left of the Third Corps was soon critical. At this point Meade dispatched Warren to check out Little Round Top, and Warren was dismayed to arrive on the hill and find no one there but a couple of signalmen. Warren was able, through frantic messages to Meade and by his own initiative in diverting troops to the hill, to save Little Round Top, but only after a bloody struggle by Fifth Corps units which arrived there just ahead of the rebels.[22]

Meade worked energetically to do what could be done to save the position so foolishly jeopardized by Sickles. He ordered up George Sykes's Fifth Corps, which had been waiting in reserve back beyond the Taneytown road. Fifth Corps brigades were instrumental in securing Little Round Top, while other Fifth Corps units, fighting in the area of the Wheatfield, in support of Birney, were less effective.

Hancock was directed to send Caldwell's division, the leftmost of his corps, to the aid of Sykes, to help in saving the army's left. The removal of Caldwell's brigades from the Cemetery Ridge line opened up even further the gap in the Union line, but it could not be helped; the Third Corps was being rapidly chewed up by Longstreet, and support was desperately needed. As it turned out, Caldwell's division did not report to Sykes at all but wound up in the Wheatfield where Birney's brigades under Ward and Colonel Philippe Regis de Trobriand were nearly fought out. Caldwell's first brigade, under the invaluable Colonel Edward E. Cross, headed for Devil's Den. Cross had been with the Fifth New Hampshire from the beginning of the war; a lanky, bald, eccentric old soldier with red whiskers, he had fought in the Mexican War and was a rigid disciplinarian. "If Colonel Cross ever knew fear," Morgan wrote, "no one ever discovered it." He knew no fear, but he did have a premonition about this fight: when Hancock told him that his general's star was sure to come this time, Cross replied that it was too late. The brigade drove the rebels back across the Wheatfield, but Cross was gunned down and killed.[23]

To the right of Cross came the Irish Brigade under Colonel Patrick Kelly. Before the advance, Father William Corby, the brigade's chaplain, had given a general absolution to all of its members, in a brief but solemn ceremony witnessed by Hancock and other officers. The brigade then moved, under heavy fire, across the Wheatfield and into the woods to the south of it. Next in line to the right was the brigade of Samuel Zook, which

moved forward at double time into a storm of fire and smoke, until Zook too
was mortally wounded and the lines of rebels and Federals became so
intermingled that the advance came to a standstill. Brooke's brigade came
up from reserve and advanced as far as any could in that field of carnage,
pushing across the bloody Wheatfield and into Devil's Den. The First
Division of the Second Corps, Hancock's old division, had acquitted itself
admirably; Hood's veterans had been roughly handled. Just then, however,
while Caldwell was looking for a way to establish a connection with the
Third Corps off to the right, everything collapsed. Charles K. Graham's
brigade of Birney's division, holding the apex of the salient in the Third
Corps line, was hammered by an attack of McLaws's division coming
through the Peach Orchard and gave way. Caldwell came upon these
troops, flying in confusion, followed by the triumphant Confederates, who
were soon on his right and rear. To avoid the capture of his division,
Caldwell was forced to order its hasty retreat, back across the Wheatfield,
back across Plum Run, back across the Taneytown road, back behind a
stone wall, where he was able to reform it. Caldwell lost heavily in his attack
and retreat, both in men and in nearly irreplaceable officers. Sykes subsequently told Hancock that the division had not behaved well; Hancock
found this hard to believe, and when he learned that its retreat was caused
solely by the sudden turning of its flank, he was satisfied that it had
performed with its customary bravery and competence.[24]

The Confederates who had turned Caldwell's division were also on the
flank of Humphreys's division, out there by itself on the Emmitsburg road.
Gibbon advanced a couple of regiments out toward Humphreys, but otherwise the division was pretty much on its own. At about this time, Meade
advised Hancock that Sickles had been wounded (he lost a leg, which
sacrifice probably kept him from being court-martialed); he placed Hancock
in command of the Third Corps as well as of his own, effectively giving
Hancock charge of the entire battle area. It is to be regretted that Meade did
not take this step much earlier; the situation would likely never have
reached the crisis stage it was in when Hancock took command. One
eminent historian of the battle suggests that Meade's recollection of Howard's loud complaints at being superseded by a junior in rank the day before
may have inhibited him from doing the same thing with the touchy Dan
Sickles.[25]

Humphreys's division, with the Second Corps regiments, gave ground,
slowly, stubbornly, but inexorably, and was driven back from its advanced
position. With the army's left in mortal danger late on that afternoon of July
2, the time had come for Winfield Scott Hancock, with his presence, his
military skill, his superhuman energy in rallying and placing troops, to save
the Army of the Potomac. He first pulled Willard's brigade out of Hays's
division and led it personally to a place where it could cover the retreat of
Birney's division. When Hancock got there, he found Birney but no division;

Birney told him his troops had all scattered to the rear. Almost immediately the enemy was upon Willard's brigade. Willard and half his men went down, but his veteran troops held on and forced the Confederates, the Mississippians of William Barksdale, flushed with their success in the Peach Orchard, back. Barksdale himself was killed. One menacing rebel thrust was contained.[26]

Once satisfied that Willard's brigade had matters in hand, Hancock galloped off to the right, where he soon came upon a large body of Confederate infantry advancing unopposed toward the undefended crest of Cemetery Ridge. The general at first thought these were Union troops retreating from the advanced front, but a volley of shots which wounded his aide Captain W. D. W. Miller soon revealed the truth. He then spied a Federal regiment of about three hundred men coming up from the rear. Spurring over to them, Hancock shouted to their colonel, "Do you see those colors? Take them!" It was clearly a suicidal mission, but Colonel William Colville and his 1st Minnesota hesitated not a moment. Charging at top speed with bayonets leveled, they tore into the enemy force, the brigade of Cadmus Wilcox of A. P. Hill's corps, and brought it to a halt. They took fearful losses—well over two-thirds of their number—but they did their job. They stopped cold a rebel advance which threatened to break the Union line in two, and they gave Hancock the time he needed to gather reinforcements in this area. The charge of the 1st Minnesota at Gettysburg has become one of the most famous of the whole war.[27]

One of the units with which Hancock reinforced the gallant Minnesotans was the 13th Vermont, a regiment of green nine-month men who had joined Doubleday's division in the First Corps only the day before. When their colonel, Francis V. Randall, brought them up, Hancock pointed to a battery which the rebels had just seized and asked Randall whether he could recapture it. Randall said he was "willing to try," and he ordered the charge. The Vermonters attacked so rapidly that they surprised and captured many Confederates. Hancock was so pleased by the audacity and success of the regiment that he told Randall to keep his men going and he himself would take care of the prisoners.[28]

And now, in the gathering darkness, on the left and center of Hancock's line, the Union army braced, held, and then pushed their enemy back. Humphreys's men, all that was left of the Third Corps as a fighting unit, regrouped and rallied, joined by several brigades of Gibbon's division and units of the First and Twelfth corps. The crisis had passed, and the left wing of the army was stitched back together, although at great cost, including the virtual destruction of one army corps. Abner Doubleday later wrote that Hancock "was indefatigable in his vigilance and personal supervision, 'patching the line' wherever the enemy was likely to break through. His activity and foresight probably preserved the ridge from capture." Indeed, Hancock was a magnificent figure in those hours, appearing everywhere, observing everything, sending in a body of soldiers at just the right moment to forestall disaster. Without Hancock, the rudderless left of the army would have collapsed.[29]

Even then, with the Cemetery Ridge line preserved, Hancock's contributions for the day were not complete. As he rode toward the right of the Second Corps, nearing Cemetery Hill, he heard the sound of heavy firing on Howard's front. Somehow it did not sound good to him, so he sent word to Gibbon to dispatch Sprigg Carroll's brigade, of Hays's division, to see if it could be of any help to Howard. Carroll was a fierce fighter with a booming voice that could be heard in any battle, and he was just the man for this assignment. When he arrived in Howard's sector, the Eleventh Corps lines were under a strong night assault. Carroll sent his men pelting in, struck the Confederate attackers, and turned them around. Chasing the rebels back down the hill, Carroll's men captured a number of them, and Cemetery Hill was safe for the night. At about the same time, Hancock heard more firing, which he estimated came from Culp's Hill, where Slocum's Twelfth Corps had been weakened to throw reinforcements into the Cemetery Ridge line. So Hancock sent two regiments to the relief of Slocum as well.[30]

That night, while the firing in the Culp's Hill area continued, Meade summoned all of his corps commanders to his headquarters for a review of the situation. They met for about two hours in the little front room of the house in which Meade was quartered, a room some ten feet square lighted by a single candle on a table in the middle. In this crowded room, filling with cigar smoke, they went over the events of the day and described the condition of their commands. After the general discussion, Butterfield, the chief of staff, converted the gathering into a council of war by posing formal questions for consideration: whether the army should remain in its present position or retire to a better one; whether it should attack or await the enemy's attack; and, if it should await the enemy's attack, for how long. There was general unanimity that the existing position should be held and that the Army of the Potomac should not attack but await Lee's assault, with differences of opinion only as to how long it should wait. Meade said, in a manner which indicated his own agreement, "Such, then, is the decision," and the council broke up. Hancock, Gibbon, and John Newton, now commanding the First Corps, found the Second Corps headquarters ambulance nearby, and all three crawled in and went to sleep.[31]

Early the next morning, July 3, the Twelfth Corps and Ewell's corps engaged in a fierce struggle which resulted in the Confederates' being driven out of the position they had seized on Culp's Hill the night before. On Cemetery Ridge the morning was quiet. At the close of the meeting the night before, however, Meade had predicted to Gibbon that Lee's attack on the third day would be against the Second Corps front. Asked why, Meade replied, "Because he has made attacks on both our flanks and failed and if he concludes to try it again, it will be on our centre." The men of Gibbon's and Hays's divisions spent the morning trying to prepare for whatever the day should bring. They boiled their coffee and chewed on their hard bread and then set to work to do what they could about their positions. There was a low stone wall which ran south from Ziegler's Grove near the crest of the ridge, angled out to the west a hundred feet or so, then again ran south. It was not much of a wall, but it offered some protection. The soldiers improved it as well as they could with fence rails and earth and anything else they could find to make it safe against musketry. Where the stone wall disappeared, they tried to take advantage of the contours of the ground for protection. The two divisions, with Hays on the right, included about 5,500 men, holding a line some 2,000 feet long. Adjoining Gibbon's division on the left was Doubleday's division of the First Corps, and then the remaining division of the Second Corps, Caldwell's sadly decimated brigades. Below Caldwell, two Sixth Corps brigades carried the line down to the Round Tops, where Sykes's Fifth Corps was well entrenched. Seventy-seven guns stood among the Federal units, and Henry Hunt worked to get these into shape for the day's affair. It was a hot and humid day, and every exertion brought forth torrents of perspiration.[32]

At about 9 a.m., Meade rode up to Hancock, who was up at the line, working on his dispositions. Meade had changed the opinion which he had voiced to Gibbon the night before; he now told Hancock he expected Lee's attack on the left. The center of the Union line was admittedly somewhat thin and not as strongly held as other positions; Meade felt that he could probably reinforce the center if an attack should come there. Hancock simply smiled; he felt his veterans could handle whatever might come.[33]

In front of Hays, and about midway between the Union line and that of the Confederates on Seminary Ridge, about three-fourths of a mile to the west, stood a barn and some smaller outbuildings of the Bliss farm. There had been some fighting over them the day before, and now they became the focus of sharp skirmishing through the morning. The barn was originally held by the Federals, but rebel skirmishers had driven them out and furnished a place for sharpshooters to hole up and harass the main Union line. As Hays prepared to send a force down the hill to recapture the barn, Hancock, who did not want to precipitate a general engagement over these insignificant farm buildings, directed him to burn them down when he recaptured them. This was done, and, with their trophy gone, the opposing lines settled down once again.[34]

About eleven o'clock a feeling of tense expectancy gripped the front. Soon, the Federals observed a huge concentration of artillery along the Confederate line opposite them. It became clear that Lee was bringing together almost all his guns and putting them into position across from the Cemetery Ridge line.

Late in the morning one of Gibbon's servants had taken possession ("no doubt without due process of law," Gibbon said) of a tough old rooster and, with the help of some potatoes, turned it into a stew. Gibbon and Hancock, sitting on a couple of odd stools, joined Gibbon's staff in pitching into this rare delight. Soon Meade and one of his staff, and then Newton and Pleasonton, with aides, happened along, and that rooster stew, like the loaves and fishes of old, sufficed to feed them all. The generals then settled under a small tree, lit up cigars, and discussed the battle of the day before and what was likely for that day. Meade still thought an attack on the left the most likely, while Hancock expected it to hit the Second Corps. After a lazy hour or so, Meade, Newton, and Pleasonton went off on their own business. At about five minutes to one, the report of a single gun from the Confederate line was heard, quickly followed by the start of the greatest artillery barrage ever witnessed on the American continent to that time. "[T]he whole air above and around us was filled with bursting and screaming projectiles . . . ," Gibbon recalled.[35]

Robert E. Lee's plans for the day's activities had matured: he was indeed going to strike the Union center—the line of Cemetery Ridge held by two divisions of the Second Corps. Standing on Seminary Ridge, Lee had looked across the shallow valley intervening and picked out a "clump of trees" standing within the angle of the stone wall as the point on which the Confederate attack should be centered. Longstreet would command it, and it would be made by about 15,000 men from Pickett's division (Longstreet's corps) and Heth's division of Hill's corps, temporarily commanded by James J. Pettigrew, Heth having been wounded on July 1. The assault would be preceded by a heavy artillery bombardment, designed to knock out the Union guns and to soften up and demoralize the Union infantry. Porter Alexander, temporarily serving as Longstreet's artillery chief, organized the rebel guns and, at about one o'clock, started the barrage.[36]

The bombardment was a fearsome thing. The Confederates had more than 125 guns trained on their adversaries, and the shelling made a deafening noise, intensified when the 77 Union pieces started to answer. Hunt, who was conscious of some depletion in his supply of ammunition, had his gunners wait for fifteen minutes before firing back. Many of the Confederate artillerists aimed their pieces a bit high, with the result that the major destruction took place on the back slope of Cemetery Ridge, behind the Second Corps line, where a heavy toll was exacted among stragglers, horses, provost guards, medics, and support personnel. Still, enough shells landed on or near the waiting infantry to cause these doughty veterans to hug the ground or a rock or anything else which might provide a little shelter. Suffering severely were the Union batteries, the specific targets of their counterparts on Seminary Ridge. The Union gunners retaliated with deadly volleys aimed at the Confederate guns. The bombardment lasted for about two hours. After it had gone on for some time, Hunt decided that he could conserve ammunition for the infantry attack which was sure to follow by slackening his guns' fire, or stopping it altogether. In making this determination Hunt ran head-on into the belief of Winfield Hancock that the morale of infantrymen under an artillery barrage is best maintained by a heavy and vigorous counterbarrage by one's own artillery. Hancock ordered the guns of the Second Corps to keep firing, and he took it upon himself to order batteries near his position but not under his command to do the same. Lieutenant Colonel Freeman McGilvery, a tough old sea captain from Maine, commanding these batteries, told Hancock he had no authority over them and that they would obey Hunt's orders. A brief but noisy and profane argument ensued, but McGilvery's guns did not fire. The question of Hunt's and Hancock's authority over and actions regarding the artillery at this time became the subject of a rather acrimonious debate in the postwar period, but Hancock had no time to dwell on it at this moment.[37]

While the Confederate bombardment was at its height, Hancock mounted his horse and, with his staff and his corps pennant behind him, rode slowly along the front of his line, as shot and shell flew all about him, from near the Taneytown road on the right, all the way to the extreme left of his position, where he remained with Brooke until the rebel advance began. It was a dangerous and gallant act, but it helped to give heart to his men, clutching desperately to the ground, and to nerve them for the ordeal which still lay before them. It was an act which the veterans of the Second Corps would never forget.[38]

Meade and Hunt eventually ordered all of their batteries to cease fire, and the Confederate generals, hoping that this cessation meant they had silenced the guns of their foes, ordered their infantry forward. Between twelve and fifteen thousand gray-clad men emerged from the woods behind the Confederate artillery and started moving toward Cemetery Ridge. The attacking force was six brigades wide, consisting from left to right of J. M. Brockenbrough's brigade, Joseph R. Davis's, Pettigrew's, and James J. Archer's, all of Heth's division, now led by Pettigrew, and then Garnett's and Kemper's brigades of Pickett's division. In support a hundred yards behind the front line were two brigades of William D. Pender's division and Armistead's brigade of Pickett's. Also moving forward, off to the right and rear, were two brigades of Anderson's division, but they at no time managed to become part of the main attack. The determined advance of the Confederates excited feelings of respect, and even awe, among the Union defenders; "their lines were formed," Hancock later wrote, "with a precision and steadiness that extorted the admiration of the witnesses of that memorable scene." The long-range shells of the Union artillery started to tear gaps in the rebel lines, but still they moved ahead. The Second Corps artillery, it might be noted, did not participate in this shelling; having expended all of its long-range ammunition, it would wait until the advance moved into canister range.[39]

As the Confederates moved forward, silent, without their wonted rebel yell, Hancock was galloping back and forth along his line, making sure that everything was ready and being cheered by a couple of regiments as he passed. He noted with approval that Hays had judiciously placed two regiments on his right out in front of the general line, and he observed with interest that two regiments of George Stannard's Vermont brigade (of the First Corps), at the left of the Second Corps line, were "posted in a little grove in front of and at a considerable angle with the main line." The Confederates came closer, and the force on Hays's right faced about to the left and shattered the brigades of Brockenbrough and Davis with an enfilading fire, effectively destroying the left of the rebel advance. On the Union left, the fire of the Vermont regiments combined with artillery fire from Little Round Top caused the Confederate right to drift toward the center—toward the "clump of trees" which Lee had initially selected as his target. It was at about this time that General Richard B. Garnett, commanding one of Pickett's brigades, was killed, having come a long way to this hillside in Pennsylvania from that sad farewell party at the Hancock home in Los Angeles.[40]

Hays and the Third Division held their own quite nicely, repulsing what was left of the Confederate left with deadly and well-aimed volleys from behind their stone wall. On the other end of the line, William Harrow's and Norman J. Hall's brigades of Gibbon's division blasted away at the Confederate right, further accentuating the drift to the center and funneling almost all of the remaining rebels toward the clump of trees. Here, however, the Federals nearly suffered disaster. Here, where the stone wall in front of the trees had an angle which was in effect a bulge in the line, was a potential weak point—a thinly held salient—and here was where the full weight of Pickett's attack hit, against Alexander Webb's Philadelphia Brigade. Obscured momentarily by the smoke of the battle, the Confederates were able to penetrate to the wall and climb over it. When they did, the 71st Pennsylvania broke and moved hastily to the rear. They were rallied and reformed by Webb and by Lieutenant Frank Haskell, of Gibbon's staff, behind the crest of the hill, but the breach in the line had been made. Led by Lewis Armistead, the only southern general left in the advance (Pickett was back by the Emmitsburg road), the Confederates poured over the wall, capturing the artillery pieces posted there.[41]

Just at that point Hancock appeared before Colonel Arthur F. Devereux of the 19th Massachusetts, in Hall's brigade. Devereux asked permission to move to the threatened point, and Hancock promptly dispatched his regiment and the 42d New York, the next on the right, to help repair the break. Shortly after, Hall moved his whole brigade to the right toward the clump of trees, and the redress in numbers between the Confederate attackers and Webb's outweighed brigade began.[42]

Hancock, meanwhile, galloped over to Stannard to have his Vermonters make a flanking attack. Stannard had something like that in mind as well, and Hancock was pleased to see the orders given. Hancock had just given some directions to Colonel Randall of the 13th Vermont when a rebel ball tore into his groin. The Vermonters assisted the stricken general from his horse and stretched him out on the ground. Hancock insisted that he remain there until the battle was over, and he propped himself up on one elbow to watch its progress.[43]

As Hancock watched, Colonel Wheelock G. Veazey, an old friend and now commander of the 16th Vermont, passed by. Hancock called him over, grasped his hand, and cried, "Go in, Colonel, and give it to them on the flank." In the Vermonters went, and with Hall, and Webb, and Harrow, and with all the common soldiers who had rushed to close up the break in the Union line, they shattered the "High Water Mark of the Confederacy," as Armistead's penetration has long been called. Armistead was shot down as he took possession of a Federal cannon, and after a fierce hand-to-hand fight of some ten minutes' duration, the Union men overwhelmed their foes. Of those Confederates who were not shot or clubbed to the ground, many surrendered and the rest fled. The great assault was over, Pickett's charge had failed, and Gettysburg was a Union victory.[44]

Captain Henry Bingham went to Lewis Armistead, lying mortally wounded only a couple of hundred yards from where his old friend Hancock lay similarly (but not fatally) wounded, told Armistead that he was an officer on Hancock's staff, and would see to the delivery of any personal effects that the dying general might wish forwarded to his family. Armistead, exhausted and broken in spirit, looked up and murmured, "Say to General Hancock for me, that I have done him, and you all, a grievous injury, which I shall always regret." He too had come far from Los Angeles, and Mexico City, and West Point, to die under the guns of one of his closest friends. The war of brother against brother, of professional soldiers using their shared skills and training to kill or maim their closest friends, had reached a poignant climax on Cemetery Ridge. But it was far from over. Thousands more would follow Hancock and Armistead to the hospital or the grave.[45]

Once he was assured that the victory was won, Hancock permitted himself to sink to the ground and to be ministered to by the corps surgeon, Alexander N. Dougherty. Mitchell came up, and Hancock sent him to Meade with news of the victory. Parker and Bingham, his aides, rode up, as did his brother John, chief of staff of the First Division. Mitchell came back with an ambulance, and they started to move the severely wounded general back to the rear. After a few minutes, however, Hancock ordered the ambulance to stop, so that he could dictate to Doctor Dougherty a dispatch to Meade, carrying out to the end his responsibility as a corps commander:

> I have never seen a more formidable attack, and if the Sixth and Fifth Corps have pressed up, the enemy will be destroyed. The enemy must be short of ammunition, as I was shot with a tenpenny nail. I did not leave the field till the victory was entirely secured and the enemy no longer in sight. I am badly wounded, though I trust not seriously. I had to break the line to attack the enemy in flank on my right, where the enemy was most persistent after the front attack was repelled. Not a rebel was in sight upright when I left. The line should be immediately restored and perfected. General Caldwell is in command of the corps, and I have directed him to restore the line.[46]

The reference to the Fifth and Sixth corps concerned a possible counter-attack after the repulse of the Confederates. Hancock and Meade had discussed such a possibility earlier, and Hancock later told the Committee on the Conduct of the War "that our lines should have advanced immediately, and I believe we should have won a great victory." Such a belief, of course, was very much a matter of conjecture, and Meade, who had the actual responsibility for throwing his battered troops back across the same ground that Pickett had had to cross, jeopardizing the victory he already had in hand, chose not to take the risk. Meade was much criticized for his failure to counterattack, and Hancock's words were often cited in that criticism. But history has been kinder to George Gordon Meade than his contemporaries were, and he is generally given the benefit of the doubt for his decision.[47]

Even without a counterattack, Gettysburg was a substantial Union victory, and Winfield Scott Hancock had a major hand in it. Had he perished at Gettysburg, dying of his wound rather than being disabled by it for a time, his fame would have been secure and the country in his debt. On each of the three days of the battle he played a significant role—rallying the beaten forces on July 1 and selecting the battlefield, redressing the Sickles blunder the next day and saving the left wing of the army, and finally beating back the last and greatest assault of the Army of Northern Virginia. When on July 3 Mitchell came to Meade from the wounded Hancock with news of the victory, Meade asked Mitchell to thank his chief "for the country and for myself for the service he has rendered today." Well might he have expressed that thanks, not just for that day, but also for the two preceding. Gettysburg was Hancock's field.[48]

THIRTEEN

The Invalid

Shot with a tenpenny nail, Hancock had told Meade, seeing in the cause of his wound a hopeful sign that the Confederacy was running low on ammunition. In fact, the nail had come from the pommel of his saddle. Doctor Dougherty probed the ugly-looking wound with his finger as Hancock lay behind Cemetery Ridge. He withdrew the nail and bits of wood from the general's thigh, very near the groin, and managed to stanch the heavy flow of blood, observing with relief that the femoral artery had been narrowly missed. Dougherty then had Hancock loaded into an ambulance and transported to the makeshift corps hospital, where other wounded soldiers crowded around the general, cheering and manifesting their admiration and affection. Hancock tried to address them, but the effort was too exhausting for a man weak from pain and loss of blood, and he fainted into the arms of his attendants.[1]

Hancock telegraphed Allie daily when the Army of the Potomac was in action, so that she would know he was safe. That morning he had wired to her, at her mother's home in St. Louis: "I am all right, so far." Now, critically and possibly fatally wounded, he dictated a message to her from the hospital: "I am severely wounded, not mortally. Join me at once in Philadelphia." The doctor suggested that the critical nature of the general's condition should be revealed. Hancock demurred; Allie had a long trip to make, and she should make it without knowing just how badly hurt her husband was.[2]

In excruciating pain, Hancock was evacuated the next day to Baltimore, clattering over bumpy roads in an ambulance until it reached the railhead at Westminster. He was then moved to Philadelphia, where he was established in the LaPierre House on Broad Street. On July 6 his father came down from Norristown to visit him, and in due course Allie and the children arrived. The intense summer heat of Philadelphia added to Hancock's discomfort, and the wound, over the next several weeks, continued to drain and showed no signs of healing. He was under the care of the eminent Dr. D. H. Agnew, a specialist in gunshot wounds, who probed for foreign bodies, but nothing seemed to help. Finally, on July 27, the patient was moved to Norristown, on the theory that the cooler air outside the city might alleviate his suffering. A contingent of Philadelphia firemen bore Hancock to the city depot, and a detail of the Invalid Corps carried his stretcher from the Norristown station to his parents' home on Swede Street. The local paper reported Winfield "in good spirits" but mentioned that an intended public demonstration was canceled at the patient's request.[3]

Even as he lay wounded, Hancock had to attend to army business. On July 22 he wrote to the adjutant-general's office to secure a thirty-day extension of his leave of absence, and each month he procured a physician's certificate attesting to his condition. After Hancock reached Norristown, Stanton wired him a request that he suggest a temporary commander for the Second Corps. Hancock recommended Gouverneur Warren, who was also Meade's preference, and Warren was chosen not long after.[4]

Hancock was more comfortable in Norristown than he had been in the sweltering city, but the agony of his unhealed wound persisted. One day a Dr. Louis W. Read came to visit him. Read, a native of Norristown, was an army surgeon who was in charge of an army hospital in Baltimore. Home on leave, he paid a courtesy call on the town's most illustrious patient. He was shocked to find Hancock looking pale and emaciated and talking of death. The general said he had been probed and tortured so much that death would be a relief. As Read arose from the bedside, Hancock said, "Goodbye, Doctor, I may never see you again." Read had made his way to the door when Hancock had another thought: "See here, Doctor, why don't you try to get this ball out. I have had all the reputation in the country at it [Agnew and his colleagues in Philadelphia]; now let's have some of the practical."

Read noted that Hancock was lying in bed with his right leg flexed; all of the probing "had been done with his leg bent at right angles." Yet he had been hit while in the saddle, with his legs extended. The doctor felt he might find the ball if he could get Hancock's leg into the same position it had been in when he was shot. With an aide he managed to straighten the limb and had Hancock straddle a chair placed on top of the dining room table. From across the room Read sighted the probable trajectory of the bullet and then inserted his probe into the wound entrance at the angle so sighted. The probe, Read said, "dropped fully eight inches into the channel and struck the ball, which was imbedded in the sharp bone which you sit upon." He was then able to extract a large Minié ball.[5]

With the foreign object removed, Hancock's recovery began, and within a week he was out of bed, moving about on crutches. Two weeks later he was able to attend a Masonic meeting, and shortly thereafter he decided it was time to leave Norristown. In mid-September he visited New York City and West Point. From there he traveled on to St. Louis, having sent Allie and the children on ahead, and stayed at Longwood, the Russell home outside the city. Hancock's recuperation at Longwood lasted six weeks; he spent some time in trimming trees and planting bushes, but mostly he sat or stretched out.

On October 12 Winfield wrote a letter to his father which proved to be both accurate and overoptimistic:

I threw aside my crutches a few days after my arrival, and now walk with a cane. I am improving, but do not yet walk without a little "roll." My wound is still unhealed, though the doctors say it is closing rapidly. I find some uneasiness in sitting long on a chair, and cannot yet ride. The bone appears to be injured, and may give me trouble for a long time. I hope, however, I may be well enough in two weeks to join my Corps.[6]

Without the regimen of constant physical activity to which he had been accustomed, Hancock soon put on a great deal of weight and seemed to undergo a considerable physiological change. One of his aides wrote that Hancock suffered "a permanent loss of some portion of his former activity and elasticity." He was never again the tall, slim young general he had been; although he was still not yet forty, he never lost the weight he gained during his convalescence. One soldier, seeing the general at Spotsylvania, wrote: "If, as has been asserted, 'all flesh is grass,' General Hancock may be said to be a load of hay." With the added weight, though, Hancock became even more stately looking, substantial and dignified. He was still the man the Army of the Potomac called "the superb."[7]

While he was recuperating, Hancock was very conscious that the Confederacy was still unsubdued. Back in Virginia, Meade's army was engaged primarily in a war of maneuver during the months after Gettysburg, with the only significant fighting being the action at Bristoe Station, where the Second Corps, temporarily under Caldwell, badly mauled A. P. Hill's corps. This was followed by the abortive Mine Run campaign, at the conclusion of which Meade retreated rather than attack a strongly fortified position. He then went into winter quarters around Culpeper, but his enemies in Washington criticized him so fiercely for the retreat that he felt sure his relief was imminent. Hancock and Gibbon sent Meade supportive letters, but even these did little to lift the army commander's gloom. Rumors reached Meade that Hancock was being considered as his successor. Young Theodore Lyman, a new staffer at Meade's headquarters, ticked off all the potential candidates and decided that Hancock was the only one possible: "he belongs in this army, is popular, and has an excellent name." Meade wrote to Hancock on December 11, saying that with the pressures on the army from Washington, "its command is not to be desired by any reasonable man, nor can it be exercised with any justice or satisfaction to yourself. While, therefore, I should be glad to see you promoted to a high command as a friend and well-wisher, with my experience I cannot say I could congratulate you if you succeed me."[8]

Hancock followed the back-and-forth movements of the armies with a mounting sense of frustration, and, just about as soon as he could walk again, he was back in Washington, to see about rejoining the war. He saw a doctor in the capital on December 12 but could not procure permission to go back on duty until the twenty-fourth. Meanwhile, Meade's letter of December 11 caught up with him, and he was quick to respond. "I am no aspirant," Hancock wrote to his friend, and I never could be a conspirator, had I other feelings towards you than I possess. I would sooner command a corps under you than have the supreme command. I have faith in you. . . . I have always served faithfully, and so I intend to do. I would always prefer a good man to command that army than to command it myself. If I ever command it, it will be given to me as it was to you. I shall never express or imply a desire to command, for I do not feel it.[9]

On December 27, still in considerable pain, Hancock reported to Meade and two days later resumed command of the Second Corps. It was a false start. Even though the army was holed up for the winter, Hancock was physically unable to carry out his duties as he felt he should. He requested a commission to examine his absence from July 3 to December 24, "with the view," as he wrote Seth Williams, "of removing any disability that may attach to me as to pay." The commission, consisting of Pleasonton, Williams, and Hunt, met on January 8, 1864, found that Hancock's absence was "satisfactorily accounted for" and declared that he could "hardly be regarded as yet fit for duty." The same day, Hancock was sent north again, to resume his convalescence, and to help with recruiting. Warren once more took over the corps.[10]

While he was in Culpeper, however, Hancock had a long talk with Meade, filling him in as best he could on what was going on in Washington. Hancock said that it had been intimated to him that he would replace Meade in command of the army. When he reported to Washington, however, Halleck told him that Meade would stay on and that he, Hancock, could go back to his old corps. Apparently Meade's report on Mine Run saved his job—for the time being. Verily, the command of the Army of the Potomac, with its umbilical cord to the political center in Washington, was a difficult and unrewarding position; the hypersensitive Meade suffered continual miseries of apprehension and suspicion of what was being done to him behind his back. For someone in Hancock's position, too, there was great difficulty in maintaining loyalty to his commander without irremediably blighting his own career prospects.[11]

On January 6, 1864, Stanton, who was well aware of Hancock's physical condition, had written to Meade, asking if he could spare his Second Corps commander "to report to me as soon as convenient with a view to performing temporary special duty, but not to interfere with his command in your army." After Hancock reached Washington, a special order assigned him "to recruit and fill up the Second Army Corps . . . to the number of 50,000 men." Such a number was wildly unrealistic, of course; the bloom was off the rose of an apparently unending war, and only the vastly unpopular draft had much effect in procuring new men for the Union army. Hancock settled in Harrisburg and concentrated on raising new troops in his native Pennsylvania. He attended rallies and made speeches in an effort to make the young men of his state recognize that the war was far from over. In February, Hancock was hailed with receptions, ovations, and resolutions in Philadelphia, New York, Albany, and Boston, and he responded with pleas for more soldiers. But even Hancock's great prestige was unable to raise anything like the number of new recruits envisioned by Stanton. When the army headed into the Wilderness to start the 1864 campaign, the Second Corps had a strength of about 27,000 men.[12]

Winfield Scott Hancock made one very important acquisition when, on January 26, 1864, Brigadier General Francis Channing Barlow was assigned to the Second Corps and directed to report by letter to Hancock at Harrisburg for recruiting purposes. Barlow was an unlikely general. He was born in Brooklyn in 1834, son of a minister and a descendant of the prominent Channing family of Boston and Cambridge, a distinguished clan of Unitarian ministers, poets, philosophers, and pacifists. Barlow was raised in Brookline, Massachusetts, was graduated first in his class from Harvard in 1855, and practiced law in New York City until the start of the war. Enlisted as a private in the 12th New York, Barlow was mustered out with his unit after three months. He reenlisted as lieutenant colonel of the 61st New York, and his distinguished service resulted in his rise to general rank. He was severely wounded at Antietam, and at Gettysburg, commanding a division in the Eleventh Corps, he was wounded so critically on the first day of battle that he was left for dead. Taken prisoner by the Confederates, he was exchanged and hospitalized in the North. Slender and clean-shaven, Francis Barlow looked more like a Harvard patrician than a tough, aggressive fighter, but in fact he was both. He was later singled out by Palfrey as one of the few officers in the Army of the Potomac who actually took a fierce joy in fighting—Hancock was another—instead of simply doing his duty in performing a disagreeable but necessary task. Hancock had spotted Barlow earlier as the kind of subordinate he would like to have; after Chancellorsville, he told Barlow that he would be delighted to have him, and he later wrote to Meade's chief of staff asking for Barlow as a division commander. Now, for the 1864 campaign, Hancock would have him.[13]

An unnecessary controversy flared up in January 1864, when Congress passed a joint resolution giving thanks for the victory at Gettysburg to Meade, Hooker, and Howard. An odder enactment was probably never made. Hooker, of course, was nowhere near Gettysburg during the battle, but he *had* commanded the army until a few days before the fight, and he did still have many friends in Congress. Howard's name had been added to the resolution by Senator James Grimes of Iowa, and there were apparently no members alert enough or sufficiently aware of the facts to object. But the partisans of the other corps commanders, particularly those of Hancock, were quick enough to raise their voices after Lincoln signed the resolution on January 28. A letter signed "Truth," which appeared in the *Army and Navy Journal* on February 20, was typical: "But by what strange process of reasoning or distortion of facts is the name of Major General Howard placed in this resolution?" The letter recited the achievements of Hancock and the failings of Howard, and asserted that Hancock was, next to Meade, "the prominent man at Gettysburg. The Army gave to him the credit which

Congress has given to Major General Howard." It concluded: "Happily his [Hancock's] reputation is fixed on too substantial a basis to be dependent on any action of Congress."[14]

Instead of letting the matter drop, Howard for some reason chose to react to a pro-Hancock article in the *Philadelphia Evening Bulletin,* and he wrote to Hancock about it. "I would not, on any account enter into a newspaper controversy," he wrote, "and care little about the article, except so far as it accuses me, for some political reasons, of accepting what belongs to you, i.e. of being a willing party to your detriment. I trust this is not your sentiment." Howard went on to say that he thought Hancock, too, deserved the thanks of Congress for Gettysburg: "No man was more welcome than you, when you joined me on that famous cemetery height. No man could have worked harder, or have effected more."[15]

Hancock's response to Howard was frosty:

> I have not written anything for the press concerning the battle of Gettysburg, nor am I responsible for anything that has been written. As to the article in the Evening Bulletin concerning which you made reference in your letter, I can state that I never saw it, nor was I aware of its publication until a week afterwards. I then only learned the author. I have my views concerning the battle of Gettysburg, but I have not yet put them in print, nor shall I do so, so far as I know now. I have seen many things in print which I consider unjust, but I do not think it wise to reply to them.

> I do consider that an act of injustice was done by Congress, in singling out any corps commander at Gettysburg for his services there. . . . I thought myself the act of Congress might have been induced by a desire on the part of the administration to make you prominent, to have an effect in case it would be thought wise or advisable to use your name and reputation in the coming Presidential or Vice Presidential campaign. It was a thought of mine, and has not been borne out by anything I have heard since from people who ought to know. . . .

> My temperament is such that the fact that Congress chose to thank you for services in a battle where I had a like command, and did not do the same for me, could not cause me to cease speaking of your gallantry, nor would I consider it a matter personal between ourselves, should I think my services had been over-looked by any tribunal having the authority to judge, and that yours had not been.[16]

But Howard was in Tennessee, away from the Army of the Potomac, so he was no longer any immediate concern of Hancock. Getting back to his corps was. As January passed into February, and February into March, George Gordon Meade began chafing at Hancock's absence. He had ideas for a major reorganization of the Army of the Potomac, and he was anxious to get on with it. On March 15, he wrote to John Gibbon, asking, "What has become of Hancock? . . . It is impossible to reorganize till he arrives, as certain points can only be decided after consultation with him as corps commander." Then he mentioned that he had given Hancock's name to the Committee on the Conduct of the War as a witness on his behalf in the inquisition the committee was currently holding on Meade's actions at Gettysburg, an investigation inspired by Sickles. Indeed, one of the reasons why Hancock had not yet returned to the Army of the Potomac was his scheduled appearance before the committee on March 22.[17]

Hancock testified before the Committee on the Conduct of the War as scheduled, giving the congressmen his views of the battles of Chancellorsville and Gettysburg. To the disappointment, no doubt, of the committee members, who were largely friends of Hooker, Sickles, and Dan Butterfield, and hostile to Meade, Hancock's testimony was unfavorable to Hooker and favorable, on the whole, to Meade. His only criticism of Meade was for the failure to launch a counterattack after the repulse of Pickett, and he tempered this by saying he understood Meade had ordered something like that but the troops of the Fifth and Sixth corps were so slow in gathering that the remaining hours of daylight passed away. The members of the committee treated Hancock himself with complete cordiality and respect.[18]

Finally, on the next day, March 23, Hancock returned to the Army of the Potomac, staying at Meade's headquarters at Culpeper before going on to join his corps on March 24. Also on March 23, the War Department issued General Orders No. 115, the reorganization of the eastern army by the reduction of the number of corps to three, the Second, the Fifth, and the Sixth. Because of the immense difficulty of keeping existing units up to effective strength, it was decided to abolish the First and Third corps, transferring their units into the remaining corps. The First Corps divisions were incorporated into the Fifth Corps, and the first and second divisions of the Third Corps moved over to the Second Corps, with the last division of the Third Corps going to the Sixth. (The Eleventh and Twelfth corps had been sent to Tennessee the previous September, so that they were no longer part of the Army of the Potomac.) Hancock of course continued as commander of the Second Corps and John Sedgwick as commander of the Sixth, and Gouverneur Warren was named to head the Fifth Corps. Part of the fallout from the reorganization was the detachment from the Army of the Potomac of such veteran generals as George Sykes, William H. French, John Newton, Alfred Pleasonton, and John Caldwell, but one of the unspoken reasons for the big shakeup was the suspicion that Meade's army suffered from a shortage of competent corps commanders, and these generals had been found wanting.[19]

Hancock took over the Second Corps on March 24 and the next day announced its new organization. The old Second Corps regiments were all consolidated into two divisions, with Francis Barlow commanding the first and John Gibbon the second. Barlow's brigades were led by Nelson Miles, Thomas A. Smyth, Paul Frank, and John Brooke. Gibbon's brigade commanders were Alexander Webb, Joshua T. Owen, and Sprigg Carroll. What had been the First Division, Third Corps, now became the Second Corps's

Third Division, under David B. Birney, with J. H. Hobart Ward and Alexander Hays leading its brigades, and the Fourth Division was the former Second Division of the Third Corps. It was planned to have Brigadier General Joseph B. Carr command this division, but his promotion had run into trouble in the Senate; if it failed of approval, Carr would be outranked by one of his brigade commanders, Gershom Mott, and of course that would not be permitted. As things turned out, Carr did not get his promotion, so Mott took over the division right before the start of the campaign.[20]

The commander of the new Third Division, David B. Birney, found himself in a precarious situation. A cold and ambitious man, he had many enemies but was a competent general. One of his major motivating forces was the advancement of his own military career, but he had just made a big misstep. A Philadelphia lawyer before the war, Birney had supported the cause of Dan Sickles, his former corps commander, when Sickles commenced a political vendetta against Meade after Gettysburg. Now a new campaign was about to begin, and Birney found himself still in Meade's army. Indeed, his new corps commander was Meade's close friend. So, early in April, Birney went to see Hancock, to disavow any connection with Sickles and to see whether Meade would let him come and explain himself. Meade, hearing this, told Hancock that he was not aware of any need for explanation on Birney's part. Finally, on April 18, Birney got his meeting with Meade, who listened coolly as Birney squirmed to get into the commander's good graces. When Birney was finished, Meade simply said he had never heard that Birney had any unfriendly feelings toward him. David Birney no doubt walked out of Meade's tent with the feeling that he would not get many second chances if he made any mistakes.[21]

Meade's army had about five weeks to shake down its new organization before the start of the year's campaign. The men of the disbanded corps, in many cases following the lead of their officers, did much grumbling and complaining about the consolidation and the loss of their units' identities, even though they were allowed to continue wearing their old corps and division insignia. One soldier from Maine wrote: "It was a heavy blow to veterans of the old 3rd Corps to sink their identity in another body, but . . . there are no troops in the Army of the Potomac who wouldn't feel proud to fight under Hancock. . . ." In addition, since the old Third Division of the Second Corps was also broken up, Alexander Hays and the men of that division were unhappy. "The enemies of our country have . . . assailed it in vain," Hays wrote his wife, "and now it dissolves by the action of our own friends." For his part, Hancock soon found fault with the old Third Corps units now under his command, writing on March 26 that they performed picket duty very poorly. In truth, the Third Corps under Sickles had become a slipshod outfit; at one point, Humphreys, the only military professional in its top leadership, wrote a friend about its shortcomings, exclaiming, "You see how things were managed in the Third Corps." Hancock hoped to straighten them out; unfortunately, he would not have the assistance of Humphreys, who had become Meade's chief of staff.[22]

Those five weeks were precious to Hancock, for they represented all the time that was available to whip his corps into shape after its winter layover. He was not much worried about the veteran Second Corps soldiers; he was concerned about the new recruits, new regiments, and transferred units that were now part of his corps, particularly those organizations with new commanders. Hancock made sure that all of his men were drilled and maneuvered and drilled some more, so that all of them would know what to do when ordered and would do it promptly. The Second Corps had a high reputation, and Hancock wanted no doubt about his men's ability to uphold it. In the latter part of April he reviewed his divisions, and on April 22 the whole corps was reviewed by the new commanding general of all the Union armies, the hero of Vicksburg and Chattanooga, Lieutenant General Ulysses S. Grant. Barlow wrote home afterwards: "It was the best and most complete Review of such a body of men that I ever saw and is so considered here. It beat the 6th Corps. . . ." Hancock's headquarters put on a luncheon reception, complete with champagne, after the review, and the whole affair was considered a great success.[23]

Grant chose to make his headquarters with the Army of the Potomac because it was accessible to the capital without being at the capital. His presence, of course, badly compromised the position of Meade. How the two-headed Union leadership would work out was yet to be seen, but Grant was eager to take on Robert E. Lee. On April 9, 1864, while he was still undecided whether to cross the Rapidan above or below the Confederates, Grant wrote to Meade: "Lee's Army will be your objective point. Wherever Lee goes there you will go also." As April came to an end and the Army of the Potomac prepared to march, that was to be the mark of the 1864 campaign.[24]

FOURTEEN

The Wilderness

The Second Corps marched at midnight, May 3, 1864. Barlow's division was in the lead, followed by Gibbon, Birney, and Mott. Barlow was instructed, verbally by Hancock and in writing by Morgan, that the head of his column was to be at Ely's Ford on the Rapidan by 6 a.m., May 4. The last campaign of the Army of the Potomac was under way.[1]

For the first time, the Army of the Potomac would not be marching alone. Grant had directed that all of the field armies of the United States move simultaneously, so that the Confederacy would be under pressure all along the line and its leaders would not be able to move forces from points not under attack to those spots that were endangered. The other principal attack besides that of the Army of the Potomac was to be Sherman's movement from Chattanooga toward Atlanta. In addition, Nathaniel P. Banks in Louisiana, Franz Sigel in the Shenandoah Valley, and Benjamin F. Butler at Fort Monroe were ordered to move.

The advance of Butler's Army of the James was supposed to be of particular consequence to that of Meade's army. Moving up the James River partway by steamer and after that on land, Butler was to seize City Point and then threaten Richmond from the south side of the river. It was anticipated that this menace might actually pull troops away from Lee's army; it would certainly mean that Lee could draw no reinforcements from the Richmond garrisons. But Butler was another political general—a War Democrat with much strength in Massachusetts and in the North generally—who was a military incompetent. He so bungled his advance that he neglected to capture Petersburg, never got closer to Richmond than Drewry's Bluff, and managed to get his army bottled up on a neck of land between the James and the Appomattox rivers, where it was effectively out of the campaign.

The Army of the Potomac, however, as it prepared to cross the fords of the Rapidan, appeared to be powerful enough to handle whatever it might encounter. As April ended, Meade had just under 100,000 men and officers in his command, with 274 guns. The Second Corps was the largest of the three infantry corps, followed by Warren's Fifth Corps and Sedgwick's Sixth. The cavalry, now under Grant's protégé, the short and swarthy Philip Sheridan, numbered 12,525. In addition, the Ninth Corps under Burnside had been refitted at Annapolis and was now ordered by Grant to report for passage of the Rapidan. Burnside's corps was not part of the Army of the Potomac and was therefore responsible only to Grant, not to Meade. It was a further refinement of the anomalous command structure the eastern army took into its 1864 campaign.[2]

Just before the campaign got under way, Winfield Hancock took care of a personal matter. On May 1 he wrote to Seth Williams, at Meade's headquarters: "I request that I may be permitted to ride in a spring wagon when I find it necessary. . . . This concession only to continue until my wound is healed. I may not require it, but I should like to have the authority." Unfortunately, Hancock would be forced to use the ambulance for transportation throughout the campaign, as his unhealed wound kept him in almost constant pain. When a fight was in progress, of course, he would leave the ambulance and ride his horse, to keep track of the battle and to be seen by his men. "I suffer agony on these occasions," he wrote to Allie, "but must go into action on horseback or ask to be relieved."[3]

The Army of Northern Virginia had been concentrated for the winter around Orange Court House, south of the Rapidan and about eighteen miles southwest of the Union crossings. Longstreet's corps was at Gordonsville, nine miles or so farther south. Grant's plan was to cross the Rapidan with two columns and move through and out of the Wilderness before encountering Lee's army, if possible getting between Lee and Richmond. Grant had no intention of fighting in the Wilderness, that great tangle of scrub oak, alders, willows, and moss-shrouded pines in which Hooker had come to grief a year earlier. It was a second-growth jungle, for the primeval forest had been converted into charcoal over a century earlier to feed the iron furnaces which dotted the countryside. The soil was poor, and the trees were stunted and scrubby and surrounded by a thick underbrush. The region was broken up by a number of small streams, dank little rivulets arched over by foliage which kept the sun from penetrating their fastnesses. Ironically, at the time Grant's army entered the Wilderness, its customary gloom was brightened by flowering dogwoods, huckleberry bushes, and wild roses. Still, these were mere flashes of brilliance in the prevailing obscurity. The Wilderness was no place for a battle—unless one's numbers were substantially smaller than one's opponent's. The difficult, almost impossible conditions could serve as a great equalizer.

The Fifth and Sixth corps crossed the Rapidan at Germanna Ford, while Hancock's corps crossed at Ely's Ford, several miles downstream. The Fifth Corps was to bivouac at the Old Wilderness Tavern, where the Germanna Plank Road intersected the Orange and Fredericksburg Turnpike; the Sixth was to camp on the heights beyond the ford. The Second Corps was directed to stop for the night on the old battlefield of Chancellorsville, an eerie place with its scattering of unburied bones of men and horses from the earlier fight. Each corps reached its assigned stopping point relatively early on the afternoon of May 4, most of Hancock's men being in camp by 1:40 p.m. Each of the three corps could have pushed on much farther that day and been that much closer to getting out of the Wilderness. The problem, however, and the reason why the army halted as it did on May 4, was protection of the lengthy and lumbering column of wagons which made up the army's supply train. The train had to cross the Rapidan after the infantry columns and, on the morning of May 5, could have been vulnerable to attack if the infantry corps had moved too far beyond the river. Nevertheless, the fact that Meade's infantry was still in the Wilderness on the morning of May 5 was to be of critical importance.[4]

Grant was relieved to be across the Rapidan without opposition; he was unaware that half of Lee's army, that evening of May 4, was camped within five or six miles of Warren and Sedgwick. Lee, whose army of 62,000 was little more than half the force under Grant's command, had no intention of letting the Army of the Potomac get out of the Wilderness unscathed. Hill and Ewell had hurried their corps east over the turnpike from Orange Court House, and Longstreet was under orders to move his corps the much greater distance from Gordonsville. Longstreet was still a long way off, but Ewell and Hill would be ready to attack in the morning.

Because the Wilderness was so densely wooded, the few roads through it became of paramount importance. It may be recalled, from the description of the 1863 fighting around Chancellorsville, that there were two principal roads running in a general east-west direction. One of these was the Orange and Fredericksburg Turnpike, an old post road from stagecoach days, and the other was the Orange Plank Road, a few miles south of the turnpike, a relic of the plank-road fashion of about 1845. Both of these roads were, in 1864, in rundown and forlorn condition, but they were at least hard-earth roads, and they facilitated, to a degree, east-west movement. The only north-south road of equivalent condition was the Germanna Plank Road, which angled southeast from Germanna Ford on the Rapidan, crossing the turnpike at Wilderness Tavern. The other roads in the area were of poorer quality, narrow footpaths through the woods which deserved the appellation "roads" only in contrast to the surrounding jungle. Among these were the road from Ely's Ford to Chancellorsville, which the Second Corps had traversed on May 4; a road which branched off from it south of Chancellorsville, called the Furnace Road; a narrow road which meandered southwesterly through the woods from the turnpike to the plank road at Parker's Store; and a road which ran south from the turnpike, crossed the Orange Plank Road, and then ran southeast to Todd's Tavern and on to Spotsylvania Court House. This last was called the Brock Road, and it was to figure strongly in the story of the Wilderness.

The evening of May 4, Grant wired Halleck: "The crossing of Rapidan effected. Forty-eight hours now will demonstrate whether the enemy intends giving battle this side of Richmond." Grant was about to become acquainted with Robert E. Lee, and he would not have to wait forty-eight hours. At 5 a.m. on May 5, the Union force was in motion again. The Sixth Corps was to move down the Germanna Plank Road to Wilderness Tavern, the Fifth Corps was ordered to march along Wilderness Run to Parker's Store, and Hancock's corps was headed down the Furnace Road, to Todd's

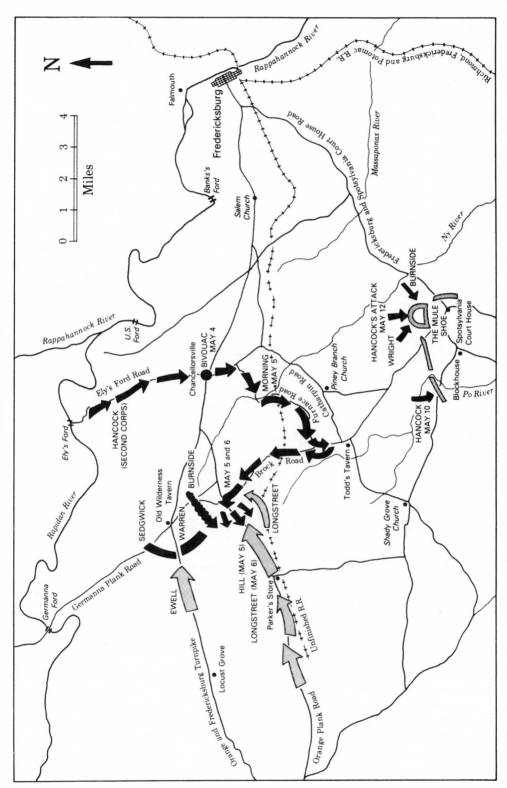

The Wilderness and Spotsylvania

Tavern, from where it was to follow another road off to the southwest toward Shady Grove Church. At this place, the Second Corps would have been in position to turn the Confederate right.

At about 6 a.m., Warren, who was preparing to pull in his pickets from the turnpike, was astonished to learn of rebel infantry on the turnpike preparing for battle. He sent word to Meade, who received the message shortly before arriving at Warren's headquarters about 7:30. Meade ordered Warren to halt the march of his corps and to attack the enemy on the turnpike with his full strength. At the same time, Meade sent word to Hancock that the Confederates were on the turnpike "in some force" and directed, "until the matter develops," that the Second Corps halt at Todd's Tavern. By the time Hancock received this order, at 9 a.m., Gibbon's division was already a mile or two beyond Todd's Tavern and had to be recalled.

It is interesting to imagine what would have happened if Meade had permitted Hancock to continue his turning movement, already well advanced, instead of halting him. Presumably the Fifth and Sixth corps could have held their own against such of Lee's forces as were present until Hancock struck the Confederate rear, an assault which should have caused great damage and confusion. This can only be speculation, of course, since Meade brought the turning movement to a halt. It must be inferred that Meade did not have full confidence in the original plan. Hancock waited in the vicinity of Todd's Tavern until 11:40 a.m., when he received an order from Meade to "move up the Brock road to the Orange Court-house plank road, and report your arrival at that point and be prepared to move out the plank road toward Parker's Store." Hancock immediately replied that he would promptly move back up the Brock Road to the Orange Plank Road.[5]

Meade knew that Hancock moved as rapidly as any commander in the army, and from that fact and from Hancock's message that he was moving to execute Meade's order, the general commanding drew an incorrect picture of the location of the Second Corps. When Hancock reversed direction at 11:40, Birney's and Gibbon's divisions were spread out along the Brock Road near Todd's Tavern, Birney being on the more northerly side. Mott's division was still on the Furnace Road where it intersected the Brock Road, and Barlow's division had been halted far back on the Furnace Road, at Catharine Furnace. The Second Corps column occupied nearly six miles of road. Birney promptly faced his division around and moved up the Brock Road, but it would be quite a while before the Second Corps as such would be on the plank road in force.

It was on the plank road that the concern of Meade and his superior, Grant, now centered. Warren had attacked Ewell on the turnpike, but the brigades and divisions of the Fifth Corps had stumbled around in the dense woods without accomplishing much more than a stalemate. On the plank road, however, Hill's corps had crashed through an ineffective Union cavalry screen and was advancing toward the Brock Road. If Hill could secure this intersection he would effectively interpose his corps between Hancock's command and the rest of the army; the Second Corps would be cut off. Grant found Getty's division of the Sixth Corps at Wilderness Tavern, and he promptly dispatched it to the area of the Brock and plank roads, to attack out along the plank road, with support from Hancock when he arrived.[6]

Getty arrived with his division at the crucial intersection just ahead of Heth's division of Hill's corps. Getty was able to hold the crossroads, but he was not strong enough to push the Confederates back to Parker's Store, as his orders contemplated. A meaningful attack had to await the arrival of the Second Corps. And, of course, the Second Corps did not begin to move toward the plank road until 11:40 a.m. Nevertheless, when Meade was informed at 1:30 p.m. that Hancock, riding ahead of his divisions with his headquarters party, had reached Getty at the plank road, he made the totally incorrect assumption that Hancock's *corps* was there with him, ready to attack. At noon, he had sent orders to Hancock to drive the enemy out the plank road beyond Parker's Store and to unite with Warren on the right. Now, at 1:30, Meade repeated: "attack them; Getty will aid you. . . . Push out on the plank road and connect with Warren." These orders bore no relation to the reality of the situation on the plank road. Hill was out there, with two big divisions. Getty could not attack them with his division, and all Hancock had at the moment was his headquarters party. In addition, Warren was nowhere near the plank road.[7]

At 2:40, Hancock reported to headquarters that he had just received both the noon and the 1:30 messages. This was the first he knew that he was expected to launch an immediate attack; until then he had ordered Birney's men to entrench as they arrived, since Getty had told him he expected a rebel attack. "I am forming my corps on Getty's left, and will order an advance as soon as prepared," he told Meade, adding that he would attack with two divisions, presumably Getty's and Birney's, with Mott's in reserve. He advised that the ground over which his attack would pass was very bad—"a perfect thicket." By this time Birney's division was up and Mott's was arriving. One of Birney's soldiers commented that "the most awful confusion" prevailed at the road junction; "there were more troops than could be utilized." Hancock and Morgan and the staff set to work sorting them out. At 3 o'clock Hancock sent word to Meade that he had just received a 2:15 dispatch advising that Warren was no longer near the plank road. Getty and two Second Corps divisions (one in reserve), Hancock said, would attack as soon as the troops got into position. At 3:15, Meade, obviously goaded by the impatient Grant, fired off another directive to Hancock, "that Getty attack at once, and that you support him with your whole corps, one division on his right and one division on his left, the others in reserve. . . ." At 4:05 Hancock reported receipt of this message and said that, in order to comply with the mandated formation, he had pulled Birney out of place and sent his division to Getty's right; "he will soon be there." Hancock neglected to mention that the divisions which were to constitute his reserve were still toiling their way up the Brock Road. He was not interested in making excuses; he now had sufficient strength in hand to make the attack demanded by headquarters, and the attack would be made.[8]

Between 4:15 and 4:30, Getty, ordered to attack independently of Hancock, pushed off with his assault, on the right and the left of the plank road, even though Birney's units were not yet in place. Birney had to move part of his division from the left of Getty around to the right while Getty's men were moving forward, making a connection difficult. Mott's men had to move from their entrenchments to those just abandoned by Birney and then forward to catch up with Getty. As a result, both Second Corps divisions were moving forward at odd angles, and Getty's flanks were far from secure. Getty's troops advanced less than a half-mile before they came face to face with Heth's veterans, and a devastating exchange of musketry commenced. The brigade of red-haired Alexander Hays came stomping through the woods on Getty's right, up and down the ridges and swales, and stirred up a frightful response. Hays sent word back to Hancock, asking for reinforcements. Hancock, who was sending troops in as fast as they arrived, said, "I will send him a brigade in twenty minutes. Tell him to hold his ground. He can do it; I know him to be a powerful man." Hays, who was absolutely fearless in battle, rode along his line, badly disordered by the blind advance through the woods, and tried to get it straightened; while he did so, a rebel put a Minié ball through his brain. Hancock's old friend and classmate toppled dead from his saddle, but the brigade held its position. Birney sent Ward's brigade to support Getty's left, and this bolstering stabilized the Union line in that sector.[9]

Farther to the left, Hancock ordered Mott's two brigades forward. They came out of their breastworks along the Brock Road and moved into the tangled woods, William R. Brewster's Excelsior Brigade on the left and Robert McAllister's Jerseymen on the right. To the inevitable problem of keeping lines straight in the dark and overgrown forest was added the further difficulty of Getty's line's stretching farther to the left than expected. McAllister's men had to move to the left, where they bunched up with Brewster's. The units of the division were thus jumbled, often separated from their officers, when the unseen Confederates suddenly opened with a fierce volley from directly in front. A feeble return fire did little good, and another heavy rebel volley killed large numbers of men and forced the others back. Apparently, the Excelsior Brigade broke first, but it was soon joined in flight by McAllister's men.[10]

A dramatic scene unfolded back at the Brock Road intersection, where Winfield Scott Hancock had established his headquarters. A courier from Meade reported the vision of Hancock on his horse—"a glorious soldier indeed." Hancock, deeply affected by the sight of the stretcher bearing the lifeless body of Hays, persevered, as a soldier must, with no time for grief. To Meade's courier: "Report to General Meade that it is very hard to bring up troops in this wood, and that only a part of my Corps is up, but I will do as well as I can." An officer rode up to tell him that Getty was hard pressed and low on ammunition. "Tell him to hold on," Hancock shouted, "and General Gibbon will be up to help him." Another officer reported that Mott's division had broken. "Tell him to stop them, sir!" roared Hancock. When Mott's men started coming out of the woods, Hancock rode among them: "Halt here! Halt here! Form behind this rifle-pit." Shortly, Sprigg Carroll came riding up the Brock Road, "calm as a May morning," his excellent brigade behind him. With hardly a pause, Hancock faced them to the left and sent them charging up the plank road to help Getty. Webb's brigade, moving up behind Carroll, arrived and was sent to relieve the routed Fourth Division. Owen's brigade, bringing up the rear of Gibbon's division, was sent out the plank road behind Carroll. With the arrival of Gibbon's division, the crisis was over and the initiative passed again to the Union forces.[11]

Carroll's advance took place about 4:30 and Owen's twenty or thirty minutes later. The weary troops of Getty's division fired off what was left of their ammunition and let Gibbon's relieving soldiers pass through their lines. Carroll's men hit the enemy with their accustomed ferocity along the plank road and drove them back; Carroll was wounded but stayed at the front. Owen's brigade, off to the left in the deep woods, was unable to make comparable progress, and a violent rebel counterattack brought it to a halt. The fighting in the woods on either side of the plank road was savage. The front seemed to sway back and forth without either side's gaining a decided advantage; it was impossible to maintain continuous lines in the dense foliage. The totals of dead and wounded mounted.

Late in the afternoon, shortly before 7 o'clock, with no decisive edge yet gained by either side in the struggle along the plank road, Hancock directed a movement by brigades in Barlow's division, holding the far left end of the Union line, to strike the right flank of Hill's force. About 7 p.m. Barlow moved forward with a heavy attack which gradually pushed the Confederate flank back. Hill's last reserve, the North Carolina brigade of James Lane, was thrown in against Barlow, and the Confederate line held, but barely. North of the plank road, Grant had ordered the Fifth Corps division of James Wadsworth forward into the gap between the Fifth and the Second corps, to strike Hill on his other flank. Wadsworth arrived just after dark, when visibility in the Wilderness had totally disappeared, so that he had to hold back his assault. The same darkness cut short Barlow's attack just as it was starting to make good progress.[12]

With the coming of darkness, the fighting stopped. The results of the first day in the Wilderness appeared to be a standoff: off and on through the day, Sedgwick and Warren had fought Ewell without decisive results, and Hancock and Hill were still on the plank road, not too far from where they had started. But appearances were deceiving, at least on the left. Hancock's forces had attained a commanding position. Hill's troops were fought out; another half-hour or so of daylight would most likely have brought them to disaster, with Barlow and Wadsworth executing a double envelopment of the exhausted Confederates. But those additional minutes of light were not available, and the battle would be rejoined the next day.[13]

Grant gave orders that the attack should be renewed at 4:30 a.m. on May 6. Meade asked that this hour be changed to 6, because of the condition of the terrain, the fatigued state of the men, and necessity of having some daylight; Grant permitted him to change the time to 5 a.m., but no later, as he did not want the enemy to take the initiative. Meade mentioned to Grant his apprehensions about Longstreet, who was known to be hurrying toward the field, and said, "I have notified Hancock to look out for his left."[14]

Longstreet! The specter of Longstreet's corps had been hanging over the Union generals during the first day's fighting and would continue to do so on the next. At 6:14 p.m. on May 5, Hancock had reported hearing "a new line of fire" on his left and said he would pull Gibbon out to face it if other firing was heard. Nothing came of it—Longstreet was still far off—but the reaction demonstrates that in these spooky woods an unseen force could exert a tangible influence on even so stalwart a general as Winfield Scott Hancock. Actually, the missing Confederate units were two divisions of Longstreet's corps, under Joseph Kershaw and Charles W. Field, and the third division, that of Richard H. Anderson, of Hill's corps. Nevertheless, three fresh divisions of well-led and veteran troops, whenever they should appear, would have a considerable impact. On paper, there was a comparable Union force approaching the battlefield as well, the Ninth Corps under Ambrose E. Burnside, but it is doubtful if anyone in either army would have considered that corps, newly recruited with green and untested troops and led by one of the most consistent bumblers in the Union army, the equal of the body of men that Longstreet was leading to the battle. The certainty that Longstreet was approaching and the uncertainty as to when and where he would strike combined to give the Union high command a bad case of jitters.[15]

Hancock's orders for the next day, received at 10 p.m., read as follows: "You are required to renew the attack at 4:30 o'clock tomorrow morning, keeping a sharp lookout on your left. Your right will be relieved by an attack made at the same time by General Wadsworth's division, and by two divisions of General Burnside's corps." At the same time, Getty was formally placed under Hancock's command. Burnside's orders from Grant directed him to start "punctually" at 2 a.m., so that his two divisions, closing the gap between Warren and Hancock, would be in position to move on the enemy at 4:30 a.m., simultaneously with the Army of the Potomac. The time for the attack, of course, was later moved back to 5 a.m.[16]

Hancock prepared for the next morning's fight with his usual meticulous attention to every contingency, while Lee and A. P. Hill, somehow assuming that the latter's battered divisions would be relieved by Longstreet and Anderson before morning, did next to nothing. They did not entrench or regroup; they did not even sort out the jumbled units. Hill permitted his men to fall asleep where they were, and he paid a fearful price for it in the morning.[17]

Hancock, ordered by Meade to keep "a sharp lookout" on his left for Longstreet, pulled Barlow's troops back from their position on Hill's flank and gave them to Gibbon for disposition back down the Brock Road, at some distance from the rest of the corps. Here Gibbon, with Barlow's brigades (but not his own) and with the corps artillery, would cover the left for the possibility of Longstreet's appearing up the Brock Road or along a path leading up from the Catharpin Road farther south. Indeed, another report came to Hancock that Longstreet was actually on the Catharpin Road. With the provisions made, the left of the corps was protected, but at a high price: one of the very best divisions in the army, Hancock's old division, the brigades which had charged for Caldwell across the Wheatfield at Gettysburg, were taken from the striking force which would move up along the plank road. From the position of his units, Hancock had little choice but to take Barlow for the duty of watchful inactivity on the Brock Road, but already the fear of Longstreet's unseen force had taken a toll.[18]

In fact, Longstreet had intended to come up by way of the Brock Road. Shortly after 5:00 p.m. on May 5, Longstreet was met by Lee's chief of staff and told to come on the plank road. After a rest, the Confederates resumed their march at midnight, a feeling of urgency having come over them from the change in the direction of their march. They could not reach the front in time to save A. P. Hill.[19]

Hancock's attack kicked off at 5:00 a.m. as ordered. Sedgwick and Warren were directed to move also at 5 o'clock, but their attacks were designed to serve as holding actions to keep Ewell's troops in place; Hancock's attack, with five divisions (plus Barlow's division watching the Brock Road), was the principal movement. Birney was placed in command of the assault column, which consisted of his own and Mott's divisions along with Getty's division, now led by General Frank Wheaton after the wounding of Getty the day before. Carroll's and Owen's brigades, both of Gibbon's division, followed behind, while Webb's brigade was held in reserve. At the same time, Wadsworth's division moved forward from its position on Hill's left flank. The Union assault quickly struck the enemy, and the fighting at once became fierce and bloody. After initial resistance, however, Hill's ill-prepared troops gave way, and Hancock's assault became irresistible. One after the other, Hill's brigades were overwhelmed and broke to the rear. In little over an hour, the Confederates were driven about a mile and a half, almost to their wagon trains and to Lee's headquarters. One of Birney's men exulted that they "had turned the Rebs right out of their blankets."[20]

It was at this time that a courier from Meade arrived at the crossroads and found a beaming Hancock. "We are driving them, sir," he exclaimed; "tell General Meade we are driving them most beautifully. Birney has gone in and he is just cleaning them out be-eau-ti-fully!" The courier was then required to give Hancock the unhappy news that Burnside had not arrived to carry out his part of the attack plan. At this fresh confirmation of Burnside's well-known slowness, Hancock said, "I knew it! Just what I expected. If he could attack *now,* we would smash A. P. Hill all to pieces!"[21]

Not only was Burnside nowhere near where he was supposed to be; Longstreet and Anderson now arrived on the plank road, passed through Hill's beaten troops, and hit the advancing Federals. Hancock's assault was slowing down just at that time by reason of its very success. Lines had become broken in the dense and tangled forest, men were tired and separated from their officers, and units were jumbled together. Wadsworth's division, pressing in from the right flank toward the road, had gotten mixed up with Birney's force, and Birney had called a halt to get everyone straightened out. It was at about 6:20 a.m. that Longstreet's fresh corps, with Field's division on the north side of the plank road and Kershaw's on the south, slammed into the weary Union attack column. A fierce and desperate struggle ensued as the Federals tried to keep up their earlier momentum, but they were unable to do so. Longstreet's charge brought the Union infantry to a standstill and than started to push it back, especially north of the road, where William F. Perry's Alabama brigade struck Wadsworth so fiercely that the division buckled in confusion, some members racing back through the woods to the Wilderness Tavern, others surging back along the plank road. South of the road, too, Kershaw forced the Union left, which had made the farthest penetration, back even with the center of Birney's advance.[22]

At 6:30, a few minutes after encountering the rebel reinforcements, Meade's courier wired: "General Hancock requests that Burnside may go in as soon as possible. As General Birney reports, we about hold our own against Longstreet, and many regiments are tired and shattered." At 7 a.m. Humphreys, Meade's chief of staff, advised Hancock that the only reserve of the army, Thomas G. Stevenson's Ninth Corps division, was there at headquarters and would be sent to him if he called for it, but to do so "only in case of the last necessity." Ten minutes later Hancock wired back that "they are pressing us on the road a good deal. If more force were here now I could use it; but I don't know whether I can get it in time or not." He hesitated to ask for Stevenson's reserve, much as he wanted it, because he knew he had not reached "the last necessity." Besides, he did have an additional force he could call on.[23]

At this point occurred one of those incidents which proved to be a source of controversy after the war. Hancock, in his report of the battle, stated:

> At 7 a.m., I sent a staff officer to General Gibbon, commanding the left of my line, informing him of our success on my right, and directing him to attack the enemy's right with Barlow's division, and to press to the right toward the Orange plank road. This order was only partially carried out. Frank's brigade, of Barlow's divison, was sent to feel the enemy's right, and after an obstinate

contest succeeded in forming a connection with the left of Mott's division. I do not know why my order . . . was not more fully carried out, but it was probably owing to the apprehended approach of Longstreet's corps on my left about that time; but, had my left advanced as directed by me in several orders, I believe the overthrow of the enemy would have been assured.[24]

Gibbon, many years after the war, took exception to this statement and strongly denied that he had ever received any such order. "I never received the order referred to nor ever heard of the charge connected with it until years after that report was written," Gibbon wrote in his memoirs, and he then devoted twenty-four pages to an attempted refutation. He printed correspondence with Humphreys, Barlow, the reporter William Swinton, Hancock, and W. D. W. Miller, Hancock's former aide, and all he demonstrated was his continued claim that he never received the order. John Gibbon, of course, was in the unfortunate position of trying to prove a negative, made more difficult by Hancock's letter to him of June 28, 1883, stating positively that Mitchell, then deceased, delivered the order to Gibbon and that a follow-up was delivered by another aide, who turned out to be Miller. Miller, whose recollections were somewhat dim by the time of his exchange with Gibbon in 1884, stated that Mitchell had, a few years before his death, confirmed to Miller the details of his delivery of the order to Gibbon. Mitchell also had told him that while on the way back to Hancock he, Mitchell, had met Miller carrying a similar order to Gibbon.[25]

That there is no copy of the supposed order would appear to weaken Hancock's case. However, in his dispatch to Humphreys of 7:10 a.m., Hancock said: "Barlow is putting in a brigade on the enemy's right flank [Frank's brigade], and I will follow it up, if necessary, and have so directed." Gibbon, in his book, made much of the circumstance that Hancock's report on the Wilderness was written nine months after the fact. The note to Humphreys, however, would appear to be nearly contemporaneous confirmation—ten minutes later—that he sent to Gibbon (then commanding Barlow's troops) something very close to what he described in his report. The "if necessary" implies a certain discretion in the direction to Gibbon, but since an attack from Gibbon's force certainly became "necessary," the discretion implied was more apparent than real. One participant expressed later his regret that Barlow was not moved as Hancock wanted, "for another story would certainly have had to be written."[26]

There were indeed serious consequences from the failure of Gibbon to attack: the destruction of Hill's corps was not completed; Longstreet's charge was able to stop Hancock's assault; and, most serious of all, the gap between Gibbon and the rest of Hancock's force invited the devastating flank attack which Longstreet made around 11 o'clock. As Hancock put it in his report, "an attack on the enemy's right by the troops of Barlow's division would have prevented the turning of the left of Mott's division, which occurred later in the day."[27]

But that was still some three or four hours in the future. Hancock was still trying to contain Longstreet's attack and to revive that of his own command. He seemed to be getting more hindrance than help from army headquarters. At 8 a.m. Hancock received a message from Meade placing Wadsworth's division under his orders and telling him that Burnside's two divisions were "nearly to Parker's Store" and would attack at any moment. Wadsworth's division, however, had been severely mauled by Longstreet and was of questionable value at that time. And Hancock waited in vain for the sound of Burnside's attack. At 8:45 Meade advised Hancock that Sheridan's cavalry had been directed to attack Longstreet's flank and rear "by the Brock road." This was shocking news, because Hancock knew that Longstreet was on the plank road in front of him. Could Longstreet's third division, that of Pickett, have arrived and be marching up the Brock Road? He then heard the sound of rifle fire from the vicinity of Todd's Tavern, down the Brock Road, and received another report of unidentified infantry moving toward him in the same area. To the hard-pressed Birney, who was trying to revitalize the attack on the plank road, Hancock sent orders to detach a brigade and send it to Gibbon; Henry L. Eustis, of Getty's division, was sent. Meade finally released Stevenson's reserve division to Hancock, who immediately sent one of its brigades to Gibbon. And he told Sprigg Carroll to send a regiment.[28]

At 9:45 Hancock got word from Meade that there was a break in Warren's left and that he, Hancock, should send troops to plug the gap. Birney promptly sent off two brigades to connect with Warren's left. Shortly before, Hancock had received another message from Meade, reminding him that he was to attack simultaneously with Burnside. Trouble on the left, trouble on the right, and headquarters wanted him to attack with Burnside! There can be little wonder that Birney's attack up the plank road, though fierce and producing more bloody fighting, failed to crack Longstreet's two divisions, strengthened by Hill's regrouped units. The four brigades taken from his force made it impossible for Birney to hammer the rebels with strength enough to make a break. Ironically, as the morning went on, it became only too evident that all three of the urgencies with which Meade's headquarters had vexed Hancock were naught but chimera. There was no enemy infantry on the Brock Road; a body of several hundred Union convalescents was following the route of the Second Corps from Chancellorsville, and *they* were the infantry who had been thought to be Pickett's veterans; the firing from Todd's Tavern had been a clash between Custer's horsemen and rebel cavalry. There was no break in Warren's lines, and, of course, there could be no simultaneous attack with Burnside for, as one observer wrote, "Burnside was nowhere near attacking, simultaneously or otherwise."[29]

By 10 o'clock it was clear that Birney's renewed offensive had not succeeded, and the firing along the plank road stopped. But Hancock's troubles for that morning were not over. The Confederates had discovered the cut of an unfinished railroad line running generally west to east between a few hundred to a thousand yards south of the plank road, before it bent off to the southeast. This railroad cut gave the Confederates an opportunity to move onto the left flank of Birney's assaulting column without having to struggle through the tangled forest. Longstreet sent four brigades down the railroad cut until they were in position to hit the Union flank. At about 11 o'clock, the Confederates charged up out of the cut, through the woods, and onto the startled Union soldiers. The brigades of Frank and McAllister first felt the force of this attack and, unable to change front in time, were simply driven away. In succession the other brigades of Mott's and Birney's divisions received the attack, broke from their lines, and ran to the rear. In each case, tired soldiers, weary after fighting back and forth on this field since 5 a.m., found the enemy on their left flank and rear, the covering unit on their left giving way, and themselves unable to put up adequate resistance under the circumstances. Hancock at first thought he could reform his troops along the plank road with a pulled-back left, but Birney advised him that the disorganization was so great that such a formation was not possible; the troops were ordered back to the breastworks along the Brock Road, at least those troops who had not already arrived there.[30]

North of the plank road, Field renewed his attack and, as the Union supports on the other side of the road melted away, pressed it hard. Wadsworth, a man of great personal bravery and audacity with little concept of military tactics, urged the 20th Massachusetts, of Webb's brigade, forward into a suicidal charge. When the regimental commander hesitated, Wadsworth personally led the charge, galloping far ahead of his troops and into the Confederate lines, where he was shot from his horse and mortally wounded. The Union forces north of the road soon conformed to the order to retire to the Brock Road.[31]

Some years later, Hancock met Longstreet and discussed with him the flank attack along the Orange Plank Road; "you rolled me up like a wet blanket," Hancock said, "and it was some hours before I could reorganize for battle." While it might have been some hours before he was fully reorganized, of course, Winfield Scott Hancock set to work immediately to prepare his men for the inevitable new assault.[32]

At this point, when things looked bleak for the Union cause and for the hard-pressed commander of the Union left, a case of history repeating itself gave the Federals a sorely needed respite. Longstreet and his chief engineer devised a complex plan for striking the far left of Hancock's forces—the stationary troops under John Gibbon—after pulling his attacking brigades out of line by an intricate procedure called a "movement by inversion." At the same time, he would deliver a frontal assault by Field and Kershaw on the Brock Road breastworks. It is highly unlikely that such a complicated maneuver could have succeeded, in those woods and with troops who were, as usual, tangled up by the very success of their attack; history will never know. Longstreet and a brigade commander, General Micah Jenkins, were riding down the plank road when a volley rang out from beneath the trees, fired by Confederates who had somehow mistaken the horsemen for a Federal counterattack. Jenkins and two of his aides were killed, and Longstreet was seriously wounded. Unlike Jackson at Chancellorsville, Longstreet was not killed, but he was lost to Lee for many crucial months.[33]

Lee, upon learning of the shooting of his corps commander, rushed to the front and took charge. He called off the proposed movement against Gibbon and began the process of aligning his forces for a full frontal assault. This took time, time which was of the utmost value to Hancock, his aides, and his subordinate commanders, pulling together a defensive position along the Brock Road. Between 1 and 2 p.m., the wandering divisions of Ambrose E. Burnside finally made their long-awaited appearance on the left of Field's division. The Ninth Corps attacked, gained an initial advantage by reason of surprise, and then was quickly driven back. Burnside withdrew and entrenched, and that was that.[34]

A member of Meade's staff told of meeting Hancock at this time, alone since all of his own aides were out reordering his troops. He was back of the Brock Road, and he was very tired as he asked the young officer to sit down under the trees. Hancock said all of his troops had rallied, but they too were tired, their formations mixed, and in no condition to advance. Reorganizing them was difficult, he added, since so many of their field officers had been killed or wounded.[35]

At 2:15 p.m., Meade ordered another attack; he told Hancock, "Should Burnside not require any assistance and the enemy leave you undisturbed, I would let the men rest till 6 p.m., at which time a vigorous attack made by you, in conjunction with Burnside, will, I think, overthrow the enemy. I wish this done." At 3 p.m., upon receipt of this order, Hancock responded that the partially disorganized condition of his force would make it difficult to "make a really powerful attack. I will, however, do my best and make an attack at that hour in conjunction with General Burnside."[36]

The attack was never made. At 4:15 p.m. Lee launched his last effort against Hancock's command. With some thirteen or so brigades, the Confederates pushed ahead to the edge of the abatis, about one hundred paces from the first Union line, and formed a firing line. They met a heavy response from behind the breastworks, and every effort to charge across the fallen trees and to gain a foothold in the Union line was beaten back. After a half-hour of this, an unexpected development brought about another crisis in the Federal ranks. The woods had been on fire for some hours, with the underbrush smoldering here and blazing there, incinerating many of the wounded lying on the ground. Suddenly, the rising late afternoon wind fanned the fire in Mott's front and blew it across the abatis to the logs which made up his breastworks. As the wind drove the heat, smoke, and flames into the faces of the defenders, they were at some points forced to abandon the works. The attackers came through the fire like diabolical visitors, their bayonets flashing, and the men of Mott's division, for the third time in two days, broke and ran. On either side, though, Getty's, Birney's, and Barlow's men held firm, and the fortuitous breach could not be widened. Hancock and his officers pushed themselves to a last mighty effort to throw troops into the breach. Captain Edwin Dow's battery of Maine artillerists fired into the onrushing Confederates with double-shotted canister. John Brooke's brigade was brought up from the left flank. Sprigg Carroll's brigade sprang forward from its reserve position, got to the gap ahead of Brooke, and quickly swept the Confederates back, pursuing them to the edge of the woods. Lee retreated in defeat, and the fighting on the left in the battle of the Wilderness was over. Meade, not surprisingly, called off the projected 6 p.m. attack.[37]

The battle of the Wilderness was a dreadful fight. There were more than 25,000 casualties in the two armies for those two days, with a disproportionate number of them coming on the left, where Hancock battled Hill and Longstreet. Theodore Lyman of Meade's staff, an acute observer, called Getty and Hancock "the stars of the Wilderness," praising Hancock for his vigor on May 5 in bringing his men up through difficult country, his skill in pushing them into action, "his punctual and dashing advance on the 6th, and his cheerful courage under reverse." Unfortunately, the inspirational leadership of such men as Hancock and Hays and Carroll had less effect in a dismal jungle like the Wilderness, where their troops could not see them twenty yards away. The net result of the fighting was a tactical stalemate. But the battle, and its aftermath, demonstrated that the Army of the Potomac would henceforth grasp Robert E. Lee and his army like a bulldog, hanging on and chewing until there was no more to chew. "Little Mac" and "Fighting Joe" and McDowell and Pope and so many others were all left behind, and Ulysses S. Grant was determined to end the war. A corps commander such as Hancock was a perfect instrument for him.[38]

The two armies adjusted their lines on May 7, fired a few shots in each other's direction, and rested. Grant that day ordered a night march, to be led by Warren's Fifth Corps, in the direction of Spotsylvania Court House. The men of Hancock's corps did not know where the army was going that night when Warren's vanguard came down the Brock Road, behind the Second Corps breastworks. Hancock's men *did* know that, if the Fifth Corps turned eastward on the plank road, its doing so would signal another retreat, back across the river. When Warren's column headed straight across the intersection, continuing south on the Brock Road, Hancock's men cheered so loudly that Confederate pickets shot off their muskets to warn of a possible attack. This, then, was the campaign from which there would be no retreat.

FIFTEEN

The Spotsylvania Campaign

Hancock's corps was ordered to follow the Fifth Corps on the march down the Brock Road. The Second Corps did not move until after daybreak on May 8 because of a traffic jam that developed on the road. No harm was done by the delay, however, and Hancock reached his assigned destination of Todd's Tavern without incident, the head of his column arriving there at about 9 a.m. Advised that he could expect an attack, Hancock spread his corps out to cover the Brock and Catharpin roads, with pickets, entrenchments, and scouting parties. His adjutant later wrote: "I do not remember ever to have known Hancock appear so anxious . . . as he did this day. His preparations were unceasing and betokened the expectation of a severe struggle." Hancock assumed that Lee would take one more crack at the Federals before they got out of the Wilderness. The only fighting in which his corps engaged, however, was by Miles, who stirred up the rebels during a reconnaissance westward out the Catharpin Road. Miles handled the attacks with his usual style, inflicting heavy losses upon the enemy. But there was nothing else; the anticipated battle of Todd's Tavern never took place.[1]

While the Second Corps moved to Todd's Tavern, the Fifth Corps lost the race for Spotsylvania Court House to Anderson's Confederates, who quickly entrenched themselves across the path of the Army of the Potomac. The fighting at Spotsylvania over the next ten days was essentially Grant's continuing effort to turn Lee's flanks, punctuated by a series of frontal assaults. Although the Confederates, on the defensive, were generally successful in repelling their opponents (with one conspicuous exception), they started to realize that Grant, as he wrote to Halleck on May 11, planned "to fight it out on this line if it takes all Summer."[2]

By midday May 9, the two armies once again confronted each other, with the Army of Northern Virginia occupying a semicircle facing north, northwest, and northeast, with the little town of Spotsylvania Court House at its rear. The Fifth Corps under Warren occupied the Federal right, the Sixth Corps was in the center, and Burnside's Ninth Corps was on the extreme left. The Second Corps was still back at Todd's Tavern. The Sixth Corps had suffered a grave loss that morning when its commander, Sedgwick— beloved as "Uncle John" by his men—had been killed by a rebel sharpshooter; Horatio G. Wright had assumed the corps command.

During the late afternoon of May 9, about 6 p.m., Hancock left Mott's division at Todd's Tavern and with his other three divisions crossed the Po River, far to the left of the Confederate lines. The Po was a narrow, deep, and heavily wooded stream, one of four which combined to form the Mattapony River. Where Hancock encountered it, the Po flowed from west to east, but it soon turned sharply south. The difficulty of the Second Corps's movement was due more to natural features than to the desultory Confederate defense. Brooke's brigade of Barlow's division pushed across and chased away the rebel cavalry and guns which had contested the passage. Birney's and Gibbon's divisions passed over the stream with minimal resistance. Once over, Hancock directed the building of bridges at the three spots where his corps had crossed and then moved his men rapidly along the Blockhouse Road, toward the bridge over the southerly stretch of the river. This crossing would put the Second Corps on or behind the left flank of the Confederate army. It proved impossible, however, to reach the bridge in force before darkness closed down on the corps, bringing with it in those dense woods the customary total lack of visibility. Grant's first flanking move was placed on hold until the morning.[3]

By next morning, Lee had taken steps to protect his left. William Mahone's division was dispatched to the Blockhouse bridge, and Heth's division was sent across the river farther down to come up on the Second Corps's right. Hancock reconnoitered the bridge and quickly recognized that the entrenched Confederates would make a passage nearly impossible. He did, however, send Brooke's brigade to cross the river below the bridge, a movement which was carried out successfully. At about this time Grant decided to terminate the movement south of the Po, reasoning that Lee's moves to counter Hancock must have weakened the Confederate center. He recalled the divisions of Gibbon and Birney to join in an attack by the Fifth Corps in the late afternoon. Since Hancock was designated to lead the attack, he accompanied the two divisions. When, however, it became apparent that Barlow, now alone south of the Po, was being attacked by superior enemy forces, Hancock went back across the river to supervise the withdrawal of Barlow's division. One aide recounted seeing Hancock ride up, entirely alone, in the midst of the attack, to direct Barlow's withdrawal. The movement was one of great difficulty, to withdraw a badly outnumbered force, under attack, over a river, but it was carried out with great skill. Twice Heth's men attacked what they thought was a retreating opponent, and twice they were thrown back with heavy casualties. Finally, with the woods on fire around them, Barlow's brigades were able to move back across the Po in good order, taking up the bridges behind them.

Harry Heth, with Lee's concurrence, published an order to his troops, congratulating them on their valor in driving the Federals from entrenched lines. Hancock snorted at this presumption on the part of his old friend: "Had not Barlow's fine division (then in full strength) received imperative orders to withdraw, Heth's division would have had no cause for congratulations."[4]

Grant received criticism for the movement across the Po, mainly for starting it late on the afternoon of May 9, when Lee could counter it before the next morning, instead of sending Hancock across early on May 10, when he might well have succeeded in turning the Confederate flank. Grant was also criticized for abandoning the turning movement in favor of the frontal assault in Warren's sector and for the general muzziness of his plan.[5]

The frontal attack was unsuccessful. Actually, two attacks were made, one at 3:45 p.m., led by Warren and made up largely of Fifth Corps units, the second at 7 p.m., led by Hancock, with Birney's and Gibbon's divisions and some units of the Fifth Corps. The results were the same each time, with well-entrenched defenders driving back the assault. The attackers lost heavily in these two efforts.[6]

At the far left of the Union line, a young Sixth Corps officer named Emory Upton led a successful penetration of the Confederate works. This local victory came to naught, however, because the support troops who were supposed to follow up and exploit the gap in the rebel line, Mott's Second Corps division, failed to do so, being stopped simply by artillery fire. The Sixth Corps commander, Wright, stormed in to Meade that night and said, "General, I don't *want* Mott's men on my left; they are not a support; I would rather have no troops there." This failure was the fourth dismal showing by Mott's division since the start of the campaign.[7]

May 11 was a rainy, gloomy day, and there was little fighting of any consequence. At 4 p.m. Hancock received orders to prepare for an early morning assault on the Confederate line by moving Birney's and Barlow's divisions, under cover of darkness, by the rear of Warren's and Wright's corps, to a point opposite the right center of the rebel position. Gibbon was moved up also, in reserve. The attack was to be made on a large salient in the Confederate line, called, by reason of its shape, the "Mule Shoe." The Second Corps was ordered to attack the tip of the salient while Burnside's Ninth Corps struck it from the left.

The rain continued and the weather became raw and disagreeable after dark. At about 10 p.m., Hancock set his troops in motion to the left of the Sixth Corps, massing them near the house of a man named Brown. In the murky darkness, Grant's staff people were unable to fix an accurate route of attack. Finally, in desperation, as Hancock wrote, the direction of the advance was fixed by a line drawn on a map "from the Brown house toward a large white house known to be inside the enemy's works, near the point we wished to strike." Barlow, being led with his division into position, said to Morgan, "At least face us in the right direction, so that we shall not march away from the enemy, and have to go round the world and come up in their rear." Since it had not been possible to reconnoiter the ground over which the troops were to move, Barlow asked sarcastically whether he could be assured at least that there was not a ravine a thousand feet deep between himself and the enemy. When Grant's staff could not even give him this assurance, he decided that he was being asked to lead what he called "a forlorn hope," a suicidal desperation attack, and he turned his valuables over to a friend.[8]

Nevertheless, Hancock had his orders and he prepared for the assault. It would be made in a massed formation, with Barlow to the left and Birney to the right, Mott's division in the rear of Birney, and Gibbon, technically in reserve, behind Barlow. The attack was called for 4 a.m., but a heavy fog at that hour caused a delay until 4:35, when the order to move forward was given. The distance to the Confederate lines was some 1,200 to 1,500 yards, over ground that sloped up hill and was heavily wooded to about 400 yards from the rebel lines, where a clearing opened that extended to the field-works. The Federals moved quickly up the hill, overran the startled Confederate pickets without firing a shot, broke into a run when they reached the clearing, and let out a mighty cheer as they approached the enemy line.[9]

Meanwhile, within the salient, a story of another kind had just been played out. Holding the Mule Shoe was a division under Major General Edward Johnson, in Ewell's corps. Johnson, an old army man, known as "Old Allegheny," was a Kentuckian, a West Pointer, and a prewar friend of Hancock, with whom he had shared a mess in Mexico. He limped from a wound sustained earlier in the war, but he was a good soldier. The night before, some scouts had picked up the sound of Hancock's corps moving away from its position, and Lee interpreted this as signaling a retreat to Fredericksburg by the Union army. He gave orders that the Confederate artillery should be made ready to pursue, and somewhere down the line this was translated into an order to remove the guns from the Mule Shoe. Armistead Long, the commander of Ewell's artillery, pulled twenty-two of the thirty guns out of the salient, and he neglected to inform Allegheny Johnson. When Johnson learned of the departure of his artillery, at the same time that he heard reports of a possible Federal attack on his line, he demanded that Ewell order the guns back. Ewell did so, but there was a delay before Long received the order. With the exquisite timing which history sometimes dictates, the guns arrived back in the salient at just about the time that Hancock's soldiers were racing up the hill toward the Confederate breastworks.[10]

The Federal attackers, "almost a solid rectangular mass of nearly 20,000 men," as Mitchell put it, pulled the works apart with their bare hands, and surged over the barricades. With bayonets and clubbed muskets they quickly overwhelmed the enemy, swarmed over the newly arrived artillery pieces (which were captured before they could fire a round), and subdued Johnson's whole division. Some of the defenders broke and ran but most were immediately made prisoner. The Second Corps took more than 2,800 prisoners, including Allegheny Johnson and George H. Steuart, an arrogant brigadier from Maryland. The two generals were sent back to Hancock. With tears in his eyes, Johnson threw his arms around Hancock and said, "This is damned bad luck; yet I would rather have had this good fortune to fall to you than to any other man living." The encounter with Steuart was somewhat different. Hancock had seen Steuart's wife in Washington a short time before, and he wanted to give his prisoner news of her. "How are you, Steuart?" he said, extending his hand. "I am General Steuart, of the Confederate Army," came the reply, "and under present circumstances I decline to take your hand." Hancock stiffened: "And under any other circumstances, General Steuart, I should not have offered it. You should not have put an affront upon me in the presence of my officers and soldiers."[11]

Hancock's corps had won a tremendous victory. Barlow's and Birney's troops later argued over which had crushed the front of the Mule Shoe first, but Hancock in his report diplomatically said they "entered almost at the same moment." Mott's and Gibbon's men, too, had pressed up so closely that in some instances they got in ahead of the front-line troops. After the initial success, the men swept forward, chasing the retreating Confederates and losing all semblance of organization themselves. "Our troops could not be restrained after the capture of the entrenchments," wrote Hancock, "but pursued the flying enemy through the forest in the direction of Spotsylvania Court House." Hancock's mighty thrust had placed the Army of Northern Virginia in a position of great peril; if the Second Corps could regroup and push ahead, it could split the Confederate army in two. It became a matter of great urgency for Lee to turn back Hancock's drive. Lee himself was ready to lead his troops forward when General John B. Gordon, temporarily commanding Early's division, forced him to turn back and led the counterattack himself. Soon two brigades from the division of General Robert Rodes came to Gordon's support, and the disorganized Federals were pushed slowly back to the breastworks. Here they held, the Second Corps divisions fighting from behind the outer side of the works which they had earlier captured.[12]

Now there commenced one of the most incredible episodes in the annals of warfare. Wright sent in his Sixth Corps on the west face of the salient, on Hancock's right, while Burnside attacked the east face. Lee poured in troops in his desperate struggle to drive the Federals back. From 6 a.m. until after midnight, the two armies waged a fierce and unrelenting fight over the breastworks, at point-blank range, firing into each other's faces, stabbing with bayonets through gaps in the works, pulling their opponents over the piled-up logs. The cold rain kept up all day and the bodies of the dead and wounded were trampled down into the mud and the blood; trees were cut down by the incessant musketry, and still the survivors battled on. "Over that desperate and protracted conflict," the Second Corps adjutant wrote, "Hancock presided, stern, strong, and masterful, withdrawing the shattered brigades as their ammunition became exhausted, supplying their places with fresh troops, feeding the fires of battle all day long and far into the night."[13]

The angle between the north and west faces of the salient, held by the Second and Sixth corps, was the scene of particularly hideous carnage; it became known forever after as the "Bloody Angle." Hancock brought artillery up to some high ground within three hundred yards of the breastworks and had the guns firing just over the heads of his own men into the Confederates jammed within the salient; at one point he even sent a battery of guns right up to the works and poured canister into the rebels until the cannoneers were all shot and the guns silenced. The infantrymen's lips were encrusted with powder from "biting cartridge," and their shoulders and hands were caked with mud that had stuck to the butts of their rifles. Finally, sometime after midnight, the Confederates retired to a new line which Lee had constructed in their rear during the day, and the Union army held the field.[14]

Humphreys tallied up the Union losses for May 12 at about 6,000 and estimated the Confederate casualties at between 4,000 and 5,000. To this, of course, must be added the bag of prisoners and the twenty guns taken by the Second Corps. One correspondent, looking back on the battle of the Mule Shoe, wrote that "Hancock's success had an excellent moral effect on the army, and was worth all it cost."[15]

The next morning, however, the sight which greeted the Union soldiers on either side of the captured breastworks was an appalling one. Gibbon wrote his wife that it "looks like a slaughter pen, & is a sight to make any one sick of war." Nelson Miles called it "a spectacle of horror without a parallel." He wrote: "It was the only ground that I ever saw during the war that was so completely covered with dead and wounded that it was impossible to walk over it without stepping on dead bodies."[16]

But the war went on. The principal activity on May 13 was a reconnaissance by Gibbon's division to ascertain where the enemy had gone. Lee's new line of entrenchments was found some 300 to 500 yards behind the old one, another formidable position which could not easily be taken. Carroll received a severe wound in his arm during this reconnaissance; he was the second of Hancock's brigade commanders to be disabled in two days, Webb having been shot in the eye during the attack the morning before. Both men were highly prized by Hancock, and both, particularly the indomitable Sprigg Carroll, would be sorely missed.[17]

On the same day, Hancock consolidated Mott's division into a single brigade and assigned it to Birney's division. The reason given was the reduction in numbers due to losses in action and the expiration of terms of service of many regiments, but it was clear that Hancock was very disappointed in the performance of this unit which had come to the Second Corps in the reorganization. Some of the numerical losses of the corps were redressed on May 17 when Brigadier General Robert O. Tyler's division of heavy artillery—troops who had been garrisoning the defenses of Washington—and the Corcoran Legion, four New York regiments, were assigned to it. This represented an addition of about 8,000 men, but these basically untested soldiers could hardly be considered real replacements for the veterans who had been killed or wounded since the crossing of the Rapidan, veterans who were inured to the fatigues and hardship of camp and march and the trials and horrors of combat.[18]

From May 13 through May 17, the Second Corps passed the time in relative inactivity. It participated in the movements ordered by Grant as the Union army gradually worked its way around to the left (eastward), attempting to get around Lee or to develop a weak spot, but this was more maneuver than fighting. On the fifteenth Birney reported with disdain that part of Mott's brigade had broken and run under artillery fire. Hancock responded that the colonels of regiments which gave way "under a little shelling and a few scattered shots had better be mustered out of service." Finally, on May 17, orders were received for an attack the next morning. Since most of the Confederate army had moved off to its right, to match Grant's movements, Grant felt that an attack on the line established by Lee after the attack on the Mule Shoe might catch the enemy off guard. The Second Corps, with support from Wright's corps, was chosen for the attempt.[19]

The attack was to be made by Gibbon's and Barlow's divisions. In preparing for the assault, the men had to cross the ground for which they had fought so heroically six days earlier; they found there many of the unburied dead of that earlier fight. The appearance of these bloated and discolored corpses was horrible, and the stench made many men violently sick as they marched over them. When they came near the Confederate works, they found the enemy strongly entrenched in rifle pits and protected by thick slashings of felled trees. The attackers were raked by musketry and well-placed artillery fire. Though Gibbon's and Barlow's men behaved well, it was obvious that the position was too strong to be taken by a frontal attack. Hancock so notified Meade, and the action was ended, at a price of about 650 men killed or wounded.[20]

Grant had given orders for a general movement of the army, by the left flank, away from Spotsylvania, on May 19. This movement was temporarily aborted, however, when Ewell led his corps out of the entrenchments which had been attacked the day before and took them north in an effort to go around the right flank of the Union army, and, if possible, to get among its supply trains. As Barlow, Birney, and Gibbon had all moved their divisions during the night of May 18, only Tyler's division of untried "heavies" remained along the road to Fredericksburg over which Ewell marched. At about 5 p.m., Ewell's corps hit Tyler's green troops at the Harris farm. Hancock heard the sound of firing and quickly ordered Birney's division to come to Tyler's rescue. Hancock himself spurred across the fields to see what he could do. When he arrived at the scene of the action, he found Tyler's troops fiercely engaged with Ewell's veterans and holding their own most creditably. He took command of the Union forces, feeding in Birney's brigades as they arrived. His troops stood their ground and ultimately drove Ewell from the field, with a Confederate loss of about 900. Hancock noted proudly that Tyler's troops, in their first engagement, "conducted themselves handsomely, firmly sustaining the shock of the enemy's attack," until help arrived.[21]

Grant postponed his planned move away from Spotsylvania for twenty-four hours, but on the night of May 20 the Army of the Potomac got away and headed south, toward the North Anna River. The campaign of Spotsylvania Court House was over. It was significant in several respects. It demonstrated to Lee and his army that Grant's purpose was to keep grinding away at his enemy, hitting and probing, flanking and attacking, but never backing away. Spotsylvania demonstrated to Grant that the Army of Northern Virginia was about done as an offensive force; aside from local sallies, Lee's army would henceforth fight on the defensive only. Finally, Spotsylvania gave to both armies convincing proof that entrenchments and defensive works could be quickly thrown up and made virtually impregnable to frontal assault. This new factor changed the character of the rest of the war on the Virginia front, although Grant was for a time reluctant to recognize it, at a cost of thousands of lives.

Spotsylvania confirmed the position of Winfield Hancock as the premier corps commander in the Army of the Potomac. While Hancock achieved the major successes of the campaign, Sedgwick was killed, Wright showed himself to be competent but unexceptional, and Warren demonstrated that command of a corps was too large a responsibility for him. Warren's hesitancy in obeying orders, which on May 12 almost resulted in his being relieved, contrasted sharply with Hancock's crisp efficiency. Burnside, of course, was not under Meade, but certainly no one ranked him near the top of the eastern generals. Hancock, still suffering the agonies of his wounded thigh, continued to demonstrate all the soldierly virtues. They would be needed, for the Virginia campaign was really just getting started.[22]

SIXTEEN

The Frustration of
General Grant

At dark on the night of May 20 the Second Corps was on the road again. Hancock's men led the way in yet another movement by the left flank, but this time there was a new wrinkle. Grant hoped to entice Lee into a fight in the open, and the Second Corps was to be the bait. The country south of Spotsylvania was of a much different character than the tangled Wilderness—more open, more cultivated, with better soil and better roads. That an army corps could move more quickly across this country was the key to Grant's plan.

The Second Corps moved south and east on May 21, to Guiney's Station, Bowling Green, and Milford Station, where it encountered a detachment of Kemper's brigade, part of Pickett's division, which was being sent north from Richmond to join Lee. The Confederates were quickly driven away, with 66 of them being taken prisoner, and the bridge over the Mattapony was secured. "A strong position was taken at once," Hancock wrote, "and so strengthened during the night that we were willing to undertake its defense against any force of the enemy." And that was the plan. Grant felt that if one corps was exposed, at some distance from the rest of the army, Lee might try to attack it before reinforcements could come up; "in which case the main army could follow Lee and attack him before he had time to intrench." The one exposed corps, of course, had to be secure enough to defend itself while the rest of the army concentrated, and Hancock had his men dig in strongly to that end.[1]

An incident here gave the soldiers of the Second Corps a good chuckle. The green troops in the heavy artillery division put up breastworks but were soon dismayed to find the enemy lobbing a few rounds of artillery over them. An officer rode back posthaste to Hancock and cried, "General, our breastwork is only bullet-proof and the rebels are shelling us!"

"Killed anybody?" asked Hancock calmly.

"Not yet, sir," said the indignant officer.

"Well, you can tell them to take it comfortably," concluded the general. "The rebels often throw shells, and I am sure I cannot prevent them."[2]

Warren's corps moved to Guiney's Station the same night, while Wright and Burnside stayed at Spotsylvania. Lee could have his choice; he could move against the two corps before him, or against Warren and Hancock, or, most tempting, against Hancock's corps alone. Grant called it "a superb opportunity," and he was disappointed that Lee failed to take advantage of it. Instead, the southern commander used his direct road to Richmond to make sure that he stayed between Grant's army and the capital; he did not feel himself strong enough to risk a major attack. And he avoided Grant's trap.[3]

The Second Corps was permitted to remain in its position on the Mattapony on May 22, getting some much needed rest, and on the twenty-third marched with the rest of the army to the North Anna River, about eleven miles south and a little west of Milford Station. The North Anna was a pretty stream, about 125 feet wide, swift and deep, and fordable in only a few places. Lee's army was already across. Hancock reached the North Anna at Chesterfield, where the Telegraph Road, the main road from Fredericksburg to Richmond, crossed the river. Warren was about four miles upstream, at Jericho Ford, where his corps crossed without opposition in the late afternoon of May 23.

Hancock had slightly more difficulty. The enemy had constructed a defensive works in front of the bridge on the north side of the river. Early in the evening, two brigades of Birney's division, those of Thomas Egan and Byron Pierce, charged from two different points across several hundred yards of open field, overpowered the defenders, and secured the bridgehead. Federal casualties were about 150 in an engagement Hancock called "very spirited and brilliant." In the morning, after being foiled in several attempts to burn the bridge, the rebels were gone from the south end of the span, so the Second Corps crossed and occupied the abandoned works. The rest of the day, aside from a brisk sally by the enemy against Gibbon's division, was occupied with reconnoitering the position which the corps had achieved.[4]

It was a peculiar position. The Fifth and Sixth corps were across the river at Jericho Ford, the Second Corps was at Chesterfield, and Lee's army was between them, its lines in the shape of an inverted V, with the tip securely anchored on the river at a spot called Ox Ford. Burnside tried to cross there but was sharply repulsed. Should either wing of the Union army attack, Lee could easily shift his troops about to reinforce a threatened spot. For either wing of the Union army to reinforce the other, however, it would have to cross the river twice. Lee's right rested on an impassable swamp, and his left was on the Little River, so that it would be difficult for Grant to turn him. Grant concluded to Halleck that "to make a direct attack from either wing would cause a slaughter of our men that even success would not justify." Besides, either of his two wings might be severely mauled if Lee should attack it with most of his force, leaving only a covering screen to face the other Union wing. Lee, however, who was ill, showed no disposition to do anything but sit and wait in his impregnable defensive position.[5]

The Second Corps was inactive May 25 and 26, while Grant confirmed in his own mind that his position was as bad as it seemed. On the evening of May 26, the delicate task of moving his army away from the enemy and back across the North Anna was accomplished, and on May 27 it moved south and east toward Hanovertown on the Pamunkey River, the Second Corps going into camp near there at about 10 p.m. The next morning Hancock had his troops on the move by 5:30, crossing the Pamunkey shortly after noon, linking up with the Sixth Corps, and moving south at a slow pace. On May 29 Grant directed that a reconnaissance in force be made by the whole army, in order to determine just where Lee's army was placed. The result of this probe was to disclose the position of the Army of Northern Virginia, strongly entrenched along the Totopotomoy Creek, a swampy, broad-bottomed waterway which flowed languidly into the Pamunkey. May 30 was taken up with nearly constant skirmishing, as Hancock's corps was moved up close to the enemy line. Late in the day the Fifth Corps got into a nasty fight, and Meade sent word to Hancock to advance his whole corps if he could find a suitable place, to relieve the pressure on Warren. It was 7 p.m. when this order arrived, and there was really no place along the line where a short-notice assault could be made successfully. Nevertheless, Hancock ordered Barlow to attack, and the First Division commander promptly complied. Brooke's brigade, advancing "over obstacles which would have stopped a less energetic commander," as Hancock wrote, carried the rebel rifle pits and effected a lodgment for the Federals. At 7:40 Meade ordered the operation to stop. The next day Birney, Gibbon, and Barlow each pushed up close to the enemy works, but the Confederate position was simply too strong for any reasonable chance of a successful attack. On the evening of June 1, after another day of skirmishing, probing, and entrenching, the Second Corps pulled back with the rest of the army, which started on another looping move to the right, south and east toward a spot called Cold Harbor, as Grant still sought a place where he could fight in the open.[6]

Sheridan's cavalry reached Cold Harbor on May 31, fought a battle with Fitz Lee's southern horsemen, and held on until reinforced by infantry. Wright's Sixth Corps was first on the scene, and later it was joined by the Eighteenth Corps of Baldy Smith, temporarily detached from Butler's Army of the James. Robert E. Lee, of course, moved his infantry down toward the Chickahominy, to stay between Grant and the southern capital. June 1 saw fighting between Smith's and Wright's corps, for the Union, and Anderson's, for the Confederates, with the Union troops achieving some local gains. In order to exploit these gains, Grant ordered that Hancock's corps make a night march to Cold Harbor so as to participate in a general attack the next morning.

Cold Harbor, sometimes called Cool Arbor, was one of the most grotesquely misnamed locations of all of those which became notorious during the Civil War. There are a number of theories on the source of its name, but there was nothing cold—or cool—about the place in early June 1864 as it baked under a hot sun. The only water anywhere near was the sluggish Chickahominy, toward which the veterans of the Peninsula campaign of two years earlier now returned with a notable lack of enthusiasm.

Quite close to Cold Harbor was the site of the earlier battle of Gaines's Mill, which was not recalled with much fondness, either. The Confederate line ran roughly south to north from the Chickahominy about five or six miles from the Richmond entrenchments, east and northeast of the city.

Hancock's march, on the night of June 1–2, was guided by one of Meade's best aides, who brought along instructions that Hancock was to make every effort to reach Cold Harbor as early as possible to reinforce the left of the Sixth Corps. "The night was dark, the heat and dust oppressive, and the roads unknown," Hancock said, but his troops still made good time. Unfortunately the guide took the lead division by a short cut and then watched the road dwindle to a path and then to nothing. The artillery could not follow, and everyone had to turn around and backtrack. The confusion and chaos of turning a whole division around, deep in the woods, and marching it back on its own track were immense. "My staff officers," Hancock said, "are entitled to great credit for reuniting the column and repairing the unfortunate mistake." The head of the Second Corps column arrived at Cold Harbor by 6:30 a.m., but the men were so exhausted by the wearing march that Grant ordered the morning's attack postponed to 5 p.m. Early in the afternoon, it was again put off to 4:30 the next morning.[7]

The Second Corps, when it arrived at Cold Harbor, moved to the far left of the Union line, closest to the Chickahominy. On its right was the Sixth Corps, and to the right of that, Smith's Eighteenth Corps. Warren and Burnside were at the far northerly end of the Union line, where they were not in direct confrontation with the enemy. The attack on the morning of June 3 was to be made by the corps of Hancock, Wright, and Smith. "The tactical movement was very simple," wrote one participant. "Each corps commander was to form his corps as he might determine, [and] a grand rush was to be made." On the Second Corps front, the divisions of Barlow and Gibbon were tapped for the assault, with Birney in reserve. At 4:30 a.m. the Federals moved forward.[8]

Barlow arranged his division in two lines, with the brigades of Miles and Brooke in the front and those of Byrnes and McDougall behind. His front line advanced to a sunken road in front of the Confederate works on Watt's Hill and, after a fierce but brief struggle, drove the enemy out, capturing a couple of hundred prisoners and three guns, which were quickly turned against the rebels. The second Union line, however, did not get up quickly enough, and a prompt Confederate counterattack drove Barlow's men out with heavy loss. They had been further handicapped when Brooke was severely wounded just as they struck the sunken road. Byrnes, too, was shot down. Instead of going back to their original line, however, Barlow's troopers took advantage of a slight crest within thirty to seventy-five yards of the rebel line, and they dug in there, using their bayonets and their bare hands to throw up a dirt protection. One regimental commander summed up the action this way: "We formed in line and charged the enemy over the earth-works, and our men fell in heaps."[9]

Gibbon's attack did not have even the slight success that Barlow's achieved. The Second Division deployed with Tyler's and Smyth's brigades in front, followed by McKeen's and Owen's. As the soldiers moved forward, they found directly in front of them a swamp, which cut the line in two. The swamp widened as it neared the rebel works, so that the attackers were forced farther and farther apart. A destructive fire from the Confederates took a heavy toll as the attack progressed; Tyler was wounded and taken from the field, and Colonel Boyd McKeen, one of those solid, dependable brigade commanders who had been with the Second Corps for a long time, was killed as he led his men forward. Frank Haskell, who as Gibbon's aide at Gettysburg had played a stalwart part in turning back Pickett's attack there, now a lieutenant colonel with his own Wisconsin regiment, was mortally wounded. Colonel James P. McMahon, of the 164th New York, charged with his regimental colors and leaped to the parapet of the rebel breastworks. He was then riddled with bullets and toppled dead inside the works. Smyth's brigade reached the breastworks but was unable to penetrate them. Gibbon's men fell back, again not to their starting position but to the closest point to the enemy where the slightest cover could be secured.[10]

"Thus ended the assault at Cold Harbor," Hancock wrote. The Second Corps, in the brief action, lost over 3,000 men, including many of its best officers. Morgan, the chief of staff, wrote that "the Second Corps here received a mortal blow, and never again was the same body of men." Even Hancock conceded that the disaster at Cold Harbor "was a blow to the corps from which it did not soon recover." The other two corps had even less success, if such the temporary occupation of the enemy's breastworks can be called, than the Second; accordingly, their losses were not as heavy. Still, the total Union loss for the brief few minutes of action at Cold Harbor was over 7,000 men, compared with probably fewer than 1,500 southerners. And it was all unnecessary. Grant had had plenty of experience, by then, of the futility of attacking Confederate entrenchments when the defenders were given sufficient time to dig in. And they had had thirty-six hours in which to make their Cold Harbor works impregnable. Apparently Grant attacked because, in frustration at his inability to engage Lee in the open, he could think of nothing else to do. In his memoirs, he commented: "I have always regretted that the last assault at Cold Harbor was ever made."[11]

Cold Harbor represented an abdication of generalship. Without adequate examination of the ground, Grant simply ordered an attack all along the line. He did not know about the swamp in front of Gibbon or the importance of Watt's Hill, where Barlow had his temporary success. There was no plan to exploit a penetration if made. Even Hancock is open to criticism here, for he let Birney's division sit in the lines vacated by Barlow and Gibbon without moving forward at all. It was a bad day.

The balance of that ghastly morning of June 3 was occupied by Meade's trying to renew the failed attack and his corps commanders' trying to make him see that such a renewal would be useless. At 6 a.m. Hancock sent

Meade a message, saying, "I shall await your orders, but express the opinion that if the first dash in an assault fails, other attempts are not apt to succeed better." At 6:35 Meade reported receipt of this dispatch but ordered, "You will make the attack and support it well." At 7:40 a.m. Meade wrote to Hancock: "I desire every effort to be made to carry the enemy's works. Of course if this is deemed impracticable, after trial, the attack should be suspended, but the responsibility for this must be on your judgment." At 8:25 a.m. Hancock received Meade's 7:40 dispatch; he told Meade he was waiting to hear from his division commanders, but "I consider that the assault failed long since." At 9 a.m. he received another note from Meade: "It is of the greatest importance no effort should be spared to succeed. Wright and Smith are both going to try again, and unless you consider it hopeless I would like you to do the same." Hancock responded by saying, "Some of my dispatches cannot have reached." He went back over the dismal results of the earlier attack and said his division commanders were not optimistic over the chances of a new attack where the original one failed. "Unless success has been gained in other points," he concluded, "I do not advise persistence here."[12]

Finally, Grant came out to speak with the corps commanders and to get from them the assessment which Meade seemed unable to comprehend. At 12:30 p.m. Grant told Meade to call off further attacks. He decreed advances "by regular approaches," that is, the commencement of a siege by the digging of advance trenches, zig zags, and parallels, a somewhat unusual procedure when the enemy's line was parallel to his own line with open country to the rear. But then General Grant may have been feeling more than a bit frustrated.[13]

The armies glared at each other from their Cold Harbor entrenchments for another nine days. It was a dreadfully uncomfortable time. The heat was intense, and the lines were so close that anyone standing up behind the entrenchments risked a Minié ball in the head. There were occasional forays from the Confederate lines against exposed Federal units, and there was frequent artillery shelling from both sides.

On June 5, at 1 p.m., Hancock asked Meade's headquarters, "Can any arrangement be made by which the wounded in front of Barlow can be removed? I understand men wounded on the 3d are still lying there." Nothing had been done to bring in the casualties of the great assault; they had been lying in the broiling sun, without water, for two days. Hancock's request initiated an exchange between Grant and Lee over a possible truce to gather the wounded, an exchange which resembled a stately gavotte marred only by the fact that men were suffering and dying while it continued. Lee, it developed, would certainly approve a truce, provided that Grant's request for it was properly that of the defeated general asking a favor. Grant balked at acknowledging that he had lost the battle, but eventually details of the truce were worked out. Unfortunately it took time to send these messages back and forth, also under flags of truce, and the cease-fire was not arranged until June 7, from 6 to 8 p.m., some 53 hours after Hancock's request. Very few wounded remained on the field by that time, although the count of corpses had necessarily increased.[14]

On the night of June 7, after the truce expired, the Confederates opened a massive artillery barrage. The men in the trenches were relatively untouched by the shelling, but Hancock's headquarters, located in what his aides thought was "unnecessarily close proximity to the line of battle," was riddled. The assistant provost marshal, Captain Alexander McCune, was killed while standing in the doorway of Hancock's tent, struck by a rebel cannon ball. A saddened Hancock next morning moved the corps headquarters back to a safer distance from the enemy line. "However he might choose to deal with his own life," his adjutant wrote, "he recognized his responsibility for the lives of the young men he had called around him." It was a responsibility he felt equally as strongly when advising Meade not to order suicidal charges.[15]

The siege at Cold Harbor was about as unpleasant as it could be, and the unpleasantness was aggravated for Hancock by the continued pain and discomfort of his unhealed wound. By June 10 he was laid low by the continuing pain, but he forced himself to get up the next day; a new movement was afoot, and the Second Corps was to play a major part in it. The Army of the Potomac was planning to leave Cold Harbor, and everyone, from the commanding general to the lowliest private, would be happy to see the last of that desolate place.[16]

SEVENTEEN

Across the James

This time Grant got away clean. He accomplished the feat of pulling his army away from close contact with the enemy in such a slick manner that for several days Lee did not know where the Army of the Potomac had gone. While Lee blinked in uncertainty, the Federals were off and running to the James River.

Grant was at a dead end at Cold Harbor. As he had moved down through Virginia since May 4, he had taken care to keep his supply lines open and handy. He had changed his base a couple of times, but the Union command of the Chesapeake and its tributaries had facilitated such changes. His base was now at White House, on the Pamunkey almost directly east of Richmond. If Grant moved again by the flank from Cold Harbor, the Confederates would be nearer his base than the Union army would be. In addition, the swamps of the Chickahominy did not invite maneuver. But it was painfully apparent that Grant was not going to reach Richmond by direct assaults upon the Confederate lines at Cold Harbor. So he conceived the bold notion of closing down his supply base at White House, marching his army away from Cold Harbor, crossing the James, and capturing Petersburg, the key to Richmond's communications with the rest of the South, without Lee's knowing what he was doing.

Grant started to put his plan into effect shortly after the debacle of June 3. The lines at Cold Harbor were pulled back slightly, straightened, and shortened to facilitate a withdrawal; boats were gathered at White House to take off the Eighteenth Corps; and pontoons were ordered to a convenient crossing point on the James River. On the night of June 12, Smith's corps was marched off to White House to be loaded on the waiting transports and carried around by water to the point where the Appomattox reaches the James, on the south side of the latter river. A pontoon bridge was erected over the Chickahominy, and Warren's corps crossed there on the morning of June 13. Hancock's corps followed Warren over the Chickahominy and was the first to reach the James, at Wilcox's Landing, at 5:30 p.m. that day. The Fifth Corps, after crossing the Chickahominy, had feinted westward, toward Richmond, screened by Wilson's cavalry division, in order to fool the Confederates. The Sixth and the Ninth corps crossed the Chickahominy lower down and marched toward the James by roads farther east. The maneuver worked perfectly. For some days Lee and the Confederate high command simply lost sight of the Union army.[1]

At 11:10 a.m. on June 14, Birney's troops started boarding the ferries which had been gathered at Wilcox's Landing for transport to the south side of the James at Windmill Point. The ferrying of the Second Corps across the river continued all day and into the night, with Gibbon's men following Birney's, and Barlow's coming across last. By 5 a.m. on June 15, the last regiment was on the south side of the river. Charles Dana, the New York newspaperman who was assistant secretary of war, was on the scene to serve as "eyes and ears" for Stanton, and he grasped the big picture: "Hancock moves out instantly for Petersburg to support Smith's attack on that place, which was to have been made at daylight." Unfortunately, the farther from headquarters and the closer to the front line one got, the more the big picture tended to blur. Smith's troops had moved out at 4 a.m., but through one delay and another were not ready to make their "daylight" attack until about 7 p.m. And Hancock's "instant" departure for Petersburg was something less than that.[2]

At 10:00 p.m. on the night of June 14, Meade wired to Hancock:

> General Butler has been ordered to send to you at Wind-Mill Point 60,000 rations. Soon as these are received and issued you will move your corps by the most direct route to Petersburg, taking up a position where the City Point railroad crosses Harrison's Creek at the cross-roads indicated on the map at this point, and extend your right toward the mouth of Harrison's Creek where we now have a work.[3]

The order to wait for rations was issued despite Hancock's assurance to Meade's staff that the Second Corps had sufficient rations and would *not* be out of food by the night of June 15, as he understood Meade to believe. Hancock would be bedeviled by the unneeded rations throughout the morning of the fifteenth. At 3:30 a.m., in a dispatch to Meade's headquarters reporting on the progress of his corps's passage across the river, he mentioned that "nothing has been heard of the rations yet." Twenty minutes later he had "no report of the rations yet" and pointed out that it would take time to issue them when they arrived, since two of his divisions were some two miles away from the landing. At 6:30 a.m. he told Meade, "no rations received yet." At 7:15 a.m. Hancock reported that the rations had arrived at the landing. Meade received this message just as he was about to send Hancock a directive to move without the rations; he amended his order to let Hancock exercise his judgment as to whether to issue the rations or to move without them, letting them catch up later. At 8:45 a.m. Major Mitchell, on the south side of the James, learned that the boats which everyone thought carried the long-awaited rations were not the ones after all; he sent a message to Hancock that "the rations have not arrived at all." Fifty-five minutes later, after Mitchell's message had been ferried across the river to where Hancock sat at the end of the telegraph line, the disgusted corps commander advised Meade that he had been deceived, the rations had not arrived, and he had ordered the corps to march. He himself crossed the river.[4]

The column was finally set in motion at 10:30 a.m. Morgan, the chief of staff, equipped with a map from Meade's headquarters, accompanied the lead division, that of Birney, as the corps marched off to find Harrison's Creek. On the map, it was between City Point and Petersburg and about four miles from the latter point. On the ground, it was nowhere to be found. Morgan soon observed that the roads shown on the map were not where they were supposed to be either. It eventually developed that Harrison's Creek was not within miles of where it was shown on Meade's map; indeed, it was within the enemy's lines. "The map," Hancock wrote later, "was found to be utterly worthless." Luckily, Morgan picked up some blacks who gave him correct information on the local geography; with this help he and Hancock were able to figure out the best way to get to Petersburg, and at 3:30 p.m. they turned Birney's division onto the proper road. It was a brutally hot day and the roads were very dusty; the men suffered for lack of water, and many of them collapsed along the road as the corps wandered blindly through the woods.[5]

At 5:25 p.m. a message was received from Grant, directing that the corps "push forward as rapidly as possible" to Petersburg to assist Smith. A few minutes later a note arrived from Smith, stating that Grant had authorized him "to call on you to hurry forward to Petersburg to aid in its capture." He asked that the Second Corps come up "in time to make an assault tonight after dark." Hancock was startled to receive these two messages; in his report he wrote that the dispatches from Grant and Smith "were the first and only intimations I had that Petersburg was to be attacked that day." Until then no one had told him that he was to aid Smith in the latter's attack.[6]

Meade, on June 27, confirmed Hancock's statement when he wrote to Grant that "had Major-General Hancock and myself been apprised in time of the contemplated movement against Petersburg, and the necessity of his co-operation, I am of the opinion he could have been pushed much earlier to the scene of operations." In other words, the two-headed command of the Army of the Potomac, which worked with difficulty in the best of circumstances, broke down completely in the presence of Butler's Army of the James, to which Smith belonged. Smith and Butler knew what was supposed to be happening, but Grant never advised Meade or, through him, Hancock, who marched back and forth over an erroneous map without even being told what he was there for.[7]

But Winfield Scott Hancock was a good soldier. Once he got word of what was expected of him, he hurried his men forward. He sent Morgan spurring ahead to advise Baldy Smith of the whereabouts of his troops and to let Smith know that he was moving to his aid with all dispatch. By 6:30 p.m. the head of Birney's division was within a mile of one of the Eighteenth Corps divisions. Hancock told Birney and Gibbon to move forward as soon as they could learn at what point their aid was required (Barlow's division had taken a wrong turn in the woods and would not arrive until morning). Hancock then rode forward to meet Smith, who, he said, "described to me the operations of the day, and pointed out as well as he could in the dusk of the evening the position of the enemy's lines he had carried." Hancock arrived after the long-delayed attack of the Eighteenth Corps had taken place at 7 p.m. The attack had been successful but had fallen far short of taking Petersburg. Hancock, who was senior in rank to Smith (his old commander on the Peninsula), was entitled to take command of all the Union forces present. However, because it was dark and Smith was familiar with the terrain while he was not, Hancock waived the prerogative of his rank and told Smith that the two Second Corps divisions now approaching the front were at the latter's disposal. Smith asked only that they be used to relieve the Eighteenth Corps troops in the line of Confederate works which his men had carried, so that if the enemy counterattacked they would meet fresh troops. This was ordered, and the relief was not completed before 11 p.m. By that time one of the great opportunities of the war had slipped past.[8]

When Baldy Smith got his corps into position at 1:30 p.m., in front of the thinly held Confederate works guarding Petersburg, he had well over 15,000 men available. Beauregard had in those works militiamen, clerks, and assorted odd lots to the number of about 2,800 men. Yet Smith, for one reason or another, did not attack until 7 p.m. Part of the time was taken up by Smith's personal reconnaissance of the rebel lines, part was lost when all of the artillery horses were taken off to be watered, part was consumed by Smith's natural caution. When the attack was made, however, it was all that a commander could wish. The troops of the Eighteenth Corps went storming forward and the misfit rebel defenders broke and ran. Smith took over a mile and a half of well-constructed entrenchments, and there was nothing between his troops and Petersburg. If Petersburg fell, there was no way to keep Richmond supplied. The Confederate capital was doomed. Smith could capture Petersburg with his own corps, but in case he needed it, the Second Corps was just behind him. Beauregard wrote that Smith "would certainly have taken Petersburg" if he had not stopped. Yet Baldy Smith stopped. "By this time darkness had set in," he wrote, "and having learned some time before that re-enforcements were rapidly coming in from Richmond, and deeming that I held important points of the enemy's line of works, I though it prudent to make no farther advance, and make my dispositions to hold what I already had." No matter that a full moon illuminated the landscape, that enemy reinforcements were not yet present, that "important points" of the enemy line meant little if Petersburg was not captured, that there were no Confederates to threaten what he had already taken. Smith had his troops hunker down in the captured trenches, waiting to be relieved by the Second Corps. The easy march into Petersburg never took place.[9]

It soon became obvious that the failure to take Petersburg on June 15 would not be passed by in silence. In any discussion of the affairs of that day, Hancock would be at a disadvantage, for Baldy Smith was an inveterate controversialist and intriguer. He had criticized his superiors throughout the war, both publicly and privately, and would continue to do so until finally shelved by Grant. His targets included Burnside, Butler, Meade, and Grant himself. Even Smith's professed friendship would not spare Hancock, for Baldy Smith in full flight knew no friends. A classic example is furnished by a gossipy letter Smith wrote to his crony General William Franklin shortly before the army embarked on its 1864 campaign:

> Meade is as malignant as he is jealous & as mad as he is either & Hancock & Warren are his right bowers now. . . . Burnside still sports on the wave of popularity & is one of those men who will never get killed in battle. Grant knows what he is but has not the nerve to put him where he belongs. Hancock is both ambitious and deceitful & now lives by Meade. . . .[10]

Smith took care to see that the newspaper correspondents with the Army of the James received the story of the attack on Petersburg from the viewpoint of the Eighteenth Corps—fighting all day, gallantly charging into the Confederate works, driving out the enemy, preparing to repel a counter-attack. The stories, which appeared in the *New York Times* on June 21 and the *New York Tribune* on June 27, also contained the charge that the attack was to have been jointly made by the Second and the Eighteenth corps, but the Second Corps was not pushed vigorously, did not arrive in time, and was thus responsible for the failure to capture Petersburg.

Hancock saw the earlier article and wrote on June 26 to Meade, asking for an investigation. Although faults were committed that day in the Second Corps, he said, "if Petersburg was garrisoned at that time only as is now believed . . . it should have been captured by the Eighteenth Corps." Hancock recited the forces available to Smith, including the two Second Corps divisions offered to him, and then went on:

> Had I arrived before dark, and been able to have seen the ground myself, I should have taken decisive action; but not knowing anything of the locality, nor what portion of the works General Smith had carried . . . and relying upon his judgment, and desiring not to interfere with his honors, as he was directed to take the place, I offered my advance troops to him, to use according to his knowledge and discretion, he having seen the position in daylight.

Had he been in perfect health, Hancock said, "and able to endure all the fatigues incident to the march," he could have corrected what errors were made. Still, he said, the Second Corps made "every effort . . . to carry out the views of the commanding general." Meade forwarded this message to Grant and commented: "I do not see how any censure can be attached to General Hancock and his corps." Grant on June 28 wrote a response to Meade, though there is some question as to whether this letter was ever sent. He said an investigation was unnecessary, as "the reputation of the Second Corps and its commander is so high, both with the public and in the army, that an investigation could not add to it." That reputation, he said, "cannot be tarnished by newspaper articles or scribblers."[11]

Hancock, in due course, saw the lengthy article William Kent published in the *New York Tribune* on June 27, again blaming the army's failure on the lack of proper "spirit and vigor" on the part of the Second Corps and on Hancock's refusal to cooperate with Smith upon his belated arrival. Infuriated, Hancock immediately requested that action be taken against the reporter, and at Meade's insistence Grant ordered Kent's arrest for "publishing false intelligence for a malicious purpose." Kent, however, fled north and avoided arrest. On July 8 Baldy Smith wrote to Hancock to express his regrets that such "unjust . . . charges" should have somehow shown up "in an article intended to do justice to the Eighteenth Corps" and his confidence that Kent "would be most anxious to repair any errors into which he had been led by mistake." Despite Smith's sanctimonious denials, when, later in the month, Grant relieved Smith of command, one of the reasons for doing so was, as Ben Butler wrote, Smith's participation "in publishing a libel upon his brother superior officer."[12]

So it was clear that Hancock's superiors did not attach any blame to him for the failure to capture Petersburg on June 15. The problems which plagued him—the wait for rations that never came, the search for a position that did not exist, the failure to tell him what his corps was wanted for—were real enough. So was his painful physical condition, which hindered his effectiveness and soon forced him out of action. A couple of days earlier, north of the Chickahominy, an officer had come upon Hancock sitting on the grass, "pouring water from a canteen on the wound inside his thigh," trying to find momentary relief. Late on June 15, when Hancock returned from his meeting with Smith, he met Gibbon, who found him "irritable, out of temper, calling me sharply to account" for infraction of a minor, inconsequential order. These actions, in the normally good-natured Hancock, look to be those of a man suffering almost constant pain, near the end of a hot, dusty day filled with frustrating activity.[13]

Still, there is a feeling of disappointment about Hancock's failure to take Petersburg on June 15, with all that it would have meant in the way of shortening the war. Certainly the *blame* for the failure goes to Smith, who should have captured the town long before the Second Corps arrived. Certainly Hancock had plenty of reasons for not attacking Petersburg. But he *could* have done it, and he did not. Theodore Lyman, a Harvard-educated naturalist serving on Meade's staff, wrote:

> Hancock got up that evening and joined the 18th Corps. Their troops were all exhausted, but oh! that they had attacked at once. Petersburg would have gone like a rotten branch. In war there is a critical instant—a night—perhaps only a half hour, when everything culminates. He is the military genius who recognizes this instant and acts upon it, neither precipitating nor postponing the critical moment.[14]

Winfield Hancock was conscientious, he was competent, he was superb—but he was not a "military genius." And this fact was demonstrated before the defenses of Petersburg on the moonlit night of June 15, 1864.

By midmorning of the next day, with the divisions of Robert Hoke and Bushrod Johnson having marched down posthaste from Bermuda Hundred, Beauregard had approximately 14,000 infantrymen in the Petersburg entrenchments, and the chance for a quick capture of the town was gone. None of Lee's army arrived until two days later, when Kershaw and Field and then Hill showed up, but 14,000 steady troops were enough to hold such a defensive position.[15]

Shortly after midnight on June 15, Hancock had sent orders to his division commanders to take possession at or before daybreak of any commanding point between their positions and the Appomattox. Neither Birney nor Gibbon had done much of anything to comply with these orders, at a time when the defenders had at most 8,000 men. Hancock later catechized the two division commanders as to exactly what they had done in response to his orders, and he left no doubt that he was not pleased with their actions.[16]

Until 2 p.m. on June 16, Hancock was in overall control of all of the troops at Petersburg; at that hour Meade arrived and took command. Hancock led, on Grant's order, a frontal attack of all three of his divisions on the rebel works at 6 p.m., supported by the Ninth and Eighteenth corps. The gallant Colonel Patrick Kelly, of the Irish Brigade, was killed in this attack, which was beaten off with heavy losses to the Federals. Again, on June 17 and 18, assaults were made on the Confederate entrenchments; these too were repulsed with severe losses to the Union attackers. It was clear that the troops were about used up; on June 16 Hancock reported that "I do not think the men attack with persistence; they appear to be wearied," and the next day Barlow said that a problem was that "there are scarcely any officers in the brigades." Charles Francis Adams, Jr., a cavalry officer, wrote to his father, the minister to England, that he had "never seen the Army so haggard and worn, so worked out and fought out, so dispirited and hopeless." Indeed, the Army of the Potomac which failed to capture Petersburg was hardly the same force which had crossed the Rapidan on May 4. The heavy losses of the Wilderness, of Spotsylvania, and of Cold Harbor had been made up, if at all, by hastily recruited, ill-trained greenhorns; it was a different army. It must be stated, too, that the generalship exhibited in the assaults at Petersburg—by Grant, by Meade, by Warren, even by Hancock, who at least had a physical excuse—was not of the highest quality. Finally, Grant acknowledged that the repeated charges against the Confederate defenses were not going to bring about anything but massive Union casualty lists. The Union army settled down for a siege.[17]

On the morning of June 17, Hancock notified Meade that he could "hardly walk or ride," and that evening, suffering great pain, he was obliged temporarily to turn over command of the corps to Birney. For several days before, fragments of bone, presumably the femur splintered at Gettysburg, had been working their way to the surface; the wound had been suppurating for over a month. Hancock later wrote that the wound had "during the entire campaign . . . given me great annoyance, and at times had prevented me from taking that active part in the movement of my troops which I desired to do." He spent the next ten days resting in his tent, chafing at the inactivity. On June 27, having, as he said, "partially recovered," he again assumed the corps command.[18]

One of the motivations for Hancock's early resumption of command was a fiasco in which the Second Corps was involved on June 22, when that corps and the Sixth Corps were pushed out past the Union left flank in an effort to reach the Weldon Railroad, one of the vital lines of communication between Richmond and the rest of the South. Birney did not handle his units well, A. P. Hill got three divisions in between the two Union corps, and the Second Corps was flanked. Grant called the embarrassing affair "a stampede," and the Federals lost nearly 2,000 prisoners. The men in the ranks knew that faulty generalship was involved; one man wrote: "General Hancock is away, or this disagreeable affair would never have taken place." When Hancock took over the corps again, he called all his generals to headquarters and raised what one officer called quaintly "such a *breeze*" about the affair of June 22, the criticism being directed mainly against Birney. He also issued a general order to be read to each regiment but not to be given to the press, expressing his chagrin that the corps had suffered a disaster which "seriously tarnished its fame." He pointed out that "the war is one of endurance" and that each man must do his duty. He directed the provost guard to shoot down those who ran away while their comrades were fighting.[19]

From Hancock's resumption of command until July 26, he later reported:

> . . . my troops were engaged in the arduous and dangerous duties incident to the siege operations in front of Petersburg; severe and almost constant labor (much of it during the night) was required from the men in erecting the formidable earth-works which were thrown up in front of that town. While performing these exhausting labors, the troops were at all times exposed to a heavy artillery fire and to the enemy's sharpshooters, from which a long list of casualties resulted daily.[20]

It was a peculiar siege. The lines of the two armies ran down from in front of Richmond, across the neck of Bermuda Hundred, and then halfway around Petersburg. The besieged were never surrounded by the besiegers, but that was not the point of the siege. Grant's aim was to extend his lines gradually westward below Petersburg, until all of the rail lines supplying Petersburg and Richmond from the south were in his hands. The two towns must then fall, and Lee's army would be forced to come out into the open to fight for its existence. The Federals already held two of the four railroad lines: an inconsequential one that went east to City Point on the James, and the Petersburg & Norfolk, running off to the southeast. The two major lines still operating were the Weldon Railroad, which ran south to Wilmington, North Carolina, the last major port still open to blockade runners, and the Southside Railroad, which went west to Lynchburg and the rest of the Confederacy. These roads were the real target of Grant's siege.

The siege was, as Hancock wrote, both a tedious and an arduous affair. There was constant digging and cutting trees and hauling logs, as the Union lines were made so strong that they could be safely held by less than the full army, giving Grant forces which could be used to probe Lee's flanks. And there was at all times the danger of rebel sharpshooters for the unwary and rebel mortar shells for those behind the lines. Both men and officers were exposed to these hazards. Barlow wrote in a letter: "Nothing can be worse than the life here." There were also, though, occasions for more relaxed get-togethers, such as one at Hancock's headquarters described by a member of Meade's staff: "Hancock lay, at full length, in a covered wagon . . . attired in a white shirt and blue flannel pantaloons, quite enough for the intensely hot day. He lies down as much as he can, to give his wounded leg rest." Meade, he said, sat down on the front seat of the wagon and lighted a cigar, "and we all knew he was fixed for an hour at least. When he gets down with Hancock they talk, and talk, and talk, being great friends." Hancock, he said, "is a very great and vehement talker but always says something worth hearing."[21]

One of the things Meade and Hancock joked about was a popularity contest being held at the Philadelphia Sanitary Fair, a fund-raising effort for the Sanitary Commission, a private organization which raised hygienic conditions in the army camps and helped to care for the wounded. The prize of the contest was a decorative sword, with votes being cast by those who made cash contributions. The two local heroes, Meade and Hancock, ran neck and neck and followed the contest with great interest. Though Meade ultimately prevailed, the size of the vote for Hancock was emblematic of the affection for him in his hometown. At about the same time, another such contest, held at the Mississippi Valley Sanitary Fair in St. Louis, resulted in a large plurality for Hancock. Accepting the sword he won there, Hancock wrote: "Having married in that city, and residing there for many years, I regard it as a home."[22]

Norristown, too, honored its famous son. The citizens of the town raised $1,650 to purchase a silver service as a tribute to Hancock. As "a testimonial from friends of my birth and boyhood" as well "as an expression of esteem for my public services," the general wrote, the gift had charms "doubly dear to me."[23]

Somewhere along the way Hancock picked up from General William French an English valet, a man named Shaw, who was the epitome of the British army manservant. "I fancy from his manner," wrote Theodore Lyman, "that he has once been a head servant or butler in some crack British regiment." Shaw it was who was responsible for Hancock's immaculate fresh linen, the clean white shirt every day. There were, of course, some drawbacks to Shaw, as Hancock related one day:

> That fellow is the most inquisitive and cool man I ever saw. Now I don't mind so much his smoking all my cigars and drinking all my liquors—which he does— but I had a bundle of most private papers which I had hidden in the bottom of my trunk, and, the other day, I came into my tent and there was Mr. Shaw reading them. And, when I asked him what the devil he meant, he said: "Oh, General, I took the liberty of looking at them, and now I am *so* interested, I hope you will let me finish the rest."[24]

Even with Shaw's help, however, Hancock was not immune from the discomforts of life in the field. One of the soldiers in Birney's division, an admirer of Hancock, reported his feeling of "profound rapture" at watching the corps commander becoming "quite animated" during lunch one day and carrying out a search-and-seizure mission on a large louse. The lice which afflicted the enlisted men occasionally got to their superiors as well.[25]

Petersburg was not, of course, all sitting and digging and generals lolling about; whenever the Army of the Potomac stayed in one place for a while, its rumormongers went to work full time, talking mostly about generals coming and going or about to go. There were stories about Meade losing the command of the army. There were rumors, subsequently confirmed, that Birney was to become commander of the Tenth Corps, in the Army of the James; Mott took over his division. The squabbling between Baldy Smith and Ben Butler continued until Smith was finally sacked.

One Second Corps general lost his job, too. Joshua Owen, the Welsh-born Philadelphia lawyer who led a brigade in Gibbon's division, was relieved of duty and mustered out of the service. Owen had been made a brigadier general for his gallant conduct at Glendale early in the war, but he had failed on three occasions in 1864 to comply with battlefield orders. He was used up, and the change had to be made.[26]

Another new general joined the Second Corps, on July 13, when Philippe Regis de Trobriand reported. The son of a French baron, Trobriand had become an American citizen before the war. He had commanded a brigade in the Third Corps at Gettysburg and had been serving for several months in New York. He later wrote that "General Hancock's welcome was most cordial. He did all I could wish by assigning me to my old division, and, like so many others, I was under the spell when I left him." Trobriand took over Ward's former brigade in the Third Division; Ward had been cashiered for being intoxicated at the Wilderness. Hancock's spell over the Frenchman would not be of long duration.[27]

Meade heard the stories about himself, and he dismissed them as "mere canards." He told his wife that the rumors of his quarreling with other generals were untrue. "Hancock is an honest man," Meade wrote, in a peculiar phrasing, "and as he always professes the warmest friendship for me, I never doubt his statements; and I am sure I have for him the most friendly feeling and the highest appreciation of his talents." Hancock himself told Meade on July 12 of a story going around that Hancock was to succeed Meade at the head of the Army of the Potomac, with Meade to be given another command. Meade dismissed this as "preposterous," but in fact something along that line was working out in Grant's mind. Since Lee had detached Jubal Early with a sizable number of troops to threaten Washington and to operate in the Shenandoah Valley, Grant had sent two Union corps to oppose Early, joining forces already there. Grant was considering naming Meade to command that theater—as a lateral move, not a demotion—with Hancock replacing him in the Army of the Potomac. Meade expected the worst and nursed his resentments. His feelings toward Hancock seemed slightly ambivalent. Should Hancock be given command of the Army of the Potomac, Meade said, he would "wish him joy of his promotion."[28]

Of course, the siege of Petersburg was also marching and fighting and dying. As usual, Hancock and the Second Corps were in the middle of all that.

EIGHTEEN

The Deep Bottom Expeditions

The real action at the siege of Petersburg was on Lee's flanks. Grant's interest was fixed on the ends of the Confederate line, for it was here that he could induce an active rebel reaction. Toward the end of July, the Second Corps marched off to the other side of the James, crossing at a place called Deep Bottom. This mission, however, was closely connected with an action in front of Petersburg.

One unit in the Ninth Corps line sitting and watching Petersburg was the 48th Pennsylvania, from the anthracite mining region near Scranton and Wilkes-Barre. Many of the soldiers in the regiment were coal miners, and some of them came up with the idea of utilizing their special talents by digging a long tunnel under the Confederate works opposite them. The end of the tunnel could be packed with powder and ignited, and if all went well a lovely hole would be blown in the rebel line. The scheme was passed up the chain of command and received the approval of Burnside, who set the men to work. Meade and Grant were less enthusiastic, but they let the operation proceed, to see what might come of it. As time passed and work on the mine went forward, Grant and Meade grew more interested, because it was soon clear that the mine offered the only prospect of direct action at Petersburg. As the mine neared completion, the expedition to Deep Bottom was planned, to draw off rebel troops from in front of Petersburg and to enhance Burnside's chance of making a major gain.

The Deep Bottom expedition was not simply a diversion, however. The force sent across the James was to be the Second Corps plus two divisions of Sheridan's cavalry, all under Hancock's command. The cavalry, if it could get around the Confederate lines, was to advance to the north of Richmond and destroy the Virginia Central Railroad from its crossing of the Chickahominy to as far north as the South Anna. The Second Corps, in the meantime, was to move toward Chaffin's Bluff, where the Confederate pontoon bridge crossed the James, and to take up a position there to prevent a rebel attempt to cut off the return of the cavalry. In addition, Grant wrote, "it is barely possible that by a bold move this expedition may surprise the little garrison of citizen soldiery now in Richmond and get in." Of course, if the Confederates reacted to the move north of the river by sending up substantial reinforcements, perhaps none of the initial aims of the expedition could be realized; then Burnside might break through. One would have to see what happened.[1]

At 4 p.m. on the afternoon of July 26, the Second Corps left its camp and marched north toward Point of Rocks, where Butler had a pontoon bridge over the Appomattox River. The column moved cautiously to avoid being spotted by the Confederates. Just after dark the corps crossed the Appomattox, headed over Bermuda Hundred behind Butler's lines, and marched up Jones' Neck to the pontoon bridge crossing the James at Deep Bottom. At 2:45 a.m. on July 27, Barlow's division started across the river, and by 6:30 a.m. the whole corps was once again north of the James. Sheridan's cavalry followed.[2]

Once the crossing was completed, Hancock pitched into the enemy, posted in a strong position near the bridge, and, with the major efforts being those of Trobriand's and Miles's brigades, drove the Confederates away. Miles captured four twenty-pound Parrott guns and their caissons. Moving on, Hancock soon discovered the Confederates, seven brigades under Kershaw and Wilcox, strongly entrenched in formidable works behind a stream called Bailey's Creek. Surprised by the strength of the enemy, Hancock realized that the chances of a successful assault here were slim, and he tried maneuvering to the right. As the day wore on, he was unable to develop any weak points or to find the enemy's flank, and the coming of night put an end to operations. The move to Chaffin's Bluff, predicated on surprise and weakly held rebel lines, was frustrated, and the cavalry was similarly unable to carry out its planned mission. During the night, Lee sent substantial reinforcements from Petersburg to prevent Hancock from making a lunge at Richmond, and on July 28 Hancock prepared to resist a possible attack. That afternoon Grant and Meade visited Hancock and instructed him to send Mott's division back to Petersburg that night, to bolster the force which would assault behind the Burnside mine. Barlow, too, departed, turning his division over to Nelson Miles when he learned of the death from typhus of his wife, working in a military hospital in Washington. Because Hancock's presence at Deep Bottom attracted such a large part of Lee's army, Grant decided to keep him there for another day. He was then to start back to Petersburg after dark on June 29. The corps got back in time to see the explosion of the mine on the morning of June 30.[3]

The Deep Bottom operation involved a great deal of marching and a small amount of fighting. Besides the struggle which took place when the Second Corps first crossed the bridge, the only serious fighting was a vigorous attack upon Sheridan on the morning of June 28. The contemplated raid against the Virginia Central Railroad was not carried out by Sheridan, and the possibility of a foray into Richmond never materialized. Nevertheless, Grant learned something of value: Deep Bottom was a very sensitive pressure point for Robert E. Lee. It was only ten miles from Richmond, and it was close enough to Chaffin's Bluff and the only usable Confederate bridge over the James that Lee had to react to a Union force there. His reaction on July 27, sending reinforcements to Kershaw at Deep Bottom, left him with only three divisions at Petersburg, just the kind of depletion Grant was hoping for in connection with Burnside's mine.[4]

Frustration and fatigue seemed to be making the Union generals a bit testy. John Gibbon wrote in his memoirs of two incidents at Deep Bottom in which, he claimed, Hancock accused him of military derelictions. The particulars of these disputes are of little importance, but Gibbon felt the accusations showed injustice on the part of Hancock. After one of the arguments, he said, Hancock made "a suitable apology." Nevertheless, Gibbon wrote, "the relations between Gen. Hancock and myself never afterwards resumed the cordiality which formerly existed." The reason for this development, he felt, was either the wear and tear of the campaign on Hancock, troubled by the reopening of his Gettysburg wound, or Hancock's disinclination to continue cordial relations. He never seemed to consider the possibility that Hancock, dismayed by the failure of Gibbon to attack when ordered in the Wilderness, might be observing his performance with a more critical eye than before.[5]

On July 31, back at Petersburg, Hancock issued a general order to his troops, expressing "his gratification with their conduct during the late movement across the James River." He cited four regiments from Miles's brigade and two from Trobriand's for their gallantry and good conduct. The corps, he felt, was "determined to maintain the high reputation they have heretofore acquired."[6]

The next day a particularly unpleasant duty devolved upon Winfield Scott Hancock, when he was directed, by Meade's Special Orders No. 205, to chair a court of inquiry looking into the disaster of Burnside's mine. The explosion of the mine, in the dawn of July 30, was a splendid success. Unfortunately, the follow-up by the Ninth Corps was an abysmal failure. The mine blew a substantial gap in the Confederate line, already weakened by the transfer of several divisions north of the James, and the road into Petersburg was open once again. The inept and pusillanimous conduct of the leaders of the Ninth Corps, Burnside and his division commanders, squandered this great opportunity; instead of moving through the gap toward Petersburg, the poorly led troops clustered in the bottom of the great crater, where they were slaughtered by the Confederates who had recovered from their initial shock. "Never, before or after, in the history of the Potomac army," wrote one observer, "was such an exhibition made of official incapacity and personal cowardice." Almost 4,000 men were lost, and an investigation became imperative. Hancock's selection to chair it may perhaps be regarded as a testimonial to the reputation for fairness he enjoyed in the eastern army—or to Meade's care to put his own friend in charge. The court convened on August 6 at Hancock's headquarters, and all orders for the mine assault were read into the record. Every officer named in those orders was directed to be notified of the proceedings. And Hancock, writing to a friend in New York, confessed that serving on this court was "not an agreeable office, I assure you."[7]

The court reconvened on August 8 and sat through the twelfth, hearing Meade and Burnside. It recessed until the twenty-ninth and then heard witnesses continuously through September 5, receiving the testimony of, among others, Grant, Warren, Mott, Humphreys, and three of the Ninth Corps division commanders. After much discussion among its members, the court issued its findings and opinions on September 9, along with ninety-three documents as an appendix."[8]

The court found five major causes of failure, from the "injudicious formation of the troops in going forward" to a lack of proper leadership of the assaulting column and "the want of a competent common head at the scene of the assault." Five officers were named as "answerable for the want of success": the corps commander, Burnside; the cowardly commander of the assault division, General James H. Ledlie; General Edward Ferrero; Colonel Z. R. Bliss of the 7th Rhode Island; and General Orlando B. Willcox, though the criticism of Willcox was less harsh than that directed to the others. Burnside was relieved from duty after the mine fiasco, and this time there was no future command for him.[9]

In the midst of all this, there were new command developments which upset Meade and Hancock. On August 1 Sheridan was given the assignment to take charge of the troops facing Early near Washington and in the Shenandoah Valley. Meade was irked, as he thought Grant had proposed him for the job. Meade had been looking forward to a command in which he would be out from under the suffocating presence of Grant. Asked about the Sheridan assignment, Grant gave Meade an evasive answer; Meade confessed himself "doubtful" but felt Grant was honest "and would not deceive me." Hancock, who of course would take command of the Army of the Potomac if Meade left, was "quite put out," Meade wrote, "and thinks some political chicanery at the bottom of it." The fact was that Grant apparently intended all along to put his favorite, Sheridan, in that command. Sheridan and Hancock were not friends—their personalities were too dissimilar—and this development did not increase Hancock's regard for the ambitious young cavalryman.[10]

The lengthy mid-August break in the proceedings of Hancock's court of inquiry was occasioned by activity against the Confederates, as Grant poked here and there around the ends of the rebel lines. On August 12 Hancock received orders to march his corps to City Point, preparatory to another movement to Deep Bottom. He promptly adjourned the court of inquiry and got ready to move out. In addition to his own corps, he was to have David Gregg's cavalry division and the Tenth Corps, now led by David Birney. The general directions for the second Deep Bottom expedition were similar to those for the first, but the reason for it was new. Grant had received information (which proved erroneous) that Lee was reinforcing Early in the Shenandoah Valley; he hoped either to force Lee to call back troops from the Valley or to exploit a weakness caused by aiding Early.[11]

The deployment to Deep Bottom had a new wrinkle. The Second Corps was to be marched onto transports at City Point and ostensibly ferried off to

Washington, from there to march after Early. After dark, however, the boats were to turn around and steam up the James to Deep Bottom, where the troops were to be disembarked over gangplanks. Someone in Grant's headquarters thought up this scheme, to fool Confederate spies, but no one checked with General Hancock about it. He had spent many years moving men from one place to another, as a quartermaster and as a combat general, and he had a strong suspicion that the gangplank idea would not work. He took General Rufus Ingalls, the chief quartermaster of the Army of the Potomac, and rode up to Deep Bottom to check out the proposed landing places. As he suspected, there were problems: many of the boats would not be able to get close enough to the shore, the banks in numerous places were not well suited to receiving gangplanks, and the operation would be even more difficult with the tide running out, as it would be. Hancock did what he could: he moved up the hour of departure from City Point to ten p.m. instead of midnight, and he sent Morgan up to Deep Bottom with a boatload of lumber to construct temporary wharves.[12]

The men of the Second Corps started boarding the sixteen steamers provided for them at noon on August 13. That morning Francis Barlow resumed command of the First Division. Gibbon was on leave, so Colonel Thomas A. Smyth, an Irishman from Delaware who had been one of the best brigade commanders in the corps since Gettysburg, took over the Second Division; Mott commanded the Third. At ten p.m. the boats started on their journey up the river, the men packed closely together on a "suffocatingly hot" night with, as Mitchell wrote, "mosquitoes infernally tormenting." At 2:30 a.m. they started the tedious job of disembarking at Deep Bottom. Because there were only three wharves, the unloading proceeded at a very slow pace; some of the boats drew so much water they could not get up to a wharf at all. The largest boat, bearing one of Barlow's brigades, ran aground in the river and had to wait several hours for a turn in the tide to float it free. The element of surprise disappeared as the soldiers of the Second Corps dribbled ashore.[13]

The Tenth Corps and Gregg's cavalry had come by land, crossing the James on the pontoon bridge, and they sat around and waited for the Second Corps. Mott's division, detailed to march to Bailey's Creek at daybreak, or as soon as it should be ashore, was about four hours behind schedule. The main attack was to be made near Fussell's Mill by the First and Second divisions, under the overall command of Francis Barlow. Not until 11:30 a.m., however, was Barlow's stranded brigade safely ashore; it was at about four p.m. that Barlow's attack was finally made. Though not expected to do so, Barlow tried to keep a connection with Mott's division. As a result he was forced to stretch out his force in a long line, and his attack strength was not what it should have been. Hancock later commented sourly that "had they been kept more compact they ought to have broken through the line, then thinly held, by mere weight of numbers."

Even more of a problem was the bad conduct of the men. The Irish Brigade, Barlow wrote, "behaved disgracefully and failed to execute my orders." Directed to attack, they crowded off into the shelter of some trees. Another brigade, Brooke's old outfit, "exhibited such signs of timidity and demoralization" that Barlow abandoned the idea of using it. Instead, he ordered the First Brigade of Smyth's division, under Colonel George Macy, to attack. Though Macy, just returned after having been wounded at the Wilderness, "did everything that a brave man and a soldier could do" before being again injured, his brigade failed to react to his leadership. The attack was a failure. The discomfort of a sleepless, tormented night on the river and the scorching heat of a dreadfully hot and humid August day doubtless had their effect on the dedication and gallantry of the troops. In addition, most of those soldiers who had served through the whole campaign were physically worn out. Regardless of the reasons, Barlow was disgusted and Hancock was frustrated. He attributed the poor conduct "to the large number of new men in the command and the small number of experienced officers." But he knew, for he had seen them at Gettysburg and elsewhere, that new men and inexperienced officers need not be insubordinate cowards. The policy of killing off the best men in frontal assaults and filling the ranks with the impressed leavings of the northern cities was coming to fruition in the fighting around Petersburg.[14]

The only positive note on August 14 was the fact that, when the Confederates were moved up to oppose Barlow, the front opposite Birney was weakened enough that the Tenth Corps was able to capture a part of the rebel line and four howitzers. Meade wrote his wife, with a touch of asperity, that "Hancock, with his usual luck," had captured the guns and colors.[15]

Over the next few days, there was a great deal of movement, a lot of skirmishing and jockeying for position, and some hard fighting, but, once Grant realized that he had been misled about Lee's reinforcements to Early, the operation at Deep Bottom was no longer a serious one. Field's and Wilcox's divisions were still at or near Deep Bottom, while Mahone's infantry division and two divisions of cavalry were sent north of the James as soon as Lee got word of Hancock's movement. The pressure point was still there. Grant chose to keep Hancock's force north of the James for several days longer because he was sending Warren's corps to the Weldon Railroad, on the far left of the Union position, and it suited his plans for Hancock to tie down three Confederate infantry and two cavalry divisions.

On August 18 illness forced Barlow to give up command of his division. Seriously wounded at Antietam and left for dead at Gettysburg, bereaved by the loss of his wife, Francis Barlow was none too robust at best. For several days, wrote Hancock's adjutant, "he had been more like a dead than a living man." Miles took over the division as Barlow went off to the hospital at City Point.[16]

One happy event at Deep Bottom was Hancock's receipt, on August 17, of a letter from the War Department informing him that he had been promoted to the rank of brigadier general in the regular army. This, of course, was a permanent rank and would be his when all the wartime brevets ended. Hancock promptly sent off a reply to Washington accepting the new rank and had the oath of office administered to him by his adjutant, Francis Walker.[17]

On the night of August 18, Hancock was ordered to send Mott's division back to Petersburg to relieve the Ninth Corps, which was going off in support of Warren. On the night of August 20, in a pouring rain which made the roads miserable, Hancock marched his other two divisions back to their old camps near Petersburg. They arrived, worn out, by daylight of August 21. The men settled down just long enough to cook breakfast, when they were ordered back on their feet and marched off toward the left of the line, where Warren was working on the destruction of the Weldon Railroad.[18]

NINETEEN

The Final Battles

Reams' Station was on the Weldon Railroad, about four miles south of Globe Tavern, where Warren's Fifth Corps had seized the railroad while Hancock faced much of Lee's infantry north of the James. Grant desired to destroy as much as possible of the railroad south from Globe Tavern so that supplies coming to Petersburg from North Carolina would have to take a long, circuitous wagon journey from the undamaged head of the railroad to the besieged town. The Second Corps, worn and ragged after its latest adventure at Deep Bottom, was the chosen instrument for this destruction.

On the afternoon of August 22, the First Division, under Miles, was moved on to the railroad, to cover the working party and to aid in the destruction effort. A two-mile stretch of track was ripped up that afternoon. The next day, with Barlow once again taking command of the division, the work of destruction was carried out as far as Reams' Station. Confederate cavalry was operating in the vicinity, but Union horse under Gregg kept it away from the railroad. The night of August 23, Barlow's men occupied the entrenchments they found at Reams' Station, entrenchments which had been thrown up hastily by the Sixth Corps back in June. No one really gave much thought to these entrenchments on August 23.[1]

Early the next morning Gibbon's division arrived at Reams' Station and relieved the First Division, which watched its commander, Francis Barlow, carried off to the hospital on a stretcher, still physically unfit for active duty. Miles resumed command. Mott's division, numerically the largest in the Second Corps, was back in the Petersburg trenches.

The men of Miles's division worked on the railroad on August 24, destroying the line for some three miles south of Reams' Station, and then came back to the entrenchments at the station that night. Gibbon's men were to take over the demolition job for the next day. At 11 o'clock that night, Hancock received a message from Meade that "large bodies of infantry" had been spotted moving south from Petersburg by roads to the west of the railroad. "They are probably destined to operate against General Warren or yourself—most probably against your operations," he was warned.[2]

Early the next morning, Gregg's horsemen were sent out to look for signs of an increased enemy presence, but as none was found Gibbon's division moved out to tear up more track. Very shortly, however, it was ascertained that Confederate infantry was in the vicinity, and Hancock recalled Gibbon to Reams' Station. With both his divisions united, Hancock had about 6,000 men, many of them green recruits. Now they all had to concern themselves with the poorly conceived works at the station.

The entrenchments were roughly in the shape of a U, with its base, about 700 yards long, facing west. The sides, running back to the east, were about 800 or 900 yards in length; they were so close together that artillery firing at the northern face could overshoot its mark and strike in the back troops defending the southern face. The worst feature of the position was that the front of the works—the west face—extended beyond the railroad. The Weldon Railroad and a road called the Halifax Road ran north and south, parallel to each other and to the front of the entrenchments, but within them. As a consequence, the two artillery batteries and infantry units which held this front, facing A. P. Hill's infantry attacks, found themselves with a low parapet in front and 20 to 30 yards behind them, the railroad, "forming here an embankment and there a cut," as one observer wrote, making it "impossible for ammunition or reserves to be brought up, except at disadvantage, or for the troops to retire without exposure to observation and to fire."[3]

Hancock did not like the position. In his report he wrote: "It is proper to say here that the defensive position at Reams' was selected on another occasion by another corps, and was, in my judgment, very poorly located, the bad location contributing very materially to the subsequent loss of the position, and particularly to the loss of the artillery." One is constrained to say, however, that there is no evidence that Hancock ordered any rectification of the position while his troops occupied it for the day or so before the fight on August 25. He was all too conscious of the overmastering fatigue of most of his men, and it appears likely that he chose to permit those units not engaged in tearing up track simply to rest rather than to work at improving a bad defensive position. It was an unfortunate decision, or lack of decision, but one for which no one seems to have criticized Hancock.[4]

The northern face of the Union works was held by the First Division, while the southern face was held by the Second. The west face, looking at the advancing Confederates, was held by two artillery batteries and the Fourth Brigade of Miles's division, under Colonel K. Oscar Broady. To the far left of Gibbon's division was Gregg's cavalry, dismounted for the fighting on the afternoon of August 25.[5]

At noon, enemy infantry under A. P. Hill drove in Miles's pickets and advanced toward the works but was driven back. At 2 p.m. a stronger attack was made against Miles—Hill had four brigades, three of Wilcox's division and one of Field's, with more on the way—but it was quickly repulsed. A short time later, another attack was made in the same area, the angle where the Union line turned to the east, and again it was driven back, the Confederates losing heavily in these attacks. Some of the enemy dead were found within three yards of the breastworks.[6]

At about this time, Hancock was advised by Meade that Mott's division had been ordered to march down to Reams' Station; Meade also authorized Hancock to withdraw if he felt that to be wise. Hancock responded at 2:45 p.m., saying, "Considering that the enemy intend to prevent any further destruction of the railroad, there is no great necessity for my remaining here . . . but I do not think, closely engaged as I am at present, I can withdraw safely at this time. I think it will be well to withdraw tonight, if I am not forced to do so before." He did not expect the latter contingency, for he went on to say, "Eveything looks promising at present." Winfield Hancock was not accustomed to thinking about retreating in the face of the enemy.[7]

At 2:45 p.m. Meade advised Hancock that he was also sending Willcox's Ninth Corps division to Reams' Station, although instead of sending it straight down the Halifax Road (a distance of four miles) he ordered it to proceed by another road, making the distance twelve miles. As a result, Willcox could not get to the station in time. Curiously, too, Meade sent this message by courier rather than by telegraph, so that Hancock did not receive it until after 4 p.m. By this time it was becoming apparent that another rebel attack was in preparation.[8]

At 3 p.m. Harry Heth had arrived with two of his own brigades and two brigades of Mahone's division. Because A. P. Hill was sick, Heth took over command of the Confederate forces, now composed of eight infantry brigades along with Hampton's cavalry. Hill sent for Heth and told him "that he *must* carry the position," considering the Confederate preponderance of numbers and the infelicitous Federal defensive position.[9]

Shortly after 5 p.m. the Confederates opened with a heavy artillery fire, which, Hancock said, "while it did little actual damage, had its effect in demoralizing a portion of the command exposed to a reverse fire," to wit, the men of Gibbon's division who were being hit from the rear. After some fifteen minutes of shelling, Heth threw forward four brigades in another attack on the northern angle of the Union works. Initial resistance was strong, and just a few minutes more of the same, said Hancock, "would have secured the repulse of the enemy, who were thrown into considerable disorder by the severity of the fire they were subjected to and the obstacles to their advance." It was not to be. In a sudden moment of panic, the Consolidated Brigade of the First Division gave way, the troops either fleeing in disorder or throwing themselves on the ground in surrender. And with this, things fell apart. A force of four Second Division regiments, held behind the lines as a reserve, was ordered forward by Miles to fill the breach; they refused to move and were shortly captured en masse by the advancing Confederates. All of the guns in the space between the railroad and the west face of the entrenchments were captured. Hancock ordered Gibbon's division forward to retrieve the lost position, "but the order was responded to very feebly by his troops," and they fell back at the first fire from the enemy. "Affairs at this juncture," Hancock wrote, "were in a critical condition."[10]

Large numbers of Gibbon's men, discouraged by the firing from their rear and not too eager in any event to give their lives for their country, surrendered without firing a shot. Others simply refused to do any serious fighting. Miles's division was broken and disordered, and almost all of the Federal guns were taken. It was a moment when the day could be saved from irretrievable disaster only by individual bravery and leadership. It was a moment made for two men who possessed those qualities in abundance: Winfield Scott Hancock and his young division commander, Nelson Miles.

Miles found a portion of his own regiment, the 61st New York, and, using it as a nucleus for other men who wished to keep fighting, led it back toward the breastworks, recapturing three of the lost artillery pieces and driving the Confederates into the railroad cut. He had only about two hundred men, but as fast as men were shot they were reinforced by more soldiers gathered up by Hancock. The corps commander's adjutant wrote that Hancock "exposed himself far more conspicuously than any private soldier, in his efforts to restore the fortunes of the day." His horse was shot, his bridle rein was split in two by a ball, the corps flag was shredded, but he was indomitable. He was all over the field, and his efforts, combined with those of Miles, Colonel Broady, some of the gunners, and Gregg's dismounted cavalry, who saved Gibbon's division by repulsing an attack by Wade Hampton's cavalry, retrieved some honor for the Second Corps and stabilized its position. As darkness came on, Hancock talked with the three division commanders, to see if they could retake their positions. Miles and Gregg promptly agreed to make the effort, but Gibbon told him that the Second Division could not do it. Since without that division the effort would be futile, Hancock directed that, after dark, the corps would retire eastward, where Willcox's approaching division would act as a rear guard.[11]

Colonel Morgan, his chief of staff, recognized Hancock's desolation at this battle, "for it was the first time he had felt the bitterness of defeat during the war." His troops had failed in the past to carry entrenched positions, "but he had never before had the mortification of seeing them driven, and his lines and guns taken, as on this occasion." The Second Corps, once the mightiest of fighting machines, was but a shadow of its former self, and Reams' Station made this clear to Hancock. Morgan saw him ride up to a staff officer in the midst of the fighting; "covered with dust and begrimed with powder and smoke, he placed his hand upon the staff officer's shoulder and said: 'Colonel, I do not care to die, but I pray to God I may never leave this field.' "[12]

The Second Corps withdrew after dark, marching back toward the Petersburg lines. Hill's Confederates, badly mauled in the fighting, withdrew at the same time. Hancock lost about 600 men killed and wounded, while the Confederates lost well over 700. But the rebels marched off with more than 2,000 prisoners, 9 guns, and 12 Federal colors.[13]

At 11 o'clock that night, Meade sent Hancock a message, assuring him that "no one sympathizes with you more than I do in the misfortunes of this evening." He explained that he had not sent direct reinforcements because he had no doubt of Hancock's ability to hold lines against a direct attack. He went on:

> I am satisfied you and your command have done all in your power, and though you have met with a reverse, the honor and escutcheons of the old Second are as bright as ever, and will on some future occasion prove it is only when enormous odds are brought against them that they can be moved. Don't let this matter worry you, because you have given me every satisfaction.

Kind words, comforting sentiments; but nothing could undo the effect of Reams' Station on Winfield Hancock. His adjutant, later his biographer, Francis Walker, wrote: "The agony of that day never passed away from the proud soldier." But for Winfield Hancock, luckily, there *would* be another day.[14]

For Hancock one of the most frustrating features of the fight at Reams' Station was that it was very nearly a tidy little victory. Before the break in the First Division, the Confederates had suffered heavy losses, and even after that they were almost as disorganized as the Federals. "Had I had but one more Brigade between 6 & 7 p.m.," Hancock wrote to a friend on August 28, "I could have won a great victory." He reiterated this in a letter to Alexander Webb a couple of days later: "We had a rough fight at Reams' Station the other day, and we ought to have won a grand victory. . . . The enemy brought everything they could rake and scrape. We ought to have whipped them."[15]

Under the circumstances, Hancock seems hardly to have been in the mood to be confronted by John Gibbon, shortly after the fight, with a demand for a complete reorganization of the corps or it "could never again do efficient service." Hancock replied, according to Gibbon, by harshly criticizing the conduct of the Second Division at Reams' Station. The First Division, after all, had repulsed three Confederate attacks before a portion of it gave way, while none of Gibbon's units put up any fight at all. Gibbon apparently failed to recognize that the conduct of the corps was a very sore point with Hancock and that it might be best to let a few days pass for the corps commander to cool down. Instead, that night, Gibbon resumed his hectoring with a letter to Hancock in the course of which he said that he himself was prepared to yield his own position "for the good of the corps." He was then "much mortified," he said, to receive a curt response from Hancock saying that perhaps it would be best for Gibbon to give up command of his division. "More than hurt at this reply," Gibbon at once fired off to corps headquarters an official application to be relieved from duty with the Second Corps. Hancock sent for him and suggested that he withdraw the application, but when Gibbon said he could take no other course in view of the "insult," Hancock flared up and terminated the interview, which took place during a break in the mine inquiry. Later that evening Hancock summoned Gibbon again, and the two men had a calm and relatively pleasant talk for two hours, going over the possibility of reorganizing the corps and finally reaching Gibbon's application for relief. Hancock told him it was a bad time to make such an application, but Gibbon stiffly refused to withdraw it, saying that Hancock's note was an insult to his reputation. Hancock asked to see the note and, reading it over, said, "I was mad when I wrote this letter." Gibbon said that made no difference. Finally Hancock said, "Suppose I withdraw this letter." Gibbon replied, "All right, General, if you withdraw it the matter is ended and I authorize you to stop my application to be relieved." Hancock then stuck his offending note in the flame of his candle and threw the burning paper in the fireplace. "We parted on tolerably good terms," Gibbon said, "but there was a soreness of feeling remaining probably on both sides which never entirely disappeared." John Gibbon was a good soldier, but his posturing, lack of tact, and extreme sensitivity to imagined slights were plainly getting under Hancock's skin. The corps commander could not have been greatly upset when, on September 4, Gibbon was named the temporary commander of the Eighteenth Corps.[16]

After Reams' Station, the Second Corps went back to the Petersburg lines, where the men were soon heavily engaged in building a formidable line of works to protect the left rear of the Union position. It was not long, indeed, before Hancock protested that enough was enough. His men were being employed on so much continuous fatigue duty, building fortifications, laying out roads, digging trenches, that they had no time to attend to normal military routine. "The men have, in fact, become day laborers," Hancock exclaimed, "and suffer in their proper character as soldiers." As a result, morale suffered, discipline lagged, and there was no opportunity to drill the many new recruits in the skills needed for battle.[17]

Another major problem was the lack of officers. On September 17 Hancock wrote to Seth Williams, at Meade's headquarters: "I consider it of the highest importance that as many as possible of the officers of the Second Corps now absent who are able to perform duty in the field be returned at once." If the corps, with its great losses, was to be relied upon, he warned, it had to have its best officers.[18]

Eventually Hancock got some of his officers back, and he was able to salvage some time away from construction work to drill some of his new recruits. In fact, when Meade asked Hancock on October 15 if he could spare any working parties, the Second Corps commander said his officers "now think their men are worked unusually hard." Besides, he said, "there are a good many recruits in the command whom we are trying to drill, and I have not allowed them to be worked within the last few days on that account." Defensive works and corduroy roads were all well and good, but Deep Bottom and Reams' Station had demonstrated that nothing replaced well-drilled, well-officered troops.[19]

Although the corps, occupying positions close to the rebel lines, was under fairly regular mortar and sharpshooters' fire, it engaged in few serious fights through September. On the night of September 9, however, Mott's division had a little struggle which "proved to be one of the most creditable operations of the siege," as the corps historian wrote. At a place called "The Chimneys" on the Jerusalem Plank Road, the rifle pits of the Confederate picket line were considered too close to the Union lines. Hancock ordered that they be taken. At 1:30 a.m. on August 10, two regiments of Trobriand's brigade rushed the enemy line and carried it with bayonets; they then "reversed" the rifle pits and incorporated the captured works into the Union line. Hancock issued a general order, expressing his thanks to Mott, to Trobriand, and to the officers and men of the two regiments.[20]

As the season moved from late summer into fall, the presidential contest became a matter of great interest. Hancock was concerned about the election because of the great bearing it would have on the future conduct of the war. Early in August he had written to a civilian friend about the peculiar-looking political picture: "It is hard to tell who is going to be president. I do not think either party knows yet who is to be their Candidate." The Republicans, of course, had already met and renominated Abraham Lincoln, but a number of their party leaders were calling for his replacement in light of the gloomy war news: long casualty lists coupled with stalemates around Richmond and Atlanta. The Democratic party met at the end of August, declared in its platform that the war was a failure, and nominated George B. McClellan.[21]

With these two candidates, the incumbent commander-in-chief and the creator of the Army of the Potomac, it was inevitable that the men and officers of the army should indulge in strenuous discussions of the merits of the candidates, the issues of the election, and the conduct of the war. Hancock took steps, in his corps, to keep such discussion from getting out of hand, having a general order read to each regiment stating that the army's duty was to stop the rebellion, not to talk about politics, and that the end of the war was the time for criticism. Until then, the soldier's duty was to obey and fight. Such an order, of course, in that army, had as much chance of stopping political discussion as Canute's gesture had of stopping the waves.[22]

One evening Trobriand was in Hancock's tent, arguing about the election with another officer who was a McClellan partisan. Hancock, Trobriand said, "preserved a diplomatic silence," which was not surprising in view of the fact that he believed in Lincoln's war policy, ultimately voting for the president, but considered McClellan a close friend. The election was painful for Hancock, a Democrat and a loyal friend, but also a soldier who recognized that the failure to retain Lincoln in office would be disastrous for the prosecution of the war and the restoration of the Union. On this occasion Trobriand foolishly chose to attack McClellan for his dispatch after Williamsburg, the one that praised Hancock but failed to mention Hooker,

Kearny, and Peck, the other generals engaged. When the Frenchman noticed that Hancock was "plainly annoyed," he tried to smooth things over with fawning words about Hancock's part in the battle. He could not, however, let it go at that. "But I appeal to yourself," he went on. "What can be thought of a general-in-chief capable of such conduct, and of such injustice towards three generals out of four?" Hancock was not soothed. "I understand," he said, according to Trobriand. "You are all alike in the old Third Corps. In your eyes, you have done everything in this war, and all others nothing."

The Frenchman felt that he had lost Hancock's good will through this ill-chosen exchange and had also "revived his prejudice against the whole Third Division." While Hancock may have wondered at Trobriand's tactless blunder, it is unlikely that he harbored a lasting grudge; it was not his nature. Trobriand, however, clearly did. He wrote a book after the war, and he took pains to denigrate Hancock with carefully honeyed barbs.[23]

In late October the last offensive before cold weather set in was planned by Grant. The Union army had been making progress in its siege. At the end of September, the Eighteenth Corps under General Edward Ord had captured Fort Harrison, one of the elements of the Richmond defensive perimeter north of the James. In addition, the Union lines had been gradually extended farther to the southwest, so that the Weldon Railroad was now under substantial Federal control and Grant could think of the remaining line coming into Petersburg, the Southside Railroad. He planned a movement which would utilize most of the Army of the Potomac: the Fifth Corps, the Ninth Corps, and two divisions of the Second.

On the morning of October 25, Hancock withdrew the Second and Third divisions from the Petersburg entrenchments, and Nelson Miles spread his division out to cover the lines previously held by the whole corps. Gibbon was again absent, and General Thomas W. Egan, a New Yorker who had been a brigade commander in the old Third Corps, led the division on this occasion. The following afternoon the Second Corps units marched southwest to Fort Dushane, on the Weldon Railroad, from which point they would set out for the operations of October 27.[24]

The plan for the Union movement was a coordinated effort of the three corps, with Hancock's being the principal striking force. The field of operations was the area to the southwest of the current lines of the two armies, beyond the earthworks and entrenchments, where there was still opportunity to march and maneuver. Hancock was to cross a stream called Hatcher's Run and then move up to the Boydton Plank Road. This road was a sensitive spot for General Lee because, with a large stretch of the Weldon Railroad in Union hands, it was over this road coming up from the south that supply wagons must move to keep Petersburg and Richmond alive. From the Boydton Plank Road, Hancock was then to move west on the White Oak Road, recross Hatcher's Run, push on for the three and a half miles to the Southside Railroad, "and endeavor to seize a commanding position on that road." Two divisions of the Second Corps, of course, could not do all this if the weight of the Confederate army should be thrown against them, but the Ninth Corps, now under General John G. Parke, was to attack early on October 27, to the northeast of the Second Corps, in the gap between the end of the Confederate entrenchments and Hatcher's Run, and Warren's Fifth Corps was to support the Ninth. The activities of these two corps were to occupy the rebels sufficiently that Hancock's force could carry out its mission.[25]

That Hancock's divisions were to be accompanied by David Gregg's cavalry was quite gratifying to the Second Corps commander. Hancock had worked closely with Gregg in several engagements before this, and he had a high regard for the modest, genial cavalryman, who was a Pennsylvanian like himself, from Huntingdon. Gregg was not one to delight in the showy, wide-ranging forays so dear to the hearts of Stuart, Sheridan, Pleasonton, and those reporters who liked to portray the cavalry in bold and vivid colors; Gregg excelled in the essential but less glamorous service of screening the army, locating its adversary, patrolling the rear, and fighting alongside the infantry. Later Hancock said of Gregg, "I can state with confidence that I have seen no officer whom I would prefer to have with me." Gregg, he said, was "cool, tenacious, brave, and judicious. I could not give higher qualities to any person." Gregg had helped to save the day at Reams' Station, and Hancock was glad to have him along at Hatcher's Run.[26]

At 3:30 a.m. on October 27, Hancock's divisions moved out toward Dabney's Mill, with Gregg's cavalry heading off to the left flank. Soon after daylight the head of Egan's column reached Hatcher's Run, and Smyth's brigade carried the enemy works on the other side of the stream. After getting his command over to the opposite bank, Hancock sent off a dispatch to Meade expressing some uneasiness that he had not heard any firing from the Ninth Corps. (How often had Hancock waited in vain to hear from the Ninth Corps?) He then moved his force on to strike the Boydton Plank Road, chasing away enemy artillery from a place called Burgess' Tavern. Soon after arriving at the plank road, Hancock was pleased to be joined by Gregg, and preparations were made to continue down the White Oak Road. At about 1 p.m., Hancock received orders from Meade to halt at the plank road, where Mott and Egan were deployed, and skirmishing continued with the rebels, who kept up an annoying artillery fire from across the stream. Shortly thereafter Meade and Grant appeared on the scene and filled Hancock in on what was happening. Parke, they said, had found that the Confederate entrenchments went farther than they had thought, extending all the way to Hatcher's Run. The Ninth Corps, therefore, had made no attack but had simply adopted a menacing attitude. With no Ninth Corps attack to support, Warren had been ordered to send just one division up along Hatcher's Run to connect with Hancock. Samuel W. Crawford's division of the Fifth Corps was consequently supposed to be working its way along the banks of the stream, and Hancock was to assist in making the connection by extending to his right, in the direction from which he could expect Crawford. The Second Corps was to hold its position until the following morning and then to withdraw over the same road it had come in on. The Union high command had decided to liquidate the operation; until Crawford came up, however, Hancock's force was in jeopardy.[27]

By the time Grant and Meade departed, it was 4 p.m. Crawford had not yet shown up, and in fact he never did; the woods along Hatcher's Run were so thick and tangled that Crawford's units became thoroughly jumbled. He finally brought everything to a halt and went to work trying to straighten out his lines. In the meantime, Hancock determined to take the high ground beyond the run from which Confederate artillery was keeping up a steady shelling. Egan had his division in position for a charge, along with McAllister's brigade from Mott, when a spurt of musketry behind him warned him that something untoward was taking place. A force of about 5,000 Confederates under Harry Heth had moved up from the run (once it was clear that Hancock had the only Union force from which any movement was to be feared) and through the woods on a blind path that the Union forces knew nothing about. Heth fell upon Pierce's brigade of Mott's division and overpowered it by weight of numbers, capturing a section of artillery. Hancock sent Major Mitchell to Egan, to direct him to face about and confront the charging Confederates, but Mitchell found that Egan had already done so without orders. Egan's men, with significant help from McAllister's Jerseymen, swept down upon Heth's flank, recaptured the lost guns, and drove the southerners from the field, back into the woods.[28]

Almost at the same time, firing off to the south told Hancock that Gregg was being attacked. He sent back to his cavalry leader all of the dismounted cavalry that had rushed up to help defeat Heth, and with this aid Gregg was able to hold off Wade Hampton's southern horsemen. Unable to send infantry to help out, Hancock said he "trusted General Gregg to hold his own, and I was not disappointed."[29]

As darkness fell, Hancock analyzed his position. When Meade was advised of the attack against the Second Corps, he directed Warren to send another division, that of Romeyn Ayres, to Hancock, but Ayres was well short of the Second Corps when darkness forced him to halt for the night. Hancock could expect that Ayres and Crawford might reach him in the morning; in light of Crawford's difficulties, of course, he could not regard that as a sure thing. Both Hancock's divisions and Gregg's were just about out of ammunition; the expedition had been ordered to march without the burden of ammunition wagons. Meade would send replenishment in the morning, but it was by no means certain that the wagons would reach them before the Confederates did. There were rebels on three sides of Hancock, with only the road back to Dabney's Mill still open for a withdrawal. Meade left to Hancock's discretion the question of staying and fighting on the morrow or withdrawing that night.[30]

Winfield Hancock never liked the idea of withdrawing from a field on which his men had fought, especially when, as here, the fight had been a successful one. He recognized, however, that the possibility of a drive to the Southside Railroad was gone and that to risk a fight with heavy rebel forces in the morning, possibly before either reinforcements or ammunition reached him, was to court a devastating defeat. "Reluctant as I was to leave the field, and by so doing lose some of the fruits of my victory, I felt compelled," he wrote, "to order a withdrawal rather than risk disaster by awaiting an attack in the morning only partly prepared." He ordered the withdrawal to begin at 10 p.m., and it was carried out without loss, though a heavy rain was falling and the woods were dark and obscure.[31]

The movement to Hatcher's Run failed to accomplish any of what Grant was hoping for, and it brought to a close active campaigning around Richmond and Petersburg for 1864. Lee's army—and the Confederacy—would survive into 1865. But Hatcher's Run was important for Hancock and the Second Corps, because it restored the pride and self-confidence of the corps after the fiasco at Reams' Station. A substantial number of officers and men had returned to the corps from sick leave, and there had been time for some training of the new recruits who filled up so many of the corps's regiments. The improvement was striking. The October 27 operation involved a hard march under difficult conditions and a surprise flank attack. Nevertheless, the Second Corps handled its problems with competence and gallantry. Egan, Hancock said, had "an unusual opportunity for distinguishing himself, and he availed himself of it to the utmost." Smyth and McAllister, too, were conspicuous for their good work. And the men in the ranks, bolstered by the return of experienced officers and the confidence engendered by some training in what was expected of them in battle, stood their ground and did their jobs. Hancock, of this his last battle, was able to write to Barlow: "We had a hard fight but beat the enemy." And they did it by themselves: "The Rebels concentrated everything against me as at Reams' Station while the rest of our troops looked on."[32]

It appeared that Hancock's days with the Second Corps were nearing their end. There was still talk of placing him in command of the Army of the Potomac—Grant had written to Stanton of the possibility on October 11, and he spoke about it with Hancock later in the month, with Meade to go to the Valley—but another prospect had piqued Hancock's interest. As he wrote to Barlow:

> When Grant told me the other day about the Veterans Corps & that it would in all probability be a separate command I told him that it would suit me—that I did not want the A.P. I do not like to leave my corps the Old Second but I would like a separate command of course. I do not like to serve ungenerous people always.

Hancock did not identify these "ungenerous people," but his only superiors were Meade, with whom he enjoyed close relations, and Grant. He may, of course, have been referring to the civilians in Washington, but he had never had any trouble with Stanton or the president. There is no evidence that he was particularly close to Grant, and he may well have been tiring of the latter's favorites. In any event, the idea of a separate command was undoubtedly a very congenial one.[33]

TWENTY

The End of the War

The idea of the corps of veterans had in fact progressed somewhat further than Hancock's letter to Barlow indicated. Not only had Grant spoken with Hancock about it; he also had cleared it with Stanton, and the plan was almost fully matured. On October 25, as Hancock and his two divisions were preparing to march toward Hatcher's Run, Stanton sent Grant a proposed order for the organization of a new army corps, of not less than 20,000 infantrymen, to be composed of able-bodied men who had served honorably for at least two years and to be led by officers who also had at least two years' service. Recruits, when accepted, were to receive a special bounty of $500 when mustered in. The proposed order concluded: "Major-General Hancock is assigned to the command of this corps when organized." Grant read the proposed order and approved it; "it will prove a success," he said, "and will give us a body of men equal to any army now in service."[1]

The corps of veterans was the culmination of serious Union concern with manpower procurement for the national armies. Long past was the enthusiasm for the Federal cause which produced men by the hundreds of thousands in the early months of the war. For the past year or so the Union authorities had relied on conscription, the hiring of substitutes, and the payment of hefty bounties to keep the armies up to strength. So far as numbers were concerned, the Federal forces were maintained, but the quality of those brought to the service in these ways was far inferior to that of the volunteers of the early years. The failures at Deep Bottom and Reams' Station amply illustrated this decline. Thus the concept of the veterans' corps was developed—a means of bringing back into the army men who had been good soldiers but who had served their time, had been mustered out, and were not subject to conscription.

There were to be two incentives to lure these veterans back into the army: a substantial bounty and the opportunity to serve under one of the most popular commanders, Winfield Scott Hancock. The $500 bounty set forth in Stanton's proposed order was eventually scaled down to $300 by the time the order was promulgated. Even so, that represented the highest peak of Federal bounties, when added to the $100 stipend up front provided by act of Congress for enlistment up to three years. Thus a man could sign up in the veterans' corps for a three-year term and receive at once $400 in Federal money plus whatever local and state bounties were available to him. Even more attractive than the money, however, was to be the name of Hancock.

Any soldier who had survived two years of service was going to be pretty choosy about the kind of man he would serve under; he would want to make sure that his commander was one who took care of his men, who led them well, and who did not get them killed off by battlefield blunders. The Union high command was agreed that they could not do better in this regard than the Second Corps commander, who had long been well known to the army for possessing just these qualities.[2]

The word was soon out around the Army of the Potomac that this was to be Hancock's new assignment. It was understood that the change would probably not come about until after the election, but when Lincoln had been safely reelected on November 8 and still nothing was done about the veterans' corps, people started getting edgy. On November 12 Andrew Humphreys, who had been told by Meade that he would receive the Second Corps command, wrote to his wife: "Hancock has received no orders yet. If he is going and if I am to command the Second Corps, I hope it may be settled at once." On November 15 Grant wired Stanton, asking what had happened to the order. The next day Stanton replied, stating that the order had been held up by the president but should be out in a day or two. Meade passed this news on to Hancock that evening.[3]

Hancock reacted badly to these tidings, suspecting (perhaps correctly) that political factors in the capital were posing difficulties. He wrote back immediately to Meade, asking for a twenty-day leave to look after his personal affairs. He felt that the veterans' corps command was probably out, "since the matter has assumed so much importance" that the president had gotten involved. "I suppose that other persons have desired the position," he said, "or the matter would not have been brought to his attention."[4]

Meade answered him the same night, telling Hancock in effect to keep his shirt on, because it was still intended that he be given the veterans' corps. Finally, on November 25, Meade dropped him a note, saying, "Your orders will be issued in a few days. In the meantime, if you wish it, you can go on leave." Hancock replied, "I will avail myself of the leave" and asked to take his aides Parker and Miller with him, Mitchell and Morgan being already on leave. He asked if he should transfer his command to Gibbon, the senior division commander, and Meade responded that Humphreys would be assigned to command of the Second Corps. On the same day, Meade's headquarters issued a special order giving twenty days' leave to Hancock and his aides and placing Humphreys temporarily in command of the corps.[5]

The next morning Humphreys arrived at Hancock's headquarters and passed a pleasant hour and a half with the departing commander, his staff, and his division commanders. Hancock gave him a copy of his farewell order, issued that day, and Humphreys prepared an order of his own assuming command. "Hancock's task was comparatively easy," Humphreys wrote, "for he had much to say of what the Corps had done during a long command of it." Toward the end of his order, after reciting the list of battles from Antietam to the Boydton Plank Road, Hancock told his men: "Conscious that whatever military honor has fallen to me during my association with the Second Corps has been won by the gallantry of the officers and soldiers I have commanded, I feel that in parting from them I am severing the strongest ties of my military life." He did not recite—though he undoubtedly had them in his mind—the names of the notable subordinates who had helped him to win great acclaim for the corps, such men as Caldwell, Webb, Brooke, Barlow, Miles, Gibbon, Zook, Mott, Birney, Hays, Meagher, Kelly, Egan, Smyth, and Carroll. A roster of heroes—some now dead, others broken in body, some separated from the corps, but all integral parts with Hancock of its illustrious history. After issuing his message, Hancock left the Second Corps forever.[6]

Hancock traveled to Washington by way of Fort Monroe, where he made arrangements to have Colonel Morgan attached to his new command. The order formally establishing the corps of veterans, to be designated the First Corps, and naming Hancock to its command, was finally issued by the War Department on November 28. A minor flap blew up a few days later when Alexander Dougherty, the corps surgeon who had been with Hancock for a long time, was moved from the Second to the new corps without Meade's being consulted. Meade said he had no objection to the transfer but felt the department should refer such questions to him before issuing the orders; he wanted to establish that the good of the service, particularly that of the unit where a vacancy was being created, was the proper criterion, especially as he understood "that a considerable number of staff and other officers were expecting orders to report to Major-General Hancock."[7]

Hancock went to work at recruiting his new corps, but the flow of veterans back into the army was hardly overwhelming. As the veteran could only be credited for the district in which he lived, he might not receive as large a bounty, even with the $400 Federal money, as someone who signed up in a different district which paid high local bounties. In addition, there were simply not that many men who, having survived two years in the army, were anxious to risk their lives all over again. A little over 4,400 men was the sum total of Hancock's recruiting.[8]

On January 16, 1865, Grant wrote to Hancock, offering the services of General Carl Schurz "to assist in raising your corps and to command a division when raised." Schurz, a participant in the German revolution of 1848 who had in the United States become a prominent politician, had been a division commander in the ill-fated Eleventh Corps. Hancock had never been impressed with any of the officers of the Eleventh Corps (except Barlow). Schurz, besides, was something of a popinjay, and Hancock was none too anxious to have him. "A sufficient number of officers who have heretofore served with me have applied to fill the prominent commands," he replied to Grant. "If the decision should be left with me, I would prefer appointing them, though I have no doubt the officer you mentioned would be of service in the Northwest in recruiting." Schurz was promptly assigned to Hancock for recruiting duty, although John Rawlins at the same time wrote Hancock that he did not have to keep the German for command when the organization of the corps was completed.[9]

Grant's original plan in assigning Hancock to recruit his 20,000-man corps of veterans was to have Hancock's force proceed up the Shenandoah Valley, when campaigning started in 1865, to help trap Lee's army when it inevitably abandoned Richmond and Petersburg. When it became clear that there would be no 20,000-man corps, Hancock was named commander of the Department of West Virginia and the Middle Military Division on February 27, 1865, relieving Sheridan, whom Grant wanted freed for active operations with his cavalry. At the same time, Hancock got three of his old subordinates: Thomas Egan, Sprigg Carroll, and John Brooke were all ordered to report to him.[10]

Hancock's predecessor as commander of the Department of West Virginia was General George Crook, a good soldier who became renowned after the war as one of the army's best Indian fighters. The occasion for Crook's relief, however, was an occurrence of great embarrassment to Crook and a tipoff to the kind of war which was taking place in the Middle Military Division. Early in the morning of February 21, Crook and General Benjamin Kelley were snatched from their beds in a Cumberland, Maryland, hotel by a force of seventy rebel cavalrymen dressed in Union uniforms. The red-faced generals were carted off to Libby Prison in Richmond.[11]

The enemy, in the Middle Military Division, was made up primarily of guerrillas, raiders, and partisans under John S. Mosby, Thomas Rosser, and William L. Jackson. The capture of Crook and Kelley, while a little more spectacular than the usual rebel raid, was typical of the kind of operation carried out in the division. The line of the Baltimore & Ohio Railroad obviously offered a prime target for Confederate horsemen. The entire division consisted of the departments of Washington, Pennsylvania, and West Virginia and the Middle Department, primarily Maryland and Delaware. In addition, Hancock's new jurisdiction included the Nineteenth Army Corps, under the command of General William H. Emory.[12]

Hancock had hardly arrived at his new headquarters in Winchester (which he soon moved to Martinsburg, West Virginia) when he received word from Stanton of a rumored guerrilla raid on Martinsburg. Later there were reports of Rosser's gathering men at Strasburg and of Mosby's men at several locations. By keeping alert and on the move, Hancock largely frustrated rebel efforts to find vulnerable spots in the Union dispositions, and he protected the railroad. And those were to be his primary functions in the Middle Military Division.[13]

George Crook was finally exchanged when Grant intervened with Stanton, who was no great admirer of the captured general, because Grant wanted to use Crook with the Army of the Potomac. Crook, however, insisted on being restored, if only for a day, to his prior command in West Virginia, the one he was kidnapped from, to show the public that he was not in disfavor with the War Department. Hancock did not like this (he now held the job, of course) because nobody consulted him about it. Rumors spread that Hancock would have Crook arrested if he showed up, but there was nothing to such stories. Crook came back to Cumberland, whence he had been abducted, was welcomed by the brigade of General Rutherford B. Hayes but not by Hancock, and then departed for Petersburg. One historian called the affair "probably the most flagrant case of military ado about nothing in the whole war."[14]

Grant wanted Hancock to stay ready in the lower Shenandoah Valley, poised to move south to cut off Lee if necessary. Hancock had his units ready—General Hayes was to command one of the columns marching up the Valley—but Lee surrendered before any marching orders came.[15]

There was some irony in the fact that one of the great fighting generals of the war was sitting in comparative inactivity at the base of the Valley while preparations were underway for the final, decisive campaign against Lee's army, and no doubt Hancock himself felt regret. But he was a soldier; he went where he was ordered, and he did the very best he could wherever he was posted. On March 25, 1865, Stanton sent him a message stating his gratification at Hancock's "energy in organizing and administering the affairs of your command, vindicating my judgment in assigning you to that position." For a soldier, such a message was some consolation for the absence from the front.[16]

On April 9 Robert E. Lee surrendered his army to Grant at Appomattox Court House. For Winfield Scott Hancock, aside from some desultory and ultimately unsuccessful efforts to persuade Mosby to surrender his rangers, the Civil War was over. At its start Hancock had told a friend that he expected to come out of the war a brevet major; at its end he was a brevet major general, a regular brigadier general, and one of the most respected soldiers in the United States.[17]

TWENTY ONE

The Execution of Mary Surratt

At the close of the war, Hancock and his newly formed force were at Winchester, Virginia, awaiting orders for a final push up the Shenandoah Valley. After Lee's surrender, Allie left Baltimore and headed for Winchester to be with her husband. Their hopes for a respite from military cares, however, were quickly crushed. The day Allie arrived, Hancock was summoned back to Washington. Abraham Lincoln had been murdered, and the new president, Andrew Johnson, wanted Hancock, whose Middle Military Division included Washington, on the scene to restore order.

The city was in a state of panic when the general arrived. Not only had Lincoln been killed but an attack had been made on Secretary of State William H. Seward; rumors circulated of a grand conspiracy, orchestrated by the vindictive leaders of the now defunct Confederacy, to destroy the top officials of the government and throw it into chaos. Gradually, as it became known that Hancock was present, the air of frenzy in the capital abated. Attorney General James Speed spoke of Hancock's "calmness and equipoise in the midst of excitement," inspiring "calmness in others." Hancock published an appeal to the black residents of Washington, calling upon them to "hunt down this cowardly assassin of your best friend as you would the murderer of your own father." On April 26 John Wilkes Booth was apprehended and killed (by soldiers, not by blacks) near Port Royal, Virginia; in the meantime arrests had been made of other alleged members of the great conspiracy.[1]

Stanton had assumed control of the campaign to bring the conspirators to justice. Stanton was a man of great talents, but he was also harsh, vindictive, mercurial, and easily panicked. These latter qualities, unfortunately, guided his conduct throughout the brief period during which the alleged perpetrators were tried and punished. Stanton pushed for an immediate trial. On May 1, after Attorney General Speed had ruled that the assassination suspects were triable before a military commission, Johnson ordered that such a court be convened. He named Major General John F. Hartranft special provost-marshal-general "for the purpose of said trial, and attendance upon said commission, and the execution of its mandates."[2]

By May 9, 1865, the commission had been established, and the next day the trial started. The defendants who were brought before the commission were Samuel Arnold, Dr. Samuel T. Mudd, Edward Spangler, Michael O'Laughlin, George B. Atzerodt, Lewis Payne, David E. Herold, and the only woman, Mary E. Surratt. As everyone knew, the actual assassin, Booth, was dead. The defendants were persons who had been connected in one way or other with Booth, some almost incidentally. Payne had made the assault on Seward; Spangler, a stagehand at Ford's Theater, had failed to prevent Booth's escape; some of the others had been involved with an earlier plot of Booth's to abduct Lincoln to Richmond in order to force a peace settlement; Doctor Mudd had set Booth's broken leg after he fled from Washington following the killing. And Mary Surratt ran the boardinghouse where Booth and several of the other defendants had lodged. Apparently her fugitive son, John, had been included in some of the Booth plotting; the government hoped to force John Surratt from hiding by trying his mother.[3]

The preparation for and conduct of the trial reflected little credit upon those responsible for it, and the whole affair was a dismal example of American criminal jurisprudence. Four of the defendants—Herold, Payne, Atzerodt, and Mary Surratt—were condemned to death, with the other four receiving sentences varying from six years to life imprisonment. The commission also attached to Mrs. Surratt's sentence a recommendation for clemency, although this was apparently concealed from the president by Stanton and Judge Advocate General Joseph Holt. On July 5 Johnson confirmed the sentences and ordered the executions for July 7.[4]

Later, when Stanton and Holt had become bitter political enemies of Andrew Johnson, the president emphatically declared that he had never seen or been told of the recommendation for clemency. Even so, Andrew Johnson cannot come out clean. The whole procedure, from the trial by military commission to the execution of a woman convicted on flimsy and circumstantial evidence, had about it such an air of drumhead justice and kangaroo court that no one with the least knowledge of Anglo-American judicial traditions should have countenanced it. Orville H. Browning, Johnson's secretary of the interior, noted in his diary on July 6, 1865: "This commission was without authority, and its proceedings void. The execution of these persons will be murder."[5]

Of these difficulties, of course, the public at large knew relatively little. But from this point events moved quickly. On July 6 the press reported the verdicts as they were made public; from here on Winfield Scott Hancock, in his capacity as division commander, was to be closely involved with the proceedings. He was the object of some criticism for his part in it, especially during the presidential campaign of 1880, though his wife defended his connection with Mary Surratt's execution as "purely military and official," as surely it was.[6]

At the end of June, Hancock had accompanied Secretary Seward to Auburn, New York, for the funeral of Seward's wife. He returned to Washington on the last day of the month as the members of the military commission were completing their deliberations. Several days later, the warrant of execution signed by Johnson was delivered to Hancock. The wheels were thus set in motion. At noon on July 6, Hancock went to the grim arsenal where the prisoners were now confined and delivered the four death warrants to Hartranft, the special provost-marshal-general. The two generals then visited the prisoners and informed them individually of the sentences and the time fixed for their deaths. Mary Surratt, upon hearing the news, was shocked and prostrated by the vision of imminent and unexpected death; she could do no more than murmur faintly as she collapsed, "I had no hand in the murder of the President." When Hancock returned to the arsenal at 11 p.m., Mrs. Surratt was under the care of a physician.[7]

Mary Surratt's lawyers labored through the night on a petition for a writ of habeas corpus, and, at 3 a.m. on July 7, Judge Andrew Wylie of the Supreme Court of the District of Columbia issued the requested writ, directed to Hancock, to produce the defendant in court at 10 a.m. that day. When court convened for the day, Hancock was not present. The marshal's return was read, stating that service was made upon the general at 8:30 a.m. The judge considered the situation and decided that his powers were inadequate to meet "the military power possessed by General Hancock." He concluded, "The court therefore must submit to the supreme physical power which now holds the custody of the petitioner, and declines to issue an attachment or to make any other order in this case." He then went on to other business.

But Mary Surratt's day in court was not quite over. A half-hour before noon, there was a bustle and a stir in Judge Wylie's courtroom, and then Winfield S. Hancock appeared, accompanied by Attorney General Speed. Speed apologized for their tardiness, attributing it to Hancock's busy schedule and his distance from the courthouse. One of Hancock's callers that morning had been Anna Surratt, the prisoner's daughter, who asked what further she might do. Hancock advised her to see the president personally to beg for her mother's life.

Hancock then, through Speed, made his response to the writ. He acknowledged "that the body of Mary E. Surratt is in my possession, under and by virtue of an order of Andrew Johnson . . . for the purposes in said order expressed." He then declined to "produce said body by reason of the order of the President of the United States indorsed upon said writ." Johnson's order specifically suspended the writ of habeas corpus in this case, directed Hancock to carry out the judgment of the military commission, and ordered him to cite this suspension in answer to the writ. Hearing this, Wylie figuratively threw up his hands, stating, "This court finds itself powerless to take any further action in the premises, and therefore declines to make orders which would be vain for any practical purpose."[8]

Interior Secretary Browning, present in the courtroom while all this was taking place, muttered darkly and later recorded his feeling that the judge should have held Hancock in contempt "and have seen whether the President would have taken him forcibly from the hands of the Court."[9]

In any event, Wylie did not do so. Hancock asked leave to depart, which the judge granted him, and he headed back to the arsenal, because, as he later wrote, "expecting that there might be other writs," he wanted to wait there to receive them. He arrived at the arsenal at 12:30 p.m. The efforts of Anna Surratt to plead personally with the president for her mother's life had been of no avail, but Hancock, who obviously had no taste for the unpleasant duty of hanging a woman, still nurtured a hope that Johnson would spare Mary Surratt. He posted mounted couriers at intervals along the route from the White House to the arsenal so that word of such a reprieve could be hastened to him with no undue loss of time.[10]

Allie Hancock later asserted that her husband personally intervened with the president on behalf of Mary Surratt; "not once, but many times, did my husband urge upon the President unanswerable reasons for granting a pardon." That may be. Allie, however, wrote at a time when it was generally accepted that Mary Surratt had been unjustly executed for a crime in which her involvement was peripheral at most. Allie wrote that the Surratt execution was "as cruel a spectacle as ever stained the escutcheon of a Nation," and she wanted to put some historical distance between her husband and Andrew Johnson. But there appears to be no other evidence of this personal solicitation by Hancock for his prisoner's life, and the claim, if for no other reason than the severely limited time frame available, must be suspect.[11]

When Hancock arrived back at the arsenal, John W. Clampitt, Mrs. Surratt's attorney, approached him and asked, "Are there any hopes?" Hancock, with a catch in his voice, replied, "I am afraid not. No; there is not." A few minutes later, obviously perturbed, the general returned and said, as Clampitt related, "I have been in many a battle, and have seen death and mixed with it in disaster and in victory. I've been in a living hell of fire, and shell, and grape-shot and—I'd sooner be there ten thousand times over than to give the order this day for the execution of that poor woman. But I am a soldier, sworn to obey, and obey I must." At 1:15 p.m., under Hancock's supervision, Hartranft led the procession from the prison to the specially erected scaffold. Some of the religious counselors to the prisoners made statements, and then Hartranft read the order for execution. The four prisoners were tied and hoods were placed over their heads, and then each had a noose slipped over the neck and tightened. At 1:25 p.m. the order to proceed was given and all four were hanged at once. The reporter for the *New York Times,* perhaps to comfort his readers, recorded that "Mrs. Surratt appeared to suffer very little." At 1:35 p.m. medical officers examined and pronounced dead the four bodies, and they were cut down. Two and a half hours later they were placed in coffins and buried.[12]

Thus died Mary Surratt. It was not long before grave doubts were abroad in the land regarding both the procedures and the outcome of the trial of the "Lincoln conspirators." Among those upon whom the odium for the "judicial murder of Mary Surratt" was cast by some was Hancock, for his participation in the execution. Political opponents in 1868 and again in 1880 seized upon the Surratt hanging in attempts to rouse popular feeling against the general. These attempts were finally laid to rest with the publication in the midst of the 1880 campaign of a long statement by John W. Clampitt, who spelled out many details of Hancock's attempts to be helpful; he concluded that Hancock "was deeply moved in her behalf and distressed on her account. . . . General Hancock afforded to Mrs. Surratt every kindness in his power, and was anxious that she should be spared by a pardon, and he hoped for it up to the very last." Lieutenant Walter Halleck, commander of the guard over the prisoners, spoke of Hancock's "humane instructions" for their treatment. Earlier, Father John A. Walter, Mary Surratt's priest, had issued a statement refuting the charge that the general had somehow prevented her from receiving spiritual consolation just prior to her death.[13]

The other charge made against Hancock is that he was wrong in failing to bring Mary Surratt before Judge Wylie and in carrying out the president's order of execution. Andrew Johnson, it was said, later regretted especially his order suspending the writ of habeas corpus in the case of Mary Surratt. But what was Hancock to do? He was a soldier, son of a lawyer, a believer to the core in the idea that the civil authority was superior to the military. His civilian commander-in-chief issued an order to him, suspending the writ, and directed that he should so answer to the court. As counsel for his appearance in court, he had the ranking civilian legal officer of the government. When his answer was made to the court, the judge accepted it and gave Hancock leave to withdraw. Was Hancock, as a military man, to rebel and interpose his will against the civil authorities? Had Judge Wylie refused to accept the general's return to the writ and directed that the prisoner be brought before him regardless, a far different question would have been presented. But Wylie acquiesced in Johnson's suspension order, and Hancock can hardly be faulted for doing the same.[14]

Similarly, the only way that Hancock could have refused to participate in the execution, in the limited role that he had as division commander, would have been to resign his commission. For a man whose entire life had been (and was to be) the military, this would have been a fateful step to take. Hancock, we must recall, had not participated in or even attended the trial of Mary Surratt and her fellow defendants, so that presumably he had no factual basis for a determination of their guilt or innocence. His feeling for Mrs. Surratt was apparently that of a warmhearted human being who was opposed to the hanging of a woman. For Hancock to throw over his career because of opposition to a policy decision on the part of his superiors in the case of a single person who, for all Hancock knew, *had* participated in Lincoln's assassination would have been absurd. And it would have been fruitless. After all, Hartranft, not Hancock, gave the order for the executions, and he would have given it just as surely in Hancock's absence as in his presence.

Hancock later wrote: "Every soldier was bound to act as I did under similar circumstances." One of the great strengths of this soldier's career was his clear understanding of the demarcation between military and civil authority. In the case of Mary Surratt's death, Hancock cannot be assigned the blame for the wrongheaded and arbitrary decisions of civilians, decisions which he reluctantly but dutifully carried through.[15]

TWENTY TWO

Indian Problems

Shortly after the death of Mary Surratt, the Middle Military Division was abolished, replaced on the army's organizational charts by an entity known as the Middle Military Department. Hancock commanded the new unit as he had the old. His headquarters, however, were transferred to Baltimore, where he and his wife tried, with mixed success, to mollify the chronically sore southern sympathizers of the Maryland metropolis.[1]

Nevertheless, the Hancocks enjoyed their tenure in Baltimore. The social life was satisfactory, and the army duties were not onerous. After all the excitement of the past years, it was a routine existence into which they settled: reading muster reports and troop dispositions, checking on food and supplies, taking periodic inspection trips, attending occasional dinners and receptions. With no fighting going on, there was time to look after things, time which was seldom available in combat.

Hancock had the opportunity to bind up some of the wounds of the war. He was able to intervene with the attorney general to help procure a pardon for his old friend from Los Angeles, Joseph Lancaster Brent, who had been a Confederate general and who was living briefly in Baltimore. In addition, when Harry Heth came to Baltimore, the Hancocks insisted he stay with them. After the two old soldiers spent some time arguing about the Po River and Reams' Station and Hatcher's Run and all the other fights in which they had opposed one another, Hancock said he owed Heth a thousand dollars. Heth thanked him but said he needed no charity, even though his affairs were in disorder. Hancock said it was no gift; he produced a ledger book showing their complicated mutual business dealings and investments back in the 1850s and said that by his calculations he owed Heth one thousand dollars, which he then paid him. Heth exclaimed in wonderment at the strange course of events, when they had spent the prior four years "trying our best to kill each other."[2]

Heth's Confederacy, though, was gone, and its great adversary was disappearing. The mighty Union army, developed with so much difficulty and pain into a fighting machine, was being rapidly dismantled. It had always been, of course, an army of civilians in uniform, and now the civilians were going home. They had whipped the rebels, and it was time to get back to a more mundane existence, on the farm, or in the dry-goods store, or in the accounting office, or wherever. For most of the men of the

Union army, their days of soldiering, days of blood and grime, of fatigue and excitement, of camaraderie and danger, were done forever.

But tasks remained, tasks which would of necessity be performed by the much-reduced peacetime army. The prewar regular army, largely swallowed up by the great Union army of the Civil War, was overhauled and reorganized by an act of Congress signed by Andrew Johnson on July 28, 1866. Total strength of the army was fixed by the War Department at 54,000 men. The regular army, three times the size of its prewar predecessor but with a far greater and more complex mission, would face the problems of policing the conquered South and subduing the Indians of the West. To do so, it would in effect be made into two "armies." The first, the traditional army which fought Indians and garrisoned the posts of the North and Northwest, would be under the constitutional control of the president. The second army, the army in the South, would eventually come under the control of Congress and the commanding general and would involve itself in matters which had always been considered beyond the ken of the American military establishment.[3]

The major burden of controlling the Plains Indians fell upon General William Tecumseh Sherman, the commander of the Military Division of the Missouri. It was plain to Sherman that he had been placed in a well-nigh impossible situation, given the factors of Indians, whites, miles of unsettled prairie, and few troops. The key to the area was the Department of the Missouri, one of several departments which made up his division. The department comprised Missouri, Kansas, Colorado, and New Mexico. Its problems included the Santa Fe and Overland trails, a flood of settlers heading west, and a prairieful of unhappy, suspicious Indians. As if this were not enough, the Kansas Pacific was building a railroad due west through the heart of the department.

Sherman wanted Hancock on the plains. On March 10, 1866, he had written to Grant, the army commander, asking for "a young General, who can travel and see with his own eyes and if need be command both whites and Indians to keep the peace." He had specified Hancock—"Baltimore is no place for him"—but at that time had not been able to get him.[4]

Meanwhile, in Washington the Thirty-ninth Congress adopted a resolution on April 21, 1866, acclaiming and thanking Hancock for his great services at the battle of Gettysburg. This measure redressed to some extent the injustice of the earlier resolution thanking Hooker, Meade, and Howard. When Congress created the rank of general in the regular army, Grant was moved up to the new position, and Sherman was promoted to the vacancy at lieutenant general. This left a vacancy at major general, to be selected from among the nine current brigadier generals, and when Grant recommended him, Hancock was appointed.[5]

Finally, in August, Sherman had his way. Hancock was named commander of the Military Department of the Missouri, and he and his family headed west. The department over which Hancock assumed command was one of the focal points of plains warfare. The state of Missouri, of course, was largely free of wild Indians. The only trouble Hancock had to deal with in Missouri was a flare-up of violence by ex-Copperheads in Saline and Chariton counties; he sent a couple of companies of troops and matters calmed down. New Mexico, with its ancient Spanish settlements around Santa Fe, was too far off for Hancock to involve himself deeply there, though the warlike Comanches and Apaches were always a worry in that territory, and the Navajos were unhappy with the reservation to which they had been confined. But Kansas and Colorado presented problems enough for any commander.[6]

Kansas was sparsely settled, with most of its people located in the eastern area which had seen so much violence in the days before the Civil War. It had been admitted to statehood in 1861, but even after the war its western three quarters were still virtually unoccupied, except by stage stations and nomadic Indians. The Great Plains started in Kansas, just about where the population stopped, a vast, nearly flat sea of closely matted grass, undulating gently across the miles, sloping gradually upward as it westered, until it came to an end at the foothills of the Rocky Mountains, halfway across Colorado Territory. The region had for decades been called "the great American desert," and it was still widely thought to be uninhabitable. Two major rivers ran across the southern plains, the Arkansas to the south and the Platte to the north. In addition, a number of lesser streams watered western Kansas, creating meandering green oases of cottonwoods and other trees to break the monotony of the prairie. These included the Smoky Hill, Solomon, Saline, and Republican rivers, little streams which were important features in western geography. "A most beautiful country," wrote one local politician, "robed in green and jewelled with winding streams of living water."[7]

The eastern, high-plains half of Colorado Territory was as little populated as western Kansas. But the center of the territory, where the Rockies began, had been the site of a gold boom, starting about 1859 in the Cherry Creek and Pike's Peak areas and along Clear Creek, west of Denver. Colorado had a population of 34,000 in 1860, 39,000 in 1870, and many thousands more who came, tried their luck, and then departed during the intervening decade. But these were whites. What of the Indians who lived on the plains? They were, after all, the reason the army was there. Since the coming of Europeans to North America, the Indians had been pushed steadily back, from both the Atlantic and the Pacific coasts. From the plains, from the area between the Missouri and the Rockies, there was no longer any place to push them, without wiping them out or penning them up. On the Great Plains lived several major tribes, all of whom were to some degree disaffected from the white settlers and soldiers. In the north were the hostile Sioux, divided into several tribes, led by doughty chiefs such as Red Cloud and Spotted Tail. South of the Sioux was the great and warlike Cheyenne nation, divided into its northern and southern branches. The Cheyennes roamed through Nebraska, Kansas, and Colorado and were, like the Sioux, firmly planted across the whites' lines of travel. And in Texas, Kansas, and the Indian Territory (now Oklahoma) were the smaller but equally troublesome Kiowas and Arapahos.

The Plains Indians were dwindling in numbers, but they were still numerous enough to be an insoluble problem to planners in Washington and a murderous hazard to white travelers on the prairie. The nomadic Plains Indians, hardy and resolute, at least those not debauched by idleness and whiskey, were tough fighters and skilled horsemen. They were defending their homeland. They were prepared to contest the mastery of the plains until they were subjugated. They needed the great herds of buffalo for their subsistence and their very way of life, and the buffalo needed the broad expanse of the prairie for their survival in great numbers. The plans of policy makers in the East for use of the Great Plains were more prosaic; in 1866 large-scale population of "the great American desert" was not projected, but a safe milieu was needed for railroads and other routes of travel to the mountains and the Pacific coast beyond. And, in the circumstances, "safe" meant one thing: no Indians.

Hancock took command of the Department of the Missouri in late summer 1866 during a period of relative calm. With the war just over and many soldiers still being mustered out, travel across Kansas was relatively light in 1866. The Kansas Pacific railroad was advancing steadily westward, from Fort Riley to Fort Harker, near present-day Ellsworth, and the Indians watched it unhappily. Still, incidents were few and the plains were quiet. But recent history indicated that trouble was inevitable.

The Indians of the plains had been peaceful, on the whole, during 1862 and 1863, as the Civil War brought western migration to a virtual halt. A more aggressive policy adopted by the governor of Colorado climaxed with the infamous Sand Creek massacre in November 1864. Colorado militia under Colonel John M. Chivington treacherously attacked a peaceful village of some five hundred Cheyennes led by a chief called Black Kettle and killed, scalped, and mutilated men, women, and children in a manner hardly exceeded by any comparable Indian "outrage." Thereafter settlers, travelers, and soldiers on the plains paid a bloody price for Chivington's attack. Through the late winter, spring, and summer of 1865, the enraged Indian tribes brought fierce and bloody reprisal to the South Platte roads and settlements, as well as to other areas both to the north and to the south. Congressional pressure forced the creation of a peace commission, which set out from Washington to meet with the southern tribes at the mouth of the Little Arkansas River in October. With great difficulty a treaty was worked out with the Cheyennes and Arapahos, but the Cheyenne leaders who were pressured into signing it did so with great reluctance, for it ceded to the whites the country around the Smoky Hill River, the tribe's favorite hunting ground. After much delay the Treaty of the Little Arkansas was signed in mid-November 1866.[8]

The fact that the treaty was pending probably had much to do with the relative calm that prevailed in Kansas and Colorado in 1866. But the snags involved in having it ratified, the lack of enthusiasm for it among the tribes, and the Indians' universal reluctance to give up the Smoky Hill region made its duration problematical.

Two other factors complicated the Indian trouble for any commander, and Hancock soon encountered both. The first was the government policy which left the responsibility for handling the tribes to the Indian Bureau in the Department of the Interior; military men seethed in frustration at this state of affairs, because their troops were called in to restore order only when matters got out of hand. The other factor sprang from the first. This was the activity of white traders doing business with the Indians under licenses issued by the Indian Bureau. The traffic in arms, ammunition, and alcohol which they conducted was responsible for vast amounts of trouble for the people of the frontier, both whites and Indians. The traders were usually irresponsible drifters, looking out for the "fast buck" opportunity wherever it might occur or whomever it might jeopardize. They seldom troubled to draw a distinction between arms for the purpose of shooting game and arms for the purpose of shooting whites.[9]

In January 1867 reports of the activities of traders in western Kansas filtered in to army headquarters. First, the commander at Fort Larned wrote that white traders were peddling war materials to the Indians in his vicinity; a few days later, the commander at Fort Dodge confirmed this with stories of traders selling arms and ammunition there and at Fort Zarah. In addition, the Kiowas near Dodge were boasting of their hostile intentions and capabilities. The post commanders suspected that there would be trouble come spring.

All of these matters were in Sherman's head as he pondered the situation on the plains in 1867 and prepared his plans for Hancock's department. On December 30, 1866, he had written to his brother, Senator John Sherman, stating that "I expect to have two Indian wars on my hands." He went on gloomily: "The Sioux and Cheyennes . . . I suppose . . . must be exterminated, for they cannot and will not settle down, and our people will force us to it." Later, however, he was a bit more optimistic. The Cheyennes, the major troublemakers on the southern plains, were saying they wanted peace, so that 1867 might be no worse than 1866. Still, with all those reports of Indians being armed to the teeth by white traders, in exchange for a few buffalo robes, it might not be a bad idea to let the tribes know that the army was in no humor to be fooled with. Out of all this came the concept that was shaped into Hancock's Kansas expedition.[10]

While the plans for the Indian expedition were being formed, Winfield Hancock suffered a severe personal loss. He received word that his father, then sixty-seven years old, was ailing, and he procured permission to travel to Norristown to be with him. He arrived while his father still lived, but shortly after, on February 1, Benjamin Franklin Hancock passed away. His father had been a great influence upon Winfield, and he was shocked by the death. To the soldier, however, there is not given the opportunity for lengthy periods of mourning. Winfield helped with arrangements, comforted his mother, saw to the burial in Montgomery Cemetery, and departed. Duty required his return to Leavenworth.[11]

It had fallen to Hancock to liquidate the army's part in the controversial experiment of the Bosque Redondo. In 1863 Brigadier General James H. Carleton had received permission to try a new tack in Indian relations, moving the entire Navajo tribe (as well as the Mescalero Apaches) to a large reservation, the Bosque Redondo, on the Pecos River in east-central New Mexico, where they were protected—or restrained—by an army garrison at nearby Fort Sumner. Although some contradictions certainly existed in Carleton's motives, it appears to have been in the main a humanitarian policy, an effort to protect the Navajos from whites and to help them to become self-sufficient by learning white ways. Carleton corresponded regularly with Hancock, an old friend from California, describing conditions at the Bosque and the frustrations he suffered in trying to attain his goals for the reservation. Hancock did what he could to support Carleton, but he could not protect him against changes in policy at the capital. A decision was made there to transfer control of the Navajos at the Bosque—the Mescalero Apaches had almost all escaped—back to the Indian Bureau, and the attempt at a new departure in Indian relations came to an end. Hancock told Carleton that "the management at the Bosque Redondo has been the best effort in the direction of humanity and wisdom which has yet been inaugurated for the benefit of our Indians," but he was required to issue the orders terminating that effort.[12]

On March 8 Hancock and Sherman sat down together at the latter's headquarters in St. Louis to put the finishing touches to the Kansas operation. In order to extend the army's protection to lawfully settled citizens, mail routes, and other lines of travel through Indian country, as well as to forts, stations, and troops on the march, Sherman authorized Hancock "to organize, out of your present command, a sufficient force to go among the Cheyennes, Arapahos, Kiowas, or similar bands of Indians, and notify them that if they want war they can have it now; but if they decline the offer, then impress on them that they must stop their insolence and threats."[13]

The force Hancock put together to overawe the nomads of the southern plains was a mixed unit and, as it turned out, one of questionable utility for chasing Indians across the prairies. He had about 1,400 men altogether for his expedition, including elements of the Thirty-seventh Infantry, the newly formed Seventh Cavalry, and an artillery battery. He also took with him the makings of a pontoon bridge, though this inclusion may have indicated a certain failure to recognize the difference between the Chickahominy, for instance, and the Smoky Hill. Hancock, of course, knew little about fighting Indians. His prewar service in the trans-Mississippi West had not included such conflicts. Sherman, however, was by now supposed to be pretty good at dealing with the Indians of the plains. Presumably he had approved Hancock's dispositions for his march; it is unrealistic to think that he and Hancock did not discuss the composition of the force when they met in St. Louis on March 8. Thus the entire onus for taking an unwieldy and impractical instrument with which to coerce the Cheyennes and Kiowas should not fall on Hancock.[14]

Starting on March 22, the expeditionary force was concentrated at Fort Riley, the railhead of the Kansas Pacific, and on March 25 Hancock himself arrived there. The following day he issued the order putting his troops on the march. He was back in his own element now; one of his subordinates in the old Second Corps once wrote that Hancock "could conduct a long march, over bad roads, with artillery and trains, better . . . than any other officer of the war, Federal or Confederate." And, indeed, the march itself came off very well.[15]

The expedition moved out of Fort Riley, at Junction City, where the Republican River flows into the Kansas, and it headed due west to Fort Harker. Hancock's plan was to march from fort to fort across Kansas, giving him the opportunity to inspect these installations as he proceeded on his primary mission to show the flag to the Cheyennes, Kiowas, and Arapahos. The permanent forts in Kansas were built principally for the protection of the great western roads. Forts Zarah, Larned, and Dodge guarded the Santa Fe Trail to New Mexico, along the Arkansas River. Forts Hays and Wallace overlooked and defended the Overland route along the Smoky Hill River, leading to Denver and Colorado Territory. Fort Leavenworth, the oldest of all the military posts in Kansas, Fort Riley, and Fort Harker guarded the western road before it divided.

The commander of the Seventh Cavalry, as it moved out of Fort Riley for its initial action, was Andrew Jackson Smith, a veteran who held the brevet rank of major general and the permanent rank of colonel. Besides heading the Seventh Cavalry, Smith had additional duties as the district commander of that part of Kansas through which the expedition would move. Accordingly, the active leadership of the cavalry devolved upon Smith's second in command, the picturesque and already famous George Armstrong Custer, the former "Boy General" of the Army of the Potomac, now reduced by the postwar deflation of rank to a lieutenant colonelcy.

Four squadrons of cavalry rode out from Fort Riley, with Smith and Custer at their head, to join forces with the balance of the regiment at Forts Harker, Larned, and Dodge. They set an unhurried pace across the Kansas prairie, measuring their speed to keep from getting too far ahead of the plodding infantry and the ponderous supply train. Shortly after the expedition left Riley, it was joined by a fledgling newspaper correspondent, a twenty-five-year-old Welshman and adventurer who went by the name of

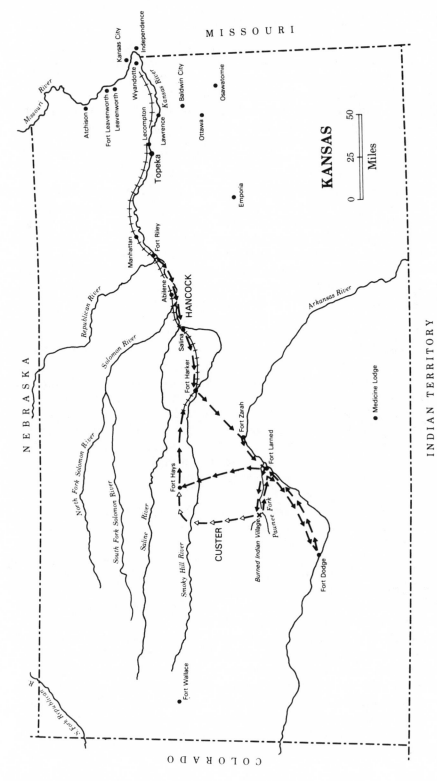

Hancock's Kansas Expedition, 1867

Henry M. Stanley. He was to report back to the *Missouri Democrat,* in St. Louis, and from there his stories would be picked up by other journals throughout the East. The evening of his arrival, Stanley was summoned by the commanding general to present his credentials. He found Hancock "a hale, hearty, and tall gentleman, in the prime of life," was gratified when Hancock bade him welcome, and was pleased to be favored with some conversation about the expedition's mission before being dismissed for the night.[16]

The expedition reached Fort Harker on April 1 and remained there two days before heading southwest over the Santa Fe Trail, arriving two days later at Fort Zarah, along the Arkansas River. At Zarah, Hancock ordered the erection of a more defensible and commodious structure and then moved his men out, toward Fort Larned. The plains, Stanley wrote, grew "more immense as civilized Kansas recedes from touch with us." On April 7 Hancock's expeditionary force reached Larned, on the Pawnee Fork, eight miles west of the Arkansas. Established in 1859, it was the most important of the Kansas forts on the trail to New Mexico. Stanley called Larned "a green oasis in the Sahara of bleached grass" and "a model of neatness."[17]

To this point Hancock had done one of the things he was famous for, and he had done it very well: he had marched his force some 150 miles across an uninviting wilderness without loss or delay. Now would commence those activities for which his previous training and experience had not prepared him; at Larned he was to meet with the chiefs of the Southern Cheyennes.

At Larned, Major Edward W. Wynkoop, the agent for the Cheyennes, Arapahos, and Plains Apaches, advised the general that he had sent runners to the Cheyenne chiefs in the vicinity, asking them to meet with Hancock at Fort Larned on April 10. Hancock agreed to wait there until the meeting, taking advantage of the break to rest his troops, somewhat worn from their march, and to inspect the post.

The day before the chiefs were due, a fierce northeast wind brought with it a crushing early-spring storm, dumping eight inches of snow as it howled and raged all day and on into the night. The snowstorm was deemed sufficient reason to postpone the start of the council. On April 11, Wynkoop received and passed on to Hancock word that the Indians, about to start toward Larned from their camp thirty miles away, had sighted a herd of buffalo and gone whooping off on a hunt. Hancock thought this very suspicious, certainly "not sufficiently important to warrant the Indians in not keeping their engagement with me more promptly," although it is questionable whether the chiefs thought they had made an "engagement." Hancock was clearly becoming edgy; first a big snowstorm, now a buffalo hunt: what were these people in this strange country really up to? Here he had marched all those soldiers all that way to put it to the Indians—peace or war—and now he could not even find a chief to whom to express his ultimatum. He determined that he would give them one more day and then march up the Pawnee Fork.[18]

The next day, April 12, there was no sign of the Cheyenne chiefs, and the general gave marching orders for the following morning. However, that evening, two chiefs, Tall Bull and White Horse, and ten or twelve braves arrived at Fort Larned. They expected to be fed and put up for the night and then to meet in the morning with this new general who had marched all his men so far to see them. They were startled and alarmed when Hancock determined to parley with them that evening. That was considered a strange and possibly hostile thing to do; councils were simply not held at night. The general brushed their fears aside as of little importance. The council was already two days late, two chiefs were a rather meager showing, and Hancock had a whole department to command, a vast area with which he was largely out of contact. He had no time to waste, and he obviously had little conception of the impact that Chivington and Sand Creek had made on this tribe of all tribes. So, he directed that the council would be held that night.

Hancock started the council by expressing his disappointment at the small Indian turnout and his intention on the morrow to march up the Pawnee Fork to the camp. He was irked at having to make his speech twice. "Now I have a great many soldiers," he said, "more than all the tribes put together. . . . I intend not only to visit you here, but my troops will remain among you, to see that the peace and safety of the plains is preserved." Then he said, "I have heard that a great many Indians want to fight. Very well; we are here, and we came prepared for war. If you are for peace, you know the conditions. If you are for war, look out for its consequences." He emphasized "the importance of keeping treaties made with us and of letting the white man travel unmolested." Finally: "I will await the end of this council, to see whether you want war or peace."

After a few moments of deep silence, Tall Bull of the Cheyennes lit his pipe preparatory to a reply. He was much briefer. "We never did the white man any harm," he said. "We don't intend to." He continued: "The buffalo are diminishing fast. The antelope, that were plenty a few years ago, are now few. When they shall all die away, we shall be hungry; we shall want something to eat, and will be compelled to come in the fort. Your young men must not fire on us." Then: "You say you are going to our village tomorrow. If you go, I shall have no more to say to you there than here. I have said all I want to say here."

Hancock interrupted to say that he was indeed going to the village the next day, then went on to emphasize again that the Indians could never expect to stop the whites in their numbers. "You must go to the white man to be taken care of," he said, "and you should cultivate his friendship. That is all I have to say."[19]

Reading the words spoken at Hancock's first encounter with the Cheyenne chiefs, one can sense the great gulf between the mind-set Hancock brought to the meeting and that of Tall Bull. True, the general had been primed by Sherman and he was carrying out instructions. But he caught little of the pathos and sense of weary inevitability expressed in the chief's words. Hancock, as a military man, aimed to the exclusion of all else to accomplish his mission, and he had no meaningful knowledge of Indians or of Indian ways to fall back on.

The next morning, April 13, Hancock marched his force up the Pawnee Fork, camping for the night about twenty-one miles from Fort Larned. During the day parties of Indians several times set fire to the grass, with a view to delaying the march or discouraging the troops from camping near their village. In the evening several Cheyenne chiefs and Pawnee Killer, chief of a band of Sioux which was sojourning with the Cheyennes, came to see Hancock and arranged that they and all of the chiefs should meet with the general the next morning.

The following morning at the appointed time, 9 o'clock, nobody showed up. At 9:30 Bull Bear, one of the Cheyenne chiefs, came in and said that the other chiefs were on the way to the camp. Hancock, however, was plainly miffed by now; he was a punctual West Pointer and he found it hard to understand how these fellows could treat dates and appointments so casually. He informed Bull Bear that he "would march up the stream nearer to their village, and would see them after we had encamped for the night." At 11 a.m. his force set out again.[20]

After going a few miles, the soldiers made out a large body of armed and mounted Indians (estimated by Stanley to be more than three hundred braves) formed in line in their front. Hancock, coming upon this host not more than a half-mile away, sent orders out to his troops to form line of battle, bringing the cavalry into line at a gallop with sabers drawn. When they were within a few hundred yards of each other, Hancock halted his force and the Indians halted also. In this tense situation, where the least untoward movement on anyone's part might have triggered a fight, Wynkoop rode out between the lines and spoke to the Indian chiefs, asking them to come forward to talk with Hancock. Some twelve Indians then rode forward, led by the famous Cheyenne warrior Roman Nose, to meet Hancock, Smith, Custer, and a few other officers. Hancock asked peremptorily whether the Indians wanted peace or war. Roman Nose responded sarcastically: "We don't want war; if we did we would not come so close to your big guns." Hancock asked him why he did not come to Fort Larned. Roman Nose replied: "My horses are poor, and every man that comes to me tells me a different story about your intentions."[21]

Hancock announced that he was resuming his march to their camp and he wished all the chiefs to visit him that night. Most of the Indians then started back toward their village. Hancock waited a bit before starting his troops off again in the same direction, because he wanted the Indian warriors to have a chance to inform the inhabitants of the village of his peaceful intentions before the command came into view. Bull Bear stayed behind with the column, and he took Wynkoop aside to tell him that it would do no good to march to the village. The women and children, he said, would be terrified. "This I communicated to General Hancock," Wynkoop said, "but he did not agree with that view of it."[22]

After proceeding another ten and a half miles, following the direction the Indians had taken, the soldiers came upon the village. Hancock was struck by the beauty of the site. "I am not surprised," he wrote Sherman, "that the Indians do not wish to give up this country and the heads of these streams." Camp was made about 2 o'clock, within a half-mile of the village, and Hancock then posted guards and issued orders that no soldier was to approach it. At about 5 p.m., several chiefs appeared at Hancock's headquarters in response to his summons and advised him that their women and children had fled the village, "being terrified by the presence of the troops, and having the 'Chivington Massacre' still fresh in their minds." Actually, by this time, they had had several hours' head start.[23]

Hancock became quite angry at this news and demanded to know why the Indians had acted so meanly toward him. It apparently never occurred to him that he had succeeded only too well in his mission of impressing the Cheyennes with his military might; those in the village on the Pawnee Fork wanted to have nothing at all to do with Hancock or his army. He ordered the chiefs to bring their people back at once. Several hours later, about 9:30 p.m., the chiefs sent word that they had decided to flee with their women and children.[24]

Hancock then summoned Custer and ordered him to take his cavalry, surround the village, and prevent the Indians from escaping. He also ordered the infantry and artillery to arms, "in case there should be any resistance on the part of the Indians." It is difficult to imagine what possible use he envisaged for the artillery battery, at night, with his own cavalry creeping toward the only conceivable target, but this order putting the artillery on alert must be regarded as fairly conclusive evidence that Hancock was by now somewhat rattled, as he had never been by the fiercest rebel charge. Custer, meanwhile, surrounded the village with his cavalry but soon found that it contained nothing but empty lodges.[25]

Poor Hancock. One of the great leaders of the Union army, he had marched across Kansas to coerce these Cheyennes into peace, with infantry, artillery, cavalry, and pontoons, and he could not even get them to stay around and talk. Now he had struck with his brand-new cavalry regiment and captured a deserted village. Their conduct, he said, convinced him that the Indians "felt guilty on account of past offenses, that they intended to make war, and that the Sioux had come down from the North to the Cheyenne village to conspire with them there against the whites." Later that night he told Wynkoop "that he intended to burn the village the next morning, as he considered that they had acted treacherously towards him, and they deserved punishment." He ordered Smith to prepare a detachment of cavalry under Custer to take off at dawn the next morning in pursuit of the fugitives.[26]

Custer's mission was a total failure. The Indians' trail simply disappeared before him as he rode to and fro about the prairie in frustration. Eventually Custer and his troopers reached the Smoky Hill River and its stage line some thirteen miles west of Downer's Station. They then headed for that station, arriving there on the night of April 16, and were advised that Indians in small parties headed north had been crossing the road since that morning. They also heard of depredations committed upon several stage posts, particularly at Lookout Station, where three men had been killed, the station burned, and horses and mules taken. Custer sent a dispatch back to Hancock stating "there is no doubt" the attack at Lookout Station was by the Indians who had fled the Pawnee Fork; Hancock received this the evening of April 17. During the following day, the general evidently wrestled with a decision regarding the Indian village; at one point he told Wynkoop that the village would not be destroyed. He wrote to Sherman: "I think we have provocation sufficient to destroy the camp; still we may not have, and by burning it we will certainly inaugurate a war which might otherwise have been avoided." Finally, however, recognizing the consequences, he decided to burn it.[27]

He ordered that, "as a punishment for the bad faith practised by the Cheyennes and Sioux who occupied the Indian village at this place, and as a chastisement for murders and depredations committed since the arrival of the command at this point," the village was to be "utterly destroyed." He acknowledged to Sherman that burning the camp was "a cheap victory," but he felt it "an imperative duty." Later, when ordered by Grant to report the reasons for his action, Hancock wrote, defensively: "If I had not felt satisfied of the wisdom and propriety of my course it is scarcely probable that I would have acted as I did." With everything happening around him, "I concluded that this must be war."[28]

On the morning of April 19, some 40 lodges and axes, kettles, crowbars, and other serviceable items of hardware were commandeered as "captured property"; everything else, first carefully inventoried, was set ablaze. About 250 lodges as well as nearly 1,000 buffalo robes and all sorts of miscellaneous items were burned. "The dry poles of the wigwams caught fire like tinder," Stanley wrote, "and so many burning hides made the sky black with smoke. Flakes of fire were borne on the breeze to different parts of the prairie, setting the prairie grass on fire. With lightning speed the fire rolled on, and consumed an immense area of grass." As the conflagration erased all trace of the Indian village, recorded Stanley, "the Indian agents cry with hands aloft, 'Oh Lord, what will become of Hancock?' " The young reporter reacted to the agents with scorn, stating that they had returned Hancock's kindness and courtesy "with acrimonious censure." But the general was in fact taking a risky step in thus destroying the lodges and artifacts of the Cheyennes and Sioux. As the flames from his fire spread across the nearby prairie, so too did Indian war spread across the prairie near and far.[29]

To the bellicose editors back in Leavenworth, near the Missouri border, this was not unwelcome news. "The Indian ball has evidently opened," wrote one. "We expect and hope the campaign of General Hancock will be effective, and that the result will not be left in doubt." Another wrote that "if an Indian cannot be tamed, he should certainly be whipped into good behavior." Out on the prairie, though, the express driver, the stationkeeper, and the lonely settler were not so quick to welcome all-out war with the Indians.[30]

It did not take long for Hancock's troubles to mount. Later in the day on April 19, while the ashes from the great fire were still smoldering, he received an additional dispatch from Custer. The cavalry commander had ridden over, the day before, to Lookout Station, to examine firsthand the atrocity on the strength of which the village at the Pawnee Fork had been fired. Custer had found three mangled bodies, half-burned and partially eaten by wolves, and had buried them. What he had failed to find was "the slightest clue as to what tribe committed the act." Custer had ascertained, however, that the attack had taken place on April 15, too early for the Cheyennes who had fled from the Pawnee Fork to have been the culprits. This inconvenient fact contributed to Hancock's embarrassment, for it robbed him of most of his justification for the destruction of the village. He was forced, in his official report, to ignore Custer's dispatch of April 19 and simply blame "the outrages on the Smoky Hill" for his decision. Besides, as he wrote to Sherman a couple of days later, whether any particular depredations could be attributed to these Indians was not "of much importance, for I am satisfied that the Indian village was a nest of conspirators." Later, too late to help Hancock, it developed that the Sioux who had been at the Pawnee Fork but who had left before the army arrived were the perpetrators of the attack at Lookout Station.[31]

After burning the village on April 19, Hancock the next day marched off to the southwest again, to Fort Dodge, to consult with the Kiowas and Arapahos. As he did so he was unaware of two developments. Custer had moved on to Fort Hays from Lookout Station; on his arrival there he had found that Hancock's order to ship sufficient forage to Hays for the cavalry units had been ignored. Custer and the cavalry which was supposed to be the army's striking force on the prairie were immobilized with barely enough sustenance to keep horses alive and none to provision them for a march. And, while Custer was shut up in camp, Indian attacks were reported from all over Kansas, up and down the stage line and along the projected route of the railroad, as the Cheyennes and Sioux reacted to word of the fire on the Pawnee Fork.

Hancock and his force reached Fort Dodge on the morning of April 22, when the general was advised of a skirmish which had taken place on the nineteenth at the Cimarron Crossing of the Arkansas. Six young Cheyennes, fleeing from the village at the Pawnee Fork, were accosted by a detachment of the Seventh Cavalry, and two of the six Indians were killed and one soldier was wounded. These two Indians, it should be noted, were the only ones killed by Hancock's force during his spring campaign on the prairie.[32]

At Fort Dodge, Hancock met with several Kiowa and Arapaho chiefs who had come in response to his summons. He urged the Indians to stay south of the Arkansas, clear of the hostile Cheyennes and Sioux. While on the road back to Larned, the expedition was overtaken by the famed war chief of the Kiowas, Satanta, a rather unsavory character—a big, bluff, roistering Indian who had participated with gusto in the murderous feuding between the Kiowas and the whites in Texas. Now, however, Satanta assured Hancock of his good heart and of his desire for peace. When the parley broke up, Hancock presented his colorful guest with the overcoat, sash, and hat of a major general; he obviously felt that such good will shown by a prominent warrior-chief augured well for the prospects of peace south of the Arkansas. Hancock was no doubt chagrined later in the summer to hear of the mercurial Satanta's leading an attack on the herds at Fort Dodge while garbed in the regalia of a major general.[33]

The next day, May 2, Hancock marched his force almost due north across the prairie to Fort Hays, arriving the afternoon of May 3. He found there the immobilized squadrons of Colonel Custer, who had been languishing at Hays since April 19. Hancock learned that his order to ship forage to Hays had been ignored, as had been several orders to march troops out from Harker and Leavenworth to take up protective positions at potentially vulnerable points. Angrily, he renewed these orders, and he deployed other units to points along the road to New Mexico and along the Smoky Hill stage route.

On May 5 Hancock left Hays to march toward Fort Harker; while en route he received a dispatch from Governor Samuel J. Crawford, stating that six civilians had been killed by Indians near the Republican River and pleading for troops to be sent there. This was one of the early salvos in a barrage of complaints, reports, and entreaties from the governor, who would ultimately badger Sherman sufficiently to win authorization to raise a regiment of Kansas volunteers. Hancock issued the appropriate orders to bring succor to Crawford's threatened constituents and resumed the march to Fort Harker, where he arrived on May 6. He stayed overnight and marched out the next evening, covering twenty-five miles to Spring Creek, the terminus of the railroad. On May 9 the general arrived back at Fort Leavenworth, his grand expedition to show the flag to the Plains Indians at an end.[34]

It is hard to discern many positive results of Hancock's expedition. He was able to make detailed inspections of the numerous forts strung out across Kansas and to prescribe additions and improvements for a number of them. But this could have been accomplished by a simple inspection tour, at much less cost in men and materials. Hancock picked up, the hard way, some experience in dealing with Indians, and his soldiers, mostly untried recruits, were hardened to the ways of campaigning on the plains. On the other hand, Hancock left an Indian war behind him where there had been at least a tenuous peace before he came. He marched 1,400 men across Kansas and back to no apparent purpose. And he failed utterly in his mission of impressing upon the Indians respect for the striking power of the United States Army.

In all this, of course, Hancock was not totally to blame. He carried out orders given to him by Sherman, apparently quite faithfully. The two men had clearly agreed upon the concept of the mission. A condescending attitude toward the Indian is clear in Hancock's talk, but such condescension was universal in white America. Hancock came to his parley with the Cheyennes with far too bellicose a frame of mind; this may have been generated by his annoyance at being trifled with, as he understood it, by the Cheyenne chiefs.

Nevertheless, for whatever reason, central and western Kansas and eastern Colorado were plagued with Indian raids, all of them laid at Winfield Scott Hancock's feet. Forgotten were the predictions that a war with the Indians was likely on the plains in 1867; Hancock's burning of the Pawnee Fork village had done it. No doubt his destruction of the village triggered the outburst, though some incident or other would have done so. The conflict between whites and Indians—now focused on the Great Plains, where the railroad, telegraph, and stage lines were usurping the buffalo range—was approaching its climax. It was Hancock's misfortune to be thrust unprepared into the midst of it.

For the balance of the spring and summer, Hancock attempted to cope with the outbreaks. Sherman had written: "Until Congress gives to the military power the right to say what Indians are at peace and what at war this conflict of races must go on. In the meantime I must leave to General Hancock to do his best." Hancock, attempting to do so, deployed small bodies of troops across the plains in attempts to cover trouble spots. But they were hardly enough to cover so vast an area.[35]

The great burden of the Indian raids was borne by civilian travelers, settlers, and railroad construction parties. In June and July, the Smoky Hill stage line to Denver stopped running. This was puzzling to Hancock, who had traveled the route on an inspection trip to Denver in late June; he advised Sherman that the stations were not harmed and that there were ample guards available to protect them. It is most likely that the owners of the stage, burdened with an unprofitable operation, were attempting to take advantage of the Indian war to lay claim on the government while bailing out of a losing proposition. There were not really many clashes between the military and the Indians, because the latter specialized in hit-and-run raids upon unsuspecting civilians. During the course of the summer, nineteen soldiers were killed—eleven of them in the ambush of Lieutenant Lyman S. Kidder and his party, sent out to find Custer—and fifty wounded, while ten Indians were killed.[36]

One of Hancock's problems, however, concerned Custer. The cavalry leader was detailed to leave Fort Hays on June 1 with six companies of his regiment, riding north toward the Platte. His orders were to scout to Fort McPherson on the Platte, looking for hostiles; here he met Sherman, who ordered him to swing southward to the headwaters of the Republican River and then west and north again to Fort Sedgwick on the Platte, near present-day Julesburg, Colorado. Here he was to regroup and take on new supplies, then ride south to the Smoky Hill and Fort Wallace. The scout was a disaster. The details of it belong more to a study of Custer than of Hancock, but it may suffice to say that virtually everything which might have been done wrong was. One officer, drinking heavily, committed suicide. Custer sorely overtaxed his poorly motivated men with numerous forced marches, resulting in a great number of desertions and Custer's direction to shoot deserters. Custer and his men missed connections with the ill-fated Kidder party, which was bringing new orders to them. Reaching Fort Wallace, Custer, without orders, leave, or authorization, left his men behind and raced off to Riley to see his wife.

Hancock ordered Custer arrested, after Colonel Smith and Captain Robert West preferred charges against him, and a court-martial was convened to try him. Custer claimed the trial was "an attempt by Hancock to cover up the failure of the Indian expedition." Custer took pen in hand and sent off three lengthy articles to a New York–based sporting journal, *Turf, Field and Farm*, in which, changing the facts to suit his thesis, he accused Hancock of single-handedly bringing about a costly Indian war through his rashness and stupidity. Nevertheless, the court-martial resulted in Custer's conviction, and, commenting on its leniency, General Grant approved the sentence—suspension from the army for one year.[37]

By the time the court-martial had taken its course, however, Hancock was gone from the plains. Similarly, he was not there for the Medicine Lodge Treaty, signed on October 27, 1867, bringing a short-lived peace to the Department of the Missouri. In midsummer Congress created a new peace commission, which was to go out to the plains and talk with the hostile Indians, to bring the fighting to a close. Sherman told Hancock to limit his troops' activities to the main routes of travel. "Do not," Sherman wrote, "invade the country south of the Arkansas River, except in pursuit of parties guilty of hostile acts. I want the deliberations of the Commissioners to be as little disturbed by acts of our troops as possible, so that the effort to settle the Indian question may have a fair chance of success."[38]

Hancock was understandably sensitive to charges that *he* had brought about the plains warfare of 1867, particularly since he had to recognize his vulnerability on the subject. By his lights, however, he had tried to give the Cheyennes on the Pawnee Fork the benefit of every doubt, and he had finally burned their village only after he felt himself pushed to that extreme by their belligerence—and by Custer's incorrect report. There is no indication that his military superiors, Sherman and Grant, were critical of Hancock's conduct, so that such heat as he felt came from nonmilitary sources. At the end of July, Hancock wrote to his friend Duncan Walker, a former staff officer in the Army of the Potomac, now a Washington editor: "I have made official reports, which had they been published would have entirely exonerated me from 'wantonness' or 'foolishness.' " At the end of August, after he had been ordered to Louisiana, Hancock wrote Walker that he was sorry to be leaving "before I have done with the Indian commission. I have some things yet to say to that body which I was anxious to file with their proceedings." Later Hancock took note of efforts on the part of some of the peace commissioners to ascribe the 1867 war to the burning of the Cheyenne village; "but the Indians invariably, when speaking of the late war, dated its commencement as prior to that event." Finally, when Hancock's report *was* published, he wrote to Walker to ask that copies be sent to each governor, army general, and bureau chief in Washington and "to each important frontier newspaper." "I consider," Hancock wrote, "this essential to a correct understanding of this important subject."[39]

The treaties which were reached by the commission, called collectively the Medicine Lodge Treaty, with the Cheyennes, Arapahos, Kiowas, Comanches, and Kiowa-Apaches, represented one more effort to negotiate a nonnegotiable question; as such the treaty was doomed to a short existence.

But all these things transpired after Hancock's jurisdiction over them had ended. On August 26, 1867, President Andrew Johnson issued an order assigning Hancock to the command of the Fifth Military District (Louisiana and Texas). Hancock's tour on the plains was over.

TWENTY THREE

Reconstruction
Commander

New Orleans was the sorest point of reconstruction. The colorful and exotic Crescent City had for decades been a focus of contending forces, French, Spanish, and British, Creole and American, now blacks, Radicals, carpetbaggers, conservatives, and unrepentant rebels. The city had fallen into Union hands in the spring of 1862 and had been occupied by an army under the command of General Benjamin F. Butler. Butler's stern rule made him infamous in the eyes of the town's citizens. His successor, General Nathaniel P. Banks, continued in somewhat milder form the government established by Butler, and the Radicals controlled the city, with the army's support. Then, the elections held in 1865 and 1866 turned many local and state offices over to former Confederates and set the stage upon which General Philip Sheridan was placed after the close of the Civil War.

New Orleans, the nation's second busiest port, with a prewar population of 170,000, had suffered with the rest of the South the privations of war. The Creoles had given way grudgingly to American immigrants during the antebellum years, and now the fortunes of war moved another element of society toward the top, those who in many cases were recent arrivals or who had been outside the ruling establishment. Into this social gumbo were mixed the emancipated former slaves and free blacks. While many of the Radicals who now claimed preeminence in Louisiana were sincerely motivated to assist the blacks in adjusting to their newly acquired status, many more were prepared to exploit the blacks for political, financial, and ultimately social power. These men sneered at Camp Street, at the prewar leaders of the community, as they schemed to replace them. Not surprisingly, these leaders were not prepared to accept with docile resignation the ascendancy of the black, the Radical, and the carpetbagger; their bitter opposition took the form of vote fraud, economic pressure, physical intimidation, and, on occasion, violence including murder. Physical violence had long been a means of resolving disagreements in Louisiana, and it became endemic in the unsettled conditions after the war.[1]

Philip Sheridan was a man of force, magnetism, and precious little subtlety. His style as a leader of the Union army had been audacity and attack; later, he was to fight Indians in the same way. When he served as commander of an occupying army, supported by Radical majorities in

Congress, however, Sheridan's nature led him into excesses of arbitrary rule. He was encouraged in this course by the local Radicals, who knew that their only hope of control in Louisiana was in the enfranchisement of the blacks. Sheridan took it upon himself to stretch to their limits the powers given him by the congressional reconstruction acts. When he combined this with insolent defiance of the president, however, his tenure came to an end.

Andrew Johnson was finally striking back at his enemies. On August 12, 1867, he suspended Secretary of War Stanton, and on August 17 he sent Grant an order naming Major General George H. Thomas to take command of the Fifth Military District (Louisiana and Texas), moving Sheridan to the Department of the Missouri and directing Hancock to replace Thomas at the Department of the Cumberland. Grant protested but, after a brief interview with the president on August 19, acquiesced, saying that Sheridan would do well with Indians.[2]

Three days later, Grant turned over to Johnson a telegram from Thomas's doctor, advising that the hero of Chickamauga was in West Virginia suffering from a liver disorder and that it would be dangerous for him to go to New Orleans, where yellow fever was prevalent. The president was overjoyed; he had wanted to send Hancock there in the first place but had picked Thomas because his known Radical views might mollify Sheridan's supporters. Grant had hoped that the disability of Thomas would keep Sheridan in place; instead, Johnson named Hancock for the Fifth District. Grant protested again, claiming that "the public interests require the retention of Gen. Hancock in Missouri." Johnson stood firm, and Grant agreed to Hancock's appointment. Sheridan was angered at the change; he was already unhappy with Hancock, whom he blamed for the punishment of his young friend Custer, and now he apparently felt that Hancock should have refused the proffered command.[3]

Grant's order directing Hancock to New Orleans, according to Allie, "was very distasteful to him"; he wrote to Grant that it was "not a desire of mine to go to . . . the south." He would, of course, obey orders. "I am expected to exercise extreme military authority over those people," he told his wife. "I shall disappoint them. I have not been educated to overthrow the civil authorities in time of peace. I intend to recognize the fact that the Civil War is at an end, and shall issue my order or proclamation accordingly. I tell you this," he added, "because I may lose my commission, and I shall do so willingly, rather than retain it at the sacrifice of a life-long principle."[4]

The conservatives in Louisiana were happy to learn of the removal of Phil Sheridan and the appointment of Hancock. The *New Orleans Times* felt "that our people will be fully satisfied with the rule of Gen. Hancock, believing that he will deal out justice impartially, unbiased by prejudice or partisan feeling." Relief for the whites of Louisiana was not yet at hand, however. Sheridan left New Orleans on September 1, turning over command to General Charles Griffin. But Griffin died of yellow fever within two weeks, and Hancock did not arrive until late November. Commanding in the interim was Major General Joseph A. Mower, a forty-one-year-old New England er who was, if anything, even more arbitrary than Sheridan. Mower removed twenty-six Louisiana officials during his brief tenure, and the natives ranked him in the same pantheon of despotism with Butler and Sheridan.[5]

In Texas, too, the local commander, Major General Joseph J. Reynolds, seemed determined to turn the government of the state completely over to the Republicans before the new district commander arrived. He consulted Governor Elisha M. Pease (himself a recent appointee of Sheridan), removed over five hundred Democrats from office, and named more than six hundred Republicans to city and state positions.[6]

Hancock was summoned by Grant and the president to Washington before he took up his new post. He dined at the White House; among the guests was Navy Secretary Gideon Welles, who recorded that "General H. talks very well, and I hope will act sensibly in Louisiana." Hancock was cheered at the theater and was tendered a testimonial dinner arranged by Colonel Amasa Cobb, one of his old regimental commanders. While in the capital, Hancock was visited in his hotel room by Grant, who told him that Johnson's policies were a menace to the country and that Hancock should continue the general tenor of military rule which then prevailed throughout the South. But Grant was not sure of his man—this accounting for his strenuous efforts to prevent Hancock's assignment to New Orleans—and the hotel interview was not satisfactory to him, either.[7]

Hancock, of course, had been pitched into the center of the conflict between Johnson and the Radical Republicans, a conflict in which the president had precious few weapons left. His veto power was meaningless, his right to remove subordinates was gone, his authority over the actions of the military governors had vanished. He retained the power of appointment and removal of the district commanders, and that power he had exercised in the Fifth Military District. Now Johnson could only wait and watch to see if his appraisal of Hancock was correct. He felt that the general from Pennsylvania, a Democrat, believed in a conservative, white-oriented restoration of the South. Johnson knew, however, that he had misjudged others of the generals he had sent south—to date, all of them had acted in accord with Grant, Stanton, and the Radicals. The president seemed not to understand that the generals, on the whole, were not prepared to see the South restored to the Union as if nothing had happened. Johnson knew only that all of the reconstruction commanders had maintained their loyalties to Grant and not to him. He hoped that Hancock would be different.

This time the president's expectations were not disappointed. Hancock was not just nominally a Democrat; he had absorbed from his father at an early age the party's doctrines on the rights of the states and the limitations on the national government. His wife had been raised in a slaveholding border state. During his years in the army before the war, most of Hancock's closest friends had been southerners—Heth, Armistead, Brent, Johnson,

Buckner, and others—and from these friendships he had developed a sympathy for the whites of the South which resurfaced once rebellion was put down. He saw no need to reconstruct the South; once insurrection was suppressed, the natural leadership of the region should resume its authority. With these views, there could be little doubt where Hancock would be found politically when he reached Louisiana.

Hancock delayed his and his wife's departure down the Mississippi until the yellow fever epidemic then rampant in New Orleans had run its course. In the latter part of November, they left St. Louis on the steamer *Mississippi*, which worked its way slowly down the river, the water being low. As they headed south, the political elements in the city prepared to meet them. "Between the 'Conservative Party' committee, and the 'Union Party' committee," wrote one commentator, "General Hancock has a fair prospect of being extensively advised." Another story warned of the "little band of the meanest rebels the sun of God ever shone upon; men who are perjurers, assassins, blackguards, pimps," proposing to "capture General Hancock." Politics, as the general would quickly learn, was played for keeps in New Orleans. At 5 p.m. on November 28, Hancock's packet docked and the new commander walked ashore in civilian dress. There was no reception, the troops having been dismissed before the boat's arrival, and he moved off to the army's headquarters.[8]

There was much speculation about Hancock's future course, speculation he quickly squelched. On his first day of command, he issued a document, officially tagged General Orders No. 40, which set forth his position on the proper role of a district commander. The general, it stated, "is gratified to learn that peace and quiet reign in this department," and he would endeavor to preserve that condition. "As a means to this end he requires the maintenance of the civil authorities and the faithful execution of the laws as the most efficient under existing circumstances." When, he went on, insurrection has been overcome "and the civil authorities are ready and willing to perform their duties, the military power should cease to lead and the civil administration resume its natural and rightful dominion. . . . [T]he great principles of American liberty are still the inheritance of this people and ever should be. The right of trial by jury, the *habeas corpus*, the liberty of the press, the freedom of speech, the natural rights of persons, and the rights of property must be preserved." Hancock's order continued: "Free institutions, while they are essential to the prosperity and happiness of the people, always furnish the strongest inducements to peace and order. Crimes and offenses committed in this district must be left to the consideration and judgment of the regular civil tribunals, and those tribunals will be supported in their lawful jurisdiction." Finally, having indicated "his purpose to respect the liberties of the people," Hancock wished "all to understand that armed insurrection or forcible resistance to the law will be instantly suppressed by arms."[9]

Hancock had composed the order on his downriver trip, though many of its ideas were doubtless suggested in his meetings in the capital with Johnson and members of his cabinet. Allie tells of coming upon him writing it one night, after 3 a.m., and his reading it to her. When she congratulated him on its message, Winfield said, "They will crucify me. I warned the President of my intentions. . . . I know I shall have his sympathy, but he is powerless to help me."[10]

The question has sometimes been raised whether Hancock was motivated by political ambition in writing this celebrated order. Certainly, he did not seek the assignment to the Fifth Military District or any other reconstruction command; he went reluctantly and with misgivings. He suspected, however, the kind of effect the order would have and promulgated it anyway, when he could have achieved something of the same result in the district by simply refusing to interfere in civil affairs, without announcing his intentions beforehand to the nation. The order placed Hancock instantly on the side of the conservative white Democrats, and he certainly understood that it would do so. His order did in fact bring him prominently to the attention of the national Democratic party, attention he clearly found not unwelcome.

General Orders No. 40 stirred a storm throughout the nation. The views expressed were contrary to the whole philosophy of the reconstruction acts passed by Congress. In addition, of course, the order presupposed a neutral "civil administration," which was an impossibility in the postwar South; both sides realized that the order placed Hancock in opposition to the Radicals. The *New Orleans Crescent* reported that no document since war's end had given such a feeling of satisfaction and assurance as had General Orders No. 40, while the *New Orleans Times* felt that "a new era has dawned in Louisiana, and it is believed results the most satisfactory will be obtained."[11]

The president, his secretary noted, called the message "manly and statesmanlike," not surprisingly, whereas Adam Badeau, one of Grant's aides, said Hancock had issued a proclamation "in direct contradiction of the spirit of the Reconstruction measures," which was certainly true. In Congress, Oliver P. Morton, the Radical senator from Indiana, attacked the order, predicting that Hancock's "laurels would wither like the tender flowers beneath the simoon of the desert."[12]

The people of Louisiana and Texas, the majority who had supported the Confederacy but recognized and accepted its defeat, who abhorred both black rule and carpetbagger rule, and who wanted simply to be left alone, as well as the minority who regarded the order as a license to increase intimidation and violence against the freedmen and their Radical allies, were pleased with the order. "Even the old French element, who had little to do with Americans," wrote Mrs. Hancock, "were most effusive in their thanks." Her time in her new home in the Garden District was taken up in returning gifts showered on the general and in acknowledging the messages of thanks. "This feeling of gratitude pervaded the entire community."[13]

In the rest of the South as well, Hancock's decree seemed to be the first glimmer of hope that reconstruction and the imposition of oversight from Washington might be nearing an end. A correspondent of Hancock's old classmate Bolivar Buckner wrote that the order might be "the commencement of a reighn [*sic*] of reason and Law throughout the South." It was a false dawn, as time would prove, but it endeared the general from Pennsylvania to the section against which he had fought so hard and so successfully.[14]

Andrew Johnson prepared a message to Congress, urging a vote of thanks to Hancock for the expression of sentiments contained in the message. After a cabinet meeting on December 17, the president showed his message to several of his ministers, winning their approval for it. Gideon Welles noted in his diary that it "will exasperate the Radicals, but it may have the effect of inducing a contrast between the action of Hancock and the other military generals." Obviously, Johnson had no notion that he would receive a favorable reaction from the House and Senate.[15]

The next day, the president submitted to both houses a copy of Hancock's order, together with his own message comparing Hancock to George Washington in his devotion to the principle of civil supremacy over the military. "I am far from saying that General Hancock is the only officer . . . influenced by the example of Washington," he continued. "But the distinguished honor belongs to him of being the first officer in high command south of the Potomac, since the close of the civil war, who has given utterance to these noble sentiments in the form of a military order." The congressional answer to this riposte was a brace of bills, introduced in the Senate by John M. Thayer of Nebraska and in the House by James A. Garfield of Ohio, to reduce the number of major generals in the army by eliminating the junior one, who happened to be Winfield Hancock. Nothing came of these bills, which were opposed by Grant and Sherman and which, in any event, were presumably put together only for their political and psychological effect. Still, it was one more worry for Hancock.[16]

Shortly after Hancock had been appointed to succeed Sheridan, on August 31, Grant had issued an order, obviously designed to hamper Hancock's administration, forbidding district commanders from appointing to civil offices any persons who had been removed from office by the commanders themselves or their predecessors. Later, however, Grant specifically authorized Hancock to revoke any of Mower's post-November 10 orders. On December 4 Hancock reversed a Mower order which had removed one P. R. O'Rourke as a parish court clerk. O'Rourke was reinstated in the office, and Hancock said that if any charges were made against O'Rourke, the courts could take "whatever action may be necessary." Others removed by Mower were also reinstated.[17]

Having countermanded Mower, the next day Hancock countermanded Sheridan. He revoked an order Sheridan had issued some three months earlier relative to the qualifications of jurors in the state courts of Louisiana.

"The administration of justice . . .," Hancock wrote, "is clogged, if not entirely frustrated," by the enforcement of the Sheridan order, which encouraged the service of freedmen while barring whites who had supported the Confederacy. "To determine who shall, and who shall not be jurors, appertains to the legislative power. . . . [I]t is deemed best to carry out the will of the people as expressed in the last legislative act upon this subject." What this meant was that henceforth the prior statute, banning black men from jury service, would govern. So few of the freedmen could read or write that their presence on juries brought the business of the courts to a standstill. That this was a serious problem few in the state denied; the Radicals, however, would bear with it in order to preserve the forward step of black qualification. Hancock would not. His solution was a pragmatic one, one which accorded as well with his strict constructionist views on civil supremacy over the military and on the rights of the states. It was also a popular solution with the majority of the white inhabitants of Louisiana.[18]

On December 18 Hancock fixed February 10–14, 1868, for a referendum in Texas on a constitutional convention, adding that "military interference with elections . . . is prohibited by law, and no soldiers will be allowed to appear at any polling place," unless as registered voters for the sole purpose of voting. This dictum was a novel one in the reconstructing South, and it excited much comment.[19]

Since his arrival, Hancock had heard from citizens throughout Louisiana who feared some kind of black uprising and requested that the general send troops to protect them. Finally, on December 23, Hancock wrote to Grant, asking for reinforcements: "A few soldiers at various posts under discreet commanders, to represent the Federal Authority and maintain the laws, are in my opinion absolutely necessary." He added that "they must be white: black troops are unsuitable for the performance of this peculiar service." This request obviously held little appeal for Grant and the Radicals in Washington, but the danger could not be ignored. Hancock hoped for a regiment but had to be satisfied with three or four companies.[20]

In the meantime, Hancock had turned his attention to the state of Texas. On December 4, having been barraged with complaints about Reynolds's conduct, Hancock required that the local commander justify his wholesale removals, make no further changes, and permit those removed who still physically held their offices to remain. Reynolds finally replied on the last day of the year, lamely explaining that the actions were taken on the recommendations of Governor Pease, the Radical whom Sheridan had installed, with little personal knowledge on his own part.[21]

A confrontation also developed with Pease, when he requested a military commission to try three prisoners accused of a murder in Uvalde County, in the western part of the state. Pease wrote that "it is not probable that they can be kept in confinement long enough even to be tried by the civil courts of that county." On December 28, 1867, Hancock's answer was fired off to Pease. "At this time the country is in a state of profound peace," he wrote.

"The state government of Texas . . . is in the full exercise of all its proper powers. The courts . . . are in existence." The state government, he said, had all the powers necessary to try the prisoners properly and promptly. "If these powers are not exercised for that purpose," Hancock went on ominously, "the failure to exercise them can be attributed only to the indolence or culpable inefficiency of the officers now charged with the execution and enforcement of the laws under the authority of the state government. . . . [I]t will then become the duty of the commander to remove the officers who fail to discharge the duties imposed on them, and to replace them with others who will discharge them."

This reply squelched Pease for the time being; it did not make a friend of the Texas governor. Hancock would hear from him again soon. The *New Orleans Times* called the answer to Pease a "magnanimous abnegation of a power which has heretofore been applied with so ruthless an indifference to the rights and feelings of the people and to the true character and principles of our Government."[22]

Two days later Hancock's headquarters communicated to the appointed governor of Louisiana, Benjamin Franklin Flanders, the general's refusal to remove summarily from office the members of the police jury of Orleans Parish, on the basis of allegations forwarded by Flanders. "These charges," Hancock wrote, "present a proper case for judicial investigation and determination." The courts, he went on, "can afford adequate relief for the wrongs complained of, if proved to exist."[23]

Still, Hancock felt, his message—that he refused to usurp the functions of the civil courts—was not getting across. The persistence of the requests for military intervention pointed out more clearly than almost anything else could how common it had been for Sheridan and Mower to interfere in the workings of the local judiciary. Hancock began 1868 with a general order, issued on New Year's Day, spelling out with even greater clarity his view that "the administration of civil justice appertains to the regular courts." The rights of litigants, he said, "are to be adjudged and settled according to the laws," not according to "the views of the general." The arbitrary power he was urged to assume had "no existence here."[24]

After four or five weeks in command, Hancock was immensely popular with the white citizens of his district. They had been encouraged by his initial order, and his subsequent policies confirmed his announced intention of permitting civil government to function without military interference. As it became clear that the rule of the Radicals was in fact at an end—at least while Hancock was in command—the normal civil life of New Orleans, and of the two states of the district, was resumed. It was hoped that Hancock had brought an end to the long period which had commenced with Butler more than five years earlier.

Not everyone was happy with the general. The Radicals were sorely discomfited by Hancock's administration, and they made the fact known, both on the scene and in communications to Washington. In an editorial entitled, significantly, "A Word to Congress," the *New Orleans Republican* wrote: "Andrew Johnson is determined that governments worse than those imposed by Jefferson Davis shall be erected in the South, through the Generals he is sending to govern it." One correspondent wrote to the commissioner of the Freedmen's Bureau, General O. O. Howard: "Hancock is avowedly with the rebels in sympathy. . . . [W]e poor old soldiers who fought with him have no show." Another wrote that Hancock "injured us seriously" and called him "a great impediment to reconstruction," giving "all the aid and comfort in his power to the Rebs." A carpetbagger wrote to Garfield that he considered Hancock "the most infamous man in America."[25]

These complaints were unfair. Hancock had repeatedly risked his life on behalf of his country, and he would have been ready to do so again if necessary. His loyalty, however, was to the Union and to the Constitution as he construed it; a conservative Democrat, he did not understand his efforts and those of the men he had led in battle to have been for the propagation of Radical tenets such as black suffrage and the remaking of southern society. He believed that the restoration of the late seceded states did not require their reconstruction once the principle of disunion was laid to rest and slavery ended. He was willing to forgo the proscription of the natural leadership of the southern communities, especially where the alternative appeared to be unlettered farmhands fresh from bondage. In these sentiments Hancock was joined by millions of other loyal citizens of the North, who opposed black suffrage and the extension of economic rights to the freedmen. The Radical ascendancy was brought about primarily by the astonishing political ineptitude of Andrew Johnson, and even so it was of relatively limited duration. History does not look kindly upon the efforts of the white South, aided by policies such as Hancock's, to keep the blacks of the region in an inferior position. Nevertheless, the position of the Democratic party in support of long-maintained constitutional principles has a certain forlorn appeal to it. These principles had been inculcated in Winfield Hancock since childhood by his father, a lawyer and a Democrat, and, isolated by his military status from many of the currents of change at large in the country, Hancock had seen no reason to modify them. Now he held to those principles, regardless of anticipated consequences, when he was suddenly injected into the midst of the reconstruction conflict.

As 1868 got under way, Hancock stirred controversy again with two major actions taken on January 11. First, since Flanders had resigned as governor of Louisiana, apparently unable to work with the commanding general, he appointed as successor an elderly planter, West Pointer, and judge named Joshua Baker, of St. Mary, a Unionist called by the *Times* "a representative Louisianian." Baker was no Radical, regarding Andrew Johnson's requirements for reconstruction as adequate. In a second major decision, Hancock revoked Sheridan's orders on voter registration. This action was an obvious sequel to his jury-eligibility decree of five weeks earlier, but the Radicals liked it no better for all that. The previous May, Sheridan had sent out to the local voter registrars "memoranda of disqualifications" and "questions to be answered by persons proposing to register," designed to disfranchise ex-Confederates. Hancock revoked the Sheridan memoranda and directed the registrars to comply with Louisiana statutory law.[26]

Under the Sheridan instructions, registration had been weighted heavily in favor of blacks; whites with any connection whatever with the Confederacy found it virtually impossible to qualify. The September 1867 election in Louisiana for constitutional convention delegates was revealing. There were for that election 127,639 registered voters, and of this total 82,907 were black. Because they regarded the electoral deck as stacked by Sheridan and the Radicals, most white voters boycotted the election. The convention was approved by a vote of 75,083 for and 4,006 against. Of the 98 delegates elected, 96 were Republicans, evenly divided, as arranged, between blacks and their white allies. "The members are below par as to intelligence," wrote one Radical, "but that is better than to be so as to loyalty."[27]

With the Sheridan memoranda revoked, the impediment to the registration of white voters was removed, though the black voters already on the rolls would remain. "Hancock's action," one authority has recently written, "speeded the recovery of the Democratic party and the eventual demise of the Republicans." Although it may have had this result in Louisiana, there is evidence that in Texas, with the blessing of Reynolds, the Republican registrars proceeded about as they had before.[28]

In the meantime, the controversy with Governor Pease of Texas flared up again. In an exchange of correspondence with Grant, Hancock's general course in Texas had been approved. Still, on January 17, Pease wrote to Hancock, dissenting vigorously from the latter's view that Texas was in a state of peace and retailing all the reasons why criminal justice could not be administered by the civil authorities. He implied that the issuance of General Orders No. 40 had been a considerable incitement to violent crime in Texas. This letter reached Hancock on January 27, having already appeared in the press.[29]

Hancock composed a long and powerful rebuttal to Pease, methodically and systematically squelching all of the complaints and contentions of the Texas governor. Pease had said that "a large majority of the white population . . . are embittered against the Government, and yield to it an unwilling obedience." Hancock rejoined that "I have been accustomed to believe that sentiments of respect or disrespect, and feelings of affection, love or hatred, so long as not developed into acts in violation of law, were matters wholly beyond the punitory power of human tribunals." Pease implied that the local laws and tribunals existing before the end of the war were now totally subject to the power of the military. Hancock replied that, excepting those relating to slavery, "they are as perfect a system of laws as may be found elsewhere, and better suited than any other to the condition of this people, for by them they have long been governed. Why should it be supposed Congress has abolished these laws?" He scored Pease's statement that there had been "a perceptible increase of crime and manifestations of hostile feeling toward the Government" since the publication of Hancock's initial order, pointing out that there had hardly been time for such an effect to make itself manifest and then reciting statistics to the contrary. And he heaped ridicule upon Pease's complaint that the civil authorities in Texas could not maintain order, asserting pointedly that this was the local government "created by military power prior to my coming here" and "composed of your personal and political friends." He called it a "profound mystery" that "your political friends, backed up and sustained by the whole military power of the United States in this district, should be unwilling to enforce the laws against that part of the population lately in rebellion, and whom you represent as the offenders." Hancock added that "I believe you are in very great error as to facts." He did not hear from Governor Pease again.[30]

In February another crisis arose, one which proved to be Winfield Scott Hancock's undoing in New Orleans. In the election of 1866, a young conservative named Arthur Gastinel was elected recorder of the Second District of New Orleans. His defeated opponent went to court, alleging Gastinel's ineligibility by virtue of being under the age required by law. Gastinel lost in the courts, and the position was declared vacant. By February 1868 Gastinel had attained legal age, and Hancock intended that the voters' choice should be honored. On February 4, however, the Board and Assistant Board of Aldermen met in joint session, for the purpose of electing a recorder. There was much acrimonious debate, because Hancock had directed the aldermen not to conduct such an election, citing a provision in the reconstruction acts that all vacancies in elective offices were to be filled by the district commander, as well as an unrevoked standing order issued by Sheridan. The aldermen resolved nevertheless to proceed with the election but were frustrated when enough members left the meeting that there was no quorum present. On February 5 Hancock appointed Gastinel to the vacancy. On the same day he fired New Orleans Streets Commissioner William Baker, a Sheridan appointee, for malfeasance and corruption in office.[31]

Two days later Hancock removed from office the three aldermen and six assistant aldermen who had voted to hold the election, "in contempt of orders from these Headquarters," and named replacements for them. Seven of the nine ousted were blacks and represented the entire black membership of the board; all had been appointed originally by Sheridan. No blacks were among the new members. The departure of the ousted members was little lamented in New Orleans, except in the Radical camp. The *Daily Picayune* remarked that the council's incompetency "was notorious," and the *Times* wrote: "[T]hat the colored population is not represented in the new board is at the same time their fault and their misfortune."[32]

Reaction in New Orleans, of course, was not as significant as that in Washington. The ousted aldermen and their allies shipped off complaints and accusations to the capital, and these soon had an effect. On February 8, having received a wire from Hancock explaining what had been done, Grant directed that the ouster order be suspended. Hancock, in restrained terms, remonstrated against ·this interference and advised that, if Grant's order stood, he would desire to be relieved from his position. On February 11 Grant wired Hancock that the removals could stay in effect while he looked into the matter. On February 14 the House directed Grant to furnish to it copies of his correspondence with Hancock. The *New Orleans Times* marveled at "what wonderfully grand and important individuals some half a dozen Aldermen . . . must be, that the whole nation should be convulsed, and the national capital turned upside down, because better men have been found for their places." Another paper predicted that Grant would value too highly the services of Hancock to place before him "the alternative of resignation or a revocation of orders so deliberately issued."[33]

Finally, after much hesitation, Grant on February 21 ordered the reinstatement of the displaced officials in New Orleans, in a letter from John Rawlins which Hancock did not receive until February 27. Grant looked slightly foolish in doing so, for the ousted aldermen had flouted an order of Phil Sheridan's as well as one of Hancock's. But, as Grant was learning, political imperatives even though unreasonable had still to be obeyed.[34]

Hancock, of course, complied with Grant's order when he got it. He did not hesitate, however, to send off his own letter, the same day, to Adjutant General Lorenzo Thomas, enclosing his request "to be relieved from the command of this Military District, where it is no longer useful or agreeable for me to serve." It was clear to Hancock that the reversal by Grant, in a matter which had assumed the proportions it had, had fatally compromised his effectiveness in the district, and a change in command was required. No doubt the sight of crowds of jeering blacks parading around his residence early in the morning confirmed Hancock in the wisdom of his decision.[35]

The white citizens of New Orleans were not happy at the thought of Hancock's departure. On Saturday evening, February 29, Hancock was accorded a standing ovation at the Opera House, and the next day the *New Orleans Times* said that the general's rumored request for relief had excited much "uneasiness and serious apprehension among our respectable and honest citizens." Nevertheless, the request stood, and on March 16 Hancock was relieved of command in the Fifth Military District and ordered by the president to come to Washington.[36]

For the people of Louisiana, the withdrawal of Hancock represented yet another change of direction. Louisiana was kept in turmoil by the continued struggle between Radicals and white conservatives. The Radicals in Washington, and their tools such as Ulysses S. Grant, would keep up the effort to impose a government based on black suffrage, against the will of the resistant white population. Such an experiment, in a state in which all the levers of economic power were held by whites, in which racism continued to run deep and strong, and in which resort to violence was a matter of common policy, was doomed to failure. The will of the Republicans of the North to support reconstruction gradually eroded, but the troops supporting carpetbag governments were not removed from Louisiana until 1877, when they left in the aftermath of the Hayes-Tilden impasse. The lamentations of the white citizens at the departure of Hancock would surely have been twice as loud had they known they were to be afflicted with nine more years of imposed rule.[37]

For Hancock, the tour of duty in the Fifth Military District, brief as it was, marked a watershed in his career. Henceforth, he was not just the hero of Cemetery Ridge and the Bloody Angle; he was now identified in the public perception as a Democratic general.

TWENTY FOUR

A Boom for President

Hancock returned to Washington from New Orleans, and on March 28 he was named commander of the Division of the Atlantic. Hancock's return resulted in a definite estrangement from Grant, although there had been hints back in Virginia in 1864 that Hancock had certain reservations about the lieutenant general. There were apparently two incidents in 1868 which brought this about. When Hancock arrived back in Washington, he reported to the commanding general's headquarters and signed the register, as was required by regulations, but did not wait for a personal interview with Grant, as was required by custom. "Under existing circumstances," he told John Rawlins when he learned that Grant was not there, "it is probably as well." He left his address but was never sent for. A day or so later, while Grant was conversing on the sidewalk with former governor Flanders of Louisiana, Hancock approached; he was said to have touched his hat to Grant in a formal manner and then passed by, although not in any attitude, as Flanders confirmed, of hostility. Grant was angered by what he considered snubs on the part of a subordinate officer, while Hancock, for his part, harbored at the time no cordial feelings toward a superior who had overruled and embarrassed him for political rather than military reasons. "I felt hurt," he wrote Sherman, "that as a soldier defending the prerogatives of my office, General Grant, my next commander, had not sustained me, but humiliated me in presence of the people whom I had been sent to govern." It was an unfortunate situation for both old soldiers, but one in which Grant certainly appeared the lesser man. For Grant to have expected Hancock to resume instantly their relationship without taking into account the embarrassment recently visited upon him was unrealistic. "I . . . was aggrieved," Hancock said, "and felt cold to General Grant." For Grant subsequently to use his superior position to deny Hancock the normal privileges of his rank was discreditable. Johnson thought that Hancock "had shown his manliness by refusing to exhibit the least cringing" before Grant; unfortunately, Johnson would soon be gone and Grant would be his successor.[1]

When the new president was inaugurated in 1869, Hancock was banished to the relatively unimportant Department of Dakota, though his major general's rank entitled him to a better post. In 1870, when George Thomas died, leaving a vacancy in the command of the Division of the Pacific, Hancock asked for that spot. Again, his rank entitled him to the position, but Grant sent John M. Schofield, who was junior. When Hancock complained to Sherman, the latter wrote back: "The President authorizes me to say to you, that it belongs to his office to select the Commanding Generals of Divisions and Departments, and that the relations you chose to assume towards him, officially and privately, absolve him from regarding your personal preferences." Hancock responded that, "as the President leads me to believe that because I have not his personal sympathies, my preferences for command will not be regarded, notwithstanding my rank, I shall not again open the subject." He pointed out, though, that it established "an unfortunate precedent" to disregard rank, in peacetime, in the assignment of general officers to commands.[2]

But all this was in the future. For the present, while Hancock took up his position in Washington, all attention in that political city was centered on the impeachment of Andrew Johnson and, what was even more important, the selection by the two parties of their candidates for the 1868 presidential election. In the proceedings against the president, the Radicals made the best effort that old Thad Stevens and Ben Butler could produce, fumed at the rulings of Chief Justice Chase, and watched in frustration as the attempt to convict fell one vote short. In any event, Johnson's tenure was now measured in months only, and the choice of his successor quickly became the overriding political question.

The Republicans met in Chicago on May 20. There was never much doubt as to the identity of their candidate, and Ulysses S. Grant was nominated by a unanimous vote on the only roll call taken, with Schuyler Colfax of Indiana chosen for the vice presidency.

For the Democrats, there was no such certainty. They were scheduled to convene in New York City on the Fourth of July, and they had a number of potential candidates. One of those most prominently mentioned was Hancock, whose activities in Louisiana had brought him favorably to the attention of many Democrats who felt that a military hero would present an attractive counter to the Republican nominee. Other possibilities included the incumbent, Andrew Johnson, former congressman George H. Pendleton of Ohio, Senator Thomas A. Hendricks of Indiana, and former governor Horatio Seymour of New York. One of the oddest developments was the potential candidacy of Chief Justice Salmon P. Chase. Chase, over the years a Whig, a member of the Liberty party, a Free Soil Democrat, and an early Republican, was an aspirant for the nomination which went to Lincoln in 1860, and he had been a Radical as secretary of the treasury in Lincoln's cabinet. As chief justice he had been a disappointment to those Republicans who expected him to be a partisan. His ambition for the presidency burned as brightly as ever, however, and the Democratic party now seemed to be the only vehicle left to him. The major obstacle to a rapprochement between Chase and the Democrats was his long-held and consistent stand in favor of black suffrage. If a suitable accommodation could be made on that issue, Chase might become a very real contender.

The range of possible candidates, particularly including Chase, made it plain that the 1868 convention was to be the Democratic party's struggle for its own soul. Few political parties had ever undergone the trauma which the Democratic party had recently endured, and it was obvious that its trial had not yet ended. There were, among the candidates, serious differences on monetary policy—the inflationist Pendleton and the hard-money Seymour were the extremes—and there were, as always, geographical differences. The crucial question for every candidate, however, was what his position had been during the war. Many Democrats had opposed Lincoln's policy in using force to coerce the South back into the Union, felt that the Federal government had had no right to interfere with the institution of slavery within the states, and deplored the unconstitutional means employed by the administraion to conduct the war. Many had sympathized openly with the Confederacy, and some had acted in ways that went beyond sympathy. Another sizable portion of the party agreed with Lincoln that the Union had to be preserved but disapproved of some of the methods used. Many others went down the line with the president in his politics throughout the war, while maintaining their belief in the principles of the Democratic party. Some had gone to the extreme of leaving their party and aligning themselves with the so-called Union party in 1864; the excesses of the Radicals had repelled them and driven them back to the Democracy. And, of course, there were those who, like Hancock, had been prominent in the prosecution of the war. In addition to these, of course, there were the Democrats of the South, who had made up a large part of the party in prewar days.

Pendleton and Hendricks were among those Democratic leaders who had grudgingly supported the war effort because they disapproved of many of the policies followed by Lincoln in prosecuting the war; they represented substantial sentiment within the party, but many party leaders were wary of presenting one of them as the candidate. Seymour, too, as war governor of New York from 1863 to 1865, had worked hard to keep up New York's contribution to the cause, but his well-publicized differences with the administration had marked out a Democratic policy and made Seymour an idol of many party regulars. Johnson, of course, had been the most conspicuous of the Union party adherents, but he was still a Democrat, with all the philosophical and historical baggage that fact entailed. Hancock, while serving loyally and most usefully in the Federal army, had kept intact his Democratic principles, seeing in them no obstacle to fighting hard to preserve the Union. Chase represented the other end of the spectrum, the former Democrat who had become a Republican and a Radical but who had now been disillusioned and, for whatever reason, sought to rejoin the Democracy.

The rise of the Republican party, the disappearance of the Whigs, and the great crisis of the Union and its preservation, all taking place within little more than a decade, had left party identification in an unusual state of flux. The schism of 1860 and the stresses of the Civil War had cost the Democratic party many of its adherents. But the Republicans had not really proved themselves able to capitalize on this weakness; harsh and bitter partisans such as Thaddeus Stevens, Benjamin F. Wade, and Edwin M. Stanton were not very attractive to the American voter. Black suffrage was not a popular issue in the North. The results of the Congressional election of 1866, bad as they were for the Democrats, were attributable to Johnson's ineptitude. There was no reason to believe that the election represented a long-term trend; the northern elections of 1867, with the issue of black suffrage in the forefront, were much more favorable to the Democrats. In 1868 the Democrats had a chance to regain control; the Republicans, obviously, felt unable safely to nominate one of their political leaders—they had to go with the war hero, Grant, whom they hoped to manage. Those in the antiwar wing of the Democracy were confident, on the evidence of the 1867 elections, that they could nominate one of their own without making any significant effort to attract voters from the opposition. Others were not so sure, faced with the preeminent hero of the Union army. The prime candidate for soliciting votes from Republicans was, obviously, Chase, if he and the Democratic party could come to terms. Otherwise, this appeal must be represented by a military figure, and of these the Democrats were in short supply. The likeliest-looking war-hero candidate the party could boast was Hancock. Unlike Chase, Hancock had never been anything but a Democrat. His war record and his record in peacetime dwarfed those of any other Democratic possibilities, such as William Rosecrans, Henry Slocum, and McClellan, who had been beloved by his troops but who had not, unfortunately, won many battles.

If the decision, however, should be to select a candidate from among those who had carried the party's banner during its period of travail, there were still choices to make. The Radical press might lump Seymour, Hendricks, and Pendleton together, but there were significant differences among them, and it would be the task of the party organs to bring these differences forth. The party organs, unfortunately, were having trouble coping with what they saw as the "Chase boom" in the weeks preceding the convention. Newspaper editors seldom acknowledge pangs of embarrassment, and few were expressed after the nonappearance of the candidacy of the chief justice. Yet the record indicates that the Chase candidacy was the merest will-o'-the-wisp, without much substance except in the nightmares of some southern delegates and the machinations of some New York leaders.

As the convention approached, it was acknowledged that Pendleton would probably have the largest number of votes on the first ballot. "Gentleman George," as he was known, handsome and wealthy, was the candidate of the soft-money forces of the West, prime advocate of the "Ohio idea," a scheme for paying the government's debts in greenbacks. There was an uneasy truce between the Pendleton and Hendricks camps; Pendleton would be allowed to run his race before Hendricks was brought forward, and Indiana would vote for Pendleton—at first. For there was much doubt that Pendleton would ever be able to win the support of enough eastern delegates to capture the nomination.[3]

The Chase movement was a curiosity from start to finish, a strange adagio performed principally by New York Democratic leaders, some of whom harbored deeper intentions of procuring the nomination of Horatio Seymour. Colonel John Dash Van Buren and Manton Marble, the editor of the *New York World,* were among the backers of Chase, feeling that the Democrats could not expect to win without attracting substantial numbers of voters from the other party. For this purpose, they felt, Chase was the best bet. James Gordon Bennett and his *New York Herald* took a similar position, as did Charles Dana in the *New York Sun.* There was a major problem: Chase had consistently avowed his belief in black suffrage, which was hardly a tenet of the orthodox Democratic faith. It was recognized that Chase and the Democrats might make common cause only if this item of prime disagreement were overcome. On May 29 August Belmont, the New York financier who was chairman of the Democratic National Committee, wrote to Chase, pledging to "use all my efforts and influence to bring about your nomination." Belmont suggested that Chase would prefer having the states vote on the question of black suffrage to having it imposed upon the southern states by Congress. In other words, if universal suffrage could be dressed up in appropriate states' rights garb, it might be acceptable to the Democratic party, at least sufficiently so to permit Chase to run as a Democrat.[4]

After some waffling, the continuing presidential ambition of the chief justice got the better of him. Chase released a statement in mid-June, saying in part, "universal suffrage is a democratic principle, the application of which is to be left under the Constitution of the United States to the States themselves." Here was the accommodation for which certain Democratic leaders had been waiting. Chase, it was felt, might now be sufficiently sanitized for a Democratic nomination.[5]

But there were some wily politicos at work in New York. The New York Democratic leaders, spiritual descendants of Aaron Burr, William Marcy, and Martin Van Buren, were often sinuous, subtle intriguers. Seymour, Samuel J. Tilden, John Pruyn of Albany, Sanford E. Church, and their colleagues had ends in mind which were not always those immediately apparent. On June 10 Church wrote to Tilden that Chase was out of the question: "we will use him well but must not think of nominating him." A few weeks earlier, on May 1, John Van Buren had written a gossipy letter to Seymour, who had denied any interest in the nomination for himself. Van Buren spoke of the "strong talk" and "loud and noisy" movement for Hancock and of the apparent preference of Hendricks to remain in the Senate. Finally, he said, "your declination is regarded in Washington as sincere. As you said to me some time ago, the next Presidency, if to be got by us, must be got by diplomacy—do you see any opening?" Clearly, there was less to the Chase movement, in these hands, than met the eye.[6]

The titular leader of the party, George B. McClellan, the 1864 candidate, wrote from France in wonderment about the Chase movement and "whether the Democratic party will survive a victory so won any better than a defeat under a well known Democrat. . . . The odd thing to me is that *Chase* should be the leader in an anti-radical crusade." The southern delegates, fearing the worst with Chase, were astonished as they arrived in New York for the convention to find how little support there was for the chief justice; they had been led to believe that his nomination was a foregone conclusion. The Democrats of Ohio were not enraptured by the candidacy of Chase; William Allen wrote: " . . . we want no disappointed negro worshipper like Chase."[7]

As matters stood, the candidacy of Winfield Hancock took on more importance. Several years later, Hancock wrote that he had become a candidate only because "accidental circumstances" made him alone "of the war men" available: "I had an opportunity which others did not have or did not take advantage of, to ingratiate myself with the 'civilian' element of the country, by showing a deference to civil law and the Constitution." Early support for the general had come from the South: the *New Orleans Times* on February 11 quoted the *Paris* (Texas) *Press* urging Hancock as the man who should be the Democratic choice. Subsequently, the *Mobile Register,* the *Richmond Enquirer,* the *Memphis Avalanche,* and the *Charleston Mercury* all supported Hancock, since his military record would appeal to the North and his service in the Fifth Military District commended him to the South. As a native son, he might carry Pennsylvania, normally very difficult for a Democrat; he had backing in Pennsylvania, including that of Senator Charles Buckalew. Hancock alone could challenge Grant for the soldier vote, and the "peace" Democrats, though they would oppose his nomination, would have no alternative to him in the fall election.[8]

In May the *Boston Post* endorsed Hancock, and Robert J. Walker, the former secretary of the treasury, wrote Tilden that Hancock was the only Democrat who could "certainly be elected." Frank Blair of Missouri, himself a hopeful, said that, "if compelled to work for somebody" besides himself, that person would be Hancock. Many of Hancock's old comrades, led by General William B. Franklin and General Thomas Kilby Smith, were pushing his cause, and it received aid from a few administration officials who recognized that Johnson's nomination was impossible. Hancock "has many elements of strength," reported the *New York World,* "and scores of earnest supporters." Among these, early on, were Senator James Doolittle of Wisconsin and the former congressman Daniel Voorhees of Indiana.[9]

Hancock was undoubtedly a major candidate, but his advocates soon found themselves in a contest for which they were little prepared. The movement was largely an amateur one, generated by admiration for the general and a recognition of the position in which his record and abilities happened to place him. The Hancock men soon learned of the subtleties and devices of big-time politics. They found the name of McClellan brought forth as more worthy of soldier support, and they could discover little strength in the West, where the "peace" men opposed him and the soft-money forces decided that Hancock was not one of them. The governor of Pennsylvania, where Hancock might have expected support, said the general might do for the second place on the ticket, and was well regarded for the first, but Pennsylvania would remain noncommital before the convention. There were whispers about his connection with the execution of Mary Surratt, and Roman Catholics were told that he had prevented that doomed woman's priest from attending her. Even Sherman thought that Hancock had "too many old charges to carry."[10]

The Pennsylvania situation particularly miffed Hancock, who felt that he might have won if the delegation had been instructed for him. Unfortunately, as he wrote later, "the delegates were appointed before I really came on the field, so that I had no voice in the matter or my friends."[11]

What it all meant, of course, was that the 1868 nomination was up for grabs going into the convention, and no one could predict the course of the meeting. Winfield Scott Hancock, amateur supporters and all, appeared to have as good a chance as any. Hancock's workers gathered at the Astor House, while the Pendleton crowd put up at the Masonic Hall and other delegations and candidates filled up the rest of Manhattan's leading hostelries.

Another element to be added to the confused picture was the Democratic Soldiers and Sailors Convention, scheduled to meet in New York at the same time as the party convention. The politicians were rather uneasy about this meeting, feeling that its aim was to stampede the party in the direction of Hancock, or McClellan, or perhaps even Frank Blair. "In whose interest is this military representation called?" Sanford Church wrote suspiciously to Tilden. "If it is gone into we had better direct it." The Hancock people certainly hoped that the presence of the veterans would help their man win. But the veterans, though hopeful of Hancock's success, were not trying to dictate a nomination; they planned to urge the selection of a candidate who had not opposed the war. The Soldiers and Sailors Convention was organized and led by Generals Gordon Granger, James Steedman, Henry Slocum, and others in an effort to keep the Republicans from winning all the veterans' votes and sweeping the northern states.[12]

As the party delegates gathered and the finishing touches were put on the new Tammany Hall, where the convention sessions would be conducted, the outlines of the struggle to come could be seen. Pendleton would have the lead at the start. Johnson would start out with a good number of votes but would then decline. Hancock would be well supported, though to what extent such support would be translated into delegate votes was not clear. Hendricks would become a factor if no choice was made early. The southern delegates, not wishing to give a candidate the burden of having been chosen by ex-rebels, would follow the lead of the North in picking a nominee. And, somewhere along the way, the Chase boom might materialize. The shadowy schemes of the New York leaders were still too obscure to fathom. Though the outline of the convention battle was discernible, its end could only be guessed at. "Very few," wrote one observer, "have the assurance to venture an opinion as to the ultimate result of the deliberations of the Convention."[13]

At 11 o'clock in the morning on the Fourth of July, the Tammany Society held a ceremony to take formal possession of its newly finished building, on 14th street between Irving Place and Third Avenue, near Union Square. As the Tammany ceremony ended, the building was filling with delegates to the Democratic convention, called for noon. At 12 o'clock August Belmont, as national chairman, banged his gavel, called the meeting to order, and welcomed the delegates to New York. He then turned the gavel over to the temporary chairman. After a brief squabble over rules, the convention was adjourned to July 6, the intervening day being a Sunday.[14]

In the meantime, in the hotel lobbies and caucus rooms, the real business of the convention was being transacted. Because of the size of New York City, the impact of the convention's presence was not so great as it would have been in another locale, and the delegates were scattered among more hotels than they would have been elsewhere. For this reason, the usual lobbying and horse trading among the different camps was more difficult. But within the individual headquarters there was much activity.

The Chase people were counting heavily on New York. Their expectation was that New York, on the first ballot, would cast its thirty-three votes for Seymour, who would rise from his seat in the delegation, decline to have his name supported, and then speak eloquently on behalf of the chief justice, thereby winning the New York delegation and—it was hoped—triggering a movement to Chase. However, matters started going awry for Chase. Seymour's agreement to serve as permanent president of the convention took him off the floor and made it impossible for New York to cast its first-ballot vote for him. The New York delegation, at its caucus on July 4, chose to pledge its votes to Sanford E. Church, who, while certainly a prominent party leader, was not dreamed of by anyone as a potential nominee. For as long as Church was kept forward, however, the New York bloc was on ice.[15]

Meanwhile, the Pendleton leaders were expressing to all who would listen their anger at what they felt was a betrayal on the part of Hendricks. He had been with Pendleton originally, they claimed, and his becoming a candidate now was unfair. Besides their pique at Hendricks, the Pendleton forces suspected deep down that if the convention had been held anywhere but in New York—in Cincinnati, say, or in Chicago—their man would have stood a much better chance of winning.[16]

Most of the political activity was concentrated at the Fifth Avenue, St. Nicholas, and New York hotels, where the most delegations were quartered.

Here what there was of wire-pulling, glad-handing, and backslapping took place as the partisans of the various candidates attempted to win converts (or second-choice commitments) for their causes. The rulers of the lobbies were gossip and rumor. Before the balloting started, all candidacies were viable. With the strong possibility of a deadlock, the backers of the favorite-son candidates, Asa Packer of Pennsylvania, Governor James English of Connecticut, Joel Parker of New Jersey, and Senator James Doolittle of Wisconsin, pushed their men as compromise choices. The New York leaders kept their own counsel; they would vote for Sanford E. Church.[17]

On Monday, July 6, the convention resumed, and the first order of business was the election of Horatio Seymour as permanent president. The assemblage then heard from two prominent Democratic generals, Henry Slocum and Thomas Ewing, Jr., representatives of the Soldiers and Sailors Convention meeting at Cooper Union. Earlier in the day, at the soldiers and sailors meeting, the veterans had presented a resolution which urged, among other things, that the Democrats nominate Hancock for president. There seemed little doubt that Hancock was the first choice of a large majority of the veteran delegates, but the introduction of this resolution stirred up a minority bloc, apparently favoring Francis Blair, which thereupon caused such turmoil, disorder, and confusion that no vote was taken on the resolution. Because the veterans' convention never formally expressed itself on the choice of a candidate, its ultimate influence on the Democrats' deliberations was less than it might otherwise have been. Obviously, Hancock's candidacy was affected *pro tanto*.[18]

July 7 saw the adoption of the party platform and the start of balloting for president. Seymour made a ruling that the two-thirds rule for selection of a candidate, already adopted, meant two-thirds of all members of the convention, not just those voting. An unexceptionable ruling, really, but it appeared to make stalemate more likely. And it was in a stalemate that the New York leaders would play their cards.[19]

When the states were called for nominations, the first to respond was Connecticut, which presented its governor, English. Next, Samuel J. Anderson of Maine nominated Hancock, who, he said, "unites in himself all the best characteristics of the most available candidates," a man who "fought well for the nation which placed him in command, but held forth the hand of mercy to the enemy when brought beneath his arms." A minority of the Maine delegation then named Pendleton, and New Jersey followed with its former governor, Joel Parker. When New York was called, Tilden presented the illustrious name of Sanford E. Church, and General George McCook of Ohio then nominated Pendleton with a one-sentence speech. Judge George W. Woodward of Pennsylvania, in an overlong speech, brought forth industrialist Asa Packer, and Tennessee presented Andrew Johnson. Finally, Senator Doolittle was put in nomination by Wisconsin, and all those that were to be formally presented had been named. The nominating-speech business was much less advanced in 1868 than it was to become, and it was all over in short order. Three prominent names, as everyone noticed, had not been mentioned—Chase, Hendricks, and Seymour.[20]

At last the time for which everyone had come to New York had arrived. All present paid close attention as the clerk called the roll of the states for the first ballot. The results showed Pendleton with 105 votes, far short of the 211½ total needed for nomination. President Johnson stood second with 65 (all but 4 from the South), followed by Church with 34, Hancock with 33½, Packer with his 26 from Pennsylvania, English 16, Parker and Doolitle 13 each, 8½ for Reverdy Johnson of Maryland, 2½ for Hendricks, and a half-vote for Frank Blair. Hancock's first ballot votes included all 7 from Louisiana and all 7 from Mississippi, 4½ from Maine, 11 out of 12 from Massachusetts, and 2 each from Missouri and New Hampshire.[21]

On the second ballot, the president's strength started to erode, as Texas switched to Hancock and Virginia to Blair. Pendleton led on this ballot with 104, showing no progress, as Johnson declined to 52 and Hancock moved up to 40½. After a motion to recess was defeated, the third ballot was taken, with Pendleton going up to 119½, Johnson falling off to 34½, and Hancock moving into the second position with 45½, having picked up 6 North Carolina votes.[22]

The clerk called the roll again for the fourth ballot, and during the course of it the North Carolina delegation caused a sensation by casting 9 votes for Horatio Seymour. There was much cheering, until Seymour came forward and said, "I must not be nominated by this convention, as I could not accept the nomination if tendered, which I do not expect. My own inclinations prompted me to decline at the outset; my honor compels me to do so now." Pendelton stayed steady at 118½, Hancock slipped a little to 43½, as 3 from Florida failed to replace the North Carolina votes lost to Seymour, and Johnson was now down to 32, one vote behind Church.[23]

Two more ballots followed, and then the convention voted to adjourn to the following day. At the end of the sixth ballot, Pendleton still led with 122½, Hancock stood second with 47, Church still had his 33 New York votes, and Hendricks was fourth with 30, having climbed slowly but steadily all day. Packer had 27 and Andrew Johnson only 21. The deadlock everyone had predicted was now clearly evident, fostered in large part by the persistence of the New York, Pennsylvania, Wisconsin, and New Jersey delegations in keeping 84 votes tied up with favorite-son candidates. It would now be seen what a night in the hotel rooms and watering holes of Manhattan would produce.[24]

The reporter for the New York World wrote that there was a general impression, when the session of July 7 ended, "that there was no chance for the nomination of Pendleton, and the idea was quite prevalent that Hendricks would be the winning man." But the Ohio men were determined that Hendricks, of all those in contention, should not be the victor, because they felt that he had played Pendleton false. There was talk that Hancock was a good bet for the second spot on the ticket, "yet his immediate supporters do not definitely admit that he cannot be selected for the first place."[25]

As the delegates gathered on the morning of July 8, there was much excitement as all waited to see whether any dramatic changes would be manifested. Before the balloting started, the Indiana delegation formally presented Thomas A. Hendricks. Then the clerk called the roll. Pendleton and Hendricks both increased their totals, the former up 15 votes to 137½, the latter up nine to 39½. Hancock fell off slightly to 42½, while Blair, Parker, and Andrew Johnson all declined. The eighth ballot started immediately, with Pendleton again gaining. By the time it was finished, "Gentleman George" was up to 156½, only 2½ short of a majority. A highly significant event took place, however, when the New York delegation returned from a caucus to switch its 33 votes from Church to Hendricks, who went up to 75. Hancock declined to 28, as his Louisiana and North Carolina votes left him.[26]

Suspicious observers felt that New York's swing to Hendricks was still part of the Chase game. They reasoned that it was too early to bring Chase forward while Pendleton was still strong and that Hendricks, as a westerner, was the man to cause attrition in the Pendleton ranks. In addition, because of the feeling of the Pendleton people against Hendricks, it was assumed that Hendricks could not achieve the two-thirds required for victory. Thus, support for Hendricks at this stage was the best way to preserve the stalemate. And stalemate would lead to Chase—or to someone else not now in contention.[27]

As it developed, the eighth ballot was George Pendleton's high-water mark. He was done in, apparently, by the continuing growth of support for Hendricks, which fact increased the bitter hostility the Pendleton men felt against the Hoosier senator. On the next ballot, Pendleton fell off 12½ votes, to 144, while Hendricks moved up to 80½ and Hancock recouped slightly, to 34½. On the next three roll calls there was little change among the three leaders, although there was some excitement in the galleries when a California delegate cast a half-vote for Chase on the twelfth ballot. Those in on the Chase intrigue apparently felt that the time for a move had not yet come, so nothing developed from the vote; New York kept on voting for Hendricks.

On the thirteenth ballot, both Pendleton and Hendricks declined. Pendleton lost 12, to 134½, his lowest total of the day, while Hendricks fell from 89 to 81. Hancock started a surge at this point, gaining from 30 to 48½ as both Virginia and North Carolina switched to him. On the fourteenth, Hancock moved up to 56 votes, while Pendleton fell to 130 and Hendricks gained slightly to 84½.[28]

On the next ballot, Pennsylvania finally abandoned Asa Packer, throwing its 26 votes to its other son, Hancock, who finished the roll call with 79½ votes, only three behind Hendricks. One observer wrote that the action of the Keystone State delegation "had something of magnetic influence, which the demonstration of New York in favor of Mr. Hendricks had failed to exert." The reason, he felt, was that there was "in the name of Hancock a prestige of success." Another reporter wrote that the Pennsylvania switch "was remarked by all as a beginning of the real work of nomination." It produced great applause. Hancock now had momentum in his favor; how far it would carry him would soon be learned.[29]

On the sixteenth ballot, Hancock jumped 34 votes, mainly from the South, to a total of 113½, moving into the first position. Pendleton fell to 107½, out of the lead for the first time, while Hendricks declined to 70½. On the next ballot, Hancock made another sizable gain, going to 137½, despite efforts by Tilden to move an adjournment—a clear indication that the New Yorkers no longer felt in control of things. Hendricks had moved into second position, with 80 votes, while Pendleton, sinking fast, fell to 70½.[30]

On the eighteenth ballot, Hancock's total increased again, to 144½, and momentum seemed to be working very well for him. Hendricks had 87, and Pendleton received on this call only 56½ votes, exactly 100 fewer than his peak of several hours earlier. Hancock seemed on his way to a nomination, when an altercation arose in the Illinois delegation, some sort of a skirmish raised by one noisy delegate over the application of the unit rule. When the squabble would not die down, another motion for adjournment was made. On the motion, it appeared that the "nays" clearly outnumbered the "ayes," but Seymour announced from the chair that the motion had carried and adjourned the convention until morning. The amazed Hancock supporters could do nothing but watch the presiding officer's back as he walked away.[31]

With Hancock now far in front of the field, a cannon in front of the hall was fired in celebration of his anticipated victory, and some New York papers announced that he had all but won. But the politicians knew that the adjournment had in all likelihood been fatal to Hancock's chances. The one eventuality the intriguers from New York had failed to provide for was a stampede in favor of Hancock. It is very likely that one or two more ballots would have brought victory to the general, and the effect of Seymour's ruling "against the fact," as one reporter put it, was to cut Hancock off from those one or two more ballots. Hancock himself, working on this day as on others at his headquarters in Washington, recognized that the adjournment was a "movement hostile to himself." One editor wrote that "the adjournment . . . was to fix up things." Or, as Gideon Welles put it, "there will be intrigue to-night."[32]

"A large part of the night was spent in scheming and bargaining," wrote one who was there. As a result, he said, "the friends of General Hancock found with dismay that the interruption of the tide of enthusiasm in favor of their candidate was fatal, and that already many who had helped to make up his last promising vote were preparing to desert him." Because the general refused to authorize any binding commitments, his friends' hands were tied. Another reporter wrote: ". . . no other names than Chase and Seymour are much talked of to-night, though some friends of Hancock believe he has still a chance."[33]

The first action of the day when the delegates reconvened on July 9 was the formal presentation of Blair's name by James Broadhead of Missouri. California then presented Justice Stephen J. Field. Finally, Clement Vallandigham withdrew the beaten Pendleton's name from further contention, and the nineteenth ballot was ready to begin. As the delegations answered the clerk's call, it was clear that Hancock was losing a little here, a little there, and not gaining enough to offset the losses. Toward the end of the ballot, he picked up Tennessee's 10 votes, which had gone to Andrew Johnson on the last ballot the day before. This gave Hancock a net of 135½ votes, down 9 votes. Hendricks rose to 107½. The big break that never came for Hancock was in the Ohio delegation. With Pendleton out of the running, Ohio cast its 22 votes for, of all people, Asa Packer, long since discarded by Pennsylvania. Had Ohio, in its wisdom, cast those 22 votes for Hancock, giving him, despite the untimely adjournment and all the nighttime dealing, a gain of 13 votes over the last ballot of the day before, the psychological boost would have been incalculable. Such a vote was not inconceivable, for on the next two ballots Hancock received 11 of the Ohio votes, with the rest going to English, whom Connecticut had dropped the day before. What the Ohioans were trying to accomplish with these votes for Packer and English remains obscure. The two nominations Ohio feared most, Hendricks and Chase, became more likely as Hancock declined. Ohio's caucus the night before had resolved that under no circumstances would it support Chase, its old-time enemy. Yet Chase still remained a likely result of stalemate, and Asa Packer and James English meant stalemate.[34]

In any event, Hancock declined on the nineteenth ballot, and this effectively ended his chances. On the twentieth ballot, he increased slightly to 142½, with the 11 Ohio votes offsetting minor losses. Hendricks, on this ballot, moved up to 121. On the next ballot, Hancock lost Arkansas to Hendricks and 6 votes from Massachusetts, 4 of them to Chase, slipping to 135½ while Hendricks pulled up to 132. At this point, Vallandigham learned that Indiana and Pennsylvania leaders were talking of pooling the Hendricks and Hancock votes to select the former for the head of the ticket and the latter for second place.[35]

Vallandigham, alarmed, went immediately to Tilden and urged that New York make its move to Chase promptly. This, he felt, was the only way to defeat Hendricks. Tilden was armed with the decision of the New York caucus made that morning, to swing the vote to Chase as soon as Hendricks began to decline; nine or ten other delegations were said to be ready to move to Chase as soon as New York did. The only problem was that Hendricks was not declining; Tilden could legitimately refuse Vallandigham's request. Besides, Tilden was no great admirer of the chief justice, and he knew that Ohio had to come up with some other plan to prevent the nomination of Hendricks. Logic dictated that this plan would be to stampede the convention for Seymour, to which Tilden would not be at all averse. Accordingly, Tilden told Vallandigham the time was not ripe for New York to drop Hendricks; the Chase coup would not take place yet.[36]

When Ohio was called on the next roll call, General George McCook rose and cast Ohio's 22 votes for Horatio Seymour, "against his inclination, but no longer against his honor." Seymour came to the front of the stage to protest the votes for him, in a rambling talk which concluded with the words, "your candidate I cannot be." He then left the stage. It was curious that, though Seymour was said to be strongly in favor of the Chase boom, he never pronounced those words which might really have taken him off the hook, "You must select Chase" or something along that line.

After Seymour left, Vallandigham said that Ohio stood by its vote and asked others to join it. Francis Kernan of Utica, one of the influential New York leaders, from Seymour's home town, said that Horatio must let the judgment of the convention prevail. After all this, curiously, the balloting continued much as it had before, with Hendricks climbing to 145½ and Hancock dropping to 103½, without much more impact from the attempted coup for Seymour. The last state, however, was Wisconsin; her delegation announced that it was dropping Doolittle, for whom it had voted unswervingly from the beginning, in favor of Seymour. That did it. Kentucky, Massachusetts, and North Carolina then switched their votes, and the rout was on. In the bedlam that followed, every state soon changed its vote to Seymour, with Tilden, at the end, rising to announce New York's vote for its former governor. "The convention," said one writer, "abandoned itself to uproar; and while some of the delegates were yet looking in each other's faces in wonder and perplexity, the announcement was made that Horatio Seymour had received the votes of every state, and the cannon in the street below began to fire. . . ."[37]

After a recess of an hour, the delegates returned, to nominate Blair for vice-president and then to adjourn *sine die*. Hancock was not considered for the second spot because Pennsylvania's proximity to New York would rob the ticket of geographical balance. It was just as well, for in Seymour the Democrats had made a strange and unwise choice.

With Grant as the Republican nominee, the last thing the Democratic party should have done was send forth a nominee whose candidacy made the prosecution of the late war an issue. Against Grant, they could never win on such an issue. Seymour was a hero within the compact ranks of his party, but his legalistic nit-picking against the policies of the Lincoln administration had given him at large the image of an opponent of the war who used his control of the largest state in the Union to frustrate the war effort in every way he could. While this was not a true picture, the Democrats took him at their risk against the hero of Vicksburg and Richmond.

Moreover, the party need not have incurred all of Seymour's liabilities. Whether the New York leaders ever seriously intended to forward Chase, or whether their game all along was the nomination of Seymour, as Gideon

Welles proclaimed in his diary, the obvious alternative was Winfield Hancock. He had no problems with Democratic orthodoxy, his war record was untouchable, and his record on reconstruction was all that any party member could ask. He was popular and he was handsome and he would at once neutralize the prime, if not only, asset of the Republican nominee. Observers at the time and later felt that Hancock, if nominated, probably would have won. The Republicans were overjoyed, first, with the nomination of Seymour and, second, with the defeat of Hancock. Carl Schurz had written, before the convention, "if a man like General Hancock shall be nominated, we shall have to work very hard." With Seymour, they could keep Grant quiet and haul out the bloody shirt.[38]

When Hancock received the news of Seymour's victory, he went to call on the president, telling reporters that he never thought the nomination was coming to him, so that he had no great feelings about it one way or the other. Later, when his friends returned from New York and reported on the late convention, he seemed convinced that he had been tricked out of the nomination by New York politicians. Indeed, there was hardly any other way to regard the action of Seymour in adjourning the convention on July 8 when the vote was against it. But, as one reporter put it, "his pride in his position as a soldier is a bulwark against political disappointment," and he kept his reactions to himself.[39]

Nevertheless, when the Republicans put out stories that the general was miffed at the outcome of the convention, Hancock took the opportunity to make his views known. A friend from St. Louis, a lawyer named Samuel T. Glover, writing to him on July 13, alluded to the assertions of the opposition that he was dissatisfied with Seymour's nomination. On July 17 Hancock wrote back: "Those who suppose that I do not acquiesce in the work of the National Democratic convention, or that I do not sincerely desire the election of its nominee, know very little of my character." He never sought the presidency for his own sake, he said. "My only wish was to promote, if I could, the good of the country and to rebuke the spirit of revolution which had invaded every sacred precinct of liberty." Had he been the nominee, he went on, "I should have considered it a tribute, not to me, but to principles which I had proclaimed and protected; but shall I cease to regard these principles, because by the judgment of mutual political friends another has been appointed to put them in execution? Never! Never!" This letter was made public, but E. L. Godkin, the editor of the *Nation,* still wrote that in Hancock the Seymour-Blair ticket would not have a very ardent supporter.[40]

As the campaign moved along, the Democratic folly in choosing Seymour became ever more clear. Former Union party adherents and War Democrats were lukewarm at best, if they were not actually supporting Grant. Seymour was thrown on the defensive, as incidents from his war governorship were dredged up. On October 1 the nominee wrote to Tilden, suggesting that Hancock and other soldiers be invited to Philadelphia for a reception. "I fear we have neglected the soldiers too much," Seymour said.

"It seems to me that some military exhibition on our side is the only thing to be done before the Pennsylvania election." Tilden sent this note on to Hancock, urging his attendance. On October 10 Hancock wrote back to Tilden, declining to become involved. His old Gettysburg wound was threatening to reopen, and he thought army officers should not participate actively in political campaigns. "Still, the crisis is of such vital moment that I might probably have acted differently," he wrote. "But neither time nor health permits me to act." The *Springfield Republican* sneered that Hancock's wound "has never kept him from doing anything which he has wanted very much to do." This comment was unfair—the old wound was in fact giving a lot of trouble at the time—but it was obvious that Hancock did not feel that trying to bail out Seymour was a matter of much moment to him.[41]

The Republicans won all four of the states holding October elections— Ohio, Indiana, Iowa, and Pennsylvania. An effort was then commenced to dump the Seymour-Blair ticket and to replace the presidential candidate with Hancock, Chase, or Hendricks. Hancock quickly squelched any use of his name in such a connection, and he urged that the movement be ended. Seymour stayed on, eventually absorbing a substantial defeat in electoral votes (though a surprisingly narrow one in popular votes) in November.[42]

The nation would have, in March 1869, a military man as its president. But it would be Ulysses S. Grant, not Winfield Scott Hancock.

TWENTY FIVE

Return to the Plains

Grant took office on March 4, 1869; Washington, with the rest of America, waited anxiously for clues to the kind of president the taciturn soldier would be. It did not have to wait long.

The new president's cabinet was a total surprise, a curious mélange of wealthy men, inconsequential men, in one case a legally ineligible man. At the same time, the nation's military leaders were confronted with a shuffling of *their* assignments. On March 5 the adjutant-general issued orders, by direction of the president, that changed the posts of nine general officers, among them Meade, back to the Division of the Atlantic, Sheridan, once again to Louisiana, and Hancock, to the Department of Dakota. In addition, in a devastating blow to Meade, Grant ignored seniority and named Sheridan to the vacancy at lieutenant general created when Sherman moved up to the general's slot left open by Grant's resignation. Meade called Sheridan's appointment "the cruelest and meanest act of injustice." He was not the only general outraged that day. The dispatch of Hancock to Dakota was a piece of vindictive pettiness. The Department of Dakota was considered a military backwater, "the least important of the three in the Division in which I was placed," wrote Hancock. The other departments in the division had two and three times the number of soldiers as were in Dakota, and both were commanded by Hancock's juniors. Besides, Grant and Sherman were well aware of Hancock's preference for the Department of the Missouri, because of Allie's home in St. Louis. Finally, as a major general, Hancock should have commanded a division rather than a department. But he had crossed Grant, and for that he would suffer. His protest of "what I deemed a want of due consideration" was ignored, and he dutifully shipped off to St. Paul.[1]

The Department of Dakota included the state of Minnesota and the territories of Dakota and Montana. Its most prominent geographical feature, other than the ranges of the Rocky Mountains in its far western reaches, was the upper Missouri River, which served as conduit, divider, and provider. One observer spoke of the beautiful river flowing "in unbroken solitude through desolate hills and silent, uninhabited prairies. . . . Herds of buffalo trampled the low banks of the broad river, and the thirsty wolf lapped unmolested the waters of its many tributaries." The river and the prairie dominated people's thinking about the region.[2]

Among the Indians located in the department were Sioux, Northern Cheyennes, Crows, Mandans, Chippewas, Poncas, Assiniboines, Flatheads, Blackfeet, Gros Ventres, and Arikaras, more than a quarter of all the Indians left in the country. Hancock found, in his entire command, covering an area that stretched almost twelve hundred miles from east to west, the grand total of 1,682 soldiers. There were, in Minnesota, two posts and three companies made up of 155 men; in Dakota, ten posts and twenty-seven companies with 1,121 men; and in huge, distant Montana, three posts and ten companies with 406 men.[3]

Though the army starved it, the Department of Dakota was not a placid command. Minnesota was peaceful enough now, but Dakota and Montana saw much conflict between the army and the Indian. Hancock immediately embarked upon an inspection trip through his far-flung department. He visited every post under his command, examined the troops, investigated the status of supply and ordnance, and drew conclusions in his mind as to how prepared his force was to accomplish its mission. He covered about 6,800 miles in his tour, which he called "a hard, toilsome, dangerous trip," traveling by boat, horseback, and stage. He was not happy with what he saw. "The number of men at each station," Hancock wrote, "I found to be so small that . . . there were too few for active service in case of an emergency requiring them to take the field, their strength being in all cases scarcely sufficient to meet a vigorous attack from hostile Indians, and in some cases too little to do so with much hope of success."[4]

On July 2 Hancock and his staff steamed into Fort Stevenson and held a council on board his boat with several chiefs of the Mandans, Gros Ventres, and Arikaras. Hancock listened sympathetically to the plight of these tribes, ravaged by disease and starvation, and took what steps he could to relieve their sufferings. Hancock had learned his lesson thoroughly from the unhappy experience in Kansas. For this council he prepared, he did his homework, and he let his own frank and kindly nature govern his actions. These peaceful tribes were most appreciative of his efforts and attitudes. One of the chiefs present that July day was to say later of his meeting with Hancock and its sequel that it was a "rift in the passing clouds in the welfare of my people—a ray of light that did not long linger."[5]

The Department of Dakota was divided into three districts, Minnesota, Montana, and the Middle District, and the independent post of Fort Buford. Buford had been built in 1866, far up the Missouri at its confluence with the Yellowstone, and the Indians hated it. "Fort Buford," Hancock said, ". . . is exceedingly offensive to the hostile Sioux." Its outposts were attacked again and again, and its stock was forever being ridden off by the Indians. The fort was, Hancock wrote, "constantly in a state of siege." The garrison was small, and the fort was far from possible reinforcement. The Sioux considered Buford an intolerable intrusion into their traditional hunting grounds, and they did what they could to force the army to remove it. The Sioux, it should be remembered, were flushed with the victory of Red Cloud in 1868, when the army agreed in the Treaty of Fort Laramie to abandon its fort in the Powder River country and to give up the Bozeman Trail to Montana. Red Cloud's warriors had shared the joy of setting a torch to Fort C. F. Smith and to Fort Phil Kearny, and they anticipated the same treatment for Buford. "It has not heretofore commanded the respect of the Indians," Hancock reported, "nor been always able to protect its herds." To see to the permanence of Fort Buford was now a part of his mission.[6]

When Hancock took over, the commander in the Middle District was Colonel David S. Stanley, while Colonel George Sykes, well known to Hancock from the Army of the Potomac, was in charge in Minnesota. In far-off Montana, just shifted from Fort Stevenson and the Middle District, was Colonel Philippe Regis de Trobriand, whom Hancock knew all too well. In early 1868 Trobriand's memoir of the war, *Quatre Ans de Campagne à l'Armée du Potomac*, had appeared in Paris; the book included an attack on Hancock as one who showed partiality and preference for those without military merit but with political influence. Though he was not responsible for the change, Hancock surely had no regrets at Trobriand's removal from Fort Stevenson to distant Fort Shaw in Montana.[7]

With the limited force at his command, Hancock faced four primary assignments: the maintenance of Fort Buford, the safety of surveying parties for the Northern Pacific Railroad, the protection of the Indian agencies along the Missouri River, and the security of the far-flung mining settlements of the Gallatin Valley of Montana. The commander's record would be judged on his success in carrying out these assignments. Before he was finished, however, Hancock would be confronted with one additional task— protecting the Black Hills against the incursions of importunate white settlers.

Hancock tried to limit the problems facing him. He recommended that the Indian reservations be located temporarily on the eastern bank of the Missouri. "The river," he said, "would then be a formidable barrier between the well and evil-disposed—not always easily passed and readily controlled." Those Indians who were friendly and ready to settle down would be protected in their efforts to farm the land. "From the experiences of the past summer," he wrote of 1868, "some of the Indians have become discouraged, and declare that they will not again, under such circumstances, try to raise crops on the western bank of the Missouri River."[8]

In writing this recommendation, General Hancock overlooked the force that would change his mission from year to year—the sheer power of the westward movement of the white settler. His 1869 report stated that "the Sioux dominate on the plains," and this was true when he wrote it. But the Sioux had met their match, as the progress of the next several years would demonstrate. As matters developed, Hancock had only to conduct a holding action along the Missouri. Once Fort Buford and the agencies near the river had been preserved from destruction by the Indians, the flow of white settlers made future dangers remote. In fact, the white settlers shortly came to dominate the plains, with the Sioux fighting a doomed rearguard action.[9]

Farther west, Hancock established a camp, manned by one company, near a town called Diamond City, to protect the mining settlements in southwestern Montana from Blackfoot raiding parties. In addition, he received permission to construct a new fort close to the border, where the Red River of the North flowed into Canada; work was started on Fort Pembina in the spring of 1870. Unsettled conditions created by the Méti Rebellion at Fort Garry (now Winnipeg) caused fears that a sizable contingent of Sioux, driven from Minnesota and Dakota in 1862 and bitterly antagonistic to Americans, might head south on the warpath, to even old scores. Fort Pembina served its purpose; the hostile Sioux stayed in Canada.[10]

In the winter of 1870, an action in Hancock's department attracted nationwide attention. Sheridan, the division commander, planned a winter expedition against bands of Blackfoot Indians, who were historically hostile to whites and who had for two or three years been raiding the settlers in the Gallatin Valley in Montana.[11] Hancock and Trobriand, commanding the district of Montana, made their dispositions for the march. Major Eugene M. Baker was placed in command of the expedition, which was kept as secret as possible. Baker left Fort Ellis, at the bend of the Gallatin River, with four companies of cavalry on January 6, 1870, headed north. Eight days later he reached Fort Shaw, on the Sun River near the present Great Falls, Montana, where he rested for five days and received reinforcements. On January 19 Baker resumed the march. On the morning of January 23, at 8 o'clock, his force surprised a Blackfoot camp on the Marias River, killing 173 Indians. Of these, 53 were women and children; 100 other women and children were captured and later released. Baker returned to Fort Ellis and arrived there on February 6, having marched six hundred miles during a month of bitter cold weather.[12]

Unfortunately, Baker and the rest of the military soon learned that what they considered a highly successful punitive mission was being trumpeted with horror through the East as "the Baker massacre." An agent for the Blackfeet got into the hands of the eastern press a report alleging that only fifteen of those killed by Baker were warriors, with the rest being women, children, and old men. Baker's report, and the army's explanation of the marauding nature of the tribe attacked, never caught up with the first sensational story of a dastardly massacre. After the attacks at Sand Creek and the Washita, people expected nothing better from the military. Baker and the army were convicted by public opinion.[13]

Sherman, Sheridan, and Hancock came to Baker's defense, but their words had little effect on the public outcry. Hancock wrote that it was unfortunate that "some women and children were accidentally killed" but that the number was greatly overstated in the newspapers. He explained that "in affairs of this kind," there is always "a certain proportion of accidental killing," especially in an early-morning attack. "It is a necessary element of success to fire into the lodges at the outset to drive the Indians out to an open contest." Considering the hardships endured by Baker and his men in getting to the camp on the Marias, Hancock said, "I think the command is entitled to the special commendation of the military authorities and the hearty thanks of the nation." Anyway, he said, "the lesson administered to the Indians has been salutary in its effects, and highly beneficial to the interests of Montana. I predict it will be a long time before serious trouble may be again apprehended from the Blackfeet."[14]

Although Hancock's participation in the Baker affair on the Marias River may have been at a great distance, he was actively involved in another Indian problem in his department, the protection of the Black Hills. The Black Hills covered an area sixty miles wide and one hundred miles from north to south in the southwestern corner of Dakota Territory. Dark and wooded outcroppings rising more than 3,000 feet above the surrounding high plains, the Black Hills were considered holy by the Sioux. Indians had long visited the hills, but they did not stay long there. Travel in the hills was not easy, for the deep canyons were clotted with dense and tangled thickets of aspen, birch, and willow and were often flooded by beaver dams. Alternating with the canyons were limestone and sandstone cliffs, while frequent violent storms, mountain lions, and grizzly bears added to the hostile nature of the Black Hills. Superstition and prudence confined the Sioux to the foothills; they had no wish to risk the displeasure of the Great Spirit, dwelling in the higher reaches of the mountains.

The Sioux could hardly hide such an outstanding geographic feature, and several white explorers passed through or observed the Black Hills. The Sioux knew there was gold in the Black Hills, and they tried to keep this knowledge from outsiders. In 1857, however, Lieutenant Gouverneur K. Warren conducted a military and scientific expedition of seventeen men to the area; his report set forth the fact that he had found gold there and his opinion that the hills would be important in any wars with the Indians of the northern plains. With this report, the Indian loss of the Black Hills became inevitable; only the timing of the white takeover was in question.[15]

Nevertheless, by the Treaty of Fort Laramie in 1868, the Black Hills, with the rest of the southern Dakota Territory west of the Missouri River, had been confirmed to the Sioux. It then became the duty of the army to keep the turbulent and assertive whites of the frontier out of the hills. Of all the missions the army was called on to perform in the nineteenth-century West, the one it usually carried out with the least success was that of protecting Indians from whites. Still, it turned away several attempts by white men out of Yankton to get to the Black Hills. But there was always another group ambitious to try its luck in finding the fabled gold of the hills.

In early 1872, recruiting for an expedition into the Black Hills under a Sioux City editor named Charles Collins was proceeding at a brisk pace in the towns along the Missouri when Winfield Scott Hancock put his foot down. On March 26 a proclamation over the commanding general's signature was issued from his headquarters in St. Paul, referring to the inquiries being received there "in regard to the reputed gold discoveries" in the Black Hills "and asking if expeditions, presumed to be now in process of organization, will be permitted to penetrate that region." The answer, Hancock stated explicitly, was "no." "The faith of the Government," he said, was pledged to protect the Black Hills "from the encroachment of, or occupation by, the whites." Accordingly, he would prevent, with his troops if necessary, any expeditions from "visiting or 'prospecting' the region."[16]

The Collins expedition then fizzled out. A group of eighteen enlisted men deserted from Fort Randall to go off and look for gold in the Black Hills, but they were quickly captured. Hancock's intervention kept the hills inviolate for 1872. It would remain for other army commanders, who did not understand the pledged faith of the government as Hancock did, to make the Black Hills available for white penetration. The famous Custer Expedition of 1874, under the aegis of Phil Sheridan, who called for "the erection of a large military post" in the region, would signal the actual opening of the Black Hills.[17]

The principal activity in 1872 on the northern plains was connected with the ongoing construction of the Northern Pacific railroad. Hancock sent out expeditions to protect surveying parties engaged in fixing the location of the line for future construction. The encounters of these parties with large numbers of Sioux and Cheyennes made it clear that railroad building was not to progress unimpeded. Hancock recommended that "to succeed in the construction of the railroad between the Missouri and Yellowstone Rivers, and along the latter to the Gallatin Valley, Montana, it will require much larger bodies of troops than we now have disposable in this department," particularly more cavalry.[18]

Hancock had now had three years' experience with the Sioux, and he felt a healthy respect for them. Building the railroad through the heart of their great hunting grounds was a direct challenge to the Sioux chieftains, and he had little doubt that, as things presently stood, they could "effectually prevent the operation of the road." Consequently, he reported, relations with the Indians must "be more clearly defined before the road is completed." Hancock's solution, "but merciful and just to the Indians as well as to the whites," was to put them on reservations "and rigidly keep them there." He wanted an end to the incredible but prevalent policy whereby "our charity to the Indians" in the form of supplies and arms became "the means of encouraging war against the troops of the Government"; supplies should be issued to families or even to individuals, and arms suitable only for the hunt should be furnished. What he contemplated was a reservation system accompanied by general and honest treatment, not the hodge-podge actually in effect of on-again-off-again reservations administered by mean-spirited, dishonest agents.[19]

Hancock played a small but significant role in another aspect of the development of the area south of the Gallatin. When Lieutenant Gustavus C. Doane of the Second Cavalry made a report of an expedition to the upper reaches of the Yellowstone, describing in detail the region of geysers, bubbling mud, deep canyons, and sulphurous waters, Hancock sent the report on to the adjutant-general, recommending that it be published. On February 24, 1871, the secretary of war communicated it to the Senate, and this was one of the influences which led to the congressional establishment in 1872 of Yellowstone as the country's first national park.[20]

While inspection tours and Indian fighting were the more eventful occurrences in a prairie command, they were the exception rather than the rule. Most of the duties Hancock described as being "of the passive character usual to times of peace on the frontier, viz, the construction and repairs of quarters and store-houses, guarding public property, and the protection of Indian officials and the various routes of travel within the limits of the department." The general had time for much correspondence of an unofficial nature. He kept up a series of letters, begun while he was at Leavenworth, to a Philadelphia artist named Peter Rothermel, who was working on a mammoth painting of the climactic moments of the battle of Gettysburg. Hancock was anxious that Rothermel should get it right, at least insofar as it pictured himself and his command. The general also kept up a lively political correspondence with trusted friends. He was clearly eager to run for president again in 1872 and wanted to do it right; "in '68," he admitted, "I allowed the matter to drift." Hancock felt that he had to have Pennsylvania "solid," and he expected much support from the South and other sections; "my friends in Missouri, Delaware, New Jersey, Minnesota, and elsewhere," he wrote, "are not *idle*." For Pennsylvania he urged that "a reliable soldier of good character" be located in each county, to set up veterans clubs for him. As it turned out, of course, Hancock did not run, but this was not for lack of interest.[21]

In November 1872 Meade died, and Hancock became the senior major general of the army. As such, according to custom, he was entitled to command of the Division of the Atlantic, in succession to Meade. Hancock's resentment at his earlier ill treatment by Grant on the question of assignments had become public in a short-lived flap in 1870, and there was apprehension that Grant would not permit the change. Sherman, however, recommended it because it would soothe Hancock while making sure he did not receive a command in the South; at the same time, the change would make Sheridan happy because it would give him a more congenial subordinate, Alfred Terry, in Dakota. Sherman's reasoning was convincing to the president, and Hancock was named on November 25 to the command which he would hold for the balance of his life.[22]

TWENTY SIX

East and an Election

On December 7, 1872, while Hancock and his family were on their way east, Sherman issued an order switching the headquarters of the Military Division of the Atlantic from Philadelphia to New York City. Meade had been permitted to maintain his headquarters in Philadelphia, his hometown, as a courtesy. The only city which had any special appeal for Hancock was St. Louis, because of Allie's family connection, so he had no objection to the order specifying New York as his base. He took command on December 16, 1872.[1]

The command of the Division of the Atlantic, presiding over the military destinies of New England, the Great Lakes area, the Middle Atlantic states, and Washington, was not, under most circumstances, an onerous one. The division was at the time split into two departments, the Department of the East, the command of which was another function of the division commander, and the Department of the Lakes, commanded from Detroit by Brigadier General Philip St. George Cooke. Unless something went seriously wrong, command of the Military Division of the Atlantic took the form of the quiet establishment and maintenance of proper administrative channels. Winfield Hancock had always been adept at processing the army's requirements of paper—orders, requisitions, reports, and so on—so that he was quickly able to take full control of his new bailiwick.[2]

Part of the process of taking control involved Hancock in a thorough inspection tour of his division. He believed that there was no substitute for personal observation, and he invariably followed assumption of a new command by taking to the road to look over the troops and posts under him. With the self-confidence which was such an integral part of his makeup, Hancock soon felt perfectly comfortable with his new command. On October 29, 1873, the War Department abolished the two departments in the division, and thereafter Hancock and his staff in New York City handled all the business previously carried out from two headquarters.[3]

Of course, Hancock's position in the nation's greatest metropolis gave him much increased visibility in the public eye, visibility which often led to political speculation. Even while he was in St. Paul, in the Department of Dakota, the general had been involved in presidential maneuvering for 1872; he wanted to check out possible obstacles, "so that when [not "if"] we run the course again we may be enabled to crush or avoid them." He and his friend Duncan Walker were busy constructing a network of correspondents to keep the Hancock name before the public and to try to get the right men chosen as delegates for 1872. He was frank with his friend Thomas Kilby Smith to warn against "the fatal policy of putting me in the 'light' of a candidate seeking for the office," but that was because such a "light" would mar the nonpolitical image which was one of his greatest assets. To James O. Broadhead, an influential Missouri Democrat, who seemed inclined toward Hancock, the general suggested that, to win, "it will be necessary if not wise, to nominate me."[4]

There is little doubt that Hancock could have gained substantial support for the 1872 Democratic nomination. In early 1870 Republican Congressman John A. Logan of Illinois, the driving force behind the powerful Grand Army of the Republic and an implacable foe of West Pointers, sponsored an army-reduction bill which was designed, Sherman felt, to force General Henry W. Halleck and Hancock out of the army. "If he succeeds," Sherman wrote his brother, "Hancock will be the next President." Congressman Samuel J. Randall of Philadelphia, late in 1871, said that Hancock was "still the central figure in Washington" as far as most Democrats were concerned. Whether he could have secured the nomination is questionable; the Democratic impulse to join in fusion with whomever the anti-Grant Republicans should put up was very strong. In any event, Hancock eventually decided to pull back. He wrote letters to his supporters, declining to be considered for 1872. As it developed, the Democrats were forced to swallow the astonishing Liberal Republican selection of Horace Greeley; all the potential Democratic choices had removed themselves from the race.[5]

Three years later Hancock was mentioned as a possible candidate for governor of Pennsylvania. The Democratic party in the Keystone State was in a condition of great confusion as the result of a violent and insoluble split between the adherents of Congressman Randall and those of Senator William Wallace. A measure of the depth of the intraparty cleavage is provided by the consideration of Hancock, whose principal attraction (since he lived in New York City and had spent no appreciable amount of time in Pennsylvania since his appointment to West Point) was his lack of connection with either side. However, the general never indicated the least interest in the position. The Hancocks' daughter, Ada, had died at the young age of eighteen on March 28, 1875; Mrs. Hancock recorded "the seclusion, gloom and depression" that filled their lives after this tragedy. The bereaved father, crushed by the loss of a beloved daughter to whom he was very close, had no taste for a political canvass. Neither Wallace nor Randall pushed him any further, and the trial balloon for the 1875 gubernatorial nomination sank as quickly as it had risen.[6]

In the following year, however, Hancock was obviously a willing aspirant for the Democratic presidential nomination. With Grant grudgingly acquiescing in the proposition that he should not seek a third term, the Republicans sprouted a wide selection of presidential hopefuls, ranging from administration stalwarts such as Roscoe Conkling of New York and

Oliver P. Morton of Indiana to the reformers' choice, Benjamin Bristow of Kentucky, with James G. Blaine of Maine somewhere in between. As none of these men looked particularly formidable, there were numerous Democrats who appeared willing to make the run.[7]

Foremost among them was Samuel J. Tilden, a canny, devious old corporation lawyer from New York City, no longer just a manipulator behind the scene but now governor of New York since his election in 1874. Widely heralded as a "reformer" after his brushes with Tammany's Tweed Ring in the city and the bipartisan thievery of the Canal Ring upstate, Tilden was in fact a veteran politician with full appreciation for the uses of organization and money in winning control of a party. He had no hesitation, however, in using his newly won reputation for purposes of advancement, and he benefited as well from the political reality that almost any governor of New York must be considered a potential nominee. Tilden would not be unchallenged, however. Among other Democrats who were seriously considered were Hancock, Hendricks, Senator Thomas F. Bayard of Delaware, and William Allen, former governor of Ohio. Other names mentioned were Allen Thurman of Ohio, Justice David Davis, Jeremiah S. Black of Pennsylvania, and Joel Parker, former governor of New Jersey.

Although the friends and supporters of all these candidates did what they could to procure support, they soon discovered that they were dealing with one of the craftiest political artists in American history. Samuel Tilden wanted the nomination, and he knew how to go about getting it. He had networks of agents who fanned out through the doubtful states, and there was no lack of money for his men to use. By the time the delegates assembled in St. Louis on June 27, the convention was all but locked up for Tilden. Hancock had written on June 14 to his friend Brent, a Louisiana delegate, that not only was he "considered a candidate" at St. Louis but that success was "quite possible." Less than two weeks later, however, he wrote Brent again, saying, "I am satisfied in my own mind that the matter in St. Louis is settled."[8]

Still, there were possibilities for General Hancock. The Republicans had broken their deadlock by naming a dark horse, the little-known governor of Ohio, Rutherford B. Hayes. Hayes's modestly successful war record received favorable comment, and many Democratic veterans felt the best way to beat a Republican soldier was with a better Democratic soldier. "Nominate Hancock," said one hopeful Mississippian, "and the bloody shirt will be folded away." There was talk of a "rising Hancock breeze" in Virginia and elsewhere in the South. Hancock's banner, one reporter wrote three days before the convention assembled, was "rapidly moving to the front," and another said that Hancock "possibly may be the coming man." On the eve of the convention, Henry Watterson, the outspokenly pro-Tilden editor of the *Louisville Courier-Journal,* had to quell a Hancock revolt in his own Kentucky delegation. Fitzhugh Lee of Virginia said that "only with Hancock can we carry this country against the Radical candidate." But an evening meeting of the leaders of the Hendricks, Bayard, Allen, Hancock, and Thurman camps failed to come up with agreement on a man to beat Tilden.[9]

The convention opened on June 27, and the Tilden forces soon showed that they were in control. Kentucky's Watterson was named temporary chairman, and a platform satisfactory to the governor of New York was adopted. Nominations were made on the second day, with the names of Bayard, Hendricks, Tilden, Allen, and Hancock being presented. Congressman Hiester Clymer of Pennsylvania made the speech in favor of Hancock, a brief one but well received. Brent from Louisiana and a delegate from Texas seconded.[10]

With the formalities of nominating out of the way, the first ballot was taken; its result confirmed what had now become apparent to all, that this was a Tilden convention. The New York governor had 417 votes, with Hendricks far behind at 140. Hancock stood third with 75, trailed by Allen, Bayard, and Joel Parker. On the second ballot, Tilden soared far past the required two-thirds vote, gaining the nomination with 535 votes, followed by Hendricks with 60, Hancock 59, Allen 54, Parker 18, Bayard 11, and Allen Thurman 7. The next day the disgruntled Indiana delegation was mollified by the selection of Hendricks for the second place on the ticket.[11]

So ended Winfield Scott Hancock's second attempt to win a presidential nomination. Though his effort appears to have been as serious a one as in 1868, Hancock's personal involvement was low-keyed and well below a level which might bring criticism to him as an officer in the United States Army. His friends, as usual, kept up the pretense that the general was not himself actively seeking the nomination. He accepted his defeat with equanimity and settled back to observe Tilden's canvass. Allie later wrote that this campaign was "the only one that I can recall that my husband followed with intense interest and anxiety," not even excepting that of 1880.[12]

The Democratic candidate managed his own campaign with skill and tenacity, confident that the Republican record of corruption and mismanagement would finally bring a Democratic victory. The Republican nominee—good, gray Governor Hayes—practically disappeared from view as his party put together a campaign based on two major thrusts. The Republican speakers assailed Tilden, in a particularly malevolent manner, with every charge, legitimate or not, which the party brain trust could conjure up; in addition, they waved, more vigorously than ever before, the bloody shirt of secession and slavery. Eleven years, however, had passed since Appomattox, and the appeal of the bloody shirt was declining. When the votes came in on election night, it became quickly apparent that the factors producing political control in America had changed. Tilden carried the northern states of New York, Connecticut, New Jersey, and Indiana, along with a solid phalanx of border and southern states for an apparent Democratic majority.

The familiar story of the machinations which made Hayes president, despite a quarter-million popular-vote plurality for the Democratic candidate—the contest in the three southern states still under military control, the venal returning boards, the "visiting statesmen," and the electoral-vote struggle in Congress—will not be rehashed here. Given the audacity of the Republican position, and the fact that the Democrats declined in the end to resort to unconstitutional means to counter it, the reversal of Tilden's apparent victory became inevitable. Yet there were from time to time signs that Democratic acquiescence might not be so complete as the opposition hoped.

Henry Watterson, as an example, made a speech in Washington on January 8, 1877, calling for 100,000 Democrats to march on the capital, and the fact that he specified unarmed citizens was soon lost in the uproar his speech produced. Even before Watterson's speech, Congressman James A. Garfield wrote a friend: "If we were to go by the talk of the Democrats, we should come to the conclusion that they really mean war, but I doubt if they have the nerve to carry out their threats." With the specter of renewed civil war, there was soon much comment and speculation about the course of the military, since the commander of the army in the East was a prominent Democrat, and a disappointed presidential hopeful at that. One story that went the rounds was that Grant would have Hancock transferred in short order to the Pacific coast, so that he would be nowhere near Washington when the crisis came. Other rumors described the various courses of action that Hancock would take, with his troops behind him, of course, to see to the inauguration of Tilden. The only problem, as can be plainly seen, was that the persons who retailed these stories surely knew little about Winfield Scott Hancock.[13]

Hancock at first gave credit to the rumors that he might be sent west. "Yes," he wrote to his wife, "I think it likely there may be some truth in the rumor that I am to be sent to California." He had had personal experience with Grant when his old commander had political ends in view, and he had no illusions about what might happen. Eventually, Sherman sent him a note telling him there was no truth to the story. Hancock was relieved, but, he told Sherman, "had it been true, I should, of course, have presented no complaint, nor made resistance of any kind."[14]

He wrote a long letter on December 28 to Sherman, keyed to the idea that "the army should have nothing to do with the selection or inauguration of Presidents." The people, he said, elect the president, Congress declares the winner, and "we of the army have only to obey his mandates." Hancock felt strongly, though, that the proposed Electoral Commission was unnecessary; he said he would be very surprised if Tilden consented to it. In the event that Congress was unable to agree that a candidate for either the presidency or vice-presidency had won a majority of the electoral college, "there is a lawful machinery already provided to meet that contingency, and to decide the question peacefully." That machinery, furnished by the Constitution, was for the House to elect the president (as it had already done on two occasions) and the Senate the vice-president. "That machinery," he said, "would probably elect Mr. Tilden president and Mr. Wheeler Vice-President." And, he went on, "that would be right enough."[15]

"I have no doubt Governor Hayes would make an excellent President," Hancock said. "For a brief period he served under my command; but as the matter stands I can't see any likelihood of his being duly declared elected by the people, unless the Senate and House come to be in accord as to that fact." Finally, he said, "what the people want is a peaceful determination of this matter, as fair a determination as possible, and a lawful one. No other determination could stand the test."[16] Clearly, Winfield Hancock was not going to be the man on horseback, leading an army of outraged Democrats in an attack upon the government. And anyone who had followed Hancock's career should have known that from the beginning of the crisis.

Tilden, of course, permitted himself to be persuaded that the Electoral Commission bill should be passed. Justice Joseph B. Bradley became the all-important fifteenth member of the commission and the deciding vote on all of the eight-to-seven decisions which gave every contested electoral vote—and the election—to Hayes. Most important, as Hancock had written, the people saw the process as a peaceful one, as the fairest possible in the circumstances, and as one with the color of legality. They acquiesced in the decision, and Hayes served his term without any serious question of his title to the office.[17]

TWENTY SEVEN

The Great Strike

In June 1876 the Department of the South, comprising primarily the Upper South, was added to Hancock's Division of the Atlantic. This department, commanded from Atlanta by Colonel Thomas H. Ruger, included the state of South Carolina, where the army's use was a source of some controversy.

Hancock, in his official report, briefly mentioned Ruger's troop movements, made "with a view to preserving order in the department during the fall of 1876 and winter of 1876–77, when a disturbed condition of affairs prevailed, resulting mainly from the elections of that period." Hancock took care to point out that the instructions under which Ruger acted went to the latter directly from Washington, bypassing his headquarters. What Hancock's decorous sentences failed to mention was that in fact Ruger's troops had been deployed throughout South Carolina at the order of the politicians in Washington to try to save the state for Hayes and for Governor Daniel H. Chamberlain, running for reelection against the immensely popular Wade Hampton. Hancock was blunter in a private letter to Sherman, written during the electoral crisis: "I was not in favor of the military action in South Carolina recently." If Ruger had sought his advice, he said, "I would have advised him not, under any circumstances, to allow himself or his troops to determine who were the lawful members of a state legislature."[1]

Warming to his subject, Hancock told Sherman that "it is no business of the Army to enter upon such questions. . . . I have not thought it lawful or wise to use Federal troops in such matters as have transpired east of the Mississippi within the last few months." He felt that the army "has been used unlawfully at times, in the judgment of the people (in mine certainly)," and as a result the army had receded considerably in the esteem of the public. "It is time," he concluded, "to stop and unload."[2]

Hancock's position, it will be noted, had not changed since the promulgation of General Orders No. 40 some nine years earlier. All that had happened in the interim had confirmed him in the correctness of his stand and demonstrated the continued folly of the Republicans in using military means to settle political controversies. "The time under our System of Government, when an army becomes political in its character . . . ," he wrote to Irvin McDowell, "is about the end of its career."[3]

In May 1877 Hancock's division received the rest of the South; the Department of the Gulf, commanded by General Christopher C. Auger at

New Orleans, was added to it. There was less to this change than meets the eye, however, because of the withdrawal by Hayes of the troops which had supported the three remaining carpetbag regimes, all of which promptly collapsed and were replaced with white Democratic administrations. A number of units were sent west, and all that were left in the Department of the Gulf were small garrisons for federal installations. Reconstruction was over, and that phase of the army's mission was done with.

Inside of a few months, however, Winfield Hancock found himself leading his troops in something utterly new to the army, something indeed new to the United States. For in July 1877, there broke out at numerous spots in the eastern and central parts of the country violent and widespread labor troubles. Only the interposition of the regular army brought the strikes and resulting riots under control.[4]

The nation was but slowly recovering from the harsh and grinding depression which followed the Panic of 1873. Throughout the economy wages had been slashed, mostly without any great protest on the part of workers, who were anxious simply to hold onto their jobs. In 1877, however, the country's major railroads determined to crack down even further on their employees. Encouraged by the end of a ruinous rate war early in June 1877, the companies soon put into effect sizable additional wage cuts; these reductions, which increased the misery and privation of the workingman and his family, provoked the turmoil which soon followed.[5]

The mighty Pennsylvania Railroad, whose president Thomas A. Scott received an annual salary of $175,000, not including dividends, led the way. In June 1877 it cut the wages of its workers, already paid less than $400 per year, by ten percent. The Erie, the New York Central, the Michigan Southern, and other roads quickly followed suit, announcing similar reductions to go into effect July 1. There was some ineffectual protest against these measures but little of any consequence. Those who complained quickly found themselves unemployed.[6]

Finally, the Baltimore & Ohio announced that, on July 16, it would cut by ten percent all wages of more than $1.00 per day. This announcement followed by one day the report by B&O president John Garrett of the "entirely satisfactory" affairs of the company and its customary 10 percent dividend to its stockholders. The firemen and brakemen who worked for the B&O issued a protest to the company but were told that the reduction stood. On the morning of July 16, resistance developed and the great railway strike of 1877 was under way. Some workers in Baltimore refused to run the trains, but they were quickly replaced by strikebreakers. In Martinsburg, West Virginia, however, a different set of circumstances prevailed: the police force was small, the citizens fervently supported the trainmen, and the workers were forcefully led. When firemen declined to work and were arrested, they were soon rescued by a large crowd of sympathizers who refused to allow replacements aboard the trains. Freight brakemen joined the firemen, and soon no freight trains were permitted through this important junction. Before long, some twelve hundred freight cars completely blocked the tracks at Martinsburg.[7]

The astonished officials of the B&O soon fired off a request to Governor Henry M. Matthews of West Virginia to call out the militia at Martinsburg. The governor was quick to comply. Two companies of militia, many of the members with friends or relatives among the strikers, made feeble and futile attempts to restore order. "Since then," a correspondent wrote, "the strikers have been masters of the field." At 3 o'clock in the morning on July 17, a freight train arriving in South Baltimore from the west was greeted by a crowd of strikers and pushed off the track, its cars wrecked, and its engine burned. No trouble was reported between Baltimore and Martinsburg, but from Martinsburg west to Wheeling the strikers soon had control of the B&O.[8]

On July 18 Governor Matthews, hard pressed by Garrett of the B&O, wired President Hayes, asking for troops. Half of his militia was already at Martinsburg, he said, "and in sympathy with the rioters." Hayes, after some initial soul searching, issued a proclamation directing all involved at Martinsburg "to disperse and retire peaceably to their respective abodes" by the following noon, and, more to the point, Secretary of War George W. McCrary ordered troops from Washington and Fort McHenry to proceed to Martinsburg at once.[9]

On the drizzly morning of July 19, the regulars, approximately 230 men under the command of Colonel William H. French, arrived at Martinsburg, and matters quieted down. At the same time, however, the strike was spreading into Ohio and New York, and hostile crowds were growing in Baltimore. In Pittsburgh employees of the Pennsylvania Railroad walked out. To the wage cut on this line had been added a doubling in length of freight trains, and finally the men had had enough. When news of the B&O strike reached Pittsburgh, the Pennsy workers simply left the trains where they were and walked off.[10]

In Baltimore the mobs erupted out of control, and Governor John Lee Carroll's militia units were attacked leaving their armories. In the shooting, burning, and rioting that took place, ten persons were killed, and Carroll called upon Hayes for federal help. Hancock, who had to that point been dispatching troops where needed from his headquarters in New York, was ordered to Baltimore to confer with Carroll and, in fact, to assume command of what was becoming a major campaign. He arrived in the Maryland metropolis at 4 a.m. on July 22, met immediately with the harried governor, and disposed his troops to the threatened points in the city.[11]

With regular troops now on the scene, matters became "tolerably quiet in Baltimore," Hancock said, but appeared to be getting out of hand in Pennsylvania. Part of Hancock's command was sent on to Cumberland, Maryland, and the general himself was ordered, around midnight of July 22, to leave for Philadelphia and "to take a sufficient force with me to restore order there." In Philadelphia, he was told, affairs were "exceedingly threatening." Some five thousand men had taken over the railroad yards. In Pittsburgh one of the most violent and turbulent riots in American history had broken out. Complicating matters was the absence, in Wyoming, of Pennsylvania's governor, John F. Hartranft, with his constitutional authority to request federal assistance, so that the actual order to Hancock directed him only "to protect United States property there against mob violence."[12]

Hancock left Baltimore the next morning, July 23, for Philadelphia, where he set up his headquarters at St. George's Hotel and met with the mayor, the collector of revenue, and, as his orders from Washington had suggested, Tom Scott of the Pennsylvania. The general ordered all units from the north and east to stop in Philadelphia before reporting to their assigned destinations. The strikers in Philadelphia had maintained possession of the Pennsylvania Railroad's depot and line for almost two days. The appearance of the regular army, however, served to disperse the crowd, as it was to do almost everywhere that the troops were sent. One observer felt that "the rioters . . . had a wholesome fear of the willingness of regular troops to obey orders and fire upon the mobs when necessary," and this fear accounted for the regulars' ability to do with their mere presence what the milita was unable to do at all. By Monday evening the area around the depot was quiet. The saloons and lager beer shops in the neighborhood were shut down, anyone found on the street was stopped and examined by the soldiers, and no one was permitted to cross the Schuylkill River bridges into West Philadelphia. Hancock was soon able to report Philadelphia "comparatively quiet." Pittsburgh was another matter completely.[13]

In Pittsburgh, where strikers had brought the Pennsylvania Railroad to a standstill, trigger-happy militia brought in from Philadelphia on July 21 responded to scattered rock throwing by firing two volleys into a crowd, killing twenty and wounding about forty more. This barrage touched off a vengeful mob which trapped the militia in the roundhouse at the railroad yards. The next morning the desperate militiamen burst out, shooting their way through the crowd, killing another twenty and suffering losses of their own as they escaped. The maddened mob spent the next twenty-four hours looting, burning, stealing, shooting, and generally terrorizing the helpless city. Locomotives, freight cars, offices, and other buildings associated with the Pennsy were the first to be set to the torch, but as the hours passed the compass of destruction moved well beyond that of railroad property alone. Nearly one hundred persons died in the Pittsburgh rioting. An eyewitness called it "the most terrible twenty-four hours in the history of Pittsburgh and among the most lawless in history of any American city."[14]

Winfield Hancock, arriving the following day in Philadelphia, about three hundred miles away, found his authority enhanced by both Governor Hartranft's formal request for help and an order from the War Department giving him full control over all troops within the division, including those in the normally independent engineer, quartermaster, and ordnance departments. "The President relies on your discretion," the order concluded, "to do all that is possible within the law to preserve peace." Hancock used this enlarged authority "to order to the principal scenes of action the entire available force of my division." Troops from the South were dispatched to Louisville and to Indianapolis, while units from as far off as Michigan, Maine, Florida and Arkansas were ordered to the scenes of disturbance. These now included Chicago, St. Louis, and Galveston, Texas, although these sites were out of Hancock's jurisdiction.[15]

In a wire to the adjutant-general on July 24, Hancock brought up a quasi-constitutional issue concerning the authority over federal troops committed to these efforts. Pointing out that United States Army units sent into Maryland had been ordered by the President to report to the governor of the state, Hancock said that he had received "no instructions concerning that matter" for the troops in Pennsylvania. Since Governor Hartranft was expected shortly, the general thought he should be instructed as to what course was to be pursued. In a long wire to Secretary of War McCrary, Hancock concluded that "when the State governments declare their inability to suppress domestic insurrection . . . and call . . . the President . . . to their assistance," that assistance should be given "by the intervention of Federal authority by military force and by the President exercising control."[16]

Still later on July 24, the adjutant-general wired Hancock to act under the orders of the governor in Pennsylvania, just as was being done in Maryland and West Virginia. The next day McCrary sent Hancock a telegram which implied that he was less than overjoyed to be faced with a jurisdictional question raised by his general commanding; "it is for the General Government to determine whether it will direct you and the troops you command to act under the direction of the State which calls for the aid of the United States." The president, he went on, "thinks you should take command of all troops" in Pennsylvania, both regular and militia. On July 26 Hancock wired off his recommendation that Governor Hartranft should be permitted to retain control, at least until he had had a chance to fail. This then was the course decided upon, and the question was settled for the time being. On July 27 Hancock sent another lengthy wire to McCrary, containing a rather turgid discussion of the strikes, their probable outcome, and federal-state relations, recommending that the time was appropriate for determining, for future purposes, how the jurisdictional issue should be handled. Since there was no further need to discuss the question at the time, of course, and no one other than Hancock seemed to be exercised about it, nothing further was done.[17]

In the meantime, Hancock had sat down to work out a plan with Governor Hartranft and with Schofield, passing through from West Point on his way to Washington, where he was to serve as an unofficial advisor to Hayes and McCrary (Sherman and Sheridan were both out west, beyond practical communications). The operation decided on was an expedition from Philadelphia to Pittsburgh, with 2,000 state militiamen under Hartranft and 500 regulars under Major John Hamilton, designated by Hancock, to open up the main line of the beleaguered Pennsylvania Railroad. This force left West Philadelphia at 11 p.m. on the night of July 26, suffered a minor derailment at Johnstown, where a switch was thrown, and arrived in Pittsburgh to restore order. By July 30 rail traffic in the state was back to near-normal operation. Hancock had also pushed forward to the Steel City nine companies of infantry which had been stopped at Chicago and Fort Wayne. The presence of federal soldiers restored Pittsburgh to a semblance of order, and the city fathers could go to work putting out fires and adding up losses.[18]

More disturbances broke out at Reading, Pennsylvania, where strikers had seized the property of Franklin B. Gowen's Philadelphia & Reading Railroad. The high-handed Gowen, completely bypassing local officials, called in the militia. In an incident which the local paper called "little better than cold-blooded murder," the militiamen on July 23 fired wantonly into a crowd composed largely of innocent bystanders, killing ten and wounding forty more. The militia were thereafter simply unable to control the infuriated city, and on July 28 it became necessary for Hancock to send help. He dispatched Major Hamilton with two hundred artillerymen to Reading, and the troubled city calmed down.[19]

Eventually, Hancock managed to locate his regular units in enough of the centers of contention that the strikes died away and the trains went back into operation. In the turbulent commonwealth of Pennsylvania, he worked closely with Governor Hartranft after the latter's return from the West and reopened the blockaded lines. On July 28 Hancock was able to wire the War Department:

> The quiet occupation of Pittsburgh and the opening of the Pennsylvania Railroad, I think, settles the question of order in this division, and the only trouble that seems to remain is that connected with the miners in certain points in the coal districts, such as Scranton. Possibly that may require similar treatment as that of the railroads.

On July 30 Hancock advised the War Department that "everything on the railroad within reach of my communications" seemed to be quiet; "a very little time and reflection, I think, will accomplish the rest."[20]

Hancock's duties in connection with the strikes were far from finished, however. Persistent troubles in the Pennsylvania hard-coal region required additional attention. Fifteen hundred workers of the Lackawanna Iron & Coal Company in Scranton struck at noon on July 24, and they were followed out that evening by trainmen at the Delaware, Lackawanna & Western and the Delaware & Hudson railroads. By Sunday July 29, all of Scranton's 35,000 workers were on strike. Other walkouts spread throughout the anthracite district. Hancock gathered up what forces he could muster and dispatched them to Scranton, Kingston, Plymouth, Wilkes-

Barre, Nanticoke, and Mauch Chunk, as well as to places in between. The disorders came to an end, but the strikes persisted; the role of the army changed materially after July 30. On August 15 Hartranft wrote to the secretary of war, conceding that "the emergency for which Federal troops were brought into this State is over" but requesting "for prudential reasons" that the troops be retained in the mining region, where he called the situation "still very critical." So, though Hancock himself returned to New York on August 16, the army stayed: virtually an army of occupation now, watching the sullen strikers as they were slowly ground down by privation and hunger. The use of the soldiers was almost exclusively for carrying out the process of United States marshals, not for the purpose for which they had been brought into Pennsylvania, and Hancock was not happy about that. He knew, as he told one questioner, that the occupation would last "practically until the miners go to work." He wrote that living conditions for the strikers were very bad, that almost 100,000 were idle, and that they were living on potatoes and wild berries. He worried about the effect of the striking miners upon his own men, who were, because of a political struggle between Hayes and the Democratic House, going without their own pay; he requested that the camps of his soldiers "be somewhat removed from the influence of the strikers and persons in sympathy with them in recent disorders." There was one advantage to the situation, which Hancock quickly seized upon. Soldiers and units were gathered in much larger concentrations than was customary for peacetime, so Hancock used the opportunity for daily tactical drills, the proper observance of ceremonials, and performance of various camp duties in accordance with regulations and approved customs. For many of the younger officers and most of the enlisted men, this was a totally new experience. Finally, the miners' strikes played out. By October 19 Hartranft had advised Hayes that the troops could be withdrawn, and on October 30 Hancock was able to pull the last of his units back from the uncongenial duty of strikebreaking.[21]

Hancock was proud that his soldiers had not gotten involved in the violence of the strikes and rioting: "wherever the troops appeared they succeeded by their presence alone in repressing the disorders." The credit for this fact is largely Hancock's; he carefully gathered his forces until he was sure that their appearance would be such that there would be no resistance and no bloodshed. The contrast, of course, with the sorry display made by the several state militias was striking. Hancock wrote to John Schofield: "It was the moral force of the United States Government that was displayed. . . . [T]he presence of the troops had a powerful effect."[22]

While Hancock was concerned primarily with the performance of his men in carrying out an assigned mission, men of property professed to see the strikes as the certain forerunner of anarchy and communism unless condign punishment were visited upon all those who took part in them. There was, however, almost no comment on the dismal precedent set by the use of military force to intervene in labor disputes. Congressman James A.

Garfield wrote: "The strike is illustrating the necessity of an army to keep the peace," overlooking the fact that the army's role had gone far beyond mere peacekeeping. Hayes, by turning his army units over to the state governors, had in effect made the army serve whatever purpose these governors wished to pursue. They were subservient to the corporate leaders within their bailiwicks—in this case the railroad presidents, canal owners, and mine operators—and the use of the army, particularly after the rioting had petered out, was for the purpose of suppressing strikes and quashing the budding workers' organizations. Hancock, as he had been directed, was in frequent contact in Pennsylvania with Scott (and later with Gowen), while his field commanders in the coal regions consulted on a daily basis with corporate officials. In the period from 1877 to the Spanish-American War, as labor became more militant and Indian conflicts died away, strike duty, invariably on the side of management, became one of the primary functions of the United States Army.[23]

Hancock for one was not happy with the army's assignment to such duties. On September 9, 1877, while his forces were occupying the anthracite region of northeastern Pennsylvania, Hancock complained to the adjutant-general that "the Regular Army . . . should not be made a police force for the state. . . ." His mind was of a practical rather than a philosophical nature, but he saw that the army's basic function was to serve as a shield of the nation against outside foes. The army could not retain the respect and goodwill of the people necessary to perform that task if it were to be used as an instrument for deciding internal political and social struggles, whether carpetbagger versus Bourbon or labor versus management. Hancock's view, however, was not that of the political leaders who would in the years to come make decisions concerning the army's utilization.[24]

In the aftermath of the disturbances of 1877, nevertheless, praise for the general commanding was widespread. Governor Hartranft expressed to Hancock the thanks of the citizens of Pennsylvania for having "done the state invaluable service, and added to the character of the army, as the final conservator of law and order." A final word came from the secretary of war: "I desire . . . emphatically to express my obligations to Maj. Gen. Winfield S. Hancock . . . for his untiring energy and great skill in directing the movements of troops."[25]

The public attention which devolved upon Hancock during the railroad strikes and riots was of great importance in fixing him in a high place in the people's affections. He was already highly respected for his wartime service, but many generals won fame and regard in the great conflict. In a nation weary of the interminable wrangling in the South, his sensible stand in New Orleans on civilian supremacy was surely more appealing in 1877 than it had been ten years earlier, with racial overtones forgotten. He had gotten some attention, but not too much, for his dealings with Indians and the advancing frontiers; other soldiers had been more prominent in this area. But the acclaim for putting down riots and tumult in the summer of 1877 was virtually Hancock's alone. Major General John Pope had been involved in the turbulence on its western fringes, but Hancock had been the principal focus of public attention. His service was viewed not so much as antilabor activity as restoration of the public peace and tranquillity. One observer ascribed to Hancock's "wise and humane forbearance in the exercise of his power" Pennsylvania's escape from further "wretched conflict" in the hard-coal region. The turbulence of that July, particularly the affairs at Baltimore, Pittsburgh, and Reading and the general strike in St. Louis, gave many citizens cause for serious alarm; to many it portended an upheaval in a long-established social order. To emerge from such turmoil as the guardian of public order clearly established Hancock as one of the most beloved of America's military leaders.[26]

TWENTY EIGHT

Hancock and the Army

Hancock was not a military theoretician, and he was never in a position to demonstrate talents as a strategist. His Civil War duties were always in a subordinate role, and he never, as Grant was wont to point out, exercised independent command. That his tactical sense was acute was proved at Gettysburg where, fortunately for Meade and the Union cause, Hancock instantly grasped the importance of seizing and fortifying Culp's Hill and Cemetery Ridge. He was not called upon, however, to formulate strategy for campaigning against Confederate armies; he was expected to place and deliver his regiments and later his corps for action in accordance with the planning of other men—men such as McClellan, Burnside, Hooker, and Grant. Hancock's great value lay in the demonstrated fact that he was reliable, aggressive, and extremely effective in carrying out the mission he was assigned. In addition, in the postwar years, because of the quirks of rank and death, Hancock never became commanding general of the army, a position in which there would have been some opportunity, within the severe constraints placed on the army by Congress, to formulate and express opinions on matters of overall military policy. It fell to Schofield, a lesser general but a more intellectual man, to succeed Sheridan as commanding general and to deal with such larger affairs. Nevertheless, from his practical experiences in the field, on the march, and in garrison, Hancock developed definite ideas on the problems of the stunted and impoverished peacetime army. He spent thirty-six years in the peacetime army—fifteen before the Civil War and twenty-one after—compared with six years of service in the two wars in which he fought. He had plenty of time to consider what was good about the army in peacetime, what was bad about it, and how it might be changed for the better.

Hancock's thinking, in the main, was on a very practical level. For example, he took the lead in the army during the 1870s in developing proficiency with the rifle among his soldiers. Because ammunition was expensive and money was scarce, there was little use of the rifle in the peacetime army until Hancock fostered an interest in it by placing strong emphasis throughout the Division of the Atlantic on rifle instruction, practice, and competition. The inspector-general of the army wrote in 1879 of Hancock's appreciation of the importance of rifle practice, his energetic action in promoting it, and the liberal facilities he made available for it. Hancock himself reported that "the interest in rifle practice is . . . on the

251

increase" and spoke of the "methods adopted to stimulate the zeal of our soldiers in this respect." One of the "methods adopted" was the general's unwavering personal involvement; he made sure to attend the army's rifle-shooting competitions, and he even served a year as president of the fledgling National Rifle Association when solicited for help to keep the organization from passing out of existence.[1]

The question of "economy" hung over everything the army did or failed to do during the long period between the end of the Civil War and the outbreak of the war with Spain in 1898. The size of the military establishment was gradually reduced until it had reached, by 1876, an effective strength of only 25,000, a level at which it stayed until the Spanish-American War. The army was widely scattered, with very small units serving in more than 200 posts, largely out of the public consciousness.

The common soldiers who made up the bulk of the force were volunteers, many foreign-born, many illiterate, who signed up for a hitch of five years. They were paid $13 per month, reduced in 1870 from the wartime rate of $16 per month. A new recruit received little training before being sent off to a unit. A large proportion of the army's strength was on the frontier. The duty was onerous and boring; the soldier on the plains spent his day escorting or protecting surveying parties, railroad workers, or traders, building structures for his post, occasionally fighting and more often chasing Indians, and combating idleness with cards and alcohol. The weather was frequently unpleasant as well, hot, dry, and dusty in the summer, bitterly cold in the winter. Poor rations, inadequate housing, and bad treatment by officers compounded the unpleasant conditions, and desertion was common.[2]

One of the areas where much conflict arose was that of military justice. Particularly troublesome were the great discrepancies in sentencing among different courts-martial for the same kind of offense. Hancock wrote that since "the military is a more arbitrary and despotic system than the civil, so is uniform and even-handed justice the more necessary in it. But we are far from securing this under our code." He advocated strengthening the army's Bureau of Military Justice and the corps of judge-advocates, at a time when both were under attack for economy reasons. In addition, he often took the initiative of reducing court-martial sentences when they seemed to him excessive or unfair.[3]

While comparatively little was done to ease the lot of the common soldier, there were movements afoot, fostered by Sherman as commanding general, to increase the professionalism of the army. Principal among these was the development of specialized schools for officers, such as the Artillery School at Fort Monroe, the Engineering School of Application, and a school for infantry and cavalry at Fort Leavenworth, which eventually became the General Service and Staff College. A parallel development was the establishment by Winfield Scott Hancock of the Military Service Institution of the United States in September 1878. This organization, which was headquartered on Governor's Island in New York Harbor, to which Hancock had moved his own headquarters on July 1, 1878, was modeled after Britain's Royal United Service Institution and was designed to encourage writing and discussion on matters of military science. Hancock served as its president. The institution was open to regular and militia officers as well as to civilians with military interests, and its quarterly journal afforded an outlet for the writings produced. Again, while Hancock himself was no theoretician, he recognized the role military science must play in the army's future and helped to create an instrument for its encouragement.[4]

In the late 1870s a debate arose over fundamental questions of American military policy; in this debate Hancock, with the ideas developed over the course of his long army career, played an important part. Substantial differences existed among military leaders as to what theory should govern the organization of the peacetime army. In enunciating these theories, Emory Upton and Hancock symbolized contending schools of thought.

Emory Upton was a young soldier from Batavia, New York, who graduated from West Point in 1861, compiled a brilliant record in the Civil War, winning a battlefield brevet as brigadier general at Spotsylvania, and had an outstanding postwar career as an instructor and administrator at the military academy. Two books which he wrote on military policy had a considerable influence upon the leaders of the army.

Upton addressed the problem of the American army, found no conscious military policy in American history, deplored civilian control over military decisions, and decried the fact that, at the start of each new conflict, the army had in effect to be re-created. Upton's solution, in which he was supported by Sherman, was the "skeleton army." Recognizing that Congress and the people would not permit the maintenance of a large standing army, he recommended that the army be organized nevertheless with the framework of a large establishment, the various units being understaffed but existent. In a time of crisis, Upton postulated, the influx of conscripts and equipment would flesh out the skeleton units and the required wartime army would emerge full-blown and virtually ready to go. The roots of Upton's theory went back to the "expansible army" advocated by John C. Calhoun when he was James Monroe's secretary of war in 1820. It had not been adopted then, had never really been tried since, but appeared to be what the army thought it was doing in practice.

Hancock felt that Upton's proposal was wrong in theory and deficient in practice. Hancock, in considering the role of the army, downplayed the needs of the Indian frontier: "The Indian furnishes only incidental duty for part of the Army. The service is of secondary importance, and is comparatively temporary in its nature." Though the major activity of the army from the Civil War to the Spanish-American War was Indian fighting, Hancock was essentially correct: the primary mission of the military establishment was the protection of the nation against a foreign enemy; the activities of hostile Indians hardly represented a threat against the country.

Hancock felt that the strength, composition, and organization of the army depended on the purpose for which it is maintained. "We rely upon creating armies from our population, when the necessity for them has actually arisen, or is impending," he said, but we also expect our small standing army "to keep pace with the progress of the profession, construct adequate and suitable national defenses," and to "be ready at a moment's notice to organize, equip, and supply, with efficiency and economy, armies of any magnitude which the occasion may call for."

The government's starvation policy, however, had made it impossible for the army to carry out the duties imposed upon it. Hancock felt that the number of enlisted men in each company had become too small for effective discipline and instruction. He recommended that infantry and cavalry companies be filled up to 100 men, while the number of companies in each regiment be reduced to eight, to avoid impinging upon the overall limit on the army's size of 25,000 men. Here, of course, was Hancock's conflict with the "skeleton" theory. He attacked it head-on:

> The concentration of enlisted men, so as to have fewer and larger companies, would be a departure from the old theory that our army in peace, especially the line, should be a *skeleton* to be filled out for war. This theory, false in principle, has always failed in practice. It involves just that lack of power so much complained of during peace—companies too small for instruction, drill, and other duty—and when war comes, in lieu of filling out the skeleton, we take entire new organizations from volunteers or militia.

"Our standing army," Hancock concluded, "should be a small, complete, compact, vigorous, healthy body, always in a thorough state of discipline and instruction, serving as a model and a standard for the national forces, and not preserved as a skeleton into which it is expected to infuse vitality, activity, and knowledge at the moment an emergency arises."[5]

In 1878 there was a flurry of congressional interest in the army, its size and its structure. A joint committee, chaired by Senator Ambrose E. Burnside of Rhode Island, erstwhile unsuccessful commander of the Army of the Potomac, was created to consider the reform and reorganization of the army. Through the summer and fall of 1878, the committee listened to the views of the army's leaders. All of the generals agreed that further cuts in army strength would be unwise, but they disagreed (as might have been expected) on the structure and purpose of the peacetime establishment. Upton and Sherman gave the committee the argument for the "skeleton" army, while Hancock reiterated his earlier views in opposition. The committee eventually rendered a report setting forth all the contentions presented to it, but the proposed bill it wrote died in Congress. The debate over a "skeleton" versus a "complete and compact" army was not really resolved, either. The structure with which the army stumbled along was closer to Upton's skeleton than to Hancock's model, though few thought that the creature really possessed the capacity to come alive required by Uptonian theory.[6]

TWENTY NINE

Off and Running for 1880

As the election of 1880 approached, Winfield Scott Hancock was again a candidate for president. There was, of course, no formal announcement of his candidacy, but there was little doubt that he was in the running. His name was mentioned from the beginning as a contender, and his emissaries were out early beating the bushes for delegate support.

Though Hancock carefully and skillfully preserved his image of a faithful soldier yielding reluctantly to the call of the people, there can be no doubt that he was ambitious to become president. Three times over a period of twelve years his name was seriously advanced in Democratic conventions, and his political supporters worked hard on his behalf. The general kept in touch with them and from time to time prodded them as to actions to be taken. As a believer in the Union and in the historic principles of the Democratic party, Hancock felt that he could lead the party to victory and, having done so, could govern the country. While he was aware that his purely military career was something of a disability, he had been an interested observer of political and governmental affairs and he was self-confident enough to believe that he could handle the presidency if it came his way. He had watched the dismal performance of Grant in the White House—Grant, with his flawed conception of the Constitution, with his complacent tolerance of bosses, sharpers, and crooks—and knew he could do better. He watched the conduct of Tilden and the Democratic leaders in Congress in 1876 and 1877, yielding however reluctantly to an extraconstitutional contrivance by which the party was counted out when a stout adherence to the Constitution should have brought victory, and he felt he could have done better. In addition, his record as a Union army hero would help to overcome the stigma of rebellion and disloyalty which in the minds of many voters still clung to the Democracy.

Hancock was not encumbered by complex political views. Several years earlier he had suggested a platform of "An honest man and the restoration of the Government," and there is little evidence that his political thinking ever went much beyond that. Hancock believed that the states should be free from interference by the central government, and he was consistently critical of Radical reconstruction. Otherwise he felt that limited government conducted honestly was a sufficient program for the nation. And he was confident that his war record and his administration of the Fifth Military District made him quite electable.[1]

Yet Hancock never let ambition get the better of him. His personal activity was always discreet and reserved, as befitted a soldier on active duty; somewhat disingenuously, he told an interviewer for the *Boston Journal* early in the year that he would not enter into "any contest or fight to secure the nomination" and moreover he was not a candidate "in the sense of being a seeker of the office of President." With the sense of detachment he was able to maintain, the disappointments visited upon him were accepted without rancor or fuss.[2]

Winfield Scott Hancock in 1880 was in his mature prime. He was fifty-six years old, vigorous and handsome. His beard and hair had whitened, and he had gained a considerable amount of weight, but he was reckoned a fine figure of a man who would present a splendid appearance to the electorate. His added weight—he was now over 240 pounds—made Hancock seem substantial rather than fat, and his serious mien gave him the air of a commander who handled grave responsibilities. The public knew him as "Hancock the Superb," the hero of Gettysburg, an Indian fighter, a reconstruction commander who tempered severity with kindness, and the preserver of public safety. He and his friends had learned from the mistakes of their earlier convention efforts, and they were prepared to profit from them. Their activities, they hoped, would be better organized and more successful, although the partisans of other candidates continued to regard Hancock's organization lightly.[3]

One thing was certain about the 1880 election: it would bring about a change in the presidency. Rutherford B. Hayes had made it clear from an early date that he would serve but one term in the White House, and there was no inclination on the part of the Republicans to seek his reconsideration of that stand. The voters of the country might have been prepared to give Hayes another term, for he had not been a bad president; the country was at peace, and the economy had just about worked its way out of the depression which followed the panic of 1873. To Republican politicos, however, Hayes had been a disaster. They despised his southern policy, by which he had pulled the troops out of the South and ended reconstruction without receiving any corresponding benefit to the Republicans of the former rebel states. They hated his sporadic attempts at civil-service reform, symbolized by his ultimately successful effort to remove the leading officers of the New York Customs House for party activities. And they scorned the liberals and reformers with whom Hayes was most comfortable. Senator Roscoe Conkling of New York sneered at the president as "Rutherfraud B. Hayes," and Conkling's senatorial colleagues such as Blaine, John A. Logan, and J. Donald Cameron counted the days until Hayes would be gone from the White House.

Blaine, the "Magnetic Man" from Maine, was an active candidate for the succession. So was John Sherman, who had served Hayes loyally enough as secretary of the treasury but who now openly schemed to replace him. But the candidate of the leading Republican bosses, the old spoilsmen such as

Conkling, Logan, and Cameron, was the man whom they had manipulated so well during his earlier eight-year tenure, Ulysses S. Grant. No one thought Grant had been a great president; few thought he had been a good one. There did not seem to be any pressing reason to resurrect him as a presidential candidate in 1880. Nevertheless, to his supporters, Grant had one shining quality. After three years of traveling around the world and being greeted by admiring crowds and the crowned heads of Europe and Asia, Grant seemed once again to be the Hero of Appomattox, the crusher of rebellion, the strong and silent general. As such, he would, they felt, be eminently electable.

Unfortunately for Grant and Conkling and the others, the effort to take the Republican nomination by storm, as it were, was not successful. The old general came home from his travels too soon. There was plenty of time for his opponents to point out that the Grant of Fort Donelson, Vicksburg, and Appomattox was also the Grant of Babcock, Belknap, and Black Friday. The heavy-handed tactics on Grant's behalf did not go unnoticed, and it soon became obvious that the former president could not win the nomination without a struggle.

The Democrats had a most peculiar situation. It had been almost universally assumed, following the fiasco of 1876–77, that the Democrats would, in 1880, offer the country "the old ticket," that is, Tilden and Hendricks, to make good the aborted victory of 1876. How better to capitalize on the Great Fraud, the theory ran, than with the Great Defrauded? This policy seemed the surest way to Democratic victory. It ignored those who had been bitterly frustrated by Tilden's apparent inactivity during the electoral deadlock, but in 1880, it was felt, Tilden would win by so much that there would be no doubt of his triumph.

But a strange thing happened along the way. In 1878 the Democrats controlling the House set up an investigating committee under Congressman Clarkson N. Potter to look into the fraudulent activities which had procured the electoral votes of Louisiana, South Carolina, and Florida for the Republicans in 1876. The committee, prodded by the editorial efforts of Tilden's friend Manton Marble of the *New York World,* turned up a number of irregularities on the part of the Republicans, and there was general rejoicing in the Tilden camp. Soon, however, it developed that a number of telegrams, in cipher, which had passed between Tilden's home at 15 Gramercy Park and code-named correspondents in the three contested states had come into the hands of the *New York Tribune.* From August through October, the *Tribune* printed the messages—still in cipher—along with tantalizing hints about the progress of its decoding efforts. Finally, having sufficiently whetted the public appetite, the paper on October 7, 1878, set forth the messages from Florida, decoded, along with an explanation of the cipher and how its experts had cracked it. The despatches, and succeeding ones from South Carolina and Louisiana, made it clear that W. T. Pelton, Tilden's nephew, Manton Marble, Smith Weed, and other Tilden confidants had engaged in efforts to buy the members of the returning boards in the contested states. From the fact that all the messages were sent from or to Tilden's home, the sizable amounts of the payments authorized, and the governor's known propensity for involving himself in details of political maneuver, it was assumed by most observers, Democrats as well as Republicans, that Tilden was quite aware of what was going on, if not actively mixed up in it. Astonishingly, in virtually every instance, some last-minute niggling over the funds at the New York end prevented the conspirators from carrying out the intended purchase; many saw in this the characteristic Tilden caution with money.

The Potter Committee was obliged to call before it Pelton, Weed, and Marble. Pelton confessed, Weed said it was "only paying money for stolen property," and Marble claimed lamely he had just been sending "danger signals" to his principal. In February 1879 the committee came to the Fifth Avenue Hotel in New York and took the testimony of the worn and haggard Tilden. In a faint, whispery voice, he denied any part in attempted bribery and said that the "futile dalliance" of his nephew, Pelton, had been merely an effort to bribe men to do what they were supposedly sworn to do anyway. Tilden's appearance was an ordeal for him, and he did not carry it off very convincingly. All of the witnesses did what they could to exonerate Tilden from personal involvement in a scheme which could no longer be denied, but his future political prospects were severely if not fatally damaged.[4]

Tilden had other problems. He was not popular in the South. He was strongly opposed by the Tammany faction in New York City. And he had legal difficulties. The Republicans had, in 1875, when Tilden's candidacy became probable, charged that he had failed to pay income taxes to the government during the Civil War. The federal government brought a blatantly political suit against him for his alleged nonpayment and kept the action alive until 1881, when it was finally forced to acknowledge its lack of a case. In the interim, however, the Republicans used the pendency of the suit as another political club with which to beat the former governor.[5]

Finally, Tilden's health was shattered by the ordeal of the contested election, with the added strain of the cipher scandal, and he never recovered it. He became palsied and arthritic, with a slow, shuffling gait and a yellowish, haggard face. "Physically, he was an old, broken man," his biographer wrote; "but his mind was still keen, and all his faculties at instant command."[6]

Tilden would be an old sixty-six in 1880, but he did not intend to be passed by. He still had many supporters within the party, and he wanted to keep them under his control for as long as he could; he himself probably did not know for sure whether he intended to be a candidate in 1880. Perhaps his friend Bigelow put it best, years later, when he wrote: "Tilden's health prevented his being wholly a candidate or wholly not a candidate."[7]

The party line of the Tildenites was that to take another candidate in 1880 was "to sanction the base conspiracy by which the people were defrauded of their choice," as Bigelow wrote. The entire strategy of the Tilden men was to keep the 1876 election the sole issue. "Old Tilden," wrote Congressman E. John Ellis of Louisiana, "don't want any new issue raised. He desires that the old fraud issue of 1876 of which he is the representative should remain undisturbed and untouched." Ellis complained that Speaker Randall's management of the House of Representatives had been aimed solely at carrying out the old man's strategy.[8]

If the Democrats could work out their Tilden problem, they stood a substantial chance of capturing the presidential prize which had so maddeningly eluded them in 1877. They had taken control of the House of Representatives in the election of 1874 and had retained that control in the subsequent elections of 1876 and 1878. In addition, when the new Congress convened in 1879, there was for the first time since before the war a Democratic majority in the United States Senate. Because the Senate's members were, prior to passage of the Seventeenth Amendment, elected by the state legislatures, control of the Senate reflected a correspondingly heavy representation in the statehouses across the country.

What the Democrats had hoped to do with their control of both houses was to write a record of opposition to the Hayes administration and the Republican party, to present themselves as an attractive alternative. Their opposition took the form of a series of riders tacked onto army appropriation bills, riders which made it a criminal offense for a president or other officer to interfere by the use of military force in any election. This effort at a symbolic repeal of reconstruction was unwise: its success would have accomplished nothing concrete, and all it really achieved was the unification, even if only temporary, of the warring Republican camps behind President Hayes. The president vetoed each measure coming to him with such a rider attached, and the Democrats were of course unable to override a veto. Hayes's stinging veto messages aroused public support for his position; Conkling in the Senate said, "The actors in this scheme have managed themselves and their party into a predicament, and unless the President lets them out they will and they must back out." He was right; the Democratic majorities ultimately passed the appropriations with the objectionable riders removed, not without some sense of embarrassment. It was not a very inspiring performance on the part of the Democratic congressional leaders, and it left a shadow in the public mind concerning the ability of the party to govern.[9]

There were other factors to be considered. The return of prosperity to the country would work to the advantage of the Republicans, whether or not they had done anything to cause it. The Democrats continued to suffer by the split in their ranks between the hard-money East and the soft-money West, but the schism between the Grant men and their opponents in the Republican party was in many ways more bitter. Finally, many people simply felt that the Republicans had been in power for so long a time that a change would be beneficial.

Where all the plusses and minuses left the two parties was of course a question which only the election in November 1880 could answer. In the meantime the selection of the parties' candidates for president and vice-president and the nature of the summer and fall campaigns would greatly influence that answer. Each party bore a burden from its past—Grant for the Republicans and Tilden for the Democrats—and how it dealt with this burden would help determine its fate in 1880.[10]

Hancock's friends were aware that the disposition of the Tilden problem would not be up to them. The party leaders, the rank-and-file members who selected delegates, the former candidate himself—from these would come the decision on a possible second Tilden nomination. If the party chose to turn its back on Tilden, most likely by an unspoken but clear consensus, because of his health, or the cipher stories, or simply disenchantment with the man, then and only then would the party seriously scan the ranks of possible successors. It was the job of Hancock's supporters to gain enough support for their man that the Democratic party would turn to him when it turned away from Tilden. This was the task that his friends set themselves to perform in the early months of 1880.

The process of selecting delegates to a national convention, although it naturally varied from state to state, began usually with the choice of party leaders on the local level, in wards, boroughs, and townships. The men thus chosen would meet at a county or other regional convention to pick delegates from among themselves to go to a state convention, which would select the delegates for the national convention. In some states, many delegates to the national convention were picked on a county or congressional-district basis, with the state convention electing delegates-at-large. The variations could be as many as there were states or territories represented, but it was usually true that those chosen were selected for their own political prominence, positions, or accomplishments, not for their specific preferences for the presidency. It became the task of presidential candidates to win support among these local party leaders who became delegates, as well as among the governors, senators, congressmen, or bosses who might control or influence them.

Of course, Hancock was not the only man hopeful of picking up the mantle of party leadership if it dropped from Samuel J. Tilden. Many of the names of his competitors were familiar ones. Thomas A. Hendricks of Indiana, former governor, seeker after the presidency in 1868 and 1876, now sixty-one years of age, had been the vice-presidential nominee on Tilden's ticket. If the party was to give the country "the old ticket," the victims of the Great Fraud, Hendricks would have to be included. But because Hendricks had his eye on the presidency, not on the second position, he discounted talk of "the old ticket" and laid out reasons why he would make a better candidate than Tilden. Eventually the Tildenites recognized that it was impossible for Tilden and Hendricks to run together again. Hendricks was a soft-money advocate, the source of much opposition to him in the East, but he was regarded as a strong contender in the West.

Ohio presented its former senator Allen G. Thurman. Thurman had been a leader of the Democrats in the Senate from 1867 to his defeat in 1879, but he was now almost sixty-seven years old and out of office. Tilden blamed him as much as anyone for the passage of the Electoral Commission bill in 1877, so that Thurman would inherit no support from the former candidate. His success was considered a rather long shot, but his loyal supporters in Ohio would stick with him. It was doubtful that he would pick up much strength elsewhere.

From the West Coast came Stephen J. Field, associate justice of the United States Supreme Court. Field was one of four celebrated brothers. Cyrus promoted the first Atlantic cable, David Dudley was a distinguished leader of the New York and American bar, and Henry was a Presbyterian clergyman and well-known author. Stephen had moved to California in his early thirties and won election to the state supreme court. In 1863 Lincoln appointed him as a Union Democrat to the federal high court, where he would serve for thirty-four years. Field's people counted on the support of the West, they hoped his states'-rights-oriented court decisions would win him adherents in the South, and they looked to his brothers' connections to develop some strength in the Northeast, where he had the support of the notorious Jay Gould, which probably did not help him. Field was not considered a favorite for the nomination, but then he had a lifetime job to fall back on in any event.

A more formidable contender was Senator Thomas Francis Bayard of Delaware. Bayard followed his father, his uncle, and his grandfather as a United States Senator. He was a vigorous fifty-two years of age and was highly respected for his idealism and starchy integrity. He followed classical Democratic principles in opposing the expansion of federal power, and he had been consistent in his denuciations of the Radical Republicans and their excesses. Bayard did have some drawbacks as a candidate. He was seen by many as haughty, pompous, and legalistic; Congressman E. John Ellis of Louisiana, a Hancock man, called Bayard "a coward and a sneak . . . dangerously ill of the presidential fever." Bayard was a defender of hard money, which cost him the hostility of the West and the suspicions of the South. He had supported the Electoral Commission bill in 1877 and thus had the firm opposition of Tilden. Most damaging of all was a speech Bayard had made on Dover Green on June 27, 1861, in which he suggested that the southern states should be permitted to withdraw from the Union, as no accommodation with them appeared feasible. Bayard's opponents took care that northern voters were reminded of the Dover Green speech from time to time, to keep fresh the picture of Bayard as a "secessionist." The conventional wisdom said that the Dover Green speech made Bayard a risky candidate in the North, but no one really knew that for sure, particularly nineteen years later. Bayard himself disposed of the Dover Green speech by saying, "I am opposed to internecine strife. I was opposed to it in 1861; I am opposed to it now." Bayard was supported editorially by the *New York Herald,* he had many friends in the Northeast, and, in a survey of eastern colleges taken in March 1880, Bayard ran far ahead of Tilden, Blaine, and Sherman. He had high hopes for the nomination.[11]

There was the usual assortment of dark horses and forlorn hopes—men such as Congressman William Morrison of Illinois, Governor James English of Connecticut, Jeremiah Black of Pennsylvania, Thomas Ewing of Ohio, even Horatio Seymour, now seventy-one, still saying "no" in such a way as to be understood to say "perhaps." There were, in addition, two other candidates, who occupied peculiarly anomalous positions. These were Henry B. Payne, a millionaire oil man from Ohio, and Speaker of the House Samuel J. Randall, the protectionist congressman from Philadelphia. Payne and Randall were considered to be the heirs of the political estate of Tilden; one or the other—or both—would be brought forward if Tilden withdrew from contention, and the rank-and-file Tildenites would be expected to support them. Until Tilden made a designation, however, Payne, Randall, and the supporters of each were left in a state of suspended helplessness; any premature move would be regarded as treachery by the old man and could be followed quickly by disinheritance.

In any assessment of strengths and weaknesses, going into the election year of 1880, Hancock came off as well as any other candidate and better than several of them. In the everlasting controversy on the currency question, Hancock had no position, because as an army officer he had never had to take one. Neither the soft-money zealots nor the gold-standard men of the money capitals held a grudge against Hancock, and he alone possessed this enviable advantage. On all sides it was conceded that Hancock would, if nominated, run on whatever currency plank the convention put into the platform; before then he need say nothing. He was also, unlike Bayard and Thurman, free of Tilden's suspicions arising from the electoral struggle, and Tilden's foes did not class Hancock as one of the former New York governor's beneficiaries. He had his sterling military record, a rarity among Democratic aspirants, and his administration in Louisiana and Texas commended him to every Democrat. His reputation as a savior of the public safety, from the railroad strikes, combined with his fine figure and demeanor to make him a very attractive candidate. Figured into his major advantages, of course, were his principal drawbacks. His foes said he had no position on the currency controversy for the same reason he had no part in the electoral crisis, which was that as a military man all his life he had no civil record whatever. The party had vigorously decried the political involvement of military men ever since the first coming of Ulysses S. Grant in 1868. "There is no other candidate for the Democratic nomination," wrote one editor, "who possesses so few of the real qualifications of a President as General Hancock, and none who can involve the Democratic party in so much inconsistency." Hancock, he went on, though no doubt a brave and accomplished soldier, "is of no more than ordinary mental calibre" and had never shown that he possessed "that qualification . . . which makes amends for many deficiencies—a sound judgment as to men."[12]

Because of his neutrality on the money question, Hancock's hopes were bounded by no geographical limitations. He anticipated a considerable amount of southern support, and there appeared no reason why he should not gather strength in the Northeast. Ohio, Indiana, and Illinois seemed to be foreclosed by their commitments to their native sons, but otherwise the Midwest could be prospected for delegates. Hancock hoped for some success in Missouri, because he and his wife had treated St. Louis as home as much as a well-traveled military couple could do. He had many friends in Minnesota, from his lengthy sojourn in the Department of Dakota, and he hoped for political support there. Finally, a key to possible victory would be the development of a sizable bloc of delegates in his native Pennsylvania. There Hancock could not avoid involvement in the virulent Wallace-Randall feud which continued to wrack the Democratic party, because so much of the party in the Keystone State as supported Randall would be for Tilden first, Randall second, and no one else beyond that. Only the Wallace faction would be available to Hancock's emissaries, and it would be necessary first to win over the wily senator. It was a worthwhile effort for Hancock to make, because Pennsylvania's was one of the largest chunks of delegate support available, and he had always been popular with the Democrats of his native state.

Many of those working for Hancock were veterans of his earlier runs for the nomination. William B. Franklin, out of the army since 1866, was vice-president and general manager of the Colt firearms establishment in Hartford, Connecticut; he dabbled in Democratic politics and set himself up as an unofficial spokesman for Hancock. Baldy Smith, long associated with Franklin, also worked for Hancock. Smith held a minor position in New York City as a Tammany functionary. Samuel T. Glover, an old friend from St. Louis, worked for the general again. Thomas Kilby Smith, who had commanded brigades and divisions in the Army of the Tennessee during the war, was a long-time supporter; later on he wrote to his son that Hancock's election was practically a *fait accompli* and that "I shall probably be regarded as one who had some hand in it." Hancock's old friend from Los Angeles, J. Lancaster Brent, worked for him in Louisiana and elsewhere, and Martin McMahon, chief of staff of the Sixth Corps in the Army of the Potomac, helped out in New York and with veterans' organizations. In Pennsylvania, St. Clair Mulholland, who had led a brigade in the Second Corps and who was now Philadelphia police commissioner, was a loyal supporter, as was B. Markley Boyer of Norristown. Boyer, who had long been a trusted counselor, was the party leader in Montgomery County, a former congressman, and a leading member of the bar.[13]

As the political year progressed, Hancock's friends buttonholed and solicited political leaders, setting out their arguments for the general's nomination. Occasionally, zeal outran good judgment. A notable instance was a party gathering which Baldy Smith addressed in Waterbury, Vermont, in April. In an effort, presumably, to demonstrate that Hancock was nothing if not a good Democrat, Smith, telling of the letter which Hancock had written to Sherman during the electoral crisis of 1876–77, stated that Hancock had expressed his intention of obeying any order Tilden might address to him after March 3, 1877, because of his belief that Tilden was the true winner of the presidential seat. While this account made for a suitably fiery speech at a political clubhouse, it did not look good in the public press, and it did reflect a measurable divergence from what Hancock had actually written to Sherman. The story did not surface publicly until after the nomination, when it caused a momentary flap that was dampened only by revelation of what Hancock really had written. Perhaps, too, it caused Hancock to waver a trifle in his faith in the discretion of Baldy Smith.[14]

Meanwhile, a development which would bring the Hancock forces a major accession of strength was taking place. Hancock, of course, was well known and popular in the Deep South since his experience as commander of the Fifth Military District in 1867–68. This fact had not heretofore translated automatically into delegate support at Democratic conventions. His southern support in 1868 and 1876 had been ephemeral at best; it must be more solidly based in 1880 for Hancock to stand a realistic chance of securing the nomination. What was needed to transform a kindly disposition toward Hancock into a substantial number of firm delegate votes was clearly a manager—a political leader, on the scene in the South, with both the inclination and the muscle to line up the region in the Hancock interest.

For 1880 such a manager was found. His name was Major Edward A. "Ned" Burke, and he was one of the most flamboyant charlatans produced by the colorful political wars of Louisiana. In 1880 Burke was state treasurer and political boss of Louisiana, but his background was, to put it mildly, obscure. Burke called himself a Kentuckian, but many observers felt that he came from farther north. His military title was almost certainly self-bestowed. He had some illicit adventures in Texas, and he arrived penniless in New Orleans in 1870, working as a day laborer in a stonecutter's yard. Within a couple of years Burke was a high executive in a small railroad, the political agent of the powerful Louisiana Lottery, and in the ascendant within the Democratic party. He became editor and publisher of the *New Orleans Democrat* and later of the consolidated *New Orleans Times-Democrat,* the mightiest voice of Bourbon Democracy. As such, he became one of the leading advocates of the economic rebirth of the New South. As the representative of Francis T. Nicholls, the apparent Democratic winner of the governorship in the disputed election of 1876, Burke had gone to Washington in the spring of 1877 and served as the guiding spirit behind the series of conferences concluding in the famous Wormley's Hotel bargain, which delivered Louisiana, Florida, and South Carolina back into the hands of the white Democrats. "There were few," writes C. Vann Woodward, "who could match his splendid audacity." A bon vivant and man about town, elected state treasurer in 1878, Ned Burke with his newspaper and lottery connections was soon undisputed ruler of the Democratic party. Burke would later, after he left office in 1889, be accused of stealing well over a million dollars from the state treasury, but by that time he had moved on to Honduras, where he lived in luxury and influence for the rest of a long and eventful life. In 1880, however, he was in a marvelous position to be of assistance to Winfield Scott Hancock.[15]

The exact mechanics of the construction of Hancock's link to Burke are still not clear, but it is probable that the first contact may have been through the good offices of Governor Nicholls of Louisiana. The governor was an oft-wounded hero of the Confederacy, a West Pointer, a conservative, and an aristocrat. After the Democrats had redeemed the state government in Louisiana, one Thomas C. Anderson, a member of the corrupt returning board which had sold out Tilden in 1876–77, was convicted of forgery and alteration of election returns and sentenced to two years at hard labor. President Hayes, obviously sensitive on the issue, sent Hancock as his personal emissary to Nicholls, to see what could be done for Anderson. Hancock arrived in Louisiana on February 8, 1878, ostensibly on an inspection tour, and was greeted effusively by the populace. "Hail to the Chief!" the *New Orleans Picayune's* editorial was headlined; it went on to say that no visitor from the North "could be more welcome than that distinguished soldier and patriot." On February 19 Hancock met with Nicholls, and on the twenty-first he left again for the North. Nicholls, Hancock later reported, promised to pardon any returning board members convicted in a state court. He was spared the necessity of doing this, however, when the state supreme court on March 18 ordered Anderson set free, on the ground that the documents he was said to have falsified were not "public records" under the forgery statute.[16]

In light of future developments, it seems reasonable to speculate that Hancock and Nicholls may have discussed more than simply the penal disposition of T. C. Anderson. With West Point as a bond between them, the two men must have reminisced about the war days, about Hancock's tenure as military governor in the Fifth District, about his past campaigns for a presidential nomination. Surely, too, they talked about Hancock's hopes for 1880 and how these hopes depended on solid support from the South. At this point, it may have been that Nicholls referred his visitor to the man who was best able to handle matters like that, Major Ned Burke. Nicholls and Burke, the aristocrat and the parvenu, were clearly very different types, and they shortly had a falling out over the question of the lottery. For a time, however, Nicholls found it convenient to utilize Burke, and it is not unlikely that he urged the same course upon Hancock.

Two years later, Hancock found himself again in the same part of the country. In March 1880 the general made a vacation visit with his son,

Russell, on the latter's plantation near Clarksdale, Mississippi. Again, we can only speculate, but it is likely that Hancock entertained political visitors while he was there. At the same time he attempted to keep his visit quiet, so that it would not be seen as "an electioneering tour."[17]

In any event, it was soon apparent that the wheels were turning for Hancock in New Orleans. Burke's paper came out strongly for the general on March 16, saying that no name "more fully commands the respect and admiration of the people of the South than that of Winfield Hancock." The next day, the *New Orleans Picayune,* in an editorial which attracted wide attention, endorsed Hancock as the only candidate who could appeal to all the factions within the Democratic party. "Bayard repels Union voters," the paper said, "by his Dover Green speech in June 1861, . . . and repels Greenback voters, not only by his extreme hard money views, but by his advocacy of the withdrawal of the greenbacks themselves." On the other hand, it went on, "Hancock attracts Union voters by his magnificent record of battles and wounds, while he will not repel Greenback voters by taking his stand on the conservative financial platform of the Cincinnati Convention." Almost all of the prominent Democratic leaders of the state—former governors Nicholls and John McEnery, Governor Louis Wiltz, Lieutenant Governor S. D. McEnery, Congressman E. John Ellis—joined Burke in support of the Hancock movement. Brent, of course, had always been for Hancock.[18]

Less than a month later, the Louisiana Democratic State Convention met on April 12 in New Orleans. Carefully controlled by Burke, the convention did exactly what the editorials of the *New Orleans Democrat* had been urging; it sent an uninstructed delegation to Cincinnati but adopted a resolution favoring Hancock for president as well as the unit rule. In this way, Burke's hands remained free but the psychological impetus was given for the general from Pennsylvania. Having nailed down his own state, Burke then went to work on his neighbors. He visited Galveston to attend the state convention in Texas, and, not surprisingly, Texas voted exactly the same: an uninstructed delegation, the unit rule, and an endorsement of Hancock.[19]

Later in April, a critical contest for Hancock developed in Pennsylvania. The presidential election was simply another opportunity for the Wallace and Randall factions to wield their knives on one another, but, while everyone knew where Randall would stand with whatever delegates he might win, no one was very clear what Wallace would do with his supporters. Randall was for Tilden, and, if Tilden were not in the running, Randall was for Tilden's designated successor, which he hoped would be Samuel J. Randall. Wallace, on the other hand, was something of an unknown quantity. All that was certain was that he was not for Tilden, he was not for Randall, and he would not be for Henry Payne or any other man to whom Tilden's favor might be shown. The two names that seemed to pass the senator's lips most frequently were those of Bayard and Hancock, though he was reported to be carrying on minor dalliances with the Hendricks and Field camps as well. One Bayard man in Philadelphia wrote that Wallace "was advocating Hancock quietly but the publicity given to it frightened him." An upstate Pennsylvanian wrote that "I am satisfied that Wallace is in earnest" for Bayard. And, as the Pennsylvania convention was opening, one of Bayard's key operatives wrote him from New York, in puzzlement: "Is Wallace still for you? They say here he favors Hancock." It was clear that the senator from Pennsylvania had no settled preference but would try to do the best he could for William A. Wallace.[20]

Wallace's plan for the Harrisburg convention in late April, provided that he could establish control of it, was to select the delegation to Cincinnati and to bind it under the unit rule, requiring the entire delegation to vote as its majority should direct. As the delegates gathered in Harrisburg on April 26, they knew not whether they were in for another of the bitter Wallace-Randall bloodlettings which had marked recent state conventions or whether some sort of compromise would patch the party together for the time being. Some of Wallace's men wanted to unite on a single candidate for president; they were becoming impatient with the senator's game of being opposed to Tilden but not squarely in favor of anyone. Mainly, they wanted to support Hancock, whose backers had done their work well. "Hancock has probably more friends in the Convention than any other candidate," wrote one reporter; another wrote: "General Hancock is about the only candidate who has anything like a boom here." Wallace, however, held to his strategy. A fight on contending delegations from Philadelphia was averted, with a compromise being stitched together. But the senator would not indicate a choice for president.[21]

In the convention itself, Wallace's unit rule was narrowly voted down 125–122. In the choice of delegates to the national convention, those selected broke down to something like 19 each for Tilden and Hancock and 20 who were uncommitted but nominally under the control of Wallace. It was technically a Tilden-Randall victory to save their 19 delegates from being submerged in a bloc of 58 votes controlled by the unit rule; E. John Ellis called "the failure of Pennsylvania to endorse" Hancock "a bad blow." This view was a trifle too gloomy; Harrisburg was a kind of victory for Hancock. The oversanguine expectations of his supporters stood in the way of recognizing it as such. There was no doubt that there would be continued strong pressure on Wallace to support Hancock or be left behind by his delegation. "It was evident," wrote an observer, "from the thunders of applause that greeted Hancock's name whenever it was mentioned that he was the favorite." One political leader said that "there was going to be a great deal of trouble," presumably for the adroit Senator Wallace, "in handling the Pennsylvania delegation."[22]

In the meantime, other state conventions were also meeting and selecting their delegates to Cincinnati. On April 20 the New York convention met in Syracuse and instructed its delegates to vote as a unit; "Mr. Tilden was unequivocally endorsed without his name being mentioned." Nevertheless, though John Kelly and his Tammany braves would have no votes at Cincinnati, it was well known that his unremitting opposition to Tilden would make carrying New York extremely difficult for the former governor. "Their hostility to him admits of no compromise," wrote one reporter, "and everybody knows that without their help neither Mr. Tilden nor any other Democrat can carry New York." In 1879 Kelly had run an independent campaign for governor and siphoned off enough votes from Tilden's man, Lucius B. Robinson, to doom his effort at reelection. No one could suppose that Kelly, who was receiving financial aid from Bayard's friends, was simply bluffing.[23]

On April 22 the Vermont Democrats met at Montpelier and chose Hancock delegates to Cincinnati. Baldy Smith had obviously done his work well in the Green Mountain State. Tilden's name brought forth polite applause, but Hancock's name produced "round after round of cheers."[24]

A curious thing appeared to be happening. While the party bigwigs worried about what they would do with Samuel Tilden, and the editors of the major papers speculated on Tilden's probable course, there were indications (ignored by the so-called political experts) that rank-and-file Democrats, when they had an opportunity to express themselves, were making Hancock their popular favorite. Certainly this aspect of the preconvention activities should not be overemphasized; popular esteem was a relatively minor factor in presidential maneuvering, and getting at public opinion was a tricky matter at best. Still, there were those stories of Democratic meetings in various towns and cities across the country which often carried the tag line "The popular favorite in the galleries appeared to be Winfield Scott Hancock of Pennsylvania"—or something like it. The phenomenon would be more pronounced at the Cincinnati convention itself; the fact that nobody noticed it in April, May, or June helps to explain why Hancock's success came as such a surprise to the experts.[25]

THIRTY

Drifting

As the national convention approached, there were few more clues to what the Democrats would do than there had been at the beginning of the year. The specter of Tilden's continuing hopes appeared to have bemused seasoned political observers as well as many of the participants in the struggle. A week before the convention, the *New York Times* editorialized: "In all the calculations that are made regarding the Democratic nomination, it is impossible to construct an equation from which the wily old man of Gramercy Park is eliminated." The questions heard everywhere concerned Tilden's strength, his intentions, and the chances of a designated successor, if Tilden stepped aside. "The Democratic party is afraid of Samuel J. Tilden," it was written, "afraid to offend him, afraid to nominate him, and . . . most of all afraid that, by hook or by crook, he will have his way, and, if he is not himself nominated, that some creature of his will become the candidate."[1]

The Republicans had met. In a bitter, contentious gathering in Chicago, a prolonged stalemate between Grant and Blaine had been broken with the nomination on the thirty-sixth ballot of a dark-horse candidate, Congressman James A. Garfield of Ohio. Even on the final ballot, the Grant forces, led by the unbending Conkling of New York, had cast 306 defiant votes for their man, while the rest of the weary delegates flocked to the surprise winner. This refusal to compromise boded no good for the party's prospects, even though Garfield and his friends picked as the vice-presidential nominee Chester Alan Arthur, chief lieutenant in Conkling's New York machine. Arthur had no visible qualifications for high national office; his most prominent position had been collector of the Port of New York, from which post he had been fired by Hayes for patronage abuses. His nomination was a gratuitous insult to the president. Garfield, too, though an attractive and personable man, had drawbacks. He had been culpably involved in the Crédit Mobilier railroad scandal, and he had later had a suspicious-looking connection with a questionable paving contract in the city of Washington. The Republicans appeared vulnerable, but no one knew, as the Democrats assembled in Cincinnati, whether the Republican weakness could be exploited.

The Democratic situation was still confused. The Tilden forces were as much bewildered as those supporting other candidates. William C. Whitney, corporation counsel for the city of New York, confidant of Tilden, and son-in-law of Henry B. Payne, one of those hoping to be Tilden's beneficiary, told a reporter in Cincinnati, "The situation is dark. It is worse. It is muddled." Whitney's understanding of Tilden's intentions, he said, differed from that of Daniel Manning, the New York chairman, "and we can't reconcile the things that have been said to each of us by the great man." Manning felt that Tilden still wanted the nomination, while Whitney, believing that Tilden intended to remove himself, was working for his father-in-law. Whitney had been in contact with Henry Tilden, Samuel's brother, who was on his way to Cincinnati with a letter from the former governor, but even Henry was unable to say whether his brother was a candidate or not. Whitney, tired of Tilden's deviousness, felt that the former governor could neither be nominated nor name the candidate. It would be Hancock, Whitney thought, although "Hancock is the man of all men that Tilden does not want."[2]

In the meantime, as Whitney, Manning, and the other Tilden leaders agonized over the course of their champion, Democrats from across the continent gathered together in the Queen City of the Ohio. The assembling took place slowly; on June 18 a reporter wrote, in some surprise: "The bars are poorly patronized, and there is very little chin music." The next day, a warm and cloudy one, the city was filling up. The center of political activity was the Grand Hotel, though Reid's, the Gibson House, and the Emory were all being used. Bayard's people were in the St. Nicholas. Burke quartered his Louisiana delegation at the "new and elegant" Hotel Emory, and he took the further precaution of lodging the Texas delegation in a suite on the same floor. Hancock's supporters fixed their headquarters at the New Central Hotel on Elm Street, and they stretched a banner bearing the general's name over the street in front of the hotel.[3]

Significantly, among those who spent several hours in the Hancock headquarters on June 19, receiving visitors and attempting to sell them on the virtues of the general as a candidate, was Senator Wallace. Baldy Smith was there, and General Franklin, who was in charge, and a number of other loyal Hancock men. St. Clair Mulholland worked hard at buttonholing individual delegates, putting his Irish charm to work for his old chief. But the important one was Wallace, who had by now yielded to the pressures in his delegation or to his own inclination and moved into the Hancock camp. As late as June 8 there had been talk of Wallace's pulling away from Hancock in favor, possibly, of Field, but it became clear that he could not deliver a substantial bloc of votes to anyone other than the general. Wallace realized this before he got to Cincinnati and was firmly for Hancock at the convention. He brought with him, of course, a sizable chunk of Pennsylvania votes, as well as a highly regarded facility for political maneuver and intrigue. In 1880, it was clear, the Hancock campaign would not be out-generaled as in 1868 or overwhelmed as in 1876. There were even two special telegraph receivers installed in the headquarters at Governor's Island, and these were kept in frequent use during the convention. "Hancock's friends," one correspondent wrote, "have a formidable organization with Wallace of Pennsylvania, chairman." The Hancock people, on June 19, claimed for their candidate 80 sure votes on the first ballot, with more coming along afterward. The next day a reporter corralled Ned Burke, whose Louisiana delegates were said to be "most enthusiastic in their support of Hancock." Burke said that Hancock would receive not less than 85 votes on the first ballot. He said it with the assurance of a man who could, if pressed, tell exactly who the 85 would be.[4]

Bayard's workers were pushing hard, particularly in the southern delegations, but his friends repeatedly came up against the hard rock of Tilden's fierce enmity, due to the Electoral Commission bill. Field's supporters claimed 180 to 210 votes for the judge on the first ballot, but such a prediction was considered a case of too much California sunshine. Horatio Seymour said once again that he was not a candidate; if he had to choose between his own funeral and a nomination, he said, he would opt for the funeral. This seemed to convince those who had been considering him that he really meant what he said. Thurman's candidacy was in trouble. Outside of Ohio he attracted little support, and a meeting was held in Columbus on June 18 in a vain effort to figure out what to do. As long as Thurman stayed in the race, of course, Henry B. Payne, if he should become a candidate, could not crack his own state's delegation. Hendricks and Morrison appeared to be holding on without gaining, and Randall's hopes were paralyzed by the indecision over Tilden and the possibility of Tilden's throwing his strength to Payne. The situation was both dark and muddled, as Whitney said.[5]

On Sunday afternoon, June 20, Henry Tilden arrived in Cincinnati, bearing the long-awaited letter from his brother. Henry wanted to have the letter held back until it could be read to the convention, presumably on instructions from his brother, but Smith Weed and Dan Manning insisted that it be read to the New York delegation "as soon as possible." That evening Manning called a caucus and read the communication from Tilden. The letter, a lengthy and craftily constructed document, on its face set forth Tilden's intention not to be a candidate in 1880. "Having now borne faithfully my full share of labor and care in the public service, and wearing the marks of its burdens," he wrote, "I desire nothing so much as an honorable discharge." He then went on to say that "in renouncing a renomination . . . I do so with no doubt in my mind as to the vote of the State of New York, or of the United States."[6]

Many of the politicians and reporters gathered in Cincinnati read the letter, however, with its recital of Tilden's great services over the years and of the Great Fraud of 1876, and discerned in it a cunning invitation to the delegates to disregard the withdrawal and to renominate the old man. Clearly, Henry Tilden, in his report to his brother the next day, was gauging the possibility of such a development. One of Bayard's men wrote that Tilden's letter was "a trick to puff his own wares and secure the nomination." Even Whitney (whose loyalty was divided between his mentor, Tilden, and his father-in-law, Payne) felt that "that letter was written to be read in the convention, and Tilden believed that if it had been the convention would have been swept into a stampede for him."[7]

What happened, of course, was nothing like that. Instead of being read to the convention, the letter was read late at night to a tired bunch of New York delegates. One of them, Augustus Schoonmaker of Ulster County, moved to accept the withdrawal in good faith and to make the letter public. The motion was passed, and that quickly Samuel J. Tilden was out of the running. Most delegates appeared to accept the ambiguous letter of withdrawal as a longed-for blessing, taking them off the hook by eliminating the necessity of actually *rejecting* the Great Defrauded.[8]

With Tilden's withdrawal, the race for the nomination took on an entirely new aspect. Tilden had asked his supporters to back Payne, but the widespread question "Who is Payne?" together with his scant chance of carrying Ohio against the popular Garfield appeared to preclude that. Bayard's people were now claiming 250 first-ballot votes, while Field's strength appeared to be on the wane. The Virginia delegates had caucused on Sunday and voted to abandon Field; although they now declared in favor of former governor English of Connecticut, that was clearly a holding action. The Bayard leaders had high hopes of these Virginia delegates, and they planned to pick up the rest of the declining Field support in the South. It was observed, however, that Hancock had as much southern strength, especially in Louisiana, Texas, and Mississippi, as anyone; Ned Burke had done his work well.[9]

Monday, June 21, was intensely hot and humid. The hotels were jammed, and the beer gardens in that very German city did a thriving business. The usual complement of gamblers, thieves, and sporting ladies showed up, and a couple of delegates reported their gold watches missing. The bands which had been hired by candidates and delegations created an air of festivity and excitement. Cincinnati was now buzzing with Democratic talk. With Tilden out of the race, there appeared no discernible pattern to events. The push for Henry Payne was not prospering, but it was keeping Speaker Randall and his friends in a state of uncertainty. At one stage, New York determined to abandon Payne and support Judge Calvin Pratt of Brooklyn. Ultimately, Judge Pratt asked that he be withdrawn, reflecting perhaps that, in comparison with *his* name, Payne's was practically a household word. The success of Bayard's efforts was hard to measure; one of his managers wired him that his strength was "good and largely diffused but we are fighting against the whole field." Later that day the same man sent the senator another wire, confessing that "old hands admit that no convention was so chaotic and so hard to form any reliable opinion about." Finally, he said, "the only thing we have to meet is the Dover speech and its supposed effect upon availability. . . ." The "only thing" for Bayard to meet, it was to prove sufficient to defeat him with a party which wanted no more of the bloody shirt.[10]

In the meantime, the Hancock effort was low-keyed, soft-spoken, a word here and there. "The Hancock plan of campaign," said one report, "appears to be to make war upon nobody and make friends." Much of the work had been done already, and Burke, Wallace, Brent, and the blond-whiskered Mulholland could be counted on to keep up the pressure where they knew they could do some good. One reporter said the Hancock canvass was "not energetic," that it lacked "enthusiasm," whereas the Associated Press correspondent, reading matters a bit more astutely, wrote: "Gen. Hancock's friends, who are many, appear to be reserving themselves until their opportunity shall develop." They kept busy passing out the general's badges, simple blue ribbons with his name inscribed on them.[11]

By this time, the party's leaders had done the essential arithmetic which was the key to the nomination. This arithmetic did not necessarily concern the number of delegates required for the two-thirds vote which would capture the nomination. It concerned the number of electoral votes which could spell victory in November. It was reasonable to expect 138 electoral votes from the South—the old Confederacy together with Delaware, Maryland, Kentucky, West Virginia, and Missouri—with no repeat of the carpetbag counts of 1876. The party would then be 47 votes shy of the required majority of 185, and the search in the convention would be for a candidate who could secure them. Nevada and California looked probable, but they provided only 9 electors between them. What it came down to was four states—New York, New Jersey, Connecticut, and Indiana—in which prospects for Democratic success seemed good and which offered 65 electoral votes. New York and any one of the other three would do it. It is in this context that Kelly's threats of Tammany vengeance against Tilden must be read; the old man's weakness in his own state made the delegates eager to take his withdrawal literally. It was in these four states that Bayard's Dover Green speech was expected to hurt. It was in these states, Hancock's men pointed out to waverers and undecideds, that the general's war record and peacetime services would win him votes among Republicans and independents while his party orthodoxy brought out the full Democratic vote.

As the clock wound down to the start of the convention, there was little doubt that the Democratic party would select a new leader, but beyond that lay uncertainty and hesitation. "The delegates," a correspondent reported the night before the convention opened, "are making tours of the beer halls and gardens and waiting for orders. . . . There is more uncertainty tonight among individual delegates than has ever been witnessed before, and when the driftwood commences to accumulate, it may pile up very fast in some unexpected corner."[12]

THIRTY ONE

The Cincinnati
Convention

Hancock did not go to Cincinnati for the Democratic convention. He remained at Governor's Island, carrying on his military routine, attempting to stay unaffected by the activities in Cincinnati's Music Hall 650 miles away, with only the clattering of the special telegraph lines betraying a special interest.

At thirty-eight minutes past noon on Tuesday, June 22, Senator William H. Barnum, the national chairman, called the convention to order. The temporary chairman, Judge George Hoadly of Ohio, delivered a somewhat tedious speech and then announced the appointment of committees on permanent organization, credentials, and resolutions, a process interrupted by John Kelly of Tammany, who rose and attempted unsuccessfully to address the chair. Shortly thereafter, the convention adjourned until the following morning.[1]

The most newsworthy event of the opening day of the convention was the decision of the New York delegation to cast its entire vote as a unit for Payne, after the withdrawal of the eminent Judge Pratt. This determination was seen as a victory of sorts for Whitney, but it remained to be seen whether many other delegates would follow New York's lead. Strenuous efforts were being made by the Payne backers with New Jersey and Connecticut. Randall was left high and dry for the time being, and, meanwhile, the *New York Times* correspondent reported that "much of Bayard's strength is going to Hancock." Apparently, this movement was occurring primarily among southern delegates, but the Hancock men were buoyant. They now predicted 140 first ballot votes, though a writer sniffed that "they are no doubt counting too fast." There were two centers of Hancock activity, one at the Emory in the Louisiana headquarters, the other at the general's headquarters in the New Central, where the Illinois and Ohio delegations came to call and were welcomed by E. John Ellis. These two states were still otherwise committed, of course, but their visits seemed to be a good sign. Tuesday evening was devoted to intrigues and maneuvers in the crowded hotel lobbies, beer gardens, and caucus rooms around Cincinnati. "The city," it was reported, "is alive tonight."[2]

On the morning of June 23, Judge Hoadly called the convention back to order at twenty minutes to eleven. The hall, packed with 10,000 people, was already hot when the credentials committee was called for its report. A long wrangle broke out over the seats in New York City disputed between Tammany and Irving halls before the majority report, permitting the Irving Hall delegates to keep their seats, was adopted. Senator John W. Stevenson of Kentucky was then elected permanent presiding officer and gave a brief address.[3]

The committee on resolutions, chaired by Henry Watterson of Kentucky, was having trouble thrashing out a platform, and it was not yet ready to report when Stevenson finished his address, so the convention proceeded to hear nominations for president. J. E. McElrath of California led off the nominations with a mediocre speech on behalf of Field, followed by Attorney General George Gray of Delaware for Bayard. Gray pleaded: "Tell the country that the sneer of Republican enemies is a lie, and that such a man as Thomas Francis Bayard is not too good a man to receive the highest honors of the Democratic party." Gray's polished address was well received, but it was doubtful that it would stop the erosion of Bayard's strength.[4]

Next up was Congressman Samuel S. Marshall of Illinois, nominating his state's favorite son, Colonel William R. Morrison, in a rambling, confused, and embarrassing speech. He was followed by the "Tall Sycamore of the Wabash," Senator Daniel W. Voorhees of Indiana, one of the party's favorite stump speakers, presenting Hendricks. Massachusetts was called, and Leverett Saltonstall rose to second the candidacy of Bayard. When New York was called, a great hubbub stirred the hall, as Tilden's name was shouted and cheers and hisses rose up on all sides. The chair admonished the gallery, and Manning then announced that New York had no nomination to make. John McSweeney of Ohio presented the name of the host state's candidate, Allen G. Thurman. The Thurman candidacy, of course, continued to stand between Payne and the votes of the Ohio delegation.[5]

Pennsylvania was next, and chairman Malcolm Hay announced that it had no candidate to present, "but a delegate wishes to advocate the claim of one of her distinguished sons." Daniel Dougherty of Philadelphia was not actually a delegate but had been substituted that day for a gentleman who had given up his seat so that Dougherty might nominate Hancock. The general's strategists felt that it was important to have an impressive nominating speech, and it was probably Wallace who came up with Dougherty. One of Dougherty's friends wrote that Dan never spoke on important occasions without careful preparation and memorizing his remarks; "he had only a few hours to prepare his address, and that doubtless gave it the merit of brevity." It was indeed brief, but it was very well received, except perhaps by the Randall man in the Pennsylvania delegation who snorted that Dougherty "hasn't voted the Democratic ticket for 20 years."[6]

"I present to the thoughtful consideration of the convention," Dougherty said, "the name of one who, on the field of battle, was styled 'The Superb' "—here there was a wild outburst of applause—"yet won still nobler renown as the Military Governor, whose first act in assuming command in Louisiana and Texas was to salute the Constitution by proclaiming, amid the joyous greetings of an oppressed people, that the military, save in actual war, shall be subservient to the civil power." More applause. "The plighted word of the soldier was proved in the deeds of the statesman." Pause for more cheering. "I name one who, if nominated, will suppress every faction, and be alike acceptable to the North and to the South, whose nomination will thrill the land from end to end, crush the last embers of sectional strife, and be hailed as the dawning of the longed-for day of perpetual brotherhood." Another outburst of cheering. "With him we can fling away our shields and wage aggressive war." The delegates loved this. "With him as our chieftain the bloody banner of the Republicans will fall from their palsied grasp. We can appeal to the supreme tribunal of the American people against the corruptions of the Republican party and its untold violations of Constitutional liberty." Dougherty paused dramatically, then continued: "Oh, my countrymen, in this supreme moment the destinies of the Republic, the imperiled liberties of the people hang breathless on your deliberations. Pause! Reflect! Beware! Make no mis-step! I nominate him who can carry every southern state—can carry Pennsylvania, Indiana, Connecticut, New Jersey, and New York—the soldier-statesman, with a record stainless as his sword." The final hesitation; then: "I nominate Winfield Scott Hancock of Pennsylvania. If elected he will take his seat." Dougherty stepped back, and the crowd went wild.[7]

For five minutes the cheering continued, while the reporters present watched and listened and realized that no other candidate had been greeted with anything like the enthusiasm which was brought forth by Hancock's name. "It was soon evident," one of them wrote, "that Gen. Hancock had secured a strong hold, not only upon the galleries, but also upon the delegates." This display of popularity "was unexpected, and had not been a factor in the calculations of the preceding day." "It was plain to be seen," wrote another, "that Gen. Hancock was the favorite of the convention."[8]

The driftwood of the convention, it appeared, was starting to pile up.

When order was restored, Wade Hampton of South Carolina seconded the nomination of Bayard, saying his man was "as brave as Hancock," but conceding that the South would feel safe in Hancock's hands "because we were safe when he had the power." He was followed by Governor Richard Hubbard of Texas, seconding Hancock. He extolled the general for reading the Constitution "as the fathers read it." He said that Hancock, "who risked his reputation, place and power in the very face and teeth of the Republican party, is a man that it will do to trust the standard of our party to."[9]

After another speech for Field, John W. Daniel of Virginia, a one-legged Confederate veteran, gave another second for Hancock. "Nominate Winfield Scott Hancock and . . . my friends, in the canvass, you will hear the hearty hurrah of the boys who wore the blue, mingling with the wild, sweet music of the rebel cheer in one grand national anthem of peace." Again, as

Dougherty and Hubbard had, Daniel found his speech enthusiastically applauded.[10]

After a final seconding speech for Thurman, the nominations were completed. The Tilden people, watching with concern the impact of the speeches and enthusiasm for Hancock, attempted to move an adjournment for the day. This was defeated, and the voting for the first ballot then commenced.

The secretary called the roll of the states, and all the fevered speculation was put aside in favor of actual votes, actual numbers, actual strength. As the balloting proceeded, Ned Burke, sitting with his Louisiana delegation, received surprise after surprise. He had counted up 148 votes for Hancock, and he had arranged for 24 of them to be held back on the first ballot so that their subsequent casting for Hancock would look like a major increase of strength. As he listened to the tally, however, he kept hearing votes for Hancock where he did not expect them. When the ballot was completed, the band played "Dixie" and "Yankee Doodle" while the numbers were added up and everyone waited for the announcement of the totals.[11]

Finally, the music stopped and the hall hushed and the secretary read the figures. Hancock had 171, Bayard had 153½, Payne 81, Thurman 68½, Field 65, Morrison 62, Hendricks 49½, Tilden 38 diehards, Thomas Ewing of Ohio 10, Horatio Seymour 8, Randall 6, and eight other men scattered 14 votes. Another loud cheer, and then a motion to adjourn was adopted. After a long session of seven and a half hours, the delegates could go back to the hotels and beer gardens, while the so-called leaders tried to sort things out.[12]

Twelve years earlier, a Democratic convention had adjourned with Winfield Scott Hancock leading the voting for president, and he had been done in in the hotel rooms and lobbies of New York City. Without doubt the power brokers of the party would set out to repeat that feat in Cincinnati. After talking with a few of them, a correspondent wrote that "there is not a well-informed politician here who will for a moment admit that Gen. Hancock's nomination is even among the possibilities. . . . Unfortunately for him, the convention now in progress here is controlled by politicians who have no sentiment other than that which they from time to time display in the palms of their hands." These men, he wrote, wanted "a trickster, a man of their own kind," and unless they should be overwhelmed by some kind of stampede, "the last man they are likely to nominate is Winfield Scott Hancock."[13]

Back in the Hancock camp, the leaders were not about to sit and wait to be overwhelmed. Instead of a few retired generals and political amateurs, as in 1868, the Hancock effort was led by a couple of those power brokers referred to, fully prepared to fight fire with fire. Analyzing the first ballot, they found that Hancock's 69 votes from the South had exactly matched Bayard's total from that region, which was supposed to be the heart of the Delaware senator's strength. Hancock had all 10 of Minnesota's votes, all 14 of Maine's, and all 10 of Vermont's. He had 6 from Massachusetts, 5 from

Michigan, 12 from Missouri, 4 from New Hampshire, 7 from Iowa, and a whopping 28 from Pennsylvania.[14]

The other candidates found gloomier reading in the first-ballot numbers. Hendricks, Field, Morrison, and Thurman appeared to be going nowhere. None of them had received other than scattered support outside of their own states. Henry Payne had gotten only 11 votes in addition to the 70 thrown him under New York's unit rule, and his cause appeared hopeless unless his home state of Ohio should switch to him. Bayard was not far behind Hancock, but he had expected to be in the lead; his cause was not surging forward. In addition, his men on the scene were still underestimating Hancock; one of them wired to Bayard: "The Hancock vote was larger than we expected because the convention got into a little furor over a speech made by Dan Dougherty." Of the others who had received votes, only Randall could be considered any sort of a threat—and then only if a number of circumstances came together for him.[15]

The wire-pullers in the hotel rooms did a great deal of talking that night, trying to break the back of the Hancock boom, which Congressman E. John Ellis called "a spontaneous movement of men free from rings and faction fights." That assessment overlooked the contributions of Burke and Wallace but was essentially correct. The wire-pullers trotted out the old stories about Mary Surratt, but no one paid much attention. They talked about Tilden but found little response to the old man's name. They talked about Payne, but, when Ohio decided to stick with Thurman a while longer, Payne became a dead issue. They talked about Randall, but, until Payne was out and New York had decided what it would do next, it was too early to float Randall seriously. They talked about Governor English of Connecticut and Senator Joseph McDonald of Indiana and former governor John M. Palmer of Illinois. None of them attracted any appreciable amount of support, and the Democratic bosses were forced to consider that old political maxim "You can't beat somebody with nobody." The bitterness of Tilden toward Bayard, Thurman, and Hendricks played its final part here, in the Cincinnati hotel lobbies, as it frustrated efforts to agree upon a consensus candidate. The Democratic bosses theoretically had votes enough to beat Hancock, but they could not concentrate them. The Hancock leaders—Burke, Wallace, the Smiths, Franklin, Ellis, Mulholland, and others—were out talking, too, and they were picking up votes here and there where they had not had them before. The strategy of making friends and not enemies was paying off.[16]

For Hancock, the opportunity was great, as was the danger. The momentum of the second day of the convention had to be utilized; the enthusiasm for the Hancock speeches, the surprise lead in the voting, the popular favor for the general—these must be capitalized upon. If the Hancock movement should falter—and it required 492 votes to win the nomination, so that 171 was just a few steps along the way—it would lose. The bosses of the party would not pick up Hancock again, and restless delegates would switch to some other likely-looking prospect. The wisdom of Burke in holding back some of his vote looked inspired, so that there would be no appearance of slipping back as the second ballot progressed. Still, it would be the additional recruits picked up overnight who would make any major gains for Hancock.

By midnight, it was becoming apparent that the Hancock leaders were having more success in winning new adherents than the anti-Hancock men were in detaching delegates from him. The same reporter who had earlier scorned the chance of Hancock's receiving the nomination now found "many indications" leading to a possible Hancock stampede on the morrow. The Hancock supporters, led by Burke, he found, had "laid their plans with a good deal of shrewdness." Burke told him they would pick up at least eighty votes on the first or second ballot on June 24. The major development the Hancock men expected was the action of Illinois in ditching Morrison in favor of the general, with Morrison then whispered for the second spot on the ticket. (When the voting for vice-president *did* come up, Morrison wired his people that he was not interested; the Hancock men did not have to deliver on whatever pledge may have been given.) The reporter still found it hard to believe: "the mass of the wire-pullers and managing politicians of the party were opposed to the movement, and . . . he has only one or two skillful men of that class on his side." A Hancock victory, he concluded, would be "a victory for the young and green portion of the party over the old and slippery veterans."[17]

June 24 dawned cloudy, and it soon became hot and sultry. "The hot air of the morning," one imaginative reporter wrote, "was freighted with Hancock whispers." One observer noticed that only Hancock badges were being purchased from the sidewalk vendors outside the hall. The old Hancock faithful—Brent, Franklin, Mulholland, and their comrades in arms—were up early, even after the busy night.[18]

Stevenson called the convention to order at 10:30 a.m., and soon Rufus Peckham of New York was on the platform. He informed the delegates of Tilden's letter of June 18—one last, forlorn effort to attract the lightning bolt for which Tilden still hoped—waited, heard nothing, and then, since Tilden had "renounced" the nomination, stated that New York was going to vote for Samuel J. Randall.[19]

The second ballot began. The hall was packed tightly, and it was hot and stifling, but the throng of ten thousand waited expectantly, ready to shout and cheer with each new development of gain or loss. Alabama led it off, and its vote of 10 for Hancock was a gain of 3; presumably, these were from Burke's reserve. A great cheer went up nevertheless. California gave Hancock 5 votes, producing another cheer. When the general's Georgia vote declined by one, there were hisses scattered with applause. Illinois was called, and it gave Hancock its entire bloc of 42 votes. "Cheering broke out like a tornado," and the issue may very well have been decided right there. Iowa gave Hancock 2 more than the day before, but its other 12 went to Randall, who was picking up scattered votes. Kansas gave Hancock its 10 votes, and again there was a burst of applause. When Watterson's Kentucky gave Hancock 10, it became clear that the Tilden votes could not be delivered intact to Randall—not at this stage of the convention. Michigan now gave Hancock 14, a gain of 9, and he picked up 5 more in Massachusetts. When Missouri was called, it cast 28 votes for Hancock, an increase of 16. It took Stevenson several minutes of hard gaveling before he could calm the ensuing demonstration. When New York gave Randall its 70, "it looked as though they were going to stem the tide." Then North Carolina dropped Bayard and gave all 20 of its votes to Hancock, and the danger of a counter-stampede had passed. Pennsylvania passed, while Randall's lieutenants worked on the Wallace men in the caucus room. Still, there were increases all along the line for Hancock. When Pennsylvania came back in, it cast 32 for Hancock and 26 for Randall—4 more votes for Hancock than on the first ballot. Senator Wallace was ecstatic, for this vote proved that Randall's men could not control their own state's delegation. As the ballot came to an end, Hancock had 310 votes. Before the total was announced, the Wisconsin chairman was up, to state that to its earlier 10 Hancock votes it was adding 10 more. This gave Hancock 320, to Randall's 129½ and Bayard's 113, with Field, Thurman, Hendricks, and English of Connecticut trailing far behind.[20]

The numbers, however, were now academic. New Jersey switched its entire vote to Hancock, and the rout was on. He had still been almost 200 votes short of the required two-thirds, and indeed was still short of a majority, but the party leaders, who knew they had no one with which to beat him, threw in their hands. They were helped along the way by Ned Burke, who had one of his Louisiana delegates take the state banner with a big portrait of Hancock on it to the platform and start waving it back and forth, to stir up whatever psychological impetus might be needed. Malcolm Hay of Pennsylvania changed all of his delegation's votes to Hancock, stating that his people were proud of both Hancock and Randall, and then Smith Weed gave Hancock the 70 votes of New York. When Ohio gave him 44 votes, it appeared that he had passed the 492 vote level. The chairman then called the roll again, and Hancock wound up with 705, to 30 from Indiana holding out for Hendricks, 2 from Maryland for Bayard, and one lonely Iowan still voting for Tilden.[21]

Winfield Scott Hancock was the Democratic party's nominee for president.

The chairman of the Indiana delegation moved that the nomination be made unanimous, and the galleries whooped and hollered some more. The obligatory love feast followed, the lion lying down with the lamb, John Kelly with the Tildenites, even Wallace with Sam Randall. Wade Hampton, George Hoadly, and Dan Voorhees each said his piece, Voorhees remarking that "there never was a nomination made which was so utterly destitute of preparation and preliminary management, as this which has been made today." Perhaps this was so, but it appears that the party professionals were

misled by the amateurish Hancock efforts of earlier conventions into underestimating the management which the leaders of the 1880 canvass
carried out so successfully.[22]

The remaining business of the convention was quickly concluded. After
the emotional outburst of the Hancock nomination, most of the delegates
wandered out of the hall. Susan B. Anthony was permitted to present a
petition on behalf of women's suffrage—received with yawning boredom by
the few delegates remaining—and then Henry Watterson presented the
party platform, which aroused little more interest and was adopted unanimously with no debate. The *Nation* wrote that "all the conventions have
now begun to treat the platform as a joke" and this one read "like a highly
inflammatory editorial" in Watterson's newspaper. No one appeared to note,
or to take cognizance of, the simple phrase "a tariff for revenue only," which
was Watterson's creation and the shortest statement on the tariff ever made
by any major party platform. The Democrats would hear much more of that
five-word phrase before November.[23]

By this time the party leaders had settled on William H. English of
Indiana, a wealthy banker who had last held office as a congressman before
the Civil War, as the choice for the vice-presidency. There was a flurry for
former governor Richard Bishop of Ohio, but he was shortly withdrawn, and
English was chosen unanimously. It was the second convention in a row in
which Indiana's holding out on the deciding ballot for the presidency had
won it the vice-presidential nomination as a sop. English would presumably
add nothing to the ticket elsewhere, but if he could help to carry his own
crucial state his selection would be vindicated. With nothing else to be done,
at 3 p.m. the convention adjourned *sine die*.[24]

How did it happen? Very few predicted that Hancock would carry off the
prize at Cincinnati, but carry it off he did. Bayard worker George Bates, who
had talked of the "little furor" stirred up by Dougherty the day before, now
wired his principal that the "whole thing has gone off in a hurrah for
Hancock." This may have been comforting to him, but its lack of perception
may help explain why Bayard slipped noticeably at Cincinnati. The *New
York Times* said that Hancock was "the candidate of sentiment," the prod-
uct of "a dire Democratic dilemma." The *Philadelphia Inquirer* simply said
that he whipped the bosses, who "have had to follow when they could no
longer lead." All of these statements contained a part of the truth, but even
without benefit of hindsight it should have been plainer than it apparently
was before the convention that Hancock was a major threat. He suffered
from none of the disabilities which afflicted the other candidates—the
hostility of Tilden, the hard- or soft-money burden, Bayard's fatal speech of
1861, the advanced ages of some contenders—and he enjoyed genuine
popularity among the people. He had been down the road a couple of times
before, so that his workers had learned a few tricks, and he took on board
several sagacious politicians. Finally, after Tilden was out of the way, the
competition was not too stern; any convention in which Stephen J. Field

was considered a major contender was surely up for grabs. Here Hancock was the beneficiary of a major blunder on the part of Tilden and his cronies: if they had pushed for Randall from the start, forgetting the impossible Payne candidacy, they might have nominated their man. Speaker Randall had connections across the country, even beyond the Tilden loyalists, and was clearly a viable candidate; the strength of his jerry-built, last-minute effort showed that. But Whitney's influence on behalf of his father-in-law, the fear generated by Wallace's hostility to Randall in his own state, and some Randall unpopularity in the South caused the fatal misstep of pushing for Payne. By the time this error was corrected, Hancock was beyond stopping.[25]

THIRTY TWO

The Campaign Begins

Winfield Hancock attempted to treat June 24, 1880, as just another day in his life, but the effort soon fell flat. He paid a visit to New York City in the morning and returned to Governor's Island at about a quarter past noon. Everyone on that small military base was well aware of what was transpiring in Cincinnati, and, when the news of the general's victory arrived, his home was soon swarming with well-wishers.

An Associated Press reporter took the little steamer out to Governor's Island and found the general on the veranda of his home surrounded by military friends. When he congratulated Hancock, the latter shook his hand but said, "Indeed, I have nothing to say at present, as I have not been officially notified of my nomination." Then, with what the reporter described as a "quizzical smile," the general said, "You know, it might all be a mistake." Obviously enjoying himself hugely, he continued by conceding that he *had* received a number of congratulatory telegrams—from Wallace, Tilden, Bayard, and others—which he showed to the correspondent.[1]

Other reporters were sent scurrying after reactions to the surprising development. The overall sentiment in Washington was that Hancock was the best candidate the Democrats could have nominated, although not many had said that before the fact. A reporter looked up General Sherman and asked him what he thought of the news from Cincinnati. Sherman said that he of course did not have anything to do with politics, "but if you will sit down and write the best thing that can be put in language about General Hancock as an officer and a gentleman, I will sign it without hesitation."[2]

The Republicans were not happy with Hancock's selection. Their newspapers quickly began to damn Hancock with faint praise. "He was a good soldier," wrote the *Philadelphia Press,* "but there his title begins and ends." The *Springfield Republican* conceded that Hancock did not represent the worst element in his party. The *St. Louis Globe Democrat* said that Hancock's nomination "no more changes the character of Democracy than a figurehead of the Virgin on Kidd's pirate craft would change it into an honest ship." The *Philadelphia Inquirer* said that "whatever knowledge he may have of our politics and public questions is as scanty and superficial as was General Taylor's." But the party leaders, in their private correspondence, told a different tale. Warner Bateman said that Hancock's nomination had taken the Republicans "with considerable surprise and some alarm," and Hayes's personal secretary wrote Garfield that the nomination was the strongest the Democrats could make. Carl Schurz commented that this development unfortunately eliminated the southern issue from the campaign.[3]

Democratic reactions varied, of course, depending on the preference of the writer. The *New Orleans Times,* pro-Bayard to the end, was sure that Hancock's nomination was "not the strongest that could have been made from the material at hand," whereas its rival, the *New Orleans Democrat,* Burke's paper, wrote: "It could not have been better." The *Atlanta Constitution* said that, with Tilden, the issue in the campaign would have been the fraud of 1876; with Hancock it was "new blood and union forever." Former Confederate general Joseph E. Johnston, now a Virginia congressman, wired Hancock: "Your nomination makes me much gladder than you."[4]

Indeed, while there can be little doubt that Hancock himself desired the nomination—and the opportunity to serve in the nation's chief executive position—there is evidence that Allie did not share this feeling. The general's son, Russell, told a reporter during the campaign, "My mother was opposed in the first place to father's allowing his name to be used as a candidate for President and in the second place her expressed desire was that he would not accept the nomination." While there can hardly have been a chance of a declination, the nomination's arrival at the Hancock household was obviously not greeted with total joy.[5]

The Bayard people pouted. Bradley Johnson of Maryland, who voted for Bayard to the very end, blamed the southerners for being "very weak-kneed" and "terribly afraid," and August Belmont ascribed Hancock's nomination to "an organized mob in the galleries." Wade Hampton assured Bayard that he was the first choice of a large majority of the delegates. This news could hardly have been comforting to the senator from Delaware, but Hampton tried to explain what happened: Bayard's southern supporters were told to scatter their votes until his northern strength could be ascertained. This, Hampton now decided, "was a great mistake. It led to the accidental position Hancock obtained & then the galleries nominated him." The *New Orleans Times* reporter on the spot, however, had a different conclusion: after describing the Hancock effort, he said, "had the Bayard boom been managed as masterly, and had Bayard's friends worked with the same zeal, the result might have been different."[6]

Tilden told a *New York Herald* reporter that he could have been nominated and elected but that he was not up to the effort that would have been required. In the meantime, however, Smith Weed was writing to the old man from Cincinnati that "it was very apparent to anyone that it was not possible to have nominated you even if you would have taken it, as I know you would not." Weed went on to say, "I feared Hancock's nomination, but did not fear it so early."[7]

Weed concluded by saying, "Barnum will tell you of the talks with Hancock people. I hope he (H.) will make it apparent that he is to be your friend, and if so that you will help him through." Curiously, Hampton had wound up his letter to Bayard by saying, "It is important that Hancock should not fall into bad hands." The Democratic leaders were suddenly facing up to the new factor in the party equation: who would advise, counsel, and try to control the surprise candidate, who was regarded as having an excellent chance of becoming president? There was much speculation on this subject, and the writer for the *Philadelphia Inquirer* expressed a common thought when he said, "There is a general impression that William A. Wallace would be the guiding genius of a Hancock administration." But no one knew.[8]

The first business of the Democratic party in gearing up for the campaign was the reorganization of the national committee, principally the election of a chairman, for this choice would give a significant indication of the realities of political heft within the party. Normally, the presidential candidate dictated this choice as a natural function of his winning control of the party at the convention. With Hancock as the nominee, however, as nonpolitical a candidate as the party had named since McClellan in 1864, there was much curiosity over, first, whether the general would attempt to impose his selection on the party and, second, who that selection might be.

The term as party chairman of William H. Barnum of Connecticut, a wealthy and experienced politico who had long been close to Tilden, expired at the close of the convention. The choice of a successor was postponed until a meeting of the national committee, called for New York on July 13, in conjunction with the official notification to Hancock of his nomination. The notification ceremony was a quaint relic of the early days of party politics in America; it presupposed that the nominee was to be taken unawares at his plow with the unexpected news that the party was calling upon him to run, while the members of the notifying committee waited in breathless anticipation to learn whether their suit would be accepted. Because the ceremony was good for a brief flurry of press coverage, it was retained.

The word coming out of Cincinnati, Washington, and New York was that the choice of national chairman would be made between Barnum and Wallace. The Pennsylvania senator was reputed to be the preference of Hancock, of course, while Barnum was the representative of the wounded but still-powerful Tilden wing. Wallace was more than just a Hancock man; it will be recalled that he had flirted with both Bayard and Field before settling down with Hancock. Wallace was preeminently anti-Tilden; his great political enemies were the Tilden Democrats of Pennsylvania, led by Sam Randall. The Bayard people, including former chairman August Belmont, were for Wallace, not particularly because he was a Hancock man but because he would sever the Tildenites' grasp on the party.[9]

Hancock let it be known that Wallace was his choice. He did not do so publicly, however, and this left him some flexibility. There was a national campaign to be waged, and the Hancock camp was a trifle shy of people who were prepared to assume its direction. Wallace, of course, could probably do so, but as his term in the Senate expired in 1881, he would have his hands full in trying to elect a friendly legislature in Pennsylvania. Besides, he had been barely able to win a majority of his delegation at Cincinnati, and he retained bitter enemies in his home state. Burke went back to Louisiana, where his interests were concentrated. He was not available for a nationwide campaign. The old generals—Franklin, Mulholland, MacMahon, and the other army friends—certainly could not lead such a campaign. Hancock, in the fortnight before the national committee meeting, started to rethink the idea of beginning the campaign with a purge of the Tilden men and the Tilden influence.

On July 1 it was reported that the anti-Tilden men were going "to make a clean sweep of the old machinery"; Barnum, it was said, "notoriously a friend of the deposed leader," could not "be trusted to conduct a campaign for the new favorite." By July 5, however, opposition was said to be growing to the idea of supplanting Barnum with Wallace. The latter, it was pointed out, "could not hope to rival Barnum . . . in collecting the large sums of money which the party so much needs."[10]

As the following week drew on, Hancock's preference for Senator Wallace was shaken by clear implications that the Tilden wing of the party would withhold both its political effort and its financial support if Barnum should be dumped. As late as the night before the meeting of the national committee, Franklin met with Belmont and some of his friends, stating that he was authorized by Hancock to express a preference for Wallace and that a similar statement would be made to the national committee the next day. The next day, however, the Hancock people threw in their hand. Franklin never appeared; Baldy Smith showed up and mentioned casually that Hancock had no choice for chairman. Barnum was easily reelected chairman, and Wallace settled for being head of the Congressional Campaign Committee.[11]

John Hunter, a New York politician closely allied to Bayard, wrote bitterly to his leader that "Hancock has completely given himself over to Tilden," but a different story was heard elsewhere. Wallace got in touch with Belmont, told him that the Congressional Campaign Committee was set up to counteract the influence of Tilden, and downplayed the significance of Barnum's reelection. "General Hancock," Wallace said, "is *utterly and absolutely uncommitted to anyone* as to the future." Hancock had been obliged to yield to the polite blackmail of the Tilden forces in the choice of national committee chairman; the campaign was only at its beginning. At its end, if Hancock should become president, he would have a much freer hand, along with four months of close observation of performance, for selecting his advisers. Nevertheless, the general's passive acquiescence in Barnum's election and his failure to assert his own prerogative was not an encouraging sign.[12]

In the meantime, the volume of traffic on the little steamer out to Governor's Island was increasing markedly. It would do so throughout the summer and fall and drive Hancock to near distraction. One welcome visitor was Harry Heth, who stayed for several days. As Heth was preparing to leave, he asked Hancock to make him a promise. Hancock quickly interrupted, saying, "Heth, I have made it a rule, by which I shall be governed, to make no promises." He told of a general in his old corps who wanted to be an ambassador. "I will not do it, for I do not think he would fill creditably the position he asks, and I am determined to appoint no man to office that I do not believe qualified to fill it." But he reassured his friend: "I have told you that I intended to look out for you and I shall do so." Heth persevered: "I am not after an appointment; the promise I wish you to make me is something personal to yourself. When you become President of the United States, you will have a great deal of entertaining to do. You will have to entertain crowned heads possibly . . . the Justices of the Supreme Court, Senators and distinguished people. I want you to promise me at these functions *not to mash your potatoes.*" The two old soldiers were young lieutenants again as Hancock roared, "To the devil with you and your potatoes!"[3]

Most of the visitors were politicians of one variety or another. W. H. English took the boat to the island on the morning of July 12, for his first meeting with his running mate. At 3 o'clock, Wallace and members of his Congressional Campaign Committee came over for an hour's talk. Both visits were concerned with discussions of the overall campaign situation and the protocol for the notification ceremony of the following day. That Hancock was able to persevere through these meetings is remarkable, for elsewhere in the house his baby grandson was desperately ill.

On the same day, Garfield's official letter of acceptance was published, eliciting groans generally from his Republican colleagues. "Very uneven," wrote the editor of the *New York Times,* and Carl Schurz, the self-proclaimed reformer who sat in Hayes's cabinet, wrote Garfield that the letter was "a great disappointment." He decried "the vagueness of your language on the financial question" as well as "the positive abandonment of ground taken . . . by the present Administration with regard to the civil service." Garfield had made an attempt to conciliate Conkling, Cameron, and the Stalwarts, hoping that the moderates in the party would recognize that he was one of them and let him get away with it. Needless to say, they did not—"a cruel disappointment," they called the letter—and Garfield found himself assailed by those whom he counted as his supporters.[14]

The next day the official notification committee, headed by Senator Stevenson of Kentucky, and accompanied by most of the other members of the national committee, took the boat over to Governor's Island as soon as Barnum's reelection was accomplished. Hancock and English met them there for the ritual, but the general was in the depths of depression and sadness. At 6 o'clock that morning, his grandchild and namesake, four-month-old Winfield Scott Hancock, had passed away. The general had been up most of the night with the sick child and its parents, but their efforts were unavailing. The sudden death cut short Hancock's joy in the visit of Russell and his family, up from their home in Mississippi since late June.

The general was as loving and doting a grandfather as he was a parent, and the presence of Russell's family had been a marvelous tonic for him in those days since the nomination for president had imposed such additional pressures. Now, that happiness was abruptly terminated, and Hancock, for the second time in five years, was stricken by the untimely death of a beloved younger family member.[15]

Hancock soldiered his way through the artificial and stilted ceremony, waiting his turn as Senator Stockton of New Jersey made a speech. Finally, Hancock advised the committee members that he did in fact accept their nomination, adding that "as soon as time permits me to give the subject that careful attention belonging to it," he would issue a formal, written reply. It was an absurd ritual, duly noted as such by the reporters present, but Hancock played his role in it as protocol demanded. At last it was over, the committee members fed and refreshed, all the hands duly shaken, and Winfield and Allie Hancock were left with their private grief.[16]

As in war, however, there would be little time for mourning. The imperatives of the campaign were not to be denied, and among these was the part to be played by the candidate. His was essentially a passive role; he would not make speeches or write articles or tour the country. He would publish his letter of acceptance and make himself available for a steady stream of visitors—party workers, celebrities of one sort and another, persons with suggestions, persons with solicitations, the curious, the ambitious, the greedy. All of these, in a never-ending flow, poured off the steamer onto Governor's Island and joined the crowd flocking around Hancock, who was obliged to be cordial and attentive to each one.

He saw very quickly that the consumption of his time would be enormous. He was still responsible for all of the posts, arsenals, and garrisons of the Military Division of the Atlantic, with the labor that entailed. There is no evidence that Hancock contemplated a leave of absence for the campaign, but he did attempt some steps to bring matters to a manageable condition. At the end of June, he asked to be relieved from further service as president of a military court of inquiry, and later he issued a circular trying to limit his availability to "see the friends who desire to call on him" to three hours a day, three days a week. This did not help much; a prospective postmaster who had come in from Ohio, for example, would hardly be pleased to be told that he had come on the wrong day to see his party's nominee. An old army friend of Hancock's came to see him one day. He found Hancock seated on his veranda, surrounded by people. The visitor asked him, "General, how do you find this thing?" "Don't find it at all," came the reply. "There is nothing congenial about this thing. These miserable devils worry me to death. They come here from all parts of the country, even from Arkansas and Texas, to tell me how many votes they can command. Worst of all, they want to exact pledges that I will give them offices for their services. Did you ever see such a hungry crowd? Hungry, hungry, hungry." He sighed and said it was worse than Gettysburg. "They take me in front and rear. They outflank me and, worst of all, they cut off my retreat." He concluded: "the locusts of old are as nothing to them."[17]

The ordeal of the campaign was hardly more pleasing to Allie, who had not welcomed her husband's candidacy in the first place: "Our home was invaded from the beginning to the end. All was turmoil, excitement and discomfort of every known kind." Seventeen weeks of such pandemonium seemed to the Hancocks like an eternity, leaving little time to weep for their grandson.[18]

Hancock, on the whole, was handled in a rather gingerly fashion by the opposition. While the Democrats proclaimed his stainless and virtuous character, his outstanding Civil War career, and his exemplary conduct while in command of the Fifth Military District, Republicans contented themselves on the whole with assailing him for his political association. There was little inclination to try to downgrade his exploits in the Civil War, but there was some sniffing at his administration in New Orleans. Mary Surratt's execution came up, briefly, until a statement by her attorney made it clear that Hancock was in no way to blame for that deplorable event. The main thrust of the attack on Hancock was that he knew nothing about politics and civil government. The *New York Times*, for example, said that Hancock had "the mind of a school-boy, just capable of grasping the conventional generalities of our politics, but utterly devoid of insight and of practical ideas."[19]

There were a few stronger attacks on the Democratic candidate. One writer said that Hancock had "attempted to nullify the reconstruction measures . . . endeavored to restore rebel civil authorities" and then "left the field of duty" because Grant frustrated his efforts. The *Chicago Tribune* started on Hancock in late June and kept up its criticism throughout the campaign, attacking him for inexperience, disloyalty, and, ultimately, military incompetence. It called him "notoriously a rough, coarse, hard officer," profane and brutal, and it said that Gettysburg would have been lost had not subordinates disobeyed Hancock's orders and thereby saved the Union cause. And a group of twenty-two Republican financial and business leaders, including Edwin D. Morgan, John Jacob Astor, J. Pierpont Morgan, and Cyrus W. Field, charged Hancock with financial ignorance.[20]

The only attack which apparently hurt Hancock personally was that of his old commander Grant. There had been a reconciliation of sorts between the two soldiers, but now Grant brutally destroyed any hope of a further relationship between them. In early October a Reverend Fowler published an account of an interview with Grant, in which the former president called Hancock "ambitious, vain, and weak." Ever since Hancock had received one vote for president in the 1864 Democratic convention, Grant said, he had "had the bee in his bonnet and shaped everything to gain Democratic and southern favor." Grant said he tried to reason with Hancock before the latter took command of the Fifth District, but Hancock simply kept repeating, "Well, I'm opposed to nigger domination." When in command in New

Orleans, Grant went on, Hancock had reinstated corrupt officers long enough to enable them to rob the state of some seven million dollars. Hancock, he said, "is crazy to be President." There was more along the same line, and it infuriated Hancock. Invited to disavow the interview, Grant could only state that he thought it was private and did not know that it would appear in the public press. He admitted that much of what he said about Louisiana was incorrect, and even Republican editors conceded that many of Grant's statements were contrary to public record. Nevertheless, Marshall Jewell, the Republican national chairman, was overjoyed; he wrote to Garfield that "Grant's utterances on Hancock are the most valuable contribution which has been made to the campaign." Only Grant, he felt, was big enough to "do Hancock justice."[21]

But Grant was no longer the darling of the people. He was, while not just another politician, at least in 1880 a disappointed officeseeker and Republican stump speaker, whose objectivity on the subject of Winfield Scott Hancock was open to serious question. Blaine said Hancock's record as a soldier was beyond criticism and that Grant was foolish to bring up personal ill-feeling. E. L. Godkin in the *Nation* lamented the episode, Grant's fame being a national possession which was suffering steady degradation, "his appearance as a loose and reckless campaign story-teller" being a long step down. The Democrats were pleased to quote Sherman's remark about Hancock after the convention, as well as the statement of Phil Sheridan, no Democratic sympathizer, certainly, and no particular friend of the candidate, who said, in the summer of 1880, "I am not in politics; but General Hancock is a great and good man." On the whole, criticism of Hancock was muted and not particularly stinging, certainly not in comparison with that of the Democrats against Garfield.[22]

Garfield's honesty and integrity were the subjects of a constant barrage of Democratic attacks. Particularly criticized were his connections with the Crédit Mobilier scandal and the DeGolyer paving contract difficulty in the city of Washington. The number "329" became a cabalistic symbol, representing the number of dollars paid to Garfield as dividends on his Crédit Mobilier stock, for which he had paid nothing. The figure was carried on banners in torchlight parades, marked on fences and walls, and emblazoned in newspaper editorials. It is doubtful that it had nearly so much influence as Democratic strategists hoped that it would. Garfield's problem was not that he was dishonest but that he was exceedingly pliable. He found himself representing the DeGolyer interests the same way that he wound up with Crédit Mobilier stock: he was very reluctant to say "no" to a suggestion for a course of action or a request for assistance. While considering himself to be firm and steadfast, Garfield was actually a classic example of a man whose conduct was determined by the chance of who spoke to him last. It was fortunate for Garfield that the public was able to discern his basic honesty without making out his real weakness.[23]

The contest of 1880, while appearing on the surface to be between a great military figure, of sterling personal character but with almost no political experience, and one of the better politicians of the country, with a few blotches on his record, was really between the two parties, almost evenly matched. The Republicans taxed their opponents with the Solid South and free trade, which they claimed would be detrimental to the maintenance of prosperity. The Democrats, needing to add very little to their southern base, attacked the Republicans as fat, corrupt, and cynical as their fifth term in control came to an end. There was much less bitterness to the campaign of 1880 than there was to those which had preceded it; party leaders found themselves unable to become emotionally overwrought at the prospect of the success either of an affable Union army hero or of an accommodating politician with whom they had worked for years in Congress.

THIRTY THREE

A Close Election

While Hancock dealt with the crowds on Governor's Island, and Garfield received visitors to his home at Mentor, Ohio, the campaign of 1880 unfolded across America. There were, besides those of Hancock and Garfield, other electoral tickets in the field. Neal Dow, for example, ran for president behind the banner of the Prohibition party, his cause encouraged by the Democrats, who knew that *they* would not lose many votes to prohibition. More important, Congressman James B. Weaver of Iowa ran as the presidential candidate of the Greenback party. The monetary principles of Weaver's party were abhorrent to the Republicans and a majority of the Democrats. Nevertheless, there were areas where Democrats and Greenbackers found it possible to make common cause in a fusion ticket. These alliances were winked at by Democratic party leaders, who, required to tolerate soft-money men within the party, reasoned that they could just as well allow deals with inflationists outside the party if electoral success might thereby be gained.

The campaign can be conveniently divided into three segments: the period from the conventions until the state election in Maine in September; the period until the state elections in the key October states of Indiana and Ohio; and the downhill run from then to the presidential election in early November.

On July 30 Hancock's letter of acceptance was published. Bland and general, it provoked scorn on the Republican side of the fence. To that point most of the Republican campaign had appeared to be the old familiar one of the bloody shirt, claiming that Hancock would be nothing but the pitiful dupe of the diabolical and clever rebel brigadiers who were lusting after control of the government. Hancock's letter, designed to refute these charges and kill the issue, recited the inviolability of the new constitutional amendments and avowed his readiness to resist any impairment of constitutional rights. One paragraph, written by Tilden at Hancock's request, called for "a wise and economical management of our governmental expenditures," a sentiment to which exception could hardly be taken. One of Hancock's friends later wrote that the letter was a good one, "not strong or great, but expressive of loyal and patriotic purposes." Republicans spoke of "the pompous platitudes of the letter," adding that "not a practical idea mars the sweet inanity of the letter." The *Nation* wrote that it read "like the opening chapter in a child's political primer." Hancock's letter was, all things considered, not much better or worse than such documents tended to be, certainly no worse than Garfield's production. Because of Hancock's lack of a political record, though, the letter of acceptance was an opportunity missed to fill in some of the blank space.[1]

Of important issues, in the campaign of 1880, there were really none. The practical differences between the two major parties had come close to disappearing. What the controlling Bourbons in the South wanted was little different from the aims of the parties in the North. The doctrines of states'-rights Democrats, evoking the shades of Jefferson, Jackson, and Cass, produced results closely similar to the fruits of Republican doctrine, since both parties were strongly leavened with the pro-business philosophy of the old Whig party. Republicans on the hustings excoriated the vices of southern secessionists, but they had no reluctance in dealing with them on terms of amity and fellowship in the halls of Congress.

Under the circumstances, the Republicans started off the campaign singing their same old song. "We hold no controversy with General Hancock," one of their circulars read, "for he is a good soldier. Our only controversy is with the party that nominated him." Another said of the Democratic party: "A new figure-head, but the same old hulk." Then the Republicans got hold of a report of Baldy Smith's overzealous speech to the Vermont Democrats that April. They charged that Hancock, far from being a professional soldier above the political wars, was so fierce a partisan and potentially disloyal to the government that he was willing to accept military orders from Tilden as president after March 4, 1877. Reference was made to Hancock's correspondence of the time with Sherman, in which the Democratic nominee was alleged to have revealed his unworthy intentions.[2]

A *New York Times* reporter intercepted the Democratic candidate on the pier at the Battery, as Hancock was boarding the steamer back to Governor's Island.

"I came to see you, General Hancock, in regard to this story about yourself, printed in the *Times* of today," opened the reporter, holding out a copy of the paper.

Hancock waved away the proffered newspaper, walked on the boat, and said, "I cannot read it. I cannot look at statements regarding me published in the newspapers."

The reporter persisted, telling the general what the story was about, but Hancock replied, "I shall not make any reply to any statement whatever. I believe I did hear about this story from a friend, but I have not read it, and do not care to make any explanations about it. I will leave that to others."

When the reporter continued to press him, Hancock sent him on his way: "I will make no explanations of newspaper stories. Let some one else explain. Why don't you go to General Sherman?"[3]

Sherman had already rebuffed the press, stating that he had known Hancock intimately and had corresponded with him for years; his personal correspondence, Sherman said, was "sacredly confidential" and his official correspondence was on file with the War Department. Ultimately, however,

Hancock authorized Sherman to make their letters available to the public; when this was done, it was quickly seen that there was no substance whatever to the allegations concerning Winfield Hancock. The *Nation* called Hancock's letter to Sherman "a sober and very sensible discussion of the situation . . . very creditable to General Hancock, both in his view of the nature of the crisis and of the relations of the Army to the civil authorities." No one took the trouble to point out that it was Baldy Smith's indiscreet tongue which had been at the base of the whole problem.[4]

Meanwhile, the Republicans hammered away at the theme that Hancock's election would mean the triumph of the Confederacy, that he would be a well-meaning but helpless captive in the hands of dissembling but unreconstructed rebels. They were helped in this effort by a clumsy statement made by Senator Wade Hampton of South Carolina. Speaking to an audience at Staunton, Virginia, Hampton said that Hancock represented the principle for which Lee and Jackson had fought. The Republicans were gleeful over the contribution, but the bloody shirt was losing its power. The war had been over for fifteen years; even the end of reconstruction was four years in the past. It is doubtful that many people really thought Hancock represented a threat to the sanctity of the Union. Ben Butler of Massachusetts, one of the most virulent of the postwar Radicals but a wartime associate of the nominee, supported Hancock, affirming that "race collisions will be at an end" with Hancock's election and that the three postwar constitutional amendments would be "carried out in their letter and spirit."[5]

The Republicans had other troubles besides trying to find the proper theme for their campaign. The major problem was Roscoe Conkling. The haughty New York boss, not propitiated by the stunning selection of Chester Arthur for the vice-presidential slot, was threatening to sit out the campaign. He did not much care for Garfield, and he detested many of Garfield's associates, such as Blaine and Schurz. On July 15 he took Arthur with him on a fishing expedition to the Thousand Islands, and it seemed clear that he was prepared to let New York—and the election—fall to the Democrats. The party leaders forced Garfield to come to New York City in the beginning of August for a meeting with Conkling's lieutenants regarding New York patronage. The New York senator then went to work in the campaign, speaking in New York State and the Midwest; without him and his mighty oratory, the Garfield campaign would have limped badly. The Hancock-English ticket was thought to be ahead, but with the Republican party united it would be a horse race.[6]

General Hancock felt good about the campaign. At the end of August, he wrote to Senator Bayard:

> Matters from every quarter look well! Of course I have letters from all quarters—the remotest district and in great detail. The people are being organized everywhere. They are in advance of the candidates, committees and politicians.

They mean a change of administration—an examination of the books—not by the old bookkeepers, but by those who are not interested in burying hastily the false entries.

The Republicans who desire change; the soldiers who are coming back to their old allegiances in political ways; the men of the new generation, all of whom wish to see the "war ended in discussion as well as in reality," will settle the question of the pending election if it is not marred by injudicious people. We ought to settle this matter and settle it *well,* in the *North.* It can be done![7]

A few days later, Hancock wrote another letter to Bayard with his views on proper campaign strategy. He said that he had nothing particular in mind. If the movement for a change in administration continued to grow, he said, it would then become necessary "to make assertions of a general character" and to meet demands "for accurate utterances on great questions." Until then, however, it was best "to let well enough alone." It was not exactly the blueprint for an aggressive campaign, but so far it seemed to be working.[8]

What was startling was that no one seemed to be taking the campaign in hand. The *Nation* spoke of the "curious lack of activity" on the part of the Democrats. Tilden was nursing his wounds, Randall was seeing to the election of congressmen favorable to his retention as speaker, Bayard was sitting home in Delaware, Barnum was tending to the housekeeping of the national committee, and Wallace was working on patronage for the future administration. English was hard at it in Indiana, but his work involved the prosaic tasks of getting the polls manned, circulating leaflets, and watching for Republican frauds, all in his home state. They all knew that Hancock had little political expertise or experience, but not one of them took over the task of planning overall strategy for the campaign. It was really Barnum's function to do so, but he provided no guidance or leadership. Watchful waiting meant that the campaign would be essentially a defensive one— surely a curious tactic for a party out of power for twenty years. Randall, in his letter of congratulations to Hancock, admonished, "Do not let our danger prove to be overconfidence." Yet that, or an incredible obtuseness, seemed to be the major characteristic of the Democratic campaign.[9]

James P. Barr, editor of the *Pittsburgh Post,* wrote that "the government will not be surrendered without a struggle and a bitter one." The Democratic National Committee's plan for conducting that struggle appeared to consist wholly of saying nasty things about Garfield and refighting the battles of the past. One politico wrote to Randall from Washington that bags of reprints of old speeches on civil service and the federal marshals bill had been sent to Indiana. "They might as well be thrown into the Potomac," he said. "Those old stories are deader than Julius Caesar." He concluded by saying, "I hope Hancock is stronger than our gross mismanagement, which has been disheartening from the start."[10]

Even in Maine, whose state election in September was being keenly contested, the national committee was performing poorly. Congressman George Ladd, after describing the efforts of the Republicans to flood the state with money and speakers, said, "Our National Committee up to this time have done nothing. Their promises to help us up to this time have raised our expectations without answering them."[11]

Maine may appear at first glance a strange place for one of the pivotal struggles of the 1880 election. It had long been considered a solid Republican state, and its Republican party boasted strong, nationally known leaders such as Blaine, Eugene Hale, William P. Frye, and Congressman Thomas B. Reed. But some funny things were happening Down East. Impoverished farmers heeded the siren song of the agrarian, soft-money Greenbackers, and Maine provided one of the most successful examples of fusion between the Greenback and Democratic parties. The fusionists had won the governor's chair in 1878, lost it, and were now contending for it once again. With the Greenback strength (mainly former Republicans) added to the Democratic minority, there were in Maine two relatively equal political forces. It made for a lively campaign.

Governor D. F. Davis was the Republican candidate for reelection, while Greenbacker Harris M. Plaisted, an ex-Republican, carried the banner for the fusionists. Each party sent speakers in from out of state, spent large amounts of money, and accused the other of electoral frauds. The Republicans were confident of victory, counting on a majority of five to ten thousand. The *New York Times* reporter in Portland wrote that "fusion" was "in a cracked and shaky condition."[12]

This feeling of confidence made what happened to the Republicans on September 13 even more shocking. When the returns came in, it quickly became clear that there would be no 10,000 majority or even a 5,000 majority. Plaisted, the fusion candidate, was elected governor by some 2,000 votes, and the fusionists captured two of the state's five congressional seats, plunging the Republicans into gloom. The Maine election, after all, was supposed to be an indicator for the presidential contest in November, and Hayes's 1876 majority of 16,000 votes appeared to have vanished. "What must be conceded to be a substantial failure in Maine," wrote the *Times*, "will be more depressing because it is unexpected."[13]

On September 14 Hancock sent off a wire to Plaisted, who had fought under him at Deep Bottom, congratulating him "on the glorious result of your campaign." Plaisted, who was supporting Weaver for president, was not overjoyed at the receipt and publication of Hancock's telegram. In addition, many northern voters—Democrats as well as Republicans—who opposed the inflationary programs of the Greenbackers failed to join Hancock in regarding Plaisted's victory as a "glorious result."[14]

From Hancock's standpoint, indeed, the Maine result turned out to have unfortunate consequences. It confirmed many Democrats in a feeling that the election was in the bag—Dana in the *Sun* crowed that the Maine election "seems to settle the destiny of the Presidential campaign"—and it caused the Republican strategists to make a marked shift in the emphasis of their campaign.[15]

Jewell wrote to Garfield that the result in Maine was definitely "a set-back" but that it should open the "purses, the pockets, and the eyes" of Republican businessmen. The appeal to the bloody shirt and fears of the Solid South had been unable to overcome pocketbook issues in Maine. Very well. The Republicans henceforth would hammer their opponents on the most basic pocketbook issue of all: national prosperity and jobs. The Democrats, courtesy of Henry Watterson, had given them the anvil: that barely noticed phrase in the platform, "a tariff for revenue only." To the very end of the campaign, Republican orators and writers would tell the American businessman and workingman that only the Republican party could be relied on to maintain the protective tariff that shielded American industries, guaranteed American jobs, and produced American prosperity. Day after day, night after night, the Republicans repeated this theme. And the Democrats let them get away with it.[16]

Economic issues would appear to have been, on their face, detrimental to the Democrats. "By 1880," one commentator had written, "the economic life of the nation had returned to a measure of stability following the excessive inflation of the Civil War years and the depressed condition of the 1873 panic." Nevertheless, even in a period of what was called "prosperity," the average skilled workingman could barely support his family on his income, while the family of the unskilled laborer could subsist only with the supplements brought in by the work of wife or children. So dissatisfaction with the economic aims and performance of the government could still benefit the Democrats, often without much indication that their policies would be very different from those of the Republicans.[17]

For a while, the Democratic leaders appeared not to have realized that the change in Republican strategy had taken place. When finally they attempted to meet the challenge, Republican arguments had already taken hold, and Democratic efforts to combat them were less than successful. The Republicans claimed credit for the return of prosperity, although their responsibility for that was passive, at most. Democratic speakers danced around the tariff question, and there were all sorts of odd attempts to explain the platform plank, none of them wholly successful. Even Hancock became involved in this, though he won marks only for valor on this field. "People dread change when they are making money," wrote one leading Democrat, "and perhaps some have been frightened by our declarations that great changes will occur." The Democrats never did establish what improvements in the body politic would take place if they were placed in power; all they really said was "Our man is better than your man."[18]

The next major battlefield after Maine, Indiana looked like a Democratic state. Tilden had carried it by 5,000 votes in 1876. It had two Democratic senators and a Democratic governor. One of its citizens held the second spot on the Democratic ticket. Another of its favorites, Thomas Hendricks, had served as both governor and senator and retained great popularity in the state. The party looked strong and confident in the Hoosier state.

Beneath the surface, however, there were problems. Party strength in Indiana was nearly equally balanced; success in elections frequently depended on colonization of voters from outside the state's borders and on outright purchase of votes. The Democratic party was sundered by the hard-soft split on the currency. The 1880 candidate for governor, inflationist Franklin Landers, was far less popular than the 1876 winner, James "Blue Jeans" Williams. The Republican candidate, Albert Porter, was a more formidable opponent than Benjamin Harrison had been four years earlier. Hendricks, denied the presidential nomination once again, was giving the ticket only lukewarm support. And English, Hancock's running mate, enjoyed little personal popularity in his home state. In addition, Indiana, while not a place where a bloody shirt campaign would have much chance, was susceptible to capture on the tariff issue.

Indiana was crucial. In the electoral college mathematics, the Democrats counted on the southern and border states with their 138 electoral votes to begin with, and then looked for the necessary additional 47 votes. New York, with its 35, was almost essential, with the balance to come from New Jersey with 9, Connecticut with 6, California with 6, Nevada with 3, Oregon with 3, and Indiana with 15. Maine's 3 votes were now a possibility as well. New York, New Jersey, Connecticut, and Indiana had been carried by Tilden, and all could be carried again in 1880. The others were close enough that hopes could be entertained for Democratic success in each. The element which made Indiana crucial was its state election in October. If the Democrats could hold the state, their prospects would be very bright; if, on the other hand, they lost a northern state which they had previously won, that fact would bode ill for November, both in Indiana and in the other doubtful states. One of the Democratic operatives in the Midwest, after assessing the problems facing the party in the Hoosier state, wrote: "The question now is whether the greater popularity of Hancock will not be more than counterbalanced by the political drawbacks I have named and make the state uncomfortably close?"[19]

Ohio's state election would take place on the same day as Indiana's, but Ohio was considered a Republican state which would likely deliver her electoral votes to her senator-elect, Garfield. What the Democratic strategists looked for in Ohio was a decline in the Republican majority from the 13,000 by which Hayes had carried his state in 1876.

To lead the campaign in the October states, the Republicans called upon Roscoe Conkling. His men having patched together a temporary alliance with Garfield, Conkling was ready to put his considerable oratorical talents to work for the party. He delivered a long address at the Academy of Music in New York on September 24 and then headed west. He spoke to huge throngs in Warren, Cleveland, and Cincinnati, Ohio, and in Richmond, Indianapolis, and Terre Haute, Indiana. The principal subject of his lengthy

speeches was the tariff and the need for protection; he barely mentioned
Garfield. Even Garfield, however, was forced to concede that the effect of
Conkling's rhetoric was a great increase in Republican strength.[20]

In the meantime, on another level, Stephen W. Dorsey, secretary of the
Republican National Committee, former carpetbag senator from Arkansas,
was working equally hard and equally effectively. Dorsey took in hand the
more practical aspects of the Indiana canvass. He handled the importation
of black voters from the Upper South, distributed money where it would do
the most good, and lined up employers to bring pressure upon their employees to vote the Republican ticket.[21]

The Democrats, of course, brought in outside speakers to try to counter
Conkling and his colleagues, and they did what they could to match
Dorsey's work. English was supposed to be an expert in this sort of secretive
maneuvering, but he found himself hopelessly outclassed by Dorsey. In
addition, the drumfire of Republican oratory, picturing closed mills, ruined
factories, and grass growing in the streets, if the Democrats should attain
control with their "tariff for revenue only," made a strong and vivid impression. Just before the election, Senator Daniel Voorhees admitted that the
Democrats in Indiana had made a bad mistake by ignoring the tariff issue.
As the election came to a close, the Republicans claimed Ohio by ten to
twenty thousand, but they conceded that Indiana would be close. The
Democrats claimed that Indiana would be theirs, probably by more than
5,000 votes. The Democratic leaders were confident. Barnum did not "think
it possible for the party to fail"; Hendricks looked for "a very respectable
majority"; Governor Williams had "not the slightest doubt" of Landers's
victory; and English saw "nothing in the way to defeat us." But Indiana was
still Indiana. It was a state where the last-minute work of party managers,
led by English on the one side and Dorsey on the other, could well be
critical. The nation waited.[22]

On October 12 the voters in the two midwestern states went to the polls
and delivered a clear verdict. Ohio went Republican by some 20,000 votes,
and Indiana was carried by the Republicans by more than 2,000. "A DEMO-
CRATIC WATERLOO," headlined the *New York Times,* and so it appeared. The
margin in Ohio was much greater than in 1876, and in Indiana the figures
had turned completely around. "The result in Indiana," wrote one correspondent from Washington, "is a surprise alike to Democrats and Republicans. The State was conceded to the Democrats by a small majority, and the
most sanguine Republicans had no expectation that there would be such a
decided reversal of the figures of former years." Charles Dana called it "an
unexpected and mortifying defeat. . . . [I]t is disastrous, and may prove
fatal."[23]

While the Republicans rejoiced, the Democrats looked for reasons. English, Landers, and Hendricks all came in for their share of blame, and there
was brief talk of dumping English from the national ticket. Tammany's
John Kelly said that Indiana had been carried by "imported niggers." The
Cincinnati Enquirer said that the Democrats lost because of the tariff

plank, because they did not work out a fusion with the Greenback party, and because Hendricks undercut English. Henry Watterson said that Indiana had been "bought right out of hand." Most Democrats were willing to concede that the party had been whipped out of its boots on the tariff issue. The question facing the party managers was whether the trend could be reversed for November. English professed himself confident that Indiana could still be carried in November, while Allen Thurman commented that Hancock was much stronger in both Indiana and Ohio "than the candidates on the state tickets." Hancock himself said that there were local issues in the state campaign which would not be involved in the voting in November.[24]

Dan Voorhees came to New York and said that Hancock was far stronger than the state ticket in Indiana; he predicted 10,000 more votes for Hancock than had been cast for Landers. So, from the disaster of October 12, it was becoming apparent that if Winfield Scott Hancock were not measurably stronger than his party in November he would be defeated. The bright hopes of summer had faded, and the Democratic party was not doing very well in 1880.[25]

With the October elections out of the way, the campaign was narrowing down. There was no realistic hope of carrying Ohio for Hancock, so the Buckeye state could now be discounted. Prospects in Pennsylvania, normally solid Republican, were gloomy; Wallace was waging an uphill fight to try to save his Senate seat. The upper midwestern states—Wisconsin, Michigan, and Minnesota—and the plains states—Kansas, Nebraska, and Iowa— were sure to go for Garfield, as was most of New England. There was a slim chance in Maine, though a slate of Weaver electors threatened the chances of the fusion ticket committed to Hancock and English. Connecticut was still a good prospect, as were the three states in the West—California, Nevada, and Oregon. Indiana could conceivably be turned around in November, so the effort would be renewed there. New Jersey was usually a Democratic state, but the party was being hurt there on the tariff issue.

Finally, there was New York. No matter what happened elsewhere, without New York's 35 electoral votes the chances of a Hancock presidency could be dismissed. Tilden had carried his home state four years earlier by some 32,000 votes, but there was no guarantee that that would be repeated. Roscoe Conkling sat out the 1876 campaign, piqued at the selection of Hayes, but he was planning a major effort to make New York Republican for 1880, and he was a formidable campaigner in his own state. The Democratic party had been severely damaged the year before by the schism between Tammany and Tilden, and it was not clear that this split could be papered over for Hancock's election. In John Kelly's eyes, Hancock had beaten Tilden at Cincinnati, so Tammany would support him, but control of the party in New York City was far more important to Kelly than the election of a president. Besides, Tilden's contribution of $25,000 to the Hancock campaign and the efforts of his followers gave credence to a report that Tilden and Hancock had made a bargain for control of New York patronage. There appears more appears to be no proof of this, but the rumor, circulated energetically by the Republican press, was not calculated to make John Kelly feel comfortable with the ticket. New York would be a problem.[26]

First, though, there was the tariff. The enigmatic phrase in the platform lent itself to such widely varying explanations, from Randall's strong protectionism to Watterson's free-trade doctrines, that it was rendered virtually meaningless. The Republicans, however, continued to press their contention that it really meant the end of protection and the end of prosperity. Finally, General Hancock undertook to deal with the issue himself. Since New Jersey was one of the states where the tariff uncertainty was apparently hurting the Democrats, Hancock submitted to an interview with a reporter from the *Paterson* (New Jersey) *Daily Guardian,* published on October 8.

The interview took place during a hack ride from the ferry landing to Union Square. After the question of rebel war claims was discussed briefly and dismissed, the reporter asked about the tariff, which he said was a major topic in Paterson. There was no great mystery about the party's tariff plank, the general said. "There had to be a certain amount—millions of dollars—raised by a tariff, that can be got in no other way, and that must necessarily give protection to the manufacturing interests of the country." The position of the two parties was really the same, and his election could make "no difference either one way or the other." He would not favor anything that interfered with the industrial interests of America. "They will have just as much protection under a Democratic administration as under a Republican administration." Finally, "the tariff question is a local question," one that was "brought up once in my native place in Pennsylvania." It was an issue, Hancock said, "that the general government seldom cares to interfere with."[27]

As an effort to put some space between himself and the free-trade interpretations of the platform, Hancock's interview might have done some good. The wretched sentence about the tariff being "a local question," however, made Hancock the object of derision and ridicule, underscoring the picture the Republicans were drawing of him as a simple soldier totally unschooled in the ways of government. Hancock knew what he meant; he later explained privately that he meant that, as the tariff "affects localities differently," "the original presentation and discussion of this question should occur among the people of the various localities" when choosing their congressmen. But he never corrected the "local question" impression from his interview, and the damage was done.[28]

While Republican editors and politicians were jeering and smirking over Hancock's gaffe, Senator Theodore Randolph of New Jersey tried to minimize the damage. He wrote a letter to the general, dated October 11, stating that Hancock had been "imperfectly understood" or "indifferently reported" in the *Guardian* interview, which, he said, "does you injustice." He invited Hancock to set the record straight.

Hancock replied the next day, disdaining to correct the earlier interview—"I thought I spoke plainly enough to satisfy our Jersey friends regarding my tariff views"—but instead amplifying it. "I am too sound an American," he wrote, "to advocate any departure from the general features of a policy that has been largely instrumental in building up our industries and keeping Americans from the competition of the underpaid labor of Europe." The need to raise revenue from a tariff would continue for "as long as human nature lasts." He thought that "all talk about 'free trade' is folly." He advocated creation of a commission of experts to eliminate "any crudities and inconsistencies existing in our present laws" and to "confirm" a system which would be just, judicious, harmonious, stable, *and* protective.[29]

Whether the Hancock-Randolph exchange did any good is problematical. The *Nation* called the letter to Randolph "nearly as mysterious as the interview." It said Hancock's discussion of the tariff "is that of a man who knows nothing about it, and who apparently, until he began to talk, had never thought about it." The "local question" image persisted, abetted by a Nast cartoon in *Harper's Weekly,* headed "A Local Question," showing Hancock whispering to Randolph at a public meeting, "Who is *Tariff,* and why is *he* for revenue *only?*" Free-trade Democrats were unhappy with Hancock for backing away from the platform plank, and the Republicans continued on their same path, predicting economic misery and dislocation should Hancock and his party come to power.[30]

Meanwhile, the problems in New York City demanded some sort of resolution. John Kelly, under pressure from the national committee and the Democratic press in New York, thought he would do what he could for the Hancock-English ticket. He agreed to sit down and talk with the leaders of Irving Hall, the so-called County Democracy, in order to achieve a unified front for the election in November. If the party could be patched up in New York City, the rest of the state would take care of itself.

The process of unification was not an easy one. The basic problem before the negotiators was the need to slate a candidate for mayor. Kelly refused to countenance the renomination of Mayor Edward Cooper, whom he cordially detested, so it was necessary for the two groups to settle upon a name agreeable to both. Through September the process dragged, with little appearance of progress. Finally, in mid-October, Kelly induced the Irving Hall negotiators to include the name of shipping executive William R. Grace on their list of acceptable candidates. The Irving Hall leaders felt sure that Kelly would not dare accept Grace, an Irish-born Roman Catholic, since no Catholic had ever run for mayor of New York. Kelly then shocked his adversaries by accepting Grace as the mayoral nominee, though there were many warnings about Grace's political unacceptability. The Republicans soon began loudly to lament the injection of religion into the campaign and to proclaim piously that they did not know for sure that Grace was planning to divert public funds for education to the parochial schools; he should be permitted to explain his stand. Of course no one listened to his explanations, and thousands of non-Catholic Democrats in New York City nervously contemplated voting Republican to keep the Pope from landing at the Battery.[31]

The campaign wound down to its final days. It was assumed that the basic structure of the canvass was now fixed and that there would be no more jolts before election day. The South was solid for Hancock; most of the Midwest and New England looked solid for Garfield. The Republicans pounded away on the tariff, while the Democrats assailed Garfield and called for change. The Catholic issue loomed large in New York, and the key states were obviously Indiana, New Jersey, Connecticut, New York, and the three western states. Hancock appeared to be stronger than his party, but that party, perhaps because of its inept leadership, seemed to be much weaker than previously supposed. Out of all this would come a president.

Then, on October 20, there came a sensational development, one which threatened to undercut all the Republican progress with workingmen on the tariff issue. A minor New York newspaper named *Truth* published in facsimile a letter signed by "J. A. Garfield" to one H. L. Morey of the Employers' Union in Lynn, Massachusetts. The letter, dated January 23, 1880, was written on congressional stationery; it addressed the question of Chinese labor, stated that "individuals or companys [*sic*] have the right to buy labor where they can get it cheapest," and advised that the present treaty with China allowing unlimited immigration should not be abrogated until the great American manufacturing interests had been consulted. The editor of *Truth* had brought the original to national Democratic headquarters, where Barnum, Randall, Congressman Abram S. Hewitt, and others examined it and pronounced themselves satisfied that the signature was genuine. In addition, Hewitt felt that the sentiments expressed were those harbored by Garfield. The question of Garfield's views on the vexing problem of Chinese immigration was one of great concern on the West Coast, where the Republican nominee's wobbly and inconsistent positions were viewed with alarm. But the Morey letter, with its specific phraseology, could, if genuine, have an impact far beyond California.[32]

Barnum thought so. He sent copies of it to every paper in the country, with his own comments: "The following was published in Truth this morning. The letter is authentic. It is General Garfield's handwriting. Denial is worse than useless. It should have the widest circulation among all classes, as it unmasks the Republican hollowness and hypocrisy on the labor question through their chief."[33]

There was much sputtering and fuming on the part of the Republicans, but from Mentor came only an ominous silence. Jewell called the Morey letter "one of the most flagrant lies which has ever been concocted by a desperate party on the eve of defeat," but Garfield waited to see what the Morey letter looked like. He may very well not have been sure whether he wrote such a letter or not, and he may have had some difficulty in recalling just what his current stand on the Chinese question was. In any event, once he saw a facsimile of the alleged letter, he felt that he could safely denounce it as a forgery, and his denial of authorship appeared on October 25, five days after the letter's initial appearance. It had by this time developed that no one in Lynn, Massachusetts, knew of a man named H. L. Morey or his Employers' Union, and the whole thing took on more and more of the character of a hoax. Some Democrats, notably Hewitt, stood by the Morey letter for an embarrassingly long time, but it was soon generally recognized that the letter *was* a concoction, though its actual author was not unmasked.[34]

One notable feature of the whole episode was that there is no evidence that anyone in the higher echelons of the Democratic party took the trouble to consult with its presidential candidate before giving the party's imprimateur to what was recognized from the beginning as a document of questionable parentage. The fallout from the Morey fiasco would certainly affect Hancock's candidacy. After the fact, Dana in the *Sun*, who had been an enthusiastic shouter for the Morey letter, contended lamely: "The fact that some pretended Democrat was base and wicked enough to forge a letter in Gen. Garfield's name affords no reason whatever for voting against Gen. Hancock. He is in no wise responsible for what every one of his faithless followers may do." It was the least that could be done for him.[35]

As the last few days of the campaign passed, Winfield Hancock seemed particularly pleased by the visit to Governor's Island of a delegation from the Welsh National Hancock & English Campaign Committee on October 28. They discussed the contributions of the Welsh to American society, and the general told them of his own descent from Jenken Jenken, the earliest Welsh settler in Montgomery County. "If any efforts of mine in the cause of truth and liberty have been due to my partly Welsh origin," he said, "I shall feel highly honored." Before leaving, his visitors sang "Land of My Fathers" to him, once in English and once in Welsh.[36]

In the meantime, a group called the Veteran Soldiers and Sailors of the Union met at Irving Hall on October 26, to hear an address signed by a number of prominent Union generals—including McClellan, Buell, Sigel, Slocum, Couch, Franklin, Smith, Butler, Rosecrans, Sickles, and Mott—urging, "Comrades, vote as you fought, with Hancock for the Union!" A report came from Democratic national headquarters that "New Jersey is absolutely safe for Hancock," and the *Sun* predicted an unprecedented majority for Hancock in the cities of New York and Brooklyn. John Kelly was more specific in this, saying that New York City would give Hancock a 60,000 majority and that the state would be carried by 30,000. Even the Democrats conceded Pennsylvania to Garfield, but they expected Indiana to be very close, despite the October debacle.[37]

One Democratic editor, seeing what he called "new life, vigor and earnestness" during the last two weeks of the campaign, felt confident enough to write: "The tide has been turned and the chances are now with Hancock." Another wrote: "The crop is ripe and ready: shall it be reaped?" The answer would soon be forthcoming.[38]

On November 2, 1880, more than nine million Americans went to the polls to vote for president, 78.4 percent of all those eligible to vote. While waiting for the verdict to be tallied, Hancock remained on Governor's Island, working at his military duties and receiving messages from around the country. The polls closed in New York at 4 o'clock, and the first returns started to filter in. The general was assured that there would be a 60,000 or 65,000 majority in the city and 25,000 in the state. These were still the projections by 9 o'clock, and Hancock was pleased. He was also, however, very tired.[39]

At 9:30 p.m. he stood up. "The results so far are very encouraging," he said, "and I hope they will continue to be so; but I am willing to wait till morning and meantime get a good night's sleep." As he left the room, he said, "I don't care to see any further despatches or be waked up." He then went to bed, leaving behind a group of dumbfounded aides, friends, and reporters.[40]

In other rooms, in other towns, party leaders pored anxiously over the returns long into the night. Strangely, the anticipated Hancock majority in New York City and Brooklyn melted away; by 10 o'clock his city majority was down to 40,000 and the state lead had disappeared. The Catholic issue combined with fainthearted support by the party "faithful" to erode normal Democratic strength. The South came through for Hancock as expected, though the ticket in such states as Florida and Bayard's Delaware had surprisingly narrow leads. New England went solidly for Garfield, with even Connecticut giving him an edge of 2,600 votes. Pennsylvania was carried substantially by the Republicans, and Hancock lost his own Montgomery County by one vote. New Jersey was extremely close, and no one could confidently claim it until almost all of the votes were in. The Midwest was Republican: Ohio went to Garfield by 35,000, Indiana by 6,500, the others not even close. The states of the West were not heard from in the early going, so the politicians settled down to watch the returns from New York. As the night wore on, Garfield crept ahead. When the returns from the West came through, showing Democratic victories in California and Nevada, and when New Jersey finally settled into Hancock's column, by just over 2,000 votes, destiny mocked the Democratic party. For Hancock had done what had to be done: he had captured enough electoral votes to add to New York and the South to give him the presidency. There was just one problem: New York was lost. John Kelly had barely managed to elect his Irish Catholic mayor; but clearly, in doing so, he had cost the Democratic party the presidency of the United States.

Garfield, up all night, knew by 3 a.m. that he had been elected. Hancock awakened at 5 a.m. and asked Allie what the news was. "It has been," she told him, with dramatic overstatement, "a complete Waterloo for you." "That is all right," the general said. "I can stand it." He then rolled over and went back to sleep.[41]

THIRTY FOUR

The Morning After

On November 3, 1880, the sun rose at its accustomed time and in the usual place. The United States of America had conducted its quadrennial trial of political strength, in another excruciatingly close election, and the results were accepted this time by the contestants with no more than the usual amount of grumbling. After all the votes were counted, more than nine million of them, Garfield's popular plurality was a miniscule 7,018 votes. The count in the electoral college was 214–155 (with one of Hancock's California electors defecting to Garfield), but if New York had gone to Hancock, the Democratic candidate would have been successful by a count of 190–179. This was a thoroughly respectable showing for the candidate of a party long out of power in a country which was enjoying the return of economic prosperity.[1]

The New York voting was very peculiar. There were complaints of election frauds in New York City, and in Brooklyn, too, there were some odd-looking returns. Barnum and Kelly claimed that there were more than 20,000 illegal Republican votes in New York City, and Hancock apparently thought that this was what had cost him the election. Most Democratic leaders, however, felt that Barnum and Kelly were trying to divert from themselves the major culpability for the Democratic defeat. Kelly managed to secure victory for his mayoral candidate by little more than 3,000 votes, and in the process he had reduced Hancock's margin to 41,376. The state had been lost by 21,000 votes, and it would have been won for the Democratic electors with anything like the normal spread in New York and Brooklyn. A southern editor wrote that Hancock was beaten by "Kelly's crowd in New York," who put up a municipal slate "which was a fearful load on the electoral ticket." There can be little doubt that New York—and the nation—would have been won had John Kelly not insisted on electing as mayor a candidate with enormous political handicaps.[2]

The other culprit was Barnum. The national chairman was a disaster, and the campaign he assumed to manage went from blunder to blunder. From the initial sublime overconfidence, which lasted well into the campaign, the failure to recognize the damage the Republicans were inflicting with the tariff issue, the decision to make the canvass solely one of defamation of the opposition candidate, and the failure to counsel with Hancock on the public issues which might have to be addressed along the way, to the final folly of the Morey letter, Barnum made one mistake after another. That with all this Hancock nearly won can be attributed to his own strength with the public and the declining vitality of the Republican party.

Well before the election, Hancock had given up the effort to get support from the national committee. He had requested that letters of his on public subjects be printed and distributed throughout the country. Barnum, who had in the early days sent out prodigious numbers of tracts on dead issues, refused, claiming poverty. Barnum's policy, one journal reported, "consisted of gasconade and slander." Even Henry Watterson, a loyal Tildenite, called the campaign "ill-planned and ill-managed, and never big with inspiration. Begun upon a low tone, it failed to give out from the first to the close one breezy, soul-stirring note, in spite of the captivating personality of Gen. Hancock."[3]

What was most unfortunate about all that, of course, was that Hancock had never wanted Barnum in the first place. He had wanted Wallace (who lost his Senate seat anyway) to run the campaign, but the genteel blackmail of the Tilden forces had frustrated him. "By accident or by instinct," the *New York Times* reported, before the election, "as events have proved, Gen. Hancock was right. His most fatal weakness has been in the Democratic Committee." No one can know what kind of a campaign Wallace would have conducted, but two things are likely: it would have been run in Hancock's interest and with Hancock's involvement, and it could hardly have been worse than Barnum's.[4]

Winfield Scott Hancock arose on the morning of November 3, 1880, had breakfast with his family, and then went off to his office by 9 a.m. A reporter was present—probably for the last time—and commented that the general "seemed in good spirits, as usual, and betrayed no indignation or disappointment." The reporter asked him what he thought about the election, and Hancock said, "If the American people can stand it, I can. If it is decreed that the will of the people shall be thwarted, it is no doubt for a wise purpose." He made it crystal clear from the outset that there was in his mind no purpose of contesting the results of the election, whether they had been brought about by fraud or not. He said he had hoped to effect many reforms, financial and otherwise, in the management of the country, had the privilege been accorded to him. Later, his old commander, George McClellan, who had been through the same experience in 1864, came to visit him, as did Franklin, Auger, and other old soldiers. "The aspiring Democratic politicians who now found no further use for Gen. Hancock," one correspondent wrote, "kept away."[5]

He was now done with politics. The idea of high civil office had been a temptation to him from 1868 on, a shining light over the next hill, a chance to be acclaimed as he certainly felt he should have been, but, even more, a chance to serve his country more fully than he could as the guardian of New York Harbor. He had had his fling now, his run with the good men, the idealists, the pragmatists, the low characters, and the charlatans who gathered around political parties and candidates, and he did not care to repeat the experience. "His defeat determined him," his wife said, "never again to permit his name to come prominently, in a political sense, before the people." A few days after the election, Hancock told Allie that he was "entirely satisfied" with the outcome: while he thought he had been elected and then defeated through fraud, "he would not exchange positions with Garfield for any earthly inducement." He had had his fill, during the campaign, of the political sycophants, pleaders, and managers who swarmed around the presidency; he was happy to leave them to a politician like Garfield.[6]

When it was over, the *New York Sun*, Charles Dana's Tildenite organ in New York, which had denigrated Hancock earlier as simply "a good man, weighing two hundred and fifty pounds," rendered a verdict on him as a candidate, even as it bewailed the failure to renominate Tilden: Hancock was everything they said of him, "even 'The Superb.' " There are those who say that it was fortunate for his reputation as a gallant soldier that Hancock was not made president; Grant, they say, is a case in point. But Hancock's intellect and political acumen appear to have been higher than Grant's, and his understanding of the nature of the government much more acute. The folly of making such judgments is pointed out by these circumstances: Garfield, the victor, a canny and experienced politician, was a presidential failure in the short time before his assassination, whereas Chester Arthur, his successor, whose training and capacity for the presidency would appear to have been much inferior to Hancock's, had a generally successful term in the White House. There were no burning issues facing the government, so that Hancock's integrity, industry, and administrative ability would likely have made him an adequate if undistinguished president. In any event, the question of how Hancock would have performed in the presidency lies, because of the performance of John Kelly's Tammany Hall, solely in the realm of speculation.[7]

As the dust from the election settled, Hancock indulged in some minor efforts at a postmortem. Piqued by the narrow loss of his home county, he wrote to a friend in Norristown, asking for a rundown of votes in the county by wards: "I am anxious to see where we had friends and where not." He wrote to a number of friends about the suspicious activities on election day in New York and Brooklyn. But this interest seems to have been solely that of a participant who desired to know exactly what had happened, with no deeper design in mind.[8]

In December Hancock wrote a chatty letter to Schofield telling him that he intended Schofield to succeed him at the Division of the Atlantic had he been elected; indeed, he even had plans for alterations to the house on Governor's Island if they were agreeable to the Schofields. But it was not to be. On February 10, 1881, after the formal certification by Congress of the election results, the general wrote complacently to his friend Duncan Walker: "Yesterday ended the presidential matter of 1880, so far as I was concerned with it. Today therefore seems a good occasion to write upon other matters."[9]

In March, Hancock, at the request of General Sherman, attended Garfield's inaugural. "I have no right to any personal feeling in the matter," he wrote; "it is clearly my duty as a soldier to obey. . . . A Democratic Congress has formally announced that the people have duly elected . . . James A. Garfield. It certainly seems that a Democratic candidate should be there to support the assertion." He concluded by saying, "The will of the majority rules, you know. What I can do in Washington, with dignity, I shall do." He went to the ceremony and observed it placidly. His erstwhile opponent had gone through four months of torment, his easygoing, vacillating personality buffeted constantly by the contentions over cabinet and other positions in the new administration, and the formal inauguration would bring him no surcease. The new president was soon embroiled in a fierce and bitter conflict with Conkling over patronage, senatorial privilege, and executive control, a conflict which led indirectly to Garfield's assassination. All of this was denied to Hancock, who returned to his peaceful routine at Governor's Island. His friend Thomas Nast, the *Harper's Weekly* cartoonist, who had been relatively easy on him during the campaign, had effectively closed this chapter in Hancock's life with a dramatic drawing of the defeated candidate, seated before a fire with his head bowed, while the spirit of Liberty places her hand on his shoulder from behind him, saying, "No change is necessary, General Hancock; we are too well satisfied with your brave record as a Union soldier."[10]

THIRTY FIVE

Down a Flight of Stairs

Life started to slow down for General Hancock in 1881. He was fifty-seven years old in February; he carried a great deal of weight on his large frame and was subject to a series of nagging and annoying illnesses. The duties of his post were not onerous, and he devoted more time to personal and private matters and less time and attention to public affairs. Gardening had long been a delight to him—he felt it an obligation to leave a post looking better than it had when he came to it—and now he was able to indulge himself in this pastime.[1]

Hancock, who had visited Norristown frequently while his mother was still living, even after she had lapsed into senility, went there less often after her death early in 1879. Still, he corresponded regularly with his lawyer and friend, B. E. Chain, and through him kept up an acquaintance with affairs in Montgomery County. He found Chain a friend in need when he was afflicted with financial difficulties, and he borrowed money from Chain on a number of occasions. The general's finances were never very good, for in addition to the normal expenses of maintaining his headquarters, he had from time to time to help out his impecunious twin brother, Hilary, whose Minneapolis law practice suffered from his addiction to alcohol. Winfield's army pay sometimes did not stretch far enough, so that Chain's assistance was much appreciated. Hancock was punctilious about paying the interest on his notes when due, together with principal, and he bristled at any indication of charity from his friend. When he asked Chain to purchase a quantity of whiskey for him, he wrote sternly to the lawyer: "Do not fail to send me that bill for the whiskey immediately; that was an order of mine which I asked you to execute, and you cannot give me that."[2]

Chain carried out for Hancock a more painful commission, that of overseeing the construction of the vault in Montgomery Cemetery which was to house the remains of the general's beloved Ada and, ultimately, of Hancock himself. Hancock designed the tomb he wanted, but, because of difficulties of time and distance, the lawyer had to supervise the actual construction. Ada had expressed the wish, while dying, that she not be buried in the ground. Her father scrupulously carried out that desire in designing the tomb, and he took care to leave room in it for his own body. He knew that Allie was determined to be buried with her family in St. Louis and that she wanted his remains to go there too. He took an equally adamant position, insisting that he be entombed with Ada in the home town of his childhood.[3]

More and more often, death was a visitor to the Hancock household. In April 1883, Allie's mother, who lived with them, died; a month later Hancock's chief of staff, General William G. Mitchell, passed away. This was a great blow to Hancock, for whom Mitchell had been an invaluable aide and inseparable friend since Williamsburg, early in the war. A key to Hancock's military success was the fact that his orders were carried out promptly and efficiently; this was largely because of Mitchell's care in seeing that there was no slipup between conception and execution. Hancock was well served by William Mitchell, returned for that service a benevolent and fatherly affection, and was shocked and bereaved when Mitchell died.[4]

A year later, on December 30, 1884, Hancock suffered a loss even more grievous than that of Mitchell. Russell died in Mississippi, at the age of thirty-four, after a brief illness. He left three children, Ada, Gwyn, and Almira. Winfield and Allie had now seen both their children die untimely deaths, along with a grandson. Russell's passing was a hard blow for the general to take.[5]

There were, in these last years of Hancock's life, a few occasions upon which he came again to public attention. One of these was the centennial celebration of the Battle of Yorktown, held in the fall of 1881. Placed in charge of the military observances, Hancock gave to the festivities the attention he would have given a major battle, even to such details as counseling on the design of special uniforms for the staff of the governor of Virginia. Hancock entertained at a grand luncheon on board the steamer *St. John* for President Arthur, leading military and civilian figures, and foreign dignitaries. Though the whole Yorktown celebration cost Hancock dearly in his straitened financial circumstances, it was a huge success. The Marquis de Rochambeau, descendant of George Washington's ally at the battle, wrote later of Hancock's luncheon: "It was easy to see that if General Hancock is a good general, he is no less a thoughtful and gracious host." Noteworthy was the fact that Hancock was the center of public attention at Yorktown, overshadowing even the president.[6]

The following year Hancock joined with the other senior officers of the army in supporting a measure then before Congress to fix an age of retirement for army officers. "In so doing," wrote John M. Schofield, "nearly all of those seniors, especially Hancock, relinquished forever all hope of rising to the command of the army." For a man with the love for the service and the sense of rank Hancock had, it was an unselfish sacrifice, grounded in his belief in the basic correctness of the retirement bill. The fires of his ambition were now substantially banked. In 1883 he declined an offer from Secretary of War Robert T. Lincoln to take command of the Division of the Missouri, which would have required a move to Chicago, and when friends asked him what he was doing to further a proposal to name Sheridan general and himself lieutenant general, he simply laughed. "I am a passenger," he said; "if the boat stops at my dock I shall get on."[7]

Hancock's last major public appearance was as supervisor of the great national obsequies which followed upon the death of Grant, who passed away at Mount McGregor, New York, on July 23, 1885. At the order of President Cleveland, Hancock was given charge of planning and directing the ceremony. Hancock stated his intention "that it should be as imposing as the Government desires and as public sentiment demands," and Governor's Island became the nerve center for a major exercise in tact and logistics: accommodating physical requirements and limitations to the wishes of myriads of Americans to view or participate in the funeral. On August 3 Hancock and his staff arrived at Mount McGregor and paid their respects to the Grant family in a stiff and formal visit of no more than ten minutes' duration; the memory of old controversies lingered. Hancock, however, was determined that the funeral rites be a tribute to the great wartime commander, rather than to the narrow partisan Grant had permitted himself to become. The next day Hancock took official custody of the body and transported it to Albany for a day and then to New York's City Hall for three days of lying in state. On August 8 he directed the great march from City Hall to the burial site on Riverside Drive, overlooking the Hudson. A four-page set of orders was issued from Hancock's headquarters, warning that "exact conformity" with the directive was "requisite." At 9 a.m. a small howitzer was fired, and the march began, led by Hancock, brilliant in dress uniform glittering with gold braid, astride a black horse. The general rode in front of his staff the eight miles of the march route, arriving at the temporary tomb after 1 p.m. President Cleveland and his cabinet, the members of the Supreme Court, senators and representatives, military leaders from both the Union and the Confederacy, numerous military and veterans' organizations, and other dignitaries and groups followed behind the bier in a lengthy but orderly procession. Grant's funeral was one of the Republic's memorable spectacles, carried off without mishap and with impressive dignity, due to the program laid out by Hancock. Grant's aide Adam Badeau later wrote: "The majestic character of those rites that attracted the attention of the world was greatly due to the tender care and chivalrous punctilio of him who thought the dead chieftain had wounded him."[8]

Aside from these few excursions into public attention, Hancock was content to carry out the routines of his command and to enjoy what Allie called "this peaceful, happy home on Governor's Island." He had long been a member of the Military Order of the Loyal Legion, and from June 5, 1879, to his death he served as commander-in-chief of the order. He continued to look after the Military Service Institution, which he had helped to found in 1878. The institute's library and museum were maintained on Governor's Island, and Hancock put in long hours working for the organization. He was elected an honorary member of the Society of the Cincinnati and joined a number of clubs in New York City. Hancock received many visits from old soldiers, delighting in seeing those who had served under him in the Second Corps, and he paid calls from time to time on old comrades who were ill or in trouble. In May 1883 he appeared at the bedside of Henry H. Sibley when that former general was confined by illness in a New York hotel room. Sibley and Hancock spent well over an hour conversing on present-day affairs as well as old times.[9]

In 1884 Grover Cleveland of New York won the presidency, the first Democrat elected since Buchanan in 1856. Hancock was highly pleased by this turn of events, but he was content to watch matters from a distance. He was among those mentioned for the post of secretary of war in the incoming cabinet, but he did nothing to encourage such a selection and was satisfied when William C. Endicott of Massachusetts was chosen for the position. People remembered Hancock's generosity as well as his past prominence in the Democratic party and attempted to take advantage of both; he was, as he wrote Chain, "overwhelmed with applications for my supposed influence." He turned them all down. One of the more painful refusals was to John W. Daniel of Virginia, who had seconded Hancock's nomination at Cincinnati in 1880; asked to "approach the President" on behalf of an aspiring office seeker, Hancock wrote to Daniel that he had consistently refused all such requests.[10]

The general was alert to questions of military history. Though he declined to contribute to the massive historical project on the Civil War conceived by *Century Magazine* in 1884, he was anxious that the Second Corps should receive its due when the story of the war came to be written; he was usually ready to comment on articles or memoirs which touched on his participation in the great struggle. When his former aide Francis A. Walker started to work on a history of the Second Corps, encouraged to do so by the general, Hancock assisted with reports, articles, references, and advice. He did the same for Alexander Webb in 1881, when that former subordinate, now president of the City College of New York, wrote a narrative of the Peninsula campaign. When Abner Doubleday's book on Gettysburg appeared, containing numerous errors about the part played by Alexander Hays, Hancock made sure that the author corrected them in the second edition. In November 1885 Hancock went to Gettysburg, for the first time in twenty years, to go over the battlefield and to clear up some matters of position and locale which had become embroiled in historical dispute. He enjoyed the trip, and he relished particularly the opportunity to relive the battle in conversations with the officers who walked the field with him.[11]

Several months later, on January 27, 1886, Hancock left for Washington on business. He was not feeling well, as he was troubled by a painful boil on the back of his neck. He had the boil lanced by a military physician, but it continued to give him much discomfort. He called upon Cleveland, Endicott, and Sheridan in the capital; among the items of business to which he gave his attention was an effort to procure a vacant brigadier generalship for one of his old brigade commanders, John Brooke. It was observed that

Hancock "seemed far from being in his usual health." He had the opportunity to meet with friends to talk about the old days, and the evening before he left he sat up with Franklin and recalled their times at West Point. Still, he stayed in his room at Wormley's except when transacting business and left Washington earlier than planned, on January 30.[12]

When he got home, the general went to see his personal physician, Dr. John H. Janeway, about his condition. Janeway had been concerned about Hancock for some time. Two years earlier, Hancock's leg had been injured and a troublesome abcess had formed. The doctor had wanted then to make a complete examination of Hancock, but the general had refused to allow it. Midway through 1885 he had again refused a similar request by Janeway. It was almost, thought the doctor, as if Hancock knew that his health was declining but did not want his suspicions confirmed.[13]

Now the doctor saw a perceptible alteration in Hancock's usual robust appearance, attributable perhaps to the loss of blood with the lancing of the boil. The boil continued to grow and soon took on the appearance of a carbuncle, suppurating constantly and causing considerable pain. On Thursday, February 4, Hancock felt very ill during the day, although his condition appeared to improve that evening. The next day he grew worse quite rapidly, lapsing into delirium at 11:30 that night. Janeway now considered his patient to be very seriously ill.

On Saturday, February 6, General Hancock took a turn for the better and rested more easily; he maintained this condition the next day. He was cheerful, hopeful of a quick recovery, and full of pleasant conversation for Allie and his grandson Gwyn, whose toys filled the sickroom. Janeway and Colonel Charles Sutherland, the post medical officer, injected Hancock from time to time with solutions of brandy and ether, whiskey and ether, and whiskey and carbonate of ammonia. The general seemed to react well to these injections, so the doctors became rather optimistic.

Through Sunday night, however, Hancock gradually weakened, and by Monday morning, February 8, he was in bad condition. The carbuncle had continued to develop, and he could not move his head without great pain. His decline through Monday afternoon was rapid, and it was felt by the doctors that he would lapse into unconsciousness before morning.

Early Tuesday morning, at about 6:15, the stricken general's wife, who had kept a constant vigil at her husband's bedside, rose to leave the room to rest for a few moments. As she walked across the room, the patient's eyes followed her. When she reached the door and looked back, he struggled to speak to her:

"O, Allie, Allie! Myra! Good—"

He was unable to finish the sentence, the last words he ever spoke. He soon became unconscious.

During the night Janeway and Sutherland made a careful analysis of Hancock's situation and admitted to puzzlement that the carbuncle was causing such dramatic and severe results. They decided that there must be some other problem which the carbuncle had aggravated. They called in a physician from the city, Dr. Daniel M. Stimson, who arrived before 10 o'clock Tuesday morning. An examination of the general's urine disclosed that he was suffering severely from diabetes. This discovery, the physicians reported, was "a great surprise" to them, although Janeway, at least, knew that Hancock's father had died a diabetic.

With this diagnosis, however, the doctors conceded that there was no chance of survival. After 1 o'clock in the afternoon, Allie was persuaded to leave the room, and the doctors and a few friends and relatives watched Hancock's last hours. At 2:30 his breathing grew labored and the muscles of his face twitched; a few minutes later he rested more calmly. Soon his breathing became more difficult again, and at 2:55 he drew a final long, deep breath, his body quivered slightly, and he then lay still.

"He is dead," said Colonel Sutherland.

Janeway later told a reporter that "the general went down to the close of his life like a person descending a flight of stairs."[14]

The nation, which had not known of Hancock's illness, was shocked and saddened to learn of his death. President Cleveland spoke truly when he wrote to Allie: "The heroism and worth of your late husband have gathered to your side in this hour of your affliction a nation of mourners." Generals, politicians, editors, simple folk both north and south, those in the seats of the mighty, and those who had been enlisted men in the ranks—all joined in the chorus of tribute to the dead soldier.[15]

Two days after the general's death, Sherman, who had been during the postwar years one of Hancock's firmest friends, delivered a simple tribute of his own. Speaking to the Ohio Loyal Legion, he talked, not about the dramatic and well-publicized days of the Civil War, but of the times when a soldier's devotion to duty was perhaps more sternly tested:

> I knew Hancock on the plains, where there was no chance for glory, no hope of fame, no desire to attract notion, nothing but abuse and hardships, the same conscientious man, anxious to do right, anxious to fulfill the orders of his government, anxious to complete a job after which he had been dispatched, and generally successful.[16]

For a soldier, it was not a bad epitaph.

THIRTY SIX

"Pure Gold"

Soon after Hancock's death an effort was set in motion to raise money for Allie to live on. "Gen. Hancock's circumstances," a reporter wrote, "and the draft upon his means of a hospitality made necessary by his official position and by calls upon his charity to which he always responded, made the movement to collect a fund for his widow eminently proper." In short, Hancock left very little estate after a lifetime in service to his country, not even a roof for Allie to keep over her head. The first two subscribers to the fund were Tilden, with $1,000, and William R. Grace, the mayor of New York whose candidacy probably cost Hancock the presidency in 1880, with $500. The fund for Allie ultimately reached $55,000, and other friends gave her a house in Washington, said to be worth $22,000. There she lived until 1891, when she spent a year in Dresden, the capital of Saxony. She returned from Europe to live in Gramercy Park, New York City, until her death on April 20, 1893. She was buried in St. Louis, in the Russell family plot.[1]

In 1887 Allie published a volume of reminiscences of her life with Winfield Scott Hancock. The book was necessarily episodic and, by its nature, partisan, though it contained some valuable glimpses of the general. Seven years after Allie's book appeared, Hancock's former aide Francis A. Walker published a biography of his old chief. From then until 1960, when a popular biography by Glenn Tucker came out, Hancock was neglected by historians, as the impact of the Civil War upon the American consciousness was diluted by other wars, other generals, other crises.

Still, Hancock was not forgotten. Statuary tributes to the general dot the American landscape, including such examples as the equestrian figure across from the National Archives building in Washington and a bust done by Wilson MacDonald, presented in 1891 to the city of New York and erected in Hancock Square, at Manhattan Avenue and 123rd Street.

Hancock's passing in 1886 followed closely upon the deaths of Grant and McClellan. Interestingly, a number of observers felt that there was more widespread grief at the loss of Hancock, perhaps because his postwar career had endeared him to the South far more than any other Union general, perhaps because he was simply a more appealing personality. "Never was public sorrow more genuine," wrote one editor, and another said, "No soldier known to this country ever approached in popularity, in wide-horizoned public favor, the man whose death is recorded . . . today."[2]

Clearly, Hancock, with his warm and manly personality, had a special effect on the American people. He was a major figure of his time, for both his wartime and his postwar service. The Civil War, of course, was the first American war that was closely covered by the daily newspapers. Hancock enjoyed, on the whole, an excellent press; he cultivated good relations with reporters—a matter, perhaps, of policy but also consonant with his open and congenial nature—and it showed. More than that, however, the army grapevine, a more accurate source of information than any journal, stressed the human qualities of Winfield Hancock. Scattered across the land after the war were old soldiers who remembered him with affection and told their friends and neighbors anecdotes about the commander of the Second Corps. They told the story of the sheep killers of the Irish Brigade, and they told the tale of the private in the 6th Maine who, with two fence rails on his shoulder, was overtaken by Hancock, when stealing fence rails was strictly against orders.

"Where are you going with those rails, sir?" Hancock barked. "Don't you know that it's contrary to orders to take them?"

The soldier dropped the rails, saluted the general, then pointed at the rails disdainfully and sneered, "And does your honor call *thim* rails?" Hancock looked at the soldier, looked at the rails, burst out laughing, and rode away.

Another favorite story was of the inexperienced aide-de-camp whom Hancock sent off with an order to a regimental commander. The young officer rode off at top speed, but in the wrong direction. When Hancock noticed this, he called out, "Come back, sir. Come back." The aide was beyond earshot, however, and kept going. As he disappeared over a hill, the general exclaimed, "There he goes! There he goes! We shall never see him again."

Congressman Henry H. Bingham, who served for much of the war on the general's staff, spoke about Hancock at the unveiling of a statue of his old chief at Gettysburg. Bingham said simply: "One felt safe when near him."[3]

In the war, Hancock was—no one said it better than McClellan—superb. He was thorough, loyal, timely, brave, and obedient. He took pains to look after the needs of his men, and they knew it. His soldiers loved him, his subordinates trusted him, and his superiors appreciated him. One of those superiors, the assistant secretary of war, said that Hancock "had more of the aggressive spirit than almost anybody else in the army." Hancock retained the respect and in most cases the affection of his fellow officers while serving for some three years in the Army of the Potomac, an organization notorious for the backbiting, backstabbing, jealousy, slander, and politicking so rife among its generals. Hancock stayed clear of all that by the simple expedient of staying out of it. He certainly had opinions about his colleagues, but he kept them to himself; at least they went no farther than to

Allie. He tried to speak ill of no man, took part in no cabals, gave unswerving loyalty to whomever the vagaries of fate put at the head of the army, and did his job, with aplomb and energetic efficiency. Hancock was a splendid soldier.[4]

In his attitudes toward the society which evolved in America after the war, Hancock was representative of the sentiment of his time. The concentration of economic power which marked the postwar years was foreign to him, as it was indeed to most Americans. He developed feelings of benevolence toward the Indian, so long as interference with the westward spread of the white settler did not result. He sympathized with the worker's efforts to earn a living wage, but he would not countenance a rupture of established patterns of commerce in that struggle. And to the black American, Hancock apparently gave little thought at all, once the institution of slavery had been crushed and the Union restored. His course in the Fifth Military District demonstrated that he was no fervent believer in black political or social equality. On the other hand, Hancock was virtually alone in the army in supporting the rights of a black cadet in a messy scandal at West Point. Clearly, on a personal level, Hancock's humanity took precedence over abstract political principles and prejudices.[5]

As standard-bearer of the Democratic party, Hancock aroused no partisan hostility in the breasts of his opponents. When one considers such generals as Andrew Jackson, Winfield Scott, or even Grant, and the strong political feelings they generated, it becomes apparent that Hancock was placed by the public in a different category. He was regarded simply as a soldier—and an admired and respected figure—who happened to be a Democrat.

A fierce and aggressive leader in wartime, Hancock was among the first to extend the hand of reunion to the defeated Confederacy. "He knew," said Walker, "too many of the men who, like his friend Armistead, had reluctantly and painfully broken the main ties of their lives in taking the other side, to indulge in cheap talk about traitors and sour-apple trees." Four years of hard and bloody war created deep and abiding rifts in the American body politic, and the course of the Radicals in reconstruction kept the wounds of conflict fresh and raw. Not the least of Winfield Hancock's contributions to his country were his efforts, as a leading Union soldier, to close up those wounds.[6]

No intellectual, and certainly not a deep or speculative thinker, Hancock thought clearly and logically about those subjects with which he was familiar. A caring, loving husband and father, Hancock was a genial man to whom the bonds of friendship were important ties to be nurtured and cherished. Winfield Scott Hancock was a good soldier who did his duty as best he could. And, as a human being—"a hot head at times, but a loving heart always . . . a strong arm but a gentle hand," as one editorialist wrote—he was comprehended and beloved by his friends and by the people.[7]

Most of all, his contemporaries talked about his character. Let the final words be those of one on the other side of the political fence, a former subordinate, ex-President Rutherford Hayes, a couple of days after Hancock's death:

> If, when we make up our estimate of a public man, conspicuous both as a soldier and in civil life, we are to think first and chiefly of his manhood, his integrity, his purity, his singleness of purpose, and his unselfish devotion to duty, we can say truthfully of Hancock that he was through and through pure gold.[8]

Notes

ABBREVIATIONS

AGO   Records of the Adjutant General's Office, War Department, National Archives.

ARH   Almira R. Hancock, *Reminiscences of Winfield Scott Hancock,* New York, 1887; Mrs. Hancock's memoir of her husband published a year after his death.

B&L   *Battles and Leaders of the Civil War,* ed. Robert Underwood Johnson and Clarence Clough Buel, 4 vols. (New York: Century, 1884–87).

DUL   Duke University Library.

HEHL   Henry E. Huntington Library.

HSP   Historical Society of Pennsylvania.

HUL   Houghton Library, Harvard University.

JCCW   Joint Committee on the Conduct of the War.

LC   Library of Congress.

LSUL   Louisiana State University Library.

MaHS   Massachusetts Historical Society.

MCHS   Montgomery County (Pa.) Historical Society.

MdHS   Maryland Historical Society.

MHSM   Military Historical Society of Massachusetts; the publisher of several volumes of papers concerning various aspects of the Civil War and the Mexican War.

MoHS   Missouri Historical Society.

MOLLUS   Military Order of the Loyal Legion of the United States.

NA   National Archives.

NYHS   New-York Historical Society.

NYPL   New York Public Library.

O.R.   *War of the Rebellion: A Compilation of the Official Records of the Union and Confederate Armies* (Washington: Government Printing Office, 1880–1901); the basic tool for anyone writing about the Civil War. All references are to series 1 unless otherwise noted.

PHMC   Pennsylvania Historical and Museum Commission, Division of Archives and Manuscripts.

UPL   University of Pennsylvania Library.

USAMHI   United States Army Military History Institute.

USMA   United States Military Academy.

WHMC   Western Historical Manuscript Collection, University of Missouri.

WSH   Winfield Scott Hancock.

YUL   Yale University Library.

ONE. HANCOCK THE SUPERB

1. Information on Hancock's funeral is from *New York Times* and *Philadelphia Inquirer,* Feb. 14–15, 1886. Both papers sent reporters to cover it. See also *Philadelphia Item,* Feb. 15, 1886.

2. *Springfield* (Mass.) *Republican,* June 19, 1880.

3. T. Lyman, "Addenda to the Paper by Brevet Lieutenant-Colonel W. W. Swan, U.S.A., on the Battle of the Wilderness," *The Wilderness Campaign, May–June 1864,* MHSM, IV, 171; U. S. Grant, *Personal Memoirs,* ed. E. B. Long, (Cleveland and New York: World Publishing Co., 1952), 582.

4. J. M. Schofield, *Forty-Six Years in the Army* (New York: Century, 1897), 456;

New York Times, Feb. 10, 1886; *Daily National Intelligencer*, June 26, 1868; E. C. Mason, "Through the Wilderness to the Bloody Angle at Spottsylvania Court House," *Glimpses of the Nation's Struggle*, 4th ser., Minnesota Commandery, MOLLUS, 299; Hugh McCulloch, *Men and Measures of Half a Century* (New York: Scribner's, 1889), 293–294.

5. *New York Evening Post*, Feb. 10, 1886.

TWO. THE LAWYER'S SON

1. Sources for the genealogical information include Hancock Griffin to Norristown Public Library, May 9, 1946, MCHS; and WSH to Virgie Wentz, in *Lancaster* (Pa.) *Intelligencer* (undated), MCHS. See also F. E. Goodrich, *Life of Winfield Scott Hancock, Major-General, U.S.A.* (Boston: Russell, 1886), 26. Several biographers have written that Benjamin served under Scott on the Canadian border in the War of 1812, but since Benjamin was just fourteen when that war ended it is not likely. See Glenn Tucker, *Hancock the Superb* (Indianapolis and New York: Bobbs-Merrill, 1960), 24.

2. J. F. Reed, ed., "Charles Sower's Diary," *Bulletin of Montgomery County Historical Society*, spring 1972, 148; WSH to Virgie Wentz.

3. "Letter from a Traveller," in Hazard's *Register of Pennsylvania*, Philadelphia, Aug. 7, 1830.

4. O. W. Davis, *A Brief Statement of the Services Rendered His Country, by Winfield S. Hancock, Major-General U.S.A.* (West Chester, Pa., 1880), 2–3; Goodrich, *Hancock*, 27; WSH to Virgie Wentz. A boyhood friend remarked years later about how the twins "at that time looked so much alike"; Goodrich, *Hancock*, 35.

5. Jos. Fornance to J. R. Poinsett, Feb. 8, 1840, and B. F. Hancock to J. R. Poinsett, Feb. 14, 1840, USMA, Cadet Application Papers, 1805–1866, AGO, NA. Chain's story is in Davis, *Hancock*, 3. For Sterigere and Bernard, see undated clipping in MCHS.

6. Jos. Fornance to J. R. Poinsett, March 21, 1840, and WSH to J. R. Poinsett, March 31, 1840, USMA, Cadet Application Papers, 1805–1866, AGO, NA.

7. F. A. Walker, *General Hancock* (New York: Appleton, 1894), 14.

8. L. Lewis, *Captain Sam Grant* (Boston: Little, Brown, 1950), 62–63, 65; O. E. Wood, *The West Point Scrap Book* (New York: Van Nostrand, 1871), 108–109; J. D. Cox, *Military Reminiscences of the Civil War* (New York: Scribner's, 1900), I, 176; Military Service Institute, *Letters and Addresses in Memory of Winfield Scott Hancock* (New York: Putnam's, 1886), 17 (this pamphlet, a treasury of reminiscences of Hancock in his early days, will hereafter be cited as *Letters and Addresses*).

9. Grant, *Memoirs*, 16.

10. Wood, *Scrap Book*, 111; Lewis, *Sam Grant*, 70–71; Walker, *Hancock*, 13.

11. R. C. Richardson, Jr., *West Point* (New York and London: Putnam, 1917), 25; Cox, *Reminiscences*, I, 177.

12. Lewis, *Sam Grant*, 70, 81.

13. G. W. Cullum, *Biographical Register of the Officers and Graduates of the U.S. Military Academy at West Point, N.Y.* (Boston and New York: Houghton Mifflin, 3rd ed., 1891), II, 192–208.

14. *Ibid.*, 162.

15. *Ibid.*, 203; *Letters and Addresses*, 17, 21.

16. J. L. Morrison, Jr., ed., *The Memoirs of Henry Heth* (Westport, Conn., and London: Greenwood Press, 1974), 24–25 (hereafter cited as *Heth Diary*); Davis, *Services*, 3.

17. Cullum, *Biographical Register*, II, 237–242, 304.

18. Lewis, *Sam Grant*, 93; Cullum, *Biographical Register*, II, 203; Walker, *Hancock*, 13; *Letters and Addresses*, 13, 21–22; G. T. Fleming, ed., *Life and Letters of*

Alexander Hays (Pittsburgh, 1919), 14–15. On Jan. 26, 1865, Hancock wrote to Hays's widow: "When I was a boy I once had a difficulty, and Alexander Hays was the first volunteer to assist me and in extracting me from my trouble became involved in aforesaid difficulty himself. I never forgot his generous action on that occasion, and hoped some day to serve him. I never had the opportunity as to the time of his death he owed his prominence to his own good qualities"; *ibid.*, 656–657.

19. WSH to John Earle, Jan. 28, 1844, Autograph File, HUL.

THREE. TO MEXICO

1. Lt. Col. Gustavus Loomis, requests for reimbursement, Jan. 17, 1846, and Sept. 28, 1846, Letters Received, AGO, Main Series, 1822–1860, NA.

2. WSH to Brig. Gen. R. Jones, June 30, 1846, Aug. 17, 1846, and Sept. 8, 1846, *ibid.*

3. Lt. Col. I. Ewing to Brig. Gen. R. Jones, Mar. 16, 1847, and April 1, 1847, and WSH to Brig. Gen. R. Jones, Apr. 7, 1847, *ibid.*

4. C. W. Denison, *Winfield, the Lawyer's Son and How He Became a Major-General* (Philadelphia, 1865), 149.

5. WSH to Lt. Col. I. Ewing, May 8, 1847, and WSH to Brig. Gen. R. Jones, May 25, 1847, with endorsement of May 31, 1847, Letters Received, AGO, Main Series, 1822–1860, NA.

6. Lt. Col. I. Ewing to Brig. Gen. R. Jones, June 21, 1847, and June 23, 1847, and Col. H. Wilson to Brig. Gen. R. Jones (from Vera Cruz), July 13, 1847, *ibid.*; K. J. Bauer, *The Mexican War, 1846–1848* (New York: Macmillan, 1974), 272.

7. WSH to Hilary Hancock, Dec. 6, 1847, in Denison, *Winfield,* 150; Bauer, *Mexican War,* 274.

8. G. H. Gordon, "The Battles of Contreras and Churubusco," *Civil and Mexican Wars 1861, 1846,* MHSM, XIII, 561–564.

9. *Ibid.,* 585; Bauer, *Mexican War,* 296–297; C. M. Wilcox, *History of the Mexican War* (Washington: Church News, 1892), 385–386.

10. Gordon, "Contreras and Churubusco," 585–586.

11. Bauer, *Mexican War,* 300; Gordon, "Contreras and Churubusco," 589–590; Goodrich, *Hancock,* 57; Cullom, *Biographical Register,* II, 201.

12. WSH to B. F. Hancock, Aug. 26, 1847, in Denison, *Winfield,* 150.

13. G. H. Gordon, "Battles of Molino del Rey and Chapultepec," *Civil and Mexican Wars 1861, 1846,* MHSM, XIII, 603–604, 609–611; Bauer, *Mexican War,* 308–310; Wilcox, *Mexican War,* 440–441; Goodrich, *Hancock,* 63.

14. WSH to Hilary Hancock, Dec. 6, 1847, in Denison, *Winfield,* 151.

15. Morrison, ed., *Heth Diary,* 56.

16. *Ibid.,* 59, 60–61.

17. Denison, *Winfield,* 151–152.

18. *Usted as me amante:* probably army Spanish for "Let me be your sweetheart."

19. Morrison, ed., *Heth Diary,* 59–60.

20. *Ibid.,* 66; order of Col. N. S. Clarke, near Jalapa, June 30, 1848, approved by Secy. of War William Marcy, July 21, 1848, Letters Received, AGO, Main Series, 1822–1860, NA.

21. Morrison, ed., *Heth Diary,* 68–69.

FOUR. BETWEEN TWO WARS

1. Morrison, ed., *Heth Diary,* 70–71.

2. *Ibid.,* 71–72.

3. *Ibid.,* 73.

4. *Ibid.,* 74.

5. For the visit with Scott, see *ibid.,* 75–77.

6. *Ibid.,* 77–78.

7. *Letters and Addresses,* 17, 22; ARH, 1. A false rumor that the bride's gown was made of spun glass produced an unruly crowd of gawkers outside the house; *ibid.,* 3.

8. Undated newspaper clippings, Wm. Clarke Breckenridge Papers, WHMC.

9. ARH, 4–5.

10. *Ibid.,* 11, 15, 17.

11. WSH to John Earle, Jr., & Co., Feb. 27, 1852, Autograph File, HUL; ARH, 7.

12. Heth said, "I thought he deserved promotion much more than I did"; Morrison, ed., *Heth Diary,* 123–124; ARH, 8.

13. *Ibid.,* 21–24.

14. *Ibid.,* 25.

15. Walker, *Hancock,* 22; Buell, in *Letters and Addresses,* 18.

16. T. M. Vincent (adjutant-general to the forces in Florida), in *ibid.,* 27; Buell, in *ibid.,* 22; ARH, 26–27.

17. *Ibid.,* 27–29; *Letters and Addresses,* 22.

18. *Ft. Myers* (Fla.) *News-Press,* Feb. 17, 1976.

19. ARH, 35–36.

20. Walker, *Hancock,* 22–23; ARH, 38–39. A broadside in the MoHS is an offer by Capt. Winf. S. Hancock to purchase "American Mules" which met certain specifications.

21. S. P. Hirshson, *The Lion of the Lord: A Biography of Brigham Young* (New York: Knopf, 1969), 181; Walker, *Hancock,* 23; ARH, 39–40.

22. WSH to ARH, Oct. 20, 1858, in ARH, 42–43; Walker, *Hancock,* 23–24.

23. *Ibid.,* 24; ARH, 46–47.

24. *Ibid.,* 45–46.

25. WSH to B. F. Hancock, Apr. 4, 1859, Drees Collection, HSP; ARH, 47–51.

FIVE. IN CALIFORNIA

1. ARH, 51–52.

2. *Ibid.,* 55, 57. "A fairly accurate census" in the summer of 1860 turned up 4,399 inhabitants; H. Newmark, *Sixty Years in Southern California, 1853–1913,* 4th ed. (Los Angeles: Zeitlin and Ver Brugge, 1970), 271.

3. Much of the information on Brent comes from his "Life in California," typescript, Brent (A&W) Collection, HEHL. For the quotation on the quiet aspect of life in Los Angeles, see *ibid.,* 2.

4. *Ibid.,* 24–25, 46, 51; J. D. Hart, *A Companion to California* (New York: Oxford U. Press, 1978), 481–482. Wilson, after whom Mt. Wilson, the observatory site, was named, was the grandfather of Gen. George S. Patton, Jr.

5. *Ibid.,* 28. For a life of Banning, though it contains some glaring errors, see Maymie Krythe, *Port Admiral: Phineas Banning, 1830–1885* (San Francisco: Calif. Historical Society, 1957).

6. Newmark, *Sixty Years,* 36–37; Hart, *Companion to California,* 176.

7. Brent, "Life in California," 54–56; Newmark, *Sixty Years,* 346. The "asphalt spring" was in all probability the La Brea Tar Pits, in downtown Los Angeles, in which many valuable fossils have been found. An earlier land venture of Hancock's was as barren of results. In the early 1850s, his West Point classmate Bolivar Buckner, stationed at Fort Snelling, Minnesota, involved Hancock in buying and selling lots in the town of Saint Anthony, which later became Minneapolis. When Hancock was sent to Florida, he sold his lots to Buckner. A. M. Stickles, *Simon*

Bolivar Buckner: Borderland Knight (Chapel Hill: U. of North Carolina Press, 1940), 31.

8. See WSH to Matthew Keller, Jan. 1, 1876, WSH to Anna E. Ogier, May 17, 1872, WSH to Benjamin D. Wilson, Mar. 30, 1870, and WSH to Jos. S. Wilson, Commissioner of General Land Office, Mar. 7, 1870, Matthew Keller Collection, HEHL.

9. Brent, "Life in California," 56; ARH, 58.

10. H. H. Goldman, "Southern Sympathy in Southern California, 1860–1865," *Journal of the West,* Oct. 1965, 577; L. P. Kibby, "California, the Civil War, and the Indian Problem: An Account of California's Participation in the Great Conflict," *ibid.,* April–July 1965, 188. Senator Lane was Breckinridge's vice-presidential candidate in 1860.

11. *Ibid.,* 191; *O.R.,* L, pt. 1, 471; G. T. Edwards, "Holding the Far West for the Union: The Army in 1861," *Civil War History,* Dec. 1968, 308–309.

12. *O.R.,* L, pt. 1, 473–474; Edwards, "Holding the Far West," 316.

13. *O.R.,* L, pt. 1, 476, 477–478.

14. *Ibid.,* 479–480.

15. *Ibid.,* 482–483, 486.

16. Brent, "Life in California," 56; J. W. Forney, *Life and Military Career of Winfield Scott Hancock* (Philadelphia: Hubbard, 1880), 51.

17. ARH, 65–66; *O.R.,* L, pt. 1, 554–555.

18. Newmark, *Sixty Years,* 301.

19. ARH, 66–67.

20. *Ibid.,* 69–70. Johnston died commanding at Shiloh, and Garnett and Armistead were both killed attacking Hancock's lines at Gettysburg, in Pickett's charge. Because of his promotion directly to brigadier general, Hancock never had any use for a major's uniform.

SIX. THE BRIGADIER

1. Tucker, *Hancock the Superb,* 55–56; Walker, *Hancock,* 28–29.

2. This thesis is developed at length in M. C. C. Adams, *Our Masters the Rebels: A Speculation on Union Military Failure in the East, 1861–1865* (Cambridge and London: Harvard U. Press, 1978).

3. ARH, 78, 80; WSH to Lorenzo Thomas, Sept. 24, 1861, Letters Received, AGO, Main Series, 1861–1870, NA.

4. *O.R.,* LI, pt. 1, 489; Davis, *Services,* 5.

5. Cullom, *Biographical Register,* II, 203; Walker, *Hancock,* 38–39.

6. *Ibid.,* 33.

7. *Ibid.,* 32.

8. *Ibid.,* 39–40; Cullom, *Biographical Register,* II, 203.

9. ARH, 81, 82–83; G. B. McClellan, *McClellan's Own Story* (New York: Charles L. Webster, 1887), 172.

10. *O.R.,* V, 20.

11. ARH, 91–92.

SEVEN. UP THE PENINSULA
WITH McCLELLAN

1. A. S. Webb, *The Peninsula: McClellan's Campaign of 1862* (New York: Scribner's, 1881), 43–44. For Keyes's report of his operations near Yorktown, see *O.R.,* XI, pt. 1, 358–360.

2. W. L. Goss, "Yorktown and Williamsburg," in *B&L*, II, 190; A. Nevins, ed., *A Diary of Battle: The Personal Journals of Colonel Charles S. Wainwright, 1861–1865* (New York: Harcourt Brace and World, 1962), 58.

3. Webb, *The Peninsula*, 54.

4. For Keyes's report, see *O.R.*, XI, pt. 1, 358–360. See also *ibid.*, 310, 390.

5. For Hancock's report for May 4, see *ibid.*, 534–535. For Smith's report, see *ibid.*, 525.

6. Webb, *The Peninsula*, 73–74.

7. J. M. Carroll, ed., *Custer in the Civil War: His Unfinished Memoirs* (San Rafael, Calif.: Presidio Press, 1977), 153.

8. J. Longstreet, *From Manassas to Appomattox: Memoirs of the Civil War in America* (Philadelphia: Lippincott, 1895; 2nd rev. ed., 1912), 77–78.

9. For Hancock's report on Williamsburg, see *O.R.*, XI, pt. 1, 533–543. For Hancock's 4:20 message to Smith, see *ibid.*, 546. See also D. S. Freeman, *Lee's Lieutenants: A Study in Command*, 3 vols. (New York: Scribner's, 1942–44), I, 180–189; and Carroll, ed., *Custer*, 155–158.

10. Freeman, *Lee's Lieutenants*, I, 188–189; McClellan, *Own Story*, 353; ARH, 92; *O.R.*, XI, pt. 1, 449. Sumner's report, interestingly, never mentions his orders to withdraw but tells of sending three regiments to reinforce Hancock, all arriving after the repulse of the enemy; *ibid.*, 451.

11. *Ibid.*, 528 (Smith), 22–23 (McClellan), 513 (Keyes).

12. Nevins, ed., *Wainwright Diary*, 60; O. O. Howard, *Autobiography of Oliver Otis Howard, Major General United States Army*, 2 vols. (New York: Baker and Taylor, 1907), I, 222; P. R. de Trobriand, *Four Years with the Army of the Potomac*, trans. G. K. Dauchy (Boston: Ticknor, 1889), 202.

13. McClellan, *Own Story*, 341–342.

14. Denison, *Winfield*, 149: Winfield's younger brother John was serving as an adjutant on his brigade staff.

15. *O.R.*, XI, pt. 2, 430; Freeman, *Lee's Lieutenants*, I, 543; W. Y. Thompson, "Robert Toombs, Confederate General," *Civil War History*, Dec. 1961, 411–412.

16. W. B. Franklin, "Rear-Guard Fighting during the Change of Base," in *B&L*, II, 369; Freeman, *Lee's Lieutenants*, I, 544–546.

17. Franklin, "Change of Base," in *B&L*, II, 375–378; Freeman, *Lee's Lieutenants*, I, 569–576; J. W. Urban, *Battle Field and Prison Pen* (n.p.: Edgewood Pub. Co., 1882), 139–141; F. A. Walker, *History of the Second Army Corps in the Army of the Potomac* (New York: Scribner's, 1886), 72–73.

18. Freeman, *Lee's Lieutenants*, I, 592–593; Webb, *The Peninsula*, 164; H. J. Eckenrode and B. Conrad, *George B. McClellan: The Man Who Saved the Union* (Chapel Hill: U. of North Carolina Press, 1941), 116; F. W. Palfrey, "The Battle of Malvern Hill," in T. F. Dwight, ed., *Campaigns in Virginia, 1861–1862*, MHSH, I, 275. Even Eckenrode and Conrad, staunch defenders of "Little Mac," concede that "it is possible that McClellan would not have continued his withdrawal if he had been fully aware of the magnitude of the success gained by his troops at Malvern Hill"; as usual, he was not on the field, so that he did not follow up for a "probable . . . great victory"; Eckenrode and Conrad, *McClellan*, 116–117.

19. *O.R.*, XI, pt. 2, 35.

EIGHT. A DIVISION AT ANTIETAM

1. W. B. Franklin, "The Sixth Corps at the Second Bull Run," in *B&L*, II, 539.

2. *Ibid.*, 540.

3. WSH to Halleck, Aug. 27, 1862, 12:20 a.m. (actually Aug. 28), signed as commanding VI Corps (in temporary absence of Franklin, Smith, and Slocum), *O.R.*, XII, pt. 3, 694; Haupt to Halleck, 1:15 a.m., *ibid.*, 695. See also *ibid.*, pt. 2, 540

(report of 2nd N.J.); H. Haupt, *Reminiscences of General Herman Haupt* (Milwaukee: Wright and Joys, 1901), 94–99; F. A. Lord, *Lincoln's Railroad Man: Herman Haupt* (Rutherford, Madison, and Teaneck, N.J.: Fairleigh Dickinson U. Press, 1969), 133; and K. P. Williams, *Lincoln Finds a General: A Military Study of the Civil War*, 5 vols. (New York: Macmillan, 1949–59), I, 303, 306–307. Because of a conflict in the dates of the various dispatches as given in *O.R.* and in Haupt's book, and probably also because Haupt was trying to reconstruct what had happened over thirty-five years earlier, Haupt's memoir gives the impression that Hancock sent out two different relief expeditions on two separate days; it appears that this is not the case.

4. S. W. Sears, *Landscape Turned Red: The Battle of Antietam* (New Haven and New York: Ticknor and Fields, 1983), 90–91.

5. *Ibid.*, 112–113; J. Gibbon, *Personal Recollections of the Civil War* (New York and London: Putnam's, 1928), 73.

6. F. W. Palfrey, *The Antietam and Fredericksburg* (New York: Scribner's, 1882), 29–30; Freeman, *Lee's Lieutenants*, II, 189.

7. W. B. Franklin, "Notes on Crampton's Gap and Antietam," in *B&L*, II, 592–594, 596; Sears, *Antietam*, 147–149. For Hancock's report on his activities, or lack of same, around Crampton's Gap, see *O.R.*, XIX, pt. 1, 405–406. He has an error of one day in the report.

8. Franklin, "Crampton's Gap and Antietam," in *B&L*, II, 596.

9. G. B. Davis, "The Antietam Campaign," *Campaigns in Virginia, Maryland and Pennsylvania, 1862–1863*, MHSM, III, 44; Freeman, *Lee's Lieutenants*, II, 192, 196.

10. McClellan, *Own Story*, 612.

11. Palfrey, *Antietam and Fredericksburg*, 91; *Letters and Addresses*, 3. For WSH's report for his brigade at Antietam, see *O.R.*, XIX, pt. 1, 406–407.

12. J. V. Murfin, *The Gleam of Bayonets: The Battle of Antietam and the Maryland Campaign of 1862* (New York and London: Yoseloff, 1965), 264; *O.R.*, XIX, pt. 2, 316, pt. 1, 279.

13. J. M. Favill, *The Diary of a Young Officer Serving with the Armies of the United States during the War of the Rebellion* (Chicago: Donnelley, 1909), 190–191; Sears, *Antietam*, 257.

14. *O.R.*, XIX, pt. 1, 279–280.

15. *Ibid.*, 280–281.

16. Favill, *Diary*, 197. For Hancock's report on the reconnaissance, see *O.R.*, XIX, pt. 2, 91–92.

17. McClellan, *Own Story*, 645–646; Gibbon, *Recollections*, 94–95; *O.R.*, XIX, pt. 2, 532, LI, pt. 1, 912–913, 916.

18. ARH, 92.

NINE. "A CHICKEN COULD NOT
LIVE ON THAT FIELD"

1. F. A. Haskell, *The Battle of Gettysburg*, ed. Bruce Catton (Boston: Houghton Mifflin, 1957), 60–61; Favill, *Diary*, 283.

2. *Letters and Addresses*, 29–30, 71; Favill, *Diary*, 223.

3. *Letters and Addresses*, 28 (W. P. Wilson), 71 (Miles); Cullom, *Biographical Register*, II, 205.

4. *Letters and Addresses*, 13.

5. *O.R.*, XL, pt. 2, 567; "An Interviewer Interviewed. A Talk with 'Gath.' " *Lippincott's Monthly Magazine*, Nov. 1891, 634. "Gath," the pen name of George Alfred Townsend of the *New York Herald*, said that Hancock told him "that he did not wish

any personal laudation" but became piqued when Gath followed his instructions too literally.

6. S. Cadwallader, *Three Years with Grant,* ed. B. P. Thomas, (New York: Knopf, 1955), 55–56, 277; B. A. Weisberger, *Reporters for the Union* (Boston: Little, Brown, 1953), 133. Hancock's major run-ins with the press (after Petersburg and Hatcher's Run) took place after Anderson joined him, so that it may be questioned how much good Anderson did him.

7. D. N. Couch, "Sumner's 'Right Grand Division,' " in *B&L,* III, 106; Palfrey, *Antietam and Fredericksburg,* 54–55. See also M. Schaff, *The Battle of the Wilderness* (Boston and New York: Houghton Mifflin, 1910), 226–227.

8. Favill, *Diary,* 202–203. Longstreet said that they did not receive information about Sumner "moving toward Fredericksburg" until Nov. 18 or 19; Sumner arrived there on Nov. 17; Longstreet, "The Battle of Fredericksburg," in *B&L,* III, 70.

9. Favill, *Diary,* 207, entry of Dec. 8, 1862.

10. Cullom, *Biographical Register,* II, 202; Walker, *Hancock,* 58–59.

11. Couch, "Sumner's 'Right Grand Division,' " in *B&L,* III, 107–108.

12. *O.R.,* XXI, 226; Walker, *Second Corps,* 148.

13. *O.R.,* XXI, 226; Couch, "Sumner's 'Right Grand Division,' " in *B&L,* III, 108–109.

14. G. F. R. Henderson, *The Civil War: A Soldier's View,* ed. Jay Luvaas (Chicago: U. of Chicago Press, 1958), 65–67.

15. Couch, "Sumner's 'Right Grand Division,' " in *B&L,* III, 109–111.

16. Longstreet, "Fredericksburg," in *B&L,* III, 79; Henderson, *Civil War,* 48; Freeman, *Lee's Lieutenants,* II, 340. McLaws, whose Confederate troops these were, wrote that "the enemy, from their position, could not see the sunken road . . . nor do I think they were aware, until it was made known to them by our fire, that there was an infantry force anywhere except on top of the hill"; L. McLaws, "The Confederate Left at Fredericksburg," in *B&L,* III, 91.

17. D. D. Zook, Jr., "A Biographical Sketch of Samuel K. Zook," *Bulletin of the Historical Society of Montgomery County, Pennsylvania,* spring 1982, 117; Henderson, *Civil War,* 46.

18. Favill, *Diary,* 211–212; Zook, "Zook," 117; *O.R.,* XXI, 227 (WSH report).

19. R. G. Athearn, *Thomas Francis Meagher: An Irish Revolutionary in America* (Boulder: U. of Colorado Press, 1949), 120; Henderson, *Civil War,* 73–75.

20. *O.R.,* XXI, 233 (Caldwell's report); *ibid.,* 129–130, 227–228, 236–237.

21. *Ibid.,* 227–228; Henderson, *Civil War,* 76–77.

22. W. Swinton, *Campaigns of the Army of the Potomac,* rev. ed. (New York: Scribner's, 1882), 225. Lee took some heat for letting his foe escape without attacking.

23. ARH, 92–93; G. A. Bruce, "The Strategy of the Civil War," *Civil and Mexican Wars 1861, 1846,* MHSM, XIII, 461–462.

24. Favill, *Diary,* 219.

TEN. THE FAILURE OF FIGHTING JOE

1. Walker, *Hancock,* 72; *Letters and Addresses,* 28–29; Favill, *Diary,* 232.

2. *Ibid.,* 223.

3. *Ibid.,* 224–226.

4. *Ibid.,* 224; Gibbon, *Recollections,* 107. The newspaper headline, on a story about the progress of one of the battles on the Peninsula, was supposed to read: "Fighting—Joe Hooker." The dash was lost and Hooker gained a nickname.

5. E. B. Coddington, *The Gettysburg Campaign: A Study in Command* (New York: Scribner's, 1968), 26–31; E. G. Longacre, *The Man behind the Guns: A*

Biography of General Henry Jackson Hunt, Chief of Artillery, Army of the Potomac (South Brunswick and New York: Barnes, 1977), 138–139; Walker, *Second Corps,* 202.

6. A. A. Humphreys to his wife, Sept. 1, 1864, Humphreys Papers, HSP; *New York Times,* Feb. 12, 1863.

7. D. N. Couch, "The Chancellorsville Campaign," in *B&L,* III, 156–157; *O.R.,* XXV, pt. 1, 171.

8. *Ibid.,* 311–312.

9. Couch, "The Chancellorsville Campaign," in *B&L,* III, 157, 159; Walker, *Second Corps,* 221; Report, JCCW, 38th Cong., 2nd sess., 66. For the possibility, before Hancock arrived, of rebel skirmishers getting on Sykes's flanks, see J. Bigelow, Jr., *The Campaign of Chancellorsville: A Strategic and Tactical Study* (New Haven: Yale, 1910), 247.

10. Couch, "The Chancellorsville Campaign," in *B&L,* III, 159.

11. Bigelow, *Chancellorsville,* 253, 256; Freeman, *Lee's Lieutenants,* II, 537.

12. Couch, "The Chancellorsville Campaign," in *B&L,* III, 161.

13. *O.R.,* XXV, pt. 1, 312; Walker, *Second Corps,* 231; N. A. Miles, *Serving the Republic* (New York: Harper, 1911), 53–54; A. Doubleday, *Chancellorsville and Gettysburg* (New York: Scribner's, 1882), 21–22, 24. Bigelow refers to "a specially vigorous attack" on Hancock at 3:15 p.m.; Bigelow, *Chancellorsville,* 284.

14. WSH testimony, Report, JCCW, 38th Cong., 2nd sess., 67.

15. *O.R.,* XXV, pt. 1, 313; Report, JCCW, 38th Cong., 2nd sess., 67. Miles, whose life was despaired of when he was wounded but who survived to fight again, won the Medal of Honor for his heroics at Chancellorsville.

16. Report, JCCW, 38th Cong., 2nd sess., 68; *O.R.,* XXV, pt. 1, 313–314; Bigelow, *Chancellorsville,* 369.

17. ARH, 93–94; Report, JCCW, 38th Cong., 2nd sess., 70–71.

18. *Ibid.,* 68–69.

19. ARH, 94–95.

20. Report, JCCW, 38th Cong., 2nd sess., 68; *O.R.,* XXV, pt. 1, 174, 308; ARH, 93–94.

21. Favill, *Diary,* 234–235.

ELEVEN. NORTH TO PENNSYLVANIA

1. Walker, *Second Corps,* 254–255; Favill, *Diary,* 236.

2. ARH, 94–95. Although Mrs. Hancock discreetly obliterated from the published version of this letter the names of the two generals whose elevation Hancock said would cause his resignation, it may be surmised that one of them was Daniel Sickles, a favorite of the New York press but not of the army. Sickles had, at the time Allie's book was published, recently participated in Hancock's funeral.

3. *Ibid.,* 182–183 (C. H. Morgan narrative).

4. Walker, *Second Corps,* 135–136; G. R. Agassiz, ed., *Meade's Headquarters, 1863–1865; Letters of Colonel Theodore Lyman from The Wilderness to Appomattox* (Boston: Atlantic Monthly, 1922), 288–289.

5. WSH to Horatio Seymour, Mar. 21, 1863, Simon Gratz Collection, HSP; WSH to Seymour, Apr. 26, 1863, Frederick H. Dearborn Collection, HUL.

6. Walker, *Second Corps,* 208; *O.R.,* XI, pt. 3, 261.

7. Coddington, *Gettysburg,* 51–53.

8. B. H. Child, "From Fredericksburg to Gettysburg," *Personal Narratives,* Soldiers and Sailors Historical Society of Rhode Island, 5th ser., no. 4 (Providence, 1895), 6; ARH, 183; Coddington, *Gettysburg,* 75, 621; *O.R.,* XXVII, pt. 3, 147.

9. *Ibid.*, 224, 247; Gibbon, *Recollections*, 125, 127–128.
10. *O.R.*, XXVII, pt. 2, 692–693.
11. Walker, *Second Corps*, 260–261.
12. *O.R.*, XXVII, pt. 3, 338; Favill, *Diary*, 241; Nevins, ed., *Wainwright Diary*, 224–225.
13. Coddington, *Gettysburg*, 36–37; *O.R.*, XXVII, pt. 1, 60.
14. *Ibid.*, 61; Gibbon, *Recollections*, 128. Gibbon mentioned that Hooker at the same time "did not appear to be in good humor at all"; *ibid.*, 129.
15. *O.R.*, XXVII, pt. 1, 367, pt. 3, 375, 395–396; Child, "Fredericksburg to Gettysburg," 8–9.
16. *O.R.*, XXVII, pt. 1, 367; Coddington, *Gettysburg*, 228, 669.
17. Lee wrote later: "It was expected that as soon as the Federal Army should cross the Potomac, General Stuart would give notice of its movement, and nothing having been heard from him since our entrance into Maryland, it was inferred that the enemy had not left Virginia"; *O.R.*, XXVII, pt. 2, 316. Of course, Lee's vague orders to Stuart had permitted the latter to stray as he did; Coddington, *Gettysburg*, 183.
18. *O.R.*, XXVII, pt. 3, 458; Coddington, *Gettysburg*, 239.
19. *O.R.*, XXVII, pt. 3, 461.
20. *Ibid.*
21. ARH, 187–188 (Morgan narrative); Coddington, *Gettysburg*, 284–285.

TWELVE. GETTYSBURG

1. Hancock's report stated that he arrived at 3 p.m.; *O.R.*, XXVII, pt. 1, 368. In his 5:25 p.m. dispatch to Meade, Hancock said that he "arrived here an hour since"; *ibid.*, 366. Later testifying before the JCCW on March 22, 1864, Hancock said that he arrived "not later than half past 3 o'clock"; Report, JCCW, 38th Cong., 2nd sess., I, 405. He mentioned the same time in a postwar magazine article; WSH, "Gettysburg. Reply to General Howard," *Galaxy*, Dec. 1876, 822–823. Howard wrote to Meade at 5 p.m. that Hancock had arrived at 4; *O.R.*, XXVII, pt. 1, 696. Doubleday later wrote that Hancock arrived "about 3:30 p.m."; Doubleday, *Chancellorsville and Gettysburg*, 150.
2. Coddington, *Gettysburg*, 266–296. See also W. W. Hassler, Jr., *Crisis at the Crossroads: The First Day at Gettysburg* (University: U. of Alabama Press, 1970), 127. For Buford's message, directed to Pleasonton, see G. Meade, *The Life and Letters of George Gordon Meade*, 2 vols. (New York: Scribner's, 1913), II, 53.
3. Haskell, *Gettysburg*, 15; H. J. Hunt, "The First Day at Gettysburg," in *B&L*, III, 283; F. A. Walker, "Meade at Gettysburg," in *B&L*, III, 408; Hassler, *Crisis at the Crossroads*, 136; Swinton, *Army of the Potomac*, 335. Gouverneur Warren, who was there, told the JCCW: "I think his personal appearance there did a great deal towards restoring order"; Report, JCCW, 38th Cong., 2nd sess., I, 377.
4. WSH, "Reply to Howard," 822.
5. O. O. Howard, "Campaign and Battle of Gettysburg, June and July, 1863," *Atlantic Monthly*, July 1876, 58.
6. *O.R.*, XXVII, pt. 1, 252 (Doubleday's report); E. P. Halstead, "Incidents of the First Day at Gettysburg," in *B&L*, III, 285.
7. *O.R.*, XXVII, pt. 1, 927 (Buford), 825 (Geary), 367–369 (Hancock report); Coddington, *Gettysburg*, 324. Hassler wrote: "Hancock's action in rallying the First and Eleventh Corps fugitives and his discerning statements sent to Meade were as superb as Howard's challenge to his authority was petty"; Hassler, *Crisis at the Crossroads*, 155.

8. Halstead, "First Day at Gettysburg," in *B&L*, III, 285; Coddington, *Gettysburg*, 330–331.

9. *O.R.*, XXVII, pt. 1, 368 (Hancock report); ARH, 191 (Morgan narrative).

10. *O.R.*, XXVII, pt. 1, 366. Meade, *Life and Letters*, II, 38–39. The next-to-last line in Hancock's message read: "Howard says that Doubleday's command gave way." When this came to light it infuriated the doughty veterans of the First Corps, who knew that they had moved back in good order while the Eleventh Corps once again broke and ran.

11. ARH, 194 (Morgan narrative). Cf. C. E. Slocum, *The Life and Services of Major-General Henry Warner Slocum* (Toledo, Ohio: Slocum Pub. Co., 1913), 102.

12. *O.R.*, XXVII, pt. 1, 696–697. Howard, known as the "Christian General" for his piety and sobersided demeanor, was more successful as a commander in the West under Sherman. His personal courage was never doubted, but in the East he was simply not a very effective leader of troops.

13. Lee's report stated: "It had not been intended to deliver a general battle so far from our base unless attacked"; *ibid.*, pt. 2, 318. WSH to Fitzhugh Lee, Jan. 17, 1878, in Fitzhugh Lee, "A Review of the First Two Days' Operations at Gettysburg and a Reply to General Longstreet," *Southern Historical Society Papers*, V, April 1878, 168.

14. Report, JCCW, 38th Cong., 2nd sess., I, 330, 348; ARH, 191 (Morgan narrative).

15. *O.R.*, XXVII, pt. 3, 466.

16. Report, JCCW, 38th Cong., 2nd sess., I, 405 (Hancock testimony); Gibbon, *Recollections*, 133–134; Haskell, *Gettysburg*, 14, 16–17. Haskell, Gibbon's adjutant, thought Hancock "the most magnificent looking General in the whole Army of the Potomac . . . [w]ith a large, well shaped person, always dressed with elegance . . . he would look as if he was 'monarch of all he surveyed' "; *ibid.*, 15.

17. *Ibid.*, 18, 20; Meade, *Life and Letters*, II, 63; Coddington, *Gettysburg*, 333.

18. Meade, *Life and Letters*, II, 70; Report, JCCW, 38th Cong., 2nd sess., I, 377 (Warren testimony); H. J. Hunt, "The Second Day at Gettysburg," in *B&L*, III, 301–302; *O.R.*, XXVII, pt. 1, 116.

19. For a comprehensive review of Sickles's long and controversial career, see W. A. Swanberg, *Sickles the Incredible* (New York: Scribner's, 1956). Sickles lived to be ninety-five, dying in 1914, and he devoted his long life to the twin task of justifying his movement of July 2, 1863, and blackening the name of George Gordon Meade.

20. Meade, *Life and Letters*, II, 77–78; Trobriand, *Four Years*, 494–495.

21. Gibbon, *Recollections*, 136; Report, JCCW, 38th Cong., 2nd sess., I, 406.

22. Meade, *Life and Letters*, II, 78–79; Coddington, *Gettysburg*, 386–387; E. G. Taylor, *Gouverneur Kemble Warren: The Life and Letters of an American Soldier, 1830–1882* (Boston and New York: Houghton Mifflin, 1932), 123.

23. Meade, *Life and Letters*, II, 86; ARH, 201, 203 (Morgan narrative); Walker, *Second Corps*, 278.

24. Child, "Fredericksburg to Gettysburg," 17–19; Favill, *Diary*, 245–246; ARH, 201–203. Zook, shot in the abdomen, lingered until 5 p.m. the next day, long enough to learn of the ultimate Union victory. "I am perfectly satisfied and ready to die," he said; Zook, "Zook," 137.

25. Gibbon, *Recollections*, 137; Walker, *Second Corps*, 282; Coddington, *Gettysburg*, 402.

26. Meade, *Life and Letters*, II, 87–88; Walker, *Second Corps*, 282–283; *O.R.*, XXVII, pt. 1, 370–371 (Hancock report). Willard went in about 7:15 p.m.

27. Walker, *Second Corps*, 283; Meade, *Life and Letters*, II, 88; W. Lochren, "The First Minnesota at Gettysburg," *Glimpses of the Nation's Struggle*, 3rd ser., Minnesota Commandery, MOLLUS, 49; A. A. Hage, "The Battle of Gettysburg as Seen by Minnesota Soldiers," *Minnesota History*, June 1963, 252–254. Hancock

wrote: "I cannot speak too highly of this regiment and its commander in its attack, as well as in its subsequent advance against the enemy"; O.R., XXVII, pt. 1, 371.

28. *Ibid.*, 351–352 (Randall's report).

29. Doubleday, *Chancellorsville and Gettysburg*, 175; Coddington, *Gettysburg*, 426.

30. O.R., XXVII, pt. 1, 372; Meade, *Life and Letters*, II, 92–93; Howard, *Autobiography*, I, 429–430; E. N. Whittier, "The Left Attack (Ewell's), Gettysburg," *Campaigns in Virginia, Maryland and Pennsylvania 1862–1863*, MHSM, III, 333. One of the two regiments sent to Slocum wound up by mistake with Howard; ARH, 205 (Morgan narrative).

31. Gibbon, *Recollections*, 140–142, 145; Meade, *Life and Letters*, II, 95–96; O.R., XXVII, pt. 1, 73–74, 126–127. After the council, Gibbon overheard Birney complaining to Meade about Hancock's being assigned over the Third Corps that afternoon. Meade answered curtly: "Gen. Hancock is your superior and I claim the right to issue the order." Gibbon, *Recollections*, 144.

32. *Ibid.*, 145; Haskell, *Gettysburg*, 69–70; Coddington, *Gettysburg*, 476–478. Though Caldwell's division was separated from the rest of the corps, Hancock did not forget about it; early in the day, reported the commander of one regiment in the Irish Brigade, Hancock came along and made adjustments in the line to improve the regiment's field of fire; O.R., XXVII, pt. 1, 392.

33. Haskell, *Gettysburg*, 74–75.

34. ARH, 195 (Morgan narrative); Haskell, *Gettysburg*, 31; Coddington, *Gettysburg*, 484–485.

35. Haskell, *Gettysburg*, 77–81; Gibbon, *Recollections*, 146.

36. Coddington, *Gettysburg*, 459–460, 462–464; Longstreet, *Memoirs*, 386–388.

37. For the cannonade, see Longacre, *Hunt*, 172–174; Gibbon, *Recollections*, 147; and Coddington, *Gettysburg*, 493–496. For the dispute between Hancock and Hunt (and McGilvery), see Longacre, *Hunt*, 174; Nevins, ed., *Wainwright Diary*, 252–253; O.R., XXVII, pt. 1, 884–885, 888; "General Hancock and the Artillery at Gettysburg," F. A. Walker, with "Rejoinder" by H. J. Hunt, in *B&L*, III, 385–387; and WSH to W. T. Sherman, Jan. 21, 1879, "Papers in Relation to the Reorganization of the Army," Senate Misc. Doc. No. 14, 46th Cong., 1st sess., 41.

38. Child, "Fredericksburg to Gettysburg," 29–30; Walker, *Hancock*, 139; WSH to P. F. Rothermel, Dec. 31, 1868, Peter Rothermel Papers, PHMC.

39. E. P. Alexander, "The Great Charge and Artillery Fighting at Gettysburg," in *B&L*, III, 364; O.R., XXVII, pt. 1, 373 (Hancock report), 239 (Hunt report); H. J. Hunt, "The Third Day at Gettysburg," in *B&L*, III, 374–375. Hunt contended, without any real evidence to support him, that if he had had control over the Second Corps artillery, the Confederates would not even have reached the Union lines; *ibid.*, 375.

40. O.R., XXVII, pt. 1, 373; WSH to P. F. Rothermel, Jan. 21, 1869, Rothermel Papers, PHMC. Randall, the commander of the 13th Vermont, said that Hancock came repeatedly to his regiment's position and gave his men "the benefit of his advice and encouragement"; O.R., XXVII, pt. 1, 352–353.

41. *Ibid.*, 374; Haskell, *Gettysburg*, 103–104.

42. O.R., XXVII, pt. 1, 443 (Devereux), 439 (Hall). Haskell was instrumental as well in getting Hall into the action quickly.

43. O.R., XXVII, pt. 1, 374–375 (Hancock), 353 (Randall).

44. Walker, *Hancock*, 143–144; O.R., XXVII, pt. 1, 440; Haskell, *Gettysburg*, 112–113.

45. Long after the war a curious controversy arose over Armistead, with allegations that he had fought on the Union side at Bull Run before joining the Confederacy (an impossibility since he had been in Los Angeles at the time) and that he had, in his dying words, recanted his allegiance to the South. Inquiries were made of

Hancock, and a letter from Bingham (then a member of Congress) to Hancock, July 19, 1882, gave Bingham's recollection of the incident. The words are certainly open to several interpretations. "Did General Armistead Fight on the Federal Side at First Manassas or Confess When Dying at Gettysburg That He Had Been Engaged in an 'Unholy Cause?' " *Southern Historical Society Papers*, X, 428.

46. WSH to P. F. Rothermel, Dec. 31, 1868, A. N. Dougherty to W. G. Mitchell, Jan. 2, 1869 (copy attested by WSH), and WSH to P. F. Rothermel, Jan. 9, 1869, Rothermel Papers, PHMC; *O.R.*, XXVII, pt. 1, 366. Caldwell commanded the Second Corps because Gibbon was also wounded in repelling Pickett's charge. Later in that day, however, Meade named General William Hays, a hard-drinking artilleryman, no relation to Alexander Hays, to command the corps; *ibid.*, pt. 3, 503.

47. Report, JCCW, 38th Cong., 2nd sess., I, 409.

48. W. G. Mitchell to WSH, Jan. 10, 1866, referred by WSH to P. F. Rothermel, Dec. 31, 1868, Rothermel Papers, PHMC. Characteristically, Hancock wanted to make sure that Webb received due credit. At a dinner later, Hancock said: "In every battle and on every important field there is one spot upon which centers the fortunes of the field. There was but one such spot at Gettysburg and it fell to the lot of Gen'l Webb to have it and to hold it and for holding it he must receive the credit due him"; Coddington, *Gettysburg*, 528.

THIRTEEN. THE INVALID

1. J. T. Riemer, M.D., "General Hancock and Dr. Read," *Bulletin of the Historical Society of Montgomery County, Pennsylvania*, spring 1972, 173; Walker, *Hancock*, 144–145, 148; Coddington, *Gettysburg*, 528.

2. ARH, 97.

3. Riemer, "Hancock and Dr. Read," 173–174; ARH, 97–99; *Norristown Herald and Free Press*, July 7, 28, 1863.

4. WSH to L. Thomas, July 22, 1863; surgeon's certificates, as follows: Dr. Geo. E. Cooper, Philadelphia, July 22, 1863, Dr. Wm. Corson, Norristown, Aug. 11, 1863, Sept. 1, 1863, Dr. E. F. Hammond, New York City, Sept. 23, 1863, Dr. John W. Randolph, Jefferson Barracks, Oct. 12, 1863, Nov. 2, 1863, and Dr. Morris, Washington, Dec. 12, 1863, Letters Received, Commission Branch, AGO, 1863–1870, NA; ARH, 99.

5. For the story of the extraction of the Minié ball, see Riemer, "Hancock and Dr. Read," 173–174; and undated clipping, *Philadelphia Times*, in MCHS's collection of Hancock items. The ball itself is now on display in MCHS.

6. Denison, *Winfield*, 214–215; ARH, 101.

7. Walker, *Hancock*, 148–149; R. L. Silliker, ed., *The Rebel Yell and the Yankee Hurrah: The Civil War Journal of a Maine Volunteer* (Camden, Me.: Down East Books, 1985), 157.

8. Meade, *Life and Letters*, II, 160–161; Agassiz, ed., *Meade's Headquarters*, 60; G. G. Meade to WSH, Dec. 11, 1863, *Letters and Addresses*, 33–34.

9. Walker, *Second Corps*, 392; WSH to Meade, Dec. 21, 1863, *Letters and Addresses*, 34.

10. *O.R.*, XXIX, pt. 1, 6; WSH to Seth Williams, Jan. 5, 1864, Ferdinand J. Dreer Collection, HSP; Special Orders No. 7, Jan. 8, 1864, and report of the commission on Hancock's absence, approved by Meade, Jan. 8, 1864, Letters Received, Commission Branch, AGO, 1863–1870, NA. For Hancock's departure from the corps, see *O.R.*, L, pt. 1, 1139; and Favill, *Diary*, 274.

11. G. G. Meade to Margaretta Meade, Dec. 28, 1863, Meade, *Life and Letters*, II, 163–164.

12. *O.R.*, XXXIII, 357, 373; Denison, *Winfield*, 221, 224.

13. *O.R.*, XXXIII, 427; Palfrey, *Antietam and Fredericksburg*, 126; F. C. Barlow to his mother and brothers, May 8, 1863, and WSH to Barlow, Dec. 12, 1863, Francis Channing Barlow Papers, MaHS. The others named by Palfrey were Sheridan, Humphreys, Kearny, and Custer. After the war, Barlow became a pillar of the New York bar, an active Republican politician, and a founder of the American Bar Association. As New York district attorney, he prosecuted the Tweed Ring.

14. J. A. Carpenter, *Sword and Olive Branch: Oliver Otis Howard* (Pittsburgh: U. of Pittsburgh Press, 1964), 63; *Army and Navy Journal*, Feb. 20, 1864.

15. O. O. Howard to WSH, Feb. 25, 1864, O. O. Howard Papers, Bowdoin College Library.

16. WSH to O. O. Howard, Mar. 14, 1864, O. O. Howard Papers, Bowdoin College Library.

17. G. G. Meade to J. Gibbon, Mar. 15, 1864, Gibbon, *Recollections*, 188; Meade to Halleck, Mar. 18, 1864, *O.R.*, XXXIII, 688.

18. Report, JCCW, I, 38th Cong., 2nd sess., 403–412; Coddington, *Gettysburg*, 532.

19. *O.R.*, XXXIII, 717–718.

20. *Ibid.*, 735–737.

21. Agassiz, ed., *Meade's Headquarters*, 266; Walker, *Second Corps*, 557–558; G. G. Meade to Margaretta Meade, Apr. 11, 1864, Apr. 18, 1864, Meade, *Life and Letters*, II, 189–190.

22. Silliker, ed., *Rebel Yell*, 139; A. Hays to Annie Hays, Mar. 25, 1864, Fleming, ed., *Hays*, 562; WSH to Seth Williams, Mar. 26, 1864, *O.R.*, XXXIII, 743; A. A. Humphreys to Archibald Campbell, Aug. 6, 1863, Humphreys Papers, HSP.

23. F. C. Barlow to Almira Barlow, Apr. 19, 1864, and F. C. Barlow to Richard Barlow, Apr. 22, 1864, Francis Channing Barlow Papers, MaHS.

24. John Y. Simon, ed., *The Papers of Ulysses S. Grant* (Carbondale: Southern Illinois U. Press, 1967–), X, 274.

FOURTEEN. THE WILDERNESS

1. *O.R.*, XXXVI, pt. 2, 356–357.

2. A. S. Webb, "Through the Wilderness," in *B&L*, IV, 152.

3. *O.R.*, XXXVI, pt. 2, 320; ARH, 101.

4. E. Steere, *The Wilderness Campaign* (Harrisburg, Pa.: Stackpole, 1960), 51–53; *O.R.*, XXXVI, pt. 2, 332, pt. 1, 318.

5. Simon, ed., *Grant Papers*, X, 397; *O.R.*, XXXVI, pt. 2, 406–407.

6. A. A. Humphreys, *The Virginia Campaign of '64 and '65* (New York: Scribner's, 1883), 25.

7. *O.R.*, XXXVI, pt. 2, 407, 409.

8. *Ibid.*, 409–410; Silliker, ed., *Rebel Yell*, 143. In his report of the battle, Hancock stated: "Owing to the fact of the Brock road being very narrow and heavily wooded on both sides, the formation of the infantry in line of battle was extremely slow"; *O.R.*, XXXVI, pt. 1, 320.

9. *Ibid.*; Schaff, *Wilderness*, 184–186; Steere, *Wilderness Campaign*, 208–212; Fleming, ed., *Hays*, 598.

10. Steere, *Wilderness Campaign*, 212–215.

11. Agassiz, ed., *Meade's Headquarters*, 91–92; Steere, *Wilderness Campaign*, 217; *O.R.*, XXXVI, pt. 1, 320.

12. Steere, *Wilderness Campaign*, 237–238.

13. Humphreys, *Virginia Campaign*, 33. The importance of Mott's earlier failure, which had delayed Hancock's offensive by at least an hour, was starkly underlined by the failing daylight; Steere, *Wilderness Campaign*, 253.

14. *O.R.*, XXXVI, pt. 2, 404–405.
15. *Ibid.*, 411.
16. *Ibid.*, 412, 425.
17. E. M. Law, "From the Wilderness to Cold Harbor," in *B&L*, IV, 123.
18. *O.R.*, XXXVI, pt. 1, 320.
19. Longstreet, *Memoirs*, 556–557.
20. Walker, *Second Corps*, 421–422; Schaff, *Wilderness*, 239–240, 242; *O.R.*, XXXVI, pt. 1, 320; Silliker, ed., *Rebel Yell*, 145.
21. Agassiz, ed., *Meade's Headquarters*, 93–94.
22. Walker, *Second Corps*, 422–423; Steere, *Wilderness Campaign*, 352–354.
23. *O.R.*, XXXVI, pt. 2, 440–441.
24. *Ibid.*, pt. 1, 320.
25. Gibbon, *Recollections*, 386–411; WSH to John Gibbon, June 28, 1883, John Gibbon Papers, MdHS.
26. *O.R.*, XXXVI, pt. 2, 440–441; Schaff, *Wilderness*, 241–242. This unfortunate dispute between two highly competent and conscientious officers was much regretted by the friends of both. It was fanned mainly by Gibbon, since Hancock did nothing about it other than to note the incident in his report—and to answer Gibbon's letters nineteen years later. Most historians have accepted Hancock's report as true, as did Grant ("Gibbon commanded Hancock's left, and was ordered to attack, but was not able to accomplish much"); Grant, *Memoirs*, 405.
27. *O.R.*, XXXVI, pt. 1, 320.
28. *Ibid.*, pt. 2, 441–443, pt. 1, 320–321; Schaff, *Wilderness*, 262–264; Steere, *Wilderness Campaign*, 366–367.
29. Schaff, *Wilderness*, 264–265; *O.R.*, XXXVI, pt. 1, 321–322.
30. Longstreet, *Memoirs*, 561–562; *O.R.*, XXXVI, pt. 1, 322.
31. Longstreet, *Memoirs*, 563; Steere, *Wilderness Campaign*, 402–403.
32. Longstreet, *Memoirs*, 568.
33. *Ibid.*, 563–564.
34. Steere, *Wilderness Campaign*, 405–406, 415.
35. Agassiz, ed., *Meade's Headquarters*, 96.
36. *O.R.*, XXXVI, pt. 2, 444–445.
37. *Ibid.*, pt. 1, 323–324.
38. Lyman, "Addenda," 171.

FIFTEEN. THE SPOTSYLVANIA CAMPAIGN

1. Walker, *Hancock*, 184; WSH report, *O.R.*, XXXVI, pt. 1, 328–329; Humphreys, *Virginia Campaign*, 61–62.
2. Simon, ed., *Grant Papers*, X, 422–423.
3. *O.R.*, XXXVI, pt. 1, 330, pt. 2, 567–568, 570; WSH to F. C. Barlow, May 9, 1864, 5:50 p.m., Barlow Papers, MaHS.
4. *O.R.*, XXXVI, pt. 1, 331–333; Favill, *Diary*, 294; Morrison, ed., *Heth Diary*, 187–188. During the withdrawal, a piece of artillery, jammed between two trees and abandoned, was the first gun ever lost by the Second Corps.
5. Humphreys, *Virginia Campaign*, 82–83; Swinton, *Army of the Potomac*, 449.
6. Humphreys, *Virginia Campaign*, 81–82; A. S. Webb, "Through the Wilderness," in *B&L*, IV, 167–168; *O.R.*, XXXVI, pt. 1, 334.
7. Agassiz, ed., *Meade's Headquarters*, 110.
8. G. N. Galloway, "Hand to Hand Fighting at Spotsylvania," in *B&L*, IV, 170; *O.R.*, XXXVI, pt. 1, 335; Walker, *Second Corps*, 468–469; F. C. Barlow, "Capture of the Salient May 12 1864," *The Wilderness Campaign, May–June 1864*, IV, 247; J. D. Black, "Reminiscences of the Bloody Angle," *Glimpses of the Nation's Struggle*, 4th

ser., Minnesota Commandery, MOLLUS, 423. Black, who was on Barlow's staff, said he never saw Barlow so depressed as he was that night before the assault on the Salient; *ibid.*

9. *O.R.*, XXXVI, pt. 1, 335; Swinton, *Army of the Potomac,* 451.

10. M. Klein, *Edward Porter Alexander* (Athens: U. of Georgia Press, 1971), 115–116; Morrison, ed., *Heth Diary,* 187.

11. *O.R.*, XXXVI, pt. 1, 358–359; ARH, 104. Because of Steuart's offensive behavior toward Hancock, the Union provost-marshals forced him to walk the distance back to Fredericksburg and captivity.

12. *O.R.*, XXXVI, pt. 1, 335–336; J. B. Gordon, *Reminiscences of the Civil War* (New York: Scribners, 1903), 278. Gordon called Hancock's charge "one of that great soldier's most brilliant achievements"; *ibid.,* 275.

13. Walker, *Second Corps,* 472–473; Walker, *Hancock,* 201–202. One writer said the soft ground turned into "a slithery maroon swamp"; Klein, *Alexander,* 116.

14. Walker, *Second Corps,* 473; Galloway, "Hand to Hand Fighting at Spotsylvania," in *B&L,* IV, 174.

15. Humphreys, *Virginia Campaign,* 104–105; Swinton, *Army of the Potomac,* 454.

16. John Gibbon to Frances Gibbon, May 13, 1864, John Gibbon Papers, MdHS; Miles, *Serving the Republic,* 67.

17. *O.R.*, XXXVI, pt. 2, 704–707; A. S. Webb, "Through the Wilderness," in *B&L,* IV, 169.

18. *O.R.*, XXXVI, pt. 1, 337; Walker, *Second Corps,* 483–484; Humphreys, *Virginia Campaign,* 109.

19. *O.R.*, XXXVI, pt. 2, 786–787, 844.

20. *Ibid.,* pt. 1, 337–338, 361–362; Walker, *Second Corps,* 485–486.

21. *O.R.*, XXXVI, pt. 2, 864–865, 869, pt. 1, 338, 362; Walker, *Second Corps,* 487–488.

22. At 10:40 a.m., May 12, Grant wired Meade: "If Warren fails to attack promptly send Humphreys to command his corps and relieve him"; Simon, ed., *Grant Papers,* X, 433.

SIXTEEN. THE FRUSTRATION
OF GENERAL GRANT

1. *O.R.*, XXXVI, pt. 1, 341; Grant, *Memoirs,* 428; Walker, *Second Corps,* 492.

2. Agassiz, ed., *Meade's Headquarters,* 120.

3. Grant, *Memoirs,* 429.

4. *O.R.*, XXXVI, pt. 1, 341; Swinton, *Army of the Potomac,* 475–476; W. P. Shreve, "The Operations of the Army of the Potomac May 13–June 2, 1864," *The Wilderness Campaign May–June 1864,* MHSM, IV, 306, 308–309.

5. *O.R,* XXXVI, pt. 1, 8–9; Grant, *Memoirs,* 432.

6. *O.R,* XXXVI, pt. 1, 343–344; Gibbon, *Recollections,* 226; Humphreys, *Virginia Campaign,* 169.

7. *O.R.*, XXXVI, pt. 1, 344; Shreve, "Operations," 315.

8. C. H. Porter, "The Battle of Cold Harbor," *The Wilderness Campaign, May–June 1864,* MHSM, IV, 333.

9. Report of Capt. James Fleming, 28th Mass., *O.R.*, XXXVI, pt. 1, 390.

10. *Ibid.,* 344–345, 366–367; Gibbon, *Recollections,* 232–233; Agassiz, ed., *Meade's Headquarters,* 144–145.

11. *O.R.*, XXXVI, pt. 1, 345–346; Walker, *Second Corps,* 522; Grant, *Memoirs,* 444.

12. *O.R.*, XXXVI, pt. 3, 525, 530–531.

13. *Ibid.,* 526.

14. *Ibid.*, 599–600, 603–604; Grant, *Memoirs*, 443–444.
15. Walker, *Second Corps*, 519–520.
16. Wright to WSH, June 10, 1864: "I am sorry to hear you are an invalid this evening"; *O.R.*, XXXVI, pt. 3, 730.

SEVENTEEN. ACROSS THE JAMES

1. *O.R.*, XXXVI, pt. 3, 598–599, 695, 745–746; Grant, *Memoirs*, 451; Nevins, ed., *Wainwright Diary*, 416; *O.R.*, XL, pt. 2, 12.
2. Mitchell's log of Second Corps activity, *ibid.*, pt. 1, 316; Dana to Stanton, June 15, 1864, 8 a.m., *ibid.*, 19–20.
3. *Ibid.*, pt. 2, 29.
4. *Ibid.*, 25, 36, 56–58.
5. *Ibid.*, pt. 1, 303–304, 316.
6. *Ibid.*, pt. 2, 59, 63, 304; W. F. Smith, *From Chattanooga to Petersburg under Generals Grant and Butler: A Contribution to the History of the War, and a Personal Vindication* (Boston and New York: Houghton Mifflin, 1893), 81.
7. *O.R.*, XL, pt. 1, 315.
8. *Ibid.*, 305.
9. Grant, *Memoirs*, 454–456; *O.R.*, XL, pt. 1, 705; P. G. T. Beauregard to C. M. Wilcox, June 9, 1874, "Letter of General Beauregard to General C. M. Wilcox," *Petersburg, Chancellorsville, Gettysburg*, MHSM, V, 120; Humphreys, *Virginia Campaign*, 215–216.
10. W. F. Smith to W. B. Franklin, Apr. 28, 1864, Wm. B. Franklin Papers, LC.
11. *O.R.*, XL, pt. 1, 313–315. Grant's unsigned original of this letter was found in his papers with Hancock's letter of June 26, but there appears to be no record of the Grant letter's being sent or received.
12. J. C. Andrews, *The North Reports the Civil War* (Pittsburgh: U. of Pittsburgh Press, 1955), 551; *O.R.*, XL, pt. 2, 567, 583, pt. 3, 89; B. F. Butler, *Butler's Book* (Boston: A. M. Thayer, 1892), 701.
13. T. Lyman, "Operations of the Army of the Potomac June 5–15, 1864," *Petersburg, Chancellorsville, Gettysburg*, MHSM, V, 19; Gibbon, *Recollections*, 243–244.
14. Agassiz, ed., *Meade's Headquarters*, 162–163.
15. Humphreys, *Virginia Campaign*, 215–216; *O.R.*, XL, pt. 2, 657.
16. Gibbon, *Recollections*, 244; *O.R.*, XL, pt. 2, 436–437, 639–642, 644; J. C. Ropes, "The Failure to Take Petersburg on June 16–18, 1864," *Petersburg, Chancellorsville, Gettysburg*, MHSM, V, 160.
17. *O.R.*, XL, pt. 2, 88–89, 90–91, 123, pt. 1, 306–307; C. F. Adams, Jr., to C. F. Adams, June 19, 1864, in *A Cycle of Adams Letters, 1861–1865*, ed. W. C. Ford, 2 vols. (London: Constable, 1921), II, 154–155.
18. *O.R.*, XL, pt. 1, 307, 318, pt. 2, 122, 162; Walker, *Second Corps*, 539. A large piece of bone came out of Hancock's wound, and he improved after that; Meade, *Life and Letters*, II, 208–209.
19. *O.R.*, XL, pt. 1, 13–14, pt. 2, 468; Silliker, ed., *Rebel Yell*, 175; J. R. C. Ward, *History of the One Hundred and Sixth Regiment Pennsylvania Volunteers* (Philadelphia: McManus, 1906), 280.
20. *O.R.*, XL, pt. 1, 307.
21. F. C. Barlow to E. Barlow, July 2, 1864, Francis C. Barlow Papers, MaHS; Agassiz, ed., *Meade's Headquarters*, 189.
22. Meade, *Life and Letters*, II, 205–206; WSH to J. E. Yeatman, June 18, 1864, in Denison, *Winfield*, 275–276. Hancock asked the St. Louis people to send the sword to Allie, then at her parents' home; *ibid.* For the appreciation of Philadelphia, see ARH, 101–102. The city councils in February 1864 passed resolutions of thanks and placed

Independence Hall at Hancock's disposal for a reception; the Union League of Philadelphia presented him with a silver medal and hung his portrait. This latter organization, objecting to Hancock's policies in New Orleans, later removed the portrait and disposed of it, treatment, Allie wrote, that "General Hancock never forgot"; *ibid.*

23. *Norristown Herald and Free Press*, July 12, Sept. 6, 1864.

24. Agassiz, ed., *Meade's Headquarters*, 191–192.

25. Silliker, ed., *Rebel Yell*, 157.

26. *O.R.*, XXXVI, pt. 1, 435–436; F. H. Taylor, *Philadelphia in the Civil War* (Philadelphia: City of Philadelphia, 1913), 87.

27. Trobriand, *Four Years*, 598; Agassiz, ed., *Meade's Headquarters*, 106.

28. Meade, *Life and Letters*, II, 212, 215; Grant to A. Lincoln, July 25, 1864, *O.R.*, XL, pt. 3, 436. On July 7 Dana wrote to Stanton his opinion that Meade would have to be relieved because his nasty temper made him impossible to deal with. He said that Grant feared he might have to let Meade go, in which case "it would be necessary to put Hancock in command"; *ibid.*, pt. 1, 35–36.

EIGHTEEN. THE DEEP
BOTTOM EXPEDITIONS

1. *O.R.*, XL, pt. 3, 437–438.

2. *Ibid.*, pt. 1, 308–309, 321.

3. *Ibid.*, pt. 1, 309–311, pt. 3, 514; Humphreys, *Virginia Campaign*, 248; *Harper's Weekly*, Aug. 13, 1864. To the divisions of Kershaw and Wilcox, Lee added those of Heth, Field, Rooney Lee, and Fitz Lee.

4. Trobriand, *Four Years*, 627; *O.R.*, XL, pt. 1, 169–170. On July 6 Lee had written to Ewell: "I do not like the continuance of the enemy on the north side of James River and the maintenance of the pontoon bridge at Deep Bottom"; *O.R.*, XL, pt. 3, 745. The "enemy" he referred to at that time was a Tenth Corps brigade which simply held the bridgehead.

5. Gibbon, *Recollections*, 247–251.

6. *O.R.*, XL, pt. 1, 324–325.

7. *Ibid.*, 171–172; Walker, *Second Corps*, 568; WSH to T. B. Myers, Aug. 6, 1864, WSH Papers, LC.

8. *O.R.*, XL, pt. 1, 44–126 (proceedings of the court of inquiry), 129–163 (appendix).

9. For the report of the court of inquiry see *ibid.*, 127–129.

10. Meade, *Life and Letters*, II, 218–219; Grant, *Memoirs*, 469.

11. *O.R.*, XLII, pt. 2, 131–132; Walker, *Second Corps*, 568; Humphreys, *Virginia Campaign*, 268.

12. *O.R*, XLII, pt. 1, 217; Walker, *Second Corps*, 569–570.

13. *O.R*, XLII, pt. 1, 217, 241, pt. 2, 148; Walker, *Second Corps*, 570.

14. *O.R.*, XLII, pt. 1, 218, 248; Walker, *Second Corps*, 572.

15. *O.R.*, XLII, pt. 1, 218; Meade, *Life and Letters*, II, 222.

16. *O.R.*, XLII, pt. 1, 249, 250; Walker, *Second Corps*, 578. Barlow and Miles in their reports, written later, say it was August 17 when the former went off to the hospital. Mitchell, in his contemporaneous log, says it was August 18; *O.R.*, XLII, pt. 1, 244.

17. WSH to L. Thomas, Aug. 17, 1864, Letters Received, Commissions Branch, AGO, 1863–1870, NA. Sherman and Sheridan received promotions at the same time, and Meade, who had been recommended for promotion at the same time as the others, did not. Meade was furious and confronted Grant, who admitted the action was his. He wanted Sherman to outrank Meade, so that he had to hold up Meade's

promotion. "The whole substance of the explanation," Meade wrote his wife, "was that he desired to advance his favorites, Sherman and Sheridan"; Meade, *Life and Letters*, II, 223–224.

18. *O.R.*, XLII, pt. 1, 222.

NINETEEN. THE FINAL BATTLES

1. *O.R.*, XLII, pt. 1, 222.
2. *Ibid.; ibid.*, pt. 2, 449. Humphreys estimated the rebel infantry to be 8,000 to 10,000 strong; *ibid.*, 452.
3. Walker, *Second Corps*, 582–583.
4. *O.R.*, XLII, pt. 1, 224. One of Hancock's battery commanders, in an excess of loyalty, wrote: "General Hancock had had no thought of a battle here, or the works would have been reformed and made tenable"; G. K. Dauchy, "The Battle of Ream's Station," *Military Essays and Recollections*, Illinois Commandery, MOLLUS (Chicago: Dial Press, 1899), III, 130.
5. Walker, *Second Corps*, 591–592.
6. *O.R.*, XLII, pt. 1, 224; Dauchy, "Ream's Station," 131.
7. *O.R.*, XLII, pt. 2, 482, 483.
8. *Ibid.*, pt. 1, 224–225, pt. 2, 483.
9. Letter from WSH to Wm. Swinton, detailing the substance of a postwar conversation with Heth, in Swinton, *Army of the Potomac*, 538.
10. *O.R.*, XLII, pt. 1, 226.
11. *Ibid.*, 226–227; Walker, *Second Corps*, 595–596; Dauchy, "Ream's Station," 136–139; W. W. Hassler, *A. P. Hill: Lee's Forgotten General* (Richmond, Va.: Garrett and Massie, 1957), 227.
12. Walker, *Second Corps*, 598–599.
13. Humphreys, *Virginia Campaign*, 283.
14. *O.R.*, XLII, pt. 2, 486; Walker, *Hancock*, 275.
15. WSH to H. C. Carey, Aug. 28, 1864, Misc. Papers, W. S. Hancock, NYPL; WSH to A. S. Webb, Aug. 30, 1864, A. S. Webb Papers, YUL.
16. Gibbon, *Recollections*, 259–262; *O.R.*, XLII, pt. 2, 691. It should be noted that all of the incidents between Gibbon and Hancock were recited from Gibbon's point of view; Hancock never seems to have mentioned any such incidents to anyone. He did, however, write to Alexander Webb to see if he would be available to command the Second Division when Gibbon was on sick leave earlier in August; WSH to A. S. Webb, Aug. 30, 1864, A. S. Webb Papers, YUL. Gibbon was an obvious candidate for a corps command soon, and bringing in someone like Webb to command his division would seem like a gentle prod to Grant and Stanton to find Gibbon an appropriate position elsewhere than the Second Corps.
17. *O.R.*, XLII, pt. 2, 993–994.
18. *Ibid.*, 886.
19. *Ibid.*, pt. 3, 238.
20. Walker, *Second Corps*, 606–607; *O.R.*, XLII, pt. 2, 774, 888. The affair at "The Chimneys" was the occasion for another flare-up between Hancock and H. J. Hunt over the issue of authority over artillery posted within the Second Corps sector. The question remained unresolved; *ibid.*, 759–761, 787.
21. WSH to T. Bailey Myers, Aug. 6, 1864, Hancock Papers, LC. McClellan, in his letter of acceptance, disowned the war plank of the platform.
22. Goodrich, *Hancock*, 195–196.
23. Trobriand, *Four Years*, 658–659.
24. *O.R.*, XLII, pt. 1, 230. Egan, a good soldier, liked his whiskey. One of his men wrote that Egan was "a firm believer in the doctrine that there is no sense in buying

meat, since half of it is bone, when one can buy whiskey with *no* bones"; Silliker, ed., *Rebel Yell*, 166.

25. *O.R.*, XLII, pt. 3, 340–341. See Hancock's report, where he stated, somewhat sourly: "The operations of the Ninth and Fifth Corps were intended, I presume, to occupy the enemy to an extent that would forbid their concentration against me"; *ibid.*, pt. 1, 231.

26. R. J. Sommers, *Richmond Redeemed: The Siege at Petersburg* (Garden City: Doubleday, 1981), 193.

27. *O.R.*, XLII, pt. 1, 231–232, pt. 3, 379, 380.

28. *Ibid.*, pt. 1, 232–234. After the war, Heth wrote: "Convinced now that Parke would make no serious assault, and Crawford remaining quiet, I withdrew one brigade . . . from my lines, and uniting it with Mahone's two brigades, I crossed over the river with this force," for the assault against Pierce; F. A. Walker, "The Expedition to the Boydton Plank Road, October, 1864," *Petersburg, Chancellorsville, Gettysburg*, MHSM, V, 349.

29. *O.R.*, XLII, pt. 1, 234–235.

30. *Ibid.*, pt. 3, 381–382.

31. *Ibid.*, pt. 1, 236.

32. Grant, *Memoirs*, 481; *O.R.*, XLII, pt. 1, 236–237; WSH to F. C. Barlow, Nov. 3, 1864, Barlow Papers, MaHS.

33. *O.R.*, XLII, pt. 3, 773; WSH to F. C. Barlow, Nov. 3, 1864, Barlow Papers, MaHS. Hancock, who hinted that he would like Barlow with him when the latter's health was restored, said, "You will have a magnificent Division in the 2nd Corps should you prefer to remain with it. It is over 7000 present for duty *now*. . . . Now our men as a mass are a *little* shaky for want of officers. But by Spring the Second Corps will be a *power*"; *ibid.* Barlow did return to command the Second Division (and, for a brief time, the Second Corps) in the spring of 1865 before returning to a distinguished legal career.

TWENTY. THE END OF THE WAR

1. *O.R.*, XLII, pt. 3, 337.

2. F. A. Shannon, *The Organization and Administration of the Union Army, 1861–1865*, 2 vols. (Cleveland: Arthur H. Clark, 1928), II, 90–91. "As Hancock is popular the Dept. hopes to make large enlistments through him"; A. A. Humphreys to Rebecca Humphreys, Nov. 6, 1864, Humphreys Papers, HSP. One veteran officer in the Army of the Potomac called the special bounty "a sort of premium offered to those who refused to re-enlist in the field"; Nevins, ed., *Wainwright Diary*, 483.

3. A. A. Humphreys to Rebecca Humphreys, Nov. 12, 1864, Humphreys Papers, HSP; *O.R.*, XLII, pt. 3, 619, 626, 628.

4. *Ibid.*, 628–629. Apparently Sickles had been making efforts to be designated to raise the corps of veterans—and Sickles had a good deal of political influence; A. A. Humphreys to Rebecca Humphreys, Nov. 23, 1864, Humphreys Papers, HSP.

5. *O.R.*, XLII, pt. 3, 629, 705. The fact that Humphreys was technically designated "temporary" commander, until Hancock was reassigned, promptly brought forth a predictable squawk from Gibbon, who said that was "a direct reflection upon me" and asked to be relieved from duty; *ibid.*, 714. Gibbon was mollified and on January 15, 1865, became commander of the Twenty-fourth Corps.

6. A. A. Humphreys to Rebecca Humphreys, Nov. 26, 1864, Humphreys Papers, HSP; *O.R.*, XLII, pt. 3, 713–714. On February 6, 1865, Longstreet still referred to the Second as "Hancock's corps"; *ibid.*, XLVI, pt. 2, 1207.

7. WSH to Gen. John A. Rawlins, ———, 1864 (probably Nov. 27), Simon Gratz Collection, HSP; *O.R.*, XLII, pt. 3, 726, 728, 769, 806.

8. Shannon, *Organization of Union Army*, II, 91.

9. *O.R.*, XLVI, pt. 2, 199, 573, 591–592.

10. *Ibid.*, 706–707. When Hancock arrived at his new command, his staff consisted of Morgan, Mitchell, Parker, and Wilson; *ibid.*, 724–725.

11. *Ibid.*, 620; ARH, 91.

12. *O.R.*, XLVI, pt. 2, 755–764.

13. *Ibid.*, 724, 863.

14. T. H. Williams, *Hayes of the Twenty-third: The Civil War Volunteer Officer* (New York: Knopf, 1965), 321.

15. *O.R.*, XLVI, pt. 3, 570–571; T. H. Williams, *Hayes*, 321–322.

16. F. A. Flower, *Edwin McMasters Stanton: The Autocrat of Rebellion, Emancipation, and Reconstruction* (Akron, Ohio: Saalfield Pub. Co., 1905), 381.

17. Mason, "Through the Wilderness to the Bloody Angle at Spottsylvania Court House," 299.

TWENTY-ONE. THE EXECUTION
OF MARY SURRATT

1. H. L. Burnett, "Some Incidents in the Trial of President Lincoln's Assassins," in *Personal Recollections of the War of the Rebellion*, ed. J. G. Wilson and T. M. Coan, 4 vols. New York Commandery, MOLLUS, I, 210; B. F. Morris, *Memorial Record of the Nation's Tribute to Abraham Lincoln* (Washington: Morrison, 1867), 117.

2. H. K. Beale, ed., *Diary of Gideon Welles*, 3 vols. (New York: Norton, 1960), II, 303 (entry of May 9, 1865); J. D. Richardson, ed., *Messages and Papers of the Presidents, 1789–1908*, 10 vols. (Washington: Bureau of National Literature and Art, 1908), VI, 334–335.

3. Special Orders, No. 211, from the Adjutant-General's Office, dated May 6, 1865, set up the tribunal, and Special Orders, No. 216, making two changes in its composition, was issued on May 9; Richardson, ed., *Messages and Papers*, VI, 335–336; D. M. DeWitt, *The Judicial Murder of Mary E. Surratt* (Baltimore: John Murphy, 1895), 28–30.

4. *Ibid.*, 97–98, 110–111. B. P. Thomas and H. M. Hyman, *Stanton: The Life and Times of Lincoln's Secretary of War* (New York: Knopf, 1962), 429–431; H. L. Burnett, "The Controversy between President Johnson and Judge Holt," in *Personal Recollections of the War of the Rebellion*, ed. Wilson and Coan, I, 220–221.

5. W. G. Moore, "Notes of Colonel W. G. Moore, Private Secretary to President Johnson, 1866–1868," *American Historical Review*, Oct. 1913, 108; J. G. Randall, ed., *The Diary of Orville Hickman Browning*, 2 vols. (Springfield: Illinois State Historical Library, 1933), II, 37. The order, dated July 5, 1865, signed by the president, directing the executions on July 7 to be carried out by General Hancock, is in Richardson, ed., *Messages and Papers*, VI, 342–348.

6. ARH, 110.

7. *New York Times*, July 1, 7, 1865.

8. *Ibid.*, July 8, 1865; A. Johnson to WSH, July 7, 1865, and WSH to Judge A. Wylie, July 7, 1865, Abraham Lincoln File, HEHL; J. S. Brisbin, *Winfield Scott Hancock* (Philadelphia: L. Lum Smith, 1880), 67–68.

9. Randall, ed., *Browning Diary*, II, 37.

10. *New York Times*, July 8, 1865; WSH to T. K. Smith, June 18, 1871, Thos. Kilby Smith Papers, USMA; Thomas and Hyman, *Stanton*, 434; McCulloch, *Men and Measures*, 225–226.

11. ARH, 109. The same limited time frame makes doubtful a statement by a Stanton biographer that Hancock went to Baltimore on Stanton's order and caused

Bishop Spalding of that see to intervene with Mary Surratt's priest to have him cease his efforts for clemency; Flower, *Stanton,* 287.

12. Forney, *Hancock,* 357; *New York Times,* July 8, 1865.

13. *New York Herald,* July 28, 1880; *Letters and Addresses,* 39. For Father Walter's statement contradicting assertions which had appeared in the *Washington Post* on Nov. 13, 1879, see *New York World,* Nov. 14, 1879.

14. McCulloch, *Men and Measures,* 226. Several years later, Hancock wrote in a private letter that the order from the president was regular and proper enough: "Had I any option? Well, there was a writ of Habeas Corpus issued. I appeared before the Court and made a return to the writ, giving a new order of the President under his signature, suspending the writ of Habeas Corpus. . . . What did the Judge do? Did he contest the order[?] Did he pursue the matter[?] No, he dismissed me and dismissed the case"; WSH to T. K. Smith, June 18, 1871, Thos. Kilby Smith Papers, USMA.

15. WSH to T. K. Smith, June 19, 1871, *ibid.,*

TWENTY-TWO. INDIAN PROBLEMS

1. Order of the President, June 27, 1865; *O.R.,* XLVIII, pt. 2, 1003–1004, and modified, *O.R.,* ser. 3, V, 512–513; Walker, *Hancock,* 296; ARH, 110.

2. WSH to J. L. Brent, June 20, 1866, and July ———, 1866, Brent (A&W) Collection, HEHL; Morrison, ed., *Heth Diary,* 200–202.

3. The act of July 28, 1866, is 14 Stat. 332–338. R. M. Utley, *Frontier Regulars: The United States Army and the Indian, 1866–1891* (New York and London: Macmillan, 1973), 10–12.

4. W T. Sherman to U. S. Grant, Mar. 10, 1866, W. T. Sherman Papers, MoHS.

5. Walker, *Hancock,* 296; Tucker, *Hancock the Superb,* 273–274. Hancock did some discreet lobbying in his own behalf, including a letter to Senator Henry Wilson of May 14, 1866, suggesting that the latter might "speak in my interest" to Johnson or Stanton; Henry Wilson Papers, DUL.

6. R. G. Athearn, *William Tecumseh Sherman and the Settlement of the West* (Norman: U. of Oklahoma Press, 1956), 65; WSH to Gov. Thos. C. Fletcher, Oct. 16 and Oct. 17, 1866, Robert T. Van Horn Papers, WHMC; mayor of Brunswick, Mo., to Fletcher, Oct. 30, 1866, Louis Benecke Papers, WHMC.

7. S. J. Crawford, *Kansas in the Sixties* (Chicago: A. C. McClurg, 1911), 231.

8. R. M. Utley, *Frontiersmen in Blue* (New York and London: Macmillan, 1967), 301–303, 337–338; D. J. Berthrong, *The Southern Cheyennes* (Norman: U. of Oklahoma Press, 1963), 241–243, 258–260, 261–264.

9. C. C. Rister, "Harmful Practices of Indian Traders of the Southwest, 1865–1876," *New Mexico Historical Review,* July 1931, 232.

10. R. S. Thorndike, ed., *The Sherman Letters: Correspondence between General and Senator Sherman from 1837 to 1891* (New York: Scribner's, 1894), 287.

11. *Norristown Herald and Free Press,* Feb. 7, 1867.

12. G. Thompson, *The Army and the Navajo* (Tucson: U. of Arizona Press, 1976), 123, 129–135; WSH to J. H. Carleton, Feb. 18, 1867, *ibid.,* 123.

13. W. T. Sherman to WSH, Mar. 14, 1867, Letters Received AGO, Main Series, 1861–1870, NA. This letter was clearly a written confirmation of the oral directions given to Hancock at the March 8 meeting in St. Louis. Berthrong, *Southern Cheyennes,* 265.

14. WSH to Sherman's HQ, Feb. 16, 1867, quoted in W. T. Sherman to U. S. Grant, Feb. 18, 1867, U. S. Grant Papers, LC. Sherman added: "I want Genl. Hancock to act just as he suggests and he is a just and fair man and would not abuse the trust."

15. F. A. Walker, "General Hancock," *Critical Sketches of Some of the Federal and Confederate Commanders,* MHSM, X, 53.

16. H. M. Stanley, *My Early Travels and Adventures in America and Asia*, 2 vols. (New York: Scribner's, 1895), I, 2. Another member of the press, Theodore R. Davis, an artist and writer for *Harper's New Monthly*, was also accredited to the expedition and caught up with it at Fort Larned.

17. WSH to W. A. Nichols, Asst. Adj. Gen., May 22, 1867, Letters Received, AGO, Main series, 1861–1870, NA (hereafter cited as WSH Report, NA); Stanley, *Travels and Adventures*, I, 19–23, 27, 28; M. H. Garfield, "The Military Post as a Factor in the Frontier Defense of Kansas, 1865–1869" *Kansas Historical Quarterly*, Nov. 1931, 54.

18. WSH Report, NA.

19. For reports of the speeches at the night council, see "Talks between Major General Hancock and the Cheyenne Chiefs Tall Bull and White Horse," Letters Received, AGO, Main Series, 1861–1870, NA; and Stanley, *Travels and Adventures*, I, 30–35.

20. G. A. Custer, *My Life on the Plains*, ed. M. M. Quaife, (Chicago: Lakeside Press, 1952), 44; WSH Report, NA. George Bird Grinnell suggested that the Indian village was actually ten miles farther away than supposed and that the chiefs were late simply because it took them longer to get there; G. B. Grinnell, *The Fighting Cheyennes* (1915; Norman: U. of Oklahoma Press, 1956), 249.

21. WSH Report, NA; T. R. Davis, "A Summer on the Plains," *Harper's New Monthly*, Feb. 1868, 295; Stanley, *Travels and Adventures*, I, 37–38.

22. *Ibid.*, 239; *Daily National Intelligencer*, Oct. 28, 1867, quoting Wynkoop's testimony to the peace commission.

23. WSH Report, NA; Stanley, *Travels and Adventures*, I, 38; WSH to Sherman, Apr. 13, 1867, in "Difficulties with Indian Tribes," House Exec. Doc. No. 240, 41st Cong., 2nd sess., 51.

24. WSH Report, NA; Grinnell, *Fighting Cheyennes*, 253. Wynkoop stated later that it was about 11 o'clock, but we may presume that Hancock was probably being precise in his report when he set the time at 9:30, particularly since it is confirmed by Custer; Custer, *My Life on the Plains*, 51. For Wynkoop's statement, see Stanley, *Travels and Adventures*, I, 240. Stanley himself thought it was 8 o'clock; *ibid.*, 38.

25. WSH Report, NA; Custer, *My Life on the Plains*, 53–59.

26. Stanley, *Travels and Adventures*, I, 240; WSH Report, NA. The *New York Times*, crediting Stanley, stated that Hancock made the decision to burn the camp on April 14, but clearly he changed his mind several times after that; *New York Times*, April 23, 1867.

27. WSH Report, NA; Berthrong, *Southern Cheyennes*, 277–278; B. W. Dippie, ed., *Nomad: George A. Custer in Turf, Field and Farm*, (Austin and London: U. of Texas Press, 1980), 132; WSH to Sherman, Apr. 17, 1867, in "Difficulties with Indian Tribes," 65.

28. Custer, *My Life on the Plains*, 96–97; WSH to Sherman, Apr. 18, 1867, in "Difficulties with Indian Tribes," 67; WSH to Grant, May 23, 1867, U. S. Grant Papers, LC.

29. Stanley, *Travels and Adventures*, I, 45–47. Hancock's destruction of their village was cited by the Cheyennes as the cause of the war, Wynkoop testified; *Daily National Intelligencer*, Oct. 28, 1867.

30. *Leavenworth Daily Conservative*, Apr. 26, 1867; *Daily Leavenworth Times*, May 2, 1867.

31. L. A. Frost, *The Court-Martial of General George Armstrong Custer* (Norman: U. of Oklahoma Press, 1968), 24; WSH Report, NA; Dippie, ed., *Nomad*, 132..

32. *Ibid.*; Berthrong, *Southern Cheyennes*, 280; Grinnell, *Fighting Cheyennes*, 254–258.

33. WSH Report, NA; Custer, *My Life on the Plains*, 102. For the transcript of the talk with the Kiowa chiefs, see "Talk between Kiowa Chiefs and Maj. Gen. Hancock

at Camp No. 17 near Ft. Dodge, April 23, 1867," Letters received, AGO, Main Series, 1861–1870, NA; for that of the talk of April 28, see "Talk Held with Little Raven, head chief of the Arapahoes," *ibid.;* and for that with Satanta, see "Proceedings of Council held by Major General Hancock, Commanding, Department of the Missouri, with the Head Chief 'Satanta' of the Kiowa tribe of Indians in Kansas, at Fort Larned, Kas., May 1, 1867," *ibid.*

34. WSH Report, NA.

35. W. T. Sherman to S. J. Crawford, June 24, 1867, in M. H. Garfield, "Defense of the Kansas Frontier, 1866–67," *Kansas Historical Quarterly,* Aug. 1932, 333.

36. Athearn, *Sherman and the West,* 170; Garfield, "Defense of the Kansas Frontier," 344.

37. G. A. Custer to Mr. Walker, Sept. 1867, in M. Merington, ed., *The Custer Story* (New York: Devin-Adair, 1950), 211; Dippie, ed., *Nomad,* 20, 22–26, 38–39. By the time Custer wrote his book in 1872, interestingly, he had completely changed his tune on Hancock's alleged culpability. Perhaps the mercurial cavalryman had been frightened by the possibility that Hancock might become president.

38. Athearn, *Sherman and the West,* 174.

39. WSH to Duncan S. Walker, July 30, 1867, Aug. 31, 1867, Dec. 11, 1867, and Dec. 25, 1867, Hancock Papers, NYHS.

TWENTY-THREE.
RECONSTRUCTION COMMANDER

1. J. G. Taylor, "Louisiana: An Impossible Task," in O. H. Olsen, ed., *Reconstruction and Redemption in the South* (Baton Rouge and London: Louisiana State U. Press, 1980), 226.

2. A. Badeau, *Grant in Peace: From Appomattox to Mount McGregor* (Hartford, Conn.: S. S. Scranton, 1887), 103; Richardson, ed., *Messages and Papers,* VI, 556–557; Moore, "Notes," 110–111; J. E. Sefton, *The United States Army and Reconstruction, 1865–1877* (Baton Rouge: Louisiana State U. Press, 1967), 156.

3. On similarity of views between Sheridan and Thomas, see Moore, "Notes," 111–113; *New Orleans Times,* Aug. 20, 1867; and *New Orleans Republican,* Aug. 23, 1867. See also *New Orleans Times,* Aug. 29, 1867; Richardson, ed., *Messages and Papers,* VI, 557; and P. A. Hutton, *Phil Sheridan and His Army* (Lincoln: U. of Nebraska Press, 1985), 130.

4. Sefton, *Army and Reconstruction,* 157; ARH, 120–122; WSH to Grant, Aug. 27, 1867, U. S. Grant Papers, LC. It must be assumed that Hancock's statement is not a verbatim quote and that he did not really declaim in such a manner in the privacy of his own quarters. Hancock had written to Duncan Walker from Fort Leavenworth that he did not like going to New Orleans: "I shall have to attend to civil as well as military affairs. . . . I hope to act as a soldier and propose to avoid political or other entangling surroundings"; WSH to Duncan Walker, Aug. 31, 1867, Hancock Papers, NYHS.

5. *New Orleans Times,* Aug. 29, 1867; Sefton, *Army and Reconstruction,* 163; J. G. Dawson III, *Army Generals and Reconstruction: Louisiana, 1862–1877* (Baton Rouge and London: Louisiana State U. Press, 1982), 68. Even Grant, at a cabinet meeting of Nov. 22, 1867, admitted that Mower "had done some things which he ought not to have done" and that Hancock should correct "any errors"; Randall, ed., *Browning Diary,* II, 166. The *New Orleans Crescent* reported on Nov. 29 a general feeling of relief that Mower's reign was at an end; F. Copeland, "The New Orleans Press and the Reconstruction," *Louisiana Historical Quarterly,* Jan. 1947. 180.

6. W. L. Richter, " 'We Must Rubb Out and Begin Anew': The Army and the Republican Party in Texas Reconstruction, 1867–1870," *Civil War History,* Dec. 1973, 336–337; C. H. Moneyhon, *Republicanism in Reconstruction Texas* (Austin and London: U. of Texas Press, 1980), 69.

7. Beale, ed., *Welles Diary,* III, 204–205; Grant to WSH, Sept. 11, 1867, U. S. Grant Papers, LC; W. B. Hesseltine, *Ulysses S. Grant: Politician* (New York: Dodd, Mead, 1935), 94.

8. *New Orleans Republican,* Nov. 26, Nov. 28, 1867; *New York World,* Nov. 29, 1867. "I have just arrived and will take command at nine (9) o'clock tomorrow"; WSH to Grant, Nov. 28, 1867, U. S. Grant Papers, LC.

9. For the text of the order, see Walker, *Hancock,* 297–298; and *The Civil Record of Major General Winfield S. Hancock during His Administration in Louisiana and Texas* (pamphlet, n.p., 1871, hereafter cited as *Civil Record*), 4–5.

10. ARH, 124. Over the years a number of men were given credit for writing this document, as well as the letter to Governor Pease, for Hancock, ranging from Johnson and Jeremiah S. Black to J. Ad Rozier, a Unionist lawyer in New Orleans. There is no real reason to think that Hancock himself did not compose it, other than a general assumption that a military man and West Point graduate would be incapable of writing it.

11. *New Orleans Crescent,* Nov. 30, 1867, in Copeland, "New Orleans Press," 180; *New Orleans Times,* Dec. 5, 1867.

12. Moore, "Notes," 113; Badeau, *Grant in Peace,* 107; Sefton, *Army and Reconstruction,* 175.

13. ARH, 125.

14. Saml. H. Hays to S. B. Buckner, Jan. 3, 1867 [actually 1868], S. B. Buckner Collection, HEHL.

15. Moore, "Notes," 114; Randall, ed., *Browning Diary,* II, 170; Beale, ed., *Welles Diary,* III, 241.

16. Richardson, ed., *Messages and Papers,* VI, 595–596; Sefton, *Army and Reconstruction,* 175; W. T. Sherman to Ellen Sherman, Jan. 23, 1868, in M. A. DeWolfe Howe, ed., *Home Letters of General Sherman* (New York: Scribner's, 1909), 367. See also Sherman to Ellen Sherman, Jan. 15, 1868: "Congress is now engaged in fabricating a bill to legislate Hancock out of service because his general course in New Orleans don't suit the extremes"; *ibid.,* 366. Garfield wrote his friend B. A. Hinsdale on Feb. 2, 1869, that his motive in introducing the bill was to show Hancock "how completely he was in our hands"; A. Peskin, *Garfield* (Kent, Ohio: Kent State U. Press, 1978), 284.

17. *New Orleans Times,* Sept. 1, Dec. 5, 1867; Grant to WSH, Nov. 29, 1867, U. S. Grant Papers, LC; Sefton, *Army and Reconstruction,* 177. On December 4, also, Hancock removed Mower as commander of the subdistrict of Louisiana and directed him to rejoin his regiment. Hancock did not, however, interfere with the commander in Texas, Reynolds, who had worked closely with the Radicals there. See also *Civil Record,* 14.

18. *New Orleans Times,* Dec. 6, 1867; *Civil Record,* 15. The *Times* spoke on December 7 of the jury order as one of "the steps he has taken to redress the wrongs inflicted upon us by Sheridan and Mower"; *New Orleans Times,* Dec. 7, 1867.

19. *Civil Record,* 16.

20. WSH to Grant, Dec. 23, 1867, C. B. Comstock to WSH, Dec. 27, 1867, Grant to WSH, Dec. 27, 1867, U. S. Grant Papers, LC: Dawson, *Generals and Reconstruction,* 72.

21. Richter, "The Army and Republican Party in Texas Reconstruction," 338.

22. *New Orleans Times,* Jan. 11, 1868; *Civil Record,* 19–21. Pease, a native of Connecticut who had come to Texas in 1836, had been Democratic governor of the state before the Civil War. After the war he switched sides and was rewarded with

Sheridan's appointment after losing the election for governor; Moneyhon, *Republicanism in Reconstruction Texas*, 43.

23. *New Orleans Times*, Jan. 4, 1868; *Civil Record*, 22.

24. *Ibid.*, 22–23.

25. *New Orleans Republican*, Jan. 8, 1868; T. W. Conway to O. O. Howard, Jan. 5, 1868, C. H. Fox to O. O. Howard, Mar. 26, 1868, and May 9, 1868, in M. Abbott, ed., "Reconstruction in Louisiana: Three Letters," *Louisiana History*, spring 1960, 154–157; Lionel Sheldon to J. A. Garfield, Apr. 22, 1868, in Peskin, *Garfield*, 284. Howard wrote to Hancock asking for copies of the Fifth Military District orders; Howard to WSH, Jan. 29, 1868, Howard Papers, Bowdoin College Library. Since the first day of Gettysburg, of course, Howard was no great friend of Hancock.

26. General Orders No. 3; *Civil Record*, 24–26; *New Orleans Times*, Jan. 12, 1868; Dawson, *Generals and Reconstruction*, 72–73.

27. J. R. Ficklen, *History of Reconstruction in Louisiana (Through 1868)* (1910; Gloucester, Mass.: Peter Smith, 1966), 193; Conway to Howard, Abbott, ed., "Three Letters," 155.

28. Dawson, *Generals and Reconstruction*, 73; Richter, "The Army and Republican Party in Texas Reconstruction," 339. One conservative historian points out that in Texas Hancock "showed no disposition to play the partisan," turning down requests of conservatives to set aside the voters' registration in Texas; C. W. Ramsdell, *Reconstruction in Texas* (New York: Columbia U. Studies in History, vol. 36, no. 1, 1910), 195. When voting registration closed in Texas in January 1868, approximately 98 percent of the male black adult population was on the rolls; Moneyhon, *Republicanism in Reconstruction Texas*, 71.

29. WSH to E. D. Townsend, Jan. 11, 1868, and Grant to WSH, Jan. 13, 1868, U. S. Grant Papers, LC; Ramsdell, *Reconstruction in Texas*, 185–187.

30. The Hancock letter to Pease, dated Mar. 9, 1868, is set out at length in Forney, *Hancock*, 236–246, and in *Civil Record*, 6–14. Ramsdell notes that the election in Texas, Feb. 10–14, 1868, for the constitutional convention "passed off more quietly than might have been expected"; Ramsdell, *Reconstruction in Texas*, 198. A more recent commentator, however, has called the same election "one of the most violent in the reconstruction period"; Moneyhon, *Republicanism in Reconstruction Texas*, 77. The president commented later that Hancock's letter to Pease "indicated more with respect to the principles of our Government than was ever in Genl. Grant's mind"; Moore, "Notes," 129.

31. *New Orleans Times*, Feb. 5, Feb. 6, Feb. 7, 1868. Hancock advised Grant of the sacking of Baker for "using his office for corrupt purposes to the public scandal"; WSH to Grant, Feb. 5, 1868, U. S. Grant Papers, LC.

32. *New Orleans Daily Picayune*, Feb. 9, 1868; *New Orleans Times*, Feb. 8, Feb. 9, 1868.

33. WSH to Grant, Feb. 7, 1868, Grant to WSH, Feb. 8, 1868, WSH to Grant, Feb. 9, 1868, Grant to WSH, Feb. 11, 1868, and WSH to Grant, Feb. 11, 1868, U. S. Grant Papers, LC; *New Orleans Times*, Feb. 12, Feb. 13, Feb. 14, Feb. 15, Feb. 20, 1868; Beale, ed., *Welles Diary*, III, 277; M. E. Mantell, *Johnson, Grant, and the Politics of Reconstruction* (New York and London: Columbia U. Press, 1973), 89–90; "New Orleans Councilmen," House Exec. Doc. No. 172, 40th Cong., 2nd sess., 1–3; *New Orleans Daily Picayune*, Feb. 12, 1868.

34. "Removal of City Council of New Orleans," House Exec. Doc. No. 209, 40th Cong., 2nd sess., 10–11; *New Orleans Times*, Feb. 28, 1868.

35. WSH to Grant, Feb. 27, 1868, U. S. Grant Papers, LC; WSH to L. Thomas, Feb. 27, 1868, Hancock Papers, LC; *Civil Record*, 31; ARH, 131–132. See also WSH to D. S. Walker, Mar. 11, 1868, Hancock Papers, NYHS.

36. *New Orleans Times*, Mar. 1, Mar. 3, 1868; *Civil Record*, 32; Grant to WSH, Mar. 14, 1868, U. S. Grant Papers, LC. He was succeeded by General Robert

Buchanan, called by Dawson "perhaps the most objective and fair-minded commander to serve in the state during the postwar years"; Dawson, *Generals and Reconstruction,* 75.

37. The new constitution was approved in a referendum, April 16–17, 1868. One writer charged that Hancock had "proved so inept" that more than 2,000 Negroes were killed or injured in that election, ignoring the fact that the election took place a month after Hancock's departure; F. M. Brodie, *Thaddeus Stevens: Scourge of the South* (New York: Norton, 1959), 328.

TWENTY-FOUR.
A BOOM FOR PRESIDENT

1. Richardson, ed., *Messages and Papers,* VI, 663; ARH, 133–134; W. T. Sherman to WSH, May 21, 1870, WSH to Sherman, July 9, 1870, and B. F. Flanders to WSH, July 1, 1870, in *Correspondence between General W. T. Sherman, U.S. Army, and Major General W. S. Hancock, U.S. Army* (St. Paul: n.p., 1871), 9–10; Moore, "Notes," 129.

2. W. T. Sherman to WSH, Apr. 14, 1870, and WSH to Sherman, Apr. 27, 1870, in *Sherman-Hancock Correspondence,* 6–7. In 1871 Grant reacted negatively when Sherman proposed adding the Department of the Platte to Hancock's command; W. T. Sherman to P. H. Sheridan, Oct. 16, 1871, Philip H. Sheridan Papers, LC.

3. The *Philadelphia Inquirer* reported from New York on July 1 that Pendleton had "many friends" among the delegates from Pennsylvania, New York, New England, and New Jersey: "Appearances to-night look much in favor of Pendleton"; *Philadelphia Inquirer,* July 2, 1868.

4. C. H. Coleman, *The Election of 1868: The Democratic Effort to Regain Control* (New York: Columbia U. Press, 1933), 58–59; Irving Katz, *August Belmont* (New York and London: Columbia U. Press, 1968), 168–169.

5. Coleman, *Election of 1868,* 121, quoting article which appeared June 18, 1868, in *New York Evening Telegram,* June 19, 1868, in *New York Herald,* and in *Cincinnati Commercial* and elsewhere.

6. Coleman, *Election of 1868,* 128; S. Mitchell, *Horatio Seymour of New York* (Cambridge: Harvard U. Press, 1938), 405. On June 24 Congressman John Pruyn told Welles that Seymour or Chase would be nominated and, if Seymour, he had "no doubt he would yield" to the demand of his party; Beale, ed., *Welles Diary,* III, 390–391.

7. G. B. McClellan to S. L. M. Barlow, June 14, 1868, McClellan Papers, LC; *Philadelphia Inquirer,* July 2, 1868; Wm. Allen to Chas. Brown, June 20, 1868, in F. A. Bonadio, *North of Reconstruction: Ohio Politics, 1865–1870* (New York: New York U. Press, 1970), 161.

8. WSH to T. K. Smith, May 8, 1871, Thos. Kilby Smith Papers, USMA; *New Orleans Times,* Feb. 11, 1868; Coleman, *Election of 1868,* 148; E. L. Gambill, *Conservative Ordeal: Northern Democrats and Reconstruction, 1865–1868* (Ames: Iowa State U. Press, 1981), 128; M. R. Dearing, *Veterans in Politics: The Story of the G.A.R.* (Baton Rouge: Louisiana State U. Press, 1952), 154.

9. *Ibid.,* 153; *New York World,* June 15, 1868; *Philadelphia Inquirer,* June 16, 1868; Gambill, *Conservative Ordeal,* 128. For Smith's description of his trips to Utica and Boston on behalf of the Hancock candidacy, see T. K. Smith to his wife, May 1, 1869 (actually 1868), T. K. Smith Collection, HEHL. Doolittle eventually became Wisconsin's "favorite son" candidate, whereas Voorhees, who prepared a pro-Hancock pamphlet, ultimately supported Hendricks, his fellow Hoosier.

10. W. T. Sherman to Ellen Sherman, June 7, 1868, in Howe, ed., *Sherman Letters,* 376; *New York World,* June 29, 1868; Gov. Wm. Bigler to S. J. Tilden, Feb. 3,

Mar. 4, 1868, in J. Bigelow, ed., *Letters and Literary Memorials of Samuel J. Tilden*, 2 vols. (New York and London: Harper, 1908), I, 216–217, 221. The *National Intelligencer*, in Washington, used its lead editorial on July 1 to deny the canard about the Surratt execution; *Daily National Intelligencer*, July 1, 1868. Certain Catholic prelates favored Hancock, but they would say or do nothing publicly; J. F. Coyle to WSH, "spring," 1868, Thos. Kilby Smith Papers, USMA.

11. WSH to T. K. Smith, May 15, 1871, Thos. Kilby Smith Papers, USMA.

12. *New York Sun*, June 29, 1868; S. Church to S. J. Tilden, June 10, 1868, in Bigelow, ed., *Tilden Letters*, I, 228.

13. *Philadelphia Inquirer*, July 4, 1868. "The north has the work to do, and the north should be allowed to select both candidate and platform"; Norvell Cobb (of Macon, Ga.) to J. L. Brent, June 1, 1868, Brent (A&W) Papers, HEHL.

14. G. Wakeman, rep., *Official Proceedings of the Democratic National Convention Held at New York, July 4–9, 1868* (Boston: Rockwell and Rollins, 1868), 3–5.

15. G. B. Woods, "The New York Convention," *North American Review*, Oct. 1868, 446, 453; Coleman, *Election of 1868*, 223–224. Some Chase workers, after the New York caucus, became "suspicious that he is being made a cat's-paw of"; *Daily National Intelligencer*, July 6, 1868.

16. *New York World*, July 2, 1868; Woods, "New York Convention," 450.

17. *Philadelphia Inquirer*, July 6, 1868.

18. Wakeman, rep., *Proceedings*, 23–26, 48–49; Mitchell, *Seymour*, 412–414; *Philadelphia Inquirer*, July 7, 1868.

19. Wakeman, rep., *Proceedings*, 58–63; Coleman, *Election of 1868*, 200–201; Woods, "New York Convention," 449.

20. Wakeman, rep., *Proceedings*, 66–73; Mitchell, *Seymour*, 422.

21. Wakeman, rep., *Proceedings*, 75–77.

22. *Ibid.*, 78–82. On July 6 the *National Intelligencer* had reported "General Clingman and a portion of the North Carolina delegation . . . active for Hancock"; *Daily National Intelligencer*, July 6, 1868.

23. Wakeman, rep., *Proceedings*, 83–85; Mitchell, *Seymour*, 424.

24. Wakeman, rep., *Proceedings*, 99–103.

25. *New York World*, July 8, 1868; Woods, "New York Convention," 456.

26. Wakeman, rep., *Proceedings*, 105–111.

27. See Woods, "New York Convention," 457.

28. Wakeman, rep., *Proceedings*, 112–121, 124–126.

29. *Ibid.*, 128–129; Woods, "New York Convention," 458; *Daily National Intelligencer*, July 9, 1868.

30. Wakeman, rep., *Proceedings*, 130–134.

31. *Ibid.*, 137–139; Coleman, *Election of 1868*, 210–211.

32. *Ibid.*, 211; *Philadelphia Inquirer*, July 9, 1868; *New York World*, July 9, 1868; Beale, ed., *Welles Diary*, III, 397.

33. Woods, "New York Convention," 460; ARH, 137; *Philadelphia Inquirer*, July 9, 1868.

34. Wakeman, rep., *Proceedings*, 141–146; Coleman, *Election of 1868*, 228. "The disappointed supporters of Pendleton in his own state refused to give their votes to the general at the very moment when their action might have brought him the nomination"; Mitchell, *Seymour*, 428.

35. Wakeman, rep., *Proceedings*, 147–151; *New York Sun*, July 11, 1868; Coleman, *Election of 1868*, 239–240.

36. *Ibid.*, 226–227, 240–242; Mitchell, *Seymour*, 428–429.

37. Wakeman, rep., *Proceedings*, 152–155; Woods, "New York Convention," 462–463.

38. See, for example, Beale, ed., *Welles Diary*, III, 400; Coleman, *Election of 1868*, 60; and Carl Schurz to Margaretta Schurz, May 24, 1868, in J. Schafer, ed., *Intimate*

Letters of Carl Schurz, 1841–1869 (Madison: State Historical Society of Wisconsin, 1928), 438. Andrew Johnson told Welles that "the Democratic party had for twelve years acted as if demented, and seemed determined to continue in error"; Beale, ed., *Welles Diary,* III, 403.

39. *Philadelphia Inquirer,* July 10, 13, 1868; *New York World,* July 10, 1868.
40. ARH, 138–139; *Nation,* Aug. 6, 1868.
41. Dearing, *Veterans in Politics,* 172; S. J. Tilden to WSH, Oct. ———, 1868, Hancock Papers, USAMHI; WSH to Tilden, Oct. 10, 1868, in Bigelow, ed., *Tilden Letters,* I, 249–250; *Springfield Republican,* Oct. 8, 1868. See John M. Schofield to WSH, Sept. 19, 1868, Hancock Papers, USAMHI, expressing sorrow at hearing "of your trouble with that old wound."
42. After the October elections, Gideon Welles wrote: "Had Hancock been on the ticket instead of Seymour, we should have carried Pennsylvania and Indiana and I think Ohio"; Beale, ed., *Welles Diary,* III, 459. Hindsight, of course, is always very acute, but Welles, at least, had been saying much the same thing before Seymour's selection.

TWENTY-FIVE.
RETURN TO THE PLAINS

1. Richardson, ed., *Messages and Papers,* VII, 19–20; Meade to his wife, Mar. 6, 1869, Meade, *Life and Letters,* II, 299–300; *Sherman-Hancock Correspondence,* 15–16; U. S. Grant to P. H. Sheridan, Dec. 24, 1868, Sheridan Papers, LC.
2. L. W. Slaughter, *Fortress to Farm, or Twenty-three Years on the Frontier,* ed. Hazel Eastman (New York: Exposition Press, 1972), 16.
3. *Record of Engagements with Hostile Indians within the Military Division of the Missouri from 1868 to 1882* (Washington: Govt. Printing Office, 1882), 4–6; "Report of the Secretary of War (1869)," House Exec. Doc. No. 1, pt. 2, 41st Cong., 2nd sess., 56. Hancock was able subsequently to acquire four companies (161 men) of the Second Cavalry, to be stationed at Fort Ellis.
4. ARH, 141; "Report of the Secretary of War (1869)," 56.
5. For the author's eyewitness description of the Fort Stevenson council, see Joseph Henry Taylor, *Sketches of Frontier and Indian Life on the Upper Missouri and Great Plains,* 4th ed. (Washburn, N. D.: author, 1932), 60–61.
6. "Report of the Secretary of War (1869)," 58.
7. P. R. de Trobriand, *Military Life in Dakota,* trans. and ed. Lucile M. Kane (St. Paul: Alvord, 1951), 284–285, 371; "Report of the Secretary of War (1869)," 57.
8. *Ibid.,* 59.
9. *Ibid.,* 65.
10. "Report of the Secretary of War (1870)," House Exec. Doc. No. 1, pt. 2, 41st Cong., 3rd sess., 28; Hancock report on Fort Pembina, in *ibid.,* 27–28. See W. D. Thomson, "History of Fort Pembina: 1870–1895," *North Dakota History,* winter 1969, 18. The major conflict experienced around Fort Pembina was the westernmost of the Fenian raids, on Oct. 5, 1871, when some 50 men led by "General" O'Neil, "General" Thomas Curley, and "Colonel" J. J. Donelly captured a Hudson's Bay Co. trading post located right at the border, only to be chased away by two companies from Fort Pembina. See also "Report of the Secretary of War (1871)," House Exec. Doc. No. 1, pt. 2, 42nd Cong., 2nd sess., 29–30; and Thomson, "Fort Pembina," 25–28.
11. P. H. Sheridan to E. D. Townsend, Oct. 21, 1869, "Expedition against Piegan Indians," House Exec. Doc. No. 197, 41st Cong., 2nd sess., 2, 5.
12. Hancock report, in "Report of the Secretary of War (1870)," 29; Baker report, dated Feb. 18, 1870, in "Expedition against Piegan Indians," 1–2.

13. For the Baker Raid, see Athearn, *Sherman and the West,* 278–281.

14. Hancock, in "Report of the Secretary of War (1870)," 29–30.

15. W. Parker, *Gold in the Black Hills* (Norman: U. of Oklahoma Press, 1966), 15–16; Taylor, *Warren,* 37. Warren, after talking with the Sioux chiefs, wrote that the only security the Indians could have in possessing their country "would be in its utter worthlessness to the whites"; *ibid.,* 41.

16. G. W. Kingsbury, *History of Dakota Territory,* 2 vols. (Chicago: S. J. Clarke, 1915), I, 874–875; Parker, *Gold in the Black Hills,* 22–23.

17. Kingsbury, *Dakota Territory,* I, 875; "Report of the Secretary of War (1873)," House Exec. Doc. No. 1, pt. 2, 43rd Cong., 1st sess., 42.

18. Hancock, in "Report of the Secretary of War (1872)," House Exec. Doc. No. 1, pt. 2, 42nd Cong., 3rd sess., 39, 40; *Record of Engagements,* 33–34; *Chronological List of Actions, &c., with Indians, from January 1, 1866, to January, 1891* (Washington: Adjutant-General's Office, 1891), 29.

19. Hancock, in "Report of the Secretary of War (1872)," 41.

20. "Report of the Secretary of War (1875)," House Exec. Doc. No. 1, pt. 2, 44th Cong., 1st sess., 28.

21. WSH letter of Oct. 23, 1871, in "Report of the Secretary of War (1871)," 25–26, 31. See WSH to P. Rothermel, Oct. 26, 1869, Mar. 26, 1870, Apr. ———, 1871, and Apr. 1, 1871, Peter Rothermel Papers, PHMC; WSH to T. K. Smith, May 8 and May 31, 1871, Thos. Kilby Smith Papers, USMA; WSH to J. L. Brent, May 21, 1871, Brent (A&W) Papers, HEHL.

22. ARH, 145, 147; W. T. Sherman to P. H. Sheridan, Nov. 16, 1872, Sheridan Papers, LC. General Order No. 100, Headquarters of the Army, assigned Hancock to the eastern command; "Report of the Secretary of War (1873)," 52.

TWENTY-SIX. EAST AND AN ELECTION

1. "Report of the Secretary of War (1873)," 52.

2. *Ibid.,* 52–53, 64–65.

3. *Ibid.,* 52–53; "Report of the Secretary of War (1874)," House Exec. Doc. No. 1, pt. 2, 43d Cong., 2nd sess., 20.

4. WSH to D. S. Walker, Jan. 14, 1870, Apr. 4, Sept. 6, Sept. 26, and Nov. 6, 1871, Hancock Papers, NYHS; WSH to T. K. Smith, May 31, 1871, Thos. Kilby Smith Papers, USMA; WSH to J. O. Broadhead, June 19, 1871, Jas. O. Broadhead Papers, MoHS.

5. W. T. Sherman to John Sherman, Mar. 21, 1870, in Athearn, *Sherman and the West,* 254–255; Randall is quoted in J. H. Hall to T. F. Bayard, Dec. 19, 1871, in C. C. Tansill, *The Congressional Career of Thomas Francis Bayard, 1869–1885* (Washington: Georgetown U. Press, 1946), 71; ARH, 144; Dearing, *Veterans in Politics,* 199, 201.

6. F. B. Evans, *Pennsylvania Politics, 1872–1877: A Study in Political Leadership* (Harrisburg: Pennsylvania Historical and Museum Commission, 1966), 172; ARH, 165–166. "The bond of earthly affection between the general and his daughter was close"; B. Perry Chain, paper, undated, Hancock Papers, MCHS. Ironically, when Jeremiah Black's daughter died, Hancock had written: "It must be especially painful for parents to lose children of promise who have arrived at the age of this young lady. Thank God I have never had such experience"; WSH to T. K. Smith, Aug. 21, 1871, Thos. Kilby Smith Papers, USMA.

7. One dispatch from Washington quoted Democrats there as being eager to match Hancock against Blaine; "it can be shown to the people that while Blaine was speculating in Spencer rifles, Hancock was using them in defense of the Government"; *New York Times,* June 15, 1876.

8. WSH to J. L. Brent, June 14 and June 25, 1876, Brent (A&W) Papers, HEHL.

9. Dearing, *Veterans in Politics*, 222–223; *Chicago Tribune*, June 19, 1876; *New York Times*, June 9, June 23, June 28, 1876; *Cincinnati Enquirer*, June 24, 1876; J. F. Wall, *Henry Watterson: Reconstructed Rebel* (New York: Oxford U. Press, 1956), 131. Wall quotes the statement of Ballard Smith, Watterson's assistant on his paper, in *Harper's Weekly,* Aug. 20, 1887, that without Watterson's intervention Kentucky would have voted for Hancock, "the other Southern States would have followed its example, and . . . General Hancock in all probability would have been the nominee. . . ." Tilden's control appears to have been too tight to permit anything like that unfolding.

10. *New York Times*, June 29, 1876.

11. Evans, *Pennsylvania Politics*, 270–271; A. K. McClure, *Our Presidents and How We Make Them* (New York and London: Harper's, 1900), 253.

12. ARH, 151.

13. Wall, *Watterson*, 149–150; J. D. Norris and A. H. Shaffer, eds., *Politics and Patronage in the Gilded Age: The Correspondence of James A. Garfield and Charles E. Henry* (Madison: State Historical Society of Wisconsin, 1970), 175, quoting letter of J. A. Garfield to C. E. Henry, Dec. 18, 1876.

14. ARH, 151–152.

15. William A. Wheeler of New York was Hayes's running mate.

16. ARH, 152–155; Bigelow, ed., *Tilden Letters*, II, 506–511.

17. Hancock considered, correctly as it turned out, that the electoral commission bill gave "to Gen. Hayes chances he did not have before"; WSH to W. T. Sherman, Jan. 19, 1877, quoted in *New York Times*, Aug. 27, 1880.

TWENTY-SEVEN. THE GREAT STRIKE

1. "Report of the Secretary of War (1877)," 90–91; WSH to W. T. Sherman, Dec. 28, 1876, in Bigelow, ed., *Tilden Letters*, II, 509. The returning board in South Carolina, of course, brought the state's vote in for Hayes, but it was unable to prevent the election of Hampton.

2. *Ibid.,* 510.

3. WSH to Irvin McDowell, Mar. 23, 1870, Otis Norcross Papers, MaHS.

4. J. A. Dacus, *Annals of the Great Strikes* (Chicago: L. T. Palmer, 1877), 17–18; J. M. Cooper, "The Army as Strikebreaker—The Railroad Strikes of 1877 and 1894," *Labor History*, spring 1977, 181.

5. R. V. Bruce, *1877: Year of Violence* (Indianapolis and New York: Bobbs-Merrill, 1959), 39–41.

6. *Ibid.,* 44.

7. Dacus, *Annals*, 20, 27–28; Bruce, *Year of Violence*, 75; P. S. Foner, *The Great Labor Uprising of 1877* (New York: Monad Press, 1977), 34.

8. *Philadelphia Inquirer,* July 18, 1877; *New York Times*, July 18, 1877.

9. *Philadelphia Inquirer,* July 19, 1877; Richardson, ed., *Messages and Papers*, VII, 447–448; "Report of the Secretary of War (1877)," xii, 87.

10. Bruce, *Year of Violence*, 93–94; *Philadelphia Inquirer*, July 20, 1877; *New York Times*, July 20, 1877.

11. "Report of the Secretary of War (1877)," 87; *New York Times*, July 23, 1877; Bruce, *Year of Violence*, 108–111.

12. "Report of the Secretary of War (1877)," 88; *New York Times*, July 23, 1877; Adjutant-General E. D. Townsend to WSH, July 22, 1877, in F. T. Wilson, "Federal Aid in Domestic Disturbances. 1787–1903," Senate Misc. Doc. No. 209, 57th Cong., 2nd sess., 320.

13. "Report of the Secretary of War (1877)," 88; *Philadelphia Inquirer*, July 24, 1877; A. K. McClure, *Old Time Notes of Pennsylvania*, 2 vols., (Philadelphia: Winston, 1905), II, 455; P. E. Mackey, "Law and Order, 1877: Philadelphia's Response to the Railroad Riots," *Pennsylvania Magazine of History and Biography*, Apr. 1972, 192–196. The telegram from the adjutant-general to Hancock on July 22 had stated: "You had better see Mr. Scott"; Wilson, "Domestic Disturbances," 320.

14. *New York Times*, July 22, 1877; *Philadelphia Inquirer*, July 23, 1877; K. E. Davison, *The Presidency of Rutherford B. Hayes* (Westport, Conn.: Greenwood Press, 1972), 147. A. K. McClure called it "a mob exasperated by pinching want"; McClure, *Old Time Notes*, II, 454. Burned in the Pittsburgh riot were 39 buildings of the Pennsylvania, 104 engines, 46 passenger cars, and over 1,200 freight cars; Foner, *Great Labor Uprising*, 64–66.

15. "Report of the Secretary of War (1877)," 88–89; E. S. Otis, "The Army in Connection with the Labor Riots of 1877," *Journal of the Military Service Institution of the United States*, Sept. 1884–June 1885, 300; Wilson, "Domestic Disturbances," 321.

16. *Ibid.*, 321–322.

17. *Ibid.*, 324–327.

18. *Ibid.*, 197–198.

19. Foner, *Great Labor Uprising*, 72–73; Wilson, "Domestic Disturbances," 198.

20. "Report of the Secretary of War (1877)," 89, 87; *New York Times*, July 29, July 31, 1877; *Philadelphia Inquirer*, July 30, 1877; Foner, *Great Labor Uprising*, 75.

21. *Ibid.*, 75–77; J. F. Hartranft to G. W. McCrary, Aug. 15, 1877, in *Pennsylvania Archives* (Harrisburg: State of Pennsylvania, 1902), 4th ser., IX, 635; WSH to Adj. General's Office, Aug. 9, 1877, in Otis, "Army in Labor Riots of 1877," 321, 318–319; Cooper, "The Army as Strikebreaker," 186.

22. "Report of the Secretary of War (1877)," 89; "S. D.," letter, *Philadelphia Inquirer*, June 30, 1880; WSH to J. M. Schofield, July 30, 1877, in J. M. Taylor, "General Hancock: Soldier of the Gilded Age," *Pennsylvania History*, Apr. 1965, 191.

23. J. A. Garfield to C. E. Henry, July 22, 1877, in Norris and Shaffer, eds., *Correspondence of Garfield and Henry*, 194; Cooper, "The Army as Strikebreaker," 186–187. One commentator has written: "Between 1877 and 1898 the U.S. Army came close to being a national police force"; B. C. Hacker, "The United States Army as a National Police Force: The Federal Policing of Labor Disputes, 1877–1898," *Military Affairs*, Apr. 1969, 261.

24. Cooper, "The Army as Strikebreaker," 186.

25. J. F. Hartranft to WSH, Oct. 19, 1877, in *Pennsylvania Archives*, 4th ser., IX, 636; "Report of the Secretary of War (1877)," xiii.

26. "S. D.," letter. Hancock paid tribute to his soldiers who carried out their orders in this difficult mission although they themselves had not been paid since June 30: "Without any pay themselves," he said, "they faithfully aided in putting down the revolutionary attempts made by others on questions of compensation arising between the employed and their employers"; "Report of the Secretary of War (1877)," 91.

TWENTY-EIGHT.
HANCOCK AND THE ARMY

1. Inspector-General N. H. Davis, Oct. 11, 1879, in "Report of the Secretary of War (1879)," House Exec. Doc. No. 1, pt. 2, 46th Cong., 2nd sess., 123; "Report of the Secretary of War (1880)," House Exec. Doc. No. 1, pt. 2, 46th Cong., 3rd sess., 165; WSH to E. S. Cleveland et al., Sept. 15, 1869, Misc. Papers, YUL; Brig. Gen. Geo. W. Wingate, N.Y. Natl. Guard, statement, in *Letters and Addresses*, 49.

2. J. D. Foner, *The United States Soldier between Two Wars: Army Life and Reforms, 1865–1898* (New York: Humanities Press, 1970), 13, 15; C. C. Rister, *Southwestern Frontier*, 68–69; Hacker, "The Army as a National Police Force," 256. "Report of a Sub-Committee of the Committee on Military Affairs relating to the Reorganization of the Army," House Misc. Doc. No. 56, 45th Cong., 2nd sess., 117–118.

3. WSH to Secretary of War J. Donald Cameron, Oct. 19, 1876, in "Report on Reorganization of the Army," 11 (this letter, a lengthy one in which Hancock touched on many matters of army organization, is hereafter cited as "Hancock-Cameron letter"); Foner, *Between Two Wars*, 47, discussing Hancock's reduction of the sentence of a private named Benson.

4. R. F. Weigley, *History of the United States Army* (New York and London: Macmillan, 1967), 273–274; J. B. Fry, "Origin and Progress of the Military Service Institution of the United States," *Journal of the Military Service Institution of the United States*, I, 1880, 20–25.

5. "Hancock-Cameron letter," 5–7.

6. "Report on Reorganization of the Army," v–x; Weigley, *History of the United States Army*, 283; "Reorganization of the Army," House Report No. 3, 45th Cong., 3rd sess. The report of the Burnside Committee is in Senate Report No. 555, pt. 2, 45th Cong., 3rd sess.

TWENTY-NINE.
OFF AND RUNNING FOR 1880

1. WSH to T. K. Smith, May 3, 1871, Thos. Kilby Smith Papers, USMA; WSH to J. O. Broadhead, June 19, 1871, Jas. O. Broadhead Papers, MoHS.

2. Quoted in *Philadelphia Inquirer*, Apr. 19, 1880.

3. Brisbin, *Hancock*, 19, The *New York Daily Graphic* spoke of Hancock as being "quite heavy . . . but he does not give one the idea of fatness"; *New York Daily Graphic*, July 6, 1880. One Bayard supporter, looking over the field, wrote: "Hancock has friends but there is no strong organization in his favor"; S. L. M. Barlow to T. F. Bayard, Aug. 14, 1879, Thomas F. Bayard Papers, LC.

4. The progress of the Potter Committee investigation and the cipher telegrams can be followed in A. C. Flick and G. S. Lobrano, *Samuel Jones Tilden: A Study in Political Sagacity* (New York: Dodd, Mead, 1939), 429–438; in A. B. Paine, *Th: Nast: His Period and His Pictures* (New York and London: Macmillan, 1904), 390–403; and in H. J. Clancy, *The Presidential Election of 1880* (Chicago: Loyola U. Press, 1958), 55–56.

5. "The South is almost as solidly opposed to his candidacy as it is opposed to that of any Republican"; *Philadelphia Inquirer*, May 19, 1880. "Mr. Tilden cannot arouse in the Southern States one spark of enthusiasm"; *New Orleans Democrat*, Mar. 13, 1880. The income tax case against Tilden is discussed in Flick and Lobrano, *Tilden*, 438–441.

6. *Ibid.*, 417. Charles Nordhoff of the *New York Herald* wrote privately: "I think Tilden weakens daily. . . . I am certain that his nomination would be fatal"; C. Nordhoff to T. F. Bayard, Oct. 12, 1879, Bayard Papers, LC.

7. Bigelow, ed., *Tilden Letters*, I, viii.

8. J. Bigelow to W. H. Peck, Feb. 28, 1879, in Bigelow, ed., *Tilden Letters*, II, 580–581; E. John Ellis to T. C. W. Ellis, May 12, 1880, Ellis Family Papers, LSUL.

9. *Congressional Record*, 46th Cong., 1st sess., 802.

10. The *Philadelphia Inquirer* commented editorially: "Grant is a candidate only of a little but powerful Senatorial clique, and Tilden of another clique of political

jobbers. Neither Grant nor Tilden has any popular following, and both, if nominated, would divide and distract their respective parties." *Philadelphia Inquirer,* Apr. 3, 1880.

11. Katz, *Belmont,* 214, 250–251; W. R. Barlow, "Cincinnati Hosts the Democrats in 1880," *Bulletin of the Cincinnati Historical Society,* July 1964, 151; E. John Ellis to T. C. W. Ellis, May 12, 1880, Ellis Family Papers, LSUL; *New Orleans Democrat,* Mar. 7, 1880; *New York Herald,* Nov. 8, 1879. Early in 1880 the *New York Sun* was able to procure a copy of the *Delaware Gazette* of 1861 and thus publish in full the text of Bayard's Dover Green speech; *New Orleans Democrat,* Feb. 28, 1880.

12. *Philadelphia Inquirer,* Apr. 23, 1880.

13. T. K. Smith to W. G. Smith, Sept. 1, 1880, in W. G. Smith, *Life and Letters of Thomas Kilby Smith, Brevet Major-General United States Volunteers 1820–1887* (New York and London: Putnam's, 1898), 461; WSH to J. L. Brent, May 15, 1880, Brent (A&W) Collection, HEHL; *Philadelphia Inquirer,* June 22, 1880; M. Auge, *Lives of the Eminent Dead and Biographical Notices of Prominent Living Citizens of Montgomery County, Pa.,* 3rd ed. (Norristown, Pa., 1879), 535–537.

14. *New York Times,* July 6, 1880.

15. J. F. Vivian, "Major E. A. Burke: The Honduras Exile, 1889–1928," *Louisiana History,* spring 1974, 180; C. Vann Woodward, *Reunion and Reaction: The Compromise of 1877 and the End of Reconstruction* (Boston: Little Brown, 1951, 1966), 192. For additional background on Burke, see W. I. Hair, *Bourbonism and Agrarian Protest: Louisiana Politics, 1877–1900* (Baton Rouge: Louisiana State U. Press, 1969), 27–29; and J. G. Taylor, *Louisiana: A Bicentennial History* (New York: Norton, 1976), 133–139, including a description of the great and malevolent influence of the Louisiana Lottery. Burke always maintained his innocence, his friends in Louisiana did what they could to clear his name, and in 1926 the New Orleans criminal court quashed the thirty-six-year-old indictments; Vivian, "Burke," 180. Burke still did not return.

16. G. W. McGinty, *Louisiana Redeemed: the Overthrow of Carpet-bag Rule, 1876–1880* (New Orleans: Pelican, 1941), 133; Hair, *Louisiana Politics,* 33; *New Orleans Picayune,* Feb. 9, Feb. 10, Mar. 18, Mar. 19, 1878. The Louisiana legislature and the New Orleans Common Council both passed resolutions of esteem and welcome when they learned that Hancock was back in town; Hancock Papers, USAMHI.

17. The *Memphis Appeal* printed the story of Hancock's effort to play down his trip to visit Russell; *Memphis Appeal,* June 25, 1880. For his travel plans see WSH to J. P. Nicholson, Feb. 29, 1880, Nicholson Papers, HEHL.

18. *New Orleans Picayune,* Mar. 17, 1880; *New Orleans Democrat,* Mar. 15, Mar. 16, 1880. See John J. Mellon to Bayard, Mar. 17, 1880, Bayard Papers, LC, complaining from New Orleans that the Hancock boom was "composed of chronic politicians" and "ex-office holders."

19. *New Orleans Democrat,* Apr. 13, Apr. 14, Apr. 22, Apr. 27, 1880.

20. J. McKibben to T. F. Bayard, Dec. 29, 1879, J. Duffy to Bayard, Feb. 23, 1880, and John Hunter to Bayard, Apr. 29, 1880, Bayard Papers, LC.

21. *Philadelphia Inquirer,* Apr. 28, 1880; *New York Sun,* Apr. 28, 1880.

22. E. John Ellis to Thos. C. W. Ellis, May 12, 1880, Ellis Family Papers, LSUL; *Philadelphia Inquirer,* Apr. 30, 1880; Dallas Sander to S. J. Randall, June 11, 1880, Randall Papers, UPL. Wallace told the *Sun*'s reporter after the convention that the delegation would probably split 38-20 against Tilden's nomination; *New York Sun,* Apr. 30, 1880.

23. *Philadelphia Inquirer,* Apr. 22, Feb. 21, 1880; Tansill, *Bayard,* 262–263; *New York Sun,* Apr. 25, 1880. For Bayard's financing of Kelly's challenge to the regular organization, see John Hunter to Bayard, Feb. 11 and Mar. 12, 1880, Bayard Papers, LC.

24. *New York Sun,* Apr. 23, 1880; *New Orleans Democrat,* Apr. 23, 1880.

25. An editorial in the *Philadelphia Inquirer* mentioned in passing that Bayard, as a candidate, was "second only to General Hancock in popularity"; *Philadelphia Inquirer,* May 26, 1880. This did not seem to be much of a factor—at that point.

THIRTY. DRIFTING

1. *New York Times,* June 17, June 18, 1880.

2. W. C. Hudson, *Random Recollections of an Old Political Reporter* (New York: Cupples and Leon, 1911), 106–109. For Tilden's view of Hancock, there does not appear to be any evidence but this unsupported statement by Whitney.

3. *New York Sun,* June 19, June 20, 1880; *New Orleans Democrat,* June 8, 1880.

4. *New York Sun,* June 20, 1880; *New York World,* June 25, 1880; *Philadelphia Inquirer,* June 8, 1880; *New Orleans Democrat,* June 21, 1880; *New York Times,* June 21, 1880. One reporter wrote that the Hancock campaign had "no cute conductors," but he may have miscalculated; *Philadelphia Inquirer,* June 19, 1880.

5. *New York Times,* June 20, 1880; *New York Sun,* June 19, 1880. The *Times,* as a Republican organ, dismissed Hancock's chances: "Gen. Hancock is that rare phenomenon, a prominent Union General, who is also a Democrat. This is his only commendation, but it gives him favor in the Southwest, where he obstructed reconstruction for a time, and to some extent elsewhere. His chance of the nomination is hardly worthy of consideration"; *New York Times,* June 17, 1880.

6. H. A. Tilden to S. J. Tilden, June 21, 1880, in Bigelow, ed., *Tilden Letters,* II, 601–602; *New York Sun,* June 21, 1880; *Philadelphia Inquirer,* June 21, 1880.

7. B. T. Johnson to T. F. Bayard, June 21, 1880, Bayard Papers, LC; Hudson, *Random Recollections,* 110. Dana, in the *Sun,* wrote even before the letter arrived that "it ought to be wholly disregarded by the convention"; *New York Sun,* June 20, 1880. Dana's editorial may give a clue to Tilden's real intentions, though it may be that Tilden, in his poor state of health, could not have said what his *real* intentions were. The reporter for the *New Orleans Times* called the letter "buncombe"; *New Orleans Times,* June 22, 1880.

8. Hudson, *Random Recollections,* 109; *New York Times,* June 21, 1880. Flick and Lobrano felt that Tilden's letter had been a bid for the endorsement of a "nomination as a personal vindication," which Tilden could then decline on the grounds of health, "without diminishing his fame or injuring the party, because it would enable him to pick his successor"; Flick and Lobrano, *Tilden,* 457. In other words, just what Tilden's enemies feared most.

9. *New York Sun,* June 21, June 22, 1880.

10. Barlow, "Cincinnati Hosts," 150; *New Orleans Democrat,* June 22, 1880. Both wires, Geo. H. Bates to Bayard, June 21, 1880, in Bayard Papers, LC. Bayard's war record, wrote one reporter, "requires defending"; a bad way to go into a campaign, felt many politicians; *New Orleans Democrat,* June 21, 1880.

11. *New York Sun,* June 22, 1880; *New Orleans Democrat,* June 22, 1880.

12. *Philadelphia Inquirer,* June 22, 1880.

THIRTY-ONE. THE CINCINNATI CONVENTION

1. Barlow, "Cincinnati Hosts," 153; E. A. Dickinson, rep., *Official Proceedings of the National Democratic Convention Held in Cincinnati, O., June 22d, 23d, and 24th, 1880* (Dayton, Ohio: 1882), 3–7; *Philadelphia Inquirer,* June 23, 1880.

2. *New York Sun, New York Times, Philadelphia Inquirer,* and *New Orleans Democrat,* June 23, 1880.

3. Dickinson, rep., *Proceedings*, 49, 62–66; Barlow, "Cincinnati Hosts," 154–155.

4. Dickinson, rep., *Proceedings*, 69–73; Barlow, "Cincinnati Hosts," 155; Tansill, *Bayard*, 280.

5. Dickinson, rep., *Proceedings*, 75–77, 79–82; Barlow, "Cincinnati Hosts," 155–156.

6. Brisbin, *Hancock*, 80; McClure, *Old Time Notes*, II, 517; *New York Times*, June 24, 1880.

7. Dickinson, rep., *Proceedings*, 85–86.

8. *New York Times, New York Sun, Philadelphia Times*, and *New Orleans Democrat*, June 24, 1880; Barlow, "Cincinnati Hosts," 157; Tansill, *Bayard*, 280.

9. Dickinson, rep., *Proceedings*, 86–89.

10. *Ibid.*, 94; *Philadelphia Times*, June 24, 1880; E. M. Daniel, ed., *Speeches and Orations of John Warwick Daniel* (Lynchburg, Va.: Bell, 1911), 159–161.

11. *New York Times*, June 24, 1880; Barlow, "Cincinnati Hosts," 157.

12. Dickinson, rep., *Proceedings*, 99.

13. *New York Times*, June 24, 1880. The *New Orleans Times*, a Bayard supporter, wrote on the same day that "the ballot cannot be said to indicate anything as to who will be the nominee"; *New Orleans Times*, June 24, 1880.

14. Dickinson, rep., *Proceedings*, 99.

15. Geo. Bates to T. F. Bayard, June 23, 1880, Bayard Papers, LC.

16. Barlow, "Cincinnati Hosts," 157; *New York Times*, June 24, 1880; *New York World* and *Philadelphia Inquirer*, June 25, 1880.

17. *New York Times*, June 24, 1880; *New York World*, June 25, 1880.

18. *New York Sun*, June 25, 1880; M. P. Breen, *Thirty Years of New York Politics* (New York, 1899), 598.

19. Dickinson, rep., *Proceedings*, 102–103. Peckham later had a distinguished career on the U.S. Supreme Court. On the morning of June 24, the New York delegates voted in caucus at first to give their bloc to Hancock, but persistent efforts by the Brooklyn leaders swung enough votes to Randall to prevail; *New York World*, June 25, 1880.

20. Dickinson, rep., *Proceedings*, 108–111; *Philadelphia Inquirer*, June 25, 1880.

21. Dickinson, rep., *Proceedings*, 111–114. A letter to the *New York Times* from W. L. Royal, a Virginia delegate, told of the Louisiana banner incident. Without it, he said, "I do not believe Gen. Hancock would have been nominated"; *New York Times*, July 3, 1880. An unlikely conclusion.

22. Dickinson, rep.,, *Proceedings*, 115–119.

23. Barlow, "Cincinnati Hosts," 160; Dickinson, rep., *Proceedings*, 127–129; *Nation*, July 1, 1880; Wall, *Watterson*, 170.

24. Dickinson, rep., *Proceedings*, 137, 142; Barlow, "Cincinnati Hosts," 160.

25. Geo. Bates to Bayard, June 24, 1880, Bayard Papers, LC; *New Orleans Democrat, New York Times*, and *Philadelphia Inquirer*, June 25, 1880. The *New Orleans Times* complained that Sam Randall had "afforded us a generous regimen of buzzard, and the enfeebled Northern Democracy almost a monopoly of the turkey"; *New Orleans Times*, June 15, 1880. But then it was a diehard Bayard organ.

THIRTY-TWO. THE CAMPAIGN BEGINS

1. For reports of Hancock's activities on the day of his nomination, see *New York Sun, New York Herald*, and *Philadelphia Inquirer*, June 25, 1880. For Bayard wire to Hancock, see Bayard Papers, LC.

2. *Philadelphia Inquirer*, June 25, 1880.

3. *Ibid.*, quoting the *Philadelphia Press* of the day before; *ibid.*, June 28, 1880;

Springfield Republican and *St. Louis Globe Democrat,* June 25, 1880, in Clancy, *Election of 1880,* 151, 175; W. M. Bateman to Wm. E. Chandler, June 28, 1880, W. K. Rogers to J. A. Garfield, June 25, 1880, Carl Schurz to Garfield, June 24, 1880, quoted in Clancy, *Election of 1880,* 149–150. *Harper's Weekly* called Hancock "a brave soldier . . . and . . . a gentleman of high personal character, but as a candidate for the Presidency he represents . . . no policy, no principle, no issue, nothing but the party which has nominated him"; *Harper's Weekly,* July 10, 1880.

4. *New Orleans Times, New Orleans Democrat,* and *Atlanta Constitution,* June 25, 1880.

5. *New Orleans Democrat,* Oct. 29, 1880.

6. B. Johnson to T. F. Bayard, June 26, 1880, A. Belmont to Bayard, June 27, 1880, and Wade Hampton to Bayard, June 26, 1880, Bayard Papers, LC; *New Orleans Times,* June 25, 1880.

7. *New York Herald,* June 26, 1880; S. M. Weed to S. J. Tilden, June 25, 1880, in Bigelow, ed., *Tilden Letters,* II, 599–600.

8. *Ibid.;* Hampton to Bayard, June 26, 1880, Bayard Papers, LC; *Philadelphia Inquirer,* June 28, 1880.

9. Katz, *Belmont,* 258–259.

10. *New York Times,* July 1, 5, 1880.

11. John Hunter to T. F. Bayard, July 17, 1880, Bayard Papers, LC; *New York Times,* July 13, 1880. The Tilden men professed to believe that Franklin's pitch for Wallace was his own idea "and not an authorized message or request from Gen. Hancock"; *New York Sun,* July 14, 1880.

12. Hunter to Bayard, July 17, 1880, Bayard Papers, LC; Katz, *Belmont,* 259. The press freely acknowledged that it would be "hazardous" for Hancock "to provoke either the active hostility or the sullen apathy of the Tilden men"; *New York Times,* July 15, 1880.

13. Morrison, ed., *Heth Diary,* 205–207.

14. *New York Times,* July 13, 1880; C. Schurz to J. A. Garfield, July 20, 1880, in F. Bancroft, ed., *Speeches, Correspondence and Political Papers of Carl Schurz,* 6 vols. (New York and London: Putnam's, 1913), IV, 1; *Nation,* July 15, 1880; *Harper's Weekly,* July 31, 1880.

15. Forney, *Hancock,* 440; *New York Sun,* July 14, 1880. For the arrival of Russell Hancock and his family, see *Philadelphia Inquirer,* June 29, 1880.

16. Dickinson, rep., *Proceedings,* 148–154; *New York Times* and *New York Sun,* July 14, 1880.

17. *New York Times* and *New York Sun,* June 30, 1880; *New York Times,* July 30, Aug. 10, 1880. The inquiry was into the conduct of Warren at the battle of Five Forks, a few days before the end of the war, when Sheridan, with Grant's authorization, relieved him from command of his corps. Hancock, as part of his military duty, frequently served on boards of inquiry and courts-martial, the most famous of which was a court-martial convened to hear charges against Grant's favorite, Orville E. Babcock, arising out of the Whiskey Ring frauds in 1875. Hancock pointed out to his colleagues that Babcock was facing identical charges in a civilian criminal court, which took precedence over a court-martial, and persuaded his reluctant fellows to yield jurisdiction to the civil court; ARH, 147–150.

18. *Ibid.,* 172.

19. *New York Times,* Aug. 2, 1880.

20. E. A. Storrs, "The Democratic Party Judged by Its History," *North American Review,* Oct. 1880, 288; Dearing, *Veterans in Politics,* 259–260; E. D. Morgan et al., "The Political Situation from a Financial Stand-point," *North American Review,* Nov. 1880, 464.

21. For the interview with Grant, which appeared the same day in the *Cincinnati Gazette,* see *New York Times,* Oct. 5, 1880. For Grant's weak attempt to backtrack,

and an editorial comment, see *ibid.*, Oct. 6, 1880. See also Badeau, *Grant in Peace,* 326, 371–372; Clancy, *Election of 1880,* 202; and M. Jewell to Garfield, Oct. 7, 1880, in Dearing, *Veterans in Politics,* 262–263. The alleged vote for Hancock in the 1864 convention was a figment of Grant's imagination; in the only ballot for president in that convention, McClellan received 174 votes, Thomas Seymour of Connecticut 38, and Horatio Seymour 12, and there was one-half vote for Charles O'Conor; J. H. Goodsell, rep., *Official Proceedings of the Democratic National Convention Held in 1864 at Chicago* (Chicago: Times Steam Book and Job Printing House, 1864), 43.

22. *Paterson Daily Guardian,* Oct. 8, 1880; *Nation,* Oct. 14, 1880; Forney, *Hancock,* 233. For acknowledgments of Sheridan's dislike for Hancock, see W. T. Sherman to Sheridan, Nov. 16, 1872, and Nov. 13, 1880, Sheridan Papers, LC.

23. On the eve of the election, the *New York Sun* wrote that "it is a disgrace to the country that the election of Garfield is even possible"; *New York Sun,* Nov. 2, 1880.

THIRTY-THREE. A CLOSE ELECTION

1. *New York Times,* July 31, 1880; Bigelow, ed., *Tilden Letters,* II, 604; Walker, *Hancock,* 306; *Nation,* Aug. 26, 1880. The *Nation* commented on the failure to make a statement of his position on political issues hitherto not addressed by Hancock; *Nation,* Aug. 5, 1880. *Harper's Weekly* spoke of "a certain child-like innocence" to the letter; *Harper's Weekly,* Aug. 21, 1880. Hancock visited Tilden and consulted with him about the letter of acceptance; WSH to Tilden, July 19 and July 27, 1880, WSH to John Bigelow, July 15, 1880, and Tilden to WSH, July 17, 1880, S. J. Tilden Papers, NYPL.

2. Dearing, *Veterans in Politics,* 257–258; *New York Times,* July 6, 1880.

3. *Ibid.,* July 7, 1880. The *Times,* which had been attacking Hancock for his lack of political knowledge or participation, charged that his letters to Sherman were not soldierly enough and showed "a restless dwelling on the partisan aspects of affairs in a troublous time" and "too much of the pettifogger and the politician"; *ibid.,* Aug. 27, 1880.

4. *Ibid.,* July 5, Aug. 27, 1880; *Nation,* Aug. 5, 1880.

5. Dearing, *Veterans in Politics,* 261; *New York Times,* Aug. 29, 1880.

6. *Ibid.,* July 16, 1880. For Garfield's problems with the senator from New York, see D. M. Jordan, *Roscoe Conkling of New York: Voice in the Senate* (Ithaca: Cornell U. Press, 1971), 349–354.

7. WSH to T. F. Bayard, Aug. 31, 1880, Bayard Papers, LC.

8. WSH to Bayard, Sept. 5, 1880, Bayard Papers, LC. One does not know quite what to make of these letters Hancock wrote to Bayard during the campaign. They appear fatuous and even silly and do not at all resemble the crisp, businesslike letters Hancock wrote when he felt sure of his subject.

9. *Nation,* Sept. 2, 1880; S. J. Randall to WSH, June 26, 1880, Randall Papers, UPL.

10. J. P. Barr to Randall, June 29, 1880, and J. E. Harvey to Randall, Aug. 22, 1880, Randall Papers, UPL.

11. Geo. W. Ladd to S. J. Randall, Aug. 23, 1880, Randall Papers, UPL.

12. *New York Sun,* Sept. 5, 1880; *New York Times,* Aug. 24, Aug. 31, 1880.

13. *Ibid.,* Sept. 14, 1880. The *Nation* called the Maine result "mixed" but conceded that "a damper" had been cast on Republican spirits; *Nation,* Sept. 16, 1880.

14. *New York Times,* Sept. 18, 1880.

15. *New York Sun,* Sept. 15, 1880. The *Sun* said there was now little doubt that Hancock would sweep all the doubtful states—and some that had not been considered possible for the Democrats, such as Wisconsin.

16. M. A. Jewell to J. A. Garfield, Sept. 14, 1880, in Clancy, *Election of 1880,* 194–195. Blaine, returning to New York from the fiasco in Maine, reportedly told a party official, "You want to fold up the bloody shirt and lay it away. It's of no use to us. You want to shift the main issue to protection"; Hudson, *Random Recollections,* 112.

17. E. Glassburg, "Work, Wages, and the Cost of Living, Ethnic Differences and the Poverty Line, Philadelphia, 1880," *Pennsylvania History,* Jan. 1979, 20. Glassburg's study shows that the average workingman's family in Philadelphia in 1880 required an income of $643.46 annually and that not many made it on the husband's income alone.

18. J. P. Barr to S. J. Randall, Sept. 9, 1880, Randall Papers, UPL.

19. M. H. Bovee to S. J. Randall, Aug. 4, 1880, Randall Papers, UPL.

20. Jordan, *Conkling,* 356–357.

21. Even Garfield involved himself in the employer-pressure business. See J. A. Garfield to Amos Townsend, Sept. 2, 1880, suggesting that John D. Rockefeller could do "immense service" in Indiana with the workingmen of the state who were dependent on him for their livelihood, in Clancy, *Election of 1880,* 194n.

22. *New York Times,* Oct. 11, 1880; *New Orleans Democrat,* Oct. 11, Oct. 12, 1880; *New York Sun,* Oct. 12, 1880.

23. *New York Times,* Oct. 14, 1880; *New York Sun,* Oct. 18, 1880.

24. *New York Times,* Oct. 14, Oct. 16, Oct. 17, 1880; *New Orleans Democrat,* Oct. 14, 1880; *Cincinnati Enquirer,* Oct. 13, 1880; *Louisville Courier-Journal,* Oct. 22, 1880; *Paterson Daily Guardian,* Oct. 13, 1880.

25. Voorhees, in *New York Sun,* Oct. 17, 1880. Hancock, the Indiana senator said, "never weakens."

26. *New York Times,* Sept. 27, 1880.

27. *Paterson Daily Guardian,* Oct. 8, 1880.

28. WSH to Jas. Doolittle, Apr. 2, 1884, quoted in Taylor, "General Hancock," 193–194. Curiously, in his 1870 campaign for reelection to Congress, Garfield, speaking about the tariff, said it was "manifest that the question has assumed a local rather than a national aspect"; R. G. Caldwell, *James A. Garfield: Party Chieftain* (New York: Dodd, Mead, 1931), 196. Unfortunately for Hancock, no one dredged up this quote to help him in the 1880 campaign.

29. *New York Times,* Oct. 16, 1880; *New York Sun,* Oct. 16, 1880. The Eaton bill to provide for the appointment of a panel of tariff experts, which Hancock said he advocated, was languishing in Congress.

30. *Nation,* Oct. 21, 1880; *Harper's Weekly,* Nov. 13, 1880.

31. *New York Sun,* Oct. 16, Oct. 19, 1880; *New York Times,* Oct. 2, 1880.

32. Allan Nevins, *Abram S. Hewitt, with Some Account of Peter Cooper* (New York and London: Harper, 1935), 436; Clancy, *Election of 1880,* 233. For a description of Garfield's wavering course on the Chinese immigration issue, see *ibid.,* 170–171.

33. *Ibid.,* 234.

34. *New York Times,* Oct. 23, 1880; Clancy, *Election of 1880,* 236–237; Nevins, *Hewitt,* 436.

35. *New York Sun,* Oct. 29, 1880.

36. *Ibid.*

37. *Ibid.,* Oct. 29, Oct. 31, Nov. 2, 1880; John Kelly to T. F. Bayard, Nov. 2, 1880, Bayard Papers, LC.

38. *Paterson Daily Guardian* and *New York Sun,* Nov. 1, 1880.

39. WSH to B. Percy Chain, Dec. 5, 1880, Hancock Papers, MCHS.

40. *Paterson Daily Guardian,* Nov. 3, 1880.

41. ARH, 172.

THIRTY-FOUR. THE MORNING AFTER

1. The popular vote count was Garfield, 4,449,053; Hancock, 4,442,035; Weaver, 308,578; and Dow, the Temperance man, 10,305. Interestingly, in the five presidential elections from 1876 through 1892, this was the only one in which the Democratic candidate did not receive the most votes. Those of 1876 and 1888, of course, are the only elections in our history in which the popular-vote winner did not receive the ultimate victory.

2. Clancy, *Election of 1880*, 243–246; M. D. Hirsch, *William C. Whitney: Modern Warwick* (New York: Dodd, Mead, 1948), 159–160. D. S. Alexander said that Kelly "wantonly sacrificed the Hancock ticket to his unscrupulous quest of local power"; D. S. Alexander, *A Political History of the State of New York*, 3 vols. (New York: Henry Holt, 1909), II, 483.

3. *New York Times*, Nov. 3, Oct. 28, 1880; *Louisville Courier-Journal*, Nov. 3, 1880. The *Memphis Avalanche* decried the "lowtoned character given to the canvass by the selection of Barnum as chairman"; *Memphis Avalanche*, Nov. 4, 1880.

4. *New York Times*, Oct. 28, 1880.

5. *New York Sun* and *New York Times*, Nov. 4, 1880.

6. ARH, 174–175.

7. *New York Sun*, Oct. 18, Nov. 3, 1880.

8. WSH to B. Percy Chain, Dec. 5, 1880, Hancock Papers, MCHS. Hancock discussed New York in *ibid.;* in WSH to Cyrus H. McCormick, Nov. 28, 1880, in Mitchell, *Seymour*, 546; and in WSH to S. S. Cox, Dec. 10, 1880, American Civil War Miscellany, U. of Chicago Library.

9. WSH to J. M. Schofield, Dec. 6, 1880, H. Barney Collection, HEHL; WSH to D. S. Walker, Feb. 10, 1881, Hancock Papers, NYHS.

10. ARH, 175; *Harper's Weekly*, Nov. 20, 1880.

THIRTY-FIVE.
DOWN A FLIGHT OF STAIRS

1. ARH, 8–9.

2. B. P. Chain, paper, undated, Hancock Papers, MCHS; WSH to B. E. Chain, May 16, 1884, July 1, 1878, Jan. 18, 1878, Apr. 8, 1878, and June 19, 1884, Hancock Papers, MCHS.

3. See WSH to B. E. Chain, July 12, 1883, Hancock Papers, MCHS. We have a good deal of information on the Hancock burial vault in Norristown because of a proposal some years later to move the general's remains to Arlington National Cemetery. Chain's son wrote a lengthy paper in opposition to the proposal, explaining in great detail about the sepulture of Hancock with Ada in Norristown; Chain, paper, undated.

4. *New York Evening Telegram*, Apr. 27, 1883; Walker, *Hancock*, 309.

5. *Ibid.*, 311; ARH, 167. Gwyn was admitted to West Point in 1894.

6. WSH to Samuel Jones, Sept. 29, 1881, F. W. M. Holliday Papers, DUL; ARH, 177; *New York Herald*, Oct. 19, Oct. 21, 1881.

7. Schofield, *Forty-Six Years*, 481; Robt. T. Lincoln to WSH, Oct. 9, 1883, Hancock Papers, USAMHI; *New York World*, Feb. 11, 1886.

8. *New York Times*, July 28, Aug. 4, Aug. 5, Aug. 6, Aug. 9, 1885; General Orders No. 13, Headquarters, Division of the Atlantic, August 6, 1885, Hancock Papers, NYHS; ARH, 178; Badeau, *Grant in Peace*, 372. Hesseltine lists Hancock as one of those who called upon the dying Grant, but no confirmation of such a visit has been found; Hesseltine, *Grant*, 451. Former Confederate general John B. Gordon told of

Hancock's insisting that he and Fitzhugh Lee ride up near the head of the procession; Gordon, *Reminiscences,* 35–36.

9. ARH, 165; MOLLUS, *In Memoriam—Winfield Scott Hancock, United States Army* (n.p., 1886), 4, 46; Taylor, "Hancock," 194. *New York Times,* July 5, 1885. See WSH to P. Sheridan, April 20, 1883, asking the latter to publish in the *Journal of the Military Service Institution* his article on Lee's surrender; Hancock Papers, DUL.

10. Dearing, *Veterans in Politics,* 309; WSH to B. E. Chain, June 18, 1885, Hancock Papers, MCHS; WSH to J. W. Daniel, May 16, 1885, John W. Daniel Papers, DUL.

11. S. Davis, " 'A Matter of Sensational Interest': The *Century* 'Battles and Leaders' Series," *Civil War History,* Dec. 1981, 340; W. G. Mitchell to F. A. Walker, Aug. 12, 1875, in J. P. Munroe, *A Life of Francis Amasa Walker* (New York: Holt, 1923), 262–263; WSH to Mrs. Annie Hays, Apr. 16, 1883, in Fleming, ed., *Hays,* 429; Walker, *Hancock,* 312. For examples of Hancock's assistance to Walker, see WHS to Francis A. Walker, Apr. 4, 1884, Jan. 15, Feb. 18, Apr. 7, and Dec. 31, 1885, MOLLUS, Massachusetts Commandery, Collection, USAMHI. WSH to A. S. Webb, June 28, Aug. 12, 1881, Webb Papers, YUL. In regard to Gettysburg, of course, Hancock continued over the years the controversy with Hunt over the use of the artillery of the Second Corps just prior to Pickett's Charge; see WSH to W. T. Sherman, Jan. 21, 1879, in "Papers in Relation to the Reorganization of the Army," Senate Misc. Doc. No. 14, 46th Cong., 1st sess., 41.

12. *New York World,* Feb. 10, 1886; *New York Tribune,* Feb. 10, 1886. For Hancock's unsuccessful efforts on behalf of Brooke, see G. W. Dorsey to J. R. Brooke, Feb. 4, 1886, and W. P. Wilson to J. R. Brooke, Feb. 22 and May 9, 1886, John R. Brooke Papers, HSP.

13. *New York Times,* Feb. 12, 1886.

14. Coverage of the general's death is primarily from long articles in the New York papers, the *Times, Herald, World, Tribune,* and *Sun,* and from the *Philadelphia Inquirer,* Feb. 10, 1886.

15. *New York Times,* Feb. 10, Feb. 11, Feb. 14, 1886.

16. *Ibid.,* Feb. 12, 1886.

THIRTY-SIX. "PURE GOLD"

1. *New York Times,* Feb. 12, 1886; Walker, *Hancock,* 313–315. Hamilton Fish, Grant's secretary of state, wrote to Hancock's niece when Allie died: "She was always so bright, so gay, so full of sunshine . . ."; Hamilton Fish to Almira R. Griffin, Oct. 31, 1893, Hancock Papers, USAMHI.

2. *New York Herald* and *New York World,* Feb. 10, 1886.

3. E. R. Jones, *Four Years in the Army of the Potomac: A Soldier's Recollections* (London: Tyne Pub. Co., n.d.), 53–54, 148–149; H. H. Bingham, *An Oration at the Unveiling of the Equestrian Statue of Major-General Winfield Scott Hancock on the Battlefield of Gettysburg, June 5, 1896* (Philadelphia, 1899), 6.

4. Dana, *Recollections,* 190.

5. Johnson C. Whittaker, one of a handful of black cadets at West Point after the war, suffered the same total ostracism which was visited by the entire corps upon each of them. In the spring of 1880, Whittaker was found tied to his bed, cut, bleeding and unconscious, but a West Point court of inquiry decided that he had done it to himself. Whittaker requested a court-martial to vindicate his name, and Hancock supported that request. Eventually, in December 1880, Hayes ordered the court-martial, which again found the young cadet guilty; J. F. Marszalek, Jr., *Court-Martial: A Black Man in America* (New York: Scribner's, 1972), 159, 238.

6. F. A. Walker, "General Hancock," *Critical Sketches of Some Federal and Confederate Commanders*, MHSM, X, 55.

7. *New York World*, Feb. 10, 1886.

8. *Ibid.*, Feb. 11, 1886, quoting from a speech Hayes delivered to a Loyal Legion banquet in Cincinnati on February 10, 1886.

Selected Bibliography

MANUSCRIPT COLLECTIONS

In addition to the collections in the National Archives in Washington, D.C., cited throughout the body of this work, the following manuscript collections were consulted and used:

American Civil War Miscellany, University of Chicago Library.
Anthony Collection, New York Public Library.
Autograph Collection, Historical Society of Pennsylvania.
Autograph File, Houghton Library, Harvard University.
Francis Channing Barlow Papers, Massachusetts Historical Society.
Barry Collection, Maryland Historical Society.
Thomas F. Bayard Papers, Library of Congress.
James Beale Papers, Massachusetts Historical Society.
Louis Benecke Papers, Western Historical Manuscript Collection, University of Missouri.
William Clark Breckinridge Papers, Western Historical Manuscript Collection, University of Missouri.
Brent (A&W) Collection, Henry E. Huntington Library.
James O. Broadhead Papers, Missouri Historical Society.
John R. Brooke Papers, Historical Society of Pennsylvania.
Bryant-Godwin Papers, New York Public Library.
Simon B. Buckner Collection, Henry E. Huntington Library.
E. A. Burke Papers, Louisiana State University Library.
E. A. Burke Papers, Tulane University Library.
Eugene A. Carr Papers, United States Army Military History Institute.
Carrington Family Papers, Yale University Library.
George W. Cullum File, United States Military Academy Archives.
John W. Daniel Papers, Duke University Library.
John F. Darby Papers, Missouri Historical Society.
Frederick M. Dearborn Collection, Houghton Library, Harvard University.
James R. Doolittle Papers, New York Public Library.
Abner Doubleday Papers, National Baseball Library.
Ferdinand J. Dreer Collection, Historical Society of Pennsylvania.
Ellis Family Papers, Louisiana State University Library.
Fessenden Family Papers, Bowdoin College Library.
William B. Franklin Papers, Library of Congress.
John Gibbon Papers, Maryland Historical Society.
Ulysses S. Grant Papers, Library of Congress.
Simon Gratz Collection, Historical Society of Pennsylvania.
Winfield S. Hancock Papers, Duke University Library.
Winfield S. Hancock Papers, Historical Society of Montgomery County, Pa.
Winfield S. Hancock Papers, Illinois State Historical Library.
Winfield S. Hancock Papers, Library of Congress.
Winfield S. Hancock Papers, New-York Historical Society.
Winfield S. Hancock Miscellaneous Papers, New York Public Library.
Winfield S. Hancock Papers, United States Army Military History Institute.
Winfield S. Hancock Papers, Special Collections Division, United States Military Academy Library.

F. W. M. Holliday Papers, Duke University Library.
O. O. Howard Papers, Bowdoin College Library.
Andrew A. Humphreys Papers, Historical Society of Pennsylvania.
Huntington Miscellaneous Collection, Henry E. Huntington Library.
C. C. Jones, Jr., Papers, Duke University Library.
Matthew Keller Collection, Henry E. Huntington Library.
Abraham Lincoln File, Henry E. Huntington Library.
George Brinton McClellan Papers, Library of Congress.
Military Division of the Missouri Papers, United States Army Military History Institute.
Military Order of the Loyal Legion of the United States, Massachusetts Commandery, Collection, United States Army Military History Institute.
Clara J. J. Morrow Papers, Duke University Library.
Mosby Family Papers, University of Virginia Library.
John P. Nicholson Collection, Henry E. Huntington Library.
Otis Norcross Papers, Massachusetts Historical Society.
Order of Indian Wars Papers, United States Army Military History Institute.
Fitz John Porter Collection, United States Military Academy Library.
Samuel J. Randall Papers, University of Pennsylvania Library.
Peter F. Rothermel Papers, Division of Archives and Manuscripts, Pennsylvania Historical and Museum Commission.
Philip Henry Sheridan Papers, Library of Congress.
William T. Sherman Papers, Missouri Historical Society.
Thomas Kilby Smith Papers, Special Collections Division, United States Military Academy Library.
Thomas Kilby Smith Collection, Henry E. Huntington Library.
James C. Stephens Papers, Western Historical Manuscript Collection, University of Missouri.
A. L. Taveau Papers, Duke University Library.
Samuel J. Tilden Papers, New York Public Library.
U.S. Army, Fifth Military District, Collection, Duke University Library.
Robert T. Van Horn Papers, Western Historical Manuscript Collection, University of Missouri.
Washburn Manuscripts, Massachusetts Historical Society.
Alexander S. Webb Papers, Yale University Library.
Henry Wilson Papers, Duke University Library.

GOVERNMENT PUBLICATIONS

Chronological List of Actions, &c., with Indians, from January 1, 1866, to January, 1891 (Office Memoranda). Adjutant General's Office, Washington, 1891.
"Difficulties with Indian Tribes," House Executive Documents No. 240, 41st Cong., 2nd session.
"Expedition Against Piegan Indians," House Executive Documents No. 185, 41st Cong., 2nd session.
"Expedition Against Piegan Indians," House Executive Documents No. 197, 41st Cong., 2nd session.
"Federal Aid in Domestic Disturbances. 1787–1903," by Frederick T. Wilson, Senate Misc. Documents No. 209, 57th Cong., 2nd session.
"Further Information respecting Armed Expeditions against the Western Indians," Senate Exec. Doc. No. 7, 40th Cong., 1st session.
"New Orleans Councilmen," House Executive Documents No. 172, 40th Cong., 2nd session.

"Papers in Relation to the Reorganization of the Army," Senate Misc. Documents No. 14, 46th Cong., 1st session.

Record of Engagements with Hostile Indians within the Military Division of the Missouri from 1868 to 1882, Government Printing Office, Washington, 1882.

"Reorganization of the Army," House Report No. 3, 45th Cong., 3rd session.

"Reorganization of the Army," Senate Report No. 555, pt. 2, 45th Cong., 3rd session.

"Removal of City Council of New Orleans," House Executive Documents No. 209, 40th Cong., 2nd session.

Report of the Joint Committee on the Conduct of the War, 3 parts, 37th Cong., 3rd session.

Report of the Joint Committee on the Conduct of the War, 38th Cong., 2nd session.

"Report of a Sub-Committee of the Committee on Military Affairs relating to the Reorganization of the Army," House Misc. Documents No. 56, 45th Cong., 2nd session.

"Report of the Secretary of War (1867)," House Executive Documents No. 1, 40th Cong., 2nd session.

"Report of the Secretary of War (1869)," House Executive Documents No. 1, pt. 2, 41st Cong., 2nd session.

"Report of the Secretary of War (1870)," House Executive Documents No. 1, pt. 2, 41st Cong., 3rd session.

"Report of the Secretary of War (1871)," House Executive Documents No. 1, pt. 2, 42nd Cong., 2nd session.

"Report of the Secretary of War (1872)," House Executive Documents No. 1, pt. 2, 42nd Cong., 3rd session.

"Report of the Secretary of War (1873)," House Executive Documents No. 1, pt. 2, v. 2, 43rd Cong., 1st session.

"Report of the Secretary of War (1874)," House Executive Documents No. 1, pt. 2, v. 1, 43rd Cong., 2nd session.

"Report of the Secretary of War (1875)," House Executive Documents No. 1, pt. 2, v. 1, 44th Cong., 1st session.

"Report of the Secretary of War (1877)," House Executive Documents No. 1, pt. 2, v. 1, 45th Cong., 2nd session.

"Report of the Secretary of War (1878)," House Executive Documents No. 1, pt. 2, 45th Cong., 3rd session.

"Report of the Secretary of War (1879)," House Executive Documents No. 1, pt. 2, 46th Cong., 2nd session.

"Report of the Secretary of War (1880)," House Executive Documents No. 1, pt. 2, 46th Cong., 3rd session.

War of the Rebellion: A Compilation of the Official Records of the Union and Confederate Armies, 128 vols., Government Printing Office, Washington, 1880–1901.

NEWSPAPERS AND JOURNALS

Daily Leavenworth (Kansas) *Times*
Daily National Intelligencer (Washington, D.C.)
Harper's Weekly
Journal of the Military Service Institution of the United States
Leavenworth Daily Conservative
Louisville Courier-Journal
The Nation
New Orleans Daily Picayune
New Orleans Democrat

New Orleans Republican
New Orleans Times
New York Daily Graphic
New York Evening Post
New York Evening Telegram
New York Herald
New York Sun
New York Times
New York Tribune
New York World
Paterson (New Jersey) *Daily Guardian*
Philadelphia Inquirer
Philadelphia Item
Springfield (Massachusetts) *Republican*

BOOKS AND ARTICLES

Not listed here are the many general works on the war by Bruce Catton, including his trilogy on the Army of the Potomac, or the eight-volume work of Allan Nevins titled generally *Ordeal of the Union*. Nevertheless, they serve as comprehensive background for anyone writing about the war.

Abbott, Martin, ed., "Reconstruction in Louisiana: Three Letters," *Louisiana History,* spring 1960.
Adams, Michael C. C., *Our Masters the Rebels: A Speculation on Union Military Failure in the East, 1861–1865,* Cambridge, Mass., and London, 1978.
Agassiz, George R., ed., *Meade's Headquarters, 1863–1865; Letters of Colonel Theodore Lyman from The Wilderness to Appomattox,* Boston, 1922.
Allan, William, "Fredericksburg," *Campaigns in Virginia, Maryland and Pennsylvania, 1862–1863,* Papers of the Military Historical Society of Massachusetts, III, Boston, 1903.
Anderson, Harry H., "A History of the Cheyenne River Indian Agency and Its Military Post, Fort Bennett, 1868–1891," *South Dakota Report and Historical Collections,* XXVIII, South Dakota Historical Society, 1956.
Andrews, J. Cutler, *The North Reports the Civil War,* Pittsburgh, 1955.
Athearn, Robert G., *Forts of the Upper Missouri,* Lincoln, Neb., 1972.
———, *Thomas Francis Meagher: An Irish Revolutionary in America,* Boulder, Colo., 1949.
———, *William Tecumseh Sherman and the Settlement of the West,* Norman, Okla., 1956.
Auge, M., *Lives of the Eminent Dead and Biographical Notices of Prominent Living Citizens of Montgomery County, Pa.,* 3rd ed., Norristown, Pa., 1879.
Badeau, Adam, *Grant in Peace: From Appomattox to Mount McGregor,* Hartford, Conn., 1887.
Bancroft, Frederic, ed., *Speeches, Correspondence and Political Papers of Carl Schurz,* 6 vols., New York and London, 1913.
Bandel, Eugene, *Frontier Life in the Army, 1854–1861,* Glendale, Calif., 1932.
Banes, Charles H., *History of the Philadelphia Brigade,* Philadelphia, 1876.
Barlow, Francis C., "Capture of the Salient May 12 1864," *The Wilderness Campaign May–June 1864,* Papers of the Military Historical Society of Massachusetts, IV, Boston, 1905.

Barlow, William R., "Cincinnati Hosts the Democrats in 1880," *Bulletin of the Cincinnati Historical Society,* July 1964.

Bates, Richard O., *The Gentleman from Ohio: An Introduction to Garfield,* Durham, N.C., 1973.

"Battle of Chancellorsville—Report of General R. E. Lee," *Southern Historical Society Papers,* III, May and June 1877.

Bauer, K. Jack, *The Mexican War, 1846–1848,* New York, 1974.

Beale, Howard K., ed., *Diary of Gideon Welles,* 3 vols., New York, 1960.

Benedict, Michael Les, *The Impeachment and Trial of Andrew Johnson,* New York, 1972.

Beringer, Richard E., Herman Hattaway, Archer Jones, and William N. Still, Jr., *Why the South Lost the Civil War,* Athens, Ga., and London, 1986.

Berthrong, Donald J., *The Southern Cheyennes,* Norman, Okla., 1963.

Bieber, Ralph P., "Some Aspects of the Santa Fe Trail, 1848–1880," *Chronicles of Oklahoma,* March 1924.

Bigelow, John, ed., *Letters and Literary Memorials of Samuel J. Tilden,* 2 vols., New York and London, 1908.

Bigelow, John, Jr., *The Campaign of Chancellorsville: A Strategic and Tactical Study,* New Haven, 1910.

Bingham, Henry H., *An Oration at the Unveiling of the Equestrian Statue of Major-General Winfield Scott Hancock on the Battlefield of Gettysburg, June 5, 1896,* Philadelphia, 1899.

Binning, F. Wayne, "Carpetbaggers' Triumph: The Louisiana State Election of 1868," *Louisiana History,* winter 1973.

Black, David, *The King of Fifth Avenue: The Fortunes of August Belmont,* New York, 1981.

Black, John D., "Reminiscences of the Bloody Angle," *Glimpses of the Nation's Struggle,* 4th ser., Minnesota Commandery, Military Order of the Loyal Legion of the United States, St. Paul, 1898.

Blakeman, A. Noel, ed., *Personal Recollections of the War of the Rebellion,* 2nd ser., New York and London, 1897.

Bodkin, Mathias, "Thomas Francis Meagher, 1822–1867," *Studies,* spring 1968.

Bonadio, Felice A., *North of Reconstruction: Ohio Politics, 1865–1870,* New York, 1970.

Bradley, Erwin Stanley, *The Triumph of Militant Republicanism: A Study of Pennsylvania and Presidential Politics, 1860–1872,* Philadelphia, 1964.

Bratton, John, "The Battle of Williamsburg," *Southern Historical Society Papers,* VII, June 1879.

Breen, Matthew P., *Thirty Years of New York Politics,* New York, 1899.

Brisbin, James S., *Winfield Scott Hancock,* Philadelphia, 1880.

Brodie, Fawn M., *Thaddeus Stevens: Scourge of the South,* New York, 1959.

Bruce, Robert V., *1877: Year of Violence,* Indianapolis and New York, 1959.

Bryan, Kirke, *Joseph Henry Taylor,* Norristown, Pa., 1953.

Butler, Benjamin F., *Butler's Book,* Boston, 1892.

Butterfield, Julia L., ed., *A Biographical Memorial of General Daniel Butterfield,* New York, 1904.

Cadwallader, Sylvanus, *Three Years with Grant,* ed., B. P. Thomas, New York, 1955.

Caldwell, Robert G., *James A. Garfield: Party Chieftain,* New York, 1931.

Campbell, Walter S., "The Cheyenne Dog Soldiers," *Chronicles of Oklahoma,* Jan. 1923.

"The Captured Guns at Spotsylvania Courthouse—Correction of General Ewell's Report," *Southern Historical Society Papers,* VII, Nov. 1879.

Carpenter, John A., "General O. O. Howard at Gettysburg," *Civil War History,* Sept. 1963.

———, *Sword and Olive Branch: Oliver Otis Howard*, Pittsburgh, 1964.

Carroll, John M., ed., *Custer in the Civil War: His Unfinished Memoirs*, San Rafael, Calif., 1977.

Catton, Bruce, *Grant Takes Command*, Boston and Toronto, 1968.

Cavanagh, Michael, *Memoirs of Gen. Thomas Francis Meagher*, Worcester, Mass., 1892.

Child, Benjamin H., "From Fredericksburg to Gettysburg," *Personal Narratives, Soldiers and Sailors Historical Society of Rhode Island*, 5th ser., No. 4, Providence, 1895.

The Civil Record of Major General Winfield S. Hancock during His Administration in Louisiana and Texas, n.p., 1871.

Clampitt, John W., "The Trial of Mrs. Surratt," *North American Review*, Sept. 1880.

Clancy, Herbert J., *The Presidential Election of 1880*, Chicago, 1958.

Clapp, Margaret, *Forgotten First Citizen: John Bigelow*, Boston, 1947.

Coddington, Edwin B., *The Gettysburg Campaign: A Study in Command*, New York, 1968.

Coffman, Edward M., *The Old Army: A Portrait of the American Army in Peacetime, 1784–1898*, New York and Oxford, 1986.

Coleman, Charles H., *The Election of 1868: The Democratic Effort to Regain Control*, New York, 1933.

Connelley, William E., "The Treaty Held at Medicine Lodge, between the Peace Commission and the Comanche, Kiowa, Arapahoe, Cheyenne and Prairie Apache Tribes of Indians, in October, 1867," *Collections of the Kansas State Historical Society*, XVII, 1928.

Cooper, Jerry M., "The Army as Strikebreaker—The Railroad Strikes of 1877 and 1894," *Labor History*, spring 1977.

Copeland, Fayette, "The New Orleans Press and the Reconstruction," *Louisiana Historical Quarterly*, Jan. 1947.

Correspondence between General Grant and Major General Hancock Relative to the Removal of Members of the City Council, New Orleans, pamphlet, n.d.

Correspondence between General W. T. Sherman, U.S. Army, and Major General W. S. Hancock, U.S. Army, St. Paul, 1871.

Coulter, E. Merton, *The South During Reconstruction, 1865–1877*, Baton Rouge, 1947.

Cox, Jacob Dolson, *Military Reminiscences of the Civil War*, 2 vols., New York, 1900.

Cox, Lawanda and John H., *Politics, Principle, and Prejudice, 1865–1866*, New York, 1963.

Crawford, Samuel J., *Kansas in the Sixties*, Chicago, 1911.

Crotty, Daniel G., *Four Years Campaigning in the Army of the Potomac*, Grand Rapids, 1874.

Cullen, Joseph P., *The Peninsula Campaign, 1862: McClellan and Lee Struggle for Richmond*, Harrisburg, Pa., 1973.

Cullum, George W., *Biographical Register of the Officers and Graduates of the U.S. Military Academy at West Point, N.Y.*, 3rd ed., Boston and New York, 1891.

Custer, George A., *My Life on the Plains*, ed. Milo M. Quaife, Chicago, 1952.

———, "War Memoirs. Yorktown and Williamsburg," *Galaxy*, Nov. 1876.

Dacus, Joseph A., *Annals of the Great Strikes*, Chicago, 1877

Dana, Charles A., *Recollections of the Civil War*, New York, 1902.

Daniel, Edward M., ed., *Speeches and Orations of John Warwick Daniel*, Lynchburg, Va., 1911.

Dauchy, George K., "The Battle of Ream's Station," *Military Essays and Recollections*, Illinois Commandery, Military Order of the Loyal Legion of the United States, III, Chicago, 1899.

Davis, George B., "The Antietam Campaign," *Campaigns in Virginia, Maryland and Pennsylvania, 1862–1863*, Papers of the Military Historical Society of Massachusetts, III, Boston, 1903.

Davis, O. Wilson, *A Brief Statement of the Services Rendered His Country, by Winfield S. Hancock, Major-General U.S.A.*, West Chester, Pa., 1880.

Davis, Theodore R., "A Stage Ride to Colorado," *Harper's New Monthly*, July 1867.

———, "A Summer on the Plains," *Harper's New Monthly*, Feb. 1868.

Davison, Kenneth E., *The Presidency of Rutherford B. Hayes*, Westport, Conn., 1972.

Dawson, Joseph G., III, *Army Generals and Reconstruction: Louisiana, 1862–1877*, Baton Rouge and London, 1982.

———, "General Phil Sheridan and Military Reconstruction in Louisiana," *Civil War History*, June 1978.

Dearing, Mary R., *Veterans in Politics: The Story of the G.A.R.*, Baton Rouge, 1952.

Dell, Christopher, *Lincoln and the War Democrats: The Grand Erosion of Conservative Tradition*, Rutherford, Madison, and Teaneck, N.J., 1975.

Denison, C. W., *Winfield, the Lawyer's Son and How He Became a Major-General*, Philadelphia, 1865.

DeWitt, David Miller, *The Judicial Murder of Mary E. Surratt*, Baltimore 1895.

Dickinson, E. B., reporter, *Official Proceedings of the National Democratic Convention Held in Cincinnati, O., June 22d, 23d, and 24th, 1880*, Dayton, Ohio, 1882.

Dinnerstein, Leonard, "The Impact of Tammany Hall on State and National Politics in the Eighteen-Eighties," *New York History*, July 1961.

Dippie, Brian W., ed., *Nomad: George A. Custer in Turf, Field and Farm*, Austin and London, 1980.

Dixon, David, "A Scout with Custer: Edmund Guerrier on the Hancock Expedition of 1867," *Kansas History*, autumn 1981.

Dixon, James W., "Across the Plains with General Hancock," *Journal of the Military Service Institution of the United States*, June 1886.

Doubleday, Abner, *Chancellorsville and Gettysburg*, New York, 1882.

Driver, William R., "Pickett's Charge at Gettysburg," *Campaigns in Virginia, Maryland and Pennsylvania, 1862–1863*, Papers of the Military Historical Society of Massachusetts, III, Boston, 1903.

———, "The Capture of the Salient at Spotsylvania, May 12, 1864," *The Wilderness Campaign, May–June 1864*, Papers of the Military Historical Society of Massachusetts, IV, Boston, 1905.

Early, Jubal A., "Reply to General Longstreet's Second Paper," *Southern Historical Society Papers*, V, June 1878.

Eckenrode, H. J., and Bryan Conrad, *George B. McClellan: The Man Who Saved the Union*, Chapel Hill, 1941.

Edwards, G. Thomas, "Holding the Far West for the Union: The Army in 1861," *Civil War History*, Dec. 1968.

Evans, Frank B., *Pennsylvania Politics, 1872–1877: A Study in Political Leadership*, Harrisburg, Pa., 1966.

Favill, Josiah M., *The Diary of a Young Officer Serving with the Armies of the United States during the War of the Rebellion*, Chicago, 1909.

Ficklen, John Rose, *History of Reconstruction in Louisiana (Through 1866)*, 1910; Gloucester, Mass., 1966.

Fleming, Geo. Thornton, ed., *Life and Letters of Alexander Hays*, Pittsburgh, 1919.

Fleming, Thomas J., *West Point: The Men and Times of the United States Military Academy*, New York, 1969.

Flick, Alexander Clarence, and Gustav S. Lobrano, *Samuel Jones Tilden: A Study in Political Sagacity*, New York, 1939.

Flower, Frank A., *Edwin McMasters Stanton: The Autocrat of Rebellion, Emancipation, and Reconstruction*, Akron, Ohio, 1905.

Foner, Jack D., *The United States Soldier between Two Wars: Army Life and Reforms, 1865–1898*, New York, 1970.

Foner, Philip S., *The Great Labor Uprising of 1877*, New York, 1977.

Ford, Worthington C., ed., *A Cycle of Adams Letters, 1861–1865*, 2 vols., London, 1921.

Foreman, Carolyn Thomas, "Col. Jesse Henry Leavenworth," *Chronicles of Oklahoma*, March 1935.

Forney, John W., *Life and Military Career of Winfield Scott Hancock*, Philadelphia, 1880.

Fox, William F., *Regimental Losses in the American Civil War, 1861–1865*, Albany, 1889.

Freeman, Douglas Southall, *Lee's Lieutenants: A Study in Command*, 3 vols., New York, 1942–44.

Frost, Lawrence A., *The Court-Martial of General George Armstrong Custer*, Norman, Okla., 1968.

Fry, James B., "Origin and Progress of the Military Service Institution of the United States," *Journal of the Military Service Institution of the United States*, I, 1880.

Fuller, J. F. C., *Grant and Lee: A Study in Personality and Generalship*, New York, 1933.

Gambill, Edward L., *Conservative Ordeal: Northern Democrats and Reconstruction, 1865–1868*, Ames, Iowa, 1981.

Garfield, James A., "The Army of the United States," *North American Review*, March–April, May–June 1878.

Garfield, Marvin H., "Defense of the Kansas Frontier, 1866–1867," *Kansas Historical Quarterly*, Aug. 1932.

———, "The Military Post as a Factor in the Frontier Defense of Kansas, 1865–1869," *Kansas Historical Quarterly*, Nov. 1931.

"Garnett's Brigade at Gettysburg," *Southern Historical Society Papers*, III, April 1877.

"General Lee's Final and Full Report of the Pennsylvania Campaign and Battle of Gettysburg," *Southern Historical Society Papers*, II, July 1876.

"General R. H. Anderson's Report of the Battle of Gettysburg," *Southern Historical Society Papers*, III, Feb. 1877.

Gibbon, John, "Another View of Gettysburg," *North American Review*, June 1891.

———, *Personal Recollections of the Civil War*, New York and London, 1928.

Gillette, William, *Retreat from Reconstruction, 1869–1879*, Baton Rouge, 1979.

Glassburg, Eudice, "Work, Wages, and the Cost of Living, Ethnic Differences and the Poverty Line, Philadelphia, 1880," *Pennsylvania History*, Jan. 1979.

Goldman, Henry H., "Southern Sympathy in Southern California, 1860–1865," *Journal of the West*, Oct. 1965.

Goodrich, Frederick E., *Life of Winfield Scott Hancock, Major-General, U.S.A.*, Boston, 1886.

Goodsell, James H., reporter, *Official Proceedings of the Democratic National Convention Held in 1864 at Chicago*, Chicago, 1864.

Gordon, George H., "Battles of Molino del Rey and Chapultepec," *Civil and Mexican Wars, 1861, 1846*, Papers of the Military Historical Society of Massachusetts, XIII, Boston, 1913.

———, "The Battles of Contreras and Churubusco," *Civil and Mexican Wars 1861, 1846*, Papers of the Military Historical Society of Massachusetts, XIII, Boston, 1913.

Gordon, John B., *Reminiscences of the Civil War*, New York, 1903.

Grant, Ulysses S., *Personal Memoirs of U. S. Grant*, ed. E. B. Long, Cleveland and New York, 1952.

Green, Horace, "General Grant's Last Stand," *Harper's Magazine*, April 1935.

Grinnell, George Bird, *The Fighting Cheyennes*, 1915; Norman, Okla., 1956.

Grossman, Lawrence, *The Democratic Party and the Negro: Northern and National Politics, 1868–92*, Urbana, Chicago, and London, 1976.

Hacker, Barton C., "The United States Army as a National Police Force: The Federal Policing of Labor Disputes, 1877–1898," *Military Affairs*, April 1969.

Hage, Anne A., "The Battle of Gettysburg as Seen by Minnesota Soldiers," *Minnesota History*, June 1963.

Hair, William Ivy, *Bourbonism and Agrarian Protest: Louisiana Politics, 1877–1900*, Baton Rouge, 1969.

Hall, Richard, *Stanley: An Adventurer Explored*, Boston, 1975.

Hancock, Almira R., *Reminiscences of Winfield Scott Hancock*, New York, 1887.

Hancock, Winfield S., "Gettysburg. Reply to General Howard." *Galaxy*, Dec. 1876.

Harsch, Joseph L., "On the McClellan-Go-Round," *Civil War History*, June 1973.

Hart, Albert Bushnell, *Salmon Portland Chase*, Boston and New York, 1899.

Haskell, Frank A., *The Battle of Gettysburg*, ed. Bruce Catton, Boston, 1957.

Hassler, Warren W., Jr., *Commanders of the Army of the Potomac*, Baton Rouge, 1962.

———, *Crisis at the Crossroads: The First Day at Gettysburg*, University, Ala., 1970.

———, "George G. Meade and His Role in the Gettysburg Campaign," *Pennsylvania History*, Oct. 1965.

Hassler, William Woods, *A. P. Hill: Lee's Forgotten General*, Richmond, Va., 1957.

Hattaway, Herman, and Archer Jones, *How the North Won: A Military History of the Civil War*, Urbana, Chicago, and London, 1983.

Haupt, Herman, *Reminiscences of General Herman Haupt*, Milwaukee, 1901.

Hebert, Walter H., *Fighting Joe Hooker*, Indianapolis and New York, 1944.

Henderson, G. F. R., *The Civil War: A Soldier's View*, ed. Jay Luvaas, Chicago, 1958.

Hesseltine, William B., *Ulysses S. Grant: Politician*, New York, 1935.

Hinckley, Ted C., "The Politics of Sinophobia: Garfield, the Morey Letter, and the Presidential Election of 1880," *Ohio History*, autumn 1980.

Hirsch, Mark D., *William C. Whitney: Modern Warwick*, New York, 1948.

Hood, John Bell, *Advance and Retreat: Personal Experiences in the United States and Confederate States Armies*, Bloomington, Ind., 1959.

House, Albert V., "Internal Conflict in Key States in the Democratic Convention of 1880," *Pennsylvania History*, April 1960.

———, "Northern Congressional Democrats as Defenders of the South During Reconstruction," *Journal of Southern History*, Feb. 1940.

Howard, Oliver Otis, *Autobiography of Oliver Otis Howard, Major General United States Army*, 2 vols., New York, 1907.

Howe, M. A. DeWolfe, ed., *Home Letters of General Sherman*, New York, 1909.

Hudson, William C., *Random Recollections of an Old Political Reporter*, New York, 1911.

Humphreys, Andrew A., *The Virginia Campaign of '64 and '65*, New York, 1883.

Hunt, Aurora, *Major General James Henry Carleton, 1814–1873: Western Frontier Dragoon*, Glendale, Calif., 1958.

Huntington, James F., "The Battle of Chancellorsville," *Campaigns in Virginia, Maryland and Pennsylvania, 1862–1863*, Papers of the Military Historical Society of Massachusetts, III, Boston, 1903.

Hutton, Paul Andrew, *Phil Sheridan and His Army*, Lincoln, Neb., and London, 1985.

Hyman, Harold M., "Johnson, Stanton, and Grant: A Reconsideration of the Army's Role in the Events Leading to Impeachment," *American Historical Review*, Oct. 1960.

Jacquette, Henrietta Stratton, *South after Gettysburg: Letters of Cornelia Hancock, 1863–1868,* New York, 1956.

Johnson, Robert Underwood, and Clarence Clough Buel, eds., *Battles and Leaders of the Civil War,* 4 vols., New York, 1884–87.

Jones, Evan R., *Four Years in the Army of the Potomac: A Soldier's Recollections,* London, n.d.

Jones, Virgil Carrington, *Ranger Mosby,* Chapel Hill, 1944.

Jordan, David M., *Roscoe Conkling of New York: Voice in the Senate,* Ithaca, N.Y., 1971.

Katz, Irving, *August Belmont,* New York and London, 1968.

Keller, Morton, *Affairs of State: Public Life in Late Nineteenth Century America,* Cambridge, Mass., and London, 1977.

Keller, Oliver J., "Soldier General of the Army: John Fulton Reynolds," *Civil War History,* June 1958.

Kennedy, Elijah R., *The Contest for California in 1861: How Colonel E. D. Baker Saved the Pacific States to the Union,* Boston and New York, 1912.

Kibby, Leo P., "California, the Civil War, and the Indian Problem: An Account of California's Participation in the Great Conflict," *Journal of the West,* April–July 1965.

Kingsbury, George W., *History of Dakota Territory,* 2 vols., Chicago, 1915.

Klein, Maury, *Edward Porter Alexander,* Athens, Ga., 1971.

Knight, Oliver, *Following the Indian Wars,* Norman, Okla., 1960.

Krythe, Maymie, *Port Admiral: Phineas Banning, 1830–1885,* San Francisco, 1957.

Langley, Lester D., "The Democratic Tradition and Military Reform, 1878–1885," *Southwestern Social Science Quarterly,* Sept. 1967.

Leckie, William H., *The Military Conquest of the Southern Plains,* Norman, Okla., 1963.

Lee, Fitzhugh, "A Review of the First Two Days' Operations at Gettysburg and a Reply to General Longstreet," *Southern Historical Society Papers,* V, April 1878.

Leech, Margaret, *Reveille in Washington, 1860–1865,* New York and London, 1941.

Lewis, Lloyd, *Captain Sam Grant,* Boston, 1950.

Lindsey, David,*"Sunset" Cox: Irrepressible Democrat,* Detroit, 1959.

Livermore, Thomas L., *Numbers and Losses in the Civil War in America, 1861–65,* Boston and New York, 1901.

———, "The Failure to Take Petersburg, June 15, 1864," *Petersburg, Chancellorsville, Gettysburg,* Papers of the Military Historical Society of Massachusetts, V, Boston, 1906.

Lochren, William, "The First Minnesota at Gettysburg," *Glimpses of the Nation's Struggle,* 3rd ser., Minnesota Commandery, Military Order of the Loyal Legion of the United States, St. Paul, 1893.

Longacre, Edward G., *The Man behind the Guns: A Biography of General Henry Jackson Hunt, Chief of Artillery, Army of the Potomac,* South Brunswick and New York, 1977.

———, ed., "The Roughest Kind of Campaign: Letters of Sergeant Edward Wightman, Third New York Volunteers, May–July 1864," *Civil War History,* Dec. 1982.

Longstreet, James, *From Manassas to Appomattox: Memoirs of the Civil War in America,* 2nd rev. ed., Philadelphia, 1912.

———, "General James Longstreet's Account of the Campaign and Battle," *Southern Historical Society Papers,* V, Jan.–Feb. 1878.

———, "General Longstreet's Second Paper on Gettysburg," *Southern Historical Society Papers,* V, June 1878.

Lord, Francis A., *Lincoln's Railroad Man: Herman Haupt,* Rutherford, Madison, and Teaneck, N.J., 1969.

Lyman, Theodore, "Addenda to the Paper by Brevet Lieutenant-Colonel W. W. Swan, U.S.A., on the Battle of the Wilderness," *The Wilderness Campaign, May–June 1864,* Papers of the Military Historical Society of Massachusetts, IV, Boston, 1905.

———, "Operations of the Army of the Potomac, June 5–15, 1864," *Petersburg, Chancellorsville, Gettysburg,* Papers of the Military Historical Society of Massachusetts, V, Boston, 1906.

McClellan, George B., *McClellan's Own Story,* New York, 1887.

———, *Report on the Organization and Campaigns of the Army of the Potomac,* New York, 1864.

McClure, Alexander K., *Old Time Notes of Pennsylvania,* 2 vols., Philadelphia, 1905.

———, *Our Presidents and How We Make Them,* New York and London, 1900.

McCulloch, Hugh, *Men and Measures of Half a Century,* New York, 1889.

McFeely, William S., *Grant: A Biography,* New York and London, 1981.

McGinty, Garnie W., *Louisiana Redeemed: The Overthrow of Carpet-bag Rule, 1876–1880,* New Orleans, 1941.

McJimsey, George T., *Genteel Partisan: Manton Marble, 1834–1917,* Ames, Iowa, 1971.

Mackey, Philip English, "Law and Order, 1877: Philadelphia's Response to the Railroad Riots," *Pennsylvania Magazine of History and Biography,* April 1972.

McKitrick, Eric L., *Andrew Johnson and Reconstruction,* Chicago, 1960.

McMurry, Richard M., *John Bell Hood and the War for Southern Independence,* Lexington, Ky., 1982.

McRae, D. K., "The Battle of Williamsburg—Reply to Colonel Bratton," *Southern Historical Society Papers,* VII, Aug. 1879.

McWhiney, Grady, and Perry D. Jamieson, *Attack and Die: Civil War Military Tactics and the Southern Heritage,* University, Ala., 1982.

Mantell, Martin E., *Johnson, Grant, and the Politics of Reconstruction,* New York and London, 1973.

Mason, Edwin C., "Through the Wilderness to the Bloody Angle at Spottsylvania Court House," *Glimpses of the Nation's Struggle,* 4th ser., Minnesota Commandery, Military Order of the Loyal Legion of the United States, St. Paul, 1898.

Maury, Richard L., "The Battle of Williamsburg and the Charge of the Twenty-fourth Virginia of Early's Brigade," *Southern Historical Society Papers,* VIII, June–July 1880.

Mayhall, Mildred P., *The Kiowas,* Norman, Okla., 1962.

Meade, George, *The Life and Letters of George Gordon Meade,* 2 vols. New York, 1913.

Mende, Elsie Porter, *An American Soldier and Diplomat: Horace Porter,* New York, 1927.

Miles, Nelson A., *Personal Recollections and Observations of General Nelson A. Miles,* Chicago and New York, 1897.

———, *Serving the Republic,* New York and London, 1911.

Military Order of the Loyal Legion of the United States, *In Memoriam—Winfield Scott Hancock, United States Army,* n.p., 1886.

Military Service Institution of the United States, *Letters and Addresses in Memory of Winfield Scott Hancock,* New York, 1886.

Millbrook, Minnie Dubbs, "Custer's First Scout in the West," *Kansas Historical Quarterly,* spring 1973.

Millis, Walter, *Arms and Men: A Study of American Military History,* New York, 1956.

Mitchell, Stewart, *Horatio Seymour of New York,* Cambridge, Mass., 1938.

Monaghan, Jay, *Custer: The Life of General George Armstrong Custer,* Lincoln, Neb., 1971.

Moneyhon, Carl H., *Republicanism in Reconstruction Texas,* Austin and London, 1980.

Montgomery, Mrs. Frank C., "Fort Wallace and Its Relation to the Frontier," *Collections of the Kansas State Historical Society,* XVII, 1928.

Moore, William G., "Notes of Colonel W. G. Moore, Private Secretary to President Johnson, 1866–1868," *American Historical Review,* Oct. 1913.

Morrison, James L., Jr., ed., *The Memoirs of Henry Heth,* Westport, Conn., and London, 1974.

Munroe, James Phinney, *A Life of Francis Amasa Walker,* New York, 1923.

Murfin, James V., *The Gleam of Bayonets: The Battle of Antietam and the Maryland Campaign of 1862,* New York and London, 1965.

Murphy, James B., *L. Q. C. Lamar: Pragmatic Patriot,* Baton Rouge, 1973.

Mushkat, Jerome, *The Reconstruction of the New York Democracy, 1861–1874,* Rutherford, N.J., 1981.

Myers, William Starr, *General George Brinton McClellan,* New York and London, 1934.

Nevins, Allan, *Abram S. Hewitt, with Some Account of Peter Cooper,* New York and London, 1935.

———, ed., *A Diary of Battle: The Personal Journals of Colonel Charles S. Wainwright, 1861–1865,* New York, 1962.

Newmark, Harris, *Sixty Years in Southern California, 1853–1913,* ed. M. H. Newmark and M. R. Newmark, 4th ed., Los Angeles, 1970.

Norris, James D., and Arthur H. Shaffer, eds., *Politics and Patronage in the Gilded Age: The Correspondence of James A. Garfield and Charles E. Henry,* Madison, Wis., 1970.

Olsen, Otto H., ed., *Reconstruction and Redemption in the South,* Baton Rouge and London, 1980.

Otis, Elwell S., "The Army in Connection with the Labor Riots of 1877," *Journal of the Military Service Institution of the United States,* Sept. 1884, June 1885.

Palfrey, Francis W., *The Antietam and Fredericksburg,* New York, 1882.

———, "The Battle of Antietam," *Campaigns in Virginia, Maryland and Pennsylvania, 1862–1863,* Papers of the Military Historical Society of Massachusetts, III, Boston, 1903.

"Papers of the Governors, 1871–1883," *Pennsylvania Archives,* 4th ser., Harrisburg, Pa., 1902.

Parker, Watson, *Gold in the Black Hills,* Norman, Okla., 1966.

Pearson, Henry Greenleaf, *James S. Wadsworth of Geneseo,* New York, 1913.

Perman, Michael, *Reunion without Compromise: The South and Reconstruction: 1865–1868,* Cambridge, Eng., 1973.

Peskin, Allan, *Garfield,* Kent, Ohio, 1978.

Peters, Joseph P., ed., *Indian Battles and Skirmishes on the American Frontier, 1790–1898,* New York, 1966.

Pitkin, Thomas M., *The Captain Departs: Ulysses S. Grant's Last Campaign,* Carbondale, Ill., 1973.

Pitman, Benn, *The Assassination of President Lincoln and the Trial of the Conspirators,* New York, 1954.

Polakoff, Keith Ian, *The Politics of Inertia: The Election of 1876 and the End of Reconstruction,* Baton Rouge, 1973.

Porter, Charles H., "The Battle of Cold Harbor," *The Wilderness Campaign May–June 1864,* Papers of the Military Historical Society of Massachusetts, IV, Boston, 1905.

Ramsdell, Charles Wm., *Reconstruction in Texas,* New York, 1910.

Randall, James G., ed., *The Diary of Orville Hickman Browning,* 2 vols., Springfield, Ill., 1933.

Report of Proceedings, Fifth Annual Reunion, Society of the Army of the Potomac, Held at New Haven, Ct., May 14, 1873.

Report of Proceedings, Sixth Annual Reunion, Society of the Army of the Potomac, Held at Harrisburg, Pa., May 12, 1874.

Richardson, James D., ed., *Messages and Papers of the Presidents, 1789–1908*, 10 vols., Washington, 1908.

Richardson, Robert C., Jr., *West Point*, New York and London, 1917.

Richter, William L., " 'We Must Rubb Out and Begin Anew': The Army and the Republican Party in Texas Reconstruction, 1867–1870," *Civil War History*, Dec. 1973.

Riemer, Joseph T., M.D., "General Hancock and Dr. Read," *Bulletin of the Historical Society of Montgomery County, Pennsylvania*, spring 1972.

Rister, Carl C., "Harmful Practices of Indian Traders of the Southwest, 1865–1876," *New Mexico Historical Review*, July 1931.

———, *The Southwestern Frontier, 1865–1881*, Cleveland, 1928.

Robertson, James I., Jr., *General A. P. Hill: The Story of a Confederate Warrior*, New York, 1987.

———, ed., *The Civil War Letters of General Robert McAllister*, New Brunswick, N.J., 1965.

Robinson, Will G., "Digest of the Reports of the Commissioner of Indian Affairs as Pertain to Dakota Indians—1869–1872," *South Dakota Report and Historical Collections*, XXVIII, 1956.

Ropes, John C., "The Battle of Cold Harbor," *The Wilderness Campaign, May–June 1864*, Papers of the Military Historical Society of Massachusetts, IV, Boston, 1905.

———, "The Failure to Take Petersburg on June 16–18, 1864," *Petersburg, Chancellorsville, Gettysburg*, Papers of the Military Historical Society of Massachusetts, V, Boston, 1906.

Sauers, Richard A., "Gettysburg: The Meade-Sickles Controversy." *Civil War History*, Sept. 1980.

Schaff, Morris, *The Battle of the Wilderness*, Boston and New York, 1910.

Schofield, John M., *Forty-Six Years in the Army*, New York, 1897.

Scott, John, *Partisan Life with Mosby*, London, 1867.

Scott, Thomas A., "The Recent Strikes," *North American Review*, Sept. 1877.

Searles, J. N., "The First Minnesota Volunteer Infantry," *Glimpses of the Nation's Struggle*, 2nd ser., Minnesota Commandery, Military Order of the Loyal Legion of the United States, St. Paul, 1890.

Sears, Stephen W., *Landscape Turned Red: The Battle of Antietam*, New Haven and New York, 1983.

Sefton, James E., *The United States Army and Reconstruction, 1865–1877*, Baton Rouge, 1967.

Shannon, Fred A., *The Organization and Administration of the Union Army, 1861–1865*, 2 vols., Cleveland, 1928.

Sharkey, Robert P., *Money, Class, and Party: An Economic Study of Civil War and Reconstruction*, Baltimore, 1959.

Sheridan, Philip H., *Personal Memoirs*, 2 vols., New York, 1888.

Sherman, William T., *Memoirs of General William T. Sherman*, 2 vols., 2nd ed., New York, 1889.

Shreve, William P., "The Operations of the Army of the Potomac May 13–June 2, 1864," *The Wilderness Campaign, May–June 1864*, Papers of the Military Historical Society of Massachusetts, IV, Boston, 1905.

Silbey, Joel H., *A Respectable Minority: The Democratic Party in the Civil War Era, 1860–1868*, New York, 1977.

Silliker, Ruth L., ed., *The Rebel Yell and the Yankee Hurrah: The Civil War Journal of a Maine Volunteer*, Camden, Me., 1985.

Slaughter, Linda W., *Fortress to Farm, or Twenty-three Years on the Frontier*, ed. Hazel Eastman, New York, 1972.

Slocum, Charles Elihu, *The Life and Services of Major-General Henry Warner Slocum*, Toledo, Ohio, 1913.

Smith, Theodore C., *The Life and Letters of James Abram Garfield*, 2 vols., New Haven, 1925.

Smith, Walter G., *Life and Letters of Thomas Kilby Smith, Brevet Major-General United States Volunteers, 1820–1887*, New York and London, 1898.

Smith, William Farrar, *From Chattanooga to Petersburg under Generals Grant and Butler: A Contribution to the History of the War, and a Personal Vindication*, Boston and New York, 1893.

———, "The Movement against Petersburg, June, 1864," *Petersburg, Chancellorsville, Gettysburg*, Papers of the Military Historical Society of Massachusetts, V, Boston, 1906.

Stampp, Kenneth M., *The Era of Reconstruction, 1865–1877*, New York, 1966.

Stanley, Henry Morton, *My Early Travels and Adventures in America and Asia*, 2 vols., New York, 1895.

Steere, Edward, *The Wilderness Campaign*, Harrisburg, Pa., 1960.

Stegmaier, Mark Joseph, "The Kidnapping of Generals Crook and Kelley by the McNeill Rangers," *West Virginia History*, Oct. 1967.

Stewart, George R., *Pickett's Charge*, Boston, 1959.

Stickles, Arndt M., *Simon Bolivar Buckner: Borderland Knight*, Chapel Hill, 1940.

Storrs, Emery A., "The Democratic Party Judged by Its History," *North American Review*, Oct. 1880.

Swanberg, W. A., *Sickles the Incredible*, New York, 1956.

Swinton, William, *Campaigns of the Army of the Potomac*, rev. ed., New York, 1882.

Tansill, Charles Callan, *The Congressional Career of Thomas Francis Bayard, 1869–1885*, Washington, 1946.

Taylor, Emerson Gifford, *Gouverneur Kemble Warren: The Life and Letters of an American Soldier, 1830–1882*, Boston and New York, 1932.

Taylor, Frank H., *Philadelphia in the Civil War*, Philadelphia, 1913.

Taylor, Joe Gray, *Louisiana: A Bicentennial History*, New York, 1976.

———, *Louisiana Reconstructed, 1863–1877*, Baton Rouge, 1974.

———, "New Orleans and Reconstruction," *Louisiana History*, summer 1968.

Taylor, John M., *Garfield of Ohio: The Available Man*, New York, 1970.

———, "General Hancock: Soldier of the Gilded Age," *Pennsylvania History*, April 1965.

Taylor, Joseph Henry, *Sketches of Frontier and Indian Life on the Upper Missouri and Great Plains*, 4th ed., Washburn, N.D., 1932.

Thomas, Benjamin P., and Harold M. Hyman, *Stanton: The Life and Times of Lincoln's Secretary of War*, New York, 1962.

Thomas, Lately, *The First President Johnson*, New York, 1968.

Thompson, Gerald, *The Army and the Navajo*, Tucson, 1976.

Thompson, Richard S., "A Scrap of Gettysburg," *Military Essays and Recollections*, Illinois Commandery, Military Order of the Loyal Legion of the United States, III, Chicago, 1899.

Thompson, William Y., "Robert Toombs, Confederate General," *Civil War History*, Dec. 1961.

Thomson, William D., "History of Fort Pembina: 1870–1895," *North Dakota History*, winter 1969.

Thorndike, Rachel Sherman, ed., *The Sherman Letters: Correspondence between General and Senator Sherman from 1837 to 1891*, New York, 1894.

Townsend, Geo. Alfred, *Campaigns of a Non-Combatant and His Romaunt Abroad during the War,* New York, 1866.

Trobriand, Philippe Regis de, *Four Years with the Army of the Potomac,* trans. Geo. K. Dauchy, Boston, 1889.

———, *Military Life in Dakota,* trans. and ed. Lucile M. Kane, St. Paul, 1951.

Tucker, Glenn, *Hancock the Superb,* Indianapolis and New York, 1960.

Urban, John W., *Battle Field and Prison Pen,* n.p., 1882.

Urwin, Gregory J. W., *Custer Victorious: The Civil War Battles of General George Armstrong Custer,* Rutherford, N. J., 1983.

Utley, Robert M., *Frontiersmen in Blue,* New York and London, 1967.

———, *Frontier Regulars: The United States Army and the Indian, 1866–1891,* New York and London, 1973.

Van de Water, Frederick F., *Glory-Hunter: A Life of General Custer,* Indianapolis and New York, 1934.

Victor, Orville J., ed., *Incidents and Anecdotes of the War,* New York, 1866.

Vivian, James F., "Major E. A. Burke: The Honduras Exile, 1889–1928," *Louisiana History,* spring 1974.

Wainwright, Nicholas B., "The Loyal Opposition in Civil War Philadelphia," *The Pennsylvania Magazine of History and Biography,* July 1964.

Wakeman, George, reporter, *Official Proceedings of the Democratic National Convention Held at New York, July 4–9, 1868,* Boston 1868.

Walker, Francis A., *General Hancock,* New York, 1894.

———, "General Hancock," *Critical Sketches of Some of the Federal and Confederate Commanders,* Papers of the Military Historical Society of Massachusetts, X, Boston and New York, 1895.

———, *History of the Second Army Corps in the Army of the Potomac,* New York, 1886.

Wall, Joseph Frazier, *Henry Watterson: Reconstructed Rebel,* New York, 1956.

Ward, Joseph R. C., *History of the One Hundred and Sixth Regiment Pennsylvania Volunteers,* Philadelphia, 1906.

Warner, Ezra J., *Generals in Blue: Lives of the Union Commanders,* Baton Rouge, 1964.

———, *Generals in Gray: Lives of the Confederate Commanders,* Baton Rouge, 1959.

Webb, Alexander S., *The Peninsula: McClellan's Campaign of 1862,* New York, 1881.

Weigley, Russell F., *History of the United States Army,* New York and London, 1967.

———, *The American Way of War: A History of United States Military Strategy and Policy,* New York and London, 1973.

Weisberger, Bernard A., *Reporters for the Union,* Boston, 1953.

Welty, Raymond L., "The Frontier Army on the Missouri River, 1860–1870," *North Dakota Historical Quarterly,* Jan. 1928.

———, "The Policing of the Frontier by the Army, 1860–1870," *Kansas Historical Quarterly,* Aug. 1938.

———, "Supplying the Frontier Military Posts," *Kansas Historical Quarterly,* May 1938.

Wharton, Clarence, *Satanta: The Great Chief of the Kiowas and His People,* Dallas, 1935.

White, Lonnie J., "The Hancock and Custer Expeditions of 1867," *Journal of the West,* July 1966.

Wilcox, Cadmus M., "General C. M. Wilcox on the Battle of Gettysburg," *Southern Historical Society Papers,* VI, Sept. 1878.

———, *History of the Mexican War,* Washington, 1892.

Wiley, Bell Irvin, *The Life of Billy Yank: The Common Soldier of the Union*, Indianapolis and New York, 1952.

Williams, Charles Richard, *The Life of Rutherford Birchard Hayes, Nineteenth President of the United States*, 2 vols., Boston and New York, 1914.

Williams, Kenneth P., *Lincoln Finds a General: A Military Study of the Civil War*, 5 vols., New York, 1949–59.

Williams, T. Harry, *Hayes of the Twenty-third: The Civil War Volunteer Officer*, New York, 1965.

———, ed., *Hayes: The Diary of a President, 1875–1881*, New York, 1964.

———, *McClellan, Sherman and Grant*, New Brunswick, N.J., 1962.

Wilson, James Harrison, *Life and Services of William Farrar Smith, Major General, United States Volunteers, in the Civil War*, Wilmington, Del., 1904.

Wilson, James Grant, and Titus M. Coan, eds., *Personal Recollections of the War of the Rebellion*, 4 vols., New York, 1891.

Wood, Oliver E., *The West Point Scrap Book*, New York, 1871.

Woods, George B., "The New York Convention," *North American Review*, Oct. 1868.

Woodward, C. Vann, *Reunion and Reaction: The Compromise of 1877 and the End of Reconstruction*, Boston, 1951, 1966.

Zook, Douglas D., Jr., "A Biographical Sketch of Samuel K. Zook," *Bulletin of the Historical Society of Montgomery County, Pennsylvania*, spring 1982.

Index

Adams, Charles Francis, Jr., 147
Adjutant-General's Department, 23–24
Agnew, D. H.: treats Hancock, 101–2
Alexander, E. Porter: Fredericksburg, 62; Gettysburg, 96
Allen, William: candidate, 238–39; on Chase, 218
Anderson, Finley: on Hancock's staff, 58, 328n
Anderson, G. T., 46
Anderson, Richard H.: Chancellorsville, 72, 74; Cold Harbor, 136; Gettysburg, 97; Spotsylvania, 126; Wilderness, 118, 120
Anderson, Robert, 35
Anderson, Samuel J., 221
Anderson, Thomas C., 265
Anthony, Susan B., 281
Antietam, battle of, 56, 58–59, 78, 105, 157, 173; described, 52–55
Antietam Creek, 52
Apaches, 184
Appomattox Court House, 257; surrender at, 65, 175
Appomattox River, 110, 147, 153
Aquia Creek, 49, 77
Arapahos, 190; expedition to, 185, 187–88, 195–96; treaty with, 199
Archer, James J., 97
Arikaras: meeting with Hancock, 230
Arkansas River, 184, 188, 190, 195–96, 198
Armistead, Lewis A.: friend of Hancock, 36, 202, 318; Gettysburg, 97–99, 325n, 332n; in Los Angeles, 33–34; in Mexico, 17, 19
Army of the James, 136, 143, 150; advance of, 110; newspaper correspondents with, 145
Army and Navy Journal, 105
Army of Northern Virginia, 65; Antietam, 52–54; Chancellorsville, 71; 1863–64 winter quarters, 111; Fredericksburg, 60; Gettysburg, 100; invasion of Maryland, 50–51; Spotsylvania, 126, 130, 133; Totopotomoy Creek, 136
Army of the Potomac, 45, 49, 57, 58, 101, 103, 105, 143, 165, 172, 188, 199, 231, 263, 317, 331n, 340n; Antietam, 52–54; approaching Richmond, 45; Burnside as commander of, 56, 59, 254; Chancellorsville, 68–73; Cold Harbor, 136–40; Crook with, 174; crossing of the James, 141; divided into corps, 38; Fredericksburg, 60–65; Gettysburg, council of war, 94, first day, 81–86, second day, 89–94, third day, 94–99; Grant with, 109; Hancock considered for command of, 155, 169; Hatcher's Run, 166–69; Hooker named to command

of, 65, 67; McClellan's command of, 51; Meade as commander of, 79, 104; Meade recommended for command of, 75; moves toward Pennsylvania, 77–79; Peninsula, 40; Petersburg, 147, 150; removal of Burnside, 65; removal of McClellan from, 56; reorganization of, 107; return of Hancock to, 107; Seven Day's battles, 46; Spotsylvania, 126–32; start of 1864 campaign of, 110; Wilderness, first day, 112–17, second day, 118–25
Army of the Tennessee, 263
Army of Virginia, 49
Arnold, Samuel, 177
Arthur, Chester Alan: president, 308; vice presidential candidate, 269, 294; at Yorktown celebration, 311
Astor, John Jacob, 289
Astor Opera House, 21
Atlanta Constitution, 284
Atzerodt, George B., 177
Auger, Christopher C., 242, 307
Ayres, Romeyn B., 168

Babcock, Orville E., 257, 357n
Badeau, Adam, 204, 312
Bailey's Creek, 153, 156
Baker, Eugene M., 232–33
Baker, Joshua, 208
Baker, William: fired by Hancock, 210, 346n
Baltimore, Md., 29, 82, 101–2, 176; Hancock residence in, 182–83; railroad strike, 243–44, 250
Baltimore & Ohio Railroad: raided by Confederates, 174; railroad strike, 243–44
Banks, Nathaniel P., 110, 200
Banks's Ford, 69, 73
Banning, Phineas, 29, 30, 32
Barksdale, William, 93
Barlow, Francis Channing, 109, 149, 173; background, 105; Cold Harbor, 137–39; death of wife, 153; Deep Bottom, 156–57; division commander, 107, 110, 114; Hancock letters to, 169, 171, 340n; illness of, 157, 159, 338n; to Petersburg, 142–43, 147; postwar career, 334n; regimental commander, 54; resumes division command, 156; Spotsylvania, 127–30, 132; Totopotomoy, 136; Wilderness, 117, 119–21, 125
Barnum, William H., 274, 284; campaign of 1880, 295, 299, 306–7; Morey letter, 303; reelected chairman, 285–87, 360n
Barr, James P., 295
Bateman, Warner, 283

379

Democratic national committee, 217, 285, 295–96, 302, 307
Democratic party, 31, 165, 204, 214–18, 226, 237, 255, 259–60, 263–66, 269, 273, 275, 285, 291–93, 296–97, 300, 305, 313, 318, 349n
Democratic Soldiers and Sailors Convention, 219, 221
Denver, Colo., 184, 188, 197
Department of Dakota, 213, 229–30, 235–36, 263
Department of the Missouri, 183, 185, 198, 201, 229
Department of the West, 24
Department of West Virginia, 174
Devereux, Arthur F., 98
Devil's Den, 84, 86, 90–92
Diamond City, Mont., 232
Division of the Atlantic, 213, 229, 235–36, 242, 251, 288, 308
Division of the Missouri, 183, 311
Division of the Pacific, 213
Dix, Morgan, 2
Doane, Gustavus C., 235
Donelly, J. J., 349n
Doolittle, James, 218, 221–22, 226, 347n
Dorsey, Stephen W., 299
Doubleday, Abner: book, 313; Gettysburg, 82–84, 88, 93, 95, 330n, 331n
Dougherty, Alexander N., 99, 101, 173
Dougherty, Daniel: nominates Hancock, 275–78, 281
Dover Green: Bayard speech, 261–62, 266, 272–73, 354n
Dow, Edwin, 125
Dow, Neal, 292, 360n
Downer's Station, 194
Drewry's Bluff, 110

Earle, John, 11
Early, Jubal A., 44, 69, 80, 82–83, 87, 130, 151, 155–57
Edwards Ferry, 78
Egan, Thomas W., 173, 339n; division commander, 166; Hatcher's Run, 167–69; North Anna, 135; rejoins Hancock, 174
Eighteenth Corps, 136–37, 141, 143–46, 164, 166
Eighth Infantry, 20
Election of 1868, 228
Election of 1876, 239–40
Election of 1880, 256, 260, 298, 305, 360n
Electoral Commission, 240–41, 261, 271
Eleventh Corps, 105, 107, 173; Chancellorsville, 69, 71; Gettysburg, 80–83, 87, 89, 94, 330n, 331
11th Ohio, 50
Eliot, William Greenleaf, 22
Ellis, E. John: on Bayard, 261; on Harrisburg

convention, 267; supports Hancock, 266, 274, 278; on Tilden, 259
El Monte, Calif., 32
Ely's Ford, 110–12
Emancipation Proclamation, 55, 58
Emmitsburg, Md., 81–82, 86, 89–90, 92, 98
Emory, William H., 174
Endicott, William C., 313
English, James, 221–22, 225, 262, 272, 278, 280
English, William H.: in Indiana, 295, 298–300; meets Hancock, 287; named for vice president, 281, 294, 302
Erie Railroad, 243
Eustis, Henry L., 122
Ewell, Richard S.: Gettysburg, 87–88, 94; Pennsylvania campaign, 77–78, 80; Spotsylvania, 129, 132; Wilderness, 112, 114, 117, 119
Ewing, Thomas, Jr., 221, 262, 277
Excelsior Brigade, 90, 116

Fair Oaks, battle of, 45–46, 67
Falmouth, Va., 60–61, 65, 69, 73, 77
Fenian raids, 349n
Ferrero, Edward, 155
Field, Charles W., 118, 120, 123, 147, 157, 160, 338n
Field, Cyrus W., 261, 289
Field, David Dudley, 261
Field, Henry, 261
Field, Stephen J.: candidate in 1880, 267, 270–72, 275–78, 280–81, 285; described, 261; in New York convention, 225
Fifth Corps, 80, 141; Antietam, 54; Chancellorsville, 68–69; Gaine's Mill, 46; Gettysburg, 91, 95, 99; Hatcher's Run, 166–67, 340n; North Anna, 135; reorganization, 107; Spotsylvania, 125–28; Totopotomoy, 136; Weldon Railroad, 159; Wilderness, 110–12, 114, 117
Fifth Military District, 199, 201–2, 204, 211–12, 218, 255, 264–65, 289, 318
5th New Hampshire, 64, 91
5th North Carolina, 44
5th Wisconsin, 36, 43
57th New York, 61
53rd Pennsylvania, 63
First Corps: abolished, 107; Antietam, 53; Gettysburg, 80–84, 93–95, 97, 330n, 331n
First Division, Second Corps, 53–54, 76, 89, 92, 99, 136, 156, 159–61, 163
First Division, Third Corps, 107
1st Minnesota, 93
Fish, Hamilton, 361n
Five Forks, battle of, 357n
Flanders, Benjamin F., 207–8
Florida, 257, 264, 305; Hancock in, 24–25, 324n
Ford's Theater, 177